Social
Issues
Primary
Sources
Collection

Family in Society

Essential Primary Sources

Social
Issues
Primary
Sources
Collection

Family in Society

Essential Primary Sources

K. Lee Lerner, Brenda Wilmoth Lerner, and **Adrienne Wilmoth Lerner,** Editors

THOMSON

GALE

Detroit • New York • San Francisco • New Haven, Conn. • Waterville, Maine • London

THOMSON
™
GALE

Family in Society: Essential Primary Sources

K. Lee Lerner, Brenda Wilmoth Lerner, and Adrienne Wilmoth Lerner, Editors

Project Editors
Dwayne D. Hayes and John McCoy

Editorial
Luann Brennan, Grant Eldridge, Anne Marie Hacht, Joshua Kondek, Andy Malonis, Mark Milne, Rebecca Parks, Mark Springer, Jennifer Stock

Permissions
Sue Rudolph, Kim Smilay, Andrew Specht

Imaging and Multimedia
Dean Dauphinais, Leitha Etheridge-Sims, Lezlie Light, Michael Logusz, Dan Newell, Christine O'Bryan, Kelly A. Quin, Denay Wilding, Robyn Young

Product Design
Pamela A. Galbreath

Composition and Electronic Capture
Evi Seoud

Manufacturing
Rita Wimberley

Product Manager
Carol Nagel

LIBRARY OF CONGRESS CATALOGING-IN-PUBLICATION DATA

Family in society : essential primary sources / K. Lee Lerner, Brenda Wilmoth Lerner, and Adrienne Wilmoth Lerner, editors.
    p. cm. — (Social issues primary sources collection)
Includes bibliographical references and index.
ISBN-10: 1-4144-0330-5 (hardcover : alk. paper)
ISBN-13: 978-1-4144-0330-4
  1. Family—History—Sources. I. Lerner, K. Lee. II. Lerner, Brenda Wilmoth. III. Lerner, Adrienne Wilmoth.

  HQ518.F335 2007
  306.8509—dc22
                                                 2006026216

This title is also available as an e-book.
ISBN-10: 1-4144-1266-5
ISBN-13: 978-1-4144-1266-5
Contact your Thomson Gale sales representative for ordering information.

Printed in the United States of America
10 9 8 7 6 5 4 3 2 1

Table of Contents

1 CONCEPTS OF FAMILY

2   MARRIAGE, PARTNERSHIP, AND DIVORCE

4 FAMILY LIFE AND FAMILY RELATIONSHIPS

6 HEALTH, HOUSING, AND FAMILY PLANNING

Advisors and Contributors

While compiling this volume, the editors relied upon the expertise and contributions of the following scholars, journalists, and researchers who served as advisors and/or contributors for *Family in Society: Essential Primary Sources*:

Steven Archambault (Ph.D. Candidate)
University of New Mexico
Albuquerque, New Mexico

William Arthur Atkins, M.S.
Normal, Illinois

Alicia Cafferty
University College
Dublin, Ireland

James Anthony Charles Corbett
Journalist
London, UK

Bryan Davies, J.D.
Ontario, Canada

Sandra Dunavan, M.S.
Saline, Michigan

Lynda Joeman
Independent Research Consultant (ex UK Home Office)
Kota Kinabalu, Sabah, Malaysia

Antoinette Johnson, MBA
Hazel Park, MI

Larry Gilman, Ph.D.
Sharon, Vermont

Amit Gupta, Ph.D.
Ahmedabad, India

Alexander Ioffe, Ph.D.
Russian Academy of Sciences
Moscow, Russia

S. Layman, M.A.
Abingdon, MD

Adrienne Wilmoth Lerner (J.D. Candidate)
University of Tennessee College of Law
Knoxville, Tennessee

Pamela V. Michaels, M.A.
Forensic Psychologist
Santa Fe, New Mexico

Caryn Neumann, Ph.D.
Ohio State University
Columbus, Ohio

Mark Phillips, Ph.D.
Abilene Christian University
Abilene, Texas

Nephele Tempest
Los Angeles, California

Melanie Barton Zoltán, M.S.
Amherst, Massachusetts

Family in Society: Essential Primary Sources is the product of a global group of multi-lingual scholars, researchers, and writers. The editors are grateful to Christine Jeryan, Amy Loerch Strumolo, Kate Kretschmann, John Krol and Judy Galens for their dedication and skill in copyediting both text and translations. Their efforts added significant accuracy and readability to this book. The editors also wish to acknowledge and thank Adrienne Wilmoth Lerner and Alicia Cafferty for their tenacious research efforts.

The editors gratefully acknowledge and extend thanks to Peter Gareffa, Carol Nagel, and Ellen McGeagh at Thomson Gale for their faith in the project and for their sound content advice. Special thanks go to the Thomson Gale copyright research and imaging teams for their patience, good advice, and skilled research into sometimes vexing copyright issues. The editors offer profound thanks to project managers Dwayne Hayes and John McCoy. Their clear thoughts, insights and trusted editorial judgment added significantly to the quality of *Family in Society: Essential Primary Sources*

Acknowledgements

Copyrighted excerpts in *Family in Society: Essential Primary Sources* were reproduced from the following periodicals:

The Atlantic Monthly, v. 271, April, 1993 for "Dan Quayle was Right" by Barbara Dafoe Whitehead. Copyright © 1993. Reproduced by permission of Writers Representatives LLC, New York, NY, on behalf of the author.—*Christian Science Monitor*, April 17, 1998; October 31, 2000. Copyright © 1998, 2000 The Christian Science Publishing Society. All rights reserved. Both reproduced by permission from *Christian Science Monitor*, (www.csmonitor.com).—*The Economist*, November 24, 2005. Copyright © 2005 The Economist Newspaper Ltd. All rights reserved. Reprinted with permission. Further reproduction prohibited. www.economist.com—*Family Relations*, v. 42, July, 1993; v. 49, April, 2000. Republished with permission of National Council on Family Relations, conveyed through Copyright Clearance Center, Inc.— *The Guardian*, February 4, 2006; March 4, 2006; March 17, 2006; March 25, 2006; April 8, 2006; April 15, 2006. Copyright Guardian Newspapers Limited 2006. All reproduced by permission of Guardian News Service, LTD.—*Journal of Economic Perspectives*, v. 139, 1996. Reproduced by permission of American Economic Association.—*The Mail on Sunday*, March 2, 2003. Reproduced by permission.—*Michigan History Magazine*, v. 66, January-February, 1982. Reproduced by permission.

National Institute on Media and the Family, 1999. © 1999 National Institute on Media and the Family. Reproduced by permission.—*National Review*, July 18, 1986. Copyright © 1986 by National Review, Inc., 215 Lexington Avenue, New York, NY 10016. Repro-duced by permission.—*The New York Times*, January 5, 1953; May 13, 1990; December 4, 2001 March 5, 2002; October 5, 2003; December 7, 2004; October 13, 2005; December 11, 2005; February 5, 2006; March 19, 2006; March 25, 2006; April 2, 2006; April 4, 2006; April 16, 2006; January 16, 2000. Copyright © 1953, 1990, 2001, 2002, 2003, 2005, 2006 by The New York Times Company. All reprinted with permission./ January 8, 1945. Copyright 1945, renewed © 1973 by The New York Times Company. Reprinted with permission.—*The Observer*, February 5, 2006. Copyright Guardian Newspapers Limited 2006. Reproduced by permission of Guardian News Service, LTD.—*Ottawa Citizen*, March 31, 1999 for "My Family will Swoosh for Nike" by James Linton. Copyright © 1999 canada.com, a division of CanWest Interactive Inc., a CanWest company. Reproduced by permission of the author.—*Parents' Press*, 1994. Copyright © 1994 Scholastic Inc. Reproduced by permission of Parents' Press.—*Refugees Magazine*, March 1, 1994; June, 2004. Both reproduced by permission of UNHCR.—*UN Daily News*, April 19, 2006. © 2006 United Nations. Reprinted with the permission of the United Nations.—*The Washington Post*, May 25, 1998; December 28, 2005. Copyright © 1998, 2005 *The Washington Post*. Both reprinted with permission./*The Washington Post*, November 6, 2005 for "Just Whom Is This Divorce 'Good' For?" by Elizabeth Marquardt. © 2005 the Washington Post Company. Reproduced by permission of the author.

Copyrighted excerpts in *Family in Society: Essential Primary Sources* were reproduced from the following books:

Dendinger, Emily. From *Family Tree*. Dramatic Publishing, 2004. © MMIV by Emily Dendinger. All rights reserved. Reproduced by permission.—Freud, Sigmund. From "Love and the Formations of Family," in *Civilization and its Discontents*. Edited and translated by James Strachey. W. W. Norton and Co., 1962, *The Standard Edition of the Complete Psychological Works of Sigmund Freud*. Edited and translated by James Strachey. Sigmund Freud Copyright, The Institute of Psycho-Analysis and The Hogarth Press, 1953. Copyright © 1961 by James Strachey, renewed 1989 by Alix Strachey. All rights reserved. Reproduced by permission of W. W. Norton & Company, Inc. In Canada by The Random House Group Ltd.—*Family Life Magazine*, November, 1977. Reproduced by permission of Pathway Publishers.—Lewin, Abraham. From "Diary of the Great Deportation," in *A Cup of Tears: A Diary of the Warsaw Ghetto*. Edited by Anthony Polonsky. Translated by Christopher Hutton. Copyright © introduction and translation of the diary, Institute for Polish-Jewish Studies 1988. Copyright © original diary, Robert and Michael Lewin. Reprinted by permission of Blackwell Publishers.

Roach, Mary. From "Two Heads are Better than Three," in *Because I Said So*. Edited by Camille Peri and Kate Moses. HarperCollins, 2005. Copyright © by Mary Roach. Reproduced by permission of the author.—Rostislavov, Dimitri Ivanovich. From "Household Work," in *Provincial Russia in the Age of Enlightenment*. Edited and translated by Alexander M. Martin. Northern Illinois University Press, 2002. © 2002 by Northern Illinois University Press. All rights reserved. Reproduced by permission.—Schor, Edward L. From *Caring for Your School-Age Child Ages 5-12*. Bantam, 1999. Copyright © 1995, 1996, 1999 by the American Academy of Pediatrics. All rights reserved. Reproduced by permission of Bantam Books, a division of Random House, Inc., and the American Academy of Pediatrics.

Photographs and illustrations appearing in *Family in Society: Essential Primary Sources* were received from the following sources:

"A. D. 1915, With Puck's Apologies to the 'Coming Woman,'" illustration by F. Opper. © Corbis.—Advertisement designed to encourage Native Americans to leave their reservations and move to urban areas, photograph. MPI/Getty Images.—Advertisement encouraging union workers to purchase only union-made clothes for their families. The Library of Congress.—Advertisement for an early-model washing machine, January 1, 1890, photograph. Hulton Archive/Getty Images.—African-American slave is being sold at an auction in South Carolina, photograph. © Corbis.—AIDS orphan Nosipho Ndlangamandla, photograph. © Gideon Mendel for The Global Fund/Corbis.—Amish family riding in open horse-drawn wagon, photograph. © Thomas B. Hollyman/Photo Researchers. Reproduced by permission.—Anti-child labor poster, photograph. © Corbis.—Austen, Jane, print.—Baby asleep in baby carrier, photograph. © Rune Hellestad/Corbis.—Baby carriage parade of husbands and firstborns, illustration. © Bettmann/Corbis.—Barras, Nancy, photograph. © Wagner, Gary/Corbis/Sygma.—Bergen, Candice, holds a newborn on the television show "Murphy Brown," photograph. © Bettmann/Corbis.—Boy drinking camel's milk in the desert, photograph. © Liba Taylor/Corbis.—Boy forcing corkscrew into car tire, photograph. © Royalty-Free/Corbis.

Boy laborers, photograph. National Archives and Records Administration.—Boy lets himself into his home, Dagenham, Kent, photo by Joseph McKeown. Joseph McKeown/Picture Post/Getty Images.—Census-taker gathers data from families, photograph. © Corbis.—Changes in American households from 1970-2003, table. Adapted by Thomson Gale from data from the US Census Bureau. Reproduced by permission of Thomson Gale.—Children play in a neglected play hut on the Lisson Green Estate, photograph. © Hulton-Deutsch Collection/Corbis.—Chinese woman uses a dispensing machine to obtain free condoms or contraceptive pills, November 26, 2004, photograph. © Reinhard Krause/Reuters/Corbis.—Civil War family from the south on their porch, photograph. © Bettmann/Corbis.—Couple in the morning, photograph. © H. Armstrong Roberts/Corbis.—Demonstrator holds a sign supporting traditional marriage during a anti-gay marriage rally on Lawyers Mall, Annapolis, Maryland, January 27, 2005, photograph. AP Images.—Divorcing couple sitting in lawyer's office, photograph. © Creasource/Corbis.—Drunkard attacks wife, illustration. © Historical Picture Archive/Corbis.—"Election Day!" poster. The Library of Congress.—English lessons for European Jewish immigrants, poster. The Library of Congress.—Family bundles scrap paper and materials for recycling during World War II, photograph. © Seattle Post-Intelligencer Collection Museum of History and Industry/Corbis.

Family Groups by Type and Selected Characteristics, table. Adapted by Thomson Gale from data from the US Census Bureau. Reproduced by permission of Thomson Gale.—Family in a fallout shelter, photograph. © Bettmann/Corbis.—Family in fall out shelter, 1955, photograph. © Bettmann/Corbis.—Family in the kitchen, photograph. © Simon Marcus/Corbis.—Family listening to news on the radio, October 8, 1939, photograph. © Bettmann/Corbis.—Family of four buying a house, photograph. © Royalty-Free/Corbis.—Family portrait, photograph. © Royalty-Free/Corbis.—Family posing with new house, photograph. © Royalty-Free/Corbis.—Family reunited in Rwanda, November 15, 1996, photograph. © Christophe Calais/In Visu/Corbis.—"Family Temperance Pledge," 1885, form. The Library of Congress.—Family tree before and after Civil War, 1880, photograph. © Corbis.—Family waiting by radio for information about the "U. S. S. Squalus," 1939, photograph. © Bettmann/Corbis.—Family with home computer, photograph. © Rob Lewine/Corbis.—Farmer John Barnett and his family, who are struggling to survive during the Great Depression on their farm, photograph. Keystone/Getty Images.—Father and Daughter in a rocking chair on the front porch reading a book, photograph. © Ariel Skelley/Corbis.—Father and son cleaning window, photograph. © Sandra Seckingerzefa/Corbis.—Father helps daughters get ready in the morning, photograph. © Brenda Ann Kenneally/Corbis.

Father punishing child, photograph. © John Springer Collection/Corbis.—Father setting the dining table with his family, photograph. © Royalty-Free/Corbis.—Father with baby, photograph. © Royalty-Free/Corbis.—Father's Day tie and accompanying card written by children, photograph. © Royalty-Free/Corbis.—Final dissolution of marriage and divorce decree document, photograph. © Royalty-Free/Corbis.—"For the Benefit of the Girl About to Graduate," cartoon, 1890. The Library of Congress.—Freud, Sigmund, fourth from left, sits at a dining table with the rest of his family, photograph. © Corbis.—"From Gold to Grey," book illustration. © Corbis.—Funeral of Charles Stewart Parnell, Glasnevin, Ireland, photograph. © Sean Sexton Collection/Corbis.—Garden Pier and beach, Atlantic City, NJ, photograph. © Corbis.—Gay dads, Brian Brantner (L) and Matt Fuller hold their 2-month-old adopted daughter, Audrey, photograph. © Tomas Van Houtryve/Corbis.—Girl being swung around, photograph. © Mark A. Johnson/Corbis.—Girl with a condition similar to spina bifida, plays catch with her sister, photograph. © Laura Dwight/Corbis.—Good parenting poster. The Library of Congress.—Graham, Robert, Dr., July, 1982, photograph. Paul Harris/Liaison/Getty Images.—Groening, Matt, with his animated creation, "The Simpsons," photograph. © Douglas Kirkland/Corbis.—Halter, Ardyn, painting marriage contract, photograph. © Robert Holmes/Corbis.

"Hanging the Washing, a Beautiful Spring Morning," painting by Helen Allingham, 1899. © Fine Art Photographic Library/Corbis.—"Hitching's Baby Cars" advertisement, illustration. © Hulton-Deutsch Collection/Corbis.—"Household Drudge and Slave," woodcut by Charles Stanley Reinhart. © Bettmann/Corbis.—Immigrant family holding landing cards, photograph. © Bettmann/Corbis.—Ingalls family from the TV Series, "Little House on the Prairie," photograph. © Bettmann/Corbis.—"It's the Little Things that Count," postcard. © Poodles/Rock/Corbis.—Jones, Christy, left, and Dr. Bradford Kolb, August 16, 2004, Pasadena, California, photograph. AP Images.—Joyce, James, and his family in their Paris home, February 7, 1934, photograph. © Bettmann/Corbis.—Ketubbah, the traditional Jewish marriage contract, photograph. Courtesy of The Library of The Jewish Theological Seminary—Large family, photograph. © Kevin Dodge/Corbis.—Levittown, New York (aerial view), photograph. © UPI/Corbis-Bettmann.—"Lincoln-Lee Legion," temperance pledge card, photograph. © Lake County Museum/Corbis.—"Low Rent Homes," poster. The Library of Congress.—Married-Couple Family Groups with Stay-at-Home Parents, 2003, table. Adapted by Thomson Gale from data from the US Census Bureau. Reproduced by permission of Thomson Gale.—Mexican immigrant children in mobile home, photograph. © Alison Wright/Corbis.—Mother administers a spanking punishment on a child while the father watches, photograph. © Bettmann/Corbis.—Mother and her baby, photograph. © A Indenzefa/Corbis.—Mother sits on the bed and reads to her two-year-old son, photograph. © Laura Dwight/Corbis.—"Mother, Sara, and the Baby," painting by Mary Cassatts. © Christies Images/Corbis.—Native Americans overlooking Chicago skyline, photograph. © Underwood & Underwood/Corbis.

"Necessity is the Mother of Invention," cartoon. © Bettmann/Corbis.—Nelson, Ozzie, (R) with Harriet Nelson and family on their TV show, October 1, 1958, photograph. Ralph Crane/Time Life Pictures/Getty Images.—Nelsons (Ozzie, Harriet, David, and Rickey) family portrait, photograph. © Bettmann/Corbis.—Neonatologist checks a newborn baby, photograph. © Jonathan Drakeepa/Corbis.—Nevada polygamist with his numerous wives and children, photograph by Nik Wheeler. © Nik Wheeler/Corbis.—New Jersey Seashore poster, photograph. © Swim Ink 2, LLC/Corbis.—Nike sports shoes rest on a table, photograph. © Bettmann/Corbis.—Nunez, Oscar, Noah Matthews and Greg Pitts, March 6, 2006, Los Angeles, CA, photograph. AP Images.—Nurse measuring a newborn baby's head, photograph. © Louis Quail/Corbis.—Nursery for the children of field workers, photograph. © Underwood & Underwood/Corbis.—Nursery workers serve tea to a group of toddlers at a day nursery, photograph. © Hulton-Deutsch Collection/Corbis.—Old photographs in picture frames, photograph. © Ute Kaiserzefa/Corbis.—"Old" and "new" washing machines displayed, 1905, photograph. © Bettmann/Corbis.—One-child family, China, photograph. © Liu Liqun/Corbis.—Osbourne family, (Ozzy, Sharon, Kelly and Jack) photograph. Frazer Harrison/Getty Images.—Pankhurst, Emmeline, photograph. © Bettmann/Corbis.

"Plant a Victory Garden," poster. © Swim Ink 2, LLC/Corbis.—Poster at a Singapore family-planning clinic, photograph. © UPI/Corbis-Bettmann.—Presidential election map of the United States made of ice in the skating rink at Rockefeller Center, November 2, 2004, New York, NY, photograph. AP Images.—Prohibition poster depicting two frightened young children, photograph. David J. and Janice L. Frent Collection/Corbis.—Reed, Sydney and Morgan, shown in the hallway of Covenant Hospital, Lubbock, Texas, February 29, 2004, photograph. AP Images.—Refugee family walks through the street, photograph. © Bettmann/Corbis.—Roosevelt, Franklin D., with WPA Administrator Harry Hopkins and his daughter, November 4, 1937, photograph. © Bettmann/Corbis.—Russian family outside their cabin, ca. 1850, photograph. © Hulton-Deutsch Collection/Corbis.—Schmeeckle, Fred, a Farm Security Administration borrower and dryland farmer, with his family, Weld County, Colorado, October, 1939, photograph. © Corbis.—School boy gets his first experience in using war ration book, photograph. © Corbis.—"Service on the Home Front," poster. The Library of Congress.—Single Parents by Sex and Selected Characteristics, table, 2003. Adapted by Thomson Gale from data from the US Census Bureau. Reproduced by permission of Thomson Gale.—Slave family, photograph by T. H. O'Sullivan. The Library of Congress.—Social worker removing children from an abusive dwelling, illustration. © Bettmann/Corbis.—Social worker surveying a filthy garbage-strewn apartment while responding to a report of child abuse at this location, photograph. Steve Kagan/Time Life Pictures/Getty Images.—Soviet Union breadline, photograph. © Bettmann/Corbis.

Spock, Benjamin, Dr., holds an infant, photograph. © Douglas Kirkland/Corbis.—Steel cabins housing individual families at a labor camp for migratory workers, Visalia, California, March, 1940, photograph. © Corbis.—Students in a learning lab set up as part of the Human Genome exhibit, photograph. © George Steinmetz/Corbis.—Students saluting the American flag, photograph. © Bettmann/Corbis.—Suffrage movement postcard, 1910. © Lake County Museum/Corbis.—Tata and one of her children, photograph. © Brenda Ann Kenneally/Corbis.—Tenement wreath makers, photograph. © Corbis.—Thai toddler orphaned by AIDS virus, standing, hugging woman's legs, photograph. © Jeremy Horner/Corbis.—"The Brady Bunch," cast, photograph. The Kobal Collection. Reproduced by permission.—"The Foolish Virgins," painting by James Tissot. © Brooklyn Museum of Art/Corbis.—"The Fruits of Intemperance," illustration. © Museum of the City of New York/Corbis.—"The Fruits of Temperance," illustration. © Museum of the City of New York/Corbis.—"The Governess," painting by Richard Redgrave. © Stapleton Collection/Corbis.—"The Shadow of Danger," prohibition poster, ca. 1919-1933, photograph. © Corbis.—"There's Cheer in the Pictures from Home," poster. The Library of Congress.

Three children enjoy their meals at a tuberculosis health camp, September 15, 1938, photograph. © Bettmann/Corbis.—Tuberculosis poster. The Library of Congress.—U. S. soldiers with cameras, photograph. © Underwood & Underwood/Corbis.—"Unfair to Babies," poster. The Library of Congress.—Union Workers cigar box label, 1898. © Museum of the City of New York/Corbis.—Unwed mothers turning over their babies to a nurse in Foundling Hospital, London, photograph. © Bettmann/Corbis.—Unwed mothers ward at hospital, photograph. © Bettmann/Corbis.—Victorian woman sits reading with a young girl, photograph. © Hulton-Deutsch Collection/Corbis.—Victorian woman with her daughter, 1910, photograph. © Poodles/Rock/Corbis.—Vietnamese-American family, photograph. © Catherine Karnow/Corbis.—Volkswagen Minibus on the beach, photograph. © Sam Diephuiszefa/Corbis.—"We Invite Your Attention to Our Family Bible," advertisement. From the Duke University Archives and the Library of Congress. The Library of Congress.—Woman baking apple pie, photograph. © Bettmann/Corbis.—Woman rests her hand on a bible at the Full Council Christian Fellowship, North Little Rock, Arkansas, photograph. Katja Heinemann/Aurora/Getty Images.

Woman taking Syphilis test, photograph. © Bettmann/Corbis.—Women and children of German families help with the war effort, photograph. © Stapleton Collection/Corbis.—Working mother taking her daughter to school, photograph. © ROB & SAS/Corbis.—Wyatt, Jane, Robert Young, Billy Gray,

Lauren Chapin, and Elinor Donahue, photograph. AP Images.—Yamada, Masahiro, at Tokyo Gakugei University, photograph. AP Images.—Young, Brigham, and his family on their way to church, illustration. © Corbis.—Young, Brigham, in a room with nine young women, one girl, and a male guest, illustration. © Bettmann/Corbis.—"Your Family Needs Protection Against Syphilis," poster. The Library of Congress.

Copyrighted excerpts in *Family in Society: Essential Primary Sources* were reproduced from the following websites or other sources:

"ACLU Disappointed the Supreme Court Will Not Hear an Appeal in Case Challenging Florida's Anti-Gay Adoption Law," *ACLU.org*, January 10, 2005. Reproduced by permission.—Garner, Abigail, "Happy Father's Day," *All Things Considered, National Public Radio*, June 14, 2001. Reproduced by permission.—*The Internet and the Family 2000: The View from Parents, The View from Kids*, May, 2000. Reproduced by permission of Annenberg Public Policy Center.—Kaye, Jeffrey, "Revisiting and Immigrant Family," *Online NewsHour*, October 26, 2005. Copyright © 2005 MacNeil/Lehrer Productions. All rights reserved. Reproduced by permission.—Ramrayka, Liza, "The Young Career," *The Guardian (Online)*, 2006. Copyright Guardian Newspapers Limited 2006. Reproduced by permission of Guardian News Service, LTD.—Riddell, Mary, "Let's Celebrate. There's Never Been a Better Time for Mothers," *The Observer (Online)*, March 26, 2006. Copyright Guardian Newspapers Limited 2006. Reproduced by permission of Guardian News Service, LTD.—"Uniform Adoption Act (1994)," *National Conference of Commissioners on Uniform State Laws*, August 5, 1994. Reproduced by permission.

About the Set

Essential Primary Source titles are part of a ten-volume set of books in the Social Issues Primary Sources Collection designed to provide primary source documents on leading social issues of the nineteenth, twentieth, and twenty-first centuries. International in scope, each volume is devoted to one topic and will contain approximately 150 to 175 documents that will include and discuss speeches, legislation, magazine and newspaper articles, memoirs, letters, interviews, novels, essays, songs, and works of art essential to understanding the complexity of the topic.

Each entry will include standard subheads: key facts about the author; an introduction placing the piece in context; the full or excerpted document; a discussion of the significance of the document and related event; and a listing of further resources (books, periodicals, Web sites, and audio and visual media).

Each volume will contain a topic-specific introduction, topic-specific chronology of major events, an index especially prepared to coordinate with the volume topic, and approximately 150 images.

Volumes are intended to be sold individually or as a set.

THE ESSENTIAL PRIMARY SOURCE SERIES

- *Terrorism: Essential Primary Sources*
- *Medicine, Health, and Bioethics: Essential Primary Sources*
- *Environmental Issues: Essential Primary Sources*
- *Crime and Punishment: Essential Primary Sources*
- *Gender Issues and Sexuality: Essential Primary Sources*
- *Human and Civil Rights: Essential Primary Sources*
- *Government, Politics, and Protest: Essential Primary Sources*
- *Social Policy: Essential Primary Sources*
- *Immigration and Multiculturalism: Essential Primary Sources*
- *Family in Society: Essential Primary Sources*

Introduction

Family in Society: Essential Primary Sources provides readings into two centuries of changes in concepts, representations, and roles of the family in society. These changes lie at the core of social evolution because changes in family structure are often the measuring stick for social change. Moreover, the study of the family in society is key to understanding the degree to which the evolution of the family mirrors social change, or drives larger social change.

The term "family" is broadly applied. From groups of organisms with similar outward physical characteristics to organisms of common genetic lineage—from nurturing and closely bound social units of parents and children to loose confederations of organized criminals, the term family is used to denote a common link among individuals. Perhaps the most expansive expression of this commonality is humanity itself. The opening clauses of the United Nations Universal Declaration of Human Rights, for example, seek to articulate the equal and inalienable rights of all members of the "human family."

The resources in *Family in Society: Essential Primary Sources* provide evidence that concepts of families change, and that these changes are not always easily accomplished. Because the concept of family is so fundamental and personal, evolution of the family—a social necessity and certainty—is often viewed with fear and skepticism that fuels passionate political and social tensions. The primary sources contained in *Family in Society: Essential Primary Sources*, however, also provide evidence that families are resilient and that changes in the structures and functions of families not only reflect social robustness, but are essential in larger struggles for human equality and dignity.

The editors intend that *Family in Society: Essential Primary Sources* provides readers with a wide-ranging and readable collection of sources designed to stimulate interest and critical thinking, and to highlight the complexity of the issues and depth of passions related to the evolving concepts of family and its essential role in society.

K. Lee Lerner, Brenda Wilmoth Lerner, & Adrienne Wilmoth Lerner, editors

Paris, London, and Jacksonville, FL.
July, 2006

About the Entry

The primary source is the centerpiece and main focus of each entry in *Family in Society: Essential Primary Sources*. In keeping with the philosophy that much of the benefit from using primary sources derives from the reader's own process of inquiry, the contextual material surrounding each entry provides access and ease of use, as well as giving the reader a springboard for delving into the primary source. Rubrics identify each section and enable the reader to navigate entries with ease.

ENTRY STRUCTURE

- Primary Source/Entry Title, Subtitle, Primary Source Type
- Key Facts—essential information about the primary source, including creator, date, source citation, and notes about the creator.
- Introduction—historical background and contributing factors for the primary source.
- Primary Source—in text, text facsimile, or image format; full or excerpted.
- Significance—importance and impact of the primary source related events.
- Further Resources—books, periodicals, websites, and audio and visual material.

NAVIGATING AN ENTRY

Entry elements are numbered and reproduced here, with an explanation of the data contained in these elements explained immediately thereafter according to the corresponding numeral.

Primary Source/Entry Title, Subtitle, Primary Source Type

---

[1] # Myth of the Perfect Family

---

[3] **Book excerpt**

[1] **Primary Source/Entry Title:** The entry title is usually the primary source title. In some cases where long titles must be shortened, or more generalized topic titles are needed for clarity primary source titles are generally depicted as subtitles. Entry titles appear as catchwords at the top outer margin of each page.

[2] **Subtitle:** Some entries contain subtitles.

[3] **Primary Source Type:** The type of primary source is listed just below the title. When assigning source types, great weight was given to how the author of the primary source categorized the source.

Key Facts

[4] **By:** Edward L. Schor

[5] **Date:** 2000

[6] **Source:** Schor, Edward L., ed. *Caring for Your School-Age Child Ages 5 to 12.* New York: Bantam Books, 2000.

[7] **About the Author:** *About the Author:* A pediatrician by training, Edward L. Schor is assistant vice-president at the Commonwealth Fund, a private foundation that supports independent research on health and

social issues and makes grants to improve health care practice and policy. He has also served on the editorial boards of several pediatric journals.

[4] **Author, Artist, or Organization:** The name of the author, artist, or organization responsible for the creation of the primary source begins the Key Facts section.

[5] **Date of Origin:** The date of origin of the primary source appears in this field, and may differ from the date of publication in the source citation below it; for example, speeches are often delivered before they are published.

[6] **Source Citation:** The source citation is a full bibliographic citation, giving original publication data as well as reprint and/or online availability.

[7] **About the Author:** A brief bio of the author or originator of the primary source gives birth and death dates and a quick overview of the person's work. This rubric has been customized in some cases. If the primary source is a written document, the term "author" appears; however, if the primary source is a work of art, the term "artist" is used, showing the person's direct relationship to the primary source. For primary sources created by a group, "organization" may have been used instead of "author." Other terms may also be used to describe the creator or originator of the primary source. If an author is anonymous or unknown, a brief "About the Publication" sketch may appear.

Introduction Essay

[8] **INTRODUCTION**

Among the most significant societal changes during the 1800s was the emergence of the urban middle-class. Prior to American industrialization, men and women typically labored on farms, sharing jobs as appropriate and making or growing most of what they needed to survive. As Americans migrated to cities and men took professional jobs in factories and offices, however, the work roles of men and women became increasingly distinct.

The role of homemaker soon became imbued with almost spiritual qualities. One perspective, known to its detractors as the cult of domesticity or the cult of true womanhood, portrayed the role of wife and mother as the highest calling a woman could heed; proponents of this philosophy also offered detailed guidance on how a woman might excel in this calling. This philosophy included four virtues that any true woman should embody: piety, purity, submissiveness, and domesticity. According to this perspective a man

might choose from thousands of occupations, but a woman was divinely intended for only one.

The specifics of domesticity were extensively discussed in women's books and magazines of the mid–1800s. The repetitive tasks of housekeeping, such as dusting furniture and making beds, were claimed to provide excellent exercise, as well as develop self-discipline. While others might refer to women's rights as something to be fought for and won, true women were encouraged to see their roles as mother, wife, cook, and housekeeper as divine rights, more than adequate for a fulfilling, though potentially overwhelming life. Writing in 1864, author and homemaker Lydia Child summarized her year's labor: In addition to daily cooking and cleaning, she had also canned fruit, cared for numerous sick children, mended clothing, and sewn linens for the home.

While the cult of domesticity bestowed a high value on a woman's daily work, it also placed upon her an inordinate amount of responsibility. Women were viewed as the sexual moderators of society and were frequently blamed for men's infidelity; an unfaithful husband was frequently assumed to have wandered due to his wife's inattention. Despite limited resources and little spending discretion women were frequently blamed if a family's clothing and general appearance were shoddy or if the house was not up to current standards. And in cases where children broke the law or otherwise strayed, their mothers, perceived to control their destinies, were frequently blamed.

Once they had been convinced of domesticity's profound value, women were given numerous suggestions as to how this ideal might be achieved. In legalistic fashion women often struggled to meet self-imposed quotas on household tasks, convinced that their family's success and their husband's happiness rested squarely on their frail shoulders.

Just as the push for domesticity was reaching full steam, reformers such as Susan B. Anthony began campaigning for women's equality—both legal and social. Thanks to their efforts, women received the right to vote in 1920. While women's rights continued to increase during the twentieth century, however, the 1950s saw a resurgence of the domesticity ideal. As marketers sought to sell new domestic tools and services, they quickly reverted to the ideals of a century before, with advertisements showing attractively dressed women in high heels vacuuming or washing dishes. Some commercials explained how much happier women would be if their houses were kept spotless, while others suggested that a husband's lack of physical interest might be his wife's fault and conveniently recommended a solution for purchase.

By the dawn of the twenty-first century, American families were more diverse than ever before; fewer than one family in five consisted of two parents and their biological children. Despite this change and over a century of advances in women's rights, some mothers still worried that they might be making a mess of their families. Ironically, some of the same myths perpetrated by nineteenth century domesticity still haunt mothers today.

[8] Introduction: The introduction is a brief essay on the contributing factors and historical context of the primary source. Intended to promote understanding and equip the reader with essential facts to understand the context of the primary source.

To maintain ease of reference to the primary source, spellings of names and places are used in accord with their use in the primary source. Accordingly names and places may have different spellings in different articles. Whenever possible, alternative spellings are provided to provide clarity.

To the greatest extent possible we have attempted to use Arabic names instead of their Latinized versions. Where required for clarity we have included Latinized names in parentheses after the Arabic version. Alas, we could not retain some diacritical marks (e.g. bars over vowels, dots under consonants). Because there is no generally accepted rule or consensus regarding the format of translated Arabic names, we have adopted the straightforward, and we hope sensitive, policy of using names as they are used or cited in their region of origin.

Primary Source

[9] PRIMARY SOURCE

The American family is a rapidly changing institution. You may have grown up in the stereotypical American family—two parents and one or more children, with a father who worked outside the home and a mother who stayed home and cared for the children and the household. Today, with the entry of so many more women into the workforce, with the increasing divorce rate, and with the growing number of single-parent households, other family structures have become more common.

If your own family is not like the one you grew up in, your situation is certainly not unusual. Currently, thirty percent of American families are now headed by single parents, either divorced, widowed, or never married. Some children live in foster families; others live in step-families or in gay and lesbian families. In more than two thirds of families, both parents work outside the home.

Even if your own family fits the more traditional mold, your children will almost certainly have some friends who live in households with different structures. From time to time you can expect your youngsters to ask questions like "Why do people get divorced?" "How come Jimmy's mother and father don't live together?" "Why does Annette's father live with another lady?" Because families are so important to children, parents need to be able to answer such questions with more than mere slogans or quick replies. By asking these questions, children are trying to understand two things about families: the different structures that families can take and the changes in structure, lifestyles and relationships that can occur.

Any group of people living together in a household can create and call themselves a family. For example, to share expenses a divorced mother with two children may live with another divorced woman with children; together, they may consider themselves a family. A grandparent who lives with her daughter, son-in-law, and grandchildren may become an integral part of their family. The variations of family structures and definition are almost endless, but they have certain qualities in common: Family members share their lives emotionally and together fulfill the multiple responsibilities of family life.

MYTH: The "nuclear family" is a universal phenomenon.

The nuclear family is generally defined as a family group made up of only a father, mother, and children. Although most people tend to think that this particular family structure has always been the dominant one, that is not the case.

The nuclear family is a relatively recent phenomenon, becoming common only within the last century. Before then, the "traditional" family was multigenerational, with grandparents often living with their children on farms as well as in urban environments, typically with other relatives living nearby. The nuclear family has evolved in response to a number of factors: better health and longer lives, economic development, industrialization, urbanization, geographic mobility, and migration to the suburbs. These changes have resulted in physical separation of extended-family members and in progressive fragmentation of the family.

MYTH: Family harmony is the rule, not the exception.

Although family life is often romanticized, it has always been filled with conflicts and tension. Difficulties between spouses are commonplace, with disagreements arising over issues ranging from how the children should be raised to how the family finances should be budgeted. Husbands and wives also often struggle with their inability to sustain romantic infatuation beyond the first few years of their marriage, thus having to learn to maintain a relationship in which partnership and companionship may become more important than passionate love.

Parent-children conflicts are commonplace too. As parents assert their authority, and children try to assert their autonomy appropriately, strife is inevitable.

While we often expect families to be above the chaos that exists in the rest of society, that outlook places unrealistic expectations upon the family. In the real world, families are not always a haven, since they, too, can be filled with conflict. Although stress and disagreements are common, they can be destructive to families, especially when conflict gets out of hand. Families are under constant stress, being pushed and pulled from many directions, often without the support systems of extended families that may have existed in the past.

MYTH: The stability of a family is a measure of its success.

Change is a part of life. Death, illness, physical separation, financial strains, divorce ... these are some of the events families have to adjust to. Consequently, stability shouldn't be the only measure of a family's success. Many families function quite well, despite frequent disruptions. In fact, one important measure of a family's success is its ability to adjust to change. Daily life is full of stresses that constantly demand accommodation from family members.

MYTH: Parents control their children's fate.

In reality, parents cannot determine how their children will turn out. Inevitably, children assert their autonomy, creating a niche for themselves separate from their parents. At the same time, many factors external to both the child and family can influence the way a child develops.

Even within the same family there can be tremendous individual variations among siblings in intelligence, temperament, mood, and sociability. Yet despite these differences, parents are responsible for imparting to each child a sense of being loved and accepted, for helping each child to succeed at various developmental tasks, and for socializing each child into respecting the rules and accepting the responsibilities society imposes. These are indeed awesome tasks.

Some parents perceive themselves as having total responsibility for their children's fate. This belief places a heavy and unrealistic emotional burden on them as well as their youngsters. If the children are having problems, they often feel a sense of failure; likewise, the children feel as though they have let their family down if they do not live up to their parents' expectations. In essence, parents can influence and shape but cannot control their children's lives.

[9] **Primary Source:** The majority of primary sources are reproduced as plain text. The primary source may appear excerpted or in full, and may appear as text, text facsimile (photographic reproduction of the original text), image, or graphic display (such as a table, chart, or graph).

The font and leading of the primary sources are distinct from that of the context—to provide a visual clue to the change, as well as to facilitate ease of reading. As needed, the original formatting of the text is preserved in order to more accurately represent the original (screenplays, for example). In order to respect the integrity of the primary sources, content some readers may consider sensitive (for example, the use of slang, ethnic or racial slurs, etc.) is retained when deemed to be integral to understanding the source and the context of its creation.

Primary source images (whether photographs, text facsimiles, or graphic displays) are bordered with a distinctive double rule. Most images have brief captions.

The term "narrative break" appears where there is a significant amount of elided (omitted) material with the text provided (for example, excerpts from a work's first and fifth chapters, selections from a journal article abstract and summary, or dialogue from two acts of a play).

Significance Essay

[10] **SIGNIFICANCE**

As American families become increasingly diverse, some traditional parenting advice has become less useful. Many Americans' perceptions of the ideal family developed from watching 1950s television shows such as *Leave it to Beaver* and *Ozzie and Harriet*, shows that even in their era portrayed a simplified, sanitized version of American family life. Given the societal changes in the half-century since these shows originally aired, their relevance to many of today's families appears quite limited. According to a 2005 survey conducted by the United States Census Bureau, for the first time in the nation's history, fewer than twenty-five percent of American households are composed of a married man and woman with their children. Since the 1970s, the number of households headed by single mothers has increased, and since the late 1990s, the number of households with at least one member of three generations of family living together is again on the rise.

Although the roles of parents continue to change and the challenges facing families are becoming more complex, today's parents have access to far more abundant resources than did their predecessors. Modern parents are typically better educated than their parents were, with access to literally hundreds of books, videos, and seminars on improving parenting skills. The modern family can never achieve perfection, but successful parents acknowledge and accept that limitation. Parenting in the twenty-first century, just as in the nineteenth, requires patience, persistence, and a willingness to make mistakes in pursuit of a healthy family life.

[10] **Significance:** The significance discusses the importance and impact of the primary source and the event it describes.

Further Resources

[11] **FURTHER RESOURCES**

Books

DuBois, Ellen Carol. *Feminism and Suffrage: The Emergence of an Independent Women's Movement in America, 1849–1869.* New York: Cornell University Press, 1978.

Safer, Jeanne. *Beyond Motherhood: Choosing a Life without Children.* New York: Pocket Books, 1996.

Warner, Judith. *Perfect Madness: Motherhood in the Age of Anxiety.* New York: Riverhead Books, 2005.

Periodicals

MacInnes, John. "Work-Life Balance in Europe: A Response to the Baby Bust or Reward for the Baby Boomers." *European Societies.* 8 (2006): 223–249.

Welter, Barbara. "The Cult of True Womanhood: 1820–1860." *American Quarterly.* 18, no. 2, part 1 (Summer 1966):151–174.

Web sites

Musee McCord Museum. "The Cult of Domesticity." June 8, 2006 <http://www.mccord-museum.qc.ca/en/keys/folders/VQ_P1_6_EN> (accessed June 17, 2006).

Public Broadcasting Service. "Cult of True Womanhood." <http://www.pbs.org/stantonanthony/resources/index.html?body=culthood.html> (accessed June 17, 2006).

[11] **Further Resources:** A brief list of resources categorized as Books, Periodicals, Web sites, and Audio and Visual Media provides a stepping stone to further study.

SECONDARY SOURCE CITATION FORMATS (HOW TO CITE ARTICLES AND SOURCES)

Alternative forms of citations exist and examples of how to cite articles from this book are provided below:

APA Style

Books:

Aikman, William. (1870). *Life at Home, or The Family and its Members.* New York: Samuel R. Wells. Excerpted in K. Lee Lerner and Brenda Wilmoth Lerner, eds., (2006) *Family in Society: Essential Primary Sources,* Farmington Hills, Mich.: Thomson Gale.

Periodicals:

Lundberg, Shelley, and Robert A. Pollak. (1996). "Bargaining and Distribution in Marriage." *Journal of Economic Perspectives.* 10, 139. Excerpted in K. Lee Lerner and Brenda Wilmoth Lerner, eds., (2006) *Family in Society: Essential Primary Sources,* Farmington Hills, Mich.: Thomson Gale.

Web sites:

U.S. Census Bureau. "America's Families and Living Arrangements: 2003 Population Characteristics." (November 2004). Retrieved from http://www.census.gov/prod/2004pubs/p20-553.pdf. Excerpted in K. Lee Lerner and Brenda Wilmoth Lerner, eds., (2006) *Family in Society: Essential Primary Sources,* Farmington Hills, Mich.: Thomson Gale.

Chicago Style

Books:

Aikman, William. *Life at Home, or The Family and its Members.* New York: Samuel R. Wells, 1870. Excerpted in K. Lee Lerner and Brenda Wilmoth Lerner, eds., *Family in Society: Essential Primary Sources,* Farmington Hills, Mich.: Thomson Gale, 2006.

Periodicals:

Lundberg, Shelley, and Robert A. Pollak. "Bargaining and Distribution in Marriage." *Journal of Economic Perspectives.* 10 (1996): 139. Excerpted in K. Lee Lerner and Brenda Wilmoth Lerner, eds., *Family in Society: Essential Primary Sources,* Farmington Hills, Mich.: Thomson Gale, 2006.

Web sites:

U.S. Census Bureau. "America's Families and Living Arrangements: 2003 Population Characteristics." November 2004. <http://www.census.gov/prod/2004pubs/p20-553.pdf> (accessed June 24, 2006). Excerpted in K. Lee Lerner and Brenda Wilmoth Lerner, eds., *Family in Society: Essential Primary Sources,* Farmington Hills, Mich.: Thomson Gale, 2006.

MLA Style

Books:

Aikman, William. *Life at Home, or The Family and its Members,* New York: Samuel R. Wells, 1870. Excerpted in K. Lee Lerner and Brenda Wilmoth Lerner, eds., *Family in Society: Essential Primary Sources,* Farmington Hills, Mich.: Thomson Gale, 2006.

Periodicals:

Lundberg, Shelley, and Robert A. Pollak. "Bargaining and Distribution in Marriage." *Journal of Economic Perspectives*. 10, 1996: 139. Excerpted in K. Lee Lerner and Brenda Wilmoth Lerner, eds., *Family in Society: Essential Primary Sources*, Farmington Hills, Mich.: Thomson Gale, 2006.

Web sites:

"America's Families and Living Arrangements: 2003 Population Characteristics." November 2004. *U.S. Census Bureau*. 24 June, 2006. <http://www.census.gov/prod/2004pubs/p20-553.pdf> Excerpted in K. Lee Lerner and Brenda Wilmoth Lerner, eds., *Family in Society: Essential Primary Sources*, Farmington Hills, Mich.: Thomson Gale, 2006.

Turabian Style

Books:

Aikman, William. *Life at Home, or The Family and its Members*. (New York: Samuel R. Wells, 1870). Excerpted in K. Lee Lerner and Brenda Wilmoth Lerner, eds., *Family in Society: Essential Primary Sources* (Farmington Hills, Mich.: Thomson Gale, 2006).

Periodicals:

Lundberg, Shelley, and Robert A. Pollak. "Bargaining and Distribution in Marriage." *Journal of Economic Perspectives* 10 (1996): 139. Excerpted in K. Lee Lerner and Brenda Wilmoth Lerner, eds., *Family in Society: Essential Primary Sources* (Farmington Hills, Mich.: Thomson Gale, 2006).

Web sites:

U.S. Census Bureau. "America's Families and Living Arrangements: 2003 Population Characteristics." available from http://www.census.gov/prod/2004pubs/p20-553.pdf; accessed 24 June, 2006. Excerpted in K. Lee Lerner and Brenda Wilmoth Lerner, eds., *Family in Society: Essential Primary Sources* (Farmington Hills, Mich.: Thomson Gale, 2006).

Using Primary Sources

The definition of what constitutes a primary source is often the subject of scholarly debate and interpretation. Although primary sources come from a wide spectrum of resources, they are united by the fact that they individually provide insight into the historical *milieu* (context and environment) during which they were produced. Primary sources include materials such as newspaper articles, press dispatches, autobiographies, essays, letters, diaries, speeches, song lyrics, posters, works of art—and in the twenty-first century, web logs—that offer direct, first-hand insight or witness to events of their day.

Categories of primary sources include:

- Documents containing firsthand accounts of historic events by witnesses and participants. This category includes diary or journal entries, letters, email, newspaper articles, interviews, memoirs, and testimony in legal proceedings.
- Documents or works representing the official views of both government leaders and leaders of terrorist organizations. These include primary sources such as policy statements, speeches, interviews, press releases, government reports, and legislation.
- Works of art, including (but certainly not limited to) photographs, poems, and songs, including advertisements and reviews of those works that help establish an understanding of the cultural milieu (the cultural environment with regard to attitudes and perceptions of events).
- Secondary sources. In some cases, secondary sources or tertiary sources may be treated as primary sources. In some cases articles and sources are created many years after an event. Ordinarily,

a historical retrospective published after the initial event is not considered a primary source. If, however, a resource contains statements or recollections of participants or witnesses to the original event, the source may be considered primary with regard to those statements and recollections.

ANALYSIS OF PRIMARY SOURCES

The material collected in this volume is not intended to provide a comprehensive overview of a topic or event. Rather, the primary sources are intended to generate interest and lay a foundation for further inquiry and study.

In order to properly analyze a primary source, readers should remain skeptical and develop probing questions about the source. As in reading a chemistry or algebra textbook, historical documents require readers to analyze them carefully and extract specific information. However, readers must also read "beyond the text" to garner larger clues about the social impact of the primary source.

In addition to providing information about their topics, primary sources may also supply a wealth of insight into their creator's viewpoint. For example, when reading a news article about an outbreak of disease, consider whether the reporter's words also indicate something about his or her origin, bias (an irrational disposition in favor of someone or something), prejudices (an irrational disposition against someone or something), or intended audience.

Students should remember that primary sources often contain information later proven to be false, or contain viewpoints and terms unacceptable to future generations. It is important to view the primary source within the historical and social context existing at its creation. If for example, a newspaper article is written within hours or days of an event, later developments may reveal some assertions in the original article as false or misleading.

TEST NEW CONCLUSIONS AND IDEAS

Whatever opinion or working hypothesis the reader forms, it is critical that they then test that hypothesis against other facts and sources related to the incident. For example, it might be wrong to conclude that factual mistakes are deliberate unless evidence can be produced of a pattern and practice of such mistakes with an intent to promote a false idea.

The difference between sound reasoning and preposterous conspiracy theories (or the birth of urban legends) lies in the willingness to test new ideas against other sources, rather than rest on one piece of evidence such as a single primary source that may contain errors. Sound reasoning requires that arguments and assertions guard against argument fallacies that utilize the following:

- false dilemmas (only two choices are given when in fact there are three or more options)
- arguments from ignorance (*argumentum ad ignorantiam*; because something is not known to be true, it is assumed to be false)
- possibilist fallacies (a favorite among conspiracy theorists who attempt to demonstrate that a factual statement is true or false by establishing the possibility of its truth or falsity. An argument

where "it could be" is usually followed by an unearned "therefore, it is.")
- slippery slope arguments or fallacies (a series of increasingly dramatic consequences is drawn from an initial fact or idea)
- begging the question (the truth of the conclusion is assumed by the premises)
- straw man arguments (the arguer mischaracterizes an argument or theory and then attacks the merits of their own false representations)
- appeals to pity or force (the argument attempts to persuade people to agree by sympathy or force)
- prejudicial language (values or moral judgments are attached to certain arguments or facts)
- personal attacks (*ad hominem*; an attack on a person's character or circumstances)
- anecdotal or testimonial evidence (stories that are unsupported by impartial facts or data that is not reproducible)
- *post hoc* (after the fact) fallacies (because one thing follows another, it is held to cause the other)
- the fallacy of the appeal to authority (the argument rests upon the credentials of a person, not the evidence).

Despite the fact that some primary sources can contain false information or lead readers to false conclusions based on the "facts" presented, they remain an invaluable resource regarding past events. Primary sources allow readers and researchers to come as close as possible to understanding the perceptions and context of events and thus, to more fully appreciate how and why misconceptions occur.

Chronology

So that the events in this volume may be placed in a larger historical context, the following is a general chronology of important historical and social events along with specific events related to the subject of this volume.

1750–1799

1772: England outlaws slavery.

1775: James Watt invents the steam engine. The invention marks the start of the Industrial Revolution.

1776: Declaration of Independence proclaims American colonies' independence from the British Empire.

1781: The thirteenth state ratifies the Articles of Confederation, creating the United States.

1785: *The Daily Universal Register*, later known as *The Times* (London), publishes its first issue.

1786: The United States establishes first Native American reservation.

1786: Britain establishes its first colony in Southeast Asia, beginning an age of European colonial expansion in Asia.

1787: The Constitutional Convention in Philadelphia adopts the U.S. Constitution.

1787: The Society for the Abolition of the Slave Trade is established in Britain.

1789: First nationwide election in the United States.

1789: Citizens of Paris storm the Bastille prison. The event ignites the French Revolution.

1789: Declaration of the Rights of Man is issued in France.

1790: The federal government established residency requirements for naturalization

1790: First U.S. census is taken.

1791: The states ratify the Bill of Rights, the first ten amendments to the U.S. Constitution.

1793: Louis XVI, King of France, is guillotined by revolutionaries.

1793: "Reign of Terror" begins in France. Almost 40,000 people face execution.

1794: The French Republic abolishes slavery.

1796: Edward Jenner administers the first vaccination for smallpox.

1798: Irish tenant farmers rebel against British landowners in the Irish Rebellion of 1798.

1798: The United States enacts the Alien and Sedition Acts making it a federal crime to "write, publish, or utter false or malicious statements" about the United States government.

1800–1849

1800: World population reaches one billion.

1801: Union of Great Britain and Ireland.

1803: Napoleonic Wars begin. Napoleon's army conquers much of Europe before Napoleon is defeated at Waterloo in 1815.

1803: The United States pays France $15 million for the Louisiana Territory extending from the Mississippi River to the Rocky Mountains.

1808: The importation of slaves is outlawed in the United States, but the institution of African slavery continues until 1864.

1812: The North American War of 1812 between the United States and the United Kingdom of Great Britain and Ireland. The war lasts until the beginning of 1815.

1814: The Congress of Vienna redraws the map of Europe after the defeat of Napoleon.

1819: Congress mandates immigration reports.

1819: South American colonial revolutions begin when Columbia declares its independence from Spain in 1819.

1820: Temperance movement begins in United States.

1821: Mexico declares independence from Spain.

1821: Jean-Louis Prévost (1790–1850), Swiss physician, jointly publishes a paper with French chemist Jean-Baptiste-André Dumas (1800–1884) which demonstrates for the first time that spermatozoa originate in tissues of the male sex glands. In 1824 they also give the first detailed account of the segmentation of a frog's egg.

1822: American Colonization Society advocates the repatriation of freed African slaves to the Colony of Liberia.

1822: Jean-François Champollion (1790–1832), French historian and linguist, deciphers Egyptian hieroglyphics using the Rosetta Stone. He is the first to realize that some of the signs are alphabetic, some syllabic, and some determinative (standing for a whole idea or object previously expressed).

1822: William Church (c.1778–1863), American-English inventor, patents a machine that sets type. Patented in Boston, his machine consists of a keyboard on which each key releases a piece of letter type that is stored in channels in a magazine.

1829: Lambert-Adolphe-Jacques Quetelet (1796–1874), Belgian statistician and astronomer, gives the first statistical breakdown of a national census. He correlates death with age, sex, occupation, and economic status in the Belgian census.

1830: Indian Removal Act forces the removal of Native Americans living in the eastern part of the United States.

1831: Charles Robert Darwin began his historic voyage on the H.M.S. *Beagle* (1831–1836). His observations during the voyage lead to his theory of evolution by means of natural selection.

1832: The advent of the telegraph.

1833: A washboard is patented in the United States. This simple wooden-framed device has a corrugated rectangular surface that is used for scrubbing clothes clean.

1835: Rubber nipples are introduced for infant nursing bottles.

1836: Johann Nikolaus von Dreyse (1787–1867), German inventor, patents the "needle" rifle with a bolt breech-loading mechanism. This gun is loaded through the rear of the barrel.

1838: More than 15,000 Cherokee Indians are forced to march from Georgia to present-day Oklahoma on the "Trail of Tears."

1838: Samuel Finley Breese Morse (1791–1872) and Alfred Vail (1807–1859) unveil their telegraph system.

1839: Theodore Schwann (1810–1882), German physiologist, extends the theory of cells from plants to animals. He states in his book, *Mikroscopische Untersuchungen*, that all living things are made up of cells, each of which contains certain essential components. He also coins the term "metabolism" to describe the overall chemical changes that take place in living tissue.

1840: John William Draper (1811–1882), American chemist, takes a daguerreotype portrait of his sister, Dorothy. This is the oldest surviving photograph of a person.

1840: Pierre-Charles-Alexandre Louis (1787–1872), French physician, pioneers medical statistics, being the first to compile systematically records of diseases and treatments.

1841: Horace Greeley (1811–1872), American editor and publisher, founds the *New York Tribune*, which eventually becomes the *Herald Tribune* after a merger in 1924.

1842: John Benne Lawes (1814–1900), English agriculturalist, patents a process for treating phosphate rock with sulfuric acid to produce superphosphate. He also opens the first fertilizer factory this year, thus beginning the artificial fertilizer industry.

1842: Samuel Finley Breese Morse (1791–1872), American artist and inventor, lays the first underwater telegraph cable in New York Harbor. It fails due to a lack of proper insulation materials.

1842: The first shipment of milk by rail in the United States is successfully accomplished.

1844: Robert Chambers (1802–1871), Scottish publisher, publishes anonymously his *Vestiges of the Natural History of Creation*. This best-selling book offers a sweeping view of evolution and although incorrect in many specifics, it does pave the way for Darwin's theory by familiarizing the public with evolutionary concepts.

1845: The potato famine begins in Ireland. Crop failures and high rents on tenant farms cause a three-year famine. Millions of Irish immigrate to flee starvation.

1846: Mexican War begins as United States attempts to expand its territory in the Southwest.

1846: Oliver Wendall Holmes (1809–1894), American author and physician, first suggests the use of the terms "anaesthesia" and "anaesthetic" in a letter to William Thomas Green Morton (1819–1868), American dentist.

1847: Claude-Felix-Abel-Niepce de Saint-Victor (1805–1870) of France first uses light sensitive materials on glass for photographs. He coats a glass plate with albumen containing iodide of potassium which, after drying, is coated with aceto-silver nitrate, washed in distilled water, and exposed.

1847: John Collins Warren (1778–1856), American surgeon, introduces ether anesthesia for general surgery. It is soon taken up worldwide as an essential part of surgery.

1847: Richard March Hoe (1812–1886), American inventor and manufacturer, patents what proves to be the first successful rotary printing press. He discards the old flatbed press and places the type on a revolving cylinder. This revolutionary system is first used by the *Philadelphia Public Ledger* this same year, and it produces 8,000 sheets per hour printed on one side.

1848: Karl Marx publishes *The Communist Manifesto.*

1848: Delegates at the Seneca Falls Convention on Woman Rights advocate equal property and voting rights for women.

1848: Series of political conflicts and violent revolts erupt in several European nations. The conflicts are collectively known as the Revolution of 1848.

1848: A group of six New York newspapers form an association or news agency to share telegraph costs. It is later called the Associated Press.

1848: The first large-scale department store opens in the United States. The Marble Dry Goods Palace in New York occupies an entire city block.

1849: Gold fever sparks mass immigration to the United States from China.

1849: First woman to receive a medical degree in the United States is Elizabeth Blackwell (1821–1910). She graduates this year from Geneva College (now a part of Syracuse University) in New York.

1849: John Snow (1813–1858), English physician, first states the theory that cholera is a water-borne disease and that it is usually contracted by drinking. During a cholera epidemic in London in 1854, Snow breaks the handle of the Broad Street Pump, thereby shutting down what he considered to be the main public source of the epidemic.

1850–1899

1850: Fugitive Slave Act passed in U.S..

1851: James Harrison, Scottish-Australian inventor, builds the first vapor-compression refrigerating machinery to be used in a brewery.

1851: James T. King of the United States invents a washing machine that uses a rotating cylinder. It is hand-powered and made for home use.

1852: Harriet Beecher Stowe's novel *Uncle Tom's Cabin* is published. It becomes one of the most influential works to stir anti-slavery sentiments.

1854: Crimean War begins between Russia and allied forces of Great Britain, Sardinia, France, and the Ottoman Empire.

1854: Violent conflicts erupt between pro-and anti-slavery settlers in Kansas Territory. The "Bleeding Kansas" violence lasts five years.

1854: Florence Nightingale (1823–1910), English nurse, takes charge of a barracks hospital when the Crimean War breaks out. Through dedication and hard work, she goes on to create a female nursing service and a nursing school at St. Thomas' Hospital (1860). Her compassion and common sense approach to nursing set new standards and create a new era in the history of the sick and wounded.

1854: Cyrus West Field (1819–1892), American financier, forms the New York, Newfoundland and London telegraph Company and proposes to lay a transatlantic telegraph cable.

1855: Alfred Russel Wallace (1823–1913), English naturalist, publishes his paper "On The Law Which Has Regulated the Introduction of New Species." Although this is written before Wallace conceives of the notion of natural selection, it shows him in the process of anticipating Darwin.

1856: *Illustrated London News* becomes the first periodical to include regular color plates.

1857: Supreme Court of the United States decision in *Dred Scott v. Sanford* holds that slaves are not citizens and that Congress cannot prohibit slavery in the individual states.

1857: The Indian Mutiny revolt against British colonial rule in India begins.

1858: The transatlantic cable is first opened with an exchange of greetings between English Queen Victoria (1819–1901) and U. S. President James Buchanan (1791–1868). Several weeks later, a telegraph operator applies too much voltage and ruins the cable connection.

1858: Mary Anna Elson (1833–1884), German-American physician, is the first Jewish woman to graduate from the Women's Medical College of Philadelphia. She practices in Philadelphia and later in Indiana.

1859: Charles Robert Darwin (1809–1882), English naturalist, publishes his landmark work *On the Origin of Species by Means of Natural Selection.* This classic of science establishes the mechanism of natural selection of favorable, inherited traits or variations as the mechanism of his theory of evolution.

1859: Ferdinand Carré (1824–1900), French inventor, introduces a refrigeration machine that uses ammonia as a refrigerant and water as the absorbent. This method becomes widely adopted.

1860: Repression in Poland sparks immigration to America.

1860: The U. S. Congress institutes the U. S. Government Printing Office in Washington, D. C.

1861: The Civil War begins in the United States.

1861: The popular press begins in England with the publication of the *Daily Telegraph.*

1862: The American Homestead Act allows any male over the age of twenty-one and the head of a family to claim up to 160 acres of land and improve it within five years or to purchase the land at a small fee.

1864: The United States legalizes importation of contract laborers.

1864: U.S. President Abraham Lincoln issues the Emancipation Proclamation, freeing the slaved in Union-occupied lands.

1865: The Civil War ends with the surrender of the secession states. The United States is reunified.

1865: President Lincoln is assassinated by John Wilkes Booth.

1865: The Thirteenth and Fourteenth Amendments to the U.S. Constitution are ratified. The Thirteenth Amendment outlaws slavery; the Fourteenth Amendment names all persons born or naturalized in the United States as U.S. citizens and extends equal protection under the law.

1867: Britain grants Canada home rule.

1868: The Fourteenth Amendment of the Constitution endows African Americans with citizenship.

1869: Japanese laborers start to arrive *en masse* in Hawaii.

1869: The first transcontinental railroad across the United States is completed.

1870: The Franco-Prussian War (1870–1871) begins.

1871: The era of New Imperialism, or "empire for empire's sake," starts a multinational competition for colonies in Africa, Asia, and the Middle East.

1871: Charles Robert Darwin (1809–1882), English naturalist, publishes his *The Descent of Man, and Selection in Relation to Sex.* This work extends his theory of evolution by applying it to humans.

1874: Thomas Alva Edison (1847–1931), American inventor, perfects his quadruplex telegraph. It is able to transmit two messages over one telegraph line or four messages in each direction over two wires.

1875: Robert Augustus Chesebrough (1837–1933), American manufacturer, first introduces petrolatum, which becomes known by its product name of Vaseline. This smooth, semisolid blend of mineral oil with waxes crystallized from petroleum becomes useful as a lubricant, carrier, and waterproofing agent in many products.

1876: Alexander Bell files for a patent for the telephone.

1876: Robert Koch (1843–1910), German bacteriologist, is able to cultivate the anthrax bacteria in culture outside the body. He then studies its life cycle and learns how to defeat it. During the next six years, Koch isolates the tubercle bacillus and discovers the cause of cholera.

1876: The American Library Association is founded in Philadelphia, Pennsylvania by American librarian, Melvil Dewey (1851–1931), the founder of the decimal system of library classification.

1877: Reconstruction, the period of rebuilding and reunification following the U.S. Civil War, ends.

1879: Albert Ludwig Siegmund Neisser (1855–1916), German dermatologist, discovers gonococcus, the pus-producing bacterium that causes gonorrhea.

1879: John Shaw Billings (1838–1913), American surgeon, and Robert Fletcher (1823–1912) of England issue the first volume of *Index Medicus.* This massive medical bibliography is initially arranged by author and subject and continues today.

1880: Difficult conditions in Italy spur start of mass immigration to America.

1880: Louis Pasteur (1822–1895), French chemist, first isolates and describes both streptococcus and staphylococcus (both in puerperal septicemia).

1882: Russian poverty and oppression spurs immigration to the United States.

1882: The Chinese Exclusion Act of 1882 temporarily halts immigration of Chinese laborers.

1883: *Journal of the American Medical Association* is first published.

1884: International conference is held at Washington, D. C., at which Greenwich, England, is chosen as the common prime meridian for the entire world.

1885: The United States bans the importation of contract laborers.

1885: Karl Benz invents in automobile in Germany.

1885: Edouard van Beneden (1846–1910), Belgian cytologist, proves that chromosomes persist between cell divisions. He makes the first chromosome count and discovers that each species has a fixed number of chromosomes. He also discovers that in the formation of sex cells, the division of chromosomes during one of the cell divisions was not preceded by a doubling.

1885: James Leonard Corning (1855–1923), American surgeon, is the first to use cocaine as a spinal anesthetic.

1885: Louis Pasteur (1822–1895), French chemist, inoculates a boy, Joseph Meister, against rabies. He had been bitten by a mad dog and the treatment saves his life. This is the first case of Pasteur's use of an attenuated germ on a human being.

1886: Richard von Krafft-Ebing (1840–1902), German neurologist, publishes his landmark case history study of sexual abnormalities, *Psychopathia Sexualis*, and helps found the scientific consideration of human sexuality.

1887: The Dawes Act passed.

1887: Theodor Boveri observes the reduction division during meiosis in *Ascaris* and confirmed August Weismann's predictions of chromosome reduction during the formation of the sex cells.

1888: First incubator for infants in the United States is built by William C. Deming.

1888: Heinrich Wilhelm Gottfried Waldeyer-Hartz (1836–1921), German anatomist, first introduces the word "chromosomes."

1889: Oklahoma land rush begins for white settlers.

1889: Francis Galton (1822–1911), English anthropologist, culminates his work on inheritance and variation with his book *Natural Inheritance*. It influences Karl Pearson and begins the science of biometrics or the statistical analysis of biological observations and phenomena.

1889: Pasteur Institute first opens in Paris.

1889: Richard Altmann (1852–1900), German histologist, isolates and names nucleic acid.

1890: The U.S. Census Bureau announces that the American frontier is closed.

1890: Herman Hollerith (1860–1929), American inventor, puts his electric sorting and tabulating machines to work on the U. S. Census. He wins this contract after a trial "run-off" with two other rival systems and his system performs in one year what would have taken eight years of hand tabulating. This marks the beginning of modern data processing.

1891: Maximilian Franz Joseph Wolf (1863–1932), German astronomer, adapts photography to the study of asteroids and demonstrates that stars appear as points in photographs while asteroids show up as short streaks. He makes the first discovery of an asteroid from photographs and during his lifetime discovers over 500 asteroids in this manner.

1891: Hermann Henking (1858–1942), German zoologist, describes sex chromosomes and autosomes.

1892: Ellis Island becomes chief immigration station of the eastern United States.

1893: Panic of 1893 triggers a three-year economic depression in the United States.

1893: Sigmund Freud (1856–1939), Austrian psychiatrist, describes paralysis originating from purely mental conditions and distinguishes it from that of organic origin.

1894: Thomas Alva Edison (1847–1931), American inventor, first displays his peep-show Kinetoscopes in New York. These demonstrations serve to stimulate research on the screen projection of motion pictures as well as entertain.

1895: John Cox is the first U. S. physician to use x-rays as an adjunct to surgery.

1896: Landmark Supreme Court of the United States decision, *Plessy v. Ferguson*, upholds racial segregation.

1896: Edmund Beecher Wilson (1856–1939), American zoologist, publishes his major work, *The Cell in Development and Heredity* in which he connects chromosomes and sex determination. He also correctly states that chromosomes affect and determine other inherited characteristics as well.

1897: Guglielmo Marconi (1874–1937), Italian electrical engineer, exchanges wireless messages across 3.5 miles of water in England.

1897: Havelock Ellis (1859–1939), English physician, publishes the first of his seven-volume work *Studies in the Psychology of Sex*. This contributes to the more open discussion of human sexuality and supports sex education.

1898: *USS Maine* sinks in harbor in Havana, Cuba; Spanish-American War begins.

1900–1949

1900: In Puerto Rico, the Jones Act grants U.S. citizenship to residents.

1901: Guglielmo Marconi (1874–1937), Italian electrical engineer, successfully sends a radio signal from England to Newfoundland. This is the first transatlantic telegraphic radio transmission and is considered by most as the day radio is invented.

1902: Clarence Erwin McClung (1870–1946), American zoologist, isolates the "x" or sex chromosome which is combined with a "y" chromosome in the male, as compared to two "x" chromosomes in the female.

1902: Ernest H. Starling (1866–1927) and William M. Bayliss (1860–1924), both English physiologists, isolate and discover the first hormone (secretin, found in the duodenum). Starling also first suggests a name for all substances discharged into the blood by a particular organ, and it is "hormones" from the Greek word meaning to "rouse to activity."

1902: The Horn & Hardart Baking Company of Philadelphia, Pennsylvania creates an early automat that offers food for a "nickel in a slot."

1903: Wright brothers make first successful flight of a controlled, powered airplane that is heavier than air.

1903: *The Great Train Robbery*, the first modern movie, debuts.

1903: Walter S. Sutton (1876–1916) of the United States writes a short paper in which he states the chromosome theory of inheritance. This important idea that the hereditary factors are located in the chromosomes is also offered independently by Theodor Boveri (1862–1915) of Germany.

1904: Russo-Japanese War (1904–1905): Japan gains territory on the Asian mainland and becomes a world power.

1904: First radical operation for prostate cancer is performed by the American urologist, Hugh Hampton Young (1870–1945).

1904: Ivan Petrovich Pavlov (1849–1936), Russian physiologist, is awarded the Nobel Prize for Physiology or Medicine for his work establishing that the nervous system plays a part in controlling digestion and by helping to found gastroenterology.

1905: Albert Einstein (1879–1955), German-Swiss-American physicist, uses Planck's theory to develop a quantum theory of light which explains the photoelectric effect. He suggests that light has a dual, wave-particle quality.

1905: Fritz Richard Schaudinn (1871–1906), German zoologist, discovers *Spirocheta pallida*, the organism or parasite causing syphilis. His discovery of this almost invisible parasite is due to his consummate technique and staining methods.

1905: Albert Einstein (1879–1955), German-Swiss-American physicist, submits his first paper on the special theory of relativity titled "Zur Elektrodynamik bewegter Korpen." It states that the speed of light is constant for all conditions and that time is relative or passes at different rates for objects in constant relative motion. This is a fundamentally new and revolutionary way to look at the universe and it soon replaces the old Newtonian system.

1905: Albert Einstein (1879–1955), German-Swiss-American physicist, publishes his second paper on relativity in which he includes his famous equation stating the relationship between mass and energy: $E = mc2$. In this equation, E is energy, m is mass, and c is the velocity of light. This contains the revolutionary concept that mass and energy are only different aspects of the same phenomenon.

1905: Hermann Walter Nernst (1864–1941), German physical chemist, announces his discovery of the third law of thermodynamics. He finds that entropy change approaches zero at a temperature of absolute zero, and deduces from this the impossibility of attaining absolute zero.

1905: Alfred Binet (1857–1911), French psychologist, devises the first of a series of tests (1905–1911) that make him the "father of intelligence testing."

1905: Edmund Beecher Wilson (1856–1939), American zoologist and Nettie M. Stevens independently discover the connection between chromosomes and sex determination. They are the first to note the X chromosome and Y chromosomes.

1905: Robert Koch (1843–1910), German bacteriologist, is awarded the Nobel Prize for Physiology or Medicine for his investigations and discoveries in relation to tuberculosis. He is one of the founders of the science of bacteriology.

1906: Marie Sklodowska Curie (1867–1934), Polish-French chemist, assumes her husband Pierre's professorship at the Sorbonne after he is killed in a traffic accident. She becomes the first woman ever to teach there.

1907: The United States and Japan agree to limit Japanese immigration to the United States.

1907: Alva T. Fisher of the United States designs the first electric washing machine. Manufactured by the Hurley Machine Corporation, it is the first washing machine that does not require an operator to crank a handle to perform the washing action.

1907: Boris Rosing, a lecturer at the Technological Institute, St. Petersburg, Russia, first introduces the idea of using a cathode ray tube as a means of reproducing a television picture. Known as "Rosing's Apparatus," he names it the "electric eye." Although this system uses an electronic receiver, it still has a mechanical camera.

1907: Clemens Peter Pirquet von Cesenatico (1874–1929), Austrian physician, and Bela Schick, Austrian pediatrician, introduce the notion and term "allergy."

1907: The first powdered soap for home use is called "Persil" and is sold by Henkel & Co. in Germany.

1908: A. A. Campbell-Swinton of England first suggests the use of a cathode ray tube as both the transmitter (camera) and receiver. This is the first description of the modern, all-electronic television system.

1909: Phoebus Aaron Theodore Levene (1869–1940), Russian-American chemist, discovers the chemical distinction between DNA (deoxyribonucleic acid) and RNA (ribonucleic acid).

1910: Charles-Jules-Henri Nicolle (1866–1936), French bacteriologist, discovers the viral origin of influenza.

1910: Harvey Cushing (1869–1939), American surgeon, and his team present the first experimental evidence of the link between the anterior pituitary and the reproductive organs.

1911: Mexican laborers are exempt from immigrant "head tax."

1912: The value of wireless at sea is demonstrated during the S.S. Titanic disaster as those who get to lifeboats are saved by rescuing vessels.

1913: California's Alien Land Law declares that aliens not eligible for citizenship are ineligible to own certain types of farm property.

1913: Alfred Henry Sturtevant (1891–1970), American geneticist, produces the first chromosome map, showing five sex-linked genes.

1914: Assassination of Archduke Franz Ferdinand of Austria-Hungary and his wife Sophie; World War I begins.

1914: Panama Canal is completed.

1914: The beginning of the massacre of 1.5 million Armenians by the Turkish government, later known as the Armenian Genocide.

1914: John Broadus Watson (1878–1958), American psychologist, launches his theory of behaviorism. This approach, which says that brain activity comprises responses to external stimuli, restricts psychology to the objective, experimental study of human behavior or human responses to stimuli.

1915: U.S. Supreme Court delivers Ozawa v. United States ruling that declares first-generation Japanese ineligible for naturalization.

1915: German U-boats sink the British passenger steamer RMS Lusitania.

1916: Easter Rising in Ireland begins fight for Irish independence.

1917: The United States enters World War I, declaring war on Germany.

1917: The United States enters World War I and anti-German sentiment grows. Names are changed to sound less Germanic.

1917: The Russian Revolution begins as Bolsheviks overthrow the Russian monarchy.

1918: World War I ends.

1918: The Great Flu: nearly twenty million perish during the two-year pandemic.

1918: The Red Terror in Russia: Thousands of political dissidents are tried and imprisoned; five million die of famine as Communists collectivize agriculture and transform the Soviet economy."

1919: The ratification of the Nineteenth Amendment to the U.S. constitution gives women the right to vote.

1919: Mahatma Gandhi initiates satyagraha (truth force) campaigns, beginning his nonviolent resistance movement against British rule in India.

1920: Red Scare (1920–1922) in the United States leads to the arrest, trial, and imprisonment of suspected communist, socialist, and anarchist "radicals."

1920: KDKA, a Pittsburgh Westinghouse station, transmits the first commercial radio broadcast.

1922: Twenty-six of Ireland's counties gain independence; the remaining six become Northern Ireland and remain under British rule.

1922: Mussolini forms Fascist government in Italy.

1922: The British Broadcasting Company (BBC) is formed.

1922: The first canned baby food is manufactured in the United States by Harold H. Clapp of New York.

1923: Max Wertheimer (1880–1943), German psychologist, publishes *Untersuchungen zur Lehre der Gestalt*, which first originates the concept of Gestalt psychology. This school of psychological thought attempts to examine the total, structured forms of mental experience.

1924: Immigration Act of 1924 establishes fixed quotas of national origin and eliminates Far East immigration.

1925: Geneva Protocol, signed by sixteen nations, outlaws the use of poisonous gas as an agent of warfare.

1925: The Scopes Monkey Trial (July 10-25) in Tennessee debates the state's ban on the teaching of evolution.

1927: Charles Lindbergh makes the first solo nonstop transatlantic flight.

1927: Lemuel Clyde McGee, American biochemist, first obtains an active extract of the male sex hormone from bull testicles.

1927: Selmar Aschheim and Bernhardt Zondek, both German physicians, devise a pregnancy test in which the subject's urine is injected subcutaneously in immature female mice. A positive reaction is marked by congestion and hemorrhages of the ovaries in the mice.

1928: Alexander Fleming discovers penicillin.

1929: The United States establishes annual immigration quotas.

1929: Black Tuesday: The U.S. stock market crashes, beginning the Great Depression.

1929: Adolf Friedrich Johann Butenandt (1903–1994), German chemist, isolates the first of the sex hormones, estrone. He obtains this female sex hormone from the urine of pregnant women.

1929: Casimir Funk, Polish biochemist, and Harrow obtain active male hormone from male urine.

1929: Edward Adelbert Doisy (1893–1986), American biochemist, first isolates estrone from the urine of pregnant women.

1930: Ronald Aylmer Fisher (1890–1962), English biologist, publishes *The Genetical Theory of Natural Selection* which, together with Sewall Wright's *Mendelian Populations* (1931), lays the mathematical foundations of population genetics.

1930: Rubber condoms made of a thin latex are introduced.

1932: Hattie Wyatt Caraway of Arkansas is the first woman elected to the U.S. Senate.

1932: Nazis capture 230 seats in the German Reichstag during national elections.

1932: Werner Karl Heisenberg (1901–1976), German physicist, wins the Nobel Prize for Physics for the creation of quantum mechanics, the application of which has led to the discovery of the allotropic forms of hydrogen.

1932: RCA (Radio Corporation of America) makes experimental television broadcasts from the Empire State Building in New York.

1933: Adolf Hitler named German chancellor.

1933: President Franklin D. Roosevelt announces the New Deal, a plan to revitalize the U.S. economy and provide relief during the Great Depression. The U.S. unemployment rate reaches twenty-five percent.

1933: U. S. President Franklin Delano Roosevelt (1882–1945) makes the first of his "fireside chats" to the American people. He is the first national leader to use the radio medium comfortably and regularly to explain his programs and to garner popular support.

1933: Christopher Howard Andrewes, English pathologist, Wilson Smith (1897–1965), English bacteriologist and virologist, and Patrick Playfair Laidlaw (1881–1940), English physician, demonstrate the viral nature of the human influenza agent by transmitting it to a ferret and then transferring the virus onto a suitable culture medium.

1934: George W. Beadle, working with Boris Ephrussi, in collaboration with A. Kuhn and A. Butenandt, worked out the biochemical genetics of eye-pigment synthesis in *Drosophila* and *Ephestia*, respectively.

1934: John Marrack begins a series of studies that leads to the formation of the hypothesis governing the association between an antigen and the corresponding antibody.

1935: Germany's Nuremburg Laws codify discrimination and denaturalization of the nation's Jews.

1935: Antonio Caetano de Abreu Freire Egas Moniz (1874–1955), Portuguese surgeon, performs the first lobotomy. This operation, which severs the patient's prefrontal lobes of the brain, opens a new field called psychosurgery. It is usually employed as a last resort and eventually is done away with once tranquilizers and other mind-affecting drugs are discovered.

1935: K. David and associates first isolate a pure crystalline hormone from testicular material and name it testosterone.

1936: Herbert McLean Evans (1882–1971), American anatomist and embryologist, and his group first isolate the interstitial cell stimulating hormone (ICSH). Also called luteinizing hormone, it is concerned with the regulation of the activity of the gonads or sex glands and is produced by the pituitary gland.

1938: Anti-Jewish riots across Germany. The destruction and looting of Jewish-owned businesses is known as *Kristalnacht*, "Night of the Broken Glass."

1938: Hitler marches into Austria; political and geographical union of Germany and Austria proclaimed. Munich Pact—Britain, France, and Italy—agree to let Germany partition Czechoslovakia.

1938: Mass hysteria among American radio listeners is caused by a dramatic reenactment of H. G. Wells' (1866–1946) novel, *War of the Worlds*. American actor, writer, and director, George Orson Welles, (1915–1985) leads many to believe that a "gas raid from Mars" is actually happening.

1939: The United States declares its neutrality in World War II.

1939: Germany invades Poland. Britain, France, and Russia go to war against Germany.

1939: The Holocaust (Shoah) begins in German-occupied Europe. Jews are removed from their homes and relocated to ghettos or concentration camps. The *Einsatzgruppen*, or mobile killing squads, begin the execution of one million Jews, Poles, Russians, Gypsies, and others.

1939: Television debuts at the World's Fair.

1940: George Wells Beadle, American geneticist, and Edward Lawrie Tatum (1909–1975), American biochemist, establish the formula "One gene = one enzyme." This discovery that each gene supervises the production of only one enzyme lays the foundation for the DNA discoveries to come.

1940: Ernest Chain and E.P. Abraham detail the inactivation of penicillin by a substance produced by *Escherichia coli*. This is the first bacterial compound known to produce resistance to an antibacterial agent.

1941: The U.S. Naval base at Pearl Harbor, Hawaii is bombed by Japanese Air Force. Soon after, the United States enters World War II, declaring war on Germany and Japan.

1941: Japanese-Americans are incarcerated on grounds of national security.

1941: The first Nazi death camp, Chelmno, opens. Victims, mainly Jews, are executed by carbon monoxide poisoning in specially designed killing vans.

1942: Executive Order 9066 orders the internment of Japanese immigrants and Japanese American citizens for the duration of World War II.

1942: Enrico Fermi (1901–1954), Italian-American physicist, heads a Manhattan Project team at the University of Chicago that produces the first controlled chain reaction in an atomic pile of uranium and graphite. With this first self-sustaining chain reaction, the atomic age begins.

1943: The Magnuson Act repeals the Chinese Exclusion Act of 1882.

1943: Penicillin is first used on a large scale by the U. S. Army in the North African campaigns. Data obtained from these studies show that early expectations for the new drug are correct, and the groundwork is laid for the massive introduction of penicillin into civilian medical practice after the war.

1945: The War Bride Act and the G.I. Fiancées Act are enacted.

1945: The United States admits immigrants based on the fact that they are fleeing persecution from their native lands.

1945: Auschwitz death camp is liberated by allied forces.

1945: World War II and the Holocaust end in Europe.

1945: Trials of Nazi War criminals begin in Nuremberg, Germany.

1945: United Nations is established.

1945: Displaced Persons (DP) camps established throughout Europe to aid Holocaust survivors. In the three years following the end of World War II, many DPs immigrate to Israel and the United States.

1945: First atomic bomb is detonated by the United States near Almagordo, New Mexico. The experimental bomb generates an explosive power equivalent to between fifteen and twenty thousand tons of TNT.

1945: RCA Victor first offers vinyl plastic records to the public.

1945: United States destroys the Japanese city of Hiroshima with a nuclear fission bomb based on uranium-235. Three days later a plutonium-based bomb destroys the city of Nagasaki. Japan surrenders on August 14 and World War II ends. This is the first use of nuclear power as a weapon.

1946: John von Neumann (1903–1957), Hungarian-American mathematician, begins work at the Institute for Advanced Study at Princeton, New Jersey to establish a digital computer project. He is soon joined by Julian Bigelow, American engineer, and American mathematician, Herman Heine Goldstein.

1948: Gandhi assassinated in New Delhi.

1948: Soviets blockade Berlin. The United States and Great Britain begin airlift of fuel, food and necessities to West Berlin. The event, the first conflict of the Cold War, became known as the Berlin Airlift (June 26-Sept 30, 1949).

1948: United Nations issues the Universal Declaration of Human Rights.

1948: Israel is established as an independent nation.

1948: American zoologist and student of sexual behavior, Alfred C. Kinsey (1894–1956) first publishes his *Sexual Behavior in the Human Male*.

1949: South Africa codifies apartheid.

1949: Soviets test their first atomic device.

1950–1999

1950: President Truman commits U.S. troops to aid anti-Communist forces on the Korean Peninsula. The Korean War lasts from 1950–1953.

1951: First successful oral contraceptive drug is introduced. Gregory Pincus (1903–1967), American biologist, discovers a synthetic hormone that renders a woman infertile without altering her capacity for sexual pleasure. It soon is marketed in pill form and effects a social revolution with its ability to divorce the sex act from the consequences of impregnation.

1952: U.S. Immigration and Nationality Act enacted

1952: First hydrogen bomb is detonated by the United States on an atoll in the Marshall Islands.

1953: Francis Harry Compton Crick, English biochemist, and James Dewey Watson, American biochemist, work out the double-helix or double spiral DNA model. This model explains how it is able to transmit heredity in living organisms.

1954: The Supreme Court delivers *Brown v. Topeka Board of Education* decision that "separate but equal" doctrine is unconstitutional.

1954: Sen. Joseph R. McCarthy begins hearings of the House Un-American Activities Committee, publicly accusing military officials, politicians, media, and others of Communist involvement.

1954: The first frozen TV dinners become available in the United States.

1955: Emmett Till, age fourteen, is brutally murdered for allegedly whistling at a white woman. The event galvanizes the civil rights movement.

1955: Rosa Parks refuses to give up her seat on a Montgomery, Alabama, bus to a white passenger, defying segregation.

1955: Warsaw Pact solidifies relationship between the Soviet Union and its communist satellite nations in Eastern Europe.

1955: Chlorpromazine and lithium are first used to treat psychiatric disorders.

1957: President Eisenhower sends federal troops to Central High School in Little Rock, Ark., to enforce integration.

1957: Soviet Union launches the first satellite, Sputnik, into space. The Space Race between the USSR and the United States begins.

1958: Explorer I, first American satellite, is launched.

1959: Cuban revolution prompts mass immigration to the United States.

1960: African American students in North Carolina begin a sit-in at a segregated Woolworth's lunch counter; the sit-in spread throughout the South.

1961: Soviet Cosmonaut Yuri Gagarin becomes first human in space.

1961: Berlin Wall is built.

1961: Bay of Pigs Invasion: the United States sponsors an overthrow of Cuba's socialist government but fails.

1962: *Silent Spring* published; environmental movement begins.

1962: Cuban Missile Crisis occurs.

1963: Rev. Martin Luther King Jr., delivers his "I Have a Dream" speech at a civil rights march on Washington, D.C.

1963: The U. S. and the Soviet Union establish a direct telephone link called the "hot line" between the White House and the Kremlin. It is intended to permit the leaders of both countries to be able to speak directly and immediately to each other in times of crisis.

1964: U.S. President Lyndon Johnson announces ambitious social reform programs known as the Great Society.

1964: Congress approves Gulf of Tonkin resolution.

1964: President Johnson signs the Civil Rights Act of 1964.

1965: U.S. Immigration Act passed.

1965: March to Selma: state troopers and local police fight a crowd of peaceful civil rights demonstrators, including the Rev. Martin Luther King Jr., as the group attempted to cross a bridge into the city of Selma.

1965: First U.S. combat troops arrive in South Vietnam.

1965: Voting Rights Act prohibits discriminatory voting practices in the United States.

1965: Watts Riots: Thirty-five people are killed and 883 injured in six days of riots in Los Angeles.

1965: François Jacob, French biologist, André-Michael Lwoff, French microbiologist, and Jacques-Lucien Monod, French biochemist, are awarded the Nobel Prize for Physiology or Medicine for their discoveries concerning genetic control of enzyme and virus synthesis.

1965: Geoffrey Harris, British anatomist, shows that sexuality is built into the hypothalamus.

1966: U.S. Cuban Refugee Act enacted.

1966: Betty Friedan and other leaders of the feminist movement found the National Organization for Women (NOW).

1966: Choh Hao Li, Chinese-American chemist and endocrinologist, describes the structure of human growth hormone and first synthesizes it (1966–1971).

1967: The new fertility drug clomiphene is introduced. Although it can result in multiple births, it proves very successful in increasing a woman's chances of getting pregnant.

1968: Rev. Martin Luther King Jr., is assassinated in Memphis, Tennessee.

1968: Cesar Chavez leads a national boycott of California table grape growers, which becomes known as "La Causa."

1969: Stonewall Riots in New York City spark the gay rights movement.

1969: The United States successfully lands a manned mission, Apollo 11, on the moon.

1970: Four anti-war demonstrators are killed when the National Guard fires into the crowd of protesters at Kent State University.

1972: Arab terrorists massacre Israeli athletes at Olympic Games in Munich, Germany.

1973: *Roe v. Wade*: Landmark Supreme Court decision legalizes abortion on demand during the first trimester of pregnancy.

1973: The American Psychiatric Association removes the classification of homosexuality as a mental disorder.

1973: Last U.S. troops exit Vietnam.

1974: U.S. President Richard Nixon resigns as a result of the Watergate scandal.

1975: As the South Vietnamese government surrenders to North Vietnam, the U.S. Embassy and remaining military and civilian personnel are evacuated.

1976: Steve Jobs and Steve Wozniak invent personal computer.

1977: Earliest known AIDS (Acquired Immunodeficiency Syndrome) victims in the United States are two homosexual men in New York who are diagnosed as suffering from Kaposi's sarcoma.

1978: Congress passes the Pregnancy Discrimination Act, stating that individuals in the workforce cannot face discrimination "because of or on the basis of pregnancy, childbirth, or related medical conditions."

1979: Three Mile Island nuclear reactor in Pennsylvania suffers a near meltdown.

1979: Iran hostage crisis begins when Iranian students storm the U.S. embassy in Teheran. They hold sixty-six people hostage who are not released until 1981, after 444 days in captivity.

1980: U.S. Refugee Act enacted.

1980: 130,000 Cuban refugees flee to the United States during the Mariel Boatlift (April 4 -October 31).

1980: President Carter announces that U.S. athletes will boycott Summer Olympics in Moscow to protest Soviet involvement in Afghanistan (Jan. 20).

1981: Sandra Day O'Connor is sworn in as the first woman justice on the Supreme Court of the United States.

1981: Urban riots breakout in several British cities, protesting lack of opportunity for minorities and police brutality.

1981: AIDS identified.

1982: Deadline for ratification of the Equal Rights Amendment to the Constitution; without the necessary votes the amendment failed.

1982: New surgical technique for prostate cancer that does not result in impotency is developed by Patrick Walsh.

1984: Steen A. Willadsen successfully clones sheep.

1986: The Immigration Reform and Control Act (IRCA) offers legalized status to aliens residing in the United States illegally since 1982.

1986: U.S. space shuttle Challenger explodes seventy-three seconds after liftoff.

1986: Chernobyl nuclear disaster in the Soviet Union contaminates large swath of Eastern Europe with radioactive fallout. The disaster is the worst nuclear accident to date.

1987: U.S. President Ronald Reagan challenges Soviet leader Mikhail Gorbachev to open Eastern Europe and the Soviet Union to political and economic reform.

1988: Civil Liberties Act provides compensation and apology to Japanese American survivors of WWII internment camps.

1988: Henry A. Erlich of the United States and colleagues develop a method for identifying an individual from the DNA in a single hair.

1989: Fall of the Berlin Wall.

1989: Tiananmen Square protest in Beijing, China.

1989: Oil tanker Exxon Valdez runs aground in Prince William Sound, spilling more than 10 million gallons of oil (March 24).

1989: The Internet revolution begins with the invention of the World Wide Web.

1989: Tim Berners-Lee invents the World Wide Web while working at CERN.

1990: *The Simpsons*, an animated satirical look at the imperfect, ideal American family, debuts on television and becomes an instant hit.

1990: Human Genome Project begins in the United States with the selection of six institutions to do the work.

1990: The U.S. Census includes question about gay couples and families.

1991: Soviet Union dissolves.

1991: Persian Gulf War (January 16 -February 28): The United States leads "Operation Desert Storm" to push Iraqi occupying forces out of Kuwait.

1991: The sex of a mouse is changed at the embryo stage.

1991: U. S. FDA (Food and Drug Administration) announces it will speed up its process for approv-

ing drugs. This change in procedure is due to the protests of AIDS activists.

1992: U.S. and Russian leaders formally declare an end to the Cold War.

1992: L.A. Riots: The acquittal of four white police officers charged with police brutality in the beating of black motorist Rodney King sparks days of widespread rioting in Los Angeles.

1992: WHO (World Health Organization) predicts that by the year 2000, thirty to forty million people will be infected with the AIDS-causing HIV. A Harvard University group argues that the number could reach more than 100 million.

1993: A terrorist bomb explodes in basement parking garage of World Trade Center, killing six.

1993: Software companies introduce programs making Internet easier to use, and several on-line information services open gateways into this "network of networks," making its popularity explode.

1993: After analyzing the family trees of gay men and the DNA of pairs of homosexual brothers, biochemists at the United States National Cancer Institute reported that at least one gene related to homosexuality resides on the X chromosome, which is inherited from the mother.

1993: U.S. military adopts the "Don't Ask, Don't Tell" policy, permitting gay individuals to serve in the military only if they do not disclose their homosexuality and do not engage in homosexual acts.; military recruiters and personnel are barred from inquiring about an individual's sexuality.

1993: The federal Family and Medical Leave Act is enacted, allowing workers to take unpaid leave due to illness or to care for a newborn or sick family member.

1994: First all-race elections in South Africa; Nelson Mandela elected President.

1996: Federal Defense of Marriage Act (DOMA) enacted; states permitted to enact legislation refusing to honor same-sex marriages entered into in another state.

1998: Terrorist attacks on U.S. embassies in Kenya and Tanzania.

1998: House of Representatives votes to impeach President William Jefferson Clinton. The Senate acquits President Clinton two months later.

1998: Torture and murder of gay college student Matthew Shepherd.

1999: NATO forces in former Yugoslavia attempt to end mass killings of ethnic Albanians by Serbian forces in Kosovo.

2000–

2000: The United Nations adopts the Millennium Declaration that results in setting eight goals (known as the Millennium Development Goals), which "promote poverty reduction, education, maternal health, gender equality, and aim at combating child mortality, AIDS and other diseases" by the year 2015.

2001: Terrorists attack the World Trade Center in New York and the Pentagon in Washington, D.C. killing 2,752.

2001: Controversial Patriot Act passed in the United States.

2001: United States and coalition forces begin War on Terror by invading Afghanistan (Operation Enduring Freedom), overthrowing the nation's Islamist Taliban regime in December of 2001.

2002: Slobodan Milosevic begins his war crimes trial at the UN International Criminal Tribunal on charges of genocide and crimes against humanity. He is the first head of state to stand trial in an international war-crimes court, but died before the trial concluded.

2002: After United States and coalition forces depose Islamist Taliban regime in Afghanistan, girls are allowed to return to school and women's rights are partially restored in areas controlled by the United States and coalition forces.

2002: The International Olympic Committee suspends gender verification procedures for the Olympics in Sydney, Australia citing potential harm to "women athletes born with relatively rare genetic abnormalities that affect development of the gonads or the expression of secondary sexual characteristics."

2002: The agricultural chemical atrazine, used in weed control, is thought to be partially responsible for the dramatic global decline in amphibians, as it is found to disturb male frog sex hormones, altering their gonads.

2003: U.S. space shuttle Columbia breaks apart upon re-entry, killing all seven crew members.

2003: Supreme Court of the United States strikes down sodomy laws in the landmark decision, *Lawrence v. Texas*.

2003: United States and coalition forces invade Iraq.

2003: The United States declares an end to major combat operations in Iraq. As of October 2006, U.S. fighting forces remain engaged in Iraq.

2003: American troops capture Iraq's former leader, Saddam Hussein.

2003: Canada recognizes same-sex marriages throughout the country.

2003: November 18, the Massachusetts Supreme Judicial court rules denying same-sex couples marriage rights violates the state constitution, legalizing same-sex marriages.

2004: Islamist terrorist bombing of commuter rail network in Madrid, Spain.

2004: Jason West, mayor of New Paltz, New York, defies state law and performs same-sex weddings. Later charged with twenty-four misdemeanor counts of performing illegal marriages, he was cleared of all charges in 2005.

2004: The California state supreme court, in a 5-2 decision, voids nearly 4,000 same-sex marriages performed in San Francisco earlier that year.

2005: U.S. House bill passes Border Protection, Antiterrorism, and Illegal Immigration Control Act (HR 4437) proposing building a fence along portions of the U.S.-Mexico border and other anti-immigration measures.

2005: U.S. House bill proposes making the provision of humanitarian assistance a felony.

2005: Islamist terrorist bombings in London: Bombs simultaneously detonate in the Underground and on a city bus.

2006: U.S. Senate passes Comprehensive Immigration Reform Act that would impose penalties on employers of illegal immigrants but that also would allow illegal immigrants who have lived in the United States for more than five years the opportunity to apply for U.S. citizenship after paying fines and taxes. Congressional leaders enter talks to try to reach compromise with House bills that would make compromise measures law.

2006: Polygamist Warren Jeffs, one of the FBI's ten most-wanted fugitives, and the subject of the documentary *The Man With 80 Wives* is arrested during a routine traffic stop in Nevada.

2006: Lawmakers in Japan set aside proposed legislation that would give females in Japan's royal family, the oldest royal family in the world, the right of succession to the throne, after Princess Kiko gives birth to the first male heir in over forty years.

1 Concepts of Family

Concepts of Family

The family can be conceptualized in numerous ways; underlying each is a fundamental idea about the structure of the family and its function in society. Some define a family purely in terms of sharing a household, a collection of individuals living together. Others define the family based on kinship. A family is a group of people who share common ancestors or a basic social unit comprised of parents and their children. Some assert that biological kinship is the defining element of family, while opponents assert that families can be a blended collection of individuals related by marriage, adoption, partnership, or friendship.

Social theorists have questioned the nature of family since the ancient times. The modern era has witnessed numerous transformations of prevailing concepts of family in Western society. "Love and the Formations of Family" discusses Sigmund Freud's concept of the family as a comprehensive social unit formed by physical, biological, emotional, and economic necessities. "Myth of the Perfect Family" introduces the cultural myth of the perfect family, then

counters the idea with a survey of diverse family structures. "'Blended Families' and Other Euphemisms" provides a personal account of the increasingly common reshaping and melding of families through divorce and remarriage. Also provided herein is demographic information on what contemporary families and households look like in the United States.

How individuals conceptualize the family is influenced by culture, religion, law, and politics. Concepts of family are diverse. Fundamental to understanding varying concepts of family are several essential questions. What makes a family? How are families created and maintained? Who are members of a family? What are the roles of members within the family? What is the role of family in society? How are families essential to society? What social forces have shaped our perceptions of family? From nuclear families to extended families, so-called traditional families to blended families, this chapter presents an overview of the different concepts of family found throughout this volume.

The Family and its Members

Life at Home

Book excerpt

By: William Aikman

Date: 1870

Source: Aikman, William. *Life at Home, or The Family and its Members*. New York: Samuel R. Wells, 1870.

About the Author: William Aikman (1824–1909) was a Presbyterian minister, a Doctor of Divinity, and an author. He was the Pastor of Hanover Street Presbyterian Church in Wilmington, Delaware. During the Civil War, Aikman wrote his most remembered article for the *Presbyterian Quarterly Review:* "The Future of the Colored Race in America," published in July 1862.

INTRODUCTION

Traditions that have shaped American cultural norms and beliefs about family have been influenced by major religious dogma and teachings, such as those of the early or medieval era Roman Catholic church leaders and counsel and their later or early modern Protestant counterparts. The Christian church exerted some influence over the formation of both canon and common law, and thereby helped to shape legislation and definition around marriage as constituting a legal agreement between a male and a female partner (in most jurisdictions in the United States), and helping to shape what became culturally, and legally, accepted norms regarding what constitutes a family.

The medieval Roman Catholic Church viewed marriage as a sacrament. A sacrament, as defined by the Roman Catholic Church, is a tangible, visible, or otherwise perceptible sign of acknowledgement of belief and participation in the rites or rituals of the Church and simultaneously acquiring elevated spiritual status. Part of the underlying philosophy of the sacrament of marriage was the notion of what constituted family; Biblical lore has it that married couples were tasked to procreate and have many children. Bearing children was therefore incorporated into the religious and cultural traditions around marriage and family. Early Catholic teachings suggested that it was "God's will" that human beings should marry in order to "be fruitful and multiply," and that having large families was beneficial in order both to serve their deity and to aid in supporting the family. Biblical literature also prescribes marriage as a means of enforcing

fidelity—which served to protect and preserve intimate relationships and reinforce the notion of the nuclear family as a central unit of society. The Catholic Church took a stance on the family that was called "naturalist," meaning that it did not discourage natural means of family planning, but enacted canon law prohibiting artificial means of birth control, as well as abortion. Until the end of the sixteenth century, most of the Western countries of Europe accepted canon law as the primary doctrine, and subordinated common law to the Church's tenets.

The Protestant Church generally took a slightly less legislative or authoritarian position on matters concerning the family. During the Protestant Reformation period occurring in the sixteenth and seventeenth centuries, the definition of marriage was shifted from the concept of "sacrament" to a more social definition, maintaining the naturalist prohibitions against artificial means of birth control and abortion, and continuing the implicit sanctions against spousal and child abuse, but redefined marriage as a voluntary union between two consenting adults. Although marriage was sanctified by the deity, it did not confer any special spiritual enhancement. Marriage was also viewed as a means of enhancing the growth and development of the community. Rather than simply being a religious ceremony, marriages were now also ratified by local legal officials, indicating that the act of marriage transcended the spiritual realm and entered that of the secular and community as well. Marriages were now registered and legally documented. With the Protestant reformation, marriage became a legalized social institution, subject to common and civil law.

PRIMARY SOURCE

…The Family is necessary for the development of the race. There can be no true development without it. The savage state knows little of the family. In the lowest types of humanity, such as the Bushmen of South Africa, it is almost unknown. Children are born, but as soon as they are able to care for their own wants, they wander off and are lost among the rest of the tribe, as a lamb is merged in the surrounding flock, and all connection between parents and their offspring is quickly lost. In tribes more elevated, but still barbaric—our American Indians may be an example—the same fact is seen; the family, such as it is in its true idea, is scarcely to be recognized. Husbands and wives may live in the same hut, and children may remain for a while near it, but all that intercourse and association which make the family is unknown. There is natural affection, often pure and deep, between individuals, but no general bond of sympathy and love holding the whole group together as a unity.

Civilization varies with the family and the family with civilization. Its highest and most complete realization is found where the enlightenment of Christianity prevails, where woman is exalted to her true and lofty place as equal with the man, where husband and wife are one in honor, in influence, in affection, and where children are a common bond of care and love. Here you have the idea of a perfect family.

Here is one of those innumerable, but powerful, because indirect and unannounced, proofs of the supernatural character of the Bible. What book of ancient times gives such pictures of the family life—what book such precepts for family government? How wonderful it is, that these old books, written many of them in those far back centuries which antedate historic records, do give us such advanced ideas! Here is a book which in this regard was clearly made not for that time alone, but for all time, not for society as it then was, but for society in its highest state—for civilization in its very best form. Paint for yourself your brightest conception of what a family should be, have husband and wife living in pure and blissful companionship; father and mother wise and loving, yet sovereign; surround the fireside with perfect children, children who are just what you would have them, affectionate, obedient, joyous; let brothers and sisters be linked together in unwavering and kindly sympathy, in love as strong and glowing as our imagination can picture; then look into the Bible. You shall find that very family set before you, you shall see all the exhortations and injunctions of this Book looking toward just such a home.

SIGNIFICANCE

The concept of marriage and family began to change with the appearance of the women's suffrage movement during the latter half of the nineteenth century. Although religious and ethno-cultural traditions still exerted considerable influence on the definition of the ideal family in American middle-class white society, the burgeoning Women's Rights movement began to effect some changes in the ways in which traditional female roles were viewed. The Temperance Movement, which occurred during the suffrage era, was also championed by women as a political and social means of reducing or eliminating the consumption of alcohol, particularly by males. Temperance was also considered a means of limiting or eradicating the domestic violence that was sometimes associated with drinking.

Those two movements had a significant impact on the appearance and the changing roles of the American family, particularly of the female members thereof, at the end of the nineteenth and the early decades of the twentieth centuries. May Wright Sewall (1844–1920), who was an activist in the suffrage movement, referred to the tasks of the senior female household member (traditionally, wife and mother) as equivalent to the work done by men outside the home. She described the process of managing home, family, and household as a business not unlike any other—it is because of that stance that she engaged in the struggle to broaden the civil rights of women.

William O'Neill, writing in the early 1970s on feminism in the era at the end of the Civil War in America, expresses his belief that the nineteenth century women's movement was unable to achieve many of its initial intents because the activists were unable to grasp (on the whole) the full extent to which they experienced a dearth of rights and freedoms, or fully understand the negative conditions under which they went about their daily business. It is his contention that the early feminist movement dissolved after suffrage was achieved as a result of its inability to come to terms with the adverse conditions imposed by the male-dominated culture in Victorian-era America. Historical writers documenting the women's movement in the United States have stated that nineteenth century feminists tended to focus on the acquisition of voting rights as a panacea for all that was wrong in American society, and failed to take adequate notice of the political, economic, and social challenges that beset them in their traditional roles. Gerda Lerner, a feminist historian, believes that the solitary focus on obtaining the vote for women prevented them from being able to see the ways in which middle-class white society oppressed women and families who were poorer or of ethnic or racial minority, as well as those with a single head of household. She refers to the leaders of the feminist movement at the end of the Civil War as "nativist, racist, and generally indifferent to the needs of working class women."

Daniel Scott Smith (writing in Hartman and Banner's *Consciousness Raised: New Perspectives on the History of Women*) views the status of women and the family during the latter half of the nineteenth century somewhat differently: he believed that there was a parallel feminist movement occurring within American households, in which women began to assert their rights and roles within the confines of what had been viewed as a traditional family constellation. He refers to this movement as "domestic feminism," and states that its centerpiece was women's taking an active role in regulating family size, and beginning to examine the means and efficacy of various types of birth control. It is his contention that women were changing the understanding of power and control within the family in a far more subtle way, within individual homes, by increasing personal autonomy, limiting family size, and shifting roles and responsibilities within the household. Political feminism, then could be viewed as taking place within the sphere of the home and family, and changes could be viewed as occurring on a small scale and gradually being accepted by the larger society.

FURTHER RESOURCES

Books

American Bible Society. *Holy Bible: King James Version.* New York: American Bible Society, 1980.

DuBois, Ellen. *Feminism and Suffrage: The Emergence of an Independent Women's Movement, 1848–1869.* Ithaca, NY: Cornell University Press, 1978.

Hartman, Mary, and Lois Banner, eds. *Consciousness Raised: New Perspectives on the History of Women.* New York: Harper & Row, 1974.

Jagger, Gill and Caroline Wright. *Changing Concepts of Family.* London: Routledge, 1999.

Lerner, Gerda. *The Majority Finds its Past: Placing Women in History.* New York: Oxford University Press, 1979.

O'Neill, William. *Everyone Was Brave: A History of Feminism in America (5th edition).* New York: Quadrangle Books, 1974.

Periodicals

DuBois, Ellen. "The Radicalism of the Woman Suffrage Movement: Notes Toward the Reconstruction of Nineteenth-Century Feminism." *Feminist Studies* 3 (Fall 1975): 63–71.

Sewall, May Wright. "Domestic Legislation." *National Citizen and Ballot Box* (September 1881): 1.

Love and the Formations of Family

Book excerpt

By: Sigmund Freud

Date: 1930

Source: Freud, Sigmund. "Love and the Formations of Family." In *Civilization and its Discontents*, edited by James Strachey. New York: W. W. Norton and Co., 1961.

About the Author: Sigmund Freud is considered the father of modern psychotherapy. While many of his ideas have since been dismissed, his groundbreaking research on the function of the unconscious mind laid the foundation for the current understanding of human motivation and behavior.

INTRODUCTION

Human behavior is often difficult to explain. Despite centuries of study, philosophizing, and scientific inquiry, the reasons for human decisions and behavior still frequently confuse or confound us. While numerous explanations for the vagaries of human choice have been proposed, none has more profoundly influenced human thinking than the work of Sigmund Freud.

Sigmund Freud lived in an age of reason and logic. Born in 1856, Freud grew up and was educated in a world where science was becoming king and rational analysis was believed to hold the key to unlocking all mysteries. Shortly after Freud's birth, Charles Darwin had published his monumental work on natural selection, and scientists and theologians the world over were debating the relationship between science and religion. The world in which Freud grew up had primed him with the expectation that any aspect of the world, even the sometimes strange behaviors of human beings, could be explained rationally and logically.

While previous philosophers had proposed and discussed the existence of a subconscious mind, Freud was responsible for bringing the concept into the public dialogue. Freud believed that human intellect is made up of three distinct parts: the id, the ego, and the super-ego. He proposed that these three aspects of the human mind co-exist in an intricate dance, seeking pleasure, meeting basic needs, and tailoring behavior to specific situations as each part pushes and tugs to achieve its own ends. Freud also believed that the id, the pleasure-seeking portion of the mind, was the largest of the three, and played a major role in determining virtually all human behavior.

In practical terms, this perspective meant that Freud saw humans as creatures constantly driven by their physical desires; Freud labeled these desires instincts, and included the desire for physical survival, the desire for sex, and the desire for death, which Freud believed all people unconsciously experience. Of the three, Freud believed that the desire for sex and sexual fulfillment was the strongest, and many of his models of human behavior hinged on this perceived drive for sex.

Sigmund Freud (fourth from left) sits at a dining table with his family. His daughter Anna, another noted psychologist, is at the far end of the table, on the right. © CORBIS.

While Freud's understanding of human thought and emotion included higher order processes such as showing compassion and the need to help others, he ultimately perceived human beings as creatures driven by the id, the basic underlying needs of the organism. Consequently, when Freud examined the structure of the human family, he observed an arrangement dictated by basic underlying drives, and he concluded that families were merely a manifestation of the basic human desires for sex and power.

PRIMARY SOURCE

One may suppose that the founding of families was connected with the fact that a moment came when the need for genital satisfaction no longer made its appearance like a guest who drops in suddenly, and, after his departure, is heard of no more for a long time, but instead took up its quarters as a permanent lodger. When this happened, the male acquired a motive for keeping the female, or, speaking more generally, his sexual objects, near him; while the female, who did not want to be separated from her helpless young, was obliged, in their interests, to remain with the stronger male. In this primitive family one essential feature of civilization is still lacking. The arbitrary will of its head, the father, was unrestricted.

I have tried to show how the way led from this family, to the succeeding stage of communal life in the form of bands of brothers. In overpowering their father, the sons had made the discovery that a combination can be stronger than a single individual. The totemic culture is based on the restrictions which the sons had to impose on one another in order to keep this new state of affairs in being. The taboo-observances were the first "right" or "law." The communal life of human beings had, therefore, a two-fold foundation: the compulsion to work, which was created by external necessity, and the power of live, which made the man unwilling to be deprived of his sexual object—the woman,—and made the woman unwilling to be deprived of the part of herself which had been separated off from her—her child. Eros and Ananke [Love and Necessity] have become the parents of human civilization too. The first result of civilization was that even a fairly large number of people were now able to live together in a community. And since these two great powers were cooperating in this, one might expect that the further development of civilization would proceed smoothly towards an even better control over the external world and towards a further extension of the number of people included in the community. Nor is it easy to understand how this civilization could act upon its participants otherwise than to make them happy.

The love which founded the family continues to operate in civilization both in its original form, in which it does not renounce direct sexual satisfaction, and in its modified form as aim-inhibited affection. In each, it continues to carry on its function of binding together considerable numbers of people, and it does so in a more intensive fashion than can be effected through the interest of work in common. The careless way in which language uses the word "love" has its genetic justification. People give the name "love" to the relation between a man and a woman whose genital needs have led them to found a family; but they also give the name "love" to the positive feelings between parents and children, and between the brothers and sisters of a family, although we are obliged to describe this as "aim-inhibited love" or "affection." Love with an inhibited aim was in fact originally fully sensual love, and it is so still in man's unconscious. Both—fully sensual love and aim-inhibited love—extend outside the family and create new bonds with people who before were strangers. Genital love leads to the formation of new families, and aim-inhibited love to "friendships" which become valuable from a cultural standpoint because they escape some of the limitations of genital love, as, for instance, its exclusiveness. But in the course of development the relation of love to civilization loses its unambiguity. On the one hand love comes into opposition to the interests of civilization; on the other, civilization threatens love with substantial restrictions.

This rift between them seems unavoidable. The reason for it is not immediately recognizable. It expresses itself at first as a conflict between the family and the larger community to which the individual belongs. We have already perceived that one of the main endeavors of civilization is to bring people together into large unities. But the family will not give the individual up. The more closely the members of a family are attached to one another, the more often do they tend to cut themselves off from others, and the more difficult it is for them to enter into the wider circle of life.

SIGNIFICANCE

While science often struggles to explain the functioning of love and other human emotions, Freud's explanation was particularly mechanistic, portraying human love and commitment in the most self-centered and calculating light possible. To Freud, families arose to satisfy the need for sex, societies arose to satisfy young men's need to overcome their fathers' dominance, and the two were destined to remain locked in eternal conflict, with family love pushing against the bonds of the larger society.

Freud's influence remains significant a century after he completed his most groundbreaking work; TIME Magazine named Freud to its list of the 100 Most Influential People of the twentieth century. Modern critics dismiss Freud's theories almost entirely, particularly his apparent obsession with the role of sexuality in behavior and motivation. They also make light of his formula for interpreting human dreams, which Freud perceived as a window into the unconscious mind, but which modern therapists attribute to a variety of causes including late-night snacking.

Freud's supporters, while acknowledging the limitations of his work, praise him for his role in crafting a new perspective on the human mind, and in particular for his efforts to explain why human beings often make such inexplicable (even to themselves) and unfortunate choices. Most men and women today acknowledge that human behavior is influenced by childhood experiences, unrecognized and unfulfilled needs, and unresolved conflict; psychoanalysis remains a common therapeutic approach within the field of psychiatry. In popular discussion, Sigmund Freud is most commonly mentioned when an individual makes a Freudian slip, such as accidentally calling a current boyfriend by the name of a previous partner. In Freud's analysis, such mistakes are not mistakes at all but are simply the subconscious mind trying to communicate its true feelings.

FURTHER RESOURCES
Books

Freud, Sigmund. *The Interpretation of Dreams*. New York: Avon (Reissue Edition), 1980.

Mitchell, Stephen A. and Margaret Black. *Freud and Beyond: A History of Modern Psychoanalytic Thought*. New York: Basic Books, 1995.

Nicholi, Armand M. *The Question of God: C.S. Lewis and Sigmund Freud Debate God, Love, Sex, and the Meaning of Life*. New York: Free Press, 2002.

Periodicals

Doidge, Normal. "The Doctor is Totally In." *Maclean's* 119 (2006): 40–42.

"Who Moved My Superego?" *Business Week* (May 29, 2006): 14.

Wong, Ting-Hong and Michael Apple. "Rethinking the Education/State Formation Connection: Pedagogic Reform in Singapore, 1945–1965." *Comparative Education Review* 46 (2002): 182–200.

Web sites

The Freud Museum of London. "1856–2006: 150th Anniversary of Sigmund Freud's Birth." 1999 <http://www.freud.org.uk> (accessed July 20, 2006).

Shippensburg University. "Sigmund Freud: 1836–1939." <http://www.ship.edu/~cgboeree/freud.html> (accessed July 20, 2006).

Problems and Strengths of Single-Parent Families

Magazine article

By: Leslie N. Richards and Cynthia J. Schmiege

Date: July 1993

Source: Richards, Leslie N., and Cynthia J. Schmiege. "Problems and Strengths of Single-Parent Families." *Family Relations*. 42(3) (July 1993).

About the Author: Leslie N. Richards, who earned a doctorate degree in human development from Cornell University, is an assistant professor in the department of human development and family sciences at Oregon State University. In addition to teaching, she has been involved in a research project involving various longitudinal aspects of human development. She has received numerous grants to fund her research and scholarly works, and has an extensive academic and scholarly publication list. Cynthia J. Schmiege is a faculty member at the Margaret Ritchie School of Family and Consumer Sciences at the University of Idaho. She received an undergraduate degree in Home Economics from the University of Minnesota, and holds master's and doctorate degrees in human development and family studies. She has published many scholarly and academic works.

INTRODUCTION

There are many types of families in America, and considerably fewer of them fit the mold of the traditional nuclear family (two parents of different genders, two children) during the twenty-first century than was the case during the middle decades of the twentieth. According to the United States Census Bureau data, roughly sixty-eight percent of family groups in America in 2003 consisted of two married parents (married to each other). Of the single parent families reported in 2003, there were roughly four and a half times as many single mothers as single fathers.

Since 1970, the number of single-parent families in America has more than tripled. A significant subgroup of single parents, particularly single mothers, report having made a deliberate decision to parent alone. Some state that they chose to adopt singly, others say that they opted to have a biological child without marriage, or became pregnant unexpectedly and decided to continue the pregnancy and raise the resulting child alone.

A growing number of "nontraditional" single-parent families are being created by gay men and lesbians who either adopt, create biological children through insemination, or have biological children through maternal surrogacy (that is often the case where a gay male employs an egg donor who undergoes artificial insemination, carries through the pregnancy to term, delivers the infant, and surrenders parental rights to the man who then raises the child).

Statistically, the largest group of single parents of either gender remains those who divorced or permanently separated from a spouse or domestic partner, and were either granted sole custody of their children or alternate custody with the other parent. Between the end of World War II and the early 1950s through the 1970s in America, the divorce rate increased. Roughly nine in one thousand marriages ended in divorce in 1960, whereas more than twenty per thousand did so by 1970. Although the rate of divorce plateaued in the late 1990s, divorced people are opting to remain unmarried for longer periods of time than they did in the past, sometimes stating that they are choosing to remain unmarried for most of their adult lives. The increasing rates of single parenthood, both by choice and by through divorce or spousal death, are also occurring in countries other than the United States. Statistics on rising single parenthood have also been published for the United Kingdom, France, and Russia, among others, although the United States remains at the forefront in terms of absolute numbers of single parents.

A 44-year-old mother, single by choice, reads to her two-year-old son. © LAURA DWIGHT/CORBIS.

PRIMARY SOURCE

Problems of Single Parents

All mothers and fathers were able to identify at least one significant problem faced when they were single parents, and many mentioned more than one....

Financial worries were pervasive. One mother who quickly remarried commented,

Financially it got pretty bad towards the end. It was like I was selling a lot of stuff like the freezer, and whatever else we had, just to keep going. It was a trying time.

Another woman, when asked to identify her three main problems, simply replied,

Money, money, and money.

As might be expected, money problems were much less common among the men in our sample. Only two

men in the sample reported difficulties with money, one because he had to reinvest too quickly to avoid capital gains tax.

Problems relating to role and task overload were also mentioned by a majority of mothers. Not having a second adult in the household to share the workload was often difficult, as was juggling work and family responsibilities. One mother of three teenagers explained,

In this day and age of child rearing it sure would be nice to be sharing the responsibility with someone else. I get tired of being a full-time policeman and everything else.

Role and task overload was also a common difficulty for single fathers (although identified somewhat less frequently by fathers than mothers). One father described cooking as a "painful task," and noted,

I would have to say that I tended to be more lenient than I should have been simply because I just didn't have the energy after I worked all day.

Difficulties coordinating a social life and parenting responsibilities were also common. Some mothers and fathers reported feelings of loneliness, while others indicated they felt out of place in social situations. One mother commented,

My social life with my friends that were married [was a problem]. Me feeling I was not fitting in coming alone with the kids.

Having a sexual relationship as a single parent can be difficult. One mother explained her feelings,

For a while, after being married for so long, it was difficult to adjust to being single, and I really...don't like the dating scene and all of that. So that was difficult to get used to. I would ask my single friends, "How do you have regular sex?" You know, what do you do? It was really major, after being with someone through my early adulthood; it was really difficult....

Strengths of Single Parents

Fifty-eight of 60 mothers and all 11 fathers were able to identify at least one parenting strength. Surprisingly, for both mothers and fathers, responses could be categorized into five general areas, with a great deal of similarity seen in the responses of both mothers and fathers. Five family strengths were identified: parenting skills, managing a family, communicating, growing personally, and providing financial support. Being supportive of the children, being patient, helping children cope, fostering independence, and so on were coded as parenting skills. Family management strengths included being well organized, dependable and able to coordinate schedules. Good communication included building a sense of honesty and trust and conveying ideas clearly to family....

Single Fathers Versus Single Mothers

Eight of the 11 single-parent fathers responded to the question of whether they thought the experiences of single fathers were different from the experiences of single mothers. Two areas of difference were noted by these men. The first, mentioned by five fathers, had to do with the recognition that fathers have real financial and career advantages over single mothers. Men mentioned the greater flexibility and income provided by their jobs, as well as feelings of security and satisfaction. One father summarized it rather well, commenting

I dated a number of single-parent women. Most of them were in terrible financial shape. They were often in that shape because they were not just single-parent women, but they were single-parent women without an outside source of income...without a career of substance they could hang onto and then milk for all the financial assistance they could get...In addition to that, there's all that ego stuff that you get from a career, and certainly that I was getting, that they weren't getting that I could see...Also, I didn't have to depend on somebody else to send me money...who could dangle me, kind of play me on a string with this, "Maybe I'll send you money, maybe I won't"

The second issue raised by single fathers was a feeling that societal perceptions of single fathers are different from those of single mothers. The four fathers who identified this as a difference felt they were treated as oddities because fathers are not commonly seen as involved and committed parents. One father who shared physical and legal custody with his former wife at first replied to the question about difference between single mothers and fathers by saying,

To tell you the truth, I don't think there is much difference...I have to make her lunch for school, I have to go over her homework, I have to make sure that her room is straightened up, she's taking care of her puppy, she's got warm clothes on, she's got her jacket, she has her books for school. To make sure that she is home and that she's safe. To make sure I know where she is and what little friends she's playing with. I have to take her to the movies on the weekend with her friends. I had to play dolls with her. I don't think there is much difference.

He went on to add, however,

My opinion is that I think most of society thinks of fathers as seeing their kids on the weekend and taking them to the amusement park and dumping them back off with their mother as opposed to actually spending time with their kids to train them and educate them, and just spend time with them. I know

when I take [my daughter] to her dance class, there is about 25 little girls...there is myself, and there is one other father in there. All the rest are mothers.

One of the fathers with sole custody had become a single-parent father in 1970, a time when men were unlikely to obtain custody. As he put it,

For the time, it was very strange. There weren't many men with kids....

SIGNIFICANCE

According to data published by the United States Bureau of the Census, families headed by single mothers increased by seven million between 1970 and 2003. Single father-headed families increased from less than five hundred thousand to more than two million during the same time period. There are significant racial and ethnic differences concerning the prevalence of single-parent families. According to the 2000 Census, nearly fifty per cent of all African American children live for most of their childhoods in single-parent families. However, there is compelling demographic data, such as that published by Bianchi, or by Ahlburg and DeVita, that more than fifty per cent of all American children will spend some significant portion of their youth living in a single-parent family.

There is considerable research on current realities and long-term outcomes for children living in single families, particularly in those families created by divorce. Although there is considerable variation, much of the sociological and psychological outcome data has been suggestive of some adjustment problems. Essentially, some children from single-parent families have been reported to have increased emotional and adjustment difficulties, and academic and school behavior problems in the short-term relative to their peers in stable two-parent families. Some published longitudinal data suggests that children who grow up in single-parent families are less likely to have stable long-term relationships, tend to marry later but have children earlier, than peers raised by two parent families. Studies published near the end of the twentieth century by Ricciuti and others opposed some of the earlier hypotheses about increased vulnerability of children growing up in single-parent families. The more recent research has suggested that what increases the vulnerability of a child to current and later potential for dysfunction may have considerably more to do with living in poverty or in households in which the primary parent is poorly educated or unemployed than it does with single parenthood per se.

Demographic data indicate that single parents who report that they are not so by choice are the poorest population category (about which census data is routinely collected), and are most likely to remain in poverty for prolonged periods of time. This is true both for the United States and for international populations. Internationally, the published data consistently indicates that children living in single-parent homes are those most likely to be raised in poverty. According to the most current census data available in the United States, more than one-third of mother-headed and more than fifteen per cent of father-headed single families exist in poverty. Although there may be many other contributing factors, growing up in poverty generally involves numerous risk factors that are likely to increase vulnerability for adverse academic and psychological outcomes, such as living in substandard and possibly unsafe housing, having the housing located in areas of transience or increased crime as a result of poverty, having inadequate or poor quality food, and lacking essential medical coverage and services. Impoverished areas generally have inadequate school systems as well. Those are all likely to increase potential for long-term negative outcome, but are attributable to poverty rather than simply to single parenthood. During the middle decades of the twentieth century, there was limited acceptance of single-parent families, regardless of financial status, and even less of mothers who chose to give birth to children while unmarried. Much had changed by the twenty-first century; single parenthood was sometimes a choice and not merely a consequence of marital dissolution or spousal death.

FURTHER RESOURCES
Books
DuPlessix Gray, Francine. *Soviet Women: Walking the Tightrope*. New York: Doubleday, 1990.

Hanson, Shirley M. H., Marsha L. Heims, and Doris J. Julina, eds. *Single-Parent Families: Diversity, Myths, and Realities*. New York: The Hawthorne Press, 1995.

Her Majesty's Stationery Office. *Annual Abstract of Statistics*. London: Her Majesty's Stationery Office, 1992.

Hobbs, Frank, and Laura Lippman. *Children's Well-Being: An International Comparison [International Population Reports Series (Series P95, Number 80)]*. Washington, D.C.: U.S. Government Printing Office, 1990.

Miller, Naomi. *Single Parents by Choice: A Growing Trend in Family Life*. New York: Insight Books, 1992.

Periodicals
Ahlburg, Dennis A., and Carolyn J. DeVita. "New Realities of the American Family." *Population Bulletin* 4 (2) (1992): 1–41.

Bock, Jane D. "Doing the Right Thing?: Single Mothers by Choice and the Struggle for Legitimacy." *Gender and Society* 14 (2000): 62–86.

Brown, Brett V. "The Single Father Family: Demographic, Economic, and Public Transfer Use Characteristics." *Marriage and Family Review* 29(2000): 203–220.

Ricciuti, Henry N. "Single Parenthood and School Readiness in White, Black, and Hispanic 6 and 7 year olds." *Journal of Family Psychology* 13 (3) (1999): 450–465.

Whitehead, Barbara Dafoe. "Dan Quayle was right." *The Atlantic* 271 (1993): 47–84.

Web sites
CHE Transitions Web Log: Alumni Letters. "Letters from Alumni: Cynthia J. Schmiege." April 14, 2005 <http://blog.lib.umn.edu/sbaugher/CHEtransitions/2005_04.html> (accessed April 15, 2006).

Oregon State University. "Curriculum Vitae: Leslie N. Richards." <http://www.hhs.oregonstate.edu/faculty-staff/> (accessed June 23, 2006).

U.S. Census Bureau. "America's Families and Living Arrangements: 2003 Population Characteristics." November 2004 <http://www.census.gov/prod/2004pubs/p20-553.pdf> (accessed June 24, 2006).

Myth of the Perfect Family

Book excerpt

By: Edward L. Schor

Date: 2000

Source: Schor, Edward L., ed. *Caring for Your School-Age Child Ages 5 to 12*. New York: Bantam Books, 2000.

About the Author: A pediatrician by training, Edward L. Schor is assistant vice-president at the Commonwealth Fund, a private foundation that supports independent research on health and social issues and makes grants to improve health care practice and policy. He has also served on the editorial boards of several pediatric journals.

INTRODUCTION

Among the most significant societal changes during the 1800s was the emergence of the urban middle-class. Prior to American industrialization, men and women typically labored on farms, sharing jobs as appropriate and making or growing most of what they needed to survive. As Americans migrated to cities and men took professional jobs in factories and offices, the work roles of men and women became increasingly distinct.

The role of homemaker soon became imbued with almost spiritual qualities. One perspective, known to its detractors as the cult of domesticity or the cult of true womanhood, portrayed the role of wife and mother as the highest calling a woman could heed; proponents of this philosophy also offered detailed guidance on how a woman might excel in this calling. This philosophy included four virtues that any true woman should embody: piety, purity, submissiveness, and domesticity. According to this perspective, a man might choose from thousands of occupations, but a woman was divinely intended for only one.

The specifics of domesticity were extensively discussed in women's books and magazines of the mid–1800s. The repetitive tasks of housekeeping, such as dusting furniture and making beds, were claimed to provide excellent exercise, as well as develop self-discipline. While others might refer to women's rights as something to be fought for and won, true women were encouraged to see their roles as mother, wife, cook, and housekeeper as divine rights, more than adequate for a fulfilling, though potentially over-whelming life. Writing in 1864, author and home-maker Lydia Child summarized her year's labor: In addition to daily cooking and cleaning, she had also canned fruit, cared for numerous sick children, mended clothing, and sewn linens for the home.

While the cult of domesticity bestowed a high value on a woman's daily work, it also placed upon her an inordinate amount of responsibility. Women were viewed as the sexual moderators of society and were frequently blamed for men's infidelity; an unfaithful husband was frequently assumed to have wandered due to his wife's inattention. Despite limited resources and little spending discretion, women were frequently

A set of family photographs. © UTE KAISER/ZEFA/CORBIS.

blamed if a family's clothing and general appearance were shoddy or if the house was not up to current standards. And in cases where children broke the law or otherwise strayed, their mothers, perceived to control their destinies, were frequently blamed.

Once they had been convinced of domesticity's profound value, women were given numerous suggestions as to how this ideal might be achieved. In legalistic fashion women often struggled to meet self-imposed quotas on household tasks, convinced that their family's success and their husband's happiness rested squarely on their frail shoulders.

Just as the push for domesticity was reaching full steam, reformers such as Susan B. Anthony began campaigning for women's equality—both legal and social. Thanks to their efforts, women received the right to vote in 1920. While women's rights continued to increase during the twentieth century, the 1950s saw a resurgence of the domesticity ideal. As marketers sought to sell new domestic tools and services, they quickly reverted to the ideals of a century before, with advertisements showing attractively dressed women in high heels vacuuming or washing dishes. Some commercials explained how much happier women would be if their houses were kept spotless, while others suggested that a husband's lack of physical interest might be his wife's fault and conveniently recommended a solution for purchase.

By the dawn of the twenty-first century, American families were more diverse than ever before; fewer than one family in five consisted of two parents and their biological children. Despite this change and over a century of advances in women's rights, some mothers still worried that they might be making a mess of their families. Some of the same myths perpetrated by nineteenth century domesticity still haunt mothers today.

■ PRIMARY SOURCE

The Myth of the Perfect Family

The American family is a rapidly changing institution. You may have grown up in the stereotypical American family—two parents and one or more children, with a father who worked outside the home and a mother who stayed home and cared for the children and the household. Today, with the entry of so many more women into the workforce, with the increasing divorce rate, and with the growing number of single-parent households, other family structures have become more common.

If your own family is not like the one you grew up in, your situation is certainly not unusual. Currently, 30 percent of

American families are now headed by single parents, either divorced, widowed, or never married. Some children live in foster families; others live in step-families or in gay and lesbian families. In more than two thirds of families, both parents work outside the home.

Even if your own family fits the more traditional mold, your children will almost certainly have some friends who live in households with different structures. From time to time you can expect your youngsters to ask questions like "Why do people get divorced?" "How come Jimmy's mother and father don't live together?" "Why does Annette's father live with another lady?" Because families are so important to children, parents need to be able to answer such questions with more than mere slogans or quick replies. By asking these questions, children are trying to understand two things about families: the different structures that families can take and the changes in structure, lifestyles and relationships that can occur.

Any group of people living together in a household can create and call themselves a family. For example, to share expenses a divorced mother with two children may live with another divorced woman with children; together, they may consider themselves a family. A grandparent who lives with her daughter, son-in-law, and grandchildren may become an integral part of their family. The variations of family structures and definition are almost endless, but they have certain qualities in common: Family members share their lives emotionally and together fulfill the multiple responsibilities of family life.

MYTH: The "nuclear family" is a universal phenomenon.

The nuclear family is generally defined as a family group made up of only a father, mother, and children. Although most people tend to think that this particular family structure has always been the dominant one, that is not the case.

The nuclear family is a relatively recent phenomenon, becoming common only within the last century. Before then, the "traditional" family was multigenerational, with grandparents often living with their children on farms as well as in urban environments, typically with other relatives living nearby. The nuclear family has evolved in response to a number of factors: better health and longer lives, economic development, industrialization, urbanization, geographic mobility, and migration to the suburbs. These changes have resulted in physical separation of extended-family members and in progressive fragmentation of the family.

MYTH: Family harmony is the rule, not the exception.

Although family life is often romanticized, it has always been filled with conflicts and tension. Difficulties between spouses are commonplace, with disagreements arising over issues ranging from how the children should be raised to how the family finances should be budgeted. Husbands and wives also often struggle with their inability to sustain romantic infatuation beyond the first few years of their marriage, thus having to learn to maintain a relationship in which partnership and companionship may become more important than passionate love.

Parent-children conflicts are commonplace too. As parents assert their authority, and children try to assert their autonomy appropriately, strife is inevitable.

While we often expect families to be above the chaos that exists in the rest of society, that outlook places unrealistic expectations upon the family. In the real world, families are not always a haven, since they, too, can be filled with conflict. Although stress and disagreements are common, they can be destructive to families, especially when conflict gets out of hand. Families are under constant stress, being pushed and pulled from many directions, often without the support systems of extended families that may have existed in the past.

MYTH: The stability of a family is a measure of its success.

Change is a part of life. Death, illness, physical separation, financial strains, divorce …these are some of the events families have to adjust to. Consequently, stability shouldn't be the only measure of a family's success. Many families function quite well, despite frequent disruptions. In fact, one important measure of a family's success is its ability to adjust to change. Daily life is full of stresses that constantly demand accommodation from family members.

MYTH: Parents control their children's fate.

In reality, parents cannot determine how their children will turn out. Inevitably, children assert their autonomy, creating a niche for themselves separate from their parents. At the same time, many factors external to both the child and family can influence the way a child develops.

Even within the same family there can be tremendous individual variations among siblings in intelligence, temperament, mood, and sociability. Yet despite these differences, parents are responsible for imparting to each child a sense of being loved and accepted, for helping each child to succeed at various developmental tasks, and for socializing each child into respecting the rules and accepting the responsibilities society imposes. These are indeed awesome tasks.

Some parents perceive themselves as having total responsibility for their children's fate. This belief places a heavy and unrealistic emotional burden on them as well as their youngsters. If the children are having problems, they often feel a sense of failure; likewise, the children feel as though they have let their family down if they do

not live up to their parents' expectations. In essence, parents can influence and shape but cannot control their children's lives.

SIGNIFICANCE

As American families become increasingly diverse, some traditional parenting advice has become less useful. Many Americans' perceptions of the ideal family developed from watching 1950s television shows such as *Leave it to Beaver* and *Ozzie and Harriet*, shows that even in their era portrayed a simplified, sanitized version of American family life. Given the societal changes in the half-century since these shows originally aired, their relevance to today's families appears quite limited.

Although the roles of parents continue to change and the challenges facing families are becoming more complex, today's parents have access to far more abundant resources than did their predecessors. Modern parents are typically better educated than their parents were, with access to literally hundreds of books, videos, and seminars on improving parenting skills. The modern family can never achieve perfection, but successful parents acknowledge and accept that limitation. Parenting in the twenty-first century, just as in the nineteenth, requires patience, persistence, and a willingness to make mistakes in pursuit of a healthy family life.

FURTHER RESOURCES
Books

DuBois, Ellen Carol. *Feminism and Suffrage: The Emergence of an Independent Women's Movement In America, 1849–1869.* Cornell University Press, 1978.

Safer, Jeanne. *Beyond Motherhood: Choosing a Life without Children.* New York: Pocket Books, 1996.

Warner, Judith. *Perfect Madness: Motherhood in the Age of Anxiety.* New York: Riverhead Books, 2005.

Periodicals

Dolev, R., *et al.* "How to Be a Good Parent in Bad Times: Constructing Parenting Advice about Terrorism." *Child Care, Health and Development.* 32 (July 2006): 467–476.

MacInnes, John. "Work-Life Balance in Europe: A Response to the Baby Bust or Reward for the Baby Boomers." *European Societies.* 8 (2006): 223--249.

Welter, Barbara. "The Cult of True Womanhood: 1820–1860." *American Quarterly.* 18, no. 2, part 1 (Summer 1966):151–174.

Web sites

Musee McCord Museum. "The Cult of Domesticity." June 8, 2006 <http://www.mccord-museum.qc.ca/en/keys/folders/VQ_P1_6_EN> (accessed June 17, 2006).

Public Broadcasting Service. "Cult of True Womanhood." <http://www.pbs.org/stantonanthony/resources/index.html?body=culthood.html> (accessed June 17, 2006).

Single Parents by Sex and Selected Characteristics

Chart

By: Jason Fields

Date: November 2004

Source: Adapted by Thomson Gale from *U.S. Census Bureau.* "America's Families and Living Arrangements: 2003 Population Characteristics." November 2004 <http://www.census.gov/prod/2004pubs/p20-553.pdf> (accessed June 24, 2006).

About the Author: Jason Fields joined the U.S. Census Bureau in 1997 as a Family Demographer in the Fertility and Family Statistics Branch of the Population Division. As a demographer in this division, Dr. Fields works extensively on child living arrangements and well-being, family formation and dissolution, unmarried couple partnerships, and grandparent/grandchild co-residence.

INTRODUCTION

The number of families headed by a single parent has been rising steadily since divorces began to increase within a decade after the end of World War II. Although this is particularly the case in the United States, the trend is international as well. According to data published by the United States Census Bureau, the last several decades have indicated a trend toward marrying later, having fewer children, and living as a single parent for longer periods of time. Single parenthood can occur in any of several different ways: divorce, death of spouse or partner, dissolution of domestic partnership or other non-married shared household arrangements, adoption by a single parent, unplanned pregnancy in which custody of the child is either maintained solely by one parent or alternately shared between both parents, or planned single parenthood through intentional pregnancy or surrogacy.

Historically, most single parents reported that they became single through death or divorce, and not by choice. During much of the latter half of the twentieth century (and still, to some extent), the statistical majority of single parents, particularly single mothers were young, poorly educated, and living in poverty.

Between 1970 and the early years of the twenty-first century, the percentage of single-parent households rose from 12 to 26 per cent for females, and from 1 to 6 per cent for males, according to reports published by the United States Census Bureau. However, much of that increase occurred between 1970 and the first years of the 1990s; the percentages have remained fairly stable since that time. There is also a significant factor contributing to the overall rise in single parent households, particularly among females, during the past two decades: The number of women who opt to become single parents without ever having been married has increased steadily since the 1970s. According to a National Vital Statistics Report published in 2000, the proportion of single females who have never been married but who have had biological children has been steadily increasing since the year 1970. Adults have also been marrying later in life than has been the case since the end of the nineteenth century, which further increases the chances for an unplanned or unmarried pregnancy and childbirth. Still, the greatest proportion of single parent families in the United States is created by divorce.

PRIMARY SOURCE

SINGLE PARENTS BY SEX AND SELECTED CHARACTERISTICS
See primary source image.

SIGNIFICANCE

Single parent households may be constituted in several different ways, and may not necessarily be composed of only one adult and her/his children. Other unrelated adults, such as domestic partners and girlfriends/boyfriends, may play roles with varying degrees of responsibility and authority. Other unrelated adults may live, or spend significant time, in the household as well. In addition, there may be related adults or others participating in the family group. It is not uncommon, particularly within Hispanic and African-American unmarried parent families, to have more than one generation, or extended family members, sharing living space. These types of living arrangements are referred to as unrelated and related subfamilies, respectively.

Single parents by sex and selected characteristics: 2003

	Single fathers					Single mothers				
		Race and ethnicity						Race and ethnicity			
		White only						White only			
Characteristic	Total	Total	Non-Hispanic	Black only	Hispanic (of any race)	Total	Total	Non-Hispanic	Black only	Hispanic (of any race)
All single parents	2,260	1,758	1,330	353	450	10,142	6,471	4,870	3,124	1,807
Type of family group										
Family household	1,915	1,506	1,176	285	346	8,139	5,155	3,690	2,591	1,357
Related subfamily	260	175	97	62	84	1,596	1,003	645	475	390
Unrelated subfamily	84	78	58	6	20	407	313	265	58	61
Number of own children under 18										
1 child	1,422	1,101	863	228	254	5,529	3,670	2,866	1,563	904
2 children	609	485	353	84	137	2,935	1,876	1,396	915	530
3 children	170	133	90	28	43	1,223	697	484	443	246
4 or more children	58	39	24	13	15	455	228	125	203	127
Presence of own children under 18										
With own children under 18	2,260	1,758	1,330	353	450	10,142	6,471	4,870	3,124	1,807
With own children under 12	1,547	1,187	846	254	360	7,417	4,624	3,385	2,391	1,405
With own children under 6	878	668	430	139	253	4,234	2,575	1,811	1,395	872
With own children under 3	530	404	261	84	152	2,287	1,364	956	789	453
With own children under 1	203	162	112	27	55	734	446	309	241	155
Education										
Less than high school	450	356	170	64	195	1,966	1,267	600	585	736
High school graduate	953	742	590	146	156	3,577	2,235	1,726	1,169	586
Some college	580	426	269	113	62	3,298	2,065	1,722	1,055	396
Bachelor's degree or higher	277	234	302	29	35	1,301	904	822	315	90
Marital status										
Never married	852	601	359	183	257	4,413	2,255	1,507	1,924	850
Married spouse absent[1]	344	264	203	53	63	1,810	1,193	773	479	480
Divorced	956	817	707	95	115	3,504	2,725	2,363	632	394
Widowed	107	76	62	22	15	416	298	228	89	83
Poverty status in 2002										
Below poverty level	357	239	142	93	100	3,268	1,849	1,214	1,237	730
At or above poverty level	1,903	1,520	1,188	260	349	6,875	4,622	3,656	1,887	1,077

[1]Married spouse absent includes separated.

SOURCE: U.S. Census Bureau, Current Population Survey, Annual Social and Economic Supplement, 2003.

PRIMARY SOURCE

Single Parents by Sex and Selected Characteristics: Statistics from the U.S. Census Bureau on single-parent families.
ADAPTED BY THOMSON GALE FROM DATA FROM THE U.S. CENSUS BUREAU.

There are racial and ethnic differences among unmarried mothers: white women are the most likely to have been married and to become single mothers as a result of divorce or marital separation, and the least likely to intentionally bear children outside of a marital relationship. African-Americans, statistically, are the most likely to have children when unmarried, or to choose not to marry at all. They are also most likely to have children when still in their teen years, and to live in multi-generational families in which other significant adults, such as parents or grandparents, are

instrumental in the raising of their children. Hispanic women who become single after having been married are the population group most likely to live in a related subfamily network, according to a Census Brief on single parent families published in 1997.

Although many people living in single-parent families exist in poverty, that relative number has decreased along with the growing trend among never married, reportedly independent, financially stable, employed, and well-educated women (and men, to a much lesser extent) who choose to become single parents, either through birth or adoption. The number of female single parents who receive public assistance, in the form of TANF (Temporary Assistance for Needy Families), Medicaid, or food stamps has decreased somewhat since the mid–1980s.

Although there are some basic similarities among single parent families, there are considerable distinctions as well. Children who live with divorce, separation, or relationship breakups experience very different stressors, particularly if there are alternating custody arrangements, or shifting blocs of time spent in more than one household, than do children who have always or only lived with a single parent. Children who lost a parent as a result of death have very different experiences than do those in divorce—although both may mourn the loss of a former way of life, there are varying degrees of permanence in the grief process.

Children who are adopted into single parent families have some similarities with the biological children of never married (and divorced, widowed, or separated) single parents, although there are unique stressors present for children who have been adopted, particularly when they transition from one culture to another (as in international adoptions) or are adopted into transracial families. Those adopted children may have more in common with adopted children in two-parent families than they do with the biological children of never married single parents.

In a statistical sample that can only look at discrete and pre-defined categories, there are groups of people who are labeled single parents when, in fact, they are living in relationships with other adults to whom they are not legally married. In most areas of the United States this describes children living in two parent families headed by gay men or lesbians. Those children may be raised in homes in which they have two full-time (living in the home, not necessarily home full-time) parents who are not able to marry. The exigencies and stressors of children growing up in households that are not legally sanctioned or socially recognized may vary considerably from, or have almost nothing in common with, those children who are growing up in "true" single parent families.

FURTHER RESOURCES
Books
Hanson, S. M., et al., eds. *Single-Parent Families: Diversity, Myths, and Realities.* New York: Hawthorne, 1995.

Hobbs, Frank, and Laura Lippman. *Children's Well-Being: An International Comparison [International Population Reports Series (Series P95, Number 80)].* Washington, D.C.: U.S. Government Printing Office, 1990.

Mason, Mary Ann, Arlene Skolnick, and Stephen D. Sugarman, eds. *All Our Families: New Policies for a New Century. 2nd edition.* New York: Oxford University Press, 2002.

Miller, Naomi. *Single Parents by Choice: A Growing Trend in Family Life.* New York: Insight Books, 1992.

O'Connell, Martin T. *Children with Single Parents—How they Fare (Census Brief).* Washington, D.C.: U.S. Census Bureau, 1997.

Periodicals
Ahlburg, Dennis A., and Carol J. DeVita. "New Realities of the American Family." *Population Bulletin* 47 (2) (1992): 1–44.

Bock, Jane D. "Doing the Right Thing? Single Mothers by Choice and the Struggle for Legitimacy." *Gender and Society* 14 (2000): 62-86.

Brown, Brett V. "The Single Father Family: Demographic, Economic, and Public Transfer Characteristics." *Marriage and Family Review* 29 (2/3) (2000): 203–220.

Ricciuti, Henry N. "Single Parenthood and School Readiness in White, Black, and Hispanic 6 and 7 Year Olds." *Journal of Family Psychology* 13 (3) (1999): 450–465.

Ventura, Stephanie, and Christina Bachrach. "Nonmarital Childbearing in the United States, 1940–1999." *National Vital Statistics Reports* 48(16) (October 2000): Table 1.

Whitehead, Barbara D. "Dan Quayle was Right." *The Atlantic* 271 (April 1993): 47–84.

Married-Couple Family Groups With Stay at Home Parents

Chart

By: Jason Fields

Date: November 2004

Source: Adapted by Thomson Gale from: Fields, Jason. *U.S. Census Bureau.* "America's Families and Living Arrangements: Married-Couple Family Groups With Stay at Home Parents." November 2004. <http://www.census.gov/prod/2004pubs/p20-553.pdf> (accessed July 22, 2006).

About the Author: Jason Fields is a family demographer and a member of the Fertility and Family Statistics Branch in the Population Division of the United States Census Bureau. The U.S. Census Bureau was established to conduct the ten-year census needed to

A family sets the table for dinner. © ROYALTY-FREE/CORBIS.

reallocate members of Congress among the states. As of 2006, the agency employs 12,000 and conducts approximately one hundred annual surveys annually in addition to the Census itself.

INTRODUCTION

Over the past half century, the typical American home has become increasingly difficult to describe. Whereas the vast majority of families in the nineteenth century consisted of two married parents and multiple children, today's families come in numerous varieties, and it has become increasingly difficult to regard any one form of family as typical.

Both cultural and medical changes have influenced this trend toward more diverse families; men and women today are more likely to postpone marriage while completing higher education. The widespread availability of inexpensive, reliable birth control has also allowed families to choose when to have children, or in some cases to forego parenthood entirely. Rising divorce rates have fueled the growth of single-parent households, and remarriages, sometimes after multiple previous marriages, have resulted in a growing population of blended families incorporating pieces of multiple previous homes.

A significant change in American attitudes occurred during the twentieth century, as women became more accepted in the workplace and husbands became less hostile to the idea of wives working. From the early 1900s to the end of the century, women moved from being an anomaly in most businesses to holding top positions in some of America's largest corporations, aided at least in part by the mass entry of women into the workforce during World War II. While most of these wartime workers returned to more traditional roles following the war, their experi-

ence gave many Americans a taste of what women could do when given the chance.

In the decades following the war, more opportunities became available to women, and a growing number chose to leave home and take outside jobs, either part-time or full-time. These opportunities, combined with falling childbirth rates and smaller families led to a gradual increase in the number of two-income families in which both parents are employed outside the home.

Despite the benefits of receiving two incomes, some families choose to live on a single income, with the other spouse remaining at home. In some families this is a transitional arrangement, maintained only while the children are small; but in other cases families choose to depend on a single earner. Because of the economic implications of living on only one income, the Census Bureau asked specific questions of these stay-at-home parents in order to better understand the reasons for their choice.

PRIMARY SOURCE

MARRIED-COUPLE FAMILY GROUPS WITH STAY AT HOME PARENTS

See primary source image.

SIGNIFICANCE

Not surprisingly, parents choose to remain at home for a variety of reasons. In the 2003 study, respondents reported staying at home due to injury, illness, or disability, while attending school, because of retirement, or due to an inability to find employment. One clear finding of the study was that men and women stay home for different reasons. In the case of men, more than forty-five percent reported staying at home due to illness or disability; for women the figure for this category was less than five percent. In comparison, men reported staying home to care for family 15.6 percent of the time, compared to more than eighty-eight percent of women who chose this response. This disparity, with women five times more likely to report staying home to care for family, suggests that despite greater workplace opportunities than ever before, women are still more likely to be the primary caregivers for children in the home.

A second finding of the study dealt with income levels and the decision to work. Fully fifty percent of the families in which the mother remained at home had an annual household income above $50,000, and more than twenty percent had incomes of $100,000 or more. This relationship suggests that staying at home

Married-couple family groups with stay-at-home parents: 2003

(in thousands)

Characteristic	Mothers		Fathers	
	Number	Percent	Number	Percent
All married-couple family groups with children under 15 years old	**23,209**	**100.0**	**23,209**	**100.0**
Labor force participation last year and stay-at-home parent families				
In labor force 1 or more weeks last year	16,371	70.5	22,199	95.6
Out of labor force all 52 weeks last year	6,838	29.5	1,009	4.3
Primary reason out of the labor force				
Ill/disabled	335	1.4	455	2.0
Retired	80	0.3	108	0.5
Going to school	227	1.0	90	0.4
Could not find work	105	0.5	111	0.5
Other	54	0.2	88	0.4
To care for home and family	6,036	26.0	157	0.7
Spouse in labor force all 52 weeks last year	5,388	23.2	98	0.4
Stay-at-home family groups	**5,388**	**100.0**	**98**	**100.0**
Type of family group				
Family household	5,276	97.9	94	95.9
Related subfamily	110	2.0	6	5.1
Unrelated subfamily	2	0.0	–	0.0
Number of own children under 15				
1 child	1,648	30.6	36	36.7
2 children	2,226	41.3	50	51.0
3 children	1,063	19.7	6	6.1
4 or more children	451	8.4	6	6.1
Presence of children				
With own children under 15	5,388	100.0	98	100.0
With own children under 12	4,883	90.6	85	86.7
With own children under 6	3,491	64.8	50	51.0
With own children under 3	2,254	41.8	28	28.6
With own children under 1	724	13.4	7	7.1
Age of stay-at-home parent				
15 to 24 years	287	5.3	4	4.1
25 to 34 years	1,795	33.3	25	25.5
35 to 44 years	2,379	44.2	46	46.9
45 to 54 years	818	15.2	19	19.4
55 to 64 years	97	1.8	4	4.1
65 years and over	12	0.2	–	0.0
Family income in 2002				
Under $10,000	126	2.3	6	6.1
$10,00–$14,999	229	4.3	3	3.1
$15,00–$19,999	318	5.9	3	3.1
$20,00–$24,999	396	7.3	11	11.2
$25,00–$29,999	416	7.7	8	8.2
$30,00–$39,999	650	12.1	17	17.3
$40,00–$49,999	508	9.4	11	11.2
$50,00–$74,999	1,043	19.4	14	14.3
$75,00–$99,999	613	11.4	17	17.3
$100,00 and over	1,089	20.2	9	9.2
Poverty status in 2002				
Below poverty level	668	12.4	13	13.3
At or above poverty level	4,720	87.6	85	86.7

– Represents zero or rounds to zero.

SOURCE: U.S. Census Bureau, Current Population Survey, Annual Social and Economic Supplement, 2003.

PRIMARY SOURCE

Married-Couple Family Groups With Stay at Home Parents: As shown by these statistics from the U.S. Census Bureau, 26 percent of married women with children do not work so that they can care for their children. Married men with children are far less likely to do so. ADAPTED BY THOMSON GALE FROM DATA FROM THE U.S. CENSUS BUREAU.

is far more common in affluent homes and that lower-income families are less able to afford the loss of income caused by a stay-at-home parent.

A final observation from the data is that stay-at-home mothers don't appear to actually stay at home all the time. Only 29.5 percent of responding mothers said they had been out of the workforce for the entire fifty-two weeks of the previous year, while the remaining 70.5 percent have worked outside the home at least one week during that time. This data paints a picture of stay-at-home mothers who devote almost all their time to caring for family but who also hold part-time jobs from time to time.

While stay-at-home dads remain the exception, with fewer than five percent of fathers staying at home for all of the previous fifty-two weeks, some research suggests that a small but growing number of men are choosing to care for the children while their wives work outside the home. Given the increasing earnings potential enjoyed by women today and a wider variety of family forms currently in existence, this trend appears likely to continue.

FURTHER RESOURCES
Books

Gill, Libby. *Stay-at-Home Dads: The Essential Guide to Creating the New Family.* New York: The Penguin Group, 2001.

Peters, Joan. *When Mothers Work: Loving Our Children Without Sacrificing Ourselves.* New York: Perseus Books, 1997.

Ramming, Cindy. *All Mothers Work: A Guilt-Free Guide for the Stay at Home Mom.* New York: Avon Books, 1996.

Periodicals

Chaker, Marie. "Business Schools Target At-Home Moms." *Wall Street Journal—Eastern Edition* 247 (2006): D1–D2.

Jayson, Sharon. "Daddy's Home to Stay." *USA Today* (June 16, 2005): D1.

"Stepping off the Mommy Track." *Money* 35 (2006): 40.

Web sites

CNN. "The stay-at-home generation." May 25, 2005. <http://edition.cnn.com/2005/WORLD/asiapcf/05/17/eyeonchina.work/index.html> (accessed July 22, 2006).

Columbia University News Service. "Stay-at-home Mothers Grow in Number." June 23, 2003. <http://www.jrn.columbia.edu/studentwork/cns/2003-06-22/316.asp> (accessed July 22, 2006).

Washington Times. "More and More Men Decide to Be Stay-at-home Fathers." April 24, 2001. <http://www.slowlane.com/articles/media/more_men_decide.html> (accessed July 22, 2006).

Households by Type: 1970–2003

Chart

By: Jason Fields

Date: November 2004

Source: Fields, Jason. *U.S. Census Bureau.* "America's Families and Living Arrangements: Households by Type: 1970–2003." November 2004. <http://www.census.gov/prod/2004pubs/p20-553.pdf> (accessed July 23, 2006).

About the Author: Jason Fields is a family demographer and a member of the Fertility and Family Statistics Branch in the Population Division of the United States Census Bureau. The U.S. Census Bureau was established to conduct the ten-year census needed to reallocate members of Congress among the states. As of 2006, the agency employs 12,000 and conducts approximately one hundred annual surveys annually in addition to the Census itself.

INTRODUCTION

The taking of a decennial census during the first year of every decade was mandated by Article 2, Section 1 of the United States Constitution: "The actual Enumeration shall be made within three years after the first meeting of the Congress of the United States, and within every subsequent term of ten years, in such manner as they shall by law direct."

When the Census formally began (population counts and descriptions had occurred informally in the USA prior to this, with the first count taking place in Virginia in the 1600s) in 1970, it was brief and quite specific, detailing just a few population characteristics for each household: number of free white males from the age of sixteen and up; number of free white males under the age of sixteen; number of free white females regardless of age; and the number of free persons of any other skin color, including an enumeration of Native American Indians who were not exempted from paying taxes. Slaves were simply counted during the first census.

At the outset, the only precise data collected concerned the name, date and place of birth, and gender of the head of the household, and this household was rather loosely defined by the person who considered himself or herself as such. The specification of males by age had to do with ascertaining areas of potential military conscription, as any free white male who had attained the age of sixteen years was eligible to be pressed into military service. The remainder of the free persons living under the same roof—figuratively speaking, as an entire plantation, with many houses and assorted staff and workers might be considered one household for the purposes of the census—were either counted or estimated, but not specifically listed out by individual identity, although they were tabulated loosely by race and gender. For the first five rounds of census-taking, this remained the case. Commencing with the sixth decennial census in 1850, the names of every member of the household were recorded, and demographic information began to be collected.

Although the questions to be asked and the types of data to be collected were relatively specific, the means by which that occurred were determined by each census taker. Printed forms for the census were not created until 1830.

PRIMARY SOURCE

HOUSEHOLDS BY TYPE: 1970–2003

See primary source image.

SIGNIFICANCE

From the outset, the census defined the nature of the household by the person who was considered to be its head, and counted the other members as subsidiary. Starting in 1800, it categorized household members, in addition to the head, by number of free white males and free white females below the age of ten, between ten and sixteen years of age, between sixteen and twenty-six, between twenty-six and forty-five, and above the age of forty-five, as well as any other persons in the household subject to taxation. Slaves were simply counted, not categorized by age or gender. In addition to the personal data, census takers also indi-

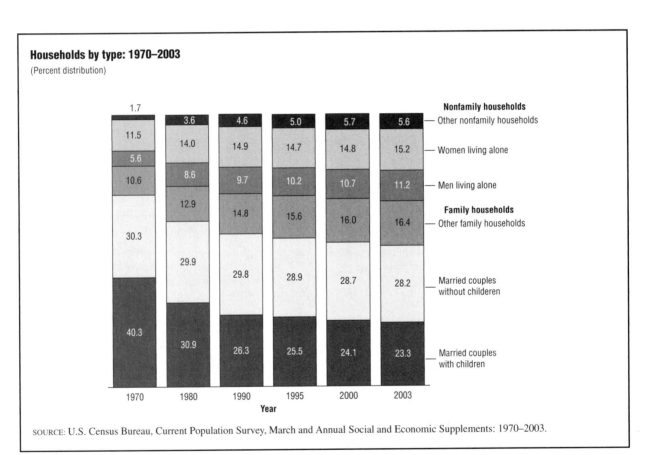

Households by type: 1970–2003
(Percent distribution)

SOURCE: U.S. Census Bureau, Current Population Survey, March and Annual Social and Economic Supplements: 1970–2003.

PRIMARY SOURCE

Households by Type: 1970–2003: U.S. Census Bureau research shows that the traditional married couple with children has declined relative to other forms of houshoulds since 1970. ADAPTED BY THOMSON GALE FROM DATA FROM THE U.S. CENSUS BUREAU.

cated the county, parish, town, township, or city in which the household lay. Starting in 1820, the census began to enumerate the free "colored" persons and slaves, distributed by age, for each household. According to the instructions given to the marshals, who were the census-takers, for the conduction of the data-gathering for the 1820 census, the head of the household was rather loosely defined—typically according to functionality or type of dwelling or business establishment. The head of household could be a shop steward, factory owner, overseer, plantation boss, or any person who was in charge of the running of the building, whether home or business establishment. For the purpose of clarity, a specific date was set for the commencement of the census, and all data gathered was to be a snapshot of reality for that day. That is, persons who were alive on the target date but died before the census was taken would be counted as living. Babies born after that date were not to be counted.

In 1830, the census underwent several significant changes: for the first time, a printed form with exact questions was used; each individual in a household was to be enumerated according to age category (the number of which were greatly expanded) and gender. Free slaves and "colored persons" were counted together; deaf and dumb persons were counted as a group, as were blind persons, without regard to race, age, or gender. White persons who were foreign-born and had not become United States citizens were also counted. Beginning in 1850, each person, not simply the head of the household, was listed by name and demographics, for the census. The population census was concerned with dwelling places; directors of institutions and wardens of correctional facilities were considered household heads, and inhabitants thereof were considered as though they were family members.

In 1850, an accounting of slaves was made, with listings of each person who held ownership rights to any individual slave listed out. Slaves were enumerated by age and gender, and assigned numbers rather than names. Family received its first formal definition for the purpose of census-taking in 1850. It was as follows: "By the term family is meant. Either one person living separately in a house, or a part of a house, and providing for him or herself, or several persons living together in a house, or in part of a house, upon one common means of support, and separately from others in similar circumstances. A widow living alone and separately providing for herself, or 200 individuals living together and provided for by a common head, should each be numbered as one family. The resident inmates of a hotel, jail, garrison, hospital, an asylum, or other similar institution, should be reckoned as one

A family portrait. © ROYALTY-FREE/CORBIS.

family." By 1880, it had been recognized that the residents of tenement or apartment houses ought to be enumerated as separate families, so long as they dwelled in distinct portions of the buildings. With the passage of time, more specificity was added to the description of the inhabitants of an abode—each person's relationship to the head of the household was to be delineated as exactly as possible, whether husband, wife, child, boarder, sister-in-law, lodger, inmate, pupil, or servant (to name but a few possibilities).

With the passage of time, changes in family composition and household definition have been created. Households are defined according to those (whether one or more) who live together in shared space. One person who is involved in the financial maintenance of the dwelling is self-designated as the "householder." Households are defined by whether they contain "family" or "non-family." "Family households" are considered those in which at least two persons, one of whom is designated as the householder, are related by birth, adoption, or marriage. "Nonfamily households" are composed either of people living alone or people sharing a dwelling who are not related to the householder. Family households have been grouped according to: married couples living together either with or without children present; other family members constituting a household; and adult women or men who live alone. The number of married-couple households has declined significantly since 1970 (from forty percent down to twenty-three percent), and the number of single-parent households or family households without spouses present has increased from eleven percent in 1970 to sixteen percent in 2003.

FURTHER RESOURCES

Books

Census and Identity: the Politics of Race, Ethnicity, and Language in National Censuses, edited by David I. Kertzer and Dominique Arel. Cambridge, UK: Cambridge University Press, 2002.

Handbook of Family Diversity, edited by David H. Demo, Katharine R. Allen, and Mark A. Fine. New York: Oxford University Press, 1999.

All Our Families: New Policies for a New Century, edited by Mary Ann Mason, Arlene Skolnick, and Stephen D. Sugarman. New York: Oxford University Press, 2002.

Periodicals

Ahlburg, D. A. and C. J. DeVita. "New Realities of the American Family." *Population Bulletin* 47, 2 (1992).

"The Changing American Family." *New York Times* (May 18, 2001): A18.

Lewin, Tamar. "Confusion Ensued After Census Report on Two-parent Families." *New York Times* (April 21, 2001): A16.

Schmitt, Eric. "For First Time, Nuclear Families Drop Below 25% of Households." *New York Times* (May 15, 2001): A1.

South Dakota Department of Labor. "From Inkwell to Internet: The History of the US Census." *Labor Market Information Center: Labor Bulletin* (May 2002): 1–4.

Web sites

U.S. Census Bureau. <http://www.census.gov> (accessed July 22, 2006).

Family Groups by Type and Selected Characteristics

Table

By: Jason Fields

Date: November 2004

Source: Fields, Jason. *U.S. Census Bureau.* "America's Families and Living Arrangements: Family Groups by Type and Selected Characteristics." <http://www.census.gov/prod/2004pubs/p20-553.pdf> (accessed July 23, 2006).

About the Author: Jason Fields is a family demographer and a member of the Fertility and Family Statistics Branch in the Population Division of the United States Census Bureau. The U.S. Census Bureau was established to conduct the ten-year census needed to reallocate members of Congress among the states. As of 2006, the agency employs 12,000 and conducts approximately one hundred annual surveys in addition to the Census itself.

INTRODUCTION

The first official United States Census was conducted in 1790. Overseen by Secretary of State Thomas Jefferson, it provided little more than a gross count of the U.S. population. Census data was collected primarily by federal marshals traveling on horseback throughout the nation.

With the basic census methodology and tools in place, additional data was relatively simple to gather, and in 1810 the government added census questions relating to manufacturing capacity and quality. Additional information was collected in subsequent years, and by 1850 the census included questions dealing with social issues including poverty, crime, and participation in religion. As both the U.S. population and the number of questions on the survey climbed, the total volume of data skyrocketed. In 1902, recognizing the need for a permanent federal agency to oversee the rapidly growing project, Congress made the Census Bureau a permanent part of government.

The Census Bureau collects data continuously, averaging more than one hundred surveys each year. The result of this ongoing effort is a detailed statistical snapshot of life in America. By collecting data on an ongoing basis, the census also allows policy makers to recognize and quantify changes in American life over time. Much of the data currently collected relates to family life and the changing face of families in the United States. In 2004, the Census Bureau published a comprehensive report on the makeup of families in America. This report, covering changes in family composition from 1970 to 2003, offered an in-depth look at what constitutes a family today in the United States.

PRIMARY SOURCE

FAMILY GROUPS BY TYPE AND SELECTED CHARACTERISTICS

See primary source image.

SIGNIFICANCE

The 2004 family report reveals several long-term trends in the makeup of American families. Notably, the report reveals that families, which the Census

Family groups by type and selected characteristics: 2003

Characteristic	Total	Married couple family groups	Other family groups Total	Other family groups Male reference person	Other family groups Female reference person
All family groups	79,210	58,586	20,624	5,001	15,623
Family type					
Family household	75,596	57,320	18,285	4,665	13,620
Related subfamily	3,089	1,232	1,856	260	1,596
Unrelated subfamily	525	34	491	84	407
Size of family group					
2 people	36,084	25,254	10,830	2,885	7,945
3 people	17,454	11,831	5,623	1,269	4,354
4 people	15,457	12,887	2,571	531	2,040
5 people	6,703	5,721	982	174	808
6 or more	3,512	2,894	618	141	477
Number of own children under 18					
No own children	40,363	32,141	8,222	2,741	5.481
1 child	17,103	10,152	6,951	1,422	5,529
2 children	14,232	10,687	3,544	609	2,935
3 children	5,490	4,096	1,393	170	1,223
4 or more children	2,022	1,509	513	58	456
Presence of own children under 18					
No own children	40,363	32,141	8,222	2,741	5,481
With own children	38,847	26,445	12,402	2,260	10,142
With own children under 12	28,557	19,593	8,964	1,547	7,417
With own children under 6	17,127	12,014	5,112	878	4,234
With own children under 3	10,023	7,206	2,817	530	2,287
With own children under 1	3,255	2,318	937	203	734
Family income in 2002					
Under $10,000	5,176	1,584	3,593	426	3,167
$10,000–$14,999	3,674	1,694	1,981	309	1,672
$15,000–$19,999	4,433	2,385	2,048	387	1,661
$20,000–$24,999	4,780	2,853	1,927	465	1,462
$25,000–$29,999	4,757	3,032	1,725	388	1,337
$30,000–$39,999	8,822	5,988	2,835	763	2,072
$40,000–$49,999	7,874	5,779	2,095	634	1,461
$50,000–$74,999	15,837	13,244	2,593	889	1,704
$75,000–$99,999	10,288	9,308	980	390	590
$100,000 and over	13,567	12,720	847	349	498
Tenure					
Owner	59,525	48,632	10,892	2,950	7,942
Renter	18,743	9,297	9,446	1,988	7,458
Occupies without payment	942	657	285	62	223

X not applicable.

SOURCE: U.S. Census Bureau, Current Population Survey, Annual Social and Economic Supplement, 2003.

PRIMARY SOURCE

Family Groups by Type and Selected Characteristics: As can be seen in this table from the U.S. Census Bureau, married couple family groups tend to be better off financially than other family groups. ADAPTED BY THOMSON GALE FROM DATA FROM THE U.S. CENSUS BUREAU.

Bureau defines as at least two related individuals living together, are less prevalent today than in the past. In 1970, eighty-one percent of all households consisted of families; by 1996 that figure had fallen to sixty-eight percent, where it remained through 2003. The remaining households consisted of individuals living alone, who accounted for more than twenty-five percent of the households in America, and those who did not fit any of the larger categories, labeled "other non-family households."

As of 2006, fewer American households include minor children. In 1970, approximately forty percent of households consisted of married couples with children; by 2003 that segment accounted for just twenty-three percent of the households in America. Families also have fewer children, on average, than their parents and grandparents did. The most common family size in America today is two individuals, and for families with minor children, the most common number is one. Very large families, those with four or more children, account for less than three percent of American families today.

Single parents also lead an increasing proportion of American families. The number of single-mother-led families jumped from three million to ten million during the years of the study, while the number of single-father headed families quadrupled to two million. These changes were driven largely be demographic and sociological shifts in American culture. More single women gave birth during the 1990s than during the 1970s, and the trend toward delaying marriage also created the opportunity for more women to become single mothers. Rising divorce rates during the years of the study expanded the number of single parents heading homes.

These changes in family makeup have important implications for the children living in these homes. Single-parent homes are far more likely to subsist below the poverty line; almost one-third of families headed by single mothers fall into that category, raising significant concerns about the welfare of children in these homes. The route to single parenthood is also an important predictor of financial security. Divorced parents are generally older and better educated, and earn higher incomes than their never-married counterparts.

The study also examined the phenomenon of stay-at-home parents. While the nuclear family of the 1950s, in which the father holds outside employment while the mother stays home, is largely forgotten, a surprising number of parents still stay at home. Of parents remaining unemployed for all of 2003, more than eighty-eight percent of mothers and more than fifteen percent of fathers gave "care for home and family" as their reason.

The 2004 family report illuminates the increasing diversity of American households. While the traditional two-parent home remains common, it is no longer the norm. Later marriages, fewer children, and fading resistance to divorce and single parenthood have combined to produce an increasingly diverse landscape of households in America. As American family forms continue to proliferate, detailed data will become increasingly important to fully understanding the workings of American family life.

FURTHER RESOURCES

Books

Greenstein, Theodore. *Methods of Family Research*. Thousand Oaks, Calif.: Sage Publishing, 2006.

Lofas, Jennifer. *Family Rules: Helping Stepfamilies and Single Parents Build Happy Homes*. New York. Kensington Publishing, 1998.

Parenting and Child Development in "Nontraditional" families, edited by Michael Lamb. New York: LEA, 1998.

Periodicals

Heaton, Tim B., et al. "Cross-national Variation in Family Influences on Child Health." *Social Science and Medicine* 60 (2005): 97–108.

Schwartz, Seth J. and Gordon Finley. "Father Involvement, Nurturant Fathering, and Young Adult Psychosocial Functioning: Differences Among Adoptive, Adoptive Stepfather, and Nonadoptive Stepfamilies." *Journal of Family Issues* 27 (2006): 712–731.

Stein, Martin T., et al. "A Difficult Adjustment to School: The Importance of Family Constellation." *Pediatrics* 114 (2004): 1464–1467.

Web sites

Alabama Cooperative Extension System. "Defining Nontraditional Families." October 7, 2002. <http://www.aces.edu/urban/metronews/vol2no1/nontrad.html> (accessed July 22, 2006).

Public Broadcasting System: Religion and Ethics Newsweekly. "Poll: Americans Idealize Traditional Family, Even as Nontraditional Families Are More Accepted." October 19, 2005. <http://www.pbs.org/wnet/religionandethics/week908/survey.html> (accessed July 22, 2006).

Manassas Changes Definition of Family

Newspaper article

By: Stephanie McCrummen

Date: December 28, 2005

Source: McCrummen, Stephanie. "Manassas Changes Definition of Family." *Washington Post* (December 28, 2005).

About the Author: Stephanie McCrummen is currently the head of the *Washington Post* African bureau in Nairobi, Kenya. She previously covered suburban and exurban issues for the *Post* from its Washington head office from 2004 until 2006. The *Washington Post* is a daily newspaper founded in 1877.

INTRODUCTION

An understanding of the Manassas, Virginia, by-law governing the nature and the number of permitted occupants in a single family residence begins with the general history of zoning by-laws.

The cities and towns that were constructed during the Middle Ages were not subject to any particular regulation concerning how lands could be used or what type of buildings could be constructed. A monarch or a local lord often dictated how they wished the locale to appear; many such cities were constructed around a prominent church or cathedral. With the rise of democratically elected governments, the planning of cities and towns fell to local municipal authorities. As a general rule in the countries of the Anglo-American legal tradition, a land owner could use land as they saw fit; the only regulation upon land use was the prospect that a neighbor might take legal action against the owner if the land usage was deemed to be a nuisance, such as the emission of a noxious product into the local environment.

A zoning by-law is defined as a regulation passed by a local government authority specifying how a particular parcel of land or a district within the municipality can be used or developed. The first zoning by-law was enacted in Frankfurt, Germany in 1891 as a means to regulate the growth of that city. The use of by-laws in Frankfurt was found to be so effective that in 1916, the City of New York became the first North American municipality to impose by-law control.

Within American cities, by-laws became the primary means by which a sense of orderly land use was created. Districts of industrial, commercial and residential use became the accepted manner in which cities were organized. With the growth of suburban developments in the vicinity of the American cities in the 1940s and 1950s, zoning regulation became a tool by which single family residential areas could be maintained as homogenous districts; as an example, zoning by-laws throughout the United States commonly prohibited the conversion of what were built as otherwise single family homes into boarding houses or other business uses.

The other form of land use control that was common from the early 1800s into the mid 1900s in the United States was the restrictive covenant contained in deeds of land. Restrictive covenants are a device where a party transferring title to a property includes a condition in the deed to the property that requires the purchaser to abide by a particular restriction as to the use of the land. Restrictive covenants concerning the ability of the new owner to subsequently sell the subject land to persons of a particular religion (such as persons of the Jewish faith) or race (such as African-Americans) were relatively common during this period. A number of appellate and Supreme Court of the United States decisions beginning in the 1950s held most such covenants to be unlawful, as a violation of the equality rights guaranteed under the constitution of the United States. In this respect the current Manassas zoning ordinance is seen as indirectly targeting immigrants in a fashion that the restrictive covenants once tackled directly.

▮ PRIMARY SOURCE

MANASSAS CHANGES DEFINITION OF FAMILY

Activists Criticize New Housing Limits

The inspector slid into his Crown Victoria, a police radio on his belt, addresses in hand. It was after 5 p.m., and he and his interpreter rolled into Manassas, down a street of benign ranch houses strung with lights. They parked, walked to a door and knocked.

"Mrs. Chavez?" Victor Purchase asked in the quiet evening.

There had been a complaint, he said. The city needed to know not just how many people lived there but how they were related. He handed Leyla Chavez a form and explained that she could be prosecuted for lying.

"Okay," she said and, in a mild state of shock, began filling it out.

There was Chavez and her husband. Their two sons. A nephew. The man who rented downstairs. His girlfriend.

"Your nephew, under our law, is considered unrelated," Purchase said, then delivered the verdict: Two people had to go.

That is because a zoning ordinance adopted this month by the city of Manassas redefines family, essentially restricting households to immediate relatives, even when the total is below the occupancy limit.

The rule, which has alarmed civil libertarians and housing activists, is among a series of attempts by municipalities across the nation to use zoning powers to deal with problems they associate with immigrants, often illegal, who have settled in suburbs, typically in shared housing to help with the rent or mortgage.

"It is not only unfair; it's racism," said Edgar Rivera, an organizer with Tenants and Workers United, a Northern Virginia group that advocates affordable housing as a solution to overcrowding. "It's basically a way to just go after certain communities."

Kent Willis, executive director of the American Civil Liberties Union of Virginia, said the new rule is "constitutionally questionable" and pointed to a 1977 Supreme Court ruling that struck down a similar law defining family passed by the city of East Cleveland, Ohio.

Even so, other municipalities have passed similar ordinances or are considering them.

Reacting to a swell of pressure from residents, the town of Herndon restricted its definition of family last year. Prince William County and Richmond are studying the Manassas ordinance. And Fairfax County is seeking authority from the state to impose criminal fines and jail time on landlords who rent houses to more than four unrelated people, typically immigrants.

In Manassas, the ordinance is one of several steps the city has taken. In October, Mayor Douglas S. Waldron (R) asked Gov. Mark R. Warner (D) to declare a state of emergency in Virginia regarding illegal immigration, as have governors in New Mexico and Arizona. The declaration, which would make localities eligible for federal homeland security dollars, was not made. Waldron also asked for expanded police powers to identify and arrest illegal immigrants.

Waldron and two city lawyers did not return several calls.

"It isn't just too many people in the house," said Manassas Vice Mayor Harry J. "Hal" Parrish II. "It's impacting parking on the streets. It's impacting the hospital and its costs, our emergency services, our schools to a great extent."

Parrish said he understands why some people might think the ordinance is racist, but he disagrees. "In my heart, I believe that is not the issue," he said. "The issue is the impact of overcrowding in our community. It looks as though that issue is a direct result of illegal immigration."

But Chavez and her husband, Juan, are U.S. citizens. They came from Honduras in the 1980s, worked more than one job—she at two laundromats, he as a cook—and eventually saved enough to buy the house on Liberia Avenue in 2003 for $270,000.

Now, faced with the loss of rental income and with a $3,500 monthly mortgage to pay, Chavez said, they are going to sell. The family will never buy a house again, she said.

Chavez, who has two nephews in the military who served in Iraq, said she could understand having some kind of rule against overcrowding.

"When it's 20 or 30 people, when there are drinkers, drugs, I say yes," she said.

Considering, though, that every house on her block more or less resembles hers, and considering that she has only seven people living in a five-bedroom house, she was suspicious about why she was singled out. As far as she knew, she and her husband were just doing what any normal family would do to make it.

"Americans live that way, too," Chavez said. "They have roommates."

In Manassas, a city of about 40,000 with a rapidly growing Latino population—it is 72 percent white, 15 percent Latino and 13 percent black—some residents see the rule as a bizarre form of social engineering. Others are indifferent, thinking they will not be subjected to the "bedroom police." The ordinance is enforced by complaint, and so far, complaints have overwhelmingly been against Latinos, Purchase said.

A vocal number of locals have welcomed the ordinance, saying they hope it will help alleviate complaints about trash, parking problems and tight school budgets as well as more general feelings of unease that somehow, the city is not theirs anymore.

New Concept in Town

The Dec. 5 town hall meeting at Round Elementary School was advertised in the usual way, without any special outreach to the Latino community. About 30 residents attended, no one objected to the ordinance, and the City Council easily adopted it. Then Brian Smith, chief building official, stood up to explain the new concept in town: consanguinity.

Under the city's old, broad definition of family, just about any group of relatives, however distantly related, was allowed to share a single-family house, along with one unrelated person.

The problem with that, Smith explained, was that when inspectors responded to a complaint, they often found houses full of aunts, uncles, cousins and extended relatives but no violations, because the total number was below the occupancy limit.

"We were stymied by families who met the existing definition," Smith said. And so the city changed the rules to break up more households.

Under the city's old zoning ordinance, there were three definitions of who could share a house: three unrelated people; two unrelated people and their children; or any combination of relatives, however extended, plus one unrelated person. It is the third definition that was changed under the new law.

"What we tried to do is define it in a way that was traditional, to make sure these peripheral people start to be winnowed out," Smith said.

According to the new definition, one unrelated person is still allowed. But everyone else must fall within the "second degree of consanguinity" from the person declared to be the head of household. Significantly, relationships are traced through the parents.

Thus, in Chavez's case, her nephew is three degrees: He is her parents' son's son and thus is considered unrelated. Under the old rule, Chavez had two unrelated people living with her—the tenant and his girlfriend—and one would have had to go. Under the new rule, though, she has three unrelated people under her roof.

The Chavezes have 30 days to comply. If they don't, they face escalating fines and, ultimately, court.

Smith said he has been surprised at how many people readily allow inspectors into their homes and how many families have complied with the rules.

From Leyla Chavez's point of view, however, the compliance stemmed more from fear than a happy sense of cooperation.

"It's like the police were here searching for murderers," she said.

If she fixed a few expensive fire code violations, and if she could find close relatives to move in, the family could perhaps stay, she realized. But it would be a hassle, she said, and one that might never end. She is hoping that things are easier in North Carolina.

"The living is cheaper there," she said. "We'll rent a little house, and we'll be comfortable."

Although safety violations often turn up during inspections, Smith said that the complaints that prompt inspection rarely have to do with safety. Typically, they are about parking or a more general suspicion that a large number of people are living next door.

Purchase, who is an assistant fire marshal, said that occasionally he will find what amounts to a rooming house full of unrelated people. More often he will find, say, eight people who were living lawfully under the old definition of family but who might now be broken up. Mostly, he said, people are living as one unit, and mostly, the houses he inspects are neat and orderly.

A Changing Area

In general, the city of Manassas is neat and orderly, too.

Crime is down again this year. The historic downtown area is doing well, with wine shops and spas and restaurants. And the city is planning more development—town-

houses and single-family homes that will bring more people.

The area is also quietly changing: *Se habla espanol* signs are hung at car dealerships. Strip malls might have a Starbucks alongside a *Mercado*. Travel agencies advertise flights to Honduras.

Along with those changes, the city has received a rising number of complaints about crowding. To help field them, an "overcrowding hotline" was established, and in October, the mayor sent two letters to Warner asking him to declare a state of emergency.

"One of the largest impacts is being felt on our once-quaint neighborhood streets, which now in many cases are littered with trash and lined with far too many vehicles due to overcrowded boarding houses and multi-family dwellings," the mayor wrote. "The situation is eroding the strong spirit of our city.... We must stress that we are not anti-immigration, rather *illegal* immigration is our concern."

Along the residential streets of Manassas, however, the sense of panic and urgency that many residents and politicians feel is not shared by everyone.

"It's definitely more diverse," said Mike Donick, a retired government worker who has lived 11 years on Abbott Road, where neighbors have complained about some houses with Latino families. "The only thing I notice is more cars around than there used to be. It hasn't really affected me."

Over on Gloxinia Way, however, Marta Horlick, a substitute teacher and translator originally from Puerto Rico, said she has had parking problems and garbage issues and has witnessed some odd scenes: In the garage of a neighbor's house one weekend, a line of men was waiting for a woman to give haircuts, for instance.

She is concerned that the city is missing out on tax dollars. She is worried about school budgets being consumed by English language programs. Really, she said, the problem is bigger than the city has the wherewithal to handle.

"I don't think it's a perfect solution," she said of the new ordinance. "But it beats doing nothing."

But Willis, of the ACLU, questioned whether the city can implement the rule without discriminating on the basis of race or national origin. "In a nation that prides itself on diversity," he said, "these kinds of ordinances are becoming part of a shameful episode in our history."

After he left Leyla Chavez's place, Purchase and his interpreter, Adriana Vallenas, got back into the Crown Victoria and headed off for the next address, a re-inspection.

They joined the streams of cars and trucks full of people coming home from work, passed Iglesia Pentecostal church, then the old white-columned houses of Grant Avenue, then Valdemar Travel Agencia de Viajes.

They pulled up to the townhouse of Oscar Cortez, a construction worker from El Salvador. A few weeks ago, he had a house full of seven tenants, all unrelated.

"We have a form for you to fill out," Purchase said to Cortez. "If you lie to me, we're going to prosecute you."

Cortez filled out the form as Vallenas explained who could live in the house he owns.

"Your brother, mother, father," she said. "No uncles, no aunts, no cousins, no nieces, no nephews."

Purchase headed upstairs to check two bedrooms that had been full before.

He pushed open the doors. This time, they were empty.

SIGNIFICANCE

An important issue raised by the Manassas zoning ordinance is what constitutes a family for the purpose of legal single-family residency in that city. The strict adherence of the Manassas legislators to a rule based upon the second degree of consanguinity is more restrictive a definition of family than that accepted in many countries of the world. Further, the modern notion of an extended family, where the family structure includes various persons who have been added to the family as a consequence of divorce, remarriage, or an alteration in a common law cohabitation arrangement is not one that will likely be consistent with the Manassas definition.

Supporters of the Manassas by-law claim it targets the problems associated with illegal immigration, including housing, street congestion and safety, and additional burdens placed upon municipal services by such immigration, such as hospitals, emergency services, garbage collection, and schools. The family that is highlighted in the primary source article is composed of legal immigrants to the United States who subsequently became citizens, persons who exist within a cultural framework where residential support to one's extended family is accepted, if not expected. The more subtle implication of the primary source article is that legal immigrants will be more likely to house illegal immigrant countrymen or family members. As of 2006, the population of the United States stood at approximately 300 million persons, of whom one in nine was an immigrant. The Manassas approach to immigrant issues is therefore one of potentially wide application to the American urban environment.

As the article notes, the Manassas zoning ordinance is one that has been mirrored in other parts of the United States; many municipalities have passed similar restrictions on single family residence occupancy. A particularly noteworthy example is that employed in Black Jack City, Missouri, where as of February 2006, three or more persons were prohibited from sharing a residence unless they were related by blood, marriage or adoption. The family challenging the Black Jack City zoning by-law is headed by common law partners of thirteen years standing, where there are also children of prior unions living in their single family residence. This type of family structure is unconnected to the immigration issues that feature in the Manassas by-law; the Black Jack City ordinance is more directly tied to the regulation of the type of families desired by local legislators to be living in a particular residential area.

In the consideration of both the Manassas and Black Jack City zoning enactments, United States federal law does not prohibit marital status as a ground of discrimination in housing arrangements. It is also to be noted that twenty-three states of the Union have enacted Fair Housing laws that might otherwise render such practices illegal as discriminatory; the federal *Fair Housing Act* "prohibits discrimination in the sale, rental, and financing of dwellings, and in other housing-related transactions, based on race, color, national origin, religion, sex, familial status (including children under the age of eighteen living with parents of legal custodians, pregnant women, and people securing custody of children under the age of eighteen), and handicap (disability)." The state of Missouri has not enacted such a law.

In such instances, the only likely relief available to an aggrieved party would be an action based upon the constitutionally protected right to both liberty and the right to privacy in family relations. A by-law that limits the number of persons in a single family home is potentially liable to attack on the same grounds approved of by the Supreme Court of the United States in *Lawrence v. Texas*, where a sodomy prosecution that originated as an act occurring within a private home was ruled unconstitutional as violating the privacy of the home.

The use of the Manassas zoning by-law and similar devices elsewhere are contrasted by the fact that aside from the homeowners illustrated in the primary source article, there are six million unmarried couples living together in the United States, of whom forty percent are raising at least one child of their union in their home. It is an open question as to when local zoning by-law intentions will collide with the dynamics and the diversity of the modern American family unit.

FURTHER RESOURCES

Books

Connerly, Charles E. *The Most Segregated City in America: City Planning and Civil Rights in Birmingham, 1920–1980*. Charlottesville, Virginia: University of Virginia Press, 2004.

Horstein, Jeffrey M. *A Nation of Realtors: A Cultural History of Twentieth Century America*. Raleigh, North Carolina: Duke University Press, 2005.

Merriam, Dwight. *The Complete Guide to Zoning*. New York: McGraw-Hill, 2004.

Web sites

Department of State Counsel's Office, State of New York. "Definition of "Family" in Zoning By-Laws and Building Codes." 2004. <http://www.dos.state.ny.us/cnsl/family.html> (accessed June 29, 2006).

'Blended Families' and Other Euphemisms

Newspaper article

By: Anne Karpf

Date: April 15, 2006

Source: Karpf, Anne. *The Guardian* (April 15, 2006).

About the Author: Anne Karpf is a British writer, journalist, and sociologist who is a regular contributor to The Guardian, a Manchester, England—based daily newspaper. Karpf writes on social, political, and Jewish issues. Karpf also appears regularly as a social commentator on various BBC television programs.

INTRODUCTION

The blended family is one of the most prominent features of the modern Western society social fabric. However, it is not a recent invention so much as an institution that has grown in prominence in the past forty years. The rise of the blended family is a product of three inter-related demographic factors: the divorce rate, the remarriage rate, and the incidence of cohabitation or common law relationships.

In earlier times throughout Western cultures, when the mortality rate was higher among adults of child rearing years than it is today, it was far more common for a family with children under the age of majority to lose a spouse or parent to death; divorce was extremely rare, due to both religious prohibitions and corresponding legal limitations. Where a spouse and parent died leaving a family behind, the Christian rule of marriage as a partnership that existed until death created the corollary acceptance of remarriage as a proper means to create stability for a family unit. In this sense, what is now termed a blended family was well accepted.

Prior to the 1960s in virtually all Western nations, cohabitation was perceived as being socially unacceptable and in some cultures there were strong religious and legal prohibitions concerning "living in sin."

The rise in the birth rate after 1945 was a factor that contributed to a liberalizing trend in a number of aspects of Western society. The divorce rate climbed dramatically from the mid 1960s to a peak in 1980 in North America and most European countries, as legislative regimes that had previously required a divorce petitioner to establish fault or adultery on the part of their spouse were replaced by less rigorous "no fault" divorce. In the United States, the 1980 rate rose to a record 22.6 divorces per 1,000 married women per year, a 500 percent increase since the end of World War II.

In lock-step with the trends in divorce, the marriage rate in the same demographic has fallen and the cohabitation rate has risen to the point where in 2006 more than 8 percent of all American households are unmarried cohabiting heterosexual couples. In countries such as Canada, Australia and Holland, the corresponding figure is in excess of 10 percent. The most telling statistic concerning the rise of the blended family from anomaly to societal institution is the fact that as of 2005, only 63 per cent of American children were being raised in the care and residence of both biological parents.

Anne Karpf notes that the expression blended family is a euphemism, as it represents a desire on the part of the newly joined parents to create a seamless and harmonious family unit from what are often several disparate parts.

■ PRIMARY SOURCE

At noon today, I'll be at a wedding. I'm not the mother of the bride but the stepmother of the groom. This means that I've acquired a delightful new step-daughter-in-law. As it's a second marriage, the old one (whom I'm still fond of) has now turned into my ex-step-daughter-in-law—at this rate the world is going to run out of hyphens.

If we were American I suppose you'd call us a blended family, though that makes it sound like we should also be rich, smooth, well-roasted, and possibly Colombian. This euphemism for stepfamilies reeks of The Brady Bunch, the 1970s American television series that tried to show step-siblings could come together harmoniously to create a wholesome nuclear family (and that American TV could find something saccharine in just about anything).

But practically none of the cliches about stepfamilies have applied to us. My stepchildren were teenagers when I first met their dad. They didn't live with him (and nor did I for the first three years). I wasn't implicated in the break-up of their parents. The guidance usually trotted out on the subject—leave the disciplining to the biological parent, don't try and compete with their real mother—simply wasn't relevant.

Of course this doesn't mean we got through without conflict. There were some pretty rough years in there. Think about mother-teenage daughter hostilities. Then add a "step" into the pot—the potential for rage increases tenfold.

Death makes it even worse. I know someone whose mother died when she was eight. Within a couple of years her father remarried an altogether saintly woman. Relieved family friends expected the girl to express gratitude. Of course she felt like killing her stepmother, and found many different ways of tormenting her. Children of that age are so awash with fantasies about the power of their feelings that the anger, to a girl whose mother had really gone and died, must have felt very dangerous.

For me and many of the other stepmothers I know, the problems have been aggravated by age difference—I'm roughly halfway in age between my stepchildren and their father, so it's been hard for them and for me to know where to place me. Surrogate parent wasn't an option, but then neither was the friend route. I've worried about them alongside their father, but never as much as I've worried about my own kids. We've had to work out the relationship as we went along, but that goes for all relationships, whatever the idealised images would have us believe.

What makes me part of a social trend is that I'm also a step-grandmother. Grandparents may have been busily throwing off the stereotypes—knitting, rocking chairs, and Madeira cake don't figure any more, but step-grandparenting is still such an emerging phenomenon that they haven't had time to create the stereotypes yet. In America step-grandparents seem exercised about what they

should be called—how many grannies can a kid reasonably be expected to have?

My teenager has made the odd attempt to orchestrate my step-grandchildren into calling me "Granny Annie" (only, of course, because she knows I'd hate it) but thankfully it hasn't caught on. I'd hate it because I don't feel old enough to be a grandmother, though biologically of course I easily am. I had my kids so late that grandparenthood is a stage I only expect to reach in my late 60s or 70s.

So I'm pretty lackadaisical in the role. I'm not bad on birthdays (though I've already forgotten one this year, on account of the house move), quite good on hugs, but I don't feel like their grandparent, and I haven't tried to simulate or manufacture it. They seem OK with that. I've got friends without children of their own, though, who've embraced the relationship with gusto, and the resulting intimacy has been a mutual gift.

In fact what I've enjoyed about being a stepmother and step-grandmother is precisely how little has been expected of me, and how little I've expected. This has made those occasions when my stepkids have spontaneously expressed affection to me (or me to them) particularly touching.

The wedding today, I've just realised, will also supply my step-grandchildren with another set of step-grandparents, along with a couple of step-aunts and a step-cousin. Bring out more hyphens.

SIGNIFICANCE

The reference to the American situation comedy "The Brady Bunch" is a common one in the literature and published commentaries concerning both the structure and the function of the modern blended family. In the television world, the blended family represented a relatively smooth and harmonious transition from two separate families to one unit. The Brady Bunch was aired from 1969 to 1974 on American network television and it was subsequently syndicated for rebroadcast in many parts of the world. Its enduring popularity as a reference point in discussions regarding the success of the blended family, more than thirty years after it ceased production, is an interesting aspect of how Western society desires the blended family to function in fact. The fictional Brady family achieved what for many blended families is a dream bordering upon the fanciful—a blended family that operated like the nuclear family depicted in an earlier generation of American television programs of the 1950s, such as "Father Knows Best" or "Leave it to Beaver."

The Brady Family from *The Brady Bunch* television program. KOBAL COLLECTION. REPRODUCED BY PERMISSION.

The Brady Bunch styled blended family, where two previously married persons join their families together might now be properly referenced as a traditional blended family, as the blended family today is just as often a creation of previously married, previously cohabited persons where children are a product of that unmarried union, or variations of each. Karpf emphasizes the modern reality of blended family actually becoming an ever expanding set of concentric family circles, where the new partner brings their own extended family unit into each relationship.

The modern definition of a blended family is such that one in three Americans is either a step-parent, step-child, step-sibling, or other member of a step-family. One in three American children can expect to be a part of a step-family before they reach the age of eighteen.

The blended family is a significant and volatile family institution because it presents a host of potential familial minefields for the new spouses, chiefly in

terms of the relationship with the other spouse's children that are brought into the union. In Western countries as many as 70 percent of second marriages that involve the introduction of a step-child into a new family unit fail. Dealing with the children themselves, the establishment of a new parental role, and the dynamics of the dealings with the new child in the face of a continuing biological parent exerting influence on the child are some of the issues that have spawned an industry. The thousands of Internet sites devoted to the dynamics of the blended family reflects the explosion in the number of information sources available to persons who are experiencing trouble with children in these structures.

Beyond the issue of the children who form a part of the blended family, the entire notion of parental and familial responsibility is altered. The extent of any duty owed to one's step-relations is not capable of precise legal definition; in many blended families expectations may exist concerning such duties that complicate the new structure.

A further significant issue associated with the rise of the blended family to societal prominence is the nomenclature used to describe the family members in the newly combined unit. The hyphenation of the names is a rather technical way in which to refer to a member of one's family; society has not yet created a distinct language with which to describe its blended family composition in a more familiar fashion.

The growth of the blended family as an institution is unlikely to decrease. As a matter of statistical probabilities alone, the more people who become a part of an blended family, the more such family members they will bring into any subsequent unions of their own.

FURTHER RESOURCES

Books

Chedekel, David. *The Blended Family Sourcebook*. Columbus, OH: McGraw-Hill, 2002.

Green, Jennifer, and Susan Wisdom. *Stepcoupling: Sustaining a Strong Marriage in Today's Blended Family*. New York: Three Rivers Press, 2002.

Massolini, Maxine. *Blended Families: Creating Harmony as You Build a New Home Life*. Chicago: Moody Press, 2000.

Shriberg, Elaine Fantle. *Blending Families*. New York: Berkley Publishers, 1999.

Web site

University of Washington. "In Touch / Blended Families." 2004 <http://www.washington.edu/admin/hr/benefits/worklife/carelink/intouch/intouch_blnded-fam.pdf> (accessed June 18, 2006).

2 Marriage, Partnership, and Divorce

Marriage, Partnership, and Divorce

In many societies, marriage is the traditional means of creating and co-mingling families. Although the rites, responsibilities, and nature of marriage may vary among different cultures or in different periods of history, the basic function of marriage is to define a new family unit—a new set of potential parents and children.

Western views of marriage have radically transformed in the modern era. From arrangements based on the management of wealth and the transfer of property, to the rise of "love matches," changes in the nature of marriage influence changes in family dynamics. The popularization of the concept of marriage based on romantic love permeated social attitudes on family life, parenting, gender roles, and childhood. "Caroline Gilman Recommends Wifely Submission," "That Terrible Question," and "An Opinion on Love Matches" provide disparate opinions, each influenced by the author's social position and historical milieu, on the value of romantic love as the basis for forming families.

Marriage is a means of granting legal recognition to family partnerships, but the dissolution of a marriage seldom severs family bonds. Parents often arrange to share child-raising duties, and remarriage blends existing families into new family relationships. While divorce may not fully sever all family bonds, it does alter them. Separation and dissolution of marriage is traumatic for all family members. Divorce has become more commonplace over the past century, but its social significance remains controversial. "Why Divorce is Bad" and "Divorces Increase by Half" provide insight into the emergence of divorce as a prominent social concern.

Today, most social theorists have expanded the concept of the nuclear family to include not only childless couples, but also same-sex partnerships. This chapter also looks at the controversy surrounding the formation of families that do not have full protection and recognition under the law, but are no less emotionally or socially valid to affected family members. The articles "Defense of Marriage Act" and "Marriage Protection Amendment" discuss the political debate over same-sex marriage. "Cohabitation, Marriage, Divorce, and Remarriage in the United States" provides a demographic look at marriage trends, but also at the growing population of couples that live together or form partnerships outside of legal marriage. Opponents of same-sex marriage and general partnership rights (for all unmarried couples) often claim that changing traditional definitions of marriage weaken family bonds and threaten social unity. Supporters assert that extending marriage and partnership rights to all who desire them will strengthen family bonds, promote equity and tolerance, and increase the number of stable families.

Caroline Gilman Recommends Wifely Submission

Book excerpt

By: Caroline H. Gilman

Date: 1838

Source: Gilman, Caroline H. *Recollections of a Southern Matron.* New York: Harper & Brothers, 1838.

About the Author: Caroline H. Gilman was a South Carolina wife and mother best known for her 1838 autobiographical novel, *Recollections of a Southern Matron.*

INTRODUCTION

Nineteenth-century Americans were romantics who dreamed of marrying for love. Unlike previous generations, they had great expectations for marriage. However, those who were already married, such as South Carolinian Caroline Gilman, warned young women against having high hopes of much happiness with their husbands.

The idea of marriage as an affectionate partnership tempted middle- and upper-class men and women beginning in the seventeenth century. Ideally, companionate marriage permitted individual choice in marriage based on personal affection and sexual attraction. It encouraged loving rather than controlling relationships between husbands and wives. Although Americans valued affection as a basis for marriage from the earliest days of settlement, colonial Americans were wary of unrestrained emotions. They sought to achieve a family life characterized by tranquility and harmony rather than by passion and desire. In colonial America, the family was organized as a mini-government, in which the relationship of husband to wife imitated that between king and subject.

The ideal of affectionate relationships became more pronounced in the revolutionary era. The attack against the king and patriarchal authority prompted Americans to view relationships as a matter of individual choice. For increasing numbers of couples, the pursuit of happiness included a quest for a marriage filled with love and respect. Abandoning such traditions as chaperones and marrying daughters off according to birth order, increasing numbers of Americans granted young men and women a degree of freedom from parental direction and supervision in order to enable them to evaluate their chances for happiness

An idealized husband and wife. © H. ARMSTRONG ROBERTS/CORBIS.

with a potential mate. Romantic love was becoming the most important factor in courtship as well as marriage by the mid-nineteenth century.

■ PRIMARY SOURCE

The planter's bride, who leaves a numerous and cheerful family in her paternal home, little imagines the change which awaits her in her own retired residence. She dreams of an independent sway over her household, devoted love and unbroken intercourse with her husband, and indeed longs to be released from the eyes of others, that she may dwell only beneath the sunbeam of his. And so it was with me. After our bustling wedding and protracted journey, I looked forward to the retirement at Bellevue as a quiet port in which I should rest with Arthur, after drifting so long on general society. The romance of our love was still in its glow, as might be inferred by the infallible sign of his springing to pick up my pocket-handkerchief whenever it fell...

For several weeks all kinds of droll associations were conjured up, and we laughed at anything and nothing. What cared we for fashion and pretension? There we were together, asking for nothing but each other's presence and love. At length it was necessary for him to tear himself away to superintend his interests. I remember when his horse was brought to the door for his first absence of two hours; an observer would have thought that he was going on a far journey, had he witnessed that parting; and so it continued for some days, and his return at each time was like the sun shooting through a three days' cloud.

But the period of absence was gradually protracted; then a friend sometimes came home with him, and their talk was of crops and politics, draining the fields and draining the revenue…I was not selfish, and even urged Arthur to go to hunt and to dinner-parties, although hoping that he would resist my urging. He went frequently, and a growing discomfort began to work upon my mind. I had undefined forebodings; I mused about past days; my views of life became slowly disorganized; my physical powers enfeebled; a nervous excitement followed; I nursed a moody discontent, and ceased a while to reason clearly. Wo to me had I yielded to this irritable temperament! I began immediately, on principle, to busy myself about my household. The location of Bellevue was picturesque—the dwelling airy and commodious; I had, therefore, only to exercise taste in external and internal arrangement to make it beautiful throughout. I was careful to consult my husband in those points which interested him, without annoying him with mere trifles. If the reign of romance was really waning, I resolved not to chill his noble confidence, but to make a steadier light rise on his affections. If he was absorbed in reading, I sat quietly waiting the pause when I should be rewarded by the communication of ripe ideas; if I saw that he prized a tree which interfered with my flowers, I sacrificed my preference to a more sacred feeling; if any habit of his annoyed me, I spoke of it once or twice calmly, and then bore it quietly if unreformed; I welcomed his friends with cordiality, entered into their family interests, and stopped my yawns, which, to say the truth, was sometimes an almost desperate effort, before they reached eye or ear.

This task of self-government was not easy. To repress a harsh answer, to confess a fault, and to stop (right or wrong) in the midst of self-defence, in gentle submission, sometimes requires a struggle like life and death; but these *three* efforts are the golden threads with which domestic happiness is woven; once beam the fabric with this woof, and trials shall not break or sorrow tarnish it.

Men are not often unreasonable; their difficulties lie in not understanding the moral and physical structure of our sex. They often wound through ignorance, and are surprised at having offended. How clear is it, then, that woman loses by petulance and recrimination! Her first study must be self-control, almost to hypocrisy. A good

wife must smile amid a thousand perplexities, and clear her voice to tones of cheerfulness when her frame is dropping with disease, or else languish alone. Man, on the contrary, when trials beset him, expects to find her ear and heart a ready receptacle…

I have not meant to suggest that, in ceasing to be a mere lover, Arthur was not a tender and devoted husband. I have only described the natural progress of a sensible, independent married man, desirous of fulfilling all the relations of society. Nor in these remarks would I chill the romance of some young dreamer, who is reposing her heart on another. Let her dream on. God has given this youthful, luxurious gift of trusting love, as he has given hues to the flower and sunbeams to the sky. It is a superadded charm to his lavish blessings; but let her be careful…

Let him know nothing of the struggle which follows the first chill of the affections; let no scenes of tears and apologies be acted to agitate him, until he becomes accustomed to agitation; thus shall the star of domestic peace arise in fixedness and beauty above them, and shine down in gentle light on their lives, as it has on ours.

SIGNIFICANCE

For those who married for love and discovered that marital bliss was an illusion, divorce became easier to acquire in the nineteenth century. Between the American Revolution and the Civil War, states passed new divorce laws that extended the grounds for divorce from adultery, desertion, and cruelty to permit the dissolution of unions ruined by neglect, jealously, and simple unkindness. As even the legal system recognized, affection had become a necessary ingredient in marriage.

The shift from patriarchy to companionship was not swift and not complete. Well into the nineteenth century, couples struggled with the contradictions of affectionate marriage. They found that their commitment to companionate marriage conflicted with their ideas about male authority. For many couples, especially those in the slave South, the persistence of male supremacy undermined the ideal of companionate marriage.

FURTHER RESOURCES
Books

Cott, Nancy F. *Public Vows: A History of Marriage and the Nation.* Cambridge, UK: Oxford University Press, 1987.

Lystra, Karen. *Searching the Heart: Women, Men, and Romantic Love in Nineteenth-Century America.* New York: Oxford University Press, 1989.

Drunkard Attacks Wife

Illustration

By: George Cruikshank

Date: 1848

Source: © Historical Picture Archive/Corbis.

About the Artist: This historical illustration is credited to George Cruikshank, and is part of the collection of the Corbis Corporation, headquartered in Seattle, with a worldwide archive of over 70 million images.

INTRODUCTION

The roles of husbands and wives throughout history have generally been governed by societal expectations. Many cultures, both past and present, practice female subordination, particularly in the context of marriage. Husbands in these cultures are typically older and better educated than their wives, giving them an intellectual advantage in the relationship; such cultures often either openly condone or simply ignore physical violence in the home, creating an environment in which men use their physical strength to control their wives.

During the nineteenth century, most Americans saw husbands as the head of the home, with wives expected to submit to their leadership. Though physical violence was generally frowned upon, it was not legally prohibited and was in many cases seen as a necessary evil while enforcing each sex's divinely ordained role. Men generally took control of their wives' financial resources; women who chose to leave an abusive marriage often found themselves penniless and unable to support themselves or their children.

Not all cultures have tolerated physical abuse. Seventeenth-century Puritans in Massachusetts passed laws strictly prohibiting spousal abuse, though these laws were offset somewhat by the fact that women were rarely allowed to divorce their husbands, even in the case of severe physical abuse. English lawmakers passed legislation in 1853 that made wife abuse a crime, specifically by prohibiting wife beating in the same terms that abuse of farm or domestic animals was already prohibited. In 1857 several American states passed laws making spousal abuse a misdemeanor punishable by fine or jail time.

As new laws began to toughen the government response to domestic abuse, other efforts were underway to minimize its causes. Though little research existed to substantiate the link, many women knew from personal experience the relationship between alcohol and violence. In response, the nineteenth-century temperance movement attempted to reduce alcohol consumption and abuse. Groups including the Anti-Saloon League and the Women's Christian Temperance Union initially used moral pressure to campaign against alcohol abuse; they later adopted political tactics to advance their cause through legislation. Though not formally connected, the temperance movement and efforts to end domestic violence had a common objective: safer lives for American women.

PRIMARY SOURCE

DRUNKARD ATTACKS WIFE

See primary source image.

SIGNIFICANCE

The temperance movement soon grew to include local organizations, reaching the zenith of its power in 1919 with the ratification of the Eighteenth Amendment to the Constitution, which prohibited the sale, purchase, production, import, or export of alcoholic beverages. While the law was lauded for its role in reducing alcohol abuse and its many resultant social ills, it faced an uphill battle. In the following years the alcohol industry reemerged, this time outside the bounds of the law and frequently in the hands of organized crime. By 1933 most Americans had concluded that the law was a mistake and it was repealed with little debate, allowing states to once again regulate the sale and consumption of alcohol.

Domestic violence laws were much slower in coming; from 1900 to 1960, little progress was made in providing legal protection to women from abuse by their spouses. The National Organization for Women (NOW), founded in 1966, along with other women's advocacy groups began to push for greater legal protections. The early 1970s saw the establishment of battered women's shelters, facilities that offered abused women a place to escape an abusive home and receive food, shelter, and support. In 1979, after extensive congressional hearings on the problem of domestic violence, President Carter established the

PRIMARY SOURCE

Drunkard Attacks Wife: Members of the temperance movement used this 1848 image, and others like it, to link poverty and abuse to alcohol consumption. © HISTORICAL PICTURE ARCHIVE/CORBIS.

federal Office on Violence against Women, a division of the Justice Department.

Despite numerous state laws prohibiting domestic violence, police departments were often reluctant to become involved in violence between husband and wife or boyfriend and girlfriend; as a result women seeking police assistance for domestic abuse were often ignored. In response, a group of women filed a 1976 class-action lawsuit against the Oakland, California, police department, charging that it failed to respond to domestic violence calls. A similar suit was filed soon thereafter in New York state. Both suits were settled when the respective law enforcement agencies agreed to modify their guidelines for responding to domestic violence complaints.

The 1980s and 1990s witnessed a flurry of state and federal legislation designed to protect women from abuse by a spouse, boyfriend, or live-in partner. Numerous programs were also launched to attack the

cause of domestic violence and prosecute offenders. A growing understanding of the scope and nature of the crime led to additional programs and services for both women and children affected by domestic violence.

In 2001, the American Institute on Domestic Violence assessed the financial costs of domestic violence, estimating that medical and mental care for victims cost more than $4 billion per year, much of it paid by employer health plans. Lost productivity and earnings added another $1.8 billion to the toll. Victims of domestic violence missed almost 8 million days of work as a result.

Despite numerous initiatives designed to reduce and punish spousal abuse, the problem remains widespread, affecting approximately 4 million American women each year. It accounts for as much as onefourth of all violent crime in the U.S., although law enforcement agencies believe that most domestic abuse cases are never reported.

LOVE · SACRIFICE · SERVICE

The Lincoln-Lee Legion

ABSTINENCE DEPARTMENT OF THE ANTI-SALOON LEAGUE

I HEREBY ENROLL WITH THE LINCOLN-LEE LEGION AND PROMISE WITH GOD'S HELP TO KEEP THE FOLLOWING PLEDGE:–

WHEREAS, THE USE OF INTOXICATING LIQUORS AS A BEVERAGE IS PRODUCTIVE OF PAUPERISM, DEGRADATION AND CRIME; AND BELIEVING IT IS OUR DUTY TO DISCOURAGE THAT WHICH PRODUCES MORE EVIL THAN GOOD, WE THEREFORE PLEDGE OURSELVES TO ABSTAIN FROM THE USE OF INTOXICATING LIQUORS AS A BEVERAGE.

NAME _____ DATE _____

THE DUPLICATE OF THIS PLEDGE IS DEPOSITED AT THE NATIONAL OFFICES OF THE LINCOLN-LEE LEGION, WESTERVILLE, OHIO

COPYRIGHT 1903, BY HOWARD H. RUSSELL   COPYRIGHT 1909, BY THE ANTI-SALOON LEAGUE OF AMERICA

A Lincoln-Lee Legion temperence pledge card. © LAKE COUNTY MUSEUM/CORBIS.

FURTHER RESOURCES

Books

Bancroft, Lundy. *Why Does He Do That? Inside the Minds of Angry and Controlling Men.* New York: Berkeley Publishing Group, 2002.

Summers, Randal W., and Allan M. Hoffman, eds. *Domestic Violence: A Global View.* Westpoint: Greenwood Press, 2002.

U.S. Department of Justice. *Criminal Victimization in the U.S., 1991.* Washington, D.C: U.S. Department of Justice, 1992.

Periodicals

Glazer, Sara. "Violence Against Women." *Congressional Quarterly.* 3, no. 8 (February 1993): 171.

Silverman, Jay, et al. "Dating Violence Against Adolescent Girls and Associated Substance Use, Unhealthy Weight Control, Sexual Risk Behavior, Pregnancy, and Suicidality." *Journal of the American Medical Association.* 286 (2001): 572–579.

Web sites

Almanac of Policy Issues. "Domestic Violence." April 2000 <http://www.policyalmanac.org/crime/archive/domestic_violence.shtml> (accessed July 4, 2006).

Binghamton University. "'The Rule of Love': Wife Beating as Prerogative and Privacy." <http://www.binghamton. edu/womhist/vawa/prologuefootnotes.htm> (accessed July 4, 2006).

U.S. Department of Justice. "Office on Violence Against Women." <http://www.usdoj.gov/ovw/> (accessed July 4, 2006).

Raziakov Family Ketubbah

Contract

By: Anonymous

Date: 1863

Source: Courtesy of The Library of The Jewish Theological Seminary.

About the Author: The Jewish Theological Seminary, based in New York City, is a center of Conservative Judaism and serves as the preeminent institution for the academic study of Judaica outside of Israel.

INTRODUCTION

A Jewish marriage contract, or ketubbah, spells out the economic responsibilities of the husband toward his wife. For centuries, the ketubbah has been an essential part of traditional Jewish marriages. It must never leave the possession of the wife for the marriage to remain valid.

The ketubbah apparently dates back two millennia to the Talmudic period in Jewish history. The main purpose of the document is to protect the married woman in the event of divorce or widowhood. Because biblical law permits the husband to divorce his wife at will, the rabbis established that prior to the wedding the husband is to undertake a written obligation to pay his wife a certain minimal sum upon the dissolution of their marriage. This financial obligation was originally termed "ketubbah," or "that which is written." The marriage contract in which the ketubbah amount was recorded was generally referred to as "sefer ketubbah" or "book of the ketubbah." In time, the entire contract became known as the ketubbah with the financial por-tion constituting the main part of the contract. A bridegroom is forbidden to cohabit with his bride following the wedding without having a ketubbah written and delivered to her before marriage. In case of the loss or destruction of a ketubbah, the husband must obtain a new one immediately.

A man who married a virgin paid twice as much as a man who married a divorcee or widow. The money amount was apparently deemed sufficient to discourage impulsive divorce and to support the divorcee or widow for a reasonable period of time. In reality, the minimum amount was often voluntarily increased in accordance with the standing of the families involved. Noble and priestly families customarily doubled the ketubbah. In addition to the financial clause, the text of the ketubbah outlined other obligations of the bridegroom. These obligations included basic traditional conjugal rights such as food, clothing, and shelter. Provisions were also made for the husband to pay all medical expenses in case his wife should be taken ill and to bear the costs related to her burial.

Ardyn Halter, an Israeli artist, paints manuscript illuminations for a Ketubah, a marriage contract in Hebrew. © ROBERT HOLMES/CORBIS.

PRIMARY SOURCE

Raziakov Family Ketubbah: A traditional Jewish marriage contract, or ketubbah, from 1863. COURTESY OF THE LIBRARY OF THE JEWISH THEOLOGICAL SEMINARY.

PRIMARY SOURCE

RAZIAKOV FAMILY KETUBBAH

See primary source image.

SIGNIFICANCE

The Raziacov family kettubah is a rare hand-decorated document. Most American kettubah were printed on standard, small sheets, which were often accompanied by miniature, printed pictures of wedding scenes. The change in kettubah design reflected a weakening of the close-knit Jewish communities that had existed for centuries in Europe and the Middle East. As Jews emigrated to the United States, and acquired a legal status equal to that given to non-Jews, the civil courts took precedent over Rabbinic courts. Jewish marriages were placed under the authority of civil courts.

Since the 1960s, more and more young couples affiliated with either the Conservative, Reform, or Reconstructionist movements have started to use an entirely new text as their marriage contract. In this text, which theoretically can be composed even by the couple themselves, both the bride and the groom take personal vows to love, cherish, and respect each other, to raise their children together, and so forth in accordance with their personal beliefs. Even in these texts, a more or less unified formula began to emerge. However, the new texts omit the financial stipulations that sparked the original creation of the ketubbah.

FURTHER RESOURCES
Books

Sabar, Shalom. *Ketubbah: The Art of the Jewish Marriage Contract.* New York: Rizzoli, 2000.

Hebrew Union College Skirball Museum. *Ketubbah: Jewish Marriage Contracts of the Hebrew Union College Skirball Museum and Klau Library.* Philadelphia: Jewish Publication Society, 1990.

That Terrible Question

Pamphlet

By: Moses Hull

Date: 1868

Source: Hull, Moses. *That Terrible Question.* Chicago: Hazlitt & Reed, 1868.

About the Author: Moses Hull (1836–1907) was a prominent Seventh-Day Adventist preacher in the mid 1800s who later converted to Spiritualism. Hull's revelation that he had committed adultery while on the lecture circuit, and that following adulterous urges was in effect obeying God's law, led some Spiritualist community members to repudiate his philosophies and writings.

INTRODUCTION

Utopian communities in the nineteenth century often deconstructed the institution of marriage, arguing against the traditional, monogamous, economic relationship and instead urging members to explore new ideas for gender roles and sexuality. John Humphrey Noyes (1811–1886) created the Oneida community in upstate New York at the end of the 1840s; his followers experienced a "radical transition in their personal lives from monogamy to celibacy, group marriage, or polygamy," according to Lawrence Foster, the author of *Religion and Sexuality: The Shakers, the Mormons, and the Oneida Community.*

Families that chose to join utopian communities changed their social structure and at times, kinship ties; couples accepted "free love" ideals to varying degrees, but within the framework of utopian community philosophy, sexual relations outside of traditional marriage was no longer taboo for these followers.

Feminists such as Susan B. Anthony (1820–1906) argued—behind the scenes—that the institution of marriage was patriarchal and inhibited women from exercising their rights; even the eighteenth century philosopher Mary Wollstonecraft (1759–1797), writer Mary Shelley's mother, argued against marriage. The utopian ideal was joined by the socialist and Marxist opinion that marriage—like capitalism—turned women and men into slaves to the institution and capitalist system that relied on marriage for private property continuation through reproduction and inheritance.

"Free love" proponents, utopians and socialists among them, argued for a wide range of actions that gave women greater freedom over their own bodies—and men greater freedom by extension. Birth control, freedom from physical discipline by one's husband, legal equality for legitimate and illegitimate children, and an end to adultery as a moral failing—these principles emerged at the same time as the Victorian Era in England. The clash between the Victorian ideals of modesty, chastity, purity, and sexual restraint and the utopian and socialist ideals was intense.

Moses Hull was a Christian preacher from the Seventh-Day Adventists who began to preach the gospel at the age of nineteen. Drawn to Spiritualism before the age of thirty, Hull believed that God was working through the spirits and trances he observed. By the mid 1860s he was a confirmed Spiritualist. Spiritualism, the belief that spirits of the dead could be contacted via people who could speak to the dead—called mediums—became a popular movement in the latter half of the nineteenth century, with prominent believers such as Victoria Woodhull (1838–1927) and Andrew Jackson Davis (1826–1910). Many Spiritualists were former Christians, disappointed with mainline Christianity's unwillingness to support women's rights reform. In 1868 Moses Hull published *That Terrible Question*; the following is an exerpt from his writings on love and marriage.

PRIMARY SOURCE

Love and Marriage

…Let those about entering wedlock know that a radical change cannot be made in an intended partner. Better try to change the spots on a leopard or the skin of an Ethiopian. Hence, we cannot too strongly urge you to know who and what the one is with whom you are about forming a copartnership for life. As soon as the sensitive partner finds that he or she has been disappointed—that the companion was wrongly *generated* on the start and cannot be *regenerated*, the feeling of disappointment together with the continual trial occasioned by the singularities of wife or husband, is such a source of trouble that the result is disease, resulting in insanity or death. How many there are now in the Lunatic Asylums who need nothing but finding the other half of themselves to restore them to sanity. Pick up almost any daily paper and read the obituaries.

"Died of consumption at the residence of her husband in—, on—. The deceased was an amiable lady—a respectable member of such a church." Sure enough, the doctor's skill is baffled and the children are left motherless. All the medicine in the world could not save her; consumption was not her disease. She died of wedlock—of being compelled to administer to the passions of a man whom she could not love. Reader, this is no fancy sketch. It is true of fifty per cent of the deaths caused by what is called consumption, liver complaint, dyspepsia, heart disease, etc.…

SIGNIFICANCE

Hull's chief complaint was that marriage, essentially forced on both parties by their parents and the need for a suitable social match in middle and upper-class society, led to unhappiness and even early death caused by malaise and resentment. Within five years, Hull's ideas on marriage and adultery would shock the Spiritualist world and provoke controversy among "free love" proponents.

In 1873, Hull published a letter in Woodhull & Claflin's Weekly in which he admitted to having an extramarital affair or repeated affairs while on the lecture circuit. Hull defended his actions by claiming that sexual urges outside of marriage are given to man by God, and that the greater sin lies in not fulfilling those urges. Hull's wife, Elvira, left him shortly after the letter was published. The "free love" aspect of utopianism and its relationship to Spiritualism was harmed; many prominent Spiritualists denounced Hull and separated themselves from the free love concept. Some more radical spiritualists, however, embraced the concept; Woodhull supported Hull's actions, and declared:

> Two persons, a male and a female, meet, and are drawn together by a mutual attraction—a natural feeling unconsciously arising within their natures of which neither has any control—which is denominated love. This a matter that concerns these two, and no other living soul has any human right to say aye, yes or no, since it is a matter in which none except the two have any right to be involved, and from which it is the duty of these two to exclude every other person, since no one can love for another or determine why another loves.

The free love movement had focused on freeing women from oppression within marriage, from coerced sexual relations, and forced marriage; with Hull's letter and the notoriety it gained, the free love movement began to look more like a justification for male adultery than a new philosophy. Free love opponents expressed concern for the family; what impact would the idea of "true marriage" proposed by Woodhull, in which sexual desire that united a man and a woman was considered a true marriage, above all legal and religious ceremonies, have on the children of such a marriage? If free love proponents believed that they could choose partners at will, as desire changed, opponents questioned what that meant for illegitimate children, property rights, and venereal disease?

By the early twentieth century, free love had migrated from the utopian communities, such as Oneida in New York and New Harmony in Indiana, into the cities. In New York City Greenwich Village was a focus of free love activity; Emma Goldman (1869–1940) and Edna St. Vincent Millay (1892–1950) were part of this urban movement. Many of the philosophical principles of free love were incorporated into society by the 1920s; women had gained a wide range of rights unavailable to them in the 1840s. While Hull's version of free love was controversial in its day, it was part of a larger ideal that aimed to restructure gender roles and sexuality within marriage and the family.

FURTHER RESOURCES
Books

Braude, Ann. *Radical Spirits: Spiritualism and Women's Rights in Nineteenth-Century America*. 2nd edition. Bloomington: Indiana University Press, 2001.

Dubois, Ellen Carol. *Feminism and Suffrage: The Emergence of an Independent Women's Movement in America, 1848–1869*. Ithaca, N.Y.: Cornell University Press, 1999.

Foster, Lawrence. *Religion and Sexuality: The Shakers, the Mormons, and the Oneida Community*. Urbana: University of Illinois Press, 1984.

Goldsmith, Barbara. *Other Powers: The Age of Suffrage, Spiritualism, and the Scandalous Victoria Woodhull*. New York: Knopf, 1998.

Hull, Moses. *The Question Settled. A Careful Comparison of Biblical and Modern Spiritualism. By Rev. Moses Hull*. Michigan Historical Reprint Series. Ann Arbor: Scholarly Publishing Office, University of Michigan Library, 2005.

An Opinion on Love Matches

Book excerpt

By: Eliza Southgate

Date: 1887

Source: Cook, Clarence, ed. *Life Eighty Years Ago: Letters of Eliza Southgate Browne*. New York: Scribner's, 1887.

About the Author: Eliza Southgate was born in 1783 in the town of Scarborough, Maine. At fourteen, she left home to attend a fashionable Boston school. She was married in 1803, but died at the age of twenty-five in 1809.

INTRODUCTION

While marriage is sometimes described as the oldest and most enduring human institution, the reasons for marrying have varied widely from era to era and culture to culture. Religious, racial, cultural, and economic factors have all played a part in determining who one could marry and the form which marriage took.

In many situations marrying has been primarily an economic decision. Monarchs sometimes arranged marriages between their children and those of other kings in order to expand their national territory, and members of royal families often found themselves constrained to other noble families when seeking a mate. In many cultures a young woman's parents were expected to provide a sizeable dowry to her suitor, while in other cultures a man's wealth was judged in part by the size of his harem and the number of wives he maintained.

Women in many cultures have found themselves playing a relatively passive role in courtship and marriage. In many ancient and some modern cultures young girls were traditionally married to older men, a choice normally made by the girl's father. In other cultures marriages were arranged by an older woman in the community, a matchmaker whose opinions were rarely disputed by the individuals involved. Historically many cultures have refused to leave the choice of a mate to the young people involved, believing that such a life-changing decision should be made by those with more experience.

The idea of romantic love as a foundation for marriage is not a recent development: The Hebrew scriptures include an entire book describing the joys of infatuation, love, and physical relations. But Western culture places unique value on the idea of love as a foundation for marriage, and on the importance of marriage in general. Particularly in the decades before women pursued educational opportunities a tremendous stigma was often attached to remaining single, the general assumption being that such a woman had been rejected by all possible suitors. For this reason women were sometimes willing to marry despite misgivings about the suitor.

■ PRIMARY SOURCE

…As I look around me I am surprised at the happiness which is so generally enjoyed in families, and that marriages which have not love for a foundation on more than one side at most, should produce so much apparent harmony. I may be censured for declaring it as my opinion that not one woman in a hundred marries for love. A woman of taste and sentiment will surely see but a very few whom she could love, and it is altogether uncertain whether either of them will particularly distinguish her. If they should, surely she is very fortunate, but it would be one of fortune's random favors and such as we have no right to expect. The female mind I believe is of a very pliable texture; if it were not we should be wretched indeed. Admitting as a known truth that few women marry those whom they would prefer to all the world if they could be viewed by them with equal affection, or rather that there are often others whom they could have preferred if they had felt that affection for them which would have induced them to offer themselves,—admitting this as a truth not to be disputed,—is it not a subject of astonishment that happiness is not almost banished from this connexion? Gratitude is undoubtedly the foundation of the esteem we commonly feel for a husband. One that has preferred us to all the world, one that has thought us possessed of every quality to render him happy, surely merits our gratitude. If his character is good—if he is not displeasing in his person or manners— what objection can we make that will not be thought frivolous by the greater part of the world?—yet I think there are many other things necessary for happiness, and the world should never compel me to marry a man because I could not give satisfactory reasons for not liking him. I do not esteem marriage absolutely essential to happiness, and that it does not always bring happiness we must every day witness in our acquaintance. A single life is considered too generally as a reproach; but let me ask you, which is the most despicable—she who marries a man she scarcely thinks well of—to avoid the reputation of an old maid, or she, who with more delicacy, than marry one she could not highly esteem, preferred to live single all her life, and had wisdom enough to despise so mean a sacrifice, to the opinion of the rabble, as the woman who marries a man she has not much love for— must make. I wish not to alter the laws of nature—neither will I quarrel with the rules which custom has established and rendered indispensably necessary to the harmony of society. But every being who has contemplated human nature on a large scale will certainly justify me when I declare that the inequality of privilege between the sexes is very sensibly felt by us females, and in no instance is it greater than in the liberty of choosing a partner in marriage; true, we have the liberty of refusing those we don't like, but not of selecting those we do. This is undoubtedly as it should be. But let me ask you, what must be that love which is altogether voluntary, which we can withhold or give, which sleeps in dullness and apathy till it is requested to brighten into life? Is it not a cold, lifeless dictate of the head,—do we not weigh all the conveniences and inconveniences which

will attend it? And after a long calculation, in which the heart never was consulted, we determine whether it is most prudent to love or not.

How I should despise a soul so sordid, so mean! How I abhor the heart which is regulated by mechanical rules, which can say "thus far will I go and no farther," whose feelings can keep pace with their convenience, and be awakened at stated periods,—a mere piece of clock-work which always moves right! How far less valuable than that being who has a soul to govern her actions, and though she may not always be coldly prudent, yet she will sometimes be generous and noble, and that the other never can be. After all, I must own that a woman of delicacy never will suffer her esteem to ripen into love unless she is convinced of a return. Though our first approaches to love may be involuntary, yet I should be sorry if we had no power of controlling them if occasion required. There is a happy conformity or pliability in the female mind which seems to have been a gift of nature to enable them to he happy with so few privileges,—and another thing, they have more gratitude in their dispositions than men, and there is something particularly gratifying to the heart in being beloved, if the object is worthy...Indeed, I believe no woman of delicacy suffers herself to think she could love any one before she had discovered an affection for her. For my part I should never ask the question of myself—do I love such a one, if I had reason to think he loved me—and I believe there are many who love that never confessed it to themselves. My pride, my delicacy would all be hurt if I discovered such unasked for love, even in my own bosom. I would strain every nerve and rouse every faculty to quell the first appearance of it. There is no danger, however. I could never love without being beloved, and I am confident in my own mind that no person whom I could love would ever think me sufficiently worthy to love me. But I congratulate myself that I am at liberty to refuse those I don't like, and that I have firmness enough to brave the sneers of the world and live an old maid, if I never find one I can love.

SIGNIFICANCE

The belief that men and women should choose their own spouses has been accepted in the U.S. for many decades. While no good comparison exists with other methods, the current system does result in a large ratio of failed marriages; roughly half of all marriages today end in divorce. And while remarriage following divorce is now widely accepted, second and third marriages have lower success rates than first unions. Statistically women who leave abusive husbands tend to choose second husbands who are also abusive.

Although many young women continue to want to eventually marry, much of the stigma surrounding singleness has vanished. Numerous women in the early twenty-first century choose to pursue advanced educations and careers, postponing or avoiding marriage entirely. With expanding career options many women now select singleness.

The practice of marrying for economic reasons remains common, as women occasionally find themselves accused of marrying for money. Ironically the reverse can occur now as well: In some cases it is the woman who brings financial resources to the relationship.

As science has expanded the understanding of personality and relationships, numerous tools have been created to help men and women identify an ideal marriage partner. Personality inventories allow trained counselors to help potential spouses understand their strengths and weaknesses, as well as what they need in a partner. Many of these tools are now employed by online services that allow participants to consider thousands of potential partners, potentially increasing the odds of identifying an ideal partner but also potentially complicating the selection process by providing an overwhelming number of options.

Just as in the 1800s, marriage in the early 2000s is a diverse arrangement, chosen by numerous couples for a multitude of varying reasons. Despite frequent criticism of marriage and its high failure rate, many men and women deeply desire to find a life partner who will love and appreciate their strengths while overlooking their weaknesses. Whether true love is as rare as this author believes is difficult to determine; what is certain is that despite difficult odds, marriage to a loving partner remains a goal for many men and women.

FURTHER RESOURCES
Books
Duby, Georges, and Michelle Perrot, eds. *A History of Women: Emerging Feminism From Revolution to World War*. Cambridge, MA.: Harvard University Press, 1993.

Perkins, Joan. *Victorian Women*. New York: New York University, 1993.

Woloch, Nancy. *Women and the American Experience*. Boston: McGraw-Hill, 2000.

Periodicals
Battan, Jesse F. "The 'Rights' of Husbands and the 'Duties' of Wives: Power and Desire in the American Bedroom,

1850–1910." *Journal of Family History*. 24 (1999): 165–186.

Malieckal, Bindu, et al. "What's Love Got to Do With It." *Newsweek*. 133(1999):18.

Web sites
Fordham University. "Internet Women's History Sourcebook." February 25, 2001 <http://www.fordham.edu/halsall/women/womensbook.html> (accessed July 17, 2006).

Human Rights Watch. "History of Rwanda." <http://www.hrw.org/reports/1999/rwanda/Geno1-3-09.htm#TopOfPage> (accessed July 12, 2006).

Stockton College. "Women in the Victorian Age." April 19, 2002 <http://caxton.stockton.edu/browning/stories/storyReader$3> (accessed July 16, 2006).

Why Divorce is Bad

Editorial

By: Margaret E. Sangster

Date: April 15, 1905

Source: *Cleveland Journal>*, April 15,1905, p. 6. Available at *Ohio Historical Center*. "Why Divorce is Bad." <http://dbs.ohiohistory.org/africanam/det.cfm?ID=3769> (accessed June 18, 2006).

About the Author: Margaret E. Sangster (1838–1912) was a nineteenth century author and editor. A deeply religious woman, she is known for her writing as well as her editorial work, including her role as editor of *Harper's Bazaar*.

INTRODUCTION

Divorce, the act of legally ending a marriage, is a common occurrence in modern America. In 2004, the United States experienced 3.7 divorces per 1,000 citizens, down considerably from 1981 when the rate peaked at a high of 5.3. However, the United States has the highest divorce rate in the industrialized world; by comparison, Canada and most Western European nations have rates of 2.0 per 1,000, and Spain's rate is only 0.6.

Divorce rates in America generally increased during the twentieth century, beginning at around 1.5 per 1,000 in the early 1900's. Numerous factors have been blamed for the rise in divorce rates. Demographics are thought to play a role; during the late nineteenth and

A divorced father gets his three daughters ready to return to their mother after spending the weekend with him, St. Louis, Missouri, August 6, 2004. © BRENDA ANN KENNEALLY/CORBIS.

early twentieth century, first-time grooms were an average of four years older than their new brides (ages twenty-six and twenty-two, respectively) and frequently had a much higher level of education. With their income potential severely limited and no government welfare programs, women had few options but to remain married.

The age difference between brides and grooms fell to three years during World War II, but from 1950 onward the age of first marriage for women steadily climbed to a 2002 level of 25.3, just below the male average of 26.9. Women marrying in the early twenty-first century are generally better educated and more financially secure, making divorce an economically realistic option for many of them. The availability of inexpensive birth control also allowed women to postpone childbearing, simplifying the decision to divorce in the early years of a marriage.

Other factors have also been blamed for rising divorce rates. Social and religious stigmas toward divorce have become less severe, and no-fault divorce laws in many states have led to newspaper ads touting inexpensive, "while-you-wait" divorces. A 1996 Census Bureau study found that the total population of divorced individuals in the United States climbed from 4 million in 1970 to 18 million in 1996, making divorced men and women a significant segment of the U.S. population.

As divorce has become increasingly common, social scientists have devoted considerable effort to assessing its impact. But decades before the effects of divorce were first scientifically investigated, some observers were already fully convinced of divorce's detrimental impact and were taking steps to curb divorces in America.

PRIMARY SOURCE

Pulpit and press and even fiction are calling attention to the widespread evil of easy divorce. A brilliant English novel, recently published, introduces no less than four misfit pairs, who, however, settle their differences in one way or another, outside the courts. Judge Grant's deeply interesting work, The Undercurrent, is a study of American life, which shows in startling colors the tendency to rush to divorce, not merely when it is, like surgery, in extreme cases necessary to save life, but when it is prompted, shall we say, by mere idleness and caprice, reinforced by a passionate desire for personal enjoyment.

In a certain ultra-fashionable set, it seems no longer to excite more than a passing comment, when A, growing tired of his wife, and coveting B's, secures a legal separation from her. In an incredibly short space of time the bond that unites the B's is probably broken and another marriage takes place; possibly two marriages take place. The thing is almost like the children's game of stagecoach, in which seats are changed with headlong haste. The evident prearrangement is shocking and awakens disgust.

This changing partners is still regarded in some conservative states of our union, notably in the south, as disgraceful, unless it be for a cause which in itself dissolves true marriage. In some of the older northern states and in some states of the newer west almost any flimsy excuse suffices to separate those who have been united by the sanction of the law and the church. Marriage is regarded by the church, or speaking strictly, by the Roman church and the Protestant Episcopal communion, as a sacrament. For the protection of society and the safeguarding of the home, it were well if this view were more generally taken. It is not very many years since it would hardly have been possible for decent people to air their quarrels and grievances in the public eye without shame and without reserve, as too frequently is now done. Nor is it very long since a slight stigma, a shadow, if not a stain, inhered in the very thought of divorce, so that respectable people shrank from it with horror and preferred to endure almost any suffering rather than have recourse to so heroic a remedy.

The worst feature of divorce is that it strikes a desperate blow at the integrity of the family. Historically speaking, the family came before the community, before the state, and before the nation. However prosperous a nation may seem to be, it cannot rise higher than the highest water-mark of its home life, nor can it be stable nor have its prosperity assured if there are rottenness and degeneracy in its homes. Divorce strikes a cruel blow at the happiness of childhood, and inflicts an unmerited reproach upon little ones who were called into the world by fathers and mothers whose self-will no longer permits them to live together in peace.

No dispassionate observer can help an extreme sorrow for children who are thus worse than orphaned in the morning of their days.

Sometimes the public is shown the spectacle of parents at strife, one or the other fighting fiercely for the possession of the offspring of both. Whichever gains the day, the father or the mother, the children have thrust upon them far too early the grief and pain which belongs only to maturity. Sensitive children suffer acutely in such circumstances. They are shamed in their own sight and in the eyes of their world of the schoolroom and the playground. Pending the decision of a stubbornly contested divorce case children are sometimes tossed about like balls in the hand of a mocking destiny, from one makeshift of a home to another, spending six months with a mother, then leaving her to pass six months with a father, both of whom adore the children, while they hate each other and are at deadly feud. No better hot-bed for the growth of everything inimical to good morals and good manners can be found than this. It stunts the good and forces the evil to rapid growth.

A curious obscurity must come over the mental vision of a father who desires to snatch his children from the mother who bore them, and a strange aberration of reason has seized the mother who would teach her children that their father is their worst enemy. No one can deny that causes exist which render legal separation a mournful necessity. Among these, infidelity, desertion, nonsupport and drunkenness must, of course, be included, and to these some thoughtful people add incompatibility of temper. In the later case it is often discovered that the incompatibility is superficial and not vital, and that it could be overcome by patience and self-control on either side. In too many instances the gist of the matter is that the infelicities of marriage spring from idleness, love of display and self-indulgence. A hard-working woman, with a more or less inebriated husband and a house full of children, once said to me: "Poor people do not go into the divorce court. They pick up their load and carry it on the best way they can. Somehow they know it will all come right at the end of the day."

The rich and the idle among women and men in this country are largely the ones who are bringing the stain of easy divorce upon the republic. It is the woman with several homes in which she does not live, haunting Europe instead, and the society man who is an idler from choice, who are most to blame. These people have grand weddings, marry with a great flourish of trumpets, and soon find the conditions of life intolerable. The next step is to establish a residence apart and through legal technicalities obtain a divorce. Next in hot haste, the wedding bells are run again. If a child has been born the trail of its misfortune seems nothing to its selfish parents.

We need not be too pessimistic. A house divided against itself is a house built on a quicksand. The ultimate good sense of the nation makes for righteousness. The nation is composed of units. The individual who scorns the right and chooses the wrong is less influential than his neighbor who stands firmly for loyalty, good faith and pure living. The nations as a nation abhors whatever mitigates against the stability of marriage and the security of home life. Our strength is in the unobtrusive, comfortable and contented home. In city and country the plain home is the bulwark of the nation. Thousands of people who never gave it a name, are living the simple life, which is also the hallowed and beautiful life. Until truth and honor are lost, and graft and corruption take their place, divorce will remain exceptional. Nevertheless, a toning up of public sentiment is needed, and if practicable, some uniformity of legal enactment should be sought for the salvation of the American home and the protection of our good name and fame.

SIGNIFICANCE

Margaret Sangster penned her editorial in an era when divorce rates were one-third of what they are today. In the century since she wrote, social scientists began to quantify the economic and social cost of divorce in America. In fiscal year 2000 the federal government spent $150 billion on aid to single-parent households, many of which are the result of a divorce. Single mothers are also far more likely to face poverty than are intact families; by one estimate up to 60 percent of all families below the poverty line consist of divorced mothers raising children.

The trauma of divorce severely impacts children. Young children experiencing divorce generally have more problems in school and are more likely to have legal trouble; they are also more likely to divorce after marrying. A 1997 study found that even adult children of divorcing parents go through a painful grieving process, despite the fact that they no longer live with their parents. A 1994 analysis of previous studies found that children in single-parent homes are from 60 to 120 percent more likely to drop out of high school; they also exhibit higher rates of asthma, speech difficulties, and general susceptibility to illness.

Alarmed at these and other discouraging findings, government, social service, and religious organizations have launched efforts to improve marriages and reduce the divorce rate. Proposals include ending no-fault divorce laws or requiring marriage counseling before a divorce is granted. Clergy in some U.S. cities have agreed that they will not perform wedding ceremonies for couples who have not completed a manda-

tory course of pre-marriage training. Both liberal and conservative politicians have endorsed efforts to strengthen families, giving the issue potential traction in Washington, D.C. As of 2006 divorce rates are holding steady or declining slightly.

Despite high divorce rates, marriage remains popular, even among the previously married, and second, third, and even fourth marriages are not uncommon. While those considering first-time marriage are frequently told they face a 50 percent chance of divorce, this statistic is somewhat skewed by serial divorcees. Further, a 2004 study funded by Rutgers University's National Marriage Project found that choices such as delaying pregnancy and childbirth until after marriage, completing some college courses, marrying after age twenty-five, and having a steady income each produced double-digit declines in projected divorce rates, making the actual chance of success for most couples much higher.

FURTHER RESOURCES

Books

Burns, Alisa, and Cathy Scott. *Mother-Headed Families and Why They Have Increased*. Hillsdale, NJ: Lawrence Erlbaum Associates, 1994.

Emery, Robert E. *Marriage, Divorce, and Children's Adjustment*. Thousand Oaks, CA: Sage Publications, 1989.

Stanton, Glenn T. *Why Marriage Matters: Reasons to Believe in Marriage in Post-Modern Society*. Colorado Spring, CO: Pinon Press, 1997.

Periodicals

Aquilino, William S. "Later Life Parental Divorce and Widowhood: Impact on Young Parents' Assessment of Parent-Child Relations." *Journal of Marriage and the Family* 56 (1994): 908–922.

Ruggles, Steven. "The Rise of Divorce and Separation in the United States, 1880–1990." *Demography*. 34 (1997): 444–466.

Smith, Jack C., et al. "Marital Status and the Risk of Suicide." *American Journal of Public Health* 78 (1988): 78–80.

Web sites

Ohio State University. "Family Life." <http://hec.osu.edu/famlife/family/index.htm> (accessed June 18, 2006).

University of California, Los Angeles. "Divorce Research Homepage." 2001 <http://jeffwood.bol.ucla.edu/> (accessed June 18, 2006).

University of Tennessee College of Law. "Tennessee Family Law/Divorce Guide." June, 2003 <http://www.law.utk.edu/library/divo2.htm> (accessed June 18, 2006).

Divorces Increase by Half

Newspaper article

By: The New York Times

Date: January 1, 1920

Source: "Divorces Increase by Half." *New York Times* (January 1, 1920).

About the Author: Published since 1851, The *New York Times* is a daily newspaper that is widely regarded as a newspaper of record in the United States.

INTRODUCTION

Divorce is defined as the legal separation of a husband and a wife that is made effective by the judgment of a court of competent jurisdiction, where the marriage is dissolved. Divorce is distinct from marital separation in that separation of two spouses is not necessarily permanent.

In the earliest days of the Christian church, there was a general prohibition against divorce. Marriage was seen as a sacred institution and one that could not be altered by man. In the 1800s, courts based in the Anglo-American judicial system began to regard marriage as having both a civil and a religion component; in their supervisory duties with regard to the civil law, courts acquired the power to terminate marriages by way of a divorce decree. In countries that have a federal constitutional structure such as the United States, individual states have the power to establish laws regarding the circumstances in which divorce will be permitted.

Many religious faiths continue to consider marriage as an inviolate contract before God. The courts have ruled, however, that even where a particular person regarded his or her vows of marriage as an inviolate part of their religious faith, the legal system has the jurisdiction to terminate the civil contract that also exists between married persons provided the appropriate grounds to do so were established.

A couple going through a divorce sits in a lawyer's office. © CREASOURCE/CORBIS.

Historically, the legal grounds upon which a court could terminate a marriage were limited to acts of spousal misconduct. Prior to the no-fault divorce (divorce by consent) regimes that became the law in many American states beginning in the 1960s, a divorce could only be granted upon the petition of one of the marriage partners to a court where the party could prove adultery or desertion (abandonment). In companion legislation to the divorce laws, courts were empowered to grant an annulment of the marriage if there existed a physical inability to consummate the marriage through sexual intercourse, or where one party had committed bigamy. New York passed legislation in 1813 that specified that both mistreated and deserted wives could petition for divorce, a law that was the most liberal in the nation at that time.

Given the strict rules by which divorce could be granted and an absence of authority to permit divorce on the basis of the desire of the parties to become divorced, collusion in the manufacture of divorce grounds was a source of common judicial complaint from the early days of the New York statute until the no-fault regime was introduced in 1966. No-fault divorce is commonly instituted upon the agreement of the parties that there exists irreconcilable differences between them, or an otherwise permanent breakdown of the marriage.

One legal feature consistent with New York divorce law in 1918 and that of the present day is the requirement of residency. At least one of the parties to the divorce action must have been resident in the state for the 12 months prior to the commencement of the proceeding.

The liberalization of divorce laws in New York and throughout the United States precipitated a significant increase in the number of claims collateral to the divorce proceeding, usually advanced by the female spouse for equalization of family property acquired during the marriage, legal proceedings that were rare in 1918. In a similar fashion, divorce proceedings may also include contests concerning child custody, child and spousal support.

■ PRIMARY SOURCE

More Than 1,400 Cases Filed in City During 1918.

Records in the County Clerk's office show that more than 1,400 divorce cases were filed in 1919, an increase of approximately 50 per cent, over the preceding year. The number was slightly more than 900. The 1918 figures were slightly lower than for several previous years.

The exact figures will be made public in a few days in the annual report of County Clerk William F. Schneider.

Supreme Court Justice Samuel Greenbaum, who has heard many divorce cases, said yesterday he believed the increase was due to the fact that "world morals are becoming more materialistic."

"Home life without families, and living in small apartments has had much to do with it," he said.

Supreme Court Justice Vernon M. Davis said that as a lay delegate to the recent convention of the Protestant Episcopal Church in Detroit, he had tried unsuccessfully to have a canon adopted forbidding the remarriage of even the innocent party in a divorce as a remedy. He attributed the increase to a lessening of the sanctity of the home.

Records of the Marriage License Bureau show that there were 11 per cent more marriages in 1919 than in 1918. In the last year City Clerk Scully has issued approximately 40,000 marriage licenses, as against 35,163 in 1918. Ex-service men predominated among the applicants.

■ SIGNIFICANCE

The rise in divorce cases that prompted the *New York Times* commentary in 1920 is of interest today because the number of divorces cited seems so modest by modern standards. The divorce rate in the United States appeared to peak statistically in 1980, when there existed the likelihood that more than 40 percent of the marriages made that year would end in divorce. Expressed as a ratio, 5.3 persons per 1,000 persons in 1983 were divorced; in 1950, the ratio was 2.6 per 1,000. Much of the 1980 peak has been attributed to the introduction of consent or no-fault divorce that took place in virtually every American state during the 1960s and early 1970s. As divorces became easier to obtain, the applications became more frequent.

A second contrast between the attitudes towards divorce as described in 1918 and the modern day is the relative stigma attached to the divorced spouses. In a fault-based divorce jurisdiction, the basis for the grant of the divorce turned on an express finding of matrimonial misconduct; divorce therefore carried both society's moral judgment as well as the legal termination of the marriage. Even where the party was successful in establishing the fault of the other spouse, the stereotypical divorcee did not enjoy the same status as a married person, having sustained a failed marriage. No-fault rules, in addition to making divorces easier to obtain, also contributed to the lessening of the stigma attached to the proceedings.

The comments attributed to Supreme Court Justice Davis in the article are inconceivable on the part of a judge today. The justice made plain his bias with respect to both the grant of divorces and the limitations that he urged upon his co-religionists of the Episcopal Church. Under modern rules concerning judicial partiality, it would be doubtful that the justice would be permitted to hear a divorce action.

The 1918 data from New York is also significant because at that time, the city was perceived by Americans to be a social bellwether, a place where trends began that might be adopted throughout the country. While divorce rates rose markedly in the late 1960s to the 1980 peak, 1918 represents the statistical commencement of a long period of steadily increasing divorce rates that was only broken by the intervention of World War II.

Although the *New York Times* article does not set out an exhaustive statistical analysis of the marriage rate for 1918, an 11 percent increase in marriage applications is noted, a function of the fact that there were large numbers of service men returning home from World War I. In 2004, 7.8 persons per 1,000 were married during that year, contrasted with 3.7 per 1,000 who were divorced.

Another prominent modern social factor that did not exist to any significant degree in 1918 is the number of persons who reside in common law relationships. Living in such a relationship in 1918 carried an even greater social stigma than being divorced; a child born out of wedlock was regarded as illegitimate in the eyes of most Christian faiths and could not be baptized. The termination of these relationships is not captured in divorce statistics.

Notwithstanding the greater frequency of divorce in modern society, coupled with the option of common law cohabitation, marriage remains a desirable option in the opinion of most persons in North American society. The divorce rate is not perceived as a deterrent for entry into first or subsequent marriages. Data in both the United States and Canada confirms that the divorce rate for second marriages is between thirty percent and fifty percent higher than that for first marriages.

FURTHER RESOURCES

Book

Friedman, Lawrence M. *A History of American Law*. New York: Touchstone, 2005.

Periodical

Hilfer, Anthony Channell. "Marriage and Divorce in America." *American Literary History* 15 (2003): 592–602.

Web site

New York Divorce and Family Law. "Divorce: History of Divorce in New York." 2006 <http://www.brandeslaw.com/grounds_for_divorce/history.htm> (accessed June 21, 2006).

Sharma v. Sharma

Kansas Appellate Court decision on First Amendment Religious Rights, 1983

Judicial decision

By: J. Richard Foth

Date: August 4, 1983

Source: J. Richard Foth. "Sharma v. Sharma." *Pacific Reporter, Second Series.* 667 (1983): 395.

About the Author: J. Richard Foth served as the Chief Judge of the Court of Appeal for Kansas from 1977 to 1985. The Court of Appeals is the highest court in the state of Kansas, empowered to hear all types of civil and criminal law appeals.

INTRODUCTION

Sharma v. Sharma is an unusually constituted divorce proceeding that was decided by the Court of Appeals for Kansas in 1983. The proceeding engaged issues not commonly adjudicated in a divorce action, namely the constitutionally protected right of freedom of religion, coupled with the relationship between a civil divorce decree and the religious consequences associated with it.

Even in a modern America that is far less homogeneous and far more culturally diverse than it was as recently as the end of the Second World War, there is a certain incongruity when a Kansas court, situated in the heart of the American Midwest, weighs the tenets of the Hindu religion against what in all other respects seems a straightforward divorce action based upon incompatibility.

The petitioner, Niranjan Sharma, sued for a grant of divorce from his wife, Mridula Sharma. Under Kansas law, as in many other American states, a person may advance a claim for divorce regardless of their nationality or citizenship; residency in the state of Kansas for the prescribed period prior to the application is the important precondition. It is for this reason that Mr. Sharma could sue for divorce even though neither he nor his wife were American citizens. Once a divorce is granted by a court of competent jurisdiction, it will invariably be recognized in all other legal jurisdictions.

The case was heard at the Court of Appeals when Mridula Sharma appealed the order after the initial trial court granted the divorce requested by her husband. He had advanced his claim for a divorce based upon the grounds of incompatibility, a broad basis for divorce that is common in all jurisdictions where the legislation permits a form of no-fault divorce. She argued that Hinduism does not recognize divorce, and granting this request would have devastating social consequences when she returned to India.

Proceedings advanced by one party or the other on the basis of incompatibility are usually uncontested; the grant of the divorce order is independent from the determination of any other property, spousal support, child support, or child custody claims. In the Sharma proceedings, the only issue before the court was the issuance of the divorce.

■ PRIMARY SOURCE

Sharma v. Sharma

FOTH, Chief Judge:

The defendant, Mridula Niranjan Sharma, appeals from an order granting a divorce to her husband, Niranjan Sharma. The parties are citizens of India and Hindus of high caste. [In Hindu culture, people are grouped into one of four social divisions known as *varna*, or castes, plus a fifth group known as the untouchables.] The wife contends that the order dissolving her marriage violates her constitutionally guaranteed right of free exercise of religion. She informs us that the Hindu religion does not recognize divorce, and that if she returns to India as a divorced woman, her family and friends will treat her as though she were dead. The husband disputes this, but even assuming that the wife's interpretation of Hindu personal law is accurate, we must affirm.

It has long been recognized that under the First Amendment of the United States Constitution, freedom of belief is absolute. The law may, however, regulate conduct prompted by religious beliefs when the individual's interest in the free exercise of religion is outweighed by a compelling state interest.

The wife contends that *Wisconsin v. Yoder*, 406 U.S. 205, 92 S.Ct. 1526, 32 L.Ed.2d 15 (1972), requires that her religious beliefs prevail. We disagree. In Yoder, the United States Supreme Court found that the State's requirement of compulsory school attendance until age

16 was in irreconcilable conflict with the religious beliefs of the Amish defendants. Formal high school education beyond the eighth grade not only exposes Amish children to values that they reject as influences that alienate man from God, but it also takes them away from the traditional training that imparts the attitudes and skills necessary for life in the Amish community. This is not such a case, for the granting of a divorce to the husband does not deny the wife her religious freedom.

We find only one case in which the present issue has been considered, *Williams v. Williams*, 543 P.2d 1401 (Okl.1975)...In response to a wife's contention that the divorce granted to her husband contravened the religious vows taken by the parties and the authority of God, the Bible, and Jesus Christ, the Oklahoma Supreme Court stated:

> The action of the trial court only dissolved the civil contract of marriage between the parties. No attempt was made to dissolve it ecclesiastically. Therefore, there is no infringement upon her constitutional right of freedom of religion. She still has her constitutional prerogative to believe that in the eyes of God, she and her estranged husband are ecclesiastically wedded as one, and may continue to exercise that freedom of religion according to her belief and conscience. Any transgression by her husband of their ecclesiastical vows, is, in this instance, outside the jurisdiction of the court....

We agree with the Oklahoma court's analysis and find it applicable here. The wife here may take such view of their relationship after the decree as her religion requires, but as a matter of law the civil contract has been dissolved.

In addition, the husband apparently does not share his wife's religious beliefs about divorce, since he sought the decree. Under these circumstances, to compel him to remain married because of the wife's religious beliefs would be to prefer her beliefs over his. Any such preference is prohibited by the Establishment Clause of the First Amendment. The government may not "aid one religion, aid all religions, or prefer one religion over another." ... We discern no constitutional infirmity in the decree dissolving the marriage.

The wife also claims that the husband is estopped [prevented] from filing for divorce because the marriage was contracted with specific reference to the parties' religious beliefs, and that there was insufficient evidence to support a finding of incompatibility. She conceded at oral argument that the estoppel claim was never presented to the trial court; therefore it is not properly before us.... Although the parties' testimony differed as to the cause and intensity of their quarrels, the record reveals competent substantial evidence that the parties were incompatible. Thus, the trial court's finding on this point must stand.

Affirmed.

SIGNIFICANCE

This decision is noteworthy for its factual and constitutional issues. *Sharma* is the only reported decision in the United States that discusses the rights of a married Hindu woman in the context of a disputed civil divorce. But for the religious question, there would be no seeming obstacle to granting the requested divorce, as the Court found that the grounds of incompatibility between the spouses were predominant.

The critical issue to be determined was the relationship between the Mridula Sharma's First Amendment rights to practice her religious beliefs, one of which is that marriage is inviolate and cannot be terminated, and those of the husband, who advanced a contrary view. The court neatly preserved the First Amendment safeguards in its finding that the civil grant of a divorce does not disturb the Sharma's ability to treat their marriage as each of them may see fit for their private religious purposes. This is consistent with a long line of American cases that speak to the division between church and state; the Court of Appeals was careful to confirm that what a Hindu or any other person who practices their religion may hold about marriage or any other concept is unquestionably their own.

The Court did not address the point advanced by the wife concerning her anticipated loss of social status in India if she were divorced, although the claimed loss of status in India is a social and not a legal consequence, as India abolished the caste system in 1949. The language of the ruling indicates little sympathy in the court, a body rendering its verdict from a relatively egalitarian American perspective, for the prospect of protecting the defendant's high-caste reputation. Such arguments clearly struck the court as far removed from the legal requirements of a divorce application in Kansas.

In cases where a court is asked to rule on a concept not within its range of knowledge or experience, an expert witness will be called by one (or both) parties to provide evidence that the court may consider. Here there was a clear conflict between the parties as to the applicable Hindu religious law regarding divorce. A plain reading of the Indian Hindu Marriage Act (1955), creates eight distinct grounds of divorce, including adultery and cruelty; no evidence of this sort was called at the initial trial proceedings to clarify the issue of whether a divorce was not permitted in Hindu religious law.

FURTHER RESOURCES

Books

Agnes, Flavia. *Women and Law in India*. New Delhi: Oxford University Press, 2004.

Basu, Monnayee. *Hindu Women and Marriage Law-From Sacrament to Contract*. New Delhi: Oxford University Press, 2004.

Periodicals

Kindregan, Charles P., Jr. "Same Sex Marriage: The Cultural Wars and the Lessons of Legal History." *Family Law Quarterly*. 38 (2004) 427.

Web sites

Washburn University School of Law. "Survey of Kansas Law: Family Law." 2004 <http://classes.washburnlaw.edu/maxw/publications/surveyoflaw1984.htm> (accessed June 19, 2006).

Bargaining and Distribution in Marriage

Journal article

By: Shelley Lundberg and Robert A. Pollak

Date: 1996

Source: Lundberg, Shelley, and Robert A. Pollak. "Bargaining and Distribution in Marriage." *Journal of Economic Perspectives*. 10 (1996): 139.

About the Author: Shelley Lundberg is a professor of economics at the University of Washington who specializes in the study of family economic relations. Robert A. Pollak is a professor of economics at Washington University in St. Louis, Missouri. The two have collaborated on a number of scholarly articles about family economics.

INTRODUCTION

The distribution of financial responsibilities between the marriage partners has undergone significant change in the past 100 years. The institution of marriage as a one-man, one-woman, lifetime proposition has given way to a multitude of variations, each with its own distinct financial considerations and responsibilities.

Until 1960, most developed countries in the world, whether they evolved from the Anglo-American legal tradition or the community property regime found in European countries such as France, had similar rules regarding the financial distributions created by marriage. All spouses were obligated to provide for one another; all parents were obligated to support the children who were the product of a marriage; all adult children were obligated to support their parents when necessary.

The general rules regarding matrimonial property in these countries were also similar to one another. Property acquired during the course of a marriage was usually deemed to be jointly owned, and all property brought into the marriage was treated as separately owned by the spouse who originally owned the property.

While the obligations of support and property division have been well defined legally, the organization of financial duties within a marriage have not been. How a marital unit used its financial resources, acquired through income or other means, or who within the marriage was responsible for financial decisions has never been regulated by the state.

In blended families, where one or both spouses may have been married previously and have corresponding financial responsibilities to either children or a former spouse, the bargaining and distribution of financial responsibilities in a second marriage can be complicated. Often the economic power of the new unit is significantly constrained by preexisting obligations, subjecting the financial viability of the new family unit to factors that cannot be controlled.

The old maxim that the man brought home the bacon and the woman cooked it has been rendered largely a historical artifact. Decisions for the modern two-wage-earner couple often include educational choices, questions regarding both the timing and the number of desired children, as well as when and if the female partner will work outside the home. Each of these decisions significantly affect how modern families determine their economic path.

PRIMARY SOURCE

Bargaining and Distribution in Marriage

In the 1970s, a proposed social welfare policy change in the United Kingdom excited considerable debate. The universal child allowance, a reduction in the amount withheld for taxes from the father's paycheck,

was to be replaced by a cash payment to the mother. An excerpt from the parliamentary debate in the *House of Commons Hansard* (May 13, 1975) expresses a popular sentiment: "[F]ar from a new deal for families, it will take money out of the husband's pocket on the Friday and put it into the wife's purse on the following Tuesday. Far from being a child benefit scheme, it looks like being a father disbenefit scheme."

Popular discussions of family policies such as the U.K. child benefit often concern their presumed effects on distribution within the family—on the relative well-being of husbands, wives and children. The economist armed only with traditional models of the family must view these discussions as naïve. Until very recently, the standard of the profession for both theoretical and empirical analysis was a "common preference" model of the family, which assumes that family members act as though they are maximizing a single utility function. A family's common preference ordering may be the outcome of consensus among family members or the dominance of a single family member, but all such models imply that family expenditures are independent of which individuals in the family receive income or control resources. Common preference models imply that all income is "pooled" and then allocated to maximize a single objective function, so that family demand behavior depends on total family income and not the incomes of individual members. This pooling of resources within the family implies that a change from child allowances paid to fathers to child allowances paid to mothers should arouse neither the ire of affected fathers nor the opposition of the parliamentary representatives....

To this end, the theoretical challenge facing family economics is to develop models in which joint family decisions are derived from the sometimes divergent interests of husbands and wives and in which the formation and dissolution of marriages provide a beginning and an end to the family allocation process. In recent years, a large number of game-theoretic models of marriage and the family have been developed, building on the seminal contributions of Manser and Brown and McElroy and Horney. In general, these modes impose fewer restrictions on observed family behavior than do common preference models, and recent theoretical contributions have been prompted, and supported, by a growing body of empirical evidence inconsistent with common preference models. The most provocative of this empirical work demonstrates a strong positive association between child well-being and the mother's relative control over family resources and has raised new questions about the potential effectiveness of policies "targeted" at specific family members.

A current snapshot of family economics would show the traditional framework under siege on both theoretical and empirical fronts. The political potency of gender issues has given a certain urgency to the development of alternatives to common preference models. However, no new theoretical framework has gained general acceptance as a replacement for common preference models, and empirical studies have concentrated on debunking old models rather than on discriminating among new ones. In this paper, we review a number of simple bargaining models that permit independent agency of men and women in marriage, discuss their implications for distribution within marriage and for observed family behavior, and present a sampling of the relevant empirical evidence.

SIGNIFICANCE

In the modern blended and multidimensional family, where the financial obligations of its members often extend in a number of directions, economic planning and decision making can be difficult. Economic strategies for the blended family stand in contrast to the traditional nuclear family, which could make financial decisions that were solely in relation to the members of the present household, usually limited to two parents and their children.

The traditional male marriage role as breadwinner with the female as homemaker has been the focus of many academic and legal analyses. One motivation for introducing property equalization and support provisions in family law was to redress the traditional imbalance in male and female economic positions if a marriage failed.

'Extended family' traditionally meant three or more generations of blood relatives—grandparent, parent, and child, for example. Today the extended family encompasses the spouse or former spouses of the family member. Unlike the blended family, with connotations that require interaction between its members to function effectively, the extended family is a clinical expression similar to the plotting of the members family positions relative to one another on a chart.

A family gathers in their kitchen. © SIMON MARCUS/CORBIS.

Blended families were a rarer and less well understood in 1975, when the British House of Commons debated the universal child allowance. The generally accepted definition is a family created through a marriage where one or both spouses have been married previously, or have lived in a common law relationship where children were born; where one or both spouses has children from the previous relationship. Today in most Western countries one child in three will be a member of a stepfamily before reaching 18.

The publication of the primary source as part of a greater body of academic literature on family economics is itself significant, given that the science of economics had no such specialties prior to 1970. Such changes in family creation and organization helped establish schools of study throughout the world devoted to the family and its economic structure: Family law practice, the study of women's issues, statistics that describe the changing demographics of family relationships, and economic issues identified through research (such as that carried out by Professors Lundberg and Pollak) now constitute a rich and vibrant interrelated field of modern university study.

With less than 25 percent of Americans now living in households comprised of a once-married pair of heterosexual spouses and children that are the product of their union alone, marriages that create a blended family are often seen in the modern world as a dispassionate social structure, as opposed to an aspect of an accepted romantic or religious institution. Most developed nations have witnessed a similar reduction in the frequency of the traditional marriage and its resulting family structure.

The blended family has altered many long-held assumptions about the family as an economically efficient structure. Traditional theory assumed that families were inherently a positive economic structure, with resources pooled and decisions made to benefit the family membership. A number of modern economists, however, suggest that the blended family may be inefficient and one that generates a negative financial outcome for its members, due to the pressures arising from obligations placed upon it by previous marriages or common law relationships.

FURTHER RESOURCES
Books

Steiner, Leslie Morgan. *Mommy Wars: Stay-at-Home and Career Moms Face off on Their Choices, Their Lives, Their Families.* New York: Random House, 2006.

Periodicals

Molloy, Alexandra Benis. "Labor Pains." *Harvard Public Health Review.* Winter 2002.

Web sites

United States Department of the Interior. "Workforce Diversity." 2005 <http://www.doi.gov/diversity/8women.htm> (accessed June 18, 2006).

European Commission. "Gender Equality." 2006 <http://www.ec.europa.eu/employment_social/gender_equality/index_en.html> (accessed June 18, 2006).

Defense of Marriage Act

Legislation

By: United States Congress

Date: January 3, 1996

Source: *Government Printing Office.* "Defense of Marriage Act." <http://frwebgate.access.gpo.gov/> (accessed June 10, 2006).

About the Author: The United States Congress is the lawmaking branch of the federal government. The Defense of Marriage Act was introduced by the 104th Congress at its second session.

INTRODUCTION

For much of U.S. history, most American families fit a similar template, consisting of a married couple and their biological children. In this arrangement the husband was the sole or primary income earner while the wife managed the house and cared for the children. The fictional Ward and June Cleaver household in the 1950's television show *Leave It to Beaver* portrayed a prototypical American family. But while the Cleaver household may not have been the norm even in the 1950's, many families of that era did resemble them, at least outwardly.

By 1990, this traditional American family was no longer the predominant household form. According to the census conducted that year households resembling the Cleavers accounted for only 16% of the total. As young people delayed marriage, more homes consisted of singles, while the growing acceptance of cohabitation led to more unmarried couples. Climbing divorce rates produced more single-parent homes, and remarriages produced blended homes combining members of several families into a new unit.

During this era homosexual rights also became a major political issue. Throughout the 1980's and 1990's, federal courts heard cases challenging state anti-sodomy laws, and several states passed legislation protecting gay rights. In 1991, three same-sex couples in Hawaii challenged the state's refusal to grant them marriage licenses. After the case was appealed to the Hawaii Supreme Court, conservative groups nationwide became concerned that the court might rule in favor of gay marriage. Their concern arose from a basic principle of federal law that requires states to recognize each other's marriages and court-authorized actions. Under this doctrine, same-sex marriages performed in Hawaii could be considered binding in other states as well.

Facing the possibility of legalized gay marriage in Hawaii, members of Congress proposed a new federal law that would limit the impact of any potential ruling in Hawaii. The act legally defined marriage as a union between one man and one woman; it also allowed each state to decide individually whether or not to recognize same-sex unions, regardless of what other states might allow. The act quickly made its way through both houses of Congress, where sponsors described it as making explicit what federal law had implied for two centuries; President Clinton signed the act into law in 1996.

■ PRIMARY SOURCE

H.R.3396

One Hundred Fourth Congress

of the

United States of America

AT THE SECOND SESSION

Begun and held at the City of Washington on Wednesday,

the third day of January, one thousand nine hundred and ninety-six.

An Act

To define and protect the institution of marriage.

Be it enacted by the Senate and House of Representatives of the United States of America in Congress assembled,

SECTION 1. SHORT TITLE.

This Act may be cited as the "Defense of Marriage Act."

SEC. 2. POWERS RESERVED TO THE STATES.

(a) IN GENERAL.—Chapter 115 of title 28, United States Code, is amended by adding after section 1738B the following:

§ 1738C. Certain acts, records, and proceedings and the effect thereof

No State, territory, or possession of the United States, or Indian tribe, shall be required to give effect to any public act, record, or judicial proceeding of any other State, territory, possession, or tribe respecting a relationship between persons of the same sex that is treated as a marriage under the laws of such other State, territory, possession, or tribe, or a right or claim arising from such relationship.

(b) CLERICAL AMENDMENT—The table of sections at the beginning of chapter 115 of title 28, United States Code, is amended by inserting after the item relating to section 1738B the following new item:

1738C. Certain acts, records, and proceedings and the effect thereof.

SEC. 3. DEFINITION OF MARRIAGE.

(a) IN GENERAL.—Chapter 1 of title 1, United States Code, is amended by adding at the end the following:

§ 7. Definition of 'marriage' and 'spouse'

In determining the meaning of any Act of Congress, or of any ruling, regulation, or interpretation of the various administrative bureaus and agencies of the United States, the word 'marriage' means only a legal union between one man and one woman as husband and wife, and the word 'spouse' refers only to a person of the opposite sex who is a husband or a wife.

(b) CLERICAL AMENDMENT.—The table of sections at the beginning of chapter 1 of title 1, United States Code, is amended by inserting after the item relating to section 6 the following new item:

7. Definition of 'marriage' and 'spouse'.

Speaker of the House of Representatives.

Vice President of the United States and

President of the Senate.

■ SIGNIFICANCE

In 1994, the Hawaiian state legislature passed a law defining marriage as a union between a man and a woman, and in 1998 that state's voters approved a state constitutional amendment defining marriage as a man-woman union. The state Supreme Court upheld this amendment in 1999.

At the federal level opponents of the Defense of Marriage Act raised several objections to the law, arguing that its scope is beyond Congress's authority and that it violates the Constitution's pledge of equal protection. Court challenges to the law in the years since its passage, however, have proven unsuccessful. A majority of states have also passed individual versions of the Defense of Marriage Act.

In 2000, Vermont became the first state to officially recognize same-sex civil unions, granting these partners the same legal rights and privileges accorded to heterosexual spouses. In 2004 the mayor of San Francisco authorized city clerks to issue marriage licenses to same-sex couples, despite a 2000 California referendum defining marriage as a heterosexual union; the state Supreme Court quickly moved to stop such issuance. That same year the Massachusetts Supreme Court ruled that civil unions were inadequate to provide equal rights for gays, effectively legalizing gay marriage in the state.

By 2006, most states had taken legal action to regulate same-sex marriage. Massachusetts was the only state allowing gay marriage, though pending court rulings offered the potential for similar rights in New Jersey, New York, and Washington. Connecticut and Vermont were the only states to recognize same-sex civil unions, while forty-one states had enacted laws prohibiting same-sex marriages and eighteen had added the same prohibition to their state constitutions. In 2006, the U.S. House of Representatives passed a proposed constitutional amendment defining marriage as a heterosexual union. The proposal failed to pass the Senate.

FURTHER RESOURCES
Books
Gerstmann, Evan. *Same-Sex Marriage and the Constitution.* Cambridge University Press, 2004.

Pinello, Daniel. *Gay Rights and American Law.* Cambridge, England, and New York: Cambridge University Press, 2003.

Richards, David. *The Case for Gay Rights: From Bowers to Lawrence and Beyond.* Lawrence, KS: The University Press of Kansas, 2005.

Periodicals
Johnson, Kirk. "4 Proposals on Same-Sex Unions Compete for Favor of Coloradans." *New York Times.* 155 (May 7, 2006): A24.

Kokoski, Paul. "Cheers and Jeers for the Proposed Gay-Marriage ban." *Christian Science Monitor.* 98 (2006): 8.

Rosenberg, Debra, et al. "Politics of the Altar." *Newsweek.* 147 (2006): 34–35.

Web sites
Associated Press. "Mass. Lawmakers Don't Address Gay Marriage." July 12, 2006 <http://hosted.ap.org/dynamic/stories/> (accessed July 11, 2006).

DOMA Watch. "Your Legal Source for Defense of Marriage Acts Information." <http://www.domawatch.org/index.html> (accessed June 15, 2006).

Stateline. "50-state Rundown on Gay Marriage Laws." November 3, 2004 <http://www.stateline.org/live/> (accessed June 15, 2006).

Declaration of Covenant Marriage

Legislation

By: Louisiana State Legislature

Date: 1999

Source: *State of Louisiana.* "House Bill 1631." 1999 <http://www.lafayetteparishclerk.com/download/pdf/hb1631.pdf> (accessed June 21, 2006).

About the Author: The Louisiana State Legislature consists of two chambers: the House, comprising 105 Representatives, and the 39-member Senate. The Legislature meets annually in the state capital, Baton Rouge.

INTRODUCTION
From 1900 to 2000, the divorce rate in America roughly doubled. As a result of this increase more children grew up in single-parent homes, making them statistically more likely to experience poverty, poor health, and problems with law enforcement. Federal spending for direct support of single-parent homes also skyrocketed, passing $150 billion per year.

Numerous factors have been blamed for the increase in divorces, including changes in state divorce laws. For most of U.S. history, state divorce laws took the traditional marriage vows of "till death do us part" literally, granting divorces only in extreme cases such as physical abuse or infidelity. Mutual dislike or a simple desire to end a marriage were not considered legal justification for divorce, making a divorce much harder to obtain. Most state laws forbade divorce unless one partner was completely at fault and the other totally innocent, a standard which if truly enforced would tend to make divorce impossible.

Despite tight restrictions on divorces, couples still found themselves seeking freedom from existing marriages. To accomplish this legal trick couples sometimes found themselves play-acting a particular script in court in order to satisfy court requirements. For example, New York State originally allowed divorce only for infidelity; historical accounts describe early twentieth century cases in which a divorcing couple hired an actress with whom the husband would stage an affair in order to obtain a divorce. This perjurious practice became known as collusive adultery.

California law initially allowed divorce for seven causes including adultery, neglect, and insanity; the ill-defined cause known as extreme cruelty quickly became the catch-all claim for couples wishing to separate, and eventually provided the legal basis for the majority of divorce filings in California. A 1966 state report criticized the system, arguing that the requirement of establishing fault in order to grant a divorce was not realistic. The result was the nation's first no-fault divorce law, which allowed divorce on the grounds of irreconcilable differences. States around the nation quickly followed suit, passing their own no-fault laws and reducing the number of hurdles standing in the path of legally ending a marriage.

Supporters and opponents of no-fault divorce disagree sharply over the law's impact. Opponents are generally critical of any measure that streamlines the process of dissolving a marriage, arguing that such measures will lead to the dissolution of marriages which might otherwise be salvaged. Supporters of the laws point out that divorce rates are not noticeably different in no-fault and at-fault divorce states, nor did divorce rates rise noticeably after no-fault laws were passed. Supporters claim these two facts suggest that even before the advent of no-fault divorce couples were finding ways to end unhappy marriages.

Marriage advocates have responded to these changes in numerous ways. Pre-marriage counseling

A women rests her hand on a Bible while listening to a sermon about Covenant Marriage at Full Council Chrisitan Fellowhip in North Little Rock, Arkansas. PHOTO BY KATJA HEINEMANN/AURORA/GETTY IMAGES.

has become far more common, with clergy in some areas requiring these sessions before performing a marriage. Marriage support groups have sprung up across the nation, and most book stores and libraries offer numerous books on marriage success. In 1999, in response to loosened divorce requirements in most states a group of Christian ministers and marriage counselors launched the Covenant Marriage Movement.

Covenant marriage requires a more rigid legal agreement than a standard marriage. Under a covenant agreement, both parties complete premarital counseling and marry for life. They also agree that they will pursue counseling before seeking a divorce, and that they will seek divorce only under very specific circumstances. In 1997, Louisiana became the first state to pass a covenant marriage law, followed by Arizona and Arkansas. Similar legislation is under consideration in several other states.

PRIMARY SOURCE

An Act

"..."

Be it enacted by the Legislature of Louisiana:

"..."

C. In cases wherein the parties intend to contract a covenant marriage, the application for a marriage license must also include the following statement completed by at least one of the two parties: both parties shall not affect the validity of the covenant marriage if the declaration of intent and accompanying affidavit have been signed by the parties.

273. Covenant marriage; contents of declaration of intent

A declaration of intent to contract a covenant marriage shall contain all of the following:

(1)A recitation signed by both parties to the following effect:

"A Covenant Marriage

We do solemnly declare that marriage is a covenant between a man and a woman who agree to live together as husband and wife for so long as they both may live. We have chosen each other carefully and disclosed to one another everything which could adversely affect the decision to enter into this marriage. We have received premarital counseling on the nature, purposes, and responsibilities of marriage. We have read the Covenant Marriage Act, and we understand that a Covenant Marriage is for life. If we experience marital difficulties, we

commit ourselves to take all reasonable efforts to preserve our marriage, including marital counseling.

With full knowledge of what this commitment means, we do hereby declare that our marriage will be bound by Louisiana law on Covenant Marriages and we promise to love, honor, and care for one another as husband and wife for the rest of our lives."

SIGNIFICANCE

While numerous states have debated mandatory waiting periods to obtain a divorce, covenant marriage is a somewhat unconventional approach to reducing the incidence of divorce. Supporters of covenant marriage cite studies showing that couples undergoing pre-marital counseling have lower divorce rates, and that troubled couples who seek marriage counseling are more likely to reconcile and less likely to divorce. They also point out that the covenant marriage process itself requires more thought and effort, forcing engaged individuals to seriously consider whether they should marry or not.

Critics of covenant marriage find several flaws in the plan, beginning with religious overtones which they see as inappropriate in a state law. They also argue that even before no-fault divorce unhappy couples found ways to separate, so a new pledge of faithfulness is unlikely to prevent divorce. Finally they point to cases of severe physical abuse as one setting in which covenant marriage might endanger a woman's life by delaying her escape from a dangerous situation.

Covenant marriage is probably not the panacea its proponents believe it to be, nor is it likely to be as impotent as its detractors claim. When offered as an alternative to a standard marriage, covenant marriage provides an alternative for couples willing to make a deeper commitment, while not hindering couples who are not willing to do so.

FURTHER RESOURCES
Books

Davis, Michelle Mwiner. *Divorce Busting: A Step-by-Step Approach to Making Your Marriage Loving Again*. New York: Simon and Schuster, 1993.

Phillips, Roderick. *Putting Asunder: A History of Divorce in Western Society*. Cambridge University Press, 1988.

Wallerstein, Judith S., et al. *The Unexpected Legacy of Divorce: The 25 Year Landmark Study*. New York: Hyperion, 2001.

Periodicals

Freed, Doris, and Timothy Walker. "Family Law in Fifty States: An Overview." *Family Law Quarterly* 18 (1985): 41.

Hakim, Danny. "Panel Asks New York to Join the Era of No-Fault Divorce." *New York Times*, February 7, 2006: A1, B7.

"Yes I really do." *The Economist* 374 (Feb 12, 20005): 31.

Web sites

California Research Bureau, California State Library. "State Grounds for Divorce." <http://www.library.ca.gov/crb/98/04/stateground.pdf> (accessed June 21, 2006).

Coalition for Marriage, Couples, and Family Education. "Can Legislation Lower the Divorce Rate?" July 1998 <http://marriage.about.com/gi/dynamic/> (accessed June 21, 2006).

Covenant Marriage Movement. "Covenant Marriage Legislation." <http://www.covenantmarriage.com/legislation/legislation.htm> (accessed June 21, 2006).

Cohabitation, Marriage, Divorce, and Remarriage in the United States

Report

By: Matthew D. Bramlett and William D. Mosher

Date: July 2002

Source: *Centers for Disease Control.* "Cohabitation, Marriage, Divorce, and Remarriage in the United States." July 2002 <http://www.cdc.gov/nchs/data/series/sr_23/sr23_022.pdf> (accessed June 19, 2006).

About the Author: Matthew Bramlett and William Mosher are researchers with the Division of Vital Statistics in the U.S. Department of Health and Human Services.

INTRODUCTION

During the twentieth century, marriage underwent sweeping changes in the United States. From 1960 to 2000, more couples opted to forego marriage entirely, and the number of unmarried couples living together increased by a factor of ten. Marriages also dissolved at an increasing pace: divorce rates more than doubled from 1.5 divorces per 1,000 residents in 1910 to 3.7 in 2004. Current U.S. divorce rates remain well above those of other industrialized nations,

including Canada (2.0 per 1,000) and Spain (0.6 per 1,000).

The total cost of failed marriages in the U.S. is difficult to quantify; however, in 2000 the federal government spent $150 billion on direct aid to single-parent households. The overwhelming majority of divorced mothers with children face financial hardship, often living below the federal poverty line. Children of divorced parents are more likely to drop out of school, experience general health problems, and enter the juvenile justice system.

Given the enormous direct and indirect costs associated with divorce in America, the federal government has significant incentive to understand why people choose to marry, live together, divorce, and remarry. In order to better understand the motivations for these choices, the U.S. Department of Health and Human Services has conducted the National Survey on Family Growth (NSFG). The 1995 edition of this survey was the fifth iteration, utilizing personal interviews with more than 10,000 women between the ages of 15 and 44. The result was a statistically intensive report detailing the impact of factors such as age, race, and income on a woman's likelihood to cohabit, marry, divorce, and remarry.

■ PRIMARY SOURCE

What are the trends? Our data show an increase in the chances that first marriages will end (in separation or divorce) for marriages that began in the 1950s through the 1970s. From the early 1970s to the late 1980s, the rates of breakup were fairly stable. The probability of remarriage following divorce has decreased slightly, and the probability that the second marriage will break up has risen from the 1950s to the 1980s.

Do the trends differ by race/ethnicity? It appears that these trends were similar for non-Hispanic white and non-Hispanic black women, but black women faced higher rates of marital breakup, lower rates of making the transition from separation to divorce, and lower rates of remarriage. Among white women, the increasing probability of first marriage breakup leveled off in the 1970s but appears to have continued rising for black women through the 1980s.

Are characteristics of communities related to success in marriage? This report shows clear evidence that community prosperity is related to successful cohabitations and marriages, and that neighborhood poverty increases the likelihood that cohabitations and marriages will fail.

Is the statistical portrait of union formation and dissolution affected if we measure unmarried cohabita-

tion and separation from marriage as well as legal divorce? One major advantage of survey data on marriage is that we are not limited to examining legal marriage and divorce. The data in this report show that the probability that an intact premarital cohabitation will result in marriage is 70 percent after 5 years; that probability is associated with the woman's race, age, education, the household's income, and the economic opportunities in the community. The data also show that a great many marriages end in legal separation but not in divorce, and that looking only at divorce greatly understates marital disruption among some groups—especially non-Hispanic black and Hispanic women.

What demographic, economic, and social factors affect the chances that marriage will succeed or fail? This report shows that a number of characteristics are closely associated with the chances that a marriage will continue or break up. For first marriages, for example, marriages are less likely to break up, and more likely to succeed, if the wife grew up in a two-parent home, is Asian, was 20 years of age or over at marriage, did not have any children when she got married, is college-educated, has more income, or has any religious affiliation.

The following highlights illustrate the kinds of findings shown in this report:

The probability of first marriage is lower for non-Hispanic black women than for other women. Getting married by the 18th birthday is more likely for Hispanic and non-Hispanic white women and less likely for non-Hispanic black and Asian women. First marriage is less likely for women who report that their religion is not important. Early marriage is more likely for women in communities with higher male unemployment, lower median family income, higher poverty and higher receipt of welfare. First marriage is more likely in nonmetropolitan areas and less likely in central cities.

The probability that an intact first premarital cohabitation becomes a marriage is higher among white women and lower among black women; higher among couples with higher incomes than for couples with lower incomes; and higher for cohabiting women with any religious affiliation than for those with no religious affiliation, especially among white women. Marriage is more likely for cohabiting white women who report that their religion is either somewhat or very important than for those who report that their religion is not important.

Cohabiting women are more likely to marry if they live in communities with lower male unemployment, higher median family income, lower poverty, and lower receipt of welfare. The male unemployment rate seems to be more important among black women than among white women.

After the first 3 years of cohabitation, **the probability that a first premarital cohabitation breaks up** is higher among black women than among Hispanic or white women and is higher among younger than older women, especially among white women. Women who have ever been forced to have intercourse before the cohabitation began are more likely to experience the breakup of their first premarital cohabitation than women who have never been forced.

Cohabiting women are more likely to experience the breakup of their first premarital cohabitation if they live in communities with higher male unemployment, lower median family income, and higher rates of poverty and receipt of welfare.

Black women are more likely to experience **first marital disruption** and Asian women are less likely to experience first marital disruption, compared with white or Hispanic women. First marriages of women who are 20 years of age or over at marriage are less likely to break up than marriages of teenaged brides; but there is no significant difference by age at marriage among Hispanic women. Women whose religion is somewhat or very important are also less likely to experience a breakup of their first marriage than those whose religion is not important. Women who lived with both parents throughout childhood are less likely to experience the breakup of their first marriage than women who were not raised with two parents throughout childhood.

SIGNIFICANCE

Interpreting the National Survey of Family Growth is challenging; the actual report spans 103 pages, of which more than half are numeric tables. While this level of detail is necessary for thorough statistical analysis, most readers are more interested in a synopsis of the findings, which is provided near the beginning of the report. In summary the report's authors conclude that divorce rates are presently stable, that marriages fail more often in poorer communities and neighborhoods, and that better education, higher age and income, and religious affiliation are associated with lower rates of divorce in a first marriage.

General findings such as these do not require exhaustive data analysis and are often available elsewhere. The value of a study such as the NSFG lies in its ability to answer very specific questions. For example, consider a social service agency attempting to reduce divorce rates in a specific urban community. The workers in this agency know that demographic factors play a role in divorce; they also understand that the specific causes of divorce vary among ethnic groups. In such cases the NSFG allows investigators to determine specific factors relevant to their community.

For example, national statistics on first marriage breakup show that divorce rates climbed more slowly during the 1970s. However, this improvement was not consistent across ethnic groups, and rates continued to rise more sharply among black women through the following decade. Such information could help the previously mentioned agency decide where to focus their efforts.

An exhaustive analysis such as the NSFG is also useful in answering some long-debated questions. Two distinct schools of thought exist regarding cohabitation, or living together while unmarried. Couples who choose to cohabitate often characterize it as a low-risk test of compatibility, potentially less risky and less complicated than a marriage and subsequent divorce. Conservative religious groups tend to be critical of such arrangements, arguing that they are emotionally unhealthy and make commitment more difficult, ultimately harming marriages.

Which perspective on cohabitation does the study data support? As often occurs in data analysis, the answer is complex. First, the relationship between premarital cohabitation and marriage is influenced by factors such as race and income level; for example, white women and those with higher incomes are more likely to move from cohabitation to marriage than black women and those earning less. In general, the study finds that after three years of cohabitation, white couples have a 60 percent chance of marrying, while the rate for Hispanics is 50 percent and the rate for blacks is 35 percent. During the first ten years of cohabitation, couples who began cohabiting while under age twenty-five face a 60 percent chance of ultimately separating.

When interpreting data from the NSFG and similar reports, care must be taken to correctly interpret the results. For example, most research on marriage and divorce measures only actual divorces and not separations. Since Americans sometimes choose to end their marriages by separating but not legally divorcing, the actual number of failed marriages is probably higher than the figures provided by the NSFG indicate. Another concern in such a study deals with social desirability bias, or the tendency for respondents to lie about socially unacceptable behaviors such as infidelity. This bias may result in inaccurate assessments of the frequencies of specific behaviors.

While the NSFG provides voluminous information on when and why Americans marry, divorce, and remarry, it does not prescribe solutions for the prob-

lems it illuminates. The study's purpose is to provide comprehensive data for use by organizations that provide solutions, allowing them to more efficiently apply their resources.

FURTHER RESOURCES
Books

Tucker, M. and C. Mitchell-Kernan. *The Decline in Marriage among African Americans*. New York: Russell Sage, 1995.

Waite, L. J. and M. Gallagher. *The Case for Marriage: Why Married People Are Happier, Healthier and Better Off*. New York: Doubleday, 2000.

Zill, N. and M. Gallagher. *Running in Place: How American Families Are Faring in a Changing Economy and an Individualistic Society*. Washington, D.C.: Child Trends, 1994.

Periodicals

Amato, P. R. "The Consequences of Divorce for Adults and Children." *Journal of Marriage and the Family* 62 (2000): 1269–1287.

Duncan, G. and S. Hoffman. "A Reconsideration of the Economic Consequences of Marital Dissolution." *Demography* 22 (1985): 485–497.

Kunz, J. "The Intergenerational Transmission of Divorce: A Nine Generation Study." *Journal of Divorce and Remarriage* 34 (2000): 169–175.

Web sites

Discovery Health. "Debunking Divorce Myths." <http://health.discovery.com/centers/loverelationships/articles/divorce.html> (accessed June 19, 2006).

Journal of Family Violence. "Divorce Related Malicious Mother Syndrome." 1995 <http://www.fact.on.ca/Info/pas/turkat95.htm> (accessed June 19, 2006).

Los Angeles County Law Library. "California Divorce Pathfinder." <http://lalaw.lib.ca.us/divorce.html> (accessed June 19, 2006).

Marriage Protection Amendment

Legislation

By: United States Congress

Date: January 24, 2005

Source: *GovTrack.us*. "S.J. Res. 1: Marriage Protection Amendment." <http://www.govtrack.us/congress/billtext.xpd?bill=sj109-1> (accessed July 26, 2006).

A demonstrator holds a sign supporting traditional marriage during an anti-gay marrriage rally on Lawyers Mall in Annapolis, Maryland, January 27, 2005. AP IMAGES.

About the Author: The United States Congress is the primary law-making branch of the federal government.

INTRODUCTION

During the 1980s and 1990s, federal courts began examining state statutes dealing with homosexuality, overturning several that outlawed homosexual practice. Several state legislatures also passed laws protecting homosexuals against employment discrimination, and in 1991 three same-sex couples sued the state of Hawaii to obtain marriage licenses. That case reached the state Supreme Court, setting the stage for a ruling that could potentially legalize gay marriage in the state. Of broader importance, U.S. law requires states to recognize legal marriages performed in other states;

such a ruling would implicitly legalize same-sex marriage throughout the United States.

Opponents of gay marriage quickly organized to avert such an occurrence. In 1996, the U.S. Congress overwhelmingly passed the Defense of Marriage Act. This bill specified that all federal legislation dealing with marriage would refer solely to heterosexual marriages. It further absolved states of any requirement to recognize same-sex unions approved by other states. President Clinton, a strong supporter of gay rights, signed the legislation into law. In the years after the act's passage, supporters and opponents of gay marriage continued to battle in the courts and through various state legislatures. In the following decade, forty-one states passed their own versions of the federal Defense of Marriage Act, and several states adopted constitutional amendments codifying marriage as an exclusively heterosexual union.

Despite these legislative decisions and the progress they represented, gay marriage opponents faced further threats. Critics of the Defense of Marriage Act claimed that Congress had overstepped its authority in passing the law, circumventing the principle of "full faith and credit" by which state legal decisions are reciprocally accepted by other states. Concerned that a federal court ruling could potentially set aside both the federal and state laws, gay marriage opponents launched a campaign to settle the issue at the Constitutional level. The proposed amendment, titled the Marriage Protection Amendment, contained fewer than one hundred words. It stated simply that marriage in the United States consists of a union between a man and a woman and that no state could redefine marriage.

Amending the U.S. Constitution is a time-consuming, difficult procedure. Amendments must first be approved by a super-majority of two-thirds in both the House of Representatives and the Senate. Following this approval, the amendment must be ratified by three-quarters of the states, with each state choosing when and if to hold its own election. A seven year time limit is typically imposed on the process, and if the proposal receives the necessary votes, it becomes part of the Constitution. Of several thousand amendments proposed to date, only twenty-seven have been enacted.

◼ PRIMARY SOURCE

109th CONGRESS

1st Session

S. J. RES. 1

Proposing an amendment to the Constitution of the United States relating to marriage.

IN THE SENATE OF THE UNITED STATES

January 24, 2005

Mr. ALLARD (for himself, Mr. INHOFE, Mr. LOTT, Mr. ENZI, Mr. DEMINT, Mr. SANTORUM, Mr. CRAPO, Mr. SESSIONS, Mr. VITTER, Mr. THUNE, Mr. ALEXANDER, Mr. FRIST, Mr. TALENT, Mr. BURR, Mrs. HUTCHISON, Mr. KYL, Mrs. DOLE, Mr. MARTINEZ, Mr. ISAKSON, Mr. MCCONNELL, Mr. HATCH, Mr. ROBERTS, Mr. CORNYN, Mr. STEVENS, and Mr. COBURN) introduced the following joint res-

olution; which was read twice and referred to the Committee on the Judiciary

May 18, 2006

Reported by Mr. SPECTER, without amendment

JOINT RESOLUTION

Proposing an amendment to the Constitution of the United States relating to marriage.

Resolved by the Senate and House of Representatives of the United States of America in Congress assembled (two-thirds of each House concurring therein), That the following article is proposed as an amendment to the Constitution of the United States, which shall be valid to all intents and purposes as part of the Constitution when ratified by the legislatures of three-fourths of the several States:

Article—

"SECTION 1. This article may be cited as the 'Marriage Protection Amendment'"

"SECTION 2. Marriage in the United States shall consist only of the union of a man and a woman. Neither this Constitution, nor the constitution of any State, shall be construed to require that marriage or the legal incidents thereof be conferred upon any union other than the union of a man and a woman."

◼

SIGNIFICANCE

Critics of the proposed marriage amendment argued that it did little to protect traditional marriage but simply relegated homosexuals to second-class status. Other opponents contended that questions regarding marriage should be reserved for the states, opposing the amendment on principles of states' rights. President Bush, who raised the issue of same-sex marriage in his reelection campaign, told an interviewer that he would not actively campaign for the amendment, because it faced almost certain defeat, though he did speak briefly in its support as the vote approached.

The Marriage Protection Act came to the floor in 2006 but received only forty-nine votes in the Senate. Supporters remarked that they had not expected the measure to pass, leading critics to question why Senate time was spent on the measure. Sponsors of the bill promised to reintroduce it the following year.

The year 2006 marked the second recent attempt to secure a constitutional amendment defining marriage. A 2003 proposal entitled the Federal Marriage Amendment contained virtually identical language and also failed to pass. As of 2006, only Massachusetts allowed gay marriages, while forty-one states prohibited gay marriage or civil unions by law or state constitutional amendment.

FURTHER RESOURCES

Books

Lehman, Jennifer M. *Gay & Lesbian Marriage and Family Reader: Analyses of Problems & Prospects for the 21st Century.* New York: Richard Altschuler & Associates, 2001.

Richards, David. *The Case for Gay Rights: From Bowers to Lawrence and Beyond.* Lawrence: The University Press of Kansas, 2005.

Stiers, Gretchen. *From This Day Forward.* New York: Saint Martins Press, 1999.

Periodicals

Killian, Mary Lou. "The Politics of Gay and Lesbian Marriage: States in Comparative Perspectives." *American Political Science Association Annual Meeting* (2002):1–23.

Kokoski, Paul. "Cheers and Jeers for the Proposed Gay-Marriage Ban." *Christian Science Monitor* 9 (June 8, 2006): 8.

McFadden, Robert. "Bloomberg is Said to Want State to Legalize Same-Sex Marriages." *New York Times* (March 6,2004): A1, B2.

Web sites

American Civil Liberties Union. "Frequently Asked Questions about the Federal Marriage Amendment and Gay Marriage." February 25, 2004 <http://www.aclu.org/lgbt/gen/11931res20040225.html> (accessed June 15, 2006).

Stateline. "50-State Rundown on Gay Marriage Laws." November 3, 2004 <http://www.stateline.org/live/> (accessed June 15, 2006).

USA Today Online. "Bush Backs Federal Marriage Amendment." June 3, 2006 <http://www.usatoday.com/news/washington/2006-06-03-gay-marriage_x.htm?csp=34> (accessed June 15, 2006).

Illinois Marriage and Dissolution of Marriage Act

Legislation

By: State of Illinois

Date: 2005

Source: *State of Illinois.* "Illinois Marriage and Dissolution of Marriage Act." April 16, 2006 <http://www.ilga.gov/legislation/ilcs/> (accessed July 11, 2006).

About the Author: The Illinois General Assembly is the state's law-making body. It is made up of a House of Representatives with 118 members and a Senate with fifty-nine members.

INTRODUCTION

The traditional Christian wedding ceremony includes language describing marriage as among the oldest human institutions. Despite this long history, numerous states have recently passed legislation formally defining marriage, largely as a result of court decisions questioning the traditional definition of marriage. A 1991 case seeking marriage licenses for same-sex couples in Hawaii reached the state's Supreme Court, raising the possibility that Hawaii might begin recognizing same-sex marriages. Because all fifty states recognize marriages legally performed in other states this ruling raised the possibility that same-sex marriages might become legally recognized throughout the United States.

Many Americans believe that marriage should remain a heterosexual arrangement; a 2006 Gallup poll found that half of all Americans support a Constitutional Amendment defining marriage as a union between one man and one woman. Consequently, following the Hawaii filing state legislatures across the country began passing legislation clarifying the definition of marriage and declining to recognize out-of-state marriages which violated state statutes.

In 2000, the state of Illinois passed the Marriage and Dissolution of Marriage Act. This comprehensive legislation addressed a number of marriage-related issues, including legal complications related to the appointment of guardians for children of divorcing parents and what paperwork was required for a marriage. And like many other state laws of the era, the statute also defined marriage as a male-female union and stated that non-conforming marriages performed in other states would not be viewed as legally valid in Illinois.

■ PRIMARY SOURCE

PART II
MARRIAGE

(750 ILCS 5/201) (from Ch. 40, par. 201)

Sec. 201. (Formalities.) A marriage between a man and a woman licensed, solemnized and registered as provided in this Act is valid in this State.

(Source: P.A. 80–923.)

(750 ILCS 5/202) (from Ch. 40, par. 202)

Sec. 202. (Marriage License and Marriage Certificate.)

(a) The Director of Public Health shall prescribe the form for an application for a marriage license, which shall include the following information:

    (1) name, sex, occupation, address, social security number, date and place of birth of each party to the proposed marriage;

    (2) if either party was previously married, his name, and the date, place and court in which the marriage was dissolved or declared invalid or the date and place of death of the former spouse;

    (3) name and address of the parents or guardian of each party; and

    (4) whether the parties are related to each other and, if so, their relationship.

(b) The Director of Public Health shall prescribe the forms for the marriage license, the marriage certificate and, when necessary, the consent to marriage.

(Source: P.A. 80–923.)

(750 ILCS 5/203) (from Ch. 40, par. 203)

Sec. 203. License to Marry. When a marriage application has been completed and signed by both parties to a prospective marriage and both parties have appeared before the county clerk and the marriage license fee has been paid, the county clerk shall issue a license to marry and a marriage certificate form upon being furnished:

    (1) satisfactory proof that each party to the marriage will have attained the age of 18 years at the time the marriage license is effective or will have attained the age of 16 years and has either the consent to the marriage of both parents or his guardian or judicial approval; provided, if one parent cannot be located in order to obtain such consent and diligent efforts have been made to locate that parent by the consenting parent, then the consent of one parent plus a signed affidavit by the consenting parent which (i) names the absent parent and states that he or she cannot be located, and (ii) states what diligent efforts have been made to locate the absent parent, shall have the effect of both parents' consent for purposes of this Section;

    (2) satisfactory proof that the marriage is not prohibited; and

    (3) an affidavit or record as prescribed in subparagraph (1) of Section 205 or a court order as prescribed in subparagraph (2) of Section 205, if applicable.

With each marriage license, the county clerk shall provide a pamphlet describing the causes and effects of fetal alcohol syndrome.

(Source: P.A. 86–832; 86–884; 86–1028.)

(750 ILCS 5/204) (from Ch. 40, par. 204)

Sec. 204. Medical information brochure. The county clerk shall distribute free of charge, to all persons applying for a marriage license, a brochure prepared by the Department of Public Health concerning sexually transmitted diseases and inherited metabolic diseases.

(Source: P.A. 86–884.)

(750 ILCS 5/205) (from Ch. 40, par. 205)

Sec. 205. Exceptions.

(1) Irrespective of the results of laboratory tests and clinical examination relative to sexually transmitted diseases, the clerks of the respective counties shall issue a marriage license to parties to a proposed marriage (a) when a woman is pregnant at the time of such application, or (b) when a woman has, prior to the time of application, given birth to a child born out of wedlock which is living at the time of such application and the man making such application makes affidavit that he is the father of such child born out of wedlock. The county clerk shall, in lieu of the health certificate required hereunder, accept, as the case may be, either an affidavit on a form prescribed by the State Department of Public Health, signed by a physician duly licensed in this State, stating that the woman is pregnant, or a copy of the birth record of the child born out of wedlock, if one is available in this State, or if such birth record is not available, an affidavit signed by the woman that she is the mother of such child.

(2) Any judge of the circuit court within the county in which the license is to be issued is authorized and empowered on joint application by both applicants for a marriage license to waive the requirements as to medical examination, laboratory tests, and certificates, except the requirements of paragraph (4) of subsection (a) of Section 212 of this Act which shall not be waived; and to authorize the county clerk to issue the license if all other requirements of law have been complied with and the judge is satisfied, by affidavit, or other proof, that the examination or tests are contrary to the tenets or practices of the religious creed of which the applicant is an adherent, and that the public health and welfare will not be injuriously affected thereby.

(Source: P.A. 94–229, eff. 1–1–06.)

(750 ILCS 5/206) (from Ch. 40, par. 206)

Sec. 206. Records. Any health certificate filed with the county clerk, or any certificate, affidavit, or record accepted in lieu thereof, shall be retained in the files of the office for one year after the license is issued and shall thereafter be destroyed by the county clerk.

(Source: P.A. 82–561.)

(750 ILCS 5/207) (from Ch. 40, par. 207)

Sec. 207. Effective Date of License. A license to marry becomes effective in the county where it was issued one day after the date of issuance, unless the court orders that the license is effective when issued, and expires 60 days after it becomes effective.

(Source: P.A. 81–397.)

(750 ILCS 5/208) (from Ch. 40, par. 208)

Sec. 208. Judicial Approval of Underage Marriages.

(a) The court, after a reasonable effort has been made to notify the parents or guardian of each underaged party, may order the county clerk to issue a marriage license and a marriage certificate form to a party aged 16 or 17 years who has no parent capable of consenting to his marriage or whose parent or guardian has not consented to his marriage.

(b) A marriage license and a marriage certificate form may be issued under this Section only if the court finds that the underaged party is capable of assuming the responsibilities of marriage and the marriage will serve his best interest. Pregnancy alone does not establish that the best interest of the party will be served.

(Source: P.A. 80–923.)

(750 ILCS 5/209) (from Ch. 40, par. 209)

Sec. 209. Solemnization and Registration.

(a) A marriage may be solemnized by a judge of a court of record, by a retired judge of a court of record, unless the retired judge was removed from office by the Judicial Inquiry Board, except that a retired judge shall not receive any compensation from the State, a county or any unit of local government in return for the solemnization of a marriage and there shall be no effect upon any pension benefits conferred by the Judges Retirement System of Illinois, by a judge of the Court of Claims, by a county clerk in counties having 2,000,000 or more inhabitants, by a public official whose powers include solemnization of marriages, or in accordance with the prescriptions of any religious denomination, Indian Nation or Tribe or Native Group, provided that when such prescriptions require an officiant, the officiant be in good standing with his religious denomination, Indian Nation or Tribe or Native Group. Either the person solemnizing the marriage, or, if no individual acting alone solemnized the marriage, both parties to the marriage, shall complete the marriage certificate form and forward it to the county clerk within 10 days after such marriage is solemnized.

(b) The solemnization of the marriage is not invalidated by the fact that the person solemnizing the marriage was not legally qualified to solemnize it, if either party to the marriage believed him to be so qualified.

(Source: P.A. 87–1261.)

(750 ILCS 5/210) (from Ch. 40, par. 210)

Sec. 210. Registration of Marriage Certificate. Upon receipt of the marriage certificate, the county clerk shall register the marriage. Within 45 days after the close of the month in which a marriage is registered, the county clerk shall make to the Department of Public Health a return of such marriage. Such return shall be made on a form furnished by the Department of Public Health and shall substantially consist of the following items:

(1) A copy of the marriage license application signed and attested to by the applicants, except that in any county in which the information provided in a marriage license application is entered into a computer, the county clerk may submit a computer copy of such information without the signatures and attestations of the applicants.

(2) The date and place of marriage.

(3) The marriage license number.

(Source: P.A. 85–1307.)

(750 ILCS 5/211) (from Ch. 40, par. 211)

Sec. 211. Reporting. In transmitting the required returns, the county clerk shall make a report to the Department of Public Health stating the total number of marriage licenses issued during the month for which returns are made, and the number of marriage certificates registered during the month.

(Source: P.A. 80–923.)

(750 ILCS 5/212) (from Ch. 40, par. 212)

Sec. 212. Prohibited Marriages.

(a) The following marriages are prohibited:

(1) a marriage entered into prior to the dissolution of an earlier marriage of one of the parties;

(2) a marriage between an ancestor and a descendant or between a brother and a sister, whether the relationship is by the half or the whole blood or by adoption;

(3) a marriage between an uncle and a niece or between an aunt and a nephew, whether the relationship is by the half or the whole blood;

(4) a marriage between cousins of the first degree; however, a marriage between first cousins is not prohibited if:

(i) both parties are 50 years of age or older; or

(ii) either party, at the time of application for a marriage license, presents for filing with the county clerk of the county in which the marriage is to be solemnized, a certificate signed by a licensed physician stating that the party to the proposed marriage is permanently and irreversibly sterile;

(5) a marriage between 2 individuals of the same sex.

(b) Parties to a marriage prohibited under subsection (a) of this Section who cohabit after removal of the impediment are lawfully married as of the date of the removal of the impediment.

(c) Children born or adopted of a prohibited or common law marriage are the lawful children of the parties.

(Source: P.A. 94–229, eff. 1–1–06.)

(750 ILCS 5/213) (from Ch. 40, par. 213)

Sec. 213. Validity. All marriages contracted within this State, prior to the effective date of this Act, or outside this State, that were valid at the time of the contract or subsequently validated by the laws of the place in which they were contracted or by the domicile of the parties, are valid in this State, except where contrary to the public policy of this State.

(Source: P.A. 80–923.)

(750 ILCS 5/213.1)

Sec. 213.1. Same-sex marriages; public policy. A marriage between 2 individuals of the same sex is contrary to the public policy of this State.

(Source: P.A. 89–459, eff. 5–24–96.)

(750 ILCS 5/214) (from Ch. 40, par. 214)

Sec. 214. Invalidity of Common Law Marriages. Common law marriages contracted in this State after June 30, 1905 are invalid.

(Source: P.A. 80–923.)

(750 ILCS 5/215) (from Ch. 40, par. 215)

Sec. 215. Penalty. Unless otherwise provided by law, any person who violates any provision of Part II of this Act is guilty of a Class B misdemeanor.

(Source: P.A. 80–923.)

(750 ILCS 5/216) (from Ch. 40, par. 216)

Sec. 216. Prohibited Marriages Void if Contracted in Another State. That if any person residing and intending to continue to reside in this state and who is disabled or prohibited from contracting marriage under the laws of this state, shall go into another state or country and there contract a marriage prohibited and declared void by the laws of this state, such marriage shall be null and void for all purposes in this state with the same effect as though such prohibited marriage had been entered into in this state.

(Source: P.A. 80–923.)

(750 ILCS 5/217) (from Ch. 40, par. 217)

Sec. 217. Marriage by Non-residents—When Void. No marriage shall be contracted in this state by a party residing and intending to continue to reside in another state or jurisdiction if such marriage would be void if contracted in such other state or jurisdiction and every marriage celebrated in this state in violation of this provision shall be null and void.

(Source: P.A. 80–923.)

(750 ILCS 5/218) (from Ch. 40, par. 218)

Sec. 218. Duty of Officer Issuing License. Before issuing a license to marry a person who resides and intends to continue to reside in another state, the officer having authority to issue the license shall satisfy himself by requiring affidavits or otherwise that such person is not prohibited from intermarrying by the laws of the jurisdiction where he or she resides.

(Source: P.A. 80–923.)

(750 ILCS 5/219) (from Ch. 40, par. 219)

Sec. 219. Offenses. Any official issuing a license with knowledge that the parties are thus prohibited from intermarrying and any person authorized to celebrate marriage who shall knowingly celebrate such a marriage shall be guilty of a petty offense.

(Source: P.A. 80–923.)

SIGNIFICANCE

The Illinois law is one of numerous federal and state statutes defining marriage in its traditional form. At the national level Congress passed the 1996 Defense of Marriage Act, which defined marriage for federal purposes as a male-female union. The act also granted the states the right to individually determine their own standards for marriage, and gave them the option not to recognize marriages performed in other states that did not meet their own state requirements.

States also passed numerous laws intended to define marriage in its traditional sense. In 2004 same-sex marriages were legalized in Massachusetts, making it the first state to allow such arrangements. State elections the following November approved constitutional amendments in eleven states defining marriage in its traditional form and providing greater protection against court ordered changes to existing state laws.

The debate over the form of marriage remains an emotionally charged conflict. Advocates of traditional marriage describe it as one of the pillars on which modern American society rests. They claim that recognizing other relationships and granting them the title of marriage will cheapen and dilute the existing institution of marriage. For many Americans, marriage also has religious implications and some find acceptance of non-traditional marriages immoral and offensive.

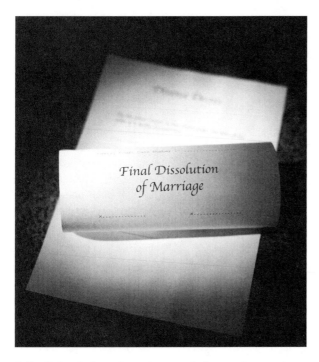

A final dissolution of marriage and divorce decree document. © ROYALTY-FREE/CORBIS.

As of 2006 forty-nine states and the federal government continue to define marriage as a union between one man and one woman. Numerous corporations extend health and other benefits to domestic partners. A 2006 effort to amend the U.S. Constitution to define marriage in the traditional sense failed to receive the needed votes in the U.S. Senate.

FURTHER RESOURCES

Books

Coontz, Stephanie. *Marriage, a History: How Love Conquered Marriage.* New York: Viking, 2005.

Lehman, Jennifer M. *Gay & Lesbian Marriage and Family Reader: Analyses of Problems & Prospects for the 21st Century.* New York: Richard Altschuler & Associates, 2001.

Richards, David. *The Case for Gay Rights: From Bowers to Lawrence and Beyond.* Lawrence: The University Press of Kansas, 2005.

Periodicals

Frieden, Joyce. "Group Sees Harm to Kids in Marriage Amendment." *Pediatric News* 39 (2005): 49.

Pinsof, William. "Marriage in the Twentieth Century in Western Civilization: Trends, Research, Therapy, and Perspectives." *Family Process* 41 (2002): 1.

Web sites

CNN. "GOP Renews Fight Against Gay Marriage." June 6, 2006 <http://www.cnn.com/2006/POLITICS/06/05/same.sex.marriage/index.html> (accessed July 10, 2006).

DuPage County Bar Association. "Significant Amendment of the Illinois Marriage and Dissolution of Marriage Act Should Alleviate Role Confusion." 2000 <http://www.dcba.org/brief/mayissue/2000/art20500.htm> (accessed July 11, 2006).

Stateline. "50-state rundown on gay marriage laws." November 3, 2004 <http://www.stateline.org/live/> (accessed June 15, 2006).

Advocates of non-traditional marriage argue that allowing them to enter into a different form of marriage actually has no impact on traditional marriages, because such marriages would continue to be recognized as they currently are. These proponents also argue that labeling their unions "domestic partnerships" or some other term implies second-class status in comparison to marriage, inherently degrading the new arrangement. Finally they argue that the traditional definition of marriage is outmoded and irrelevant in modern society, and that as a result many companies discriminate against non-traditional living arrangements by providing health and other benefits to spouses but not to unmarried partners.

While same-sex marriage advocates are the best-known and most vocal group fighting for legal recognition of non-traditional marriage, numerous smaller groups express similar aspirations. A small number of Americans practice polygamy, in which a person is simultaneously married to multiple spouses. The practice is a felony in all fifty states, but continues to exist, mostly in rural areas. Polygamists cite Biblical precedent for the practice and believe it should be legalized. Other groups advocate legal recognition for common law marriages and marriages between blood relatives, which are prohibited in many states.

Just Whom is this Divorce 'Good For?'

Newspaper article

By: Elizabeth Marquardt

Date: November 6, 2005

Source: Marquardt, Elizabeth. *Washington Post*. "Just Whom is this Divorce 'Good For?'" (November 6, 2005).

About the Author: Elizabeth Marquardt is an affiliate scholar with the Institute of American Values, based in New York City. Marquardt is the author of *Between Two Worlds: The Inner Lives of Children of Divorce*.

INTRODUCTION

Divorce and the related consequences of marital breakdown were a relative rarity throughout the Western world in the period prior to World War II. Divorce proceedings carried a significant social stigma for the partcipants; in religious faiths such as Roman Catholicism, divorce was discouraged. Divorce was not available to spouses on a consensual or on a no-fault basis, the platform upon which the modern 'good' divorce phenomenon is constructed. The custody and day-to-day care for the children of the marriage fell to the wife, almost by default. Societal and legal expectations concerning the care of children after divorce assumed that the mother was naturally most suitable custodial parent.

The central issue that is stated by all sides as the premise for estranged spouses to seek a friendly and non-confrontational divorce resolution is the preservation of the welfare and the emotional stability of the children of the marriage. As the American divorce rate climbed in the late 1960s, an increase that was closely connected to the increased availability of divorce on a no-fault basis, the issues related to the impact of the divorce upon the children of the marriage became more prominent. The custody, visitation rights, and support to be paid for the children after the divorce frequently became bitterly contested issues between the spouses.

While the divorce rate in the United States crested in 1980, divorce remains a common legal consequence of American marriages. A number of statistical analyses of recent census data confirm that the median length of a first marriage is 8 years; the likelihood of a 2006 marriage ending in divorce carries a probability of approximately 40 per cent. The number of children who are a part of a marriage ending in divorce totals over one million children every year in the United States.

It was against this statistical backdrop that the theory of the 'good' divorce was advanced by a number of American social scientists and psychologists in the period following 1980. The most notable exponent of this concept is Constance Ahron, the author of the best selling book, *Good Divorce* published in 1994.

Ahron's thesis was that children could be protected from the potential emotional damage of their parent's divorce if the parents worked to minimize conflict between themselves.

Good divorce has been the subject of considerable study since the publication of the Ahron text; the research of Elizabeth Marquardt forms a prominent part of that body of research. A 'bad' divorce is generally defined as one where the spouses wage a protracted emotional war that is visible and experienced by their children. It is Marquardt's thesis that, while a 'bad' divorce will invariably hurt the children's emotional well-being, no divorce is ever good in their eyes.

PRIMARY SOURCE

Sunday, November 6, 2005

It happens to about 1 million American children every year. Their parents sit them down and deliver the news that they're divorcing. But not to worry, they say, they're parting amicably and assuming joint custody. The scene might go something like this:

"We're splitting up the week, alternating days," announces the dad.

"How are you splitting up seven days?" demands the son, reeling and confused.

"I've got Tuesday, Wednesday and Saturday, and every other Thursday," says Dad reassuringly. "That was your father's idea," notes Mom proudly.

"Well," the son asks anxiously, "what about the cat?" A pause. "We didn't discuss the cat," says Mom with some consternation.

This scene, as it happens, is from a new movie, "The Squid and the Whale"—36-year-old director Noah Baumbach's wry take on his own parents' divorce when he was a teen. But for those of us in the first generation to grow up in an era of widespread divorce, it perfectly captures the emotional havoc wrought on children when their parents convince themselves that if they can work out the details of divorce—who goes where on what days—without rancor, they can reduce the pain for the children and pursue their own happiness without a lot of guilt.

Before the divorce rate began its inexorable rise in the late 1960s, the common wisdom had been that, where children are concerned, divorce itself is a problem. But as it became widespread—peaking at almost one in two first marriages in the mid-1980s—popular thinking morphed into a new, adult-friendly idea: It's not the act of divorcing that's the problem, but simply the way that parents handle it. Experts began to assure parents that if only they conducted a "good" divorce—if they both stayed involved with their children and minimized conflict, the kids would be fine.

It was a soothing tonic, and it was swallowed eagerly by many angst-ridden parents. But it was also, it turns out, a myth. No matter how happy a face we put on it, the children of divorce are now saying, we've been kidding ourselves. An amicable divorce is better than a bitter one, but there is no such thing as a "good" divorce.

That's a tough sell, I know. Today, praises of the good divorce abound. Countless newspaper articles, television reports and books quote therapists and academics arguing on its behalf. A holiday article last year in Newsweek, titled "Happy Divorce," featured divorced families who put their conflicts aside to spend Christmas together. Researchers, it said, "have known for years that how parents divorce matters even more than the divorce itself."

Many parents have bought it. In 2002, The Washington Post Magazine featured a cover story about Eli and Debbie, a handsome, smiling, divorced couple with three preteen daughters. Although their marriage was, according to Debbie, "all in all, an incredibly functional" one, they divorced when she became troubled by their "lack of connection." Three years later, Eli continues to come to Debbie's house every morning to get the girls ready for school and reassure them "that even though Mommy and Daddy aren't married, we're still your parents, we're still there for you, and we still love you." He and Debbie are confident that their "good" divorce will keep their daughters from suffering unnecessarily.

But they're most likely wrong.

Many people incorrectly assume that most marriages end only when parents are at each other's throats. But the reasons can often be far less urgent, like boredom or the midlife blahs. Research shows that two-thirds of divorces now end low-conflict marriages, where there is no abuse, violence or serious fighting. After those marriages end, the children suddenly struggle with a range of symptoms—anxiety, depression, problems in school—that they did not previously have. The waxing and waning cycles of adult unhappiness that characterize many marriages are often not all that obvious to children. For the children of low-conflict marriages, divorce is a massive blow that comes out of nowhere.

Of course, sometimes divorce is necessary, and when it does happen it is certainly better for children not to lose significant relationships entirely, nor to be drawn into bitter, unending fights. But when you talk to the children themselves, you find that rampant "good divorce" talk mainly reflects the wishes of adults, while silencing the voices of children. The divorce debate has long been conducted by adults, for adults, on behalf of the adult

point of view, but now the grown children of divorce are telling their own, very different stories.

As a 35-year-old whose parents split up when I was 2, I know that we've barely scratched the surface when it comes to investigating how divorce shapes the inner lives and identities of children. So, along with University of Texas sociology professor Norval Glenn, I recently conducted the first nationally representative study of the grown children of divorce. We surveyed 1,500 young adults 18 to 35 years old, half from divorced families and half from intact families. I also interviewed another 71 young adults in person in four areas of the country.

We found that children of so-called "good" divorces often do worse even than children of unhappy low-conflict marriages—they say more often, for example, that family life was stressful and that they had to grow up too soon; and they are themselves more likely to divorce and that they do much worse than children raised in happy marriages. In a finding that shatters the myth of the "good" divorce, they told us that divorce sowed lasting inner conflict in their lives even when their parents did not fight. No matter how "good" their parents were at it, the children of divorce were travelers between two very different worlds, negotiating often vastly different rules and roles.

Although only one-fifth told us that their parents had "a lot" of conflict after splitting up, the children of divorce said, over and over, that the breakup itself made their parents' worlds seem locked in lasting conflict. Two-thirds said their parents seemed like polar opposites in the years following the divorce, compared to just one-third of young adults with married parents. Close to half said that after the divorce they felt like a different person with each of their parents—something only a quarter of children from intact families said. Half said their divorced parents' versions of truth were different, compared to just a fifth of those with married parents. More than twice as many children of divorce as children of intact families said that after the divorce they were asked to keep important secrets—and many more felt the need to do so, even when their parents did not ask them to.

Children of divorce feel like divided selves, and at no time more so than when their parents get together amicably on special occasions—as they are often urged to do by experts advocating the "good" divorce. As one friend told me: "When I was a kid it would really stress me out when my divorced parents were in the same room together…because I didn't know who to be." When they come of age, children of divorce struggle with being their whole, true selves around anyone. Writing in a book of essays, Gen X poet Jen Robinson recalled having to be a different person around each of her parents—who'd had a "good" divorce—to the point that when she left for college, she found that she made friends easily, "but always in distinct groups that seldom interacted. When they did, I felt internally pressured to please both groups and at the same time to negotiate the interaction between them." Finally, she realized that "I needed to reintegrate myself, to let myself be the whole of who I was with everyone who knew me."

Those of us who grew up in the first era of widespread divorce have a new sobriety about it. Yes, sometimes divorce is necessary, but the uncomfortable truth our culture has been hiding for too long is that often it's not, and there is definitely no such thing as a "good" divorce. If parents must divorce, it's good to get along afterward. But people in high-conflict marriages aren't usually successful at "good" divorce (divorce doesn't typically bring out great new communication and cooperation skills). Couples in low-conflict marriages may manage a so-called "good" divorce, but many of them could also manage to, well, stay married and spare themselves and their children a lot of pain.

This sobriety is emerging in movies, in studies, on blogs. I'm convinced there's more to come. Our generation's story needs to be told, because our society still strongly wants to deny just how devastating divorce really is. Too many people imagine that modern divorce is another variation on ordinary family life. Sure, there may be some discomfort, but doesn't childhood stay basically the same?

The answer is no. The evidence is piling up and the message from our generation is clear: Divorce divides and shapes children's identities well into young adulthood. It frees adults at the expense of forcing their children to grow up too soon. It has lasting consequences even when divorced parents do not fight.

SIGNIFICANCE

The proponents of the 'good' divorce concept as beneficial to the children of a failed marriage contrasts sharply with the viewpoint of commentators such as Elizabeth Marquardt. There is no question that the demographic group that is under consideration is sizeable, as twenty-five percent of all young adults in the United States are the product of divorced parents.

A 'good' divorce scenario is one that is highly attractive to persons that are a part of an apparently failing marriage. The best approaches to secure such a divorce result are expounded in hundreds of web sites, self-help books and other resources; the notion of a 'good' divorce with its purportedly reduced stresses and positive outcomes for all concerned is cast as an ideal method for marriage termination.

This understanding of divorce is challenged in Marquardt's article in two distinct angles. The first implicit presumption held by the divorcing parties who seek a 'good' divorce is that if they as parents feel relatively good about themselves after divorce, the children will feel good as well. The second and related presumption is that if the parents either maintain a fiction of civility, or where the parents genuinely feel no enmity to their divorced spouse, the children will be insulated from negative emotional impacts.

These parental attitudes may be the root of the emotional damage to children that the researchers found to be a common product in 'good' divorces, as the most significant goal of this divorce process is the enhancement of the parents emotional well-being; their respective abilities to move ahead with their lives is their objective.

It is the 'sleeper effect' of this approach that its critics have described as the most profound impact of these seemingly friendly, non confrontational divorces. The research of American psychologist and researcher Judith Wallerstein that has been published since 2001 suggests that approximately 25 percent of all children of divorce sustain serious emotional scars no matter how the divorce may handled by their parents. She concluded in a fashion consistent with the Marquardt view that the later ability of divorced children to trust their own marriage partner or to otherwise maintain a positive image of marriage is reduced, creating a greater likelihood of unhappiness in their own marriages.

Marquardt advances the related proposition that in some instances, the parties (and undoubtedly the children of the marriage) would be better off in attempting to correct the difficulties of their marriage, as opposed to embarking upon a divorce that will demand considerable energy to make it a 'good' one for the children. It is estimated that two thirds of divorce proceedings are used to end what are referred to as low-conflict marriages

It is important to understand the distinction between the concept of a 'good' divorce and the principles of collaborative justice that are employed to resolve divorce issues. Collaborative justice is a process where the parties to a prospective divorce agree to resolve all issues on a shared, non-confrontational basis, without resort to the traditional adversarial processes of the courts. Collaborative justice is often hailed as being less emotionally demanding of the children involved. In contrast, a 'good' or a 'bad' divorce are possible outcomes of whatever process may be employed to resolve the legal issues arising on marriage breakup.

FURTHER RESOURCES

Books

Ahron, Constance. *The Good Divorce*. New York: Harper Paperback, 1998.

Blakeslee, Sandra, and Judith S. Wallerstein. *What About the Kids? Raising Your Children before, during, and after Divorce*. New York: Hyperion, 2003.

Wallerstein, Judith S. *The Unexpected Legacy of Divorce*. New York: Hyperion, 2001

Web sites

University of Texas. "The Divorce Dilemma." 2006 <http://www.utexas.edu/features/2006/divorce/> (accessed June 26, 2006).

Fredericksburg Free Lance-Star. "Divorce is Good? Kids Don't Agree." 2003 <http://fredericksburg.com/News/FLS/2003/02203/02022003/863486/> (accessed June 26, 2006).

Familymoons ... Are the New Honeymoons

Newspaper article

By: Sarah Turner

Date: February 5, 2006

Source: Turner, Sarah. *Guardian Newspapers Limited.* "Familymoons ... Are the New Honeymoons." (February 5, 2006).

About the Author: Sarah Turner, a journalist based in the United Kingdom, contributed this article to the *Guardian*, and also writes for the *Observer* on international news and travel.

INTRODUCTION

The twentieth century brought enormous changes to daily life. While some were technological, such as television, air-conditioning, and cellular phones, many of the more profound changes involved human relationships, in particular the form of the American family.

Marriage became less permanent, with divorce rates tripling between 1900 and 1981, then declining to about double the original rate. Divorced individuals, in turn, often remarry, though second and third marriages have even higher failure rates. Since first marriages frequently produce children, couples who

remarry often have to decide how to integrate two discrete households into a blended family.

On television this process often seems relatively painless. The popular series *The Brady Bunch* portrayed a fairy-tale version of this story in which eight individuals and their housekeeper became one enormous happy family. In reality the process is often difficult; to help speed the integration process some couples have begun including their children in all wedding-related activities, including the honeymoon.

The "familymoon" is a market-driven phenomenon, as remarrying couples attempt to beat the odds and make a second or third marriage that includes a blended family succeed. Recognizing the importance of bonding among all family members, some therapists recommend a family trip rather than a couple-only honeymoon. One planning agency reported a twenty-five percent jump in such trips from 2001 to 2006.

■ PRIMARY SOURCE

Familymoons ... Are the new honeymoons

Once upon a time, when single parents got remarried, any children from the previous unions could expect to be landed with granny and grandpa while the happy couple disappeared to the New Forest or wherever for a week.

Now marketing experts are trying to convince us to fold weddings and honeymoons into each other (preferably on some tropical beach) in a series of sun-soaked Kodak moments that everyone will treasure for the rest of their lives. Caribbean resorts even have whole packages set up for the sickly notion of familymoons, where the kids come too.

But what is the reality? A teenage girl in torture at the thought of having to strip down to a bikini next to her more attractive step-sibling or a pouting page boy counting his mosquito bites? And then there is the risk of a bankrupted bride and groom because such shenanigans don't come in under £6,000. Unless, of course, the newlyweds want to share a room with their offspring. Unlikely.

SIGNIFICANCE

More than 2.5 million weddings take place in the United States each year. Average wedding costs hover near $20,000 and total annual spending on weddings is conservatively estimated at $50 billion. Honeymoons, taken by 99% of all couples, comprise about $8 billion of this total, making them an important segment of the travel business. Top destinations for honeymooners include Las Vegas and tropical locations such as Hawaii and the Caribbean. Since the revenue from an eight-person familymoon will generally exceed that from a two-person honeymoon, these enlarged trips are a potential boon for travel planners and resorts.

Modern weddings are often a curious blend of old and new. While white dresses, tuxedos, and traditional vows remain de rigueur for many couples, a growing number opt for more individuality in their ceremonies and receptions. In her book *The New American Wedding*, author Diane Delaney describes a nontraditional wedding featuring a middle-aged bride, a canine bridesmaid, and a swimming pool instead of a diamond ring as an engagement gift. Delaney's collection of such unusual weddings lends support to her contention that more mature couples, particularly those remarrying, often prefer a more individualized ceremony than younger couples typically do.

As weddings have gradually become less traditional, companies have sprung up to support the shift. While traditional engraved white invitations remain common, brides often choose invitation scrolls or notes emblazoned with symbols of other faiths and traditions. Centerpieces, traditionally consisting of arranged flowers, can now be created from candles, candy, or anything else the couple chooses. Technology plays a growing role, too, as couples create rehearsal dinner slideshows depicting their earlier lives and videographers produce customized DVDs of the event.

While some critics may decry the loss of traditional weddings, today's ceremony and traditions are actually relatively recent creations. Medieval brides rarely wore white, for example, opting instead for the brightest, boldest colors available; those wishing to

specifically symbolize purity chose blue. It was not until 1840 that England's Queen Victoria stunned onlookers by marrying in a brilliant white gown. The choice soon caught on and by 1900 the white wedding dress was considered the only appropriate choice in England and the United States. Whether the familymoon will become a new tradition, a short-lived experiment, or just one of a wide array of options remains to be seen. Given the difficulty inherent in synthesizing a new family from the remnants of two earlier ones, any arrangement which potentially smoothes the process appears worth trying.

FURTHER RESOURCES

Books

Delaney, Diane Meier. *The New American Wedding: Ritual and Style in a Changing Culture*. New York: Viking Studio, 2005.

Fields, Denise, and Alan Fields. *Bridal Bargains: Secrets to Throwing a Fantastic Wedding on a Realistic Budget*. Boulder, CO: Windsor Peak Press, 2002.

Lansdell, Avril. *Wedding Fashions, 1860–1980*. Buckinghamshire, England: Shire Publications, 1983.

Periodicals

Levere, Jane. "Skip the Toasters. Help Us Pay for a Trip to Italy." *New York Times*. 154 (November 21, 2004):8.

Martin, Courtney E. "Saying 'I Don't' to Expensive Weddings." *Christian Science Monitor*. 98 (June 15, 2006): 9.

Weinbach, Jon. "Brides Gone Wild." *Wall Street Journal, Eastern Edition*. 247 (June 2, 2006): W1–W2.

Web sites

National Review Online. "The American Way of Wedding." January 3, 2003 <http://www.nationalreview.com/comment/comment-stolba010303.asp (June 21, 2006).

Newsweek Online. "The 'Familymoon.'" <http://www.msnbc.msn.com/id/10663352/site/newsweek> (accessed June 21, 2006).

3 Parenting and Children

Parenting and Children

Parenting is an essential element of nuclear family life. Yet the title of parent is not strictly reserved for those with biological ties. Individuals become parents through adoption, marriage, or fosterage. Within this volume, "parenting" and "parents" are terms usually used to describe individuals who actively participate in childrearing. This chapter focuses on the experiences of both parents and children in various social and historical contexts.

Beginning in the early nineteenth century, it became fashionable for parents to take an increasingly personal and active role in childrearing. The concept of childhood as a distinct and treasured period of life blossomed. Over the latter half of the century emerged the Victorian ideal of hearth and home, including a sizable family with attentive parents and a structured, disciplined family structure. With the veneration of childhood and the family came a shift in ideas about motherhood and fatherhood. Parents and children were the targets of advertisements and the subjects of science journals. The social transformation of parenting continued in the twentieth and twenty-first centuries, becoming more inclusive of diverse family models from single parent households to same-sex parents.

Although gender roles within the family and the division of family labor are discussed in a later chapter, to talk about children and parenting without some discussion of motherhood and fatherhood is impossible.

While the majority of childrearing responsibilities has traditionally fallen on mothers, women's entry into the work force and feminism changed family dynamics to promote equity in family duties and responsibilities. Representations of both mothers and fathers in this chapter illustrate parenting trends as well as reflect changing notions of gender and family roles.

Featured articles on mothers and motherhood highlight both the timelessness of some motherly duties and the radical transformation of perceptions of motherhood over the past 150 years. "Mothers Giving Babies to Nurse at Foundling Home" contrasts the timelessness of nursing duties with antiquated social stigmas placed on unwed mothers. "No Creature In this World so Ignorantly Nurtured as the Average Baby," "Mothers Warned Against Neglect," and "The Education of Mothers" reflect the notion of the mother as the chief guardian of children's health and welfare as well as the emergence of "scientific parenting." Several sources celebrate—and even challenge—the current ideals of motherhood.

Just as motherhood evolved over the past decades, so too has fatherhood. The campy "Necessity is the Mother of Invention" makes light of a father's fitness to watch over a baby, while "Changin' in the Boys' Room" is an amusing representation of current social attitudes on the everyday duties of dads. "Envisioning Fatherhood" looks at the expectations and perceptions of fatherhood among single men.

Mothers Giving Babies to Nurse at Foundling Home

Drawing

By: C. J. Staniland

Date: c. 1870

Source: © Bettmann/Corbis.

About the Artist: Charles Joseph Staniland (1838–1916) was a prolific nineteenth-century illustrator of books. The photograph of this drawing resides in the Bettmann Archives of Corbis Corporation, an image group headquartered in Seattle, with a worldwide archive of more than seventy million images.

INTRODUCTION

For centuries, orphanages and foundling homes cared for millions of children who lost their parents or who did not have families able to care for them. They numbered in the hundreds and were common throughout Europe, the United States, and Latin America. Orphanages largely disappeared by the midpoint of the twentieth century as alternative forms of child care emerged.

Children came to orphanages in a variety of ways. Most full orphans, or children who had lost both parents, were brought to institutions by a relative or family friend. In the case of half orphans, or children with one surviving parent, they were usually brought by their parent who for financial or other reasons was unable to care for his or her child, at least temporarily. Women who gave birth outside of wedlock often abandoned their children at orphanages as a way to avoid the condemnation of society for being sexually promiscuous. Other children entered orphanages through the intervention of charitable agencies, such as the Society for the Prevention of Cruelty to Children, churches, or government employees.

Children left orphanages in a range of ways. Some half orphans were able to reunite with their parent after only a year or so in an institution. Other orphans were eventually taken in by relatives. In other instances, children reunited with their families only after a number of years in orphanages, once they became old enough to work and help their family financially. Full orphans were more likely than other children to stay in an orphanage for many years.

Beyond providing basic sustenance and shelter, asylums educated children. Although this education included reading, writing, and arithmetic, moral education was of greater concern to most asylum managers. Orphanages sponsored by religious institutions typically offered religious training. Public and private asylums also provided religious instruction. Asylum children were also expected to perform any number of chores around the institution, helping keep costs down as well as presumably learning the value to work and personal discipline.

PRIMARY SOURCE

MOTHERS GIVING BABIES TO NURSE AT FOUNDLING HOME
See primary source image.

SIGNIFICANCE

Orphanages fell out of favor during the first half of the twentieth century. Child welfare advocates argued that they were producing children who were unable to function outside of institutions. Nevertheless, the demand for orphanages remained high. In the second half of the twentieth century, successors to orphanages began to appear, occasionally using the same buildings once used by orphanages. These group homes and other residential institutions cared for abused, neglected, or emotionally or physically disabled children within state-operated foster care systems.

In the 1990s, government officials called for a return to orphanages because the American system of foster care seemed inadequate to deal with increasing numbers of abused, neglected, or disabled children in need of care. However, no movement to build large numbers of homes for poor children occurred. Opponents of orphanages charged that it was inhumane to house children in institutions and they won the debate. Continuing problems with foster care in the first years of the twenty-first century has not led to a renewed call for orphanages and is not expected to lead to such demands.

FURTHER RESOURCES
Books

Crenson, Matthew D. *Building the Invisible Orphanage: A Prehistory of the American Welfare System.* Cambridge, Mass.: Harvard University Press, 1998.

Hacsi, Timothy A. *Second Home: Orphan Asylums and Poor Families in America.* Cambridge, Mass.: Harvard University Press, 1997.

Mothers Giving Babies to Nurse at Foundling Home: Unwed mothers turn over their babies to sisters in Foundling Hospital, London. © BETTMANN/CORBIS.

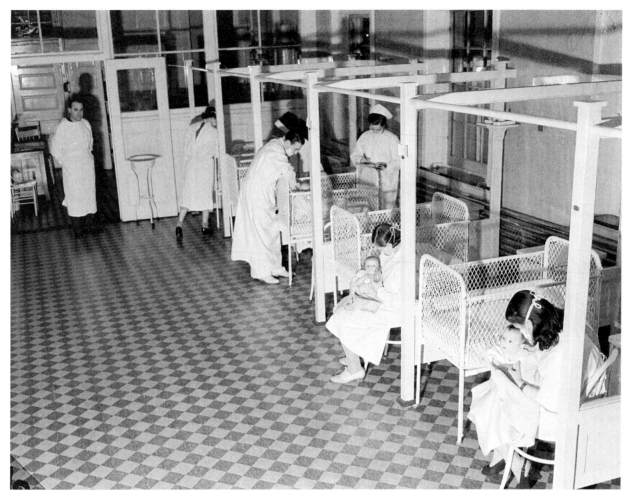

The unwed mothers ward at Misericordia Hospital in New York City, 1940s. © BETTMANN/CORBIS.

McKenzie, Richard B. *Rethinking Orphanages for the 21st Century*. Thousand Oaks, Calif.: Sage, 1999.

The Education of Mothers

Magazine article

By: Mary B. Willard

Date: June 1871

Source: Willard, Mary B. "The Education of Mothers." *The Ladies' Repository* 7 (June 1871): 448–451.

About the Author: Mary B. Wiilard wrote for *The Ladies' Repository*, a monthly periodical devoted to literature, art, and religion that was in publication from 1841 to 1876.

INTRODUCTION

Motherhood involves much more than simply bearing a child. Throughout American history, the meaning of motherhood has been debated as expectations have changed. In the nineteenth century, mothers gained political responsibilities as they became responsible for raising virtuous citizens.

At the start of the nineteenth century, Americans wondered how to produce a virtuous republic. To most people, a perfect nation required the production of moral and intelligent adults. Along with tending to the physical care of children, mothers were expected to assume more responsibility for discipline and socialization. The change diminished the role of fathers as it made mothering more intensive and the principal duty of women in the household. To fulfill their new responsibilities, mothers needed to be educated. Magazine publishers fed mothers a seemingly endless supply of stories about maternal self-sacrifice

A postcard of a Victorian woman with her daughter, 1910.
© POODLESROCK/CORBIS.

and the power of motherhood as well as advice on child-rearing.

For some women, the demands of motherhood justified their entry into male realms. There were calls for women to train as public school teachers and to graduate from medical schools. Presumably, women would use their maternal instinct to be better child-raisers and physicians than men. By the 1870s, the first generation of women's rights advocates were using motherhood to call for women to get the vote. Suffragists claimed that motherhood enabled women to make special and unique contributions to American life. As public housekeepers, women would provide for the health and safety of young children, accept responsibility for the cleanliness and comfort of other people, and clean up corruption in government. Opponents of women's rights argued that women who entered public life were attempting to overthrow the natural order in which women cared for children in the home and men provided for their families.

PRIMARY SOURCE

The scornful war-cry of the Suffragists is echoing over the land, "Woman's chief end is to get married." How horrible! To the rescue at once, "gentle Anna," and irrepressible, invincible, "Susan B." But what of motherly, silver-headed Mrs. Stanton, and deliberate, judicious Mrs. Livering and dressing into the realm of high culture and high art, I think, is Mr. Ruskins' idea, recognizing in the ministrations of food and dress fit subjects for a better education.

The woman who enters the second step of the career, wifehood, who takes a place as the joint head of the household, takes also a position in society, but at a great disadvantage when the definitions of the position have been vaguely taught her, and oftener not at all.

We come to be known as the pretty, simple-minded women, the "*real good women*" the Dorcases, the fine housekeepers, the women of intelligence, the brilliant, showy women, the intellectual and the versatile women, and so on, till the category is exhausted. What requires more special preparation and equipment than this filing one's place in society? The uneducated, even illiterate *man* often ranks higher than his more intelligent wife, and why? Because he gets by contact with business and intelligence, and what a learned Professor calls "intellectual grazing," that which now lies out of her reach and range.

Women, in this domestic sphere, have vital interest in the social and, no doubt, the political questions agitating society; and yet how trifling are they educated with reference to them! If universal suffrage ever obtains favor with a large number of women, it will be simply owing to the sense of the influence which they should exert against the existing evils of the day.

Time would fail us to tell of the many minor necessities for the particular education of women; of proper drawing out of those womanly instincts which, rightly directed and used, so greatly benefit society; of the giving of great facility in the forms, and amenities, and embellishments of life which, in such large degree, contribute to a high civilization.

Except in those schools which, to plain, sensible people, lie under the ban of fashionable schools, how seldom does one find any attention or training given to the forms and usages of polite society; and how frequently is one embarrassed and at a loss, and the whole social machinery retarded by the friction occasioned by this lack of attention!

All these are necessities which plead equally for the special education of daughter and wife. When to these are added the claims of motherhood, who shall correctly portray the need, or sufficiently forcibly illustrate the lack of preparation and discipline? When for baking and brewing one must needs draw upon Medea and Circe, Calypso and Helen, Rebeckah and the Queen of Sheba, what fountain of inspiration shall be deep and exhaustless enough to satisfy the mother's needs? Motherhood means the learning of Arete and philosophy of Hypatia, the accomplishments of Cornelia, the tenderness of Cydippe, the practical wisdom and prudence of Terentia, and the pride and ambition of Zenobia. For her emergencies she must pry out the secrets of Easculapius; she must theorize with Plato in bring out of chaos her little republic; all history must be subject to her draft for example and precedent; Bacon and Locke must teach her concerning that human understanding on which she is so skillfully to play; all poets must drop their silver speech into her ear, and Madonnas of Raphael and Correggio must breathe upon her their almost infinite tenderness.

She must be to her boys and girls now their encyclopedia, then their Mother Goose; here their improvisalrice and dreamer of dreams, there their manufacturer of babyhouses and kites. She must be such embodiment of wisdom and intelligence as to challenge all their ideals. She must be the ministering spirit at their sick-beds, and rival in nursing and skill, the well-read physician. She must be lawgiver, and judge, and advocate in one.

How shall I present to a gainsaying public the arguments for a more thorough and specific training? Arguments, however, are each day becoming less necessary. The planting and watering of public sentiment has, to a great extent, been done, and mine eyes have almost seen the lorry of an institution grounded upon these universal needs in a woman's education, and which has for its aim the specific and complete outfitting for a woman's work.

SIGNIFICANCE

For much of American history, mothers have been regarded as the main providers of child care. Accordingly, there is a lot of literature that addresses the importance of mothers and what mothers need to know to produce healthy children. In the twentieth century, medical and psychological guides to child rearing appeared in bookstores everywhere. Dr. Benjamin Spock's 1946 *Baby and Child Care* became the best known of hundreds of books promising to guide mothers through the potential pitfalls of motherhood.

By the end of the twentieth century, the working mother faced a strong and organized backlash. This often came from the camps of Christian fundamentalists who grounded their demands for the separate and complementary roles of mothers and fathers in the teachings of religion. Sometimes the opposition came from women threatened by the feminist promise of an egalitarian social order. Often with fewer educational

credentials (and fewer economic opportunities) than feminist professional women, these mothers did not see freedom and equality in the work world. For them, work represented demeaning drudgery and stay-at-home motherhood was a far more appealing alternative.

Motherhood at the start of the twenty-first century remains an institution under stress. Single parenthood, the strain involved in efforts to balance motherhood and work, and the needs of women for independence and identity separate from biology are the issues that consume contemporary debate.

FURTHER RESOURCES
Books

Mintz, Steven and Susan Kellogg. *Domestic Revolutions: A Social History of American Family Life*. New York: The Free Press, 1988.

Mothers and Motherhood: Readings in American History, edited by Rima D. Apple and Janet Golden. Columbus, Ohio: The Ohio State University Press, 1997.

Weiner, Lynn Y. *From Working Girl to Working Mother: The Female Labor Force in the United States, 1820–1980*. Chapel Hill, N.C.: University of North Carolina Press, 1985.

Mother Spanking Her Children

Editorial cartoon

By: Anonymous

Date: 1889

Source: © Bettmann/Corbis.

About the Artist: The woodcut illustration is a part of the Bettmann Collection of images maintained in the archives of the Corbis Corporation, a worldwide provider of visual content materials to such communications groups as advertisers, broadcasters, designers, magazines, media organizations, newspapers, and producers. The artist is unknown.

INTRODUCTION

The use of corporal punishment as a means of providing discipline to a child by a parent extends throughout recorded history. The most famous Biblical passage cited in support of the physical discipline of children is set out in the *Book of Proverbs* of the Old Testament: To spare the rod is to spoil the child. This admonition in favor of physical child discipline is echoed in other world religions.

The earliest settlers of the United States were almost exclusively Christians of the Protestant faith. Protestant religious practices tended to significantly influence the early American colonial legal system that was based upon the English common law. At common law, a parent or any other person with authority over a child was permitted to use reasonable force to compel a child's obedience, or to punish a child for misconduct. School teachers, near relatives and the employers of children were the most common classes of persons permitted to exercise corporal punishment upon the children in their care; the legal authority of these persons to strike a child was derived from their status as being *in loco parentis*, or standing in the place of the parent.

The term 'reasonable force' had a broad meaning in American law through the nineteenth century. Corporal punishment could be performed with a leather strap, custom crafted sticks, belts, or any other similar implement so long as serious injury did not result. Spanking, the striking of a child's buttocks with an open hand was perhaps the most common form of physical discipline in the home; the strap or the cane were the typical implements used in school settings.

At the time of the publication of this illustration in 1889, corporal punishment was not a universal disciplinary method in American schools. A number of state school boards had abolished the practice; New York State was one such jurisdiction that had done so in 1877. Corporal punishment was banned in most European schools (excepting Great Britain) by the end of the century. These educators believed that the

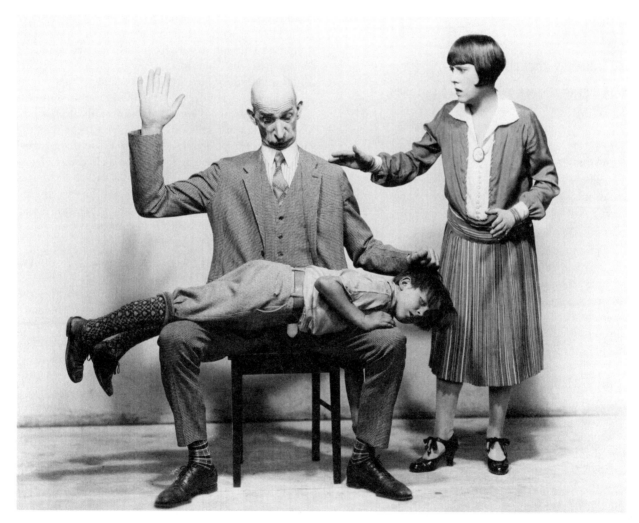

A father punishes his child. © JOHN SPRINGER COLLECTION/CORBIS.

physical punishment of students had an adverse effect upon student discipline.

In the twentieth century, corporal punishment became far less common in American schools. By the year 2000, while no state had a specific legal prohibition in place that outlawed spanking, more than thirty states had formal policies as to when such contact with a student by a teacher was permitted; corporal punishment was now retained as a disciplinary tool of last resort. In addition, the fear of civil action on the part of the subject teacher was a profound limitation on the practice.

In contrast, the use of corporal punishment within the home by a parent has remained a common aspect of American family life. It has been a hotly debated social issue for at least 150 years in the United States. Prosecutions for the excessive use of force by a parent towards a child are relatively rare. The question of whether corporal punishment hinders or helps in the emotional development of a child has remained a very contentious area of academic study.

PRIMARY SOURCE

WOODCUT OF MOTHER SPANKING HER CHILDREN
See primary source image.

SIGNIFICANCE

The 1889 illustration of a mother spanking her children is a work that combines several symbols placed within the depicted scene, each of which conveys a particular meaning.

The first important features of the illustration are the relative roles of the mother and the father to the act of spanking a child. The home appears to be an otherwise comfortable middle class residence, judging from the décor and the clothing of the characters rendered in the scene. The mother, as the homemaker, is the parent responsible for meting out punishment; the father, apparently interrupted in his reading of a newspaper, is an onlooker only.

A symbol of significance is the wall hanging that is partly obscured. The words on the wall are a clear reference to the Christian maxim 'Peace on Earth, Goodwill towards Men,' an ironic sentiment given the spanking being administered in the home.

The combination of the messages conveyed by the illustration is an encapsulation of the historic tension between the parental right to maintain order and discipline over the children resident in their home and

their corresponding obligation to use reasonable methods in their dealings with their children.

Recent public opinion polling conducted in the United States suggests that the conflicting philosophies regarding corporal punishment for children such as that portrayed in the 1889 illustration have remained a part of the modern attitude towards this practice. In a study conducted by ABC News in 2005, sixty-five percent of Americans surveyed supported in principle the right of a parent or near caregiver to spank a child. This percentage has remained relatively constant since 1990. In contrast, seventy-two percent of those polled opposed any form of corporal punishment in schools. Fifty percent of the respondents stated that they either did or would spank their child; forty-five percent stated that they would not.

Courts in the United States have traditionally given parents significant latitude in determining whether the force applied to a child was reasonable; even where the force resulted in injury or was otherwise excessive on a objective basis. Parents who have been charged with assaults arising from the application of physical discipline have frequently secured acquittals on the basis that they, in applying corrective discipline, did not intend to cause injury. The analysis of a similar Canadian law conducted in 2004 by the Supreme Court of Canada is one that is of application to all common law jurisdictions. The Court held that the provision of the Canadian Criminal Code that permits parents to use corrective force upon a child was a legitimate exception to the general law of assault so long as the force used was part of a genuine effort to educate the child and the degree of force used does not pose a risk of harm beyond that of transitory or trifling injury (such as a sore buttock or minor bruising).

In every country where the physical punishment of children is lawful, there are well organized lobbies on each side of the question. In the United States, the constituency favoring corporal punishment tends to include conservative religious groups and others who believe in the ability of parents to set appropriate rules within the family structure. On the abolition side are a diverse range of liberal groups and a significant number of experts who believe that corporal punishment is a danger to a child's long term emotional well-being.

A number of recent academic studies, including that of New Hampshire sociologist Murray Straus, suggest that the administration of corporal punishment in the home is no different than any other violent domestic conduct such as spousal assault; such studies see corporal punishment as undermining the desired notion of a non-violent home. The effects of

Woodcut of Mother Spanking Her Children: An 1889 illustration of a mother spanking her child while the father watches. © BETTMANN/CORBIS.

the physical discipline of children are seen as cumulative in terms of the later negative impact upon the self esteem and emotional health of the child.

While United States and the other nations of the common law tradition permit the physical discipline of a child in limited circumstances, the United Nations Education, Scientific, and Cultural Organization (UNESCO), in which all of these nations have representation, has pledged to work to eliminate all forms of corporal punishment used against children throughout the world.

FURTHER RESOURCES

Books

Cavanaugh, Mary M., Richard G. Gelles and Donileen R. Loseke, eds. *Current Controversies about Family Violence.* Thousand Oaks, Calif.: Sage Publications, 2005.

Straus, Murray. *Beating the Devil Out of Them.* Somerset, N.J.: Transaction Publishers, 2001.

Web sites

Canadian Department of Justice. "Section 43 Criminal Code of Canada." 2006 <http://www.justice.gc.ca/en/news/fs/2004/doc_31114.html> (accessed June 26, 2006).

University of Wisconsin. "Parenting the Preschooler." 1999 <http://www.uwex.edu/ces/flp/p/pdf/punishment.pdf> (accessed June 27, 2006).

Illustration of a Social Worker Removing a Child from an Abusive Dwelling

Illustration

By: Anonymous

Date: c. 1890

Source: © Bettmann/Corbis.

About the Artist: This illustration is part of the collection of the Bettmann Archives of Corbis Corporation, an image group headquartered in Seattle, with a worldwide archive of over seventy million images. The illustrator is not known.

INTRODUCTION

A family's treatment of their children was considered a private matter until the late 1800s in the United States. While corporal punishment was common as a

disciplinary method, the degree of physical discipline—and the line between corporal punishment and abuse—was loose and erred on the side of the parents. Child labor laws, until the 1910s, did little to protect children from abuses by employers. British and American literature from the mid- to late 1800s documented child abuse of children in orphanages, the home, the workplace, and in towns and cities; writers such as Charles Dickens detailed the plight of rich and poor children in his novels.

In England and the United States, poor children worked in mines, entering the workforce at the age of four or five, working in cramped, dark, damp mines pushing trams of coal for fourteen hours a day with no opportunity for school or church. "Free labor" came from children who lived at home with their parents, working to earn wages to help the family. Parents could withdraw their children from unsafe working conditions, but "parish labor" or "pauper labor," work done by children of the poor in workhouses, or by orphan children, was done by force. The children had no choice, and abuses against these children were extreme and widespread.

The idea of childhood as a life stage in need of protection and nurturing was not prevalent until the 1840s and 1850s, when middle-class women began to view their roles as women being dependent on children's roles as innocent beings in need of proper treatment and care. The cult of domesticity or "true womanhood" emerged as the concept of childhood formed; a mother's role, according to this ideal, was to teach her children to be moral human beings, to take childhood innocence and preserve that moral purity while raising a productive, ethical member of society. As this concept of childhood as a protected phase gained credence, Progressive Era reformers applied the ideal to all children and to campaigns for child labor limits, education rights, and protections for children against physical abuse that led to permanent disability and even death.

Through the 1870s, however, child abuse by adults was considered a domestic issue, as was spousal abuse. In the late 1860s, laws against cruelty to animals were passed in some states; by the early 1870s, reformers began to push for similar laws to protect children.

PRIMARY SOURCE

ILLUSTRATION OF A SOCIAL WORKER REMOVING A CHILD FROM AN ABUSIVE DWELLING

See primary source image.

PRIMARY SOURCE

Illustration of a Social Worker Removing a Child from an Abusive Dwelling: This illustration, "The Work of the Society for the Prevention of Cruelty to Children," depicts the rescue of children from a drunken mother in nineteenth century New York City. © BETTMANN/CORBIS.

SIGNIFICANCE

In 1873, the case of Mary Ellen Wilson, a nine-year-old orphan, gained the attention of nurse Etta Wheeler. Mary Ellen was being raised by a foster mother in Hell's Kitchen, one of the worst neighborhoods in New York City at that time, and the child exhibited scars and open wounds that were clearly marks of extreme abuse. While Wheeler worked to have Mary Ellen removed from her home, the police and courts told her it was a matter between parent and child. Wheeler appealed to Henry Bergh, a wealthy

businessman who had been instrumental in the formation of the American Society for the Prevention of Cruelty to Animals, and asked for his assistance.

In 1874, Henry Bergh asked lawyer Elbridge Gerry for help. Gerry pushed through the court system on Mary Ellen's behalf. Noted journalist Jacob Riis wrote about Mary Ellen's case; the girl herself stated in court that: "I am never allowed to play with other children; momma has been in the habit of whipping me almost everyday; she used to whip me with a twisted whip—a rawhide; the whip always left black

Social worker Dyane Clayborn surveys a filthy garbage-strewn apartment while responding to a report of child abuse.
PHOTO BY STEVE KAGAN//TIME LIFE PICTURES/GETTY IMAGES.

and blue marks on my body; I have now on my head two black and blue marks which were made by momma with the whip, and a cut on the left side of my forehead which was made by a pair of scissors in momma's hand; she struck me with the scissors and cut me; I have no recollection of ever having been kissed and I have never been kissed by momma: I have never been taken on momma's lap or caressed or petted; I never dared speak to anybody, because if I did I would get whipped; I have never had... any more clothing than I have on at present... I have seen stockings and other clothes in our room, but I am not allowed to put them on; whenever momma went out, I was locked up in the bedroom." Mary Ellen was removed from her home, placed in the care of a loving family, and went on to live into her nineties. Societies for child protection appeared across the country as social workers took up the cause of child welfare. By 1900, more than 161 such societies existed.

The belief that child treatment was a family matter persisted, but laws and social attitude slowly changed. While spanking as a form of discipline persisted, by

1912 Congress created the Children's Bureau, and in 1944 the United States Supreme Court affirmed the state's right to intervene in family matters in the court case *Prince v. Massachusetts*. In 1962, the concept of child abuse as a syndrome or a subject for distinct study appeared with the publication of the article "The Battered Child Syndrome" in the *Journal of the American Medical Association*. In response to the article, social workers and social policy experts crafted a policy approach to managing and controlling child abuse.

Throughout the 1980s, the role of school officials, church youth workers, and medical staff as "mandated reporters" became law. People in such roles, with close contact with children, have a legal obligation to report child abuse. While the current social work model in most states emphasizes keeping families intact, children are often removed from abusive homes, as are the children in the illustration above. In 2004, approximately nineteen percent of all child maltreatment cases ended with the child's removal from the home, though many families are reunited after parents attend counseling and complete other required steps for family reunification.

FURTHER RESOURCES

Books

Childhood in America, edited by Paula S. Fass and Mary Ann Mason. New York: New York University Press, 2000.

Heywood, Colin. *A History of Childhood: Children and Childhood in the West from Medieval to Modern Times.* Cambridge, U.K.: Polity Press, 2001.

Zelizer, Viviana. *Pricing the Priceless Child: The Changing Social Value of Children.* Princeton, N.J.: Princeton University Press, 1994.

Periodicals

Hempe, C. "The Battered Child Syndrome." *Journal of the American Medical Association* 181 (July 17, 1962): 17–24.

Web sites

New York Society for the Prevention of Cruelty to Children. <http://www.nyspcc.org> (accessed July 22, 2006).

Necessity is the Mother of Invention

Cartoon

By: Anonymous

Date: c.1890

Source: © Bettmann/Corbis.

About the Artist: Otto Bettmann (1903–1998), a librarian and curator in Berlin in the 1930s, began collecting photographs to preserve as a historical archive. Fleeing Germany with several trunks of photographs in his possession, he settled in the United States. By 1995, when Corbis acquired the Bettmann archive, his collection included more than eleven million items. This cartoon is part of the collection. The artist is not known.

INTRODUCTION

Fathers participated directly in the raising of children in the nineteenth century to a much greater extent than is commonly believed; the concept of "paternal manhood" urges fathers to take an active role in helping their wives raise and nurture the children. In rural families, the mother and father share farm chores and household chores; though gender roles were distinct in daily life, under duress and crises women performed standard "male" labor, while men performed household, cooking, and sewing work if

NECESSITY IS THE MOTHER OF INVENTION.

Mr. Bleecker.— What in thunder ?———
Mr. Brooke Lynn.— Well, I've *got* to see the ball game, and, of course, I can't get away from the baby; so I devised this rather novel arrangement. Clever, is n't it?

█ PRIMARY SOURCE

Necessity is the Mother of Invention: A late nineteenth century cartoon shows a young Brooklyn father's protected baby carriage, designed to make it safe to take his baby with him to the ballgame. © BETTMANN/CORBIS.

their wives were sick, away, or otherwise unable to perform such work.

With industrialization and urbanization, the role of the father, like that of all family members, changed. Moving from small towns with strong community and kinship ties into the city meant a loss of personal context; the patriarchal rule, reinforced by community and standing, lessened for many families, giving rise to a host of social changes including higher rates of illegitimacy, increased women's rights, greater spread of venereal disease, and an increased reliance of women's and children's wages in poorer families. The balance of power shifted.

While men had always been involved in childbirth to some extent—either as the direct support for wives birthing at home, or waiting outside the room on call to seek help or provide assistance—the increasing use of family planning information and devices in the late 1800s and early 1900s gave men an insight into reproduction and women's health that men had previously lacked. The father's involvement in infant and toddler care varied with each family; the family's class or status also played a part in father involvement. Historical evidence gleaned from diaries, letters, literature and nonfiction books shows that many middle class fathers were involved in their children's emotional lives, achievements, and academic progress, while fathers in working class families engaged in day-to-day feeding, toileting, and play with their children.

This cartoon, drawn and published around 1890, demonstrates one father's solution to his need to care for his baby and his desire to watch a baseball game.

■ PRIMARY SOURCE

NECESSITY IS THE MOTHER OF INVENTION

See primary source image.

■

SIGNIFICANCE

The tongue-in-cheek illustration reflects the playful tone this father sets—he can fill his fatherly duties, please his wife, and see the New York-Brooklyn game all at once, with some ingenuity and invention. The cartoon pokes fun at the lengths to which this father will go to watch the game, but at the same time offers a glimpse into urban fatherhood; that this father is expected to attend to his child's needs at all demonstrates social expectations placed on fathers in this sector of society.

Class played a large role in the degree to which fathers were involved in the daily lives and emotional development of their children. Upper class fathers tended to have a fairly small role in their children's lives, as did mothers in the same class; the fathers were the ultimate authority in deciding academic issues, marriage matches, and career paths. Poor and working class fathers were often, by necessity, involved in child care or arranging apprenticeships and jobs for their older children, though most working class fathers worked fourteen hours per day, six days per week; the paucity of extra time meant that the father was not available to his children for many hours each week. In

This 1905 postcard shows a father caring for his large family. © POODLESROCK/CORBIS.

addition, mothers in poor and working class families experienced frequent pregnancies and births; the weight of gestating, birthing, nursing, and raising a child took its toll on the mother's health. Fathers in the poor and working classes faced the greater likelihood of becoming a widower with many children, in need of a partner for help. While maternal deaths were common in the late 1800s—four to five per 1000 births—the poor and working class experienced maternal mortality at higher rates.

The middle class father was often engaged and involved, actively interested in infant and toddler growth, working with children on academic development, and easing into an adult relationship with his children as they grew. While child care of the nature depicted in this cartoon would have been less common for middle class fathers, the caricature symbolizes the changing expectations on fathers at the turn of the century, as social reformers and women's rights proponents argued for changes in gender roles and ideals of childhood and innocence.

FURTHER RESOURCES

Books

La Rossa, Ralph. *The Modernization of Fatherhood: A Social and Political History*. Chicago: University of Chicago Press, 1996.

Frank, Stephen M. *Life with Father: Parenthood and Masculinity in the Nineteenth-Century American North*. Baltimore and London: Johns Hopkins University Press, 1998.

Johansen, Shawn. *Family Men: Middle-Class Fatherhood in Early Industrializing America*. London: Routledge, 2001.

Peters, H. Elizabeth, and Gary W. Peterson, eds. *Fatherhood: Research, Interventions, and Policies*. Bingamton, N.Y.: Haworth Press, 2000.

Periodical

Atkinson, Maxine, and Stephen Blackwelder. "Fathering in the 20th Century." *Journal of Marriage and the Family.* 55 (1993): 975–986.

Advertisement for Hitching's Baby Cars

Advertisement

By: Anonymous

Date: 1897

Source: © Hulton-Deutsch Collection/Corbis.

About the Artist: This image is part of the collection of the Corbis Corporation, headquartered in Seattle, with a worldwide archive of over seventy million images. The artist is not known.

INTRODUCTION

Throughout history, new mothers have faced the challenge of carrying their young children. While the smallest babies can be easily held in the arms for short distances, longer journeys often require more elaborate arrangements, and mothers in various cultures have created numerous tools for this purpose. The modern aluminum and nylon baby backpack is surprisingly similar in form and function to the wooden papoose boards used by native American women to carry infants on their backs.

The advent of sidewalks and surfaced roads paved the way for a new type of baby conveyance, the stroller. The first ancestor of the modern baby stroller was created in the 1700's for an English Duke and his family. Less a stroller than a miniature carriage, this first design was intricately decorated, rested on a spring suspension, and was designed with a harness so it could be pulled by a large dog or a pony. The novel contraption soon caught on and wealthy families throughout Europe began buying them for their own children, though they were far more useful for play than for practical conveyance.

In the following years, the carriage gradually evolved, with the most important change being the addition of handles so the carriage could be pushed by an adult. While carriages slowly gained popularity, they remained something of a novelty until around 1840, when England's Queen Victoria purchased three. Though still somewhat unstable and hard to maneuver, carriages quickly became fashionable accessories, sporting royal-sounding names like Duchess and Princess. Like many new developments, the carriages were not universally accepted and some localities initially banned them from public sidewalks, though these bans were soon lifted.

A turning point in the history of baby carriages came in 1889, as William Richardson patented several changes that made the traditional baby carriage far more like its modern counterpart. Richardson's design included a rotating joint that allowed the baby to ride facing forward or backward, as well as independently rotating wheels that permitted the carriage to turn in a much smaller radius. The years following Richardson's work witnessed a flurry of design improvements, and by the 1920s, carriages with foot brakes and numerous other features were widely available at prices affordable to most families.

■ PRIMARY SOURCE

ADVERTISEMENT FOR HITCHING'S BABY CARS
See primary source image.

■

SIGNIFICANCE

During the twentieth century, baby carriages continued to improve, evolving from heavy wood and steel construction to lightweight metal frames with plastic handles and air-filled tires. Despite these improvements in weight and usability, the traditional carriage remained bulky and difficult to transport, limiting its practical use to areas near home. In 1965, a tinkering engineer created the first lightweight folding stroller, known as an umbrella stroller, which weighed just a few pounds, folded into a small cylinder, and could carry children of many sizes in comfort and safety. The umbrella stroller quickly replaced the traditional carriage for most families.

As the twentieth century neared its end, manufacturers created an ever-expanding assortment of strollers. Some offered additional convenience features such as larger wheels for better handling, while others appealed to specific niche markets, including strollers designed to carry twins or triplets. As the run-

■ PRIMARY SOURCE

Advertisement for Hitching's Baby Cars: An advertisement for Hitching's Baby Cars from the late nineteenth century magazine *Gentlewoman's Record.* © HULTON-DEUTSCH COLLECTION/CORBIS.

Georges Barbier's a "Baby Carriage Parade of Husbands and Firstborns," 1914. © BETTMANN/CORBIS.

ning craze of the 1970s swept the nation, joggers found that traditional strollers were poorly suited to the new pastime. In 1980, one enterprising runner began experimenting with bicycle tires mounted on a traditional stroller, eventually settling on a three-wheeled design that became the standard for jogging strollers. Many road races include parents pushing a child using one of these devices.

Modern strollers are available in numerous standard styles and can be ordered in a multitude of custom models. With Americans postponing child-raising until later in life, they generally have more income to spend on their children; as a result, baby and child care products take up a sizeable section of most grocery and discount stores, with new variations on old products continually hitting shelves. By 2005, Americans were spending more than $6 billion just on essentials such as diapers, wipes, formula and baby food, and teething toys. With U.S. birthrates relatively level, manufacturers have been forced to inno-

vate, creating new products in order to steal market share from competitors. Several hundred years after the first luxury baby carriages were created, wheeled baby carriers are considered essential equipment by most parents.

FURTHER RESOURCES

Books

Gordon, Sandra. *Best Baby Products*, 8th edition. New York: Consumer Reports, 2006.

Iovine, Vick,i and Peg Rosen. *Girlfriends' Guide to Baby Gear*. New York: Perigee Books, 2003.

Runkel, Hal . *ScreamFree Parenting: Raising Your Kids by Keeping Your Cool*. Duluth, Georgia: Oakmont Publishing, 2005.

Periodicals

Abramovitz, Robert. "Parenthood in America." *Journal of Clinical Child Psychology* 5 (1976): 43–46.

Hardin, Amy. "First Comes the Baby Carriage." *New York Times* (October 13, 2005): G1–G2.

Tucker, Nicholas. "Boon or Burden? Baby Love in History." *History Today* 43 (September 1993):28–35.

Web sites

Congress of History of San Diego and Imperial Counties. "Beautiful Baby Clothes on Display in Lakeside Museum." <http://congressofhistory.org/docs/a0507-baby-clothes-lakeside.html> (accessed July 16, 2006).

Victoriana. "The Golden Age of Carriages." <http://www.victoriana.com/lady/buggy.html> (accessed July 16, 2006).

No Creature in this World So Ignorantly Nurtured as the Average Baby

Poster

By: Erik Hans Krause

Date: 1936–1938

Source: *Library of Congress, Prints and Photographs Division.* "By the People, For the People: Posters from the WPA, 1936–1943."

About the Artist: Erik Hans Krause (1899–1990) was born in Halle-Salle, Germany, attended the Academy of Decorative Arts and Crafts in Dresden, and emigrated to the United States in 1923. A commercial artist, designer, printmaker, and book illustrator, Krause was a supervisor and designer for Federal Art Project, a division of the WPA (the Works Progress Administration, renamed the Work Projects Administration in 1939) in Rochester, New York, during the period 1936–1939. The Federal Art Project employed more than 5,000 artists who created murals, paintings, and sculptures, and produced more than two million posters from around 35,000 original designs to advertise the different types of work performed by the WPA in 1936–1943. About 900 of these posters are preserved in the Library of Congress in the Prints and Photographs collection. Eight of Erik Hans Klause's posters promoting public health in New York state from 1936 to 1938, including the silkscreened poster shown here, are in this collection. After the Depression, Krause taught design and illustration at the Rochester Institute of Technology. He specialized in botanical illustration and had exhibits at the Smith-sonian and the National Audubon Society before he died in New York.

INTRODUCTION

Erik Hans Krause' poster was part of the WPA campaign to improve public health, especially for children, during the last half of the Great Depression. The Federal Art Project's posters were displayed in busses, trains, stations, store windows, and other highly visible places, to inform people of government agencies offering useful services. Although one art historian notes that "an important factor in the posters' effectiveness was their nonjudgmental tone," (DeNoon 1987, p. 113), this particular poster is rather disparaging: Most parents are apparently not only ignorant, but cannot even nurture their young as well as other animals do.

In order to understand the caption on Krause's poster, it is necessary to know some of the history of parenting and to appreciate how attitudes towards mothers, raising children, and science changed in the early twentieth century. The growth of scientific parenting, also called trained motherhood or modern motherhood, closely related to medicalized motherhood, is tied to the contemporaneous development of several different fields, including home economics, sociology, psychology, child development, and pediatrics. Not coincidentally, during this period the United States government intervened in children's lives to a greater extant than ever before.

PRIMARY SOURCE

NO CREATURE IN THIS WORLD SO IGNORANTLY NURTURED AS THE AVERAGE BABY

See primary source image.

SIGNIFICANCE

Rima Apple and Julia Grant point out that the roots of scientific parenting lie in the late nineteenth century, when doctors began supplanting other mothers and religious figures as the primary authors of advice books for parents. An increase in literacy and mobility, medical advances, and decreasing birth rates made this prescriptive literature progressively more important to parents. In the early 1900s, raising children was more labor- and knowledge-intensive than ever before. The notion that motherhood was natural, a matter of common sense, or something passed from generation to generation, was definitely in decline.

PRIMARY SOURCE

No Creature in this World So Ignorantly Nurtured as the Average Baby: A 1930s poster promoting scientific parenting.
THE LIBRARY OF CONGRESS.

President Roosevelt with WPA Administrator Harry Hopkins and Hopkin's daughter, November 4, 1937. © BETTMANN/CORBIS.

A more systematic campaign for mothers' education emerged in the 1920s, fueled by the child welfare movement, the growth of kindergarten education, organized women's groups (including the National Congress of Mothers, which became the modern PTA—the Parent Teacher Association), social workers, psychologists, pediatricians, and government bureaucracy. The scientific utopianism of this period also played an important role. Trained mothering was further seen as a way to assimilate immigrant, working class, and African American families (Litt 2000). Foreshadowing some modern concerns, policy makers were also concerned that middle or upper class women might chose not to have children as women became more active in public life and many professions. By defining motherhood as "valuable work requiring extensive knowledge and training" (Grant 1998, p. 10), educators supported women who chose to stay home with their children.

Some of the main tenets of scientific parenting in the 1920s and 1930s included increased attention to hygiene, rigorous scheduling (particularly for feeding, sleeping, and toileting), vaccinations, and yearly pediatric checks. Infant and child behavior became more closely monitored than ever before, and deviation from physical or psychological norms was usually blamed on poor mothering. Although infant mortality and disease rates dropped quite drastically during 1900–1940, mothers were still routinely blamed for most illnesses and deaths amongst children. The increased poverty of the Depression did make many of the existing problems facing children more widespread or dangerous. As in recent times, the assistance of professionals from many fields was seen as crucial to good parenting. Mothers who did not want to be judged ignorant or reckless were responsible for seeking out the appropriate experts, like those at the New York state Health Bureau advertised by Krause's poster.

FURTHER RESOURCES

Books

Apple, Rima. *Perfect Motherhood: Science and Childrearing in America.* New Brunswick, N.J.: Rutgers University Press, 2006.

DeNoon, Christopher. *Posters of the WPA.* Los Angeles: The Wheatley Press, 1987.

Grant, Julia. *Raising Baby by the Book: The Education of American Mothers.* New Haven, Conn.: Yale University Press, 1998.

Litt, Jacquelyn S. *Medicalized Motherhood: Perspectives from the Lives of African-American and Jewish Women.* New Brunswick, N.J.: Rutgers University Press, 2000.

Web site

National Archives and Records Administration. "A New Deal for the Arts." <http://www.archives.gov/exhibits/new_deal_for_the_arts/index.html> (accessed June 11, 2006).

Mothers Warned Against Neglect

Newspaper article

By: Anonymous

Date: January 8, 1945

Source: "Mothers Warned Against Neglect." *New York Times* (January 8, 1945).

About the Author: This article was published without a byline, and was written by a staff writer for the *New York Times*, a daily newspaper with a circulation of over one million readers worldwide.

INTRODUCTION

The United States' entry into World War II brought enormous changes to life in America. As the war expanded, increasing numbers of civilian men were drafted and sent overseas, leaving their families to fend for themselves. Back home, basic commodities such as coffee, gasoline, and rubber were rationed, and new car production ceased as automobile factories were converted to produce bombers and battle tanks. As the nation began to flex its economic muscle, an urgent labor shortage began to develop. With several million men fighting overseas, businesses began struggling to fill their labor needs.

In response to the developing labor shortage, the War Department and U.S. industry took the unprecedented step of recruiting women. Although 250,000 women already served in the armed forces, most women in the 1940s did not work outside their homes, and those that did typically held non-industrial jobs. In order to overcome cultural expectations that women should remain at home, the Pentagon launched an extensive campaign to recruit women for wartime labor positions.

The campaign, featuring characters such as the famous Rosie the Riveter, encouraged women to join the workforce for several reasons. Patriotism was a primary motivation, and women were encouraged to do their part so that the war would end quickly and fewer soldiers would die. The campaign also reassured women that the work was temporary, and that their primary responsibility remained to their homes and children. Specific ads also targeted husbands, reassuring them that a working wife did not reflect poorly on their ability to provide for their families. The campaign portrayed women as talented and competent, able to get just as greasy as the men during the day but remain feminine in the evenings.

The campaign to recruit women was successful; by war's end the number of women in the U.S. workforce had climbed from twelve million to eighteen million. Many of these female workers continued to hold unskilled and low-paying jobs, freeing men for other tasks, however in many factories men and women worked side-by-side on the assembly lines, building airplanes and other equipment. Women were particularly suited to some jobs due to their generally smaller size. As the war progressed, the government began encouraging even women with small children to take jobs, raising public fears of increased juvenile delinquency among unsupervised children. In some cases, women who took jobs were criticized for allegedly abandoning their parenting responsibilities.

■ PRIMARY SOURCE

Mothers who neglect their children for war work seriously menace the present and future welfare of this country, the Rev. Thomas A. Donnellan, assistant chancellor of the Archdiocese of New York, declared yesterday at solemn mass in St. Patrick's Cathedral, marking the observance of the Feast of the Holy Family.

Saying that the home is where children must be educated and disciplined with the school existing only "to help," he predicted that a lost generation will be the product of denial of a mother's care for today's children.

Children play in a neglected play hut on the Lisson Green Estate. © HULTON-DEUTSCH COLLECTION/CORBIS.

"Marriage, the family, has for its chief purpose the generation and education of children," he said. "The war-working mother, therefore, must think first of her primary duty. The mother who works in a war plant and neglects her children isn't helping this country. She is hurting it because she is putting her family in danger.

"God did not institute the League of Nations or the Chamber of Commerce. But He did institute marriage and the family. It is the divine institution of society, the cell around which all society is built.

"It preceded the State and therefore it is evident it has rights and duties independent from the State. Education is one of these. The parents are the educators; the school exists only to help them. Whenever a State takes upon itself that right there is a long war. That's what happened in Germany. It is an important thing for us to remember in wartime conditions here."

Instead of being discouraged and worried about juvenile delinquency and similar problems, society should take the constructive step of emulating the ideal family, which came into being on Christmas Day, Father Donnellan said.

SIGNIFICANCE

Fears that mothers would abandon domestic life en masse for the workplace proved unfounded, and the vast majority of mothers remained at home or worked only temporarily during the war. Women entering the workforce for the first time often found that they were treated as second-class employees, frequently being assigned only menial tasks and generally earning lower pay than men received for identical work. Not until the passage of the Equal Pay Act of 1963 would this practice of routinely paying men more become a violation of federal labor law.

Newly hired women also faced resistance from organized labor. Industrial unions were particularly powerful during the mid-twentieth century, with leaders opposing any change that might threaten job security for members. By potentially expanding the supply of available labor, women represented just such a threat, and unions generally resisted the hiring of women to replace union members called away by military duty.

Following the war most women returned to their homes and resumed their original roles; many were undoubtedly grateful to do so as they often were often expected to retain their home responsibilities while also working in industry. Those who remained in the workforce generally held clerical or similar lower-level positions and despite the nation's experience during the war, traditional workplace norms quickly reasserted themselves. Many years would pass before women would be treated as equals in the workplace, and even fifty years after the war some industries remained somewhat hostile to female employees.

In 2005 the U.S. Department of Labor reported that women made up forty-six percent of the domestic workforce, a number projected to grow to forty-seven percent by 2014; seventy-five percent of employed women worked full-time. Women headed major corporations, including several of the Fortune 500, the largest publicly traded firms in the United States. Women were also active in politics, with several having served in the United States Senate and many others holding cabinet level posts.

Barriers to women in the workplace still remain. In 2004, a federal judge expanded a gender discrimination suit against the world's largest retailer, Wal-Mart, to include 1.6 million women employed by the company since 1988. The suit claimed that Wal-Mart systematically discriminated against women in promotion and pay practices. Wal-Mart was expected to aggressively fight the suit; experts said a loss in the case could cost the company several billion dollars.

FURTHER RESOURCES

Books

Anderson, Karen. *Wartime Women: Sex Roles, Family Relations, and the Status of Women During World War II.* New York: Berkley Books, 2001.

Gluck, Sherma B. *Rosie the Riveter Revisited: Women, the War, and Social Change.* Boston: Twayne Publishers, 1987.

Yalin, Emily. *Our Mother's War: American Women at Home and at the Front During World War II.* New York: Free Press, 2004.

Periodicals

Gillies, Val. "Working Class Mothers and School Life: Exploring the Role of Emotional Capital." *Gender & Education* 18 (1006): 281–293.

Rickman, Sarah. "Barbara Erickson: From 'Rosie the Riveter' to B–17 Pilot." *Air Power History* 52 (2005): 4–11.

Rupp, Leila J. "From Rosie the Riveter to the Global Assembly Line: American Women on the World Stage." *OAH Magazine of History* 18 (2004): 54–57.

Web sites

Columbia University. "Children of Mothers Working Full-Time in the First Year of Life Show Lower Cognitive, Verbal Development." January 29, 2004. <http://www.columbia.edu/cu/news/media/02/jeanneBrooksGunn/index.html> (accessed July 22, 2006).

Eli Lilly and Company. "Lilly Recognized as 'One of 100 Best Companies for Working Mothers." 2005. <http://www.lilly.com/about/awards/mothers.html> (accessed July 22, 2006).

Medical News Today. "Working Mothers Healthier Than Full-Time Housewives." May 15, 2006. <http://www.medicalnewstoday.com/healthnews.php?newsid=43421> (accessed July 22, 2006).

Correcting Child Vandalism

Newspaper article

By: Anna M. Grass

Date: December 30, 1952

Source: Grass, Anna M. "Correcting Child Vandalism." The *New York Times,* Dec 30, 1952.

About the Author: Anna Grass wrote extensively on issues related to social welfare during the 1950s and 1960s.

INTRODUCTION

Raising children can be one of life's more difficult tasks. Long viewed as simply smaller versions of adults, children are now understood to have their own unique set of motivations and needs, some of which can be quite different from those of adults. Child discipline, and how best to achieve it, is a topic of continuing debate, with some authorities advocating

A boy vandalizes a car. © ROYALTY-FREE/CORBIS.

rules-based systems and others favoring relationship-based coaching.

While debates on proper child discipline remain largely the domain of sociologists and family counselors, the question of society's response to misbehaving children often becomes the subject of public policy debate. The criminal justice system's proper treatment of child offenders remains a contentious topic, sparking heated discussion in situations such as when a minor is arrested for murder and faces the possibility of being tried as an adult and potentially executed.

Juvenile delinquency is defined as an offense committed by a minor that would, if committed by an adult, be considered a crime. The United States adopted a system of law for dealing with juvenile offenders in 1899, and the system has been extensively revised and expanded in the years since. The system was originally conceived to provide an alternative to incarcerating juveniles in adult prisons, a situation which often resulted in abuse. It was also hoped that young offenders might be rehabilitated more easily than their older counterparts. As of 2005 the annual cost of incarcerating a youth in the United States was approximately $43,000.

Another aspect of the juvenile criminal justice system deals with restitution, or repayment for crimes committed by children. Because children rarely possess the financial resources to make repayment for their offenses the legal system in some cases demands that parents or guardians be held financially responsible for damage caused by their children. The intent of such laws is two-fold. First, they provide for the repair of destruction caused by the child, restoring what was damaged. Second, the laws function as financial incentive for parents to control their children's behavior, because the parents can expect to pay for a child's

criminal misbehavior. Beginning in the mid 1900s states began passing laws to force parental payment for their children's crimes.

PRIMARY SOURCE

Opposition to Proposed Measure to Fine Parents is explained

Park Commissioner Moses has proposed, and the City Council has disposed of, a measure designed to protect city parks.

The bill, Council-approved 16 to 8, providing for the fining up to $25 of parents for park damage done by their children, seems to citizens and civic agencies concerned with protecting children as well as parks to have turned the clock back in the field of community effort for child delinquency prevention.

It is disturbing to note that some members of New York City's law-making body fail to evaluate realistically the park vandalism problem. They are unmindful of a fund of accredited modern knowledge of child crime causation that specifies that park vandalism, not unlike school truancy, pilfering, hopping trucks and other forms of misconduct, be but a symptom and not the causes of anti-social behavior.

Moreover, experts in the field hold that because maladapted behavior in youngsters derives in large measure from poor parent-child relations and disruption in family life the "correctional" provision to fine the parents may not only fail to correct but even backfire. Such a course would tend to disrupt increasingly family relations, making fertile ground for more problem behavior.

As the Council park vandalism bill goes again to he Board of Estimate, where earlier it had been blocked by a tie vote of 8 to 8, citizens and lawmakers concerned with child delinquency prevention and child protection will need to measure accurately what price park protection.

Finally, in any child crime-elimination program there will be need also to weigh the adoption of this measure with its negative approach versus the positive community approach of extending facilities that affect the health, education, welfare and recreation of New York City's children.

Anna M. Grass.
New York, Dec. 30, 1952

SIGNIFICANCE

By modern standards, the 1952 New York statute fining parents for their children's vandalism would be considered quite mild. As of 2005, a majority of states make parents liable for vandalism committed by their children, even beyond the penalties assessed in civil court; some states place limits on this liability, while others do not. In a recent Georgia case a child set a fire that destroyed an apartment complex; the child's parents were held financially liable for the entire cost of reconstruction.

Child violence can also cost parents: California law allows the victim of violence by a minor to recover up to $10,000 from the child's parents, who may also be assessed another $10,000 as a reward to the person who turned the child in. In some situations California state officials are empowered to file a lien against the home or other property of a delinquent's parents in order to collect monetary damages.

Other states have devised even more creative solutions. Parents in Louisiana can be jailed for up to thirty days if their child joins a street gang. In Washington State, a pre-teen who stole a $3,000 bicycle must repay the full amount before he becomes an adult; otherwise the act will become part of his credit history, destroying his credit rating. As of 2005, more than a dozen states had passed laws holding parents liable if they fail to adequately supervise a child they know to be delinquent.

Numerous options are available to parents wishing to regain control of a rebellious child, and some states offer financial assistance to parents wishing to seek assistance. Options begin with support groups, counseling, and drug rehabilitation programs, many of which are partially covered by medical insurance. More extreme solutions include boot camps—thirty- to sixty-day programs that teach self-discipline using military-style techniques—and private military schools at which students live for an entire semester. The cost of these expensive options is generally not reimbursed by insurers.

In the year 2000, there were 2.4 million juvenile arrests. While crime rates overall in the United States have fallen in the years since, much of this decline is attributed to falling juvenile populations rather than law enforcement initiatives. In 2005, the U.S. Supreme Court ruled 5-4 that the death penalty, when applied to offenders under the age of eighteen, violates the Constitutional ban on cruel and unusual punishment. Thirty-six states currently apply the death penalty.

FURTHER RESOURCES
Books

Bartollas, Clemens. *Juvenile Delinquency*. New York: Allyn & Bacon, 2002.

Heilbrun, Kirk, et al., eds. *Juvenile Delinquency: Prevention, Assessment, and Intervention*. New York: Oxford University Press, 2005.

Lahey, Benjamin, et al., eds. *Causes of Conduct Disorder and Juvenile Delinquency*. New York: Guilford Press, 2003.

Periodicals

Neuman, Clayton. "The Thin Blue Line at MySpace." *Time* (June 30, 2006): 18.

Nickoletti, Patrick, and Heather Taussig. "Outcome Expectancies and Risk Behaviors in Maltreated Adolescents." *Journal of Research on Adolescence*. 16 (2006): 217–228.

Williams, Patricia J. "Felonious Intent." *Nation* 282 (2006): 9.

Web sites

American Prospect. "I Plead the Sixth." July 30, 2002 <http://www.prospect.org/print/V13/14/polakow-suransky-s.html> (accessed June 24, 2006).

Center for Delinquency Prevention. "Preventing Juvenile Delinquency." <http://www.delinquencyprevention.org/> (accessed June 22, 2006).

Juvenile Justice FYI. "History of America's Juvenile Justice System." <http://www.juvenilejusticefyi.com/history_of_juvenile_justice.html> (accessed June 24, 2006).

Non-Custodial Mothers Developing Strategies of Support

Journal article

By: Joyce A. Anditti and Debra A. Madden-Derdich

Date: 1993

Source: Anditti, Joyce A. and Debra A. Madden-Derdich. "Non Custodial Mothers Developing Strategies in Support." *Family Relations: Interdisciplinary Journal of Applied Family Studies* 42 (1993): 305—314.

About the Author: The journal *Family Relations* has been published since 1951 by the National Council on Family Relations (NCFR), based in Minneapolis, Minnesota. The stated mission of the NCFR is to promote family well-being through the dissemination of knowledge about families and family relationships.

INTRODUCTION

In the United States through the early 1900s, the only law that generally governed the breakdown of a marital relationship was the law of divorce. Divorce carried with it a significant social and religious stigma; in many religious faiths a divorced person was not permitted to re-marry with the blessing of his or her church. Divorce laws in virtually every American state in 1920 provided that the issuance of a divorce decree was restricted to the proof of fault by one marriage partner; adultery and desertion were the most commonly advanced grounds.

At the same time, married women had few advanced educational and employment opportunities beyond the confines of the family structure, a circumstance that significantly limited the ability of women to leave a marriage that was unhappy or otherwise contrary to their private interests.

There was also a corresponding expectation that in the event of a divorce being granted, the custody of the children of the marriage inevitably would be the responsibility of the mother. It was expected that the mother would simply continue the chief parenting duties that had been discharged by her during the marriage. Custody claims by the father were rare.

The broadening of divorce availability in the 1960s to include grounds that acknowledged the consent of the marriage partners, otherwise known as no-fault divorce, was a significant impetus to the development of family law as a distinct legal discipline and area of academic study. The rise of feminism, an increase in the number of persons living in common law relationships, the blending of families through remarriage, and the legislative promotion of equality in both the provision of support and the division of matrimonial property between divorced spouses also contributed to this legal development.

With the increase in the divorce rate in the United States into the 1980s (the statistical peak in the divorce rate was reached in 1980), there was a parallel expansion in the number of circumstances where the father of the subject children advanced a custody claim. The rise of two income families contributed to making the notion of the custodial father more

Tata, a mother of five, huddles in the hallway of her apartment building. She is addicted to crack cocaine and her children have been placed in the custody of her common-law husband. © BRENDA ANN KENNEALLY/CORBIS.

socially acceptable. A number of child custody cases litigated the issue of whether mothers were inherently better caregivers and custodial candidates than fathers, with no clear precedent ever established on the point in the face of significant and often contradictory scientific data. Most jurisdictions enacted laws that entrenched the legal proposition that the 'best interest of the child' was the operative test to determine child custody in such cases. A child's best interests could include virtually any factor that impacted upon the child's general well being, including financial, social, residential, and educational circumstances; the relationship with each parent and the respective parents plans for the ongoing care of the child were at the heart of this legal test.

Kramer v. Kramer was the critically acclaimed American film produced in 1979 that epitomized the nature of the custodial battles in which parties to a divorce action became engaged. *Kramer v. Kramer* was a particularly topical work, made at a time when divorce had become an accepted outcome of marriage.

▮ PRIMARY SOURCE

Although the overwhelming majority of custody awards are made to mothers, increasingly, more mothers are losing legal and physical custody of their children after divorce. Approximately 10% of fathers retain custody of their children after divorce, and this number is growing.

There are several reasons for increases in the number of noncustodial mothers and custodial fathers. First, even if a mother is initially awarded sole custody, custodial arrangements are subject to change according to changes in a parent's circumstances or children's wishes as they grow older....

Custody and Relinquishment

...The most common reasons reported for relinquishing custody were: the children's choice intimation, court decisions, and financial problems. These reasons reflect a lack of choice on the mother's part and a sense of helplessness, supporting the notion that these mothers feel marginalized and oppressed. Two mothers explain their lack of control over the process:

He [ex-husband] agreed on joint custody... then he went behind my back and got me to move out and filed [for divorce] on desertion.

They [the children] did not want to leave their home. He [ex-husband] told me that no matter what the judge said, he would take the kids and run with them.

Mothers felt their children were greatly influenced by their fathers—either by guilt or money or both. A mother of three talks about her youngest son:

I believe that George [her son] is greatly intimidated by his father... Ted [her ex-husband] started telling George, "You no longer have to listen to your mother." Ted started telling George that I was without power in his life. So Ted took George away from me before I even left the home.

Another mother believes her children live with their father because:

Their dad bought them [the children]. Stacy left because she though he needed her, and when she wanted to come back, he put them on a guilt trip.

For several mothers, the children's well-being was of paramount importance regarding the decision to relinquish. A 38-year-old mother with two school-aged children said:

Once the court decided on temporary custody, I didn't want to put the kids through the fight. I felt like he would have manipulated the kids more if I had custody.

Another mother whose children are now grown explains:

I don't regret not fighting for custody—I didn't want to force the children to stay with me. I felt like I had to get myself on my feet first... my relationship with my children is better now.

This 48-year-old mother of two teenagers, a boy and a girl, hopes that her daughter's move to the father's home will keep her out of trouble:

She [her 16 year-old-daughter] decided I had too many rules, and the children were visiting their father on occasion, and she felt he would let her do more of what she wanted to do. She was having a lot of trouble at school... hanging around with the wrong crowd, and I think I felt maybe she would be better off trying a different situation.

A 47-year-old mother whose daughter, now 20, went to live with her ex-husband recounts:

I am torn between saying "How could you go live with your Dad when you hated him and I was always there for you," but I don't want to make her (daughter) feel guilty... I am trying to get away from manipulation.

A lack of financial resources is an important contributor for mothers' inability to fight back and get what they want from a system that seems uncaring and unmovable. An inability to secure the best legal resources was seen by one mother as a major factor as to why she lost custody:

> I had a legal aid lawyer—he had a *good* lawyer.

Another woman explains how her inability to secure financial assistance forced her to give up her children:

> I had gone to the welfare department to get help. They said I would have to move out of my house, sell my car, quit my job, and wait six months for help. At that point, I decided to give up custody due to financial problems.

Mothers reported being moderately dissatisfied with the custody arrangements while perceiving their former spouses as being very satisfied with custody arrangements. This is the same pattern documented for noncustodial fathers.... Mothers were relatively uncomfortable with their current parenting arrangements, felt guilty about not having custody of their children, and perceived that others viewed them somewhat negatively because of their noncustodial status. Several mothers perceived a lack of support and negative reactions on the part of others:

> People react negatively when you say you don't have custody—it really affects your self-esteem.

This 41-year-old mother with two school-aged sons painfully recalls:

> When we separated, my parents made me feel that I wasn't welcome. I lost friends over the situation. They [i.e., the family] have learned to live with it. They aren't happy with it but we learned to live with it. I even had friends say that I deserted my children.

Another woman talks about the lack of understanding on the part of her mother. She explains why she believes her mother is unable to support her:

> Older women have less understanding because they still think losing your children is one of the worst things.

Interestingly, one woman perceived other women as being jealous of the freedom that is believed to be connected to the noncustodial status:

> I came across women who were envious...they were very interested in my situation and would comment "I wish I could do what I wanted."

In general, mothers had difficulty dealing with their discomfort and guilt over the noncustodial status. This mother acknowledges her feelings of being different:

> It's abnormal—a mother and child not being together. I think it's an injustice what's been done [to us]

Another mother explains how difficult it is to deal with her guilt:

> I just have so many guilt feelings [over noncustodial status] that sometimes I just get really depressed about it.

This mother of a teenage daughter admits:

> I wish I could be a parent without feeling the guilt of not being perfect. I wish I would have known myself and been strong enough not to be manipulated and used... I always felt responsible and at fault for their [her daughters'] unhappiness....

SIGNIFICANCE

The above excerpt sets out the explanations tendered by a number of women as to why they had either not pursued or had relinquished child custody to their former spouses. In every case, it is apparent that the decision was not imposed by a court after the hearing of evidence as to the best interests of the child or children concerned. The decisions reflected in the excerpt are instead motivated by extra-legal factors, including the alleged manipulation of the children by their father, a lack of financial resources on the part of the non-custodial mother, and family pressures.

Since the publication of the article in 1993, the percentage of non-custodial mothers in American family structures has remained fairly constant at approximately 10 percent. The exact percentage cannot be determined due to the number of relationships, both legal marriages and those created by common law, where custody, access and child support issues are settled informally and are not the subject of a court order. While there are significant income tax consequences regarding the deductibility of child support payment from the payer's taxable income that motivate a formal court order or legal agreement, its is estimated that the custody of approximately five percent of all children whose parents are separated is governed informally.

The emotional impact of divorce and child custody disputes upon the litigants has driven the rise of alternative methods of dispute resolution since 1993, where the parties agree to attempt to settle their legal action without trial. Mediation has been a popular route to resolve child custody matters throughout North America for two general reasons. It is first a means of sparing the expense, disruption, and potential embarrassment to the litigants that is commonly associated with a public court battle. Secondly, mediations are often a useful forum in which to privately air before an independent nominee the types of issues described in the excerpt as the reasons why the mother did not pursue custody, such as suggested intimidation, "guilt trips" imposed upon on the children, and other potentially emotional issues.

Collaborative divorce is a further extension of the alternatives to divorce litigation developed in North America that have gained widespread acceptance since 2000. A collaborative divorce process is generally a cross-disciplinary approach and it may engage the services of lawyers, financial planners, child psychologists, and other experts to assist the parties in reaching an entirely negotiated resolution of all issues arising from the end of their marriage, including child custody, access, and support. The proponents of collaborative divorce refer to the process as family-based; it is evident from the excerpt that no matter who was legally correct respecting the child custody issue, the lingering emotional damage to the non-custodial mother remained.

No matter how an agreement is achieved between the parties regarding child custody, all common law jurisdictions provide that the agreement will be incorporated into the final court order governing custody. As a general rule of family law, such orders can only be revised where the parties enter into a further consent agreement or where a judge determines that there has been a material change in the circumstances of the parents or the child to warrant a change in the custodial status. Such actions are traditionally difficult to maintain as the longer a child has resided with a custodial parent, the less inclined courts are to alter the arrangements.

For these reasons, the difficulties mentioned by the non-custodial mothers in the excerpt are unlikely to ever form an appropriate basis to revise their non custodial parent status. Absent misconduct by the custodial father, the wishes of the child expressed as the child grows older is the most common basis to rework child custody arrangements.

FURTHER RESOURCES
Books

Boland, Mary L., and Brette McWhorter Sember. *Visitation Handbook*. Naperville, Ill.; Sourcebooks, 2002.

Schepard, Andrew I. *Children, Courts and Custody*. New York: Cambridge University Press, 2006.

Periodicals

Ellis, Elizabeth M. "What Have We Learned from 30 Years of Research on Families in Divorce Conflict." *Trowbridge Foundation Report* 2 (3) (2001).

Web site

Department of Justice Canada. "Overview and Assessment of Approaches to Access Enforcement." 2001 <http://www.justice.gc.ca/en/ps/pad/reports/2001-FCY-8/nature2.html> (accessed June 20, 2006).

Dr. Spock's Last Interview

Newsletter

By: Lynne Verbeek

Date: Autumn 1994

Source: Verbeek, Lynne. "Dr. Spock's Last Interview." *Parents' Press*, 1994.

About the Author: Lynne Verbeek writes for the monthly newspaper-styled publication *Parents' Press*, which is headquartered in Berkeley, California. The publication averages a circulation of about 75,000 readers in the California counties of Alameda, Contra Costa, San Francisco, Marin, and southern Solano.

INTRODUCTION

American pediatrician, educator/author, and political activist Benjamin McLane Spock (1903–1998) was a nationally known authority on child care. After establishing a private pediatrics practice in New York City, Spock wrote his first book *The Common Sense Book of Baby and Child Care* in 1946. Based on its popularity, Spock gained notoriety in the United States when he advised parents to show affection to their children and to raise them in a loving environment rather than using the authoritarian practices that was favored by most parenting authors.

Spock based his child-care advice on his studies of psychoanalysis—in which he tried to understand children's needs and how they fit into the dynamics of the family—and parental information—which he received from talking and listening to parents across the country. Basically, Spock felt that parents knew how to raise their children better than the so-called experts.

Among Spock's other writings are *A Baby's First Year*, *Feeding Your Baby and Child* (coauthored), *Decent and Indecent*, *A Teenager's Guide to Life and Love*, *Dr. Spock on Vietnam*, *A Better World for Our Children: Rebuilding American Family Values*, and *Raising Children in a Difficult Time*. Spock co-wrote his autobiog-

Pediatrician and author Dr. Benjamin Spock, holding a baby, 1988. © DOUGLAS KIRKLAND/CORBIS.

raphy, *Spock on Spock: A Memoir of Growing Up with the Century*, in 1989.

In one of his last interviews, the late Dr. Benjamin Spock spoke with Parents' Press about sex, marriage, children, and the common values than can unite and strengthen a diverse America.

Parents' Press: The term family values has so many different interpretations. What do you think are the most important values?

Dr. Benjamin Spock: There are basic values that are universal: love of family, honesty, respect of other people, and a sense of idealism that inspires people to strive for greatness. I think that the Golden Rule—treating other people with the same respect you expect for yourself—is the basis of every religious or spiritual value system the world has ever known.

Are you advocating a return to religion?

I think that the children and adults in families that adhere to a specific religion (as I don't) or a firm set of moral

standards (as I do) are fortunate. Most human beings, by their nature, want to live by some set of spiritual beliefs, whether or not they're part of a formal religion. Most societies around the world have established religions, based on similar moral precepts. It gives people's lives a firm framework, explains the mysteries of nature, and tells people clearly what their God and their fellow human beings expect of them.

What should parents model for or teach their children?

I think the most important value by far is to bring up children excited about helping other people, first in their family, and then other people outside. More than anything else, children want to help—it makes them feel grown up. That includes simple things like being able to set the table. Parents say, "Oh, I can do it quicker myself," but that misses the point. Children should be encourged to help, to be kind and loving to other people. I think these are the spiritual values that are quite obvious, But we're not paying enough attention to them.

So many kids are brought up to think of themselves first. I've heard fathers say to their sons, "You're in the world to get ahead, kid," I want to demystify the idea of spirituality by showing that it comes down to specifics like helping your parents at home, or imagining how you can grow up to be a helpful person to the world, rather than focusing on making a big pile of dough, or achieving some position in a company.

Anthropology studies from all over the world show that children can be taught any set of values that their parents and their group truly believe in. If children worship material success rather than truth or compassion, it is because they have absorbed those values from others.

We should not let children grow up believing that they are in the world primarily to acquire possessions or to get ahead. If we give them no spiritual values to live by, they are wide open to the materialism pounded in by television programs, music videos and other commercial huckersterism.

What do you think of the influence of television on our society?

Studies show that today, many children and young people get their standards **primarily** from movies and television. These media are so powerful that only forceful parents with firm beliefs can counteract the amoral or immoral values they often present. Yet objections to the glorification of violence and casual sex in television and the movies are met with protestations by civil rights activists about the chilling effect of censorship, as if that were the only issue.

To reduce violence in our society, we must eliminate violence in the home and on television. Parents should stop their children from watching inappropriate sex and violence—no excuse by parents is really valid.

I think a lot of parents are also really concerned about the constant emphasis on sex that our children are bombarded with.

Sexuality has been depersonalized and coarsened in our society. Children can see crass music videos in their homes, television sitcoms built around bathroom jokes, soap operas and TV dramas that celebrate casual sex and marital infidelity.

I think that the sex education movement itself has contributed to this problem. Sex education tries to eliminate the ignorance, fear and shame that was regularly taught to children in the past. But without presenting the spiritual and emotional aspects of sexuality, it teaches pure anatomy. If children are only taught the physical aspects of sex, they have no reason not to experiment.

Partly as a result, I think, many teenagers today regard sex not as any part of a spiritual relationship, but as a game of conquest or simply a sensual indulgence. I remember a 13-year-old girl who said to me, "Listen, sex is a perfectly normal instinct meant to be enjoyed."

It is meant to be enjoyed, but just as important, it needs to be cultivated. You need to be thinking of the other person, not just of yourself. I think we need to bring in the spiritual aspects that marriage is not for personal gratification, it is wanting to live the rest of your life with somebody, helping them, and raising fine children.

How do you explain sex to a young child, say in the 3 to 6 age group?

Children begin to ask about why boys and girls are different around the age of 2 1/2. By 3 or 3 1/2, they want to know where babies come from. The child wants a simple answer, like, the baby grows in the mother's abdomen. It may be a couple more years before the child says, by the way, what's a father for, or why do you need to be married?

Answer your child's questions simply but, I also want to say, not so simply that you leave out the spiritual aspect. I think that every time a child asks a question related to sex, parents should explain that sex is part of what makes a man and woman fall in love, want to get married, help each other, take care of each other, and take care of children together.

The depth and details depend on your child's age, but I think that love, consideration and kindness should always be emphasized.

My upbringing was full of mystery and shame and embarrassment about sexuality, and that was good to get rid of. But getting rid of the shame should be compensated by talk about the spiritual aspects of loving each other and helping each other, and what the purpose of marrying and having children really is.

One issue that's caused some discussion among our readers recently is the ideal spacing between siblings—some say three years is ideal, some say closer is better because they play together. What are your thoughts on that?

There's really no predicting ahead of time how things are going to turn out. Two years apart is one of the commonest spaces. Some are happy relationships, others are fiercely rivalrous. Parents shouldn't expect that there won't be any rivalry just because one child is three or four years older.

You try to ameliorate the rivalry by preparing the child ahead of time, letting him feel the abdomen, letting him see mom deal with other children in the neighborhood. With a 2-year-old, you have to be a little bit ingenious.

You have to not be too excited about the baby. I think that some parents, in trying to prepare the child, get so excited and ask the child to get so excited that the child says there's going to be hell to pay here.

With the holiday season coming up, do you have any suggestions about how parents can downplay the materialistic and commercial aspects?

I think greeting cards are an abomination. When birthdays and special holidays come around, children should be encouraged to make their own cards and gifts. I still remember how excited I was in about third grade to make a blotter pad for my parents for Christmas, lacing the pieces of paper together with a ribbon, and drawing a special picture of a house with smoke spiraling out of the chimney. That was many years ago, and I remember that wonderful feeling of excitement and anticipation, waiting for my mother and father to open the gift.

I want to stretch this idea by saying it's more enjoyable to give than to receive, but people won't believe me. so I'll say, I think it's as enjoyable.

SIGNIFICANCE

The ideas of Dr. Benjamin Spock with respect to parenting did not agree with the rigid methods experts traditionally proposed for raising children in the 1940s and earlier. Parents were told—as had many previous generations of parents—to strictly discipline children. For example, experts told parents not to hold their children when they cried because it would teach them to cry when wanting attention and not to display affection because children would grow up weak and dependent. When Spock introduced his now-common sense/then-radical ideas to the people of the United States, reactions of approval and controversy resulted.

Spock contended that giving children affection and love in a relaxed environment would make them happier and more likely to become secure, mature individuals. He also advised parents to be more flexible in how they raised their children and to enjoy their time together. Spock said that the advice of experts, which was generally a one-approach-fits-all attitude, was incorrect. He felt parents knew better how to raise their children than did authors of previous child-rearing books. Child-care professionals condemned and criticized Spock's ideas because they disagreed with his views. Specifically, his ideas countered what they had said for years, making their traditional methods of teaching more difficult to promote.

Many of the children of these 1940s parents revolted against the U.S. establishment during the 1960s. The perceived breakdown of society's ethics and morals and the disrespect shown of its laws and traditions were often blamed partially on Spock and his child-rearing techniques. Some people also became critical of Spock's ideas due to his opposition and protest with the Vietnam War.

Also, in the 1960s, feminists criticized Spock's books because mothers were made responsible for most of child-rearing. In the 1970s, Spock revised his books to include fatherly involvement and to refer to children using both masculine and feminine pronouns (such as him and her) rather than using only the traditional masculine ones to refer to both sexes.

Although experts criticized Spock's book *The Common Sense Book of Baby and Child Care*, parents liked what Spock said and bought his book in droves. It sold nearly one million copies annually and remained a popular book in the United States for decades after its first publication. By 1998 (the year of Spock's death), the book had sold more than fifty million copies and had been translated into thirty-nine languages. Its sales numbers make it the second best selling nonfiction book in the United States.

Spock's success is considered to have come from two basic ideals that he held. First, he listened to, and respected, parents and asked them questions on how they were raising their children. Spock wanted to learn the psychological and emotional aspects of parenting and the dynamics of parent-child relationships. Second, Spock applied his six years of advanced psychoanalytic training to child development. After learning from parents, Spock used that advice and his psychoanalytic training to write understandable child-rearing guidebooks. Consequently, Spock's words to parents gave them confidence to raise their children according to their own feelings. Spock helped parents to love their children, to develop relationships with their children, and to enjoy the time spent together with their children. Although this advice seems common sense in the 2000s, it was revolutionary in the 1940s.

Spock's ideas, which were given in a friendly and commonsense approach, directly influenced several generations of parents to raise children in more flexible and caring ways. In his day, most people considered Spock the most trusted pediatrician in the country. He continues to influence current generations of parents, as many child-care professionals and developmental psychologists now support many of his ideas of child-rearing.

FURTHER RESOURCES
Books

Bloom, Lynn Z. *Doctor Spock: A Biography of a Conservative Radical*. Indianapolis, IN: Bobbs-Merrill, 1972.

Maier, Thomas. *Dr. Spock: An American Life*. New York: Harcourt Brace, 1998.

Spock, Benjamin. *A Better World for Our Children: Rebuilding American Family Values*. Washington, DC: National Press Books, 1994.

Spock, Benjamin. *Dr. Spock's The First Two Years: The Emotional and Physical Needs of Children from Birth to Age Two*. Edited by Martin T. Stein. New York: Pocket Books, 2001.

Spock, Benjamin. *Raising Children in a Difficult Time: A Philosophy of Parental Leadership and High Ideals*. New York: Norton, 1974.

Spock, Benjamin. *A Teenager's Guide to Life and Love*. New York: Simon and Schuster, 1970.

Spock, Benjamin, and Michael B. Rothenberg. *Baby and Child Care*. New York: Pocket Books, 1985.

Spock, Benjamin, and Miriam E. Lowenberg. *Feeding Your Baby and Child*. New York: Duell, Sloan, and Pearce, 1955.

Web sites

The Dr. Spock Company. "Dr. Spock (The home page of The Dr. Spock Company)." <http://www.drspock.com/> (accessed July 12, 2006).

MacNeil/Lehrer Productions, Public Broadcasting Service. "Remembering Dr. Spock." March 16, 1998 <http://www.pbs.org/newshour/bb/health/jan-june98/spock_3–16.html> (accessed July 12, 2006).

Parents' Press. "Home page of Parents' Press." <http://www.parentspress.com/> (accessed July 12, 2006).

The Uniform Adoption Act of 1994

Legislation

By: National Conference of Commissioners on Uniform State Laws

Date: 1994

Source: *National Conference of Commissioners on Uniform State Laws.* "Uniform Adoption Act of 1994." 2002 <http://www.law.upenn.edu/bll/ulc/fnact99/1990s/uaa94.htm> (accessed June 23, 2006).

About the Author: The National Conference of Commissioners on Uniform State Laws was begun in 1892. With appointed representatives from all fifty states it works to develop and promote uniform legislation across the country.

INTRODUCTION

Children left homeless by the death of a parent, abandonment, or legal proceedings face many difficulties, and numerous approaches to their care have been considered and tried. During the nineteenth century, New York City was home to thousands of homeless and abandoned children, most of whom lived on the streets and sold rags or newspapers to survive. Charles Brace, a Christian minister, became convinced that these children needed a new start. In 1853 he formed the Children's Aid Society to relocate New York street children to rural areas and new homes.

Over the following seventy-five years the society moved more than 100,000 homeless children to rural areas where local residents were invited to consider adopting them. Many of the children were taken in by farm families, though the society was able to do little screening of prospective parents.

In 1851 Massachusetts passed the Adoption of Children Act, the first law acknowledging that the needs of children should take precedence in the adoption process. The law instructed judges to make cer-

tain that adoption arrangements were handled appropriately, though it gave no indication of exactly what this might mean. Massachusetts was also in the forefront of the move from institutional care to in-home placement and in 1869 began paying for children's care in private homes. The state also funded regular visits to foster homes to insure quality care, making it the first state in the nation to do so. In the following decades most states passed laws designed to ensure the safety and welfare of children without parents.

Although legal adoption became more common during the early twentieth century, few detailed records were kept. Specialized adoption agencies were first created during this era, offering support to adoptive parents and those wishing to give up a child for adoption. Many adoptions were also completed through private placements, in which the birth mother and her family played the primary role in arranging an adoptive placement. The 1935 Social Security Act began providing aid for dependent children, making foster care an option for many more children.

Before 1950 most adoptive parents requested children of their own race and without major health problems. The next decade brought extensive efforts to expand placement options for other children. The Urban League and similar agencies began promoting adoption for African-American children, while social service agencies began attempting adoptions involving children with physical and mental disabilities. A 1958 initiative encouraged adoption of Native American orphans, and in 1961 Congress passed legislation specifically setting conditions for the adoption of international children by U.S. citizens.

By 1994 adoption was a widely accepted practice in the United States, with 130,000 occurring annually. Roughly half these involved adoptions of children by relatives or stepparents, while as many as 10,000 involved foreign children adopted domestically and about one-fourth involved infant adoption by an unrelated adult. While adoption had made great strides, both in terms of its acceptance and in the number of children being helped, numerous legal headaches still plagued the process. Complicating difficulties within individual states were the sometimes significant differences in adoption law from state to state. In an effort to harmonize these divergent standards and encourage adoption, the National Conference of Commissioners on Uniform State Laws (NCCUSL), a century-old agency dedicated to harmonizing state laws across the nation, proposed the Uniform Adoption Act of 1994. The excerpt below, from the Act's Prefatory Note, summarizes the provisions of the Act and the principles behind them.

UNIFORM ADOPTION ACT (1994)

PREFATORY NOTE

The guiding principle of the Uniform Adoption Act is a desire to promote the welfare of children and, particularly, to facilitate the placement of minor children who cannot be raised by their original parents with adoptive parents who can offer them stable and loving homes. The Act is premised on a belief that adoption offers significant legal, economic, social and psychological benefits not only for children who might otherwise be homeless, but also for parents who are unable to care for their children, for adults who want to nurture and support children, and for state governments ultimately responsible for the well-being of children.

The Act aims to be a comprehensive and uniform state adoption code that: (1) is consistent with relevant federal constitutional and statutory law; (2) delineates the legal requirements and consequences of different kinds of adoption; (3) promotes the integrity and finality of adoptions while discouraging "trafficking" in minors; (4) respects the choices made by the parties to an adoption about how much confidentiality or openness they prefer in their relations with each other, subject, however, to judicial protection of the adoptee's welfare; and (5) promotes the interest of minor children in being raised by individuals who are committed to, and capable of, caring for them.

The most striking characteristic of contemporary adoptions is the variety of contexts in which they occur. Of the 130,000 or more adoptions that are granted each year, over half are adoptions of minor children by stepparents or relatives. Perhaps another 15–20% or more are of older children, many of whom have previously been shunted back and forth between their birth families and foster care. Many of these children come to their adoptive parents with serious psychological or physical problems that will require years of treatment and loving parental attention. Approximately 7,000–10,000 adoptions of foreign born children occur annually despite the intricate web of domestic and foreign regulations that adoptive parents have to contend with in order to complete their families. In recent years, no more than 25–30% of all adoptions involve infants adopted by unrelated adults. ...

At present, the legal process of adoption is complicated not only by the different kinds of children who are adopted and the different kinds of people who seek to adopt, but also by an extraordinarily confusing system of state, federal, and international laws and regulations. Despite allegedly common goals, state adoption laws are not and never have been uniform, and there now appear to be more inconsistencies than ever from one state to another. There are no clear answers to such basic questions as who may place a child for adoption, whose consent is required and when is consent final, how much money can be paid to whom and for what, how much information can or should be shared between birth and adoptive families, what makes an individual suitable as an adoptive parent, and what efforts are needed to encourage the permanent placement of minority children and other children with special needs who languish in foster care. Hundreds of thousands of children in this country need permanent homes, and hundreds of thousands of adults have at least some interest in adoption but are often discouraged by the confusing laws and procedures as well as by high financial and emotional costs.

To reduce this confusion—which confounds consensual adoptions and not only the relatively small number that are contested—the National Conference of Commissioners on Uniform State Laws has approved a Uniform Adoption Act to enable the States to respond more flexibly and reasonably to the changing social, economic, and constitutional character of contemporary adoption practice....

The Act meets the changing psychosocial and economic aspects of contemporary adoptions by addressing the many different kinds of adoption that now occur and the different functions they serve. Adoptions may be characterized according to the kind of individuals being adopted—minors or adults, born in this country or foreign born, with or without special needs, with or without siblings. They may also be characterized according to the kind of individuals who are adopting—married couples, single individuals, stepparents, individuals previously related or unrelated to an adoptee. Another way to characterize adoptions is according to the type of placement—direct placement by a birth parent with an adoptive parent selected by the birth parent with or without the assistance of a lawyer or an agency, or placement by a public or private agency that has acquired custody of a minor from a birth parent through a voluntary relinquishment or an involuntary termination of parental rights. A fourth way to characterize adoptions is by the nature of the proceeding—contested or uncontested.

The Act goes beyond existing statutory laws to create a coherent framework for legitimizing and regulating both direct-placement and agency-supervised adoptions. The Act will facilitate the completion of consensual adoptions and expedite the resolution of contested adoptions. By promoting the integrity and finality of adoptions, the Act will serve the interests of children in establishing and maintaining legal ties to the individuals who are committed to, and capable of, parenting them. More specifically:

(1) The Act protects minor children against unnecessary separation from their birth parents, against placement with unsuitable adoptive parents, and against harmful delays in determination of their legal status.

(2) The Act protects birth parents from unwarranted termination of their parental rights. Minor children may not be adopted without parental consent or appropriate grounds for dispensing with parental consent. The Act attempts to ensure that a decision by a birth parent to relinquish a minor child and consent to the child's adoption is informed and voluntary. Once that decision is made, however, and expressed before a judge or another individual who is not implicated in any actual or potential conflict of interest with the birth parent, the decision is final and, with very few exceptions, irrevocable.

Involuntary as well as voluntary termination proceedings conform to constitutional standards of due process, but an individual's biological ties to a child are not alone sufficient to bestow full parental rights on that individual. The Act protects the parental status of biological parents who have actually functioned as a child's parents.

(3) The Act protects adoptive parents and adopted children by providing them with whatever information is reasonably available at the time of placement about the child's background, including health, genetic, and social history, and by providing access in later years to updated medical information.

(4) The Act discourages unlawful placement activities within and across state and national boundaries by keeping track of minor children once they have been placed for adoption, distinguishing between lawful and unlawful adoption-related expenses and activities, insisting that agencies, lawyers, and other providers of professional services explain their adoption-related services and fees to people considering adoption, requiring judicial approval of adoption-related expenses, and imposing sanctions against unlawful activities.

(5) The Act encourages different kinds of people to adopt. No one may be categorically excluded from being considered as an adoptive parent. Nonetheless, preplacement (except in stepparent adoptions and when waived by a court for good cause) as well as post-placement evaluations of prospective adoptive parents are required, whether initiated by an agency or directly by a birth parent, in order to determine the suitability of particular individuals to be adoptive parents.

(6) Individuals who have served as a minor child's foster or de facto parents are given standing to seek to adopt the child, subject to the particular child's needs. Agencies receiving public funds are required actively to recruit prospective adoptive parents for children who are considered difficult to place because of their age, health, race,

ethnicity, or other special needs. The Act prohibits the delay or denial of a child's adoptive placement solely on the basis of racial or ethnic factors. A child's guardian ad litem [court-appointed representative] as well as other interested persons may seek equitable and other appropriate relief against discriminatory placement activities.

(7) The Act requires expedited hearings for contested adoptions and the appointment of a guardian ad litem for minor children whose well-being is threatened by protracted or contested proceedings. During a proceeding, courts are authorized and encouraged to make interim custody arrangements to protect minors against detrimental disruptions of stable custodial environments. Good faith efforts must be made to notify any parent or alleged parent whose rights have not previously been relinquished or terminated of the pendency of an adoption of the parent's child.

(8) The Act clarifies the relationship to adoption proceedings of the Uniform Child Custody Jurisdiction Act, the federal Parental Kidnapping Prevention Act, and the Interstate Compact on the Placement of Children. The Act supports the finality of adoption decrees by strictly limiting the time for appeals or other challenges and by presuming that a final order terminating parental rights or granting an adoption is valid. A final adoption may not be challenged by anyone for any reason more than six months after the order is entered. Even if a challenge is begun within that time, the adoption may not be set aside unless the challenger proves with clear and convincing evidence that the adoption is contrary to the child's best interests.

(9) The Act permits mutually agreed-upon communication between birth and adoptive families before and after an adoption is final. It also ensures that, except for consensual contacts, the privacy and autonomy of adoptive and birth families will be fully protected. The Act's mutual consent registry is a "user friendly" approach to the issue of whether and when to release identifying information among birth parents, adoptees, and other members of an adoptee's birth and adoptive families. This balanced and uniform procedure can be the basis of a national interstate network for the consensual disclosure of identifying information.

(10) The Act clarifies the legal and economic consequences of different types of adoption so that, within these formal structures, the emotional and psychological aspects of adoptive parent and child relationships can flourish.

SIGNIFICANCE

The proposed Uniform Adoption Act followed a series of attempts to harmonize state adoption laws. While the scope of the act was broad, major issues covered included special needs adoptions, preplacement home studies, the time allowed for a birth mother to change her mind about an adoption, and the rights of unmarried fathers. One of the more contentious aspects of the act dealt with privacy and whether adopted children should be allowed to obtain information about their birth parents. The commission eventually approved the use of mutual consent registries which provide information if both the birth parent and the adopted child (who has reached adult age) request it.

Advocates of the Uniform Adoption Act argue that any law simplifying the adoption process is welcome. They also favor reducing interstate differences in adoption law in the hope that such improvements will lead to increases in adoption. Critics of the UAA say that the act, while frequently discussing the "best interests" of the child involved never actually defines this phrase, leaving many important aspects of the adoption decision to the court or attorneys. They also believe mutual consent registries do not provide enough information to adult adoptees, particularly those whose birth parents do not register.

Like many such proposals, the Uniform Adoption Act is broad enough in scope that it has faced difficulty gaining widespread adoption. Since its completion in 1994 the act has been endorsed by the American Bar Association and the American Academy of Adoption Attorneys; as of 2006, however, only the state of Vermont had actually adopted it.

FURTHER RESOURCES

Books

Evan B. Donaldson Adoption Institute. *Benchmark Adoption Survey: Report on the Findings.* New York: Evan B. Donaldson Institute, 1997.

Martin, Deborah L., ed. *An Annotated Guide to Adoption Research: 1986–1997.* Washington, D. C.: Child Welfare League of America, 1999.

Steinberg, Gail, and Beth Hall. *Inside Transracial Adoption.* Indianapolis: Perspective Press, 2000.

Periodicals

Bachrach, C. A., et al. "On the Path to Adoption: Adoption Seeking in the U.S." *Journal of Marriage and the Family.* 53, no. 3 (1998): 705–718.

Clemetson, Lynette. "Adopted in China, Seeking Identity in America." *New York Times.* 155 (March 23, 2006): A1, A18.

D'Andrade, Amy, and Jill Berrick. "When Policy Meets Practice: The Untested Effects of Permanency Reforms in Child Welfare." *Journal of Sociology and Social Welfare.* 33 (2006): 31–52.

Web sites

Evan B. Donaldson Adoption Institute. "Benchmark Adoption Survey: First Public Opinion Survey on American Attitudes toward Adoption." 1997 <http://www.adoptioninstitute.org/survey/baexec.html> (accessed June 23, 2006).

National Adoption Day. "Adoption Statistics." 2003 <http://www.nationaladoptionday.org/2005/media/materials/Background/Adoption%20Statistics%20Factsheet.doc> (accessed June 23, 2006).

National Conference of Commissioners on Uniform State Laws. "Adoption Act." 2002 <http://www.nccusl.org/Update/ActSearchResults.aspx> (accessed June 23, 2006).

Envisioning Fatherhood: A Social Psychological Perspective on Young Men without Kids

Journal article

By: William Marsiglio, et al.

Date: April 2000

Source: Marsiglio, William, et al. "Envisioning Fatherhood: A Social Psychological Perspective on Young Men without Kids." *Family Relations* 49 (2000):138–139.

About the Author: William Marsiglio is a professor of Sociology at the University of Florida, where he has been part of the faculty since 1988. His research interests include fatherhood, human sexuality, families and primary relationships, gender, and social psychology. Marsigilo is the author of *Stepdads: Stories of Love, Hope, and Repair* (2004).

INTRODUCTION

The role of fathers has varied widely in different eras. In patriarchal societies a father might produce dozens of children with numerous wives, limiting his individual interactions with his children. In Colonial America fathers generally taught their children how to write and frequently instructed them in a trade. In most agrarian societies fathers and their children worked side-by-side in the fields.

As Americans migrated from farms to factories in the early twentieth century, the roles of fathers and mothers began to diverge. With fathers at the office or jobsite each day, much of the daily responsibility for managing the household and raising the children passed to mothers. The rise of feminism and its emphasis on the value of women and mothers coincidentally minimized the perceived importance of fathers in children's lives.

As divorce rates climbed during the twentieth century, researchers began examining how the experience of growing up in a single-parent home might impact children. Extensive research in the United States soon identified numerous disadvantages faced by children growing up in a single-parent home: These children experience more problems in school, are sick more often, and are more likely to violate the law. But recent research suggests that the specific effect of losing a parent may depend on which parent is lost. Specifically a 1998 study found that male children living without fathers were far more likely to become criminals than those living without mothers, suggesting that the influence of a father on children may be quantifiably different than the influence of a mother, and that the two probably play complimentary roles in raising children.

PRIMARY SOURCE

Envisioning Fatherhood

...When asked about the importance of fathering their own biological children, most men were quick to point out that being genetically related to children they might "father" in the future was an important feature of what they would consider to be their ideal fathering experience. Marcus, for example, indicated that biological paternity was important to him. "Cuz it's gonna be my seed. It's gonna be me. I made that being, that human being, that person. And I'm going to father it jis like my father fathered me." Meanwhile, Justin stressed his affinity for the intergenerational connection by first commenting on how proud his parents were when he graduated high school, and he noted:

> I see children as, it's like you're passing on your genes, you're passing on your hereditary information... it's like you get to a certain point in your life where you're not going to achieve much more. You're just at a stand still and you can bring up a child who can achieve great things and continue on the family.

In Justins' everyday words, he associates his desire for biological paternity and social fathering with what theorists of adult development refer to as generativity—the need to nurture and guide younger generations....

While most participants focused, as Justin did, on the relationship between themselves as a father and their potential children when evaluating the importance of biological paternity, Jerry accentuated the shared experience among prospective parents that can accompany a pregnancy.

> Just the whole thing that you and your wife will go through. Just her becoming pregnant, going to the doctors with her, and when she has her checkups, and just the whole experience pretty much. Going to the hospital with her and, being there in the delivery...

Jerry's comments reflect his appreciation for a type of collaborative approach to the prebirth process that he associates with the ideal fatherhood experience; fathering is made special by sharing the gestation process with the prospective mother....

While economic provisioning was mentioned by a number of men, participants were quick to stress the importance of fathers spending time with their kids and their desire to be actively involved in their own children's lives. Responding to what being a father meant to him, Antoine, a 19-year-old African American offered a reply that reflects the sentiments of a number of participants.

> ...Always there, no matter what you do, right or wrong, thick and thin, whatever. Somebody that's not just a provider, not just put a roof over you head, but taking care of you, gives you advice. Just your mentor and everything, friend, best friend.

Using glowing language, Reynaldo reinforced Antoine's comment by noting how his father can be a good father even while he is unemployed:

> ...my dad is a real man right now 'cause, he can support us even though he's unemployed right now, but you know, whenever he had a job, he was doing good. And he supported us and right now he is showing how he can get us through tough times right now.

Thus, for many in our sample, the essence of being a good father involved being present, approachable, a friend, and a dispenser of measured discipline.

During the course of the interviews, this general conception of the "good father" appeared to be closely related to how participants assessed their own fathers. Whether they described their fathers as positive or negative role models, the benchmark against which they articulated their assessments amounted to a fairly consistent ideal. Typically, their fathers' contributions as disciplinarians and providers were appreciated, but the men wanted these necessary roles balanced with direct involvement and emotional concern. Not surprisingly, those facets in which particular men found their own fathers lacking were the ones which they seemed most eager to improve on when they become fathers, and those qualities that the men most appreciated were the ones they hoped to emulate. At one extreme, men who felt their fathers were absent physically vowed not to leave their children fatherless. The comments of Warren, a 23-year-old African American, were representative of this small, but important group:

> I was just thinking that I didn't want to have children in X number of cities and also have a wife who wasn't the mother of those children [pause] cause that's pretty much how, what it was with my father... I never felt cheated out of a father, 'cause I think my life turned out a little better, but at the same time I would have liked to [have] known him.

At the other end of the spectrum, some men praised their fathers for developing a strong emotional connection with them or knowing how to provide just the right amount of discipline and supervision:

> I'd be a very loving father like my father was. And I would try to model myself as he raised me... I'd be firm but I'd never hit the child. I'd be very loving and supportive no matter what. Just be his best friend. [Mitchel, White, 22 years old]

> Like my father is good, so I'm gonna pretty much be the same way that he is to me. You know, not strict but having a level head and keeping me down and not letting me get out of control really. Giving me a little bit of line but not too much. [Reynaldo, Hispanic, 17 years old]

Men whose experiences fell somewhere in between these two poles presented a similar dynamic. For instance, David, who is 28 years old and White, praised his father's achievement of the provider ideal, but sees himself being emotionally closer to his children:

> Well he was a good provider. You know, he worked full time and he brought home the money, paid the bills but he wasn't like real affectionate. It didn't seem like he made an effort to like go out of his way to do things with his kids...I think I would be a lot closer to my kids than he was.

Talking about their fathers, then, became an opportunity for these men to refine their visions of themselves as future fathers by reflecting on what they valued or missed in their experience of being fathered....

SIGNIFICANCE

The 1998 study was among a flood of research studies on the impact of fathers in childrearing. Numerous findings confirmed that fathers and mothers play complimentary but distinct roles in the parenting process, and that children with both a father and a mother in the home achieve better outcomes, despite federal direct assistance of $150 billion per year for single-parent families.

Refuting contentions that fathers play a minor role in parenting, a 1997 study published by the U.S. Department of Education found that fathers play a more significant role in children's school success than mothers, and that greater father involvement in school activities led to higher grades, greater enjoyment, and fewer suspensions.

Without fathers present, self-destructive behavior becomes much more likely. Children who live apart from their fathers are four times as likely to begin smoking; the U.S. Department of Health and Human Services says they are also at dramatically greater risk of later drug and alcohol abuse. That same 1993 report noted that fatherless children are twice as likely to drop out of school, while other studies found that fatherless children had higher absenteeism.

Research has also established alarming links between fatherlessness and crime. While poverty is generally considered an accurate predictor of crime within a neighborhood, a 1988 study (Smith and Jarjoura) found that the proportion of single-parent homes in a neighborhood is actually a far more accurate predictor. A statistical analysis of incarcerated rapists and juvenile murderers found that two-thirds of them had grown up in homes without fathers present. In 1994 the American Journal of Public Health reported that children who behaved violently at school were eleven times as likely to live in a home without a father.

As the importance of fathers has become more evident and the cost of federal assistance to single mothers has skyrocketed, numerous government efforts have been launched to improve fathering in America. The U.S. Department of Health and Human Services funds an ongoing initiative to improve fathering; the effort focuses on and providing education resources to help men become better fathers. In 2004, Senators Evan Bayh and Rick Santorum cosponsored the Responsible Fatherhood Act, a federal law authorizing grants to help men become more effective fathers and to promote two-parent families. That same year President George W. Bush requested $50 million for fatherhood projects in his federal budget proposal.

FURTHER RESOURCES

Books

Blankenhorn, David. *Fatherless America: Confronting our Most Urgent Social Problem.* New York: Basic Books, 1995.

McLanahan, Sara, and Gary Sandefur. *Growing up with a Single Parent: What Hurts, What Helps.* Cambridge, Mass.: Harvard University Press, 1994.

Nappa, Mike. *Growing Up Fatherless: Healing from the Absence of Dad.* New York: Revell, 2003.

Periodicals

Denton, Rhonda E., and Charlene M. Kampfe. "The Relationship Between Family Variables and Adolescent Substance Abuse: A Literature Review." *Adolescence* 114 (1994): 475–495.

Gallagher, Maggie. "Fatherless Boys Grow Up into Dangerous Men." *Wall Street Journal* (Dec 1, 1998): A22–23.

Poponoe, David. "American Family Decline, 1960–1990: A Review and Appraisal." *Journal of Marriage and Family* 55 (3) (1993): 527—542.

Smith, Douglas, and G. Roger Jarjoura. "Social Structure and Criminal Victimization." *Journal of Research in Crime and Delinquency* 25 (1988): 27–52.

Web sites

Department of Health and Human Services. "Promoting Responsible Fatherhood." June 9, 2006 <http://fatherhood.hhs.gov/Parenting/hs.shtml> (accessed June 19, 2006).

National Fatherhood Initiative. "NFI Research." <http://www.fatherhood.org/research.asp> (accessed June 19, 2006).

ScienCentral. "Daddy's Brain." June 16, 2006 <http://www.sciencentral.com/articles/> (accessed June 19, 2006).

Ranks of Latchkey Kids Approach Seven Million

Newspaper article

By: Laurent Belsie

Date: October 31, 2000

Source: Belsie, Laurent. "Ranks of Latchkey Kids Approach Seven Million." *Christian Science Monitor* 92 (2000): 38.

About the Author: Laurent Belsie is a staff writer for the *Christian Science Monitor.* Founded in 1908, the newspaper covers U.S. and international news and social issues.

INTRODUCTION

Prior to the Industrial Age, parents frequently lived and worked in the same place, either on the farm or in the family trade. In the few cases where children attended formal schools they normally returned home after classes to find one or both parents waiting for them. As Americans gradually migrated to the cities, their lifestyles changed, with more fathers working in factories or offices. In many of these homes the mother remained at home, ready to welcome and care for children returning from school; in cases where the mother could not be at home, a nearby relative or neighbor could frequently fill this role.

In the late twentieth century, as two-income families became more common and extended families began living farther apart, after-school childcare presented a challenge, particularly to single parents. While most experts agreed that more children were spending time alone after school, little was known about the extent of the phenomenon. Two studies, released in 1995 and 1997, quantified the problem, revealing that a large segment of the child population spent time alone each day.

■ PRIMARY SOURCE

St. Louis—A generation ago, almost all children spent their after-school hours under the watchful eye of parents or neighbors. These days, as both parents increasingly work full time, many kids aren't supervised by anybody.

It's something that has nagged parents and policymakers for years, but only now are they getting comprehensive data to uncover how widespread the practice is. While various programs and initiatives have helped working parents provide day care for preschool children, new research suggests that attention to the needs of school-age children has lagged.

According to a Census report released today, almost half of all kids ages 12 to 14 spent just under seven hours home alone, and roughly 1 of every 10 elementary-school children spends 4-1/2 hours a week unsupervised by an adult. Some of them are as young as five years old.

With almost no historical data, comparisons with the past are problematic, and experts are unsure whether the ranks of so-called latchkey children are growing. But they agree that the numbers are a cause for concern—especially because the afternoon hours are the peak time for juvenile crime.

"We've given attention to child care and early childhood, but kids don't magically disappear when they turn 3 or 5 or 12," says Nancy Rankin of the National Parenting Association in New York. "In many ways, children's needs grow more complicated as adolescents."

Today's US Census Bureau report concludes that 6.9 million school children—nearly 20 percent of those between the ages of 5 and 14—regularly cared for themselves without an adult around. Most of those were 12 or older. But even among younger children, the numbers proved significant.

Some 2 percent of the nation's five-year-olds spent an average of 4½ hours a week unsupervised by an adult (although they may have been with an older sibling). It's this group of children—aged 5 to 11—that is causing the greatest consternation.

"We feel concerned about the younger children," says Kathryn Tout, research associate with Child Trends, a nonprofit research group in Washington. "It's a missed opportunity for them to be in a setting that's more developmentally appropriate. But also it could be potentially dangerous."

The Census numbers are somewhat outdated, since they report 1995 figures. But a Child Trends report released last month shows much the same phenomenon. Using 1997 data from the Urban Institute, the group found that some 4 million children aged 6 to 12 who had working mothers spent time home alone. If anything, these figures may underestimate the situation, Ms. Tout adds, because parents are reluctant to report that they leave their children unsupervised.

The reasons parents are letting their kids fend for themselves are not surprising. The biggest factor is that parents lack time because more of them are employed and work longer hours than they did a generation ago.

The percentage of married mothers who work outside the home nearly doubled between 1969 and 1996. As a result, the average family today has 22 fewer hours each week to spend at home than families had 30 years ago, says the Council of Economic Advisers. That's nearly a day less per week; more than two years by the time a child graduates from high school.

That time deficit explains much. Grade-school children with working parents are more than twice as likely to spend part of the day caring for themselves than those whose parents don't, says Kristin Smith, author of the Census report. The general pattern holds true in single-parent as well as dual-parent households. Even mothers who work part-time are far more likely to rely on their children for self-care than mothers who don't work, she adds.

Beyond that, however, the trends get murky. The poorest families are least able to pay for child care. Yet the Census data show they're far less likely to leave their children at home than families who earn at least twice the poverty income. Of course, families that work more, earn more, says Ms. Smith, and they're more likely to live in better neighborhoods where they would feel comfortable leaving children unsupervised.

Another potential factor for children home alone is the rising cost of child care. In 1995, parents paid an average $85 a week for such care—about 50 percent more than they spent a decade earlier, even after adjusting for inflation. And based on further analysis not yet published, Smith says, it appears these child-care costs are a big reason many families choose to leave even five- to eight-year-olds to care for themselves a few hours a week.

Because the research is so new, no one is certain which way the trend is going.

Some researchers suggest that welfare reform, which pushed many poor people into the work force, may be causing the numbers to rise. Others say the numbers of home-alone children may be falling, because of funding boosts from the Clinton administration and private efforts such as the Boys & Girls Clubs of America to increase the number of after-school programs in the United States.

In the end, today's mothers have been able to spend about as much time with their children as mothers in the 1960s, mostly by spending less time on housework and adjusting work schedules. Mothers in both eras spent about 5.5 waking hours each day with their children, says Suzanne Bianchi, a sociology professor at the University of Maryland at College Park.

But many researchers wonder whether parents' current pace is sustainable. "It used to be that… society was organized so that women would be at home to take care of these needs," says Donna Lenhoff, general counsel for the National Partnership for Women and Families in Washington. "Our society is no longer organized like that. But we haven't restructured the workplace."

SIGNIFICANCE

The studies described in this article contained a mix of good news and bad news. On the positive side, mothers in the 1990s spent almost the same amount of time with their children as did mothers in the 1960s, averaging five to six hours per day. However, more children appeared to be spending significant amounts of time alone or without adult supervision in the 1990s. Particularly troubling was the study's finding that a small group of five year olds were spending

A boy lets himself into his home in Dagenham, Kent, while his mother and father are still at work, January 7, 1956. PHOTO BY JOSEPH MCKEOWN/PICTURE POST/GETTY IMAGES.

close to an hour per day without any adult supervision. These findings have fueled the efforts of advocates of state or federally sponsored after-school programs.

Additional research has demonstrated the potential value of after-school programs. A 2000 study conducted by the U.S. Department of Education found that young people who attend well-run after-school programs earn better grades and higher conduct evaluations; they are also less likely to use drugs, engage in violence, or become pregnant. A 2001 study funded by the YMCA found that 79 percent of students in after-school programs were A or B students, while teens not in such programs are five times as likely to be poor students. While this study's findings do not establish a direct link between after-school programs and higher grades, they do suggest that more positive outcomes are associated with after-school programs.

Another 2000 study looked at the impact of after-school outcomes associated with participation in Boys' Clubs and Girls' Clubs. In a simple comparison between five housing areas with clubs and five without, the five without the programs experienced 30 to 50 percent more vandalism and drug activity than those that had after-school programs. A two-year Canadian study followed the progress of a housing project that instituted after-school recreational and job-training programs. Over the course of the study, juvenile arrests fell by 75 percent from the years before the study.

While the benefits of after-school programs appear well-documented by numerous studies, such programs are frequently opposed because of their costs. After-school care for children is expensive even in its most basic forms. In 2003 the Children's Defense Fund estimated the monthly cost of full-time daycare at $250 to $1200, depending on the location and services provided. While after-school care is less expensive than full-day care, it remains unaffordable for some poor families. A 1993 study by the Census Bureau found that the average employed mother with children under age 5 spent $79.00 per week for child care.

In 2002 the state of California passed a comprehensive law expanding after-school programs for at-risk children. This act allocated an additional $433 million to expand services to almost 500,000 more students throughout the state. While the cost of the program was substantial, advocates pointed to an enormous estimated payback: for each dollar spent on the program, Californians could expect to save from $9.00 to $13.00 in other costs. While some of these savings accrued due to reduced child-care costs paid by individuals, the majority of the benefit accrued from expected reductions in crime-related costs, based on the demonstrated relationship between after-school programs and lower crime rates. The study noted that a career criminal will cost the state $1.4 to $1.7 million over his lifetime, providing tremendous financial incentive to stop teens from entering a criminal lifestyle.

After-school programs, while theoretically providing enormous financial returns, have faced opposition from several fronts. Some religious groups oppose the state's involvement in providing after-school care, believing that this is the responsibility of families. Lawmakers in general often struggle to fund programs the benefits of which are many years in the future but the costs of which occur today; politicians eager for re-election often prefer to fund programs that show short-term benefits, allowing them to trumpet their achievements to voters.

FURTHER RESOURCES

Books

Fashola, Olatokunbo S. *Building Effective Afterschool Programs*. Thousand Oaks, Calif.: Corwin Press/ Sage, 2002.

Noam, Gil G., et al. *Afterschool Education: Approaches to an Emerging Field*. Cambridge, Mass.: Harvard Education Press, 2002.

Rall, Ted and Jules Feiffer. *Revenge of the Latchkey Kids: An Illustrated Guide to Surviving the 90s and Beyond*. New York: Workman, 1998.

Periodicals

Borut, Donald J. "Cities Taking the Lead to Provide Quality Afterschool Programs." *Nation's Cities Weekly* 29 (2006): 2.

J. L. T. "After-School Programs." *Education Week* 25 (2006): 12.

Web sites

Afterschool Alliance. "Afterschool Outcomes." <http://www.afterschoolalliance.org/after_out.cfm> (accessed June 28, 2006).

Nellie Mae Education Foundation. "Critical Hours: Afterschool Programs and Educational Success." <http://www.nmefdn.org/CriticalHours.htm> (accessed June 28, 2006).

William T. Grant Foundation. "The Impact of After-School Programs: Interpreting the Results of Four Recent Evaluations." January 16, 2004 <http://www.wtgrant foundation.org/usr_doc/After-school_paper.pdf> (accessed June 28, 2006).

Happy Father's Day

Interview

By: Abigail Garner

Date: June 14, 2001

Source: *National Public Radio*. "Happy Fathers' Day." <http://damnstraight.oversampled.net/2001/06/14/happy-fathers-day/> (accessed June 15, 2006).

About the Author: Abigail Garner grew up in a home with homosexual parents and now writes and speaks on homosexual rights. She is the author of *Families Like Mine: Children of Gay Parents Tell It Like It Is*. She is creator of the website FamiliesLikeMine.com.

INTRODUCTION

As a minority, homosexuals have encountered a variety of responses throughout history. In the United States, they have been alternately ignored, mocked, attacked, and accepted. American law related to homosexuals is a complicated patchwork of prohibitions and permissions; public acceptance also varies widely. With the exception of a few strident antigay activists, most Americans ignore the reality of homosexuals living among them. In some communities homosexuality has been openly acknowledged, while in others it has remained closeted.

Despite the numerous stereotypes of gay men, many of them live in committed monogamous relationships, and a surprising number raise children. A study by the Urban Institute estimated that in 2000 approximately 250,000 children lived with one or more gay parents, although estimates from the gay community put the number much higher. Children in these families often report unique experiences as a result of living in a family that is inherently different.

■ PRIMARY SOURCE

Happy Father's Day

Once again, I am shuffling through the rows and rows of greeting cards for Father's Day. I am almost certain I won't find what I'm looking for. Actually, I already have a card for my biological father.

The card I am still looking for is for Russ, my "other father" as I sometimes refer to him. Russ has been in my life since I was five years old. Back then, I safely referred to him as my father's roommate. As I got older, I grew more comfortable referring to him as my father's lover. And somewhere along the way, the current term, "partner" became most accepted.

How ever I have described Russ over the years, he has always been an important part of my life. And I use Father's Day as an opportunity to tell him. But I'm pretty certain he already knows, because, as in other gay families, having to explain or justify what we mean to each other can be an every day occurrence.

You see, Russ and I have been "family" to each other for the past 23 years. I am used to declaring our relationship to almost everyone I meet because neither law nor society officially recognizes us as family. Because of that lack of recognition, issues that heterosexual families take for granted can become nightmares for gay families.

Our families have to create extra legal documents to make sure that we are protected in issues of custody, property and inheritance that are automatic in heterosexual families. In the event of a medical emergency, our families can only cross our fingers that we will encounter hospital staff who understand our definition of family and will allow us access to our loved ones. Those are just two examples of how children with gay and lesbian parents are continually reminded that our society questions the validity of our families.

And then there are less major, although just as annoying challenges, like finding an appropriate greeting card for my father's partner on Father's Day.

There is that small but growing section of cards under the heading "like a father" intended for mentors, uncles and male role models. But most refer to the like-a-father person as a substitute for an absent father, rather than a complementary parental unit to the father I already have.

If we relied on greeting cards to represent a cross section of our society, you'd never guess that there are more than 10 million children growing up with one or more parents who are gay or lesbian. I have yet to see a greeting card that begins with "For my second mother," or "For my daddy and my papa."

How long will it be until I can shop for TWO cards for Father's Day without the annual reminder that my family is considered to be "alternative?"

Then again, will it really be a victory when I can rely on a greeting card company to tritely summarize my relationship with Russ?

For now, these questions remain hypothetical as families like mine still linger quietly in the background of American society. And that's why, at that age of 29, I'm facing another year where I will be pulling out the construction paper and markers to create another customized Father's Day card. Just for my Russ.

SIGNIFICANCE

As homosexuality entered public dialog in the 1980s and 1990s, attention focused on the demographics of same-sex couples. The United States Census, while not explicitly asking respondents about their sexual orientation, did include questions useful in identifying homosexual couples. As of 2000, census data places the ratio of these households at approximately 1% of total households, or roughly 600,000 homes.

While same-sex couples make up only a small percentage of the nation's families, they exercise an inordinate amount of financial influence. Census Bureau data for 2003 put the mean income level for same-sex households at more than $72,000, compared to the national family average of less than $44,000. That same year 22% of same-sex couples earned more than $93,000, making them a particularly affluent market segment.

Classic Father's Day gifts. © ROYALTY-FREE/CORBIS.

Despite the rich profit potential in gay and lesbian markets, American corporations have only recently begun to target this segment. In the 1990's, gay and lesbian groups began scheduling annual gatherings at Disney World; though not officially sponsoring the event, Disney Corporation encouraged and privately supported the events, earning them criticism and a decade-long boycott from the conservative American Family Association (AFA).

Ford Motors began advertising its upscale Jaguar, Land Rover, and Volvo vehicles in predominantly gay publications in 2005, but ended two of the three campaigns following an AFA petition drive. Gay activists criticized the decision, but Ford said that its marketing decisions were based on economics rather than social policy.

Microsoft, located in socially progressive Washington state, has long prohibited sexual orientation discrimination in hiring and offers company benefits to domestic partners. In 2001 a California-based gay advocacy group recognized the company for its support of gay and lesbian rights within the company and in the community. In 2005 Washington state lawmakers considered a bill that would outlaw sexual-orientation discrimination in housing and employment, and Microsoft announced its corporate support for the bill.

In the weeks following the announcement, however, Microsoft officials received a barrage of criticism. In April company President Steve Ballmer announced a change in their position, citing division among the firm's employees. The legislation failed to pass, earning Microsoft the ire of gay rights groups.

Despite the potential pitfalls, American companies are expected to seek inroads into the affluent gay marketplace due to its sheer size: A 2002 estimate put spending by gay and lesbian parents at $22 billion.

With such enormous sums at stake, products targeted specifically at the homosexual community are likely to proliferate. American companies have a long and successful history of targeting new customer groups while deftly retaining existing buyers.

FURTHER RESOURCES

Books

Lukebill, Grant. *Untold Millions: Secret Truths about Marketing to Gay and Lesbian Consumers.* San Francisco, California: Harrington Park Press, 1999.

Schulman, Sarah. *Stagestruck: Theater, AIDS, and the Marketing of Gay America.* Durham, NC: Duke University Press, 1998.

Wardlow, Daniel L., ed. *Gays, Lesbians, and Consumer Behavior: Theory, Practice, and Research Issues in Marketing.* Binghamton, NY: The Haworth Press, 1996.

Periodicals

Kiley, David. "Ford vs. the Religious Right, Round 2." *BusinessWeek.* (March 15, 2006):14.

van der Pool, Lisa. "PR Industry Divided on How to Reach Gays." *Brandweek.* 44 (2004): 6.

Yamey, Gavin. "Gay Tobacco Ads Come out of the Closet." *British Medical Journal.* 327 (August 2, 2003): 296.

Web sites

American Public Media. "Gay Marketing: Stranger to the Closet." June 7, 2005 <http://marketplace.publicradio.org/shows/2005/06/07/PM200506071.html> (accessed June 15, 2006).

Fox News. "Fortune 500 Companies See Money in Gay Families." May 26, 2004 <http://www.foxnews.com/story/0,2933,120902,00.html> (accessed June 15, 2006).

Washington Post. "Microsoft Draws Fire for Shift on Gay Rights Bill." April 26, 2005 <http://www.washingtonpost.com/wp-dyn/content/article/2005/04/25/AR2005042501266.html> (accessed June 15, 2006).

Out of Step and Having a Baby

Newspaper article

By: Molly Jong-Fast

Date: October 5, 2003

Source: Jong-Fast, Molly. "Out of Step and Having a Baby." *New York Times* (October 5, 2003)

About the Author: Molly Jong-Fast, the daughter of best-selling author Erica Jong (*Fear of Flying*), is the author of *The Sex Doctors in the Basement* and *Normal Girl.* Her essays have appeared in the *New York Times,* *Mademoiselle,* and *Modern Bride.*

INTRODUCTION

In 2002, the average age of mothers giving birth for the first time was 25.1 years; this figure includes all mothers in the United States across all ethnic groups, incomes, education levels, and geographic areas. Meanwhile, the average number of children per woman remains at 2.1, just barely above replacement levels for the current population. Among highly educated women and women in urban centers, however, the notion of giving birth in one's twenties has become unpopular, just as families with more than two children in these sectors are considered abnormal.

Well-educated, career-oriented women in cities such as New York, Los Angeles, or Chicago have been postponing birth and motherhood from the twenties to the late thirties or forties as part of a trend that spans nearly two decades; in her 2002 book, *Creating a Life: Professional Women and the Quest for Children,* economist Sylvia Ann Hewlett created controversy among feminists with her assertion that delaying motherhood into the late thirties and early forties was playing with fire; biological clocks are very real, according to Hewlett, and the modern notion that women can finish college, spend fifteen years climbing the corporate ladder, and then focus on childbearing in their late thirties with fresh eggs ready for conception is a myth. Twenty percent of all women over the age of forty are childless; for women earning more than $100,000 per year, that figure is forty-nine percent. Fearful of the "Mommy Track" in which high achievers feel derailed and fear demotion as a result of having children, many women seek to establish themselves firmly in the professional world before having children. According to Hewlett, however, by the time many of these women are ready for kids, their reproductive systems have timed out.

The American Infertility Association agrees; by the time a woman reaches the age of forty-two, the chance of having a child with her own egg is approximately ten percent. When Hewlett's book gained media attention, feminist organizations such as the National Organization for Women denounced Hewlett's premise, arguing that it created an artificial urgency that polarized the family vs. career debate further.

A mother and her baby. © A. INDEN/ZEFA/CORBIS.

Molly Jong-Fast, the daughter of writer Erika Jong, who captured the spirit of the sexual revolution in the 1970s from a woman's perspective in her book *Fear of Flying*, found herself in the middle of this debate when, as a young professional in New York City, she found herself unexpectedly pregnant at the age of twenty-four.

■ PRIMARY SOURCE

"You don't have to be a hero here," my friend Jane said, stroking my arm. "This is your future, the rest of your life. Don't throw it all away." She took my hand solemnly. "You don't have to have this baby, you know."

It was a scene that must have played itself out in a hundred Lifetime movies: the pregnant teenager and her older, wiser friend. Except I wasn't a teenager. I was 24.

The scene took place a few months ago, and I was in my apartment drinking lemonade with Jane, who is 35. She had brought over the galleys of her novel for me to look at, and the pages were spread across my dining room table. "I mean, come on, Moll," she said in a tone that was supposed to be consoling. "Think of your parents."

My parents were gleeful at the promise of a grand-child, but the reaction of my other 30-something friends was the same as Jane's: shock, shame and pity that I was having a baby in my 20s. When I broke what I thought was the joyous news, Kim, a high-profile ad executive, childless and recently divorced, neatly explained her philosophy about children.

"They ruin your life," she said. "It's never going to be about you again. Your relationship will change, every-thing will change."

Kim believes you are not supposed to have children until you are financially stable, have a nanny ready and have had at least one book on the New York Times best-seller list. Everyone knows having a book on the Times best-seller list makes you an amazing mom.

Still, I understood where she and Jane were coming from. Almost none of my friends in their early 30s have children, let alone 10-year-olds, which is what I will have when I am their age. They have spent the last decade finishing graduate school, writing books and working 12-hour days—the kind of life I always thought I would have.

In the privileged and pampered Upper East Side, where I grew up, no one ever dropped out of school to have a baby. And no one found herself pregnant, as I had, by accident. We all saw a certain brilliant gynecologist who specialized in adolescents, who, while refusing all insurance, also refused to allow a patient out the door without several birth control options tucked safely into her monogrammed L. L. Bean backpack. As for sex education at school, the basic message was that pregnancy was just another venereal disease. (Yes, it's that dangerous!)

Finally, if—God forbid—anyone ever did get pregnant (and as far as I know, no one at the Riverdale Country School ever did), Mummy would simply take you to Paris for a few nights at the Crillon and a dose of RU-486.

After navigating both high school and college without assuming any dependents, I entered adulthood with my fear of childbearing intact. My plan was to spend my 20s working like a dog, marry, write 10 books, 3 TV shows and 40 magazine articles, finish my Master of Fine Arts degree and then maybe in 10 years think about having a baby. But then I became engaged, and within a few weeks of moving into a one-bedroom apartment with my fiancé, I learned I was pregnant.

Even though I had never seen myself as the mother type and I was (and still am) horrified at the idea of all the physical pain associated with childbirth, like a lot of women, when I saw those two red lines on the preg-nancy test stick, my whole attitude changed. So out went the numerous last-minute trips to Europe, my immediate plans to finish my M.F.A., and in came the remonstrances from my older and successful friends.

Maybe there is something wrong with me, maybe I am heading for disaster, but I am just not that scared. Sure, I worry that I will have a miscarriage or that the baby will have a collapsed lung, but I'm not afraid of a baby slowing down my career.

I am not afraid of a baby ruining my marriage. I am not afraid of a baby. Of course part of the reason I am not that afraid is because I have no idea what having a child entails. Recently when I was holding a baby who spat up, I almost threw up too. And I just learned that kids do not go to school until they are 3. I was thinking maybe 6 months.

Another reason I am not so scared of what I might miss, though, is because another fear has trumped it: being 10 years older and not having a child. I belong to a generation of people mortally afraid of becoming what the generation before it became so proudly (and documented in many ambitious and wildly amusing women-looking-for-love novels): 30-something workaholics who have devoted their lives to their jobs and are now desperate to have children but quickly losing the battle with time.

It also helps that I am in no way alone. In fact, looking around sometimes, it seems as if babies are the new Birkin bag. There is Angela Lindvall holding her enormous baby with her "notice I didn't gain any weight" pose; Kate Hudson, pregnant, getting a latte wearing only hot pants and a tiny top; Brandi documenting her labor for MTV; and Reese Witherspoon looking rosy-cheeked as she plays sleazy Becky Sharp in the forthcoming movie, "Vanity Fair." Was anyone in the Brat Pack pregnant during their "St. Elmo's Fire" years?

I am in no way comparing myself to these lovely luminaries. They have cute little pregnancy bumps and I have a truck-driver gut. They have multiple nannies and I have multiple spider veins.

But I also have friends who have had babies earlier than I will have mine. One, Nichole, married a movie star, moved to Los Angeles, and promptly had two sons, all before she was 23. My friend Sarah had a child at 23. Now the child is 3, and when Sarah pushes him around Park Slope, she is constantly asked if she is the nanny.

Of course I still had some trepidation; I was in the middle of writing a series of essays about my enormous out-of-control wedding for Modern Bride magazine. When I became pregnant, I was terrified that they would cancel my contract and tell me to hit the road. I was so nervous, I asked my agent to call with the news. But my editor didn't bat an eyelash. I guess they really are modern.

When my mother (the author Erica Jong) was pregnant with me at the age of 36, the first thing her editor at New American Library did was to take out a life insurance policy on her; not exactly a vote of confidence.

I used to think I would have my first child at 41. I used to think I would be the one making those surreptitious trips to Paris. But the truth was that I just didn't know myself at all. I hate Paris. I hate flying. Maybe having a baby will slow my career; maybe I will have to spend more time than I want at a Y.M.C.A. pool and less at the rooftop pool of Soho House. But, wait. I've never been there anyway.

SIGNIFICANCE

Arlene Rossen Cardoza, in her 1986 book *Sequencing*, defined sequencing as "having it all"—career, marriage, children—but not at the same time. Cardozo recommended sequencing life by choosing an order—college, marriage, career, children, or marriage, children, college, career—rather than trying to be a "superwoman" juggling all of the roles and mastering none.

Jong-Fast's essay notes the peer pressure from accomplished women in her social network, women in their thirties and forties who are sequencing, postponing childbirth and motherhood for the sake of graduate school or careers. Jong-Fast's pregnancy, in her social network, violates social norms as her young age is viewed by friends as a time for personal and professional development, not motherhood.

This shift in attitude between Jong-Fast's generation and her mother's generation, as evidenced by the anecdote concerning her mother's editor, demonstrates a sea change among a small sector of highly educated, urban-dwelling women in the United States. However, among women of lower education levels, lower incomes, and in more rural areas, motherhood at twenty-four would not be considered deviant or abnormal; indeed, the national average of 25.1 years for the age of the birth of one's first child includes teenage mothers as well as women over the age of fifty using in-vitro fertilization with donor eggs. It is Jong-Fast's social network that defines her becoming a mother at twenty-four or twenty-five as out of the norm.

Jong-Fast notes many of the principles outlined by both Cardoza and Hewlett's books, books that were cast in a negative light by many feminists and women who fall into Jong-Fast's peer group when first published. Those ideas have become more mainstream—as evidenced by Jong-Fast's adoption of some of the ideas and by coverage of these topics in such mainstream press outlets as *Time* magazine and *Salon*—as women struggle in the twenty-first century to balance gender role expectations, careers, motherhood, and family.

FURTHER RESOURCES

Books

Cardoza, Arlene Rossen. *Sequencing*. Minneapolis, Minn.: Brownstone Books, 1986.

Crittenden, Ann. *The Price of Motherhood: Why the Most Important Job in the World is Still the Least Valued*. New York: Owl Books, 2002.

Hewlett, Sylvia Ann. *Creating a Life: What Every Woman Needs to Know About Having a Baby and a Career*. New York: Miramax, 2002.

Maushart, Susan. *The Mask of Motherhood: How Becoming a Mother Changes Our Lives and Why We Never Talk About It*. New York: Penguin, 2000.

Warner, Judith. *Perfect Madness: Motherhood in the Age of Anxiety*. New York: Riverhead Hardcover, 2005.

Wolf, Naomi. *Misconceptions: Truth, Lies, and the Unexpected on the Journey to Motherhood*. Garden City, N.Y.: Anchor, 2003.

Periodicals

Miller, Amalia R. "The Effects of Motherhood Timing on Career Path." *Department of Economics, University of Virginia*. (July 2005).

The New Red Diaper Babies

Newpaper editorial

By: David Brooks

Date: December 7, 2004

Source: *NYTimes.com*. "The New Red-Diaper Babies." December 7, 2004 <http://www.nytimes.com/2004/12/07/opinion/> (accessed June 22, 2006).

About the Author: David Brooks has been writing a weekly column for *The New York Times* since 2003. He is also a senior editor for *The Weekly Standard*, and a contributing editor for *The Atlantic Monthly* and *Newsweek*. His media credits include commentary on National Public Radio and CNN's "Late Edition." He has authored two books, "Bobos in Paradise: The New Upper Class and How They Got There" (2000) and "On Paradise Drive: How We Live Now (And Always Have) in the Future Tense" (2004). He has described himself as a political conservative, stating that he

approaches his journalistic and political commentary from that political perspective.

INTRODUCTION

Natalists, from the Latin word for birth, believe that it is their duty to procreate and to have as many children as possible. They also believe that their primary duties are to home and family, and that raising their children to the best of their abilities is the driving force in their lives. In countries with economic problems or very small populations, natalism serves a significant purpose: bolstering population size and providing much-needed workers. The youth of developing, or largely agrarian (farming) countries, by working with or for their families, are typically paid less than unrelated (hired) help, while reducing the overall unemployment rate. Some of the more developed countries, such as Italy and France, that are facing critical decreases in population growth, have offered married couples pro-natalist financial incentives in the form of tax credits and fees paid for live births—although the latter movement was the recipient of negative commentary by the media. Much of Western Europe, many countries in Latin America, and numerous larger cities across the United States have reported significantly decreased birth rates. It is becoming progressively more common for people to marry later in life and to have fewer children, particularly among two-career couples and those who live in larger or more expensive cities (related to cost of living and real estate prices).

The natalist trend in the United States has broad demographic markers: those with larger families tend to migrate to the most rapidly growing suburbs and exurbs, primarily located across the Great Plains and central regions of the United States. Those with larger, or increasing families also tend to marry young, to begin having children within a short period of time after marriage, to be politically and fiscally conservative, to attend church or religious services regularly, to have a "stay at home mother/parent," and to seek out living areas based on child-friendliness. They tend to move to areas where housing is of increased value and affordability, where crime is low and neighborhoods are considered "safe" for children to play in. Some of those who refer to themselves as natalists state that their religious values dictate family size, citing Biblical passages commanding people to "be fruitful and multiply." For those families, quality of life is reported to be of paramount importance, along with the welfare of the nuclear family. Decisions about where to live are largely dictated by familial, rather than occupational and economic, considerations.

A family of six pose in front of their new house. © ROYALTY-FREE/CORBIS.

PRIMARY SOURCE

There is a little-known movement sweeping across the United States. The movement is "natalism."

All across the industrialized world, birthrates are falling—in Western Europe, in Canada and in many regions of the United States. People are marrying later and having fewer kids. But spread around this country, and concentrated in certain areas, the natalists defy these trends.

They are having three, four or more kids. Their personal identity is defined by parenthood. They are more spiritually, emotionally and physically invested in their homes than in any other sphere of life, having concluded that parenthood is the most enriching and elevating thing they can do. Very often they have sacrificed pleasures like sophisticated movies, restaurant dining and foreign travel, let alone competitive careers and disposable income, for the sake of their parental calling.

In a world that often makes it hard to raise large families, many are willing to move to find places that are congenial to natalist values. The fastest-growing regions of the country tend to have the highest concentrations of children. Young families move away from what they perceive as disorder, vulgarity and danger and move to places like Douglas County in Colorado (which is the fastest-growing county in the country and has one of the highest concentrations of kids). Some people see these exurbs as sprawling, materialistic wastelands, but many natalists see them as clean, orderly and affordable places where they can nurture children.

If you wanted a one-sentence explanation for the explosive growth of far-flung suburbs, it would be that when people get money, one of the first things they do is use it to try to protect their children from bad influences.

So there are significant fertility inequalities across regions. People on the Great Plains and in the Southwest are much more fertile than people in New England or on the Pacific coast.

You can see surprising political correlations. As Steve Sailer pointed out in The American Conservative, George Bush carried the 19 states with the highest white fertility rates, and 25 of the top 26. John Kerry won the 16 states with the lowest rates.

In The New Republic Online, Joel Kotkin and William Frey observe, "Democrats swept the largely childless cities—true blue locales like San Francisco, Portland, Seattle, Boston and Manhattan have the lowest percentages of children in the nation—but generally had poor showings in those places where families are settling down, notably the Sun Belt cities, exurbs and outer suburbs of older metropolitan areas."

Politicians will try to pander to this group. They should know this is a spiritual movement, not a political one. The people who are having big families are explicitly rejecting materialistic incentives and hyperindividualism. It costs a middle-class family upward of $200,000 to raise a child. These people are saying money and ambition will not be their gods.

Natalists resist the declining fertility trends not because of income, education or other socioeconomic characteristics. It's attitudes. People with larger families tend to attend religious services more often, and tend to have more traditional gender roles.

I draw attention to natalists because they're an important feature of our national life. Because of them, the U.S. stands out in all sorts of demographic and cultural categories. But I do it also because when we talk about the divide on values in this country, caricatured in the red and blue maps, it's important that we understand the true motive forces behind it.

Natalists are associated with red America, but they're not launching a jihad. The differences between them and people on the other side of the cultural or political divide are differences of degree, not kind. Like most Americans, but perhaps more anxiously, they try to shepherd their kids through supermarket checkouts lined with screaming Cosmo or Maxim cover lines. Like most Americans, but maybe more so, they suspect that we won't solve our social problems or see improvements in our schools as long as many kids are growing up in barely functioning families.

Like most Americans, and maybe more so because they tend to marry earlier, they find themselves confronting the consequences of divorce. Like most Americans, they wonder how we can be tolerant of diverse lifestyles while still preserving the family institutions that are under threat.

What they cherish, like most Americans, is the self-sacrificial love shown by parents. People who have enough kids for a basketball team are too busy to fight a culture war.

SIGNIFICANCE

Based upon United States Census data, areas of the country with rapidly growing population size and affordable housing tend to be populated more by those who vote Republican rather than by those who identify themselves as Democrats. Geographic areas in which people identify themselves as politically and fiscally conservative tend to have a larger proportion of owned than rented homes, married rather than single people, and larger (more than two children) rather than smaller families, based on reported population statistics. Those "booming" areas tend to be away from coastal regions of the United States, as it is more possible for suburban areas to continue to expand in areas that are not locked by geography, such as those bordered by water or high mountains. States with the fastest growing, most geographically spread out, suburbs have higher percentages of registered Republicans than registered Democrats. There is a strong positive correlation between ability to utilize existing open land to expand areas of home construction and the cost of housing, and a concomitant positive correlation between lower cost housing in non-urban areas and registered Republican voters.

Families with more than two children are a relative rarity in the developed, particularly the Western, world. According to the United States Census for the year 2000, heterosexual couples that choose to procreate produce an average of 1.87 children. Families with six or more children are considered an extreme rarity in the United States in the twenty-first century; they account for less than 6% of the total reporting population. The rate for family size is similar in Spain, Sweden, Italy, France, New Zealand, the Netherlands, and Australia (fewer than two children); Canada has reported that less than 1% of all families have more than five children. Much of the research done on larger families appears to have been concerned with family planning and contraception issues, as well as with reasons people cite for increased family size. There is data indicating that those who choose to have larger families may be subject to social pressure and judgments from others. As a result, they may feel pressure to relocate to areas with families that look similar to theirs (in terms of number of children or family make-up) in order to avoid perceptions of social stigma. Clusters of families with similar demographics may afford social support, shared value systems and, possibly, religious or spiritual beliefs, and familiarity—and, therefore, comfort—with exigencies of daily life. Social support, and a sense of "belongingness" or community are routinely reported to social science researchers as being integral to engendering feelings of comfort and happiness with home location or neighborhood. In relatively homogeneous communities, that is, those with many families with similar make up in terms of family size, housing costs, and income and expense levels, there are often also similar political values. Families with large numbers of children relative to income and debt ratios have little choice but to be fiscally conservative. Those who are fiscally conservative tend to follow suit with their political leanings and voting preferences.

FURTHER RESOURCES
Books

Bock, Gisela, and Pat Thane, eds. *Maternity and Gender Policies: Women and the Rise of the European Welfare States.* London: Routledge, 1991 .

Cheal, David. *New Poverty: Families in Postmodern Society.* Westport, CT: Praeger Publishers, 1996.

Gauthier, Anne Helene. *The State and the Family: A Comparative Analysis of Family Policies in Industrialized Countries.* Oxford: Clarendon Press, 1998.

Statistics New Zealand. *Demographic Trends 2003.* Wellington, New Zealand: Statistics New Zealand, 2003.

Periodicals

Clyde, A. "Is Big Beautiful?" *Family Life* (March/April 1997): 46–47.

Downey, Doug B. "Number of Siblings and Intellectual Development." *The American Psychologist* 56(6/7) (2001): 497–504.

Downey, Doug B. "When Bigger Is Not Better: Family Size, Parental Resources, and Children's Educational Performance." *American Sociological Review* 60 (5) (1995): 746–762.

Web sites

The Christian Science Monitor. "Life with a Supersized Family." September 19, 2001 <http://www.csmonitor.com/2001/0919/p15s1-lifp.html> (accessed June 23, 2006).

United States Census Bureau. "U. S. Census 2000." March 17, 2006 <http://www.census.gov/main/www/cen2000.html> (accessed June 23, 2006).

ACLU Disappointed the Supreme Court Will Not Hear an Appeal in Case Challenging

Florida's Anti-Gay Adoption Law

Vows to Ensure Families Involved in the Lawsuit Stay Together

Press release

By: American Civil Liberties Union

Date: January 11, 2005

Source: *American Civil Liberties Union.* "ACLU Disappointed the Supreme Court Will Not Hear an Appeal in Case Challenging Florida's Anti-Gay Adoption Law." January 11, 2005 <http://www.aclu.org/lgbt/parenting/12438prs20050110.html> (accessed June 20, 2006).

About the Author: The American Civil Liberties Union (ACLU) was founded in 1920 as a national legal advocacy organization to advance the protection of individual civil liberties in a wide range of circumstances.

INTRODUCTION

The legal contest over the constitutionality of a Florida law that prohibits the adoption of children by gay persons mirrors a broader national debate that has unfolded in the United States since the mid–1970s. The expression 'gay rights' is one that includes a number of issues of which gay adoption is one; same-sex marriage, in both the civil sanctioned and religious contexts, the economic consequences for partners to gay unions that are terminated, survivorship rights and pension benefits, and the criminalization of sexual relations between gay persons have each commanded significant national attention. A proposed amendment to the United States Constitution defining marriage as a union between a man and a woman was the subject of an intense national debate. The gay adoption debate has been among the most controversial, as the ability to adopt a child engages the broader state interest of child welfare, unlike other aspects of gay relations that tend to be important primarily to the partners involved.

Custody and adoption are well settled legal principles in both the United States and most other countries. Adoption evolved as an entirely statutory process, with no equivalent in common law. Individual states are generally empowered to determine the rules regarding adoption in their jurisdiction, so long as such laws are consistent with any constitutional provisions. As a general proposition, adoption is a permanent reordering of the parent-child relationship, defined as a legal process in which the rights and

Gay dads Brian Brantner and Matt Fuller hold their two-month-old adopted daughter, Audrey, in San Francisco, October 12, 2004. © TOMAS VAN HOUTRYVE/CORBIS.

duties concerning a child's natural parents are terminated and replaced with those granted to the adoptive parent(s). Such proceedings may be instituted by either individuals or various types of child placement agencies. The state must ultimately approve all adoption applications.

Custody, distinct from adoption, is a more elastic concept involving the care, control, and maintenance of a child; it is not a permanent alteration of the status of the child within the family. Foster care, in which children are placed by the state with approved families, is a form of child custody. Florida law provides that approved gay couples may act as foster parents; at the time of the January 2005 Supreme Court refusal, the state had approved numerous gay persons to act as foster parents, some of whom had cared for children for a number of years.

The ACLU press release references Anita Bryant and the 1977 Florida legislation. Bryant, a well known media figure through her work as spokesperson for the Florida citrus industry, was a conservative Christian and a champion of the anti-gay lobby. She was influential in generating political support in Florida for the ban on gay adoption, claiming that a family is an exclusively heterosexual concept. Ironically, her promotional work for the Florida orange industry was terminated due to the notoriety of her work with anti-gay organizations.

At the heart of the ACLU position in its lobby to overturn the Florida gay adoption ban is the notion that American concepts regarding what constitutes a family or a proper supportive environment for a child have been entirely redefined since the passage of the 1977 legislation. Even the nomenclature in the debate has been refined since 1977: Homosexual has been largely replaced by the broader term gay, which includes the entire side of the same-sex debate, but most references include the expression gay and lesbian.

Gay adoption has been a significant battleground in other countries as well. Canada, Great Britain, and Belgium are examples of jurisdictions where gay adoption remains a significant political issue.

ACLU DISAPPOINTED THE SUPREME COURT WILL NOT HEAR AN APPEAL IN CASE CHALLENGING FLORIDA'S ANTI-GAY ADOPTION LAW

Vows to Ensure Families Involved in the Lawsuit Stay Together

NEW YORK—The American Civil Liberties Union today said that it was disappointed by the U.S. Supreme Court's refusal to hear an appeal in its lawsuit challenging a Florida law that bans gay people from adopting. "It is disappointing that the Court will not review the earlier ruling upholding the ban. There are more than 8,000 children in Florida foster care, some of whom surely would have found permanent homes if the law had been struck down," said Matt Coles, Director of the ACLU's Lesbian and Gay Rights Project. "No judge in this case ever looked at the social science on the ability of gay people to parent. Since this case was decided, however, a court in Little Rock heard from the top experts in America and concluded that sexual orientation has nothing to do with whether someone is a good parent."

"The Florida ban flies in the face of the positions of every major child welfare organization, many of which have come out publicly against this law," added Chris Zawisza, an attorney on behalf of Florida's Children First, which is representing the children involved in the case. "This law is bad public policy that does real harm to children."

The ACLU asked the Supreme Court to hear an appeal in the case after the Federal Court of Appeals for the 11th Circuit narrowly upheld the ban. By a vote of six-to-six, the full court declined to reconsider an earlier decision by a three-member panel of the appeals court upholding the law. The law was enacted by the state legislature in 1977, in the midst of Anita Bryant's anti-gay crusade. The ACLU filed a challenge to the law in 1999.

"As far as the kids directly involved in this lawsuit are concerned, this case is far from over," said Leslie Cooper, a staff attorney for the ACLU's Lesbian and Gay Rights Project who worked on the case. "We'll fight tooth and nail through local juvenile courts to ensure these families are not torn apart." Any move by the state to change the placement of any of the children involved in the case would have to be approved by a family court or other judge, in which case the ACLU would fight vigorously to keep the families intact.

Although the state bars gay people from adopting, it has no restriction on gay people serving as foster parents. In fact, two of the three families involved in the case are raising Florida foster children. Steven Lofton and his partner Roger Croteau are raising five children, including three foster children from Florida. Although the children—two 17-year-olds and a 13-year-old—have never

known any other family, they cannot be adopted by Lofton or Croteau because of Florida's law. Wayne Smith and Dan Skahen are now foster parents to two children. A family court judge issued a novel court order in 2002 granting Smith and Skahen "permanent legal custody" to one of their two children in an effort to provide the child with greater family security. Doug Houghton has been the legal guardian for nine years of a boy who is now nearly 13 years old. Even though the child's biological father would prefer for Houghton to be the legal parent, Houghton can't adopt because of the law.

"By denying our request to hear this case," said Howard Simon, Executive Director of the ACLU of Florida, "the Supreme Court, sadly, has allowed the lives of thousands of children adrift in Florida's scandal-ridden foster care system to be governed by the ugly prejudices of legislators—not even our current legislators, but the prejudices of Florida lawmakers a generation ago."

The ACLU is committed to abolishing this law and is considering other legal options to challenge it.

SIGNIFICANCE

The ban on gay adoptions in Florida is a legal issue that has profound societal repercussions across the United States. The ACLU is committed to repealing the Florida law; conservatives, including a variety of religious organizations, see gay adoption as a part of a broader incursion against traditional moral and family values.

As with many legal challenges, the Florida ban carries both legal and practical significance. For supporters of the existing law, the legislation represents an example of the ability of a state to reflect the desires of its citizens in defining the concept of family. These groups have stated in a variety of forums that local legislatures, not the Supreme Court, should determine these rules.

The ACLU and its supporters have waged a multidimensional attack upon the Florida law, as they have done with similar enactments in other states. They point to an array of statistical information in support of its position. Child advocacy groups in the United States place the number of children currently awaiting adoption at over 120,000. The number of American children who have a gay parent is broadly estimated to be between 4 and 10 million.

The Supreme Court decision confirms the dichotomy inherent in Florida adoption law that allows approved gay persons to act as foster parents, even in long-term placements, but bars them from making an adoption application. The legal device employed to create 'permanent legal custody', as described in the primary source, is clearly a legal fiction intended to avoid the Florida adoption restrictions, as there is no such statutory power given to judges under Florida child welfare law.

One of the most significant battlegrounds in the gay adoption debate is whether children suffer adverse effects from an adoption into a gay union. Opponents of gay adoption stress a number of religious objections to such a practice, including biblical prohibitions against homosexuality, with the corollary that the exposure and deliberate inclusion of a child in such circumstances is also sinful. Islam expressly describes homosexual conduct as a mortal sin. Critics also point to ethicists in the medical community who state that while childen adopted into a gay union may be appropriately cared for, such environments are inferior to a traditional heterosexual two-parent home.

Pro-adoption forces have marshaled a significant body of scientific and sociological expertise to support their contention that children incur no psychological harm when adopted into a gay union. They point to the proposition that a child who needs nurture and support receives them from a person, not a sexual orientation. Opponents of the Florida legislation also cite the 2003 Supreme Court decision *Lawrence v. Texas* that struck down Texas criminal sanctions against sodomy. The Supreme Court will almost certainly rule on gay adoption at some time in the future, given the razor-thin margin by which the appeal was dismissed at the state level; how the issues in *Lawrence*, which governs private acts between consenting adults, relate to the clear state interest in the adoption process is of interest.

The prohibition against gay adoption is also mandated by Utah and Missouri, but the Ninth Amendment of the Constitution, which states that "The enumeration ... of certain rights, shall not be construed to deny or disparage others retained by the people," has not been litigated with the same frequency as other constitutional provisions that touch upon notions of equality. Gay adoption advocates argue that the Florida law denies a fundamental right, namely the right of an otherwise qualified person to pursue an adoption proceeding.

Advances in medical technology have also affected this issue. Procedures such as artificial insemination and surrogate parenthood allow gay persons or couples to become parents in most American states and throughout the Western world. To proponents of the repeal of the Florida gay adoption laws, it is an indefensible distinction to permit gay persons to be parents in one circumstance but not in the other.

FURTHER RESOURCES

Books

Deakin, Michelle Bates. *Gay Marriage, Real Life: Ten Stories of Love and Family*. Boston: Skinner House Books, 2006.

Pinello, Daniel R. *Gay Rights and American Law*. New York: Cambridge University Press, 2003.

Senak, Mark S. *Every Trick in the Book: The Essential Gay & Lesbian Legal Guide*. New York: M. Evans and Company, 2002 .

Web sites

PBS. "Views on Gay Adoption." 2005 <http://www.pbs.org/now/politics/fightforfamily2.html> (accessed June 19, 2006).

Data on Marriage and Births Reflects the Political Divide

Newspaper article

By: Tamar Lewin

Date: October 13, 2005

Source: Lewin, Tamar. "Data on Marriage and Births Reflects the Political Divide." *New York Times*. (October 13, 2005).

About the Author: Tamar Lewin is a journalist employed by the *New York Times*. Lewin specializes in articles that examine issues pertaining to education. The *New York Times* was first published in 1851 and is among the nation's largest daily newspapers, with a circulation of over one million copies.

INTRODUCTION

The political divide noted in the following newspaper article is not the first such division to be examined in the history of American politics. Geography has been a recurring fault line in the politics of the United States, both those running between the North and the South and later divisions arising between eastern and the western states of the Union. The North/South division in political opinion was the most prominent such feature from the beginnings of the nativist movement in the late 1840s to the civil rights campaigns that continued into the 1960s.

The particular political divide identified here is one of relatively recent origin. The description of the national political interests as being those of the red

A worker puts weights on the state of Texas in a giant presidential election map of the United States made of ice in the skating rink at Rockefelller Center in New York, November 2, 2004. The states in red went to Bush, the blue states to Kerry and the remaining white states were still undecided. AP IMAGES.

states (generally conservative voters and supporters of the Republican Party nationally) or blue states (more liberal minded voters and supporters of the Democratic Party nationally) is a type of political analysis that likely began during the 1992 presidential election campaign. Red state/blue state was a form of political pundit shorthand; it is now an expression entrenched in the language of American political commentary.

When the red state/blue state analysis is applied to the results of the 1960 and 1980 presidential elections, the context in which the contemporary political divide must be examined becomes clear. The 1960 election campaign contested between Republican Richard Nixon and Democrat John F. Kennedy ended in one of the closest results in American history, as the candidates were separated by a 0.2 percent margin of the popular vote. Kennedy carried states such as Texas, Louisiana, and Georgia, all of which are now "red" Republican areas on the electoral map. In 1980, Ronald Reagan of the Republican Party swept to power on the strength of his success in forty-four out of the fifty states. Using the modern red state/blue state analysis, it would be difficult to find any political division in the face of such a mammoth and sweeping electoral victory. Just as voter attitudes do not remain

fixed to a particular geographic area, the philosophy and the political positions of each party change from election to election.

The political divide described in the following newspaper article is one that has been established as a consequence of the similar results achieved by the Republican and the Democratic presidential candidates in the successive election campaigns of 2000 and 2004. The red states and blue states remained unchanged but for two after the 2004 election; the red states are located in the north central, central, south central, and Southern regions of the United States, with the blue regions comprised of the Northeast, upper Midwest, and West coast states.

PRIMARY SOURCE

When it comes to marriage and babies, the red states really are different from the blue states, according to a new Census Bureau analysis of marriage, fertility and socioeconomic characteristics.

People in the Northeast marry later and are more likely to live together without marriage and less likely to become teenage mothers than are people in the South.

The bureau's analysis, based on a sample of more than three million households from the American Community Survey data of 2000-3, is the first to examine the data by state.

"There are marked regional differences," said Jane Dye, the bureau researcher who did the study, with Tallese Johnson.

Generally, men and women in the Northeast marry later than those in the Midwest, West, or South. In New York, New Jersey, Connecticut, and Massachusetts, for example, the median age of first marriage is about twenty-nine for men and twenty-six or twenty-seven for women, about four years later than in Arkansas, Idaho, Kentucky, Oklahoma, and Utah. And tracking the red state-blue state divide, those in California, Illinois, Michigan, Minnesota, and Wisconsin follow the Northeast patterns, not those of their region.

Nationally, the age of first marriage has been rising since 1970. But because this is the first state-by-state analysis the Census Bureau has done, the authors of the study said, it is impossible to say whether the early-marrying states are moving in the same direction, and at the same pace, as the later-marrying ones.

"With the trend to later marriage, we were interested to find out if people were living alone longer, or living with a partner and then marrying later," Ms. Dye said. "We did find that in the states where people marry later, there is a higher proportion of unmarried-couple households. So it may be that people join in couples at the same time, but just marry later."

Generally, the study found, states in the Northeast and the West had a higher percentage of unmarried-partner households than those in the South, In Maine, New Hampshire and Vermont, unmarried couples made up more than seven percent of all coupled households, about the twice the proportion of such households in Alabama, Arkansas, and Mississippi.

On teenage births, the same differences become clear. In New York, New Jersey, and Massachusetts, about five percent of babies are born to teenage mothers, while in Arkansas, Georgia, Louisiana, Mississippi, Montana, New Mexico, South Carolina, Texas, and Wyoming, ten percent or more of all births are to teenage mothers.

The study also found that the percentage of births to unmarried mothers was highest in the South.

The new study also confirms just how big and how uneven a presence immigrants have become in American society.

Over all, it found, fifteen percent of the women who had given birth in the United States in the previous year were not citizens. But immigrant presence, too, is very much a regional phenomenon. So while noncitizens made up a third of the new mothers in California, and more than twenty percent in Arizona, Nevada, New Jersey, and Texas, there were a dozen states where less than four percent of the new mothers were not citizens.

Similarly, while twenty-one percent of all women who gave birth in California in the last year and fourteen percent in Arizona, Nevada, and Texas either did not speak English well or did not speak it at all, there were fourteen states where less than two percent of the new mothers had limited English skills or none.

The researchers said that they had looked for evidence that immigrant mothers were poorer than others but that they had not found any.

"One thing that was interesting to us is that we didn't find a correlation between language and citizenship and poverty status," Ms. Dye said.

SIGNIFICANCE

The data gathered by the United States Bureau of Census regarding birth and marriage statistics on a state-by-state basis is significant on a number of different levels. The analysis of the data by means of the 'red state/blue state" comparison begs the question of whether the moral values implicit in the birth and marriage statistics are evidence of voter attitudes, or alternatively, whether the voters were influenced by factors unrelated to moral questions, such as economic performance or homeland security. Based upon a strict cause and effect relationship between the census data and the presidential electoral results, it might be said that an unwed mother is more likely to vote Republican. This is not a sound conclusion due to the myriad of factors both personal to the voter and of broader concern that are certain to impact the result of any given election campaign.

Additional statistical analysis provided by the United States Bureau of Census places the political divide that is sought to be highlighted by birth and marriage data into a clearer focus. A salient example is the fact that nine of the ten lowest birth rates reported by the census are found in the blue or Democratic states. These regions also reported a lower divorce rate than those typically found in the red or Republican states. The blue states also reported a correspondingly higher number of married partners in family units than those found in the red states.

The political division represented by red and blue states is of particular interest when the census projections of future population growth are considered. The eight states predicted to experience the greatest degree of population growth are all currently red states, including Florida and Texas. The question for future demographic study will be whether the persons added to the populations of the current red states adopt the current voting preferences of the state to which they have migrated.

It may be argued that the entire red state/blue state analysis is a tenuous one in light of how American presidential and Congressional elections are waged in practice. Given that the American system is one based upon the principle of "first past the post", where the winner of the most votes by plurality is the electoral victor, the division does not reflect the relatively thin victory margin enjoyed by the Republican party and George Bush in both the 2000 and 2004 elections that created the political divide described in the primary source. The Democratic candidate Al Gore won approximately 500,000 more votes nationally than George W. Bush in 2000; however, by virtue of the American Electoral College system, the states carried by Bush were sufficient to win the presidency. Had a key populous state such as Florida (and its significant number of electoral college votes) gone to the blue side of the ledger in either of these elections, the Democrats may have prevailed and thus, rendered the political divide described in the primary source invisible.

Further, the red state/blue state analysis is founded upon the results of the presidential popular vote. In 2004, 60.7 percent of all eligible voters nationwide actually cast their ballot, the highest such total recorded since 1968. The red state/blue state division is one resulting from the successful presidential candidate garnering a majority of the sixty percent of the population that voted, as opposed to the census data that is reflective of the entire population. For this reason, the true political sentiments of a state may not fit the birth and marriage data from the census.

Of further significance is the fact that the marriage and birth data from the census that is contrasted against the American electoral map was never a specific campaign issue in either the 2000 or 2004 presidential elections. Birth rates, particularly among single mothers, may be, but cannot be exclusively attributed to, the larger moral questions of family planning and religious values; marriage statistics are similarly often a function of factors such as a decision to cohabit prior to making a decision to marry, or the economic choices associated with career pursuits versus marriage and family.

The impact of immigration upon birth and marriage rates is a factor that is likely to be one of continuing importance given the ever increasing influence of immigration upon American demographics. In 2006, it is estimated that the country housed over thirty-three million immigrants, or one immigrant person for every nine residents of the United States. While the modern American immigrant community is not homogeneous, it has large segments of Hispanic and south East Asian people who tend to marry and have children within a traditional family structure. The contrast between immigrant birth and marriage practices and the electoral map may become skewed in the near future, as voting rights in American presidential and Congressional elections are only permitted to full citizens of the United States.

FURTHER RESOURCES
Books
Davis, Don. *One State, Two State, Red State, Blue State*. Shelbyville, Kentucky: Wasteland Press, 2005.

Longman, Phillip. *The Empty Cradle*. New York: Basic Books, 2004.

Wilson, James Q. *The Marriage Problem: How Our Culture has Weakened Families*. Toronto: Harper Collins Canada, 2003.

Web sites
The United States Bureau of Census. "State Population Increase Projections." 2005, <http://www.census.gov/Press-Release/www/2005/stateproj7.xls> (accessed June 29, 2006).

Putting Families First

News article

By: Anonymous

Date: November 24, 2005

Source: "Putting Families First." *The Economist*, November 24, 2005.

About the Author: *The Economist*, published since 1843, is one of Britain's premier magazines devoted to international business, finance, and politics.

INTRODUCTION

Before the advent of the foster care system, parentless or abandoned children were historically cared for by family members, community members, or left to their own devices. Many were victims of physical and sexual abuse, taken advantage of in labor settings, or became sex trade workers or thieves. The 1562,

English Poor Law required that all orphaned children work as unpaid apprentices until they reached the age of majority. This law was imported when the British settled portions of North America, and in the 1800s in Britain and the United States some children went to "pauper houses." Orphaned, abandoned, or in some cases the children of parents imprisoned in the poor house for debt, these children were raised by the state or private charities, turned out into the labor force to work in grueling conditions while their wages went to the pauper house, and faced cruelty and hardship as a result of the absence of protective parents.

Although having one or two parents was no guarantee of a life without abuse, in the 1800s, children without a parent faced a wide range of obstacles and dangers that often lead to disease and malnutrition, high crime and incarceration rates, and early death. Young girls and teenagers often became prostitutes; boys turned to muggings and robbery to support themselves. In 1853, the first organized foster care system in the United States was designed by Charles Loring Brace, the director of the New York Children's Aid Society. Concerned about the thousands of poor parentless children he saw sleeping in the streets, digging through trash for food, and selling their bodies for money to survive, Brace placed advertisements in southern and western newspapers, encouraging families to take these children in and raise them. In many instances the children were as exploited as they had been living in New York City, but Brace's program was the beginning of the modern foster care program.

Between 1854 and 1929, more than 100,000 children made the trip by car and train to the southern states and into the Midwest and western states. The children were viewed as a cheap source of labor; their welfare was secondary to that fact, though the majority of families treated their foster children reasonably well. Once the child reached the age of majority he or she was free to leave, though in many instances the foster children were considered to be family for those mothers and fathers who raised them.

The issue of child abuse gained attention in 1874, when Mary Ellen Wilson, a nine-year-old girl living in Hell's Kitchen in New York City, was found by a local nurse with extensive injuries from beatings by her foster mother. The nurse, Etta Wheeler, approached a wealthy businessman, Henry Bergh to intercede. Bergh was the leader of the New York Society for the American Prevention of Cruelty to Animals; he offered assistance with Mary Ellen's case, and the girl was removed from her home. Societies for the prevention of cruelty to children were founded in the aftermath of Mary Ellen's case; this, combined with Brace's

foster care system, converged with new notions in society about childhood.

The Victorian ideal viewed the child as a naive, guileless creature in need of proper nourishment, nurturing, and guidance from a moral mother and a hardworking, respectable father. Childhood became a separate life stage, and social workers—part of an emerging profession—worked to protect children from abuse and neglect. Child labor laws, coupled with an expansion of social work and government action such as the 1912 founding of the Children's Bureau, and the 1944 U.S. Supreme Court case *Prince v. Massachusetts*, which affirmed the government's right to intervene in family issues, changed how poor and abused children were treated as a policy issue.

The fields of social work and psychology added to research on the impact of abuse on children, and by the 1960s the concept of child abuse as a syndrome, or a damaging experience for children, was clear. The foster care system, however, struggled with funding, finding appropriate foster parents, and a host of family-stressing issues surrounding growing drug abuse that exploded in the 1980s and continued into the twenty-first century.

PRIMARY SOURCE

…Tales of missing, starved, abused and even murdered children in adopted homes and foster shelters are alarmingly common. Some escape the attention of overburdened social workers; others are shuttled from one foster-care placement to another for years on end. Last year, a Pew Commission on Children in Foster Care concluded that, because of the way federal funding works, children were plucked from their families too soon and left to fester in the system for too long. And although judges play a critical role in moving children to safety, family courts are among the most under-funded in the system, with few incentives to attract top lawyers and judges and little collaboration between the courts and child-welfare agencies. Dependency lawyers tend to be overworked and underpaid, with predictably bad results for the children they represent.

More than 500,000 children are in foster care in America, most of them black or Latino. They remain in the system for an average of three years. These children, typically placed in the state's care after suffering abuse and neglect at home, often endure a demoralising parade of indifferent caseworkers, lawyers, judges, teachers and foster parents, who offer little real support in their quest for a stable home. For those who cannot return to their birth parents, the situation is grim: in 2003, 119,000 children in America were waiting to be adopted, 67% of whom had been in foster care for more than two years, according to the Department of Health and Human Services (HHS). When such children "age out," or turn 18, as 18,000–20,000 do every year, they are suddenly cut off from all special services such as housing and counselling. Studies show that they disproportionately drop out of college, become homeless and unemployed, turn to drugs and alcohol and spend time in jail.

The federal government pays around half America's $22 billion child-welfare bill, according to the Urban Institute; the rest comes from state and local governments. But states have not been held accountable for how they spend this money. In an extensive three-year audit of state child-welfare systems, the HHS found that not a single state was in compliance with federal safety standards. When it came to the seven federal standards used to assess children's programmes, some of which are almost embarrassingly basic (eg, "Children are first and foremost protected from abuse and neglect" and "Children receive adequate services to meet their physical and mental health needs"), 16 states did not meet any of them, and no state met more than two. The federal agency is now running a second round of audits, to assess whether states are now complying with their own improvement plans.

"We are spending a great deal of money to damage children," says Marcia Robinson Lowry, director of Children's Rights, an advocacy group. There are no real consequences for states when they fail to meet federal targets, she argues, so class-action lawsuits are the only recourse. Children's Rights has represented foster children in 13 court cases in the past decade. Most of these have ended in a court-ordered settlement that sets the group as a watchdog over a state's mismanaged and overburdened social-services department.

But using the courts to solve America's child-welfare problems is expensive and inefficient. The best answer, many think, is for states to spend money on keeping families together, by investing in services such as child care and counselling, rather than putting children in care. This would require allowing states to use federal funding in different ways. Most federal dollars now begin flowing to states only when children are removed from their families, giving states a perverse incentive to keep children in foster care, explains Carol Emig, the director of the Pew Commission. Instead, the commission suggests that states need a little more federal money to cover all children, not just poor ones, and the flexibility to create a range of services that might keep children from entering care or help them leave care safely.

Such a change carries quite a price-tag: $5 billion over ten years. But advocates say it will bring long-term savings by producing better educated, less delinquent children and more united families. If states safely reduce their foster-care rolls, they can then reinvest dollars earmarked for foster care in other child-welfare services. Meanwhile, federal reviews will hold states to their programme promises. President George Bush has proposed, alternatively, that states should convert their foster-care entitlement programmes into block grants. That would give flexibility at first but, over time, it would amount to a cut in funds.

States and cities can already apply for waivers from federal funding restraints; some 20 states have waivers now. Advocates of flexible funding point to Illinois, a waiver recipient, where the foster-care population has been cut in half and adoptions have more than doubled since 1997. And in late October officials in New York City announced that the number of children in foster care has dropped to around 18,000, half of what it was six years ago. Once home to one of the worst foster-care systems in the country, the city now works to keep families intact and help them look after their children rather than taking the youngsters away. As a result, "the spigot coming into the system has been narrowed," explains David Tobis, director of the Child Welfare Fund, a local organisation. The money saved from federal entitlements—an estimated $27m in the fiscal year that began in July—will be put back into preventive services.

October also saw Arnold Schwarzenegger, California's governor, sign into law a number of bills to help the state's foster children—more than 80,000 of them. Most of the new laws will help teenagers when they turn 18, by making sure they stay in college and have somewhere to live.

Amid all the horror stories, it can be easy to lose sight of the people who make foster care work. After describing the madness of waiting all day at court to represent a client, only to receive five minutes of a distracted judge's time, one social worker goes on to describe some of the good foster parents she has met. Her voice grows tender when she describes one couple who have taken in a young, physically disabled child. "You tend to hear about the system's flaws," she explains. "But there are also so many other amazing things."

SIGNIFICANCE

With more than half a million children in foster care, and a patchwork system of state policies, each differing from the next, many politicians and child development researchers consider the foster care system to be in crisis, with children "aging out" and living on the streets, children placed in questionable foster care homes, and a focus on family reunification that often leaves the child in limbo for years.

In 2002, five-year-old Rilya Wilson, a foster child in the Florida system, could not be found. Her caretaker, Geralyn Graham, claimed that a Florida state social worker had taken her in 2000 upon request by Graham, but authorities had no such record of that interaction. At the same time, Florida child welfare officials admitted that they had not been keeping good records on social worker interactions with children and foster parents; as of 2006 Rilya Wilson remains missing. A 2006 follow-up to Rilya Wilson's disappearance revealed that more than 652 children in Florida in the foster care system were missing; among them "one-year-old Destiny Booth, one-year-old Geraldo Duarte, two-year-old Angelica Rodriguez, 18-month-old Sheena Ruiz-Lopez-Meeks, two-year-old Mackenzie Spears-Bennett, one-year-old Noah Samuel Varble-Rhoads, and one-year-old Louanne Wise." While the vast majority of missing children are teenagers, whom officials presume are runaways, the Florida Department of Children and Families has come under sharp criticism for losing track of so many children.

Methamphetamine abuse, extremely widespread throughout the Great Plains and portions of the west, has created a sudden and dramatic strain on foster care systems in such states as Nebraska, Kansas, and Minnesota. Unlike heroin or cocaine, "meth" can be made for very little money, and meth abuse has led thousands of parents to abandon or severely neglect their children. As Chip Ammerman, a case worker manager for Cass County in Minnesota notes, ""Before, it [meth] was one or two percent of the cases, now it's about 25 to 30 percent of the cases we're getting involved in," and the strain on the foster care system—with babies removed for testing positive for meth at birth—is echoed in bordering states' foster care rolls as well.

In the 1990s, approximately 20,000–30,000 children were adopted out of the foster care each year, 5% of the total within the system. In 1997 President William J. Clinton signed legislation that made the child's safety more important than family reunification and cut the time required in foster care before adoption from eighteen months to twelve months. The law also provides states with bonus money for each adoption above set goals.

Since the passing of the legislation, adoptions from foster care have risen steadily, to more than 51,000 in 2004. Each year more than 20,000 teenagers "age out" of the system as well, receiving no further support from the state. With 70,000 children leaving the foster care system, but nearly 300,000 entering each year (for short and long term foster care), the foster care system continues to expand and manage the lives of more and more American children.

FURTHER RESOURCES
Books

Askeland, Lori, ed. *Children and Youth in Adoption, Orphanages, and Foster Care: A Historical Handbook and Guide.* Westport, Conn.: Greenwood Press, 2005.

Hegar, Rebecca L., and Maria Scanapieco. *Kinship Foster Care: Policy, Practice, and Research.* New York: Oxford University Press, 1998.

Murphy, Patrick T. *Wasted: The Plight of America's Unwanted Children.* Chicago: Ivan R. Dee Publisher, 1997.

Web sites

Bradenton Herald. "Number of Florida Foster Kids, Who Are Vanishing, Is Skyrocketing." June 6, 2006 <http://www.bradenton.com/mld/bradenton/news/breaking_news/14752222.htm> (accessed July 9, 2006).

Minnesota Public Radio. "Methamphetamine Use Driving an Increase in Foster Care." May 3, 2005 <http://news.minnesota.publicradio.org/features/2005/03/31_rehab_methfoster/> (accessed July 10, 2006).

New York Society for the Prevention of Cruelty to Children. <http://www.nyspcc.org/> (accessed July 7, 2006).

Changin' in the Boys' Room

News article

By: Andrew Adam Newman

Date: February 5, 2006

Source: Newman, Andrew Adam. "Changin' in the Boys' Room." *New York Times* (February 5, 2006).

About the Author: Andrew Adam Newman is a writer for the *New York Times* covering contemporary American culture and society.

INTRODUCTION

The role of fathers in the United States has come a long way from the 1950s archetype in the television series *Father Knows Best* and *Leave it to Beaver*. The cardigan-wearing, all-wise father figure who came home from a long day at the office to a wife in a starched dress and heels, bearing a martini and slip-

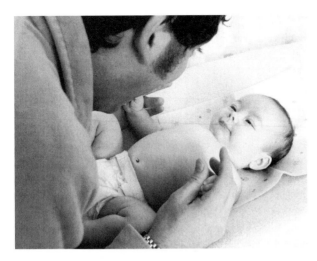

A father plays with his baby while on changing table. © ROYALTY-FREE/CORBIS.

pers for her husband, while the children adoringly greeted dear old dad was, in fact, a media creation, but one that etched itself into the collective unconscious in American culture. In the 1950s, four percent of all children born in the U.S. were born to single mothers; in 2000 that figure stood at thirty-three percent. The average age of marriage for women in the 1950s was twenty; by 2000 the average age was twenty-five. Women's participation in the workforce, however, has had the greatest impact on men as fathers—in 2000 nearly eighty percent of all women of childbearing age were part of the workforce, and while only eleven percent of mothers with children under the age of six were part of the workforce in 1950, by 2002 that figure had risen to fifty-five percent.

While the late 1960s and 1970s saw the emergence of a "new" woman, who could work, be a devoted partner and a loving mother, the "superwoman" image—stereotyped in a well-known 1970s television commercial for a perfume, in which a mother figure can "bring home the bacon/fry it up in a pan/and never let you forget you're a man/'cause I'm a woman," all with children happily vying for mom's attention—quickly fell apart under scrutiny. Women began to ask why they needed to be superwoman—in other words, where were the supermen?

A July 12, 1982 article in *Time* magazine asked "How Long Till Equality?" and examined women's political, economic, and social progress. Fatherhood and traditional two-parent nuclear families came into play: only twenty-eight percent of all families in 1982 were "traditional," and that number dropped to nine percent by 2000. The article noted the impact of stay-

ing at home on mothers' careers and examined the possibility of stay-at-home fathers: "There are not many executives who can appreciate or allow that the skill, say, of time management at home might be applied to office management, just as there are still very few corporations with personnel departments set up to accommodate the needs of the new work force and the flexible family." By 2000, "flex time" and "family friendly" were buzzwords, and fathers were expected to step up to the plate and work with their working wives to manage two careers, an average of 2.1 children, and to juggle home life, childrearing, and work expectations.

■ PRIMARY SOURCE

Did you hear the one about the guy who wheels his toddler into Hooters and asks if they have a diaper-changing table in the men's room?

It's not a joke. It happened to Greg Allen on a recent Saturday at the Hooters on West 56th Street in Manhattan. And it goes something like this:

The hostess, a perky brunette wearing wristband-size shorts and a plunging Hooters T-shirt, explained to Mr. Allen that the restaurant's only changing table was in the women's room. Then her manager said:

"If you really want to change her, maybe we can watch the women's room for you. We're very family friendly."

But Mr. Allen did not need a changing table.

He was doing field research.

Mr. Allen, 38, is compiling a list of public men's rooms in New York equipped with changing tables and using Google maps to pinpoint their locations on his blog, daddytypes.com. So far he's found 32 men's rooms that have them. It is, as far as anyone can tell, the first time anyone has used shoe leather and geospatial mapping technology for this particular purpose.

For Mr. Allen and his readers who send him restroom dispatches—Craig Winkelman reported that the newer Metro-North trains have changing tables, but warned "about a sudden deceleration, which might send your little one sliding into the toilet"—changing tables have become a sort of modern litmus test: has society evolved to embrace a new kind of fatherhood, or hasn't it?

So far the answer seems to be maybe.

A filmmaker and writer whose family shuttles between New York and Washington, Mr. Allen approaches his issue with equal parts mock indignation and indignant mockery. The manifesto introducing the list on his blog—which also devotes significant space to the small but growing dad-gear market—leads with two points: "1. Most men's rooms don't have changing tables, or even counter space big enough to change a diaper on. 2. Apparently, in addition to changing tables, many women's restrooms have gigantic lounges, with sofas and eunuchs scattering rose petals at their feet."

Earlier that Saturday, at ABC Carpet on Broadway near Union Square, which has a changing table in the women's room, Mr. Allen found none in the men's room. (Subsequently contacted by this reporter, an ABC Carpet spokeswoman said that no one had ever commented on it before but that the store would install a unit in the men's room soon.)

"From the father's perspective, you kind of assume there isn't going to be a changing table, so you improvise," said Pierre Kim, a New Yorker with a 15-month-old daughter. "I've changed her on my lap sitting on the toilet in a men's room stall." Mr. Kim, who has his own blog, metrodad.typepad.com, checks for the tables whether his daughter needs changing or not, and it reminds him and the other fathers in her play group of a less wholesome preoccupation. "We joke around about how 10 years ago you'd look and see if there was a stall where you could do a line of coke," Mr. Kim said. "And now we look, and if we see a diaper table: score!"

The commercial changing table industry itself is practically in its infancy. The oldest and largest manufacturer, Koala Bear Kare, was started in the early 1990s. David Leigh, the company's sales and marketing director, said that it "makes a case to business owners that accommodating families with small children is just good business."

According to a national survey commissioned by Koala, 77 percent of parents with kids under 6 have used changing stations; among them, 34 percent hoist their children onto one six or more times a month.

John Helmsderfer, founder of changing-table maker Brocar Products, estimates that 60 percent of all public restrooms have them today. In the early days of the industry, only about 10 percent of sales were to clients who put one in the men's room as well as the women's. Today, he said, it is "unheard of" to get an order for just women's rooms.

"When anyone calls asking for one, we say, 'so what are you going to put in the ladies' restroom, then?'" joked Mr. Leigh.

Sue Frech, vice president for marketing for Safe-Strap Company, which makes the Diaper-Depot changing table, said that these days "all of our major customers"—which include Barnes & Noble, Babies 'R'Us, Toys 'R'Us and Whole Foods—put them in both.

For Mr. Allen, a dyed-in-the-cashmere metrosexual, large chain retailers account for most of the changing-

table-equipped men's rooms on his list, which suits him about as well as a pair of Dockers. "they're generally a scourge," he said of the stores. "they're homogenizing and suburbanizing New York, which seemed to do fine without them."

Manufacturers say that contractors are most likely to order a changing table for new construction or major renovations. So older businesses often have the units exclusively in women's rooms until they remodel.

Or are sued.

"Plaintiff John William Ellis is not toilet-trained and wears diapers," states a suit filed in 1994 in New York Supreme Court in Manhattan by the toddler's father, Andrew Dwyer, a lawyer, against Lord & Taylor. "While in the Fifth Avenue store, plaintiff Andrew William Dwyer determined that plaintiff John William Ellis needed to have his diaper changed."

O.K., so it's not John Grisham, but Mr. Dwyer claimed that under the state's public accommodation law, providing changing stations solely in the store's women's room was gender discrimination.

Mr. Dwyer said recently that after he filed suit, someone from Lord & Taylor telephoned and said, "'What are you doing to us?' I said: 'I don't want money. I want justice.'"

In settling the case, the department store agreed to provide changing stations in men's rooms in all locations where it does so for women. Though the settlement pre-empted a ruling on the gender discrimination charge, Michael C. Dorf, a professor at the Columbia University School of Law, said the argument had merit on the grounds that "you have to provide equal facilities for women and men."

For some, changing tables as a civil rights issue does not pass the straight-face test. In a 1995 column about Mr. Dwyer's lawsuit, then pending, Ann Landers wrote: "This country has gone litigation goofy. No case is so cuckoo that a lawyer won't take it. Others may view this as democracy at work, but in my opinion, we need to get the nut cases dismissed or settled and keep them from tying up the courts."

Laws requiring that new or renovated public bathrooms (for both genders) be equipped with changing tables passed in San Francisco and in Miami-Dade County. A similar proposal for New York City in 2002 never made it out of—sorry, gentlemen—the Women's Issues Committee. A California bill requiring changing tables in all of the state's fast-food restaurants also died.

Still, Chuck Ault, who lives in Denver and is the national training director of Boot Camp for New Dads, an organization that prepares fathers-to-be in the practical and emotional aspects of parenthood, saw the tide shifting seven or eight years ago: "I was in Home Depot with my youngest, who's now 9, and she had a blow-out, and I thought, 'I'm in this store for power-tool-loving males, what am I going to do?' So I went back to the men's room, and they had a changing table. In this big manly store."

Several years ago Mr. Ault began noticing something on newer airplanes. The signs on the restrooms' changing tables, which previously had a triangle-shaped-dress character hovering over the baby, now featured a gender-neutral figure. It made the skies seem a little friendlier.

"I think those airplane signs are really symbolic and interesting," Mr. Ault said. "I think universal symbols are powerful indicators of what is believed."

SIGNIFICANCE

By 1993, *Time* magazine's coverage of modern-day fatherhood had shifted to coverage of fathers who experience severe tension between home and work expectations. One reported poll showed that in 1979, just twelve percent of fathers reported feeling stress over work-life tensions, but by 1989 that figure had risen to seventy-two percent. The change in expectations for fathers was fast and clear.

The need for changing tables in men's restrooms—and the message that the lack of such tables sends to fathers and society in general—is a symbol of the mixed messages American society sent to fathers in the late twentieth century and into the twenty-first century. While fathers, like mothers, are expected to participate in housework, childrearing, and the workforce, at the same time more than thirty percent of all children were born to single mothers in the year 2000, and groups such as Single Mothers By Choice organized to support women—largely professional, well-educated women in urban centers with ticking biological clocks—who chose to have children without a participating father.

By 2003, the first year the census began recording such figures, there were 98,000 self-reported stay-at-home fathers, compared to 5.4 million mothers in the same role. Some researchers place this figure far higher; At Home Dad, a support and advocacy group for at-home fathers, claims that between two and three million fathers provide more than thirty hours per week of childcare for their own children. The changing table issue and fathers' demands for such equipment represent the widespread involvement of fathers in the drudgery of child care. Changing diapers, feeding infants and toddlers, managing naps and preschool schedules and doctors' visits, however, still remain largely in the hands of mothers. While fathers have increased their time spent with children from 1.8 hours per weekday to 2.7 hours between 1981 and 2006, mothers who work outside the home still do ten hours more of housework per week than do their comparably employed husbands.

In recent polls, forty-four percent of fathers say they would take a pay cut to spend more time with their children, and twenty-eight percent claim that work negatively affects their relationship with their children. Grassroots efforts for changing tables in men's restrooms—and retailers, restaurants, and other public facilities that meet the demand—represent a new phase in gender roles and parenting in American society.

FURTHER RESOURCES

Books

Fatherhood: Research, Interventions, and Policies, edited by H. Elizabeth Peters and Gary W. Peterson. Binghamton, N.Y.: Haworth Press, 2000.

Periodicals

Atkinson, Maxine and Stephen Blackwelder. "Fathering in the 20th Century." *Journal of Marriage and the Family* 55 (1993): 975–986.

Cocks, Jay. "How Long Till Equality?" *Time* (July 12, 1982).

Web sites

At Home Dad. <http://www.athomedad.com> (accessed July 22, 2006).

National Fatherhood Initiative. <http://www.fatherhood.org> (accessed July 22, 2006).

Time.com. "Bring on the Daddy Wars." <http://www.time.com/time/nation/article/0,8599,1168125,00.html> (accessed July 22, 2006).

The Seven Ages of an Only Child

Newspaper article

By: Joanna Moorhead

Date: March 4, 2006

Source: Moorhead, Joanna. "The Guardian." *The Seven Ages of an Only Child.* (March 4, 2006).

About the Author: Joanna Moorhead is a staff writer for *The Guardian*, one of the largest circulating daily newspapers in England.

INTRODUCTION

Many aspects of how a person chooses a job and a mate, relates to co-workers, and relates to family members are linked to that individual's placement in his or her birth family. Only children were once rarities. By the late twentieth century, they had become common. The different life pattern of onlies can be seen in every major life event.

The first child in a family usually identifies with the values of the parents and works at becoming what they want. Guardians of the status quo, eldest children do not like change. Since parents emphasize achievement with a first-born; these children tend to be tenser, more serious, more reserved, and less playful than others. An eldest brother of brothers may find it difficult to work with women, while an eldest sister of brothers may be quite comfortable exercising authority over male employees.

The next child, unable to compete with the eldest, often gets recognition by becoming a rogue, the very opposite of the firstborn. While they benefit from the more relaxed atmosphere that accompanies later births in families, middle children are often displaced by a new baby. As adults, they are sensitive to being left out or slighted. Middle children are less pressured by the parents to succeed and show fewer tendencies to take initiative or think independently. Adept at dealing with all kinds of people, they are skilled negotiators. Youngest children often remain dependent on others and are more than likely than their siblings to be undisciplined in their personal lives. The youngest tend to procrastinate continually, be risk takers and are happiest in jobs that involve social interaction. With no experience caring for others, youngest children tend to be less attentive parents.

Only children show some of the characteristics of oldest children yet are likely to remain childlike into adulthood. They have a higher self-esteem than the eldest ones, with less need to control others. Since they did not have to negotiate with siblings, onlies do not understand the necessity of sharing control. Very

A girl is swung by her hands. © MARK A. JOHNSON/CORBIS.

comfortable living alone and lacking experience with children, onlies are the least likely birth order to enjoy marriage and the most likely to remain childless. Onlies have trouble adjusting to the different personalities of too many peers at the same time and generally prefer occupations that allow them to work alone.

■ PRIMARY SOURCE

THE SEVEN AGES OF AN ONLY CHILD

Alex Healey, 10

When my mum's friend had a baby it made me think about being an only child for the first time. I thought, would I like brothers and sisters? But to be honest, my friend's sister looked quite a hassle—he was always having to watch her. I thought, I'm better off on my own—especially as brothers and sisters seem to fight a lot, that's something I've noticed.

There are other good things, too. I get my privacy, and I like that: some of my friends have to share a bedroom and I know that will never happen to me. And there's no one to mess my stuff up, either. Plus I get time on my own with Mum and Dad, and that's special.

One thing I am pleased about is that my friend Thomas lives really close by, so it's easy for me to go and play with him. When I grow up I'd be happy to have just one child, but I'd always make sure we lived close to other kids.

Zoe Spencer-Silver, 15

One of the bad things about being an only child is the reaction you get from other people. They think you're spoilt—you see that look in their eyes. And then you have to prove you're not spoilt, although you know you're not and nor are most only children.

When I was little my friends thought I was lucky being an only one, but now when I tell friends I can tell they're thinking, that must be hard. She's not got a sister to go shopping with, or a brother to help with her homework. All my friends have brothers and sisters. It can be a bit lonely—like when your parents go out and you're on your own with no one to talk to. I spend a lot of time chatting to my friends on the phone, and going on MSN. And I like it when one of my grannies comes over when my parents are out, because then I've got someone to talk to. I suppose, in general, I think there are more negatives than positives, but on the other hand it's all I've known and I'm OK with it.

Sarah Lee, 29

I went to boarding school when I was seven, and the hardest thing I found was making friends. Because I was an only child, I just didn't know how to do it. The thing is

that when you're an only child you spend a lot of your time with grown-ups, you're not in a very child-centric home and you're often the only child in a gathering of adults. You're more of an appendage to your parents' lives than central to it: they can go on living more or less the sort of life they've always lived, only now you tag along too.

I found being an only child interesting, in that it gave me a place at the grown-ups' table and gave me a view into their world that children in a big family might not get. And I know it has, at least partly, moulded me into the person I am: I never like the idea of being one of a group, for example. If I'm pulled into a group I'm much more likely to go off and do something on my own, or with just one other person—I'm not comfortable with being one of a gang.

My parents are divorced now and my mother lives in the US and my father in the UK. I do feel very responsible for them—I feel responsible for their happiness, in a funny kind of way. I'm the closest relative in the world to each of them, and I am very aware of that.

Lorraine Mason, 36

I was a happy child: I had the undivided love and attention of two people, and it made me very confident and secure. I know some only children feel stifled by their parents, but that wasn't my experience. I found it enriching, which I think is mainly because we get on so well.

Because my childhood was happy, my instinct was to replicate it in my own family, and have just one child myself. I might have done that, but then a few years ago a close friend, who like me was an only child, was killed in an accident. It was devastating for all of us, but of course especially for his parents. It's a double blow for parents when they lose an only child: firstly because they were so close, and secondly because there's no one to go on for.

I came away from the funeral knowing I could never survive what that couple were going through, and it made me decide to have more than one child. My eldest daughter is four and a half, and my second child is 12 weeks old. I suppose the big age gap reflects the fact that I wanted to give my elder daughter that "only child" experience for as long as possible.

I do find having two children scary. The problem is I've absolutely no experience of this kind of situation: nothing in my past has prepared me for having to divide myself between the needs of these two little people, and the guilt is hard when I feel I've not been there enough for one of them. And on a practical level, things like sibling rivalry are going to be a whole new ball game.

Ann Richardson, 49

I always felt a little odd, and assumed it was something about me. It was only in my 30s, when I was training to be a psychotherapist, that I found myself with a group of only children, describing our experiences. It was a revelation because it made me realise that other people felt many of the same things.

Growing up in a small unit means the experience is intense, so we can be rather intense, especially in relationships. Paradoxically, we also need space and quiet, which can cause problems with partners, who might misinterpret it as rejection. We're often socially mature and present a confident exterior that hides a lot of turmoil and insecurity.

There isn't another child that you can watch, compare yourself with and compete against. It's a missing experience. I think that does leave disadvantages in adult life: you feel other people know better how to "do" relationships with peers, how to negotiate, how to be part of a group. But there are pluses too. Time alone helps you become resourceful, develop your imagination and creativity. I think the ability to operate on your own can sometimes give you the impetus to really go for something.

Geoff Allinson, 60

When I was 13 my father died, and what sticks in my mind is how, at his funeral, a neighbour put her hand on my shoulder and said, "You're the man of the house now, Geoff. You've got to look after your mother."

That responsibility weighed on me: I was only a boy. We were very close, as you are when there's just the two of you: but I also felt trapped because, like all teenagers, I wanted to start looking beyond my home to the big wide world.

Three years later Mum married again, and I remember feeling such relief, because now I could live my own life.

Over the following decades I was married and raising my own three children—I always wanted more than one—but there was always this worry in the back of my mind that one day my mother would be on her own again, and I'd be the only person there for her. Then six years ago, my stepfather died.

I was living down south and my mum was in Leeds, so there was a big distance involved and that made things hard. It was very draining, not having anyone else to share it all with; not just the practical stuff, but the worry too. In the end I decided to give up my job to care for her, and I moved her down to live with me.

I'm pleased to think that, in the years ahead, my kids have one another to share the difficulties with. In my experience, that will make a difference.

Anne Parker, 68

I'm single and I've never had children, so as I was an only child I've got no family now. And there are times when you think, it would be nice to have a gorgeous, kind brother or some lovely nieces or nephews who'd come over and help me out or just be around. But that's the most negative I could be about it, really. On the whole I'm pretty contented; I've got a lot of great friends and neighbours, and you don't miss what you've never had.

I don't suppose my parents set out to have a family with only one child in it but the war intervened: my father went off to fight when I was four, at precisely the moment when they might have had a second child. When he came back I do remember saying to both of them that I wanted a sister and it was always maybe, maybe. But it never happened. I would have welcomed a sibling, though, at that point: I know that.

But there have been lots of advantages to being an only child. I grew up being very good at occupying myself, very self-sufficient, and that's always stood me in good stead.

And a lot of the opportunities for arguments are removed when you're an only child: when my second parent died, for example, the whole issue over inheritance was completely straightforward. I've seen terrible rows between siblings over inheritance, so I was spared all that.

SIGNIFICANCE

As each child enters a family, the roles and expectations for children within that family change. These differences, as Sigmund Freud was the first psychotherapist to note, mean that each child is treated in a different way and each will establish a distinct identity by using different behaviors to get approval and attention. All other things being equal, birth order traits develop on the basis of five circumstances of birth: the order of birth, the sex of the child, the number of years between the births of siblings, the sex of siblings, and the birth order of the parents.

The average family size in developed nations has shrunk dramatically since the mid-twentieth century. For generations upon generations, families consisted of numerous children. Such offspring played a vital role in running the family farm or otherwise helping to provide for the family. Parents who wished to limit their family size were often unable to do so because effective birth control was not available. By the 1960s, children were no longer needed to supplement the family income and birth control had become both readily available and reliable. Additionally, the rise of the welfare state in Europe meant that Europeans did not need children to care for them in old age. For these reasons, the number of births dropped. Only children, once a rarity, have become common.

The societal impact of these children of the baby boomers is not yet fully known. However, psychologists have already noted the phenomenon of "helicopter" parents who hover over their children and wrap them in overprotectiveness. With just one child, parents can focus all their hopes, dreams, and anxieties on the one.

FURTHER RESOURCES

Books

Richardson, Ronald W. and Lois A. Richardson. *Birth Order and You*. North Vancouver, B.C.: Self Counsel Press., 1990.

Toman, Walter. *Family Constellation: Its Effects on Personality and Social Behavior*. New York: Springer, 1976.

Web sites

BeingAnOnly.com. <http://www.onlychild.icom43.net> (accessed July 22, 2006).

It was a Selfish Decision but I Never Regretted It

Newspaper article

By: Fiona McIntosh

Date: March 17, 2006

Source: McIntosh, Fiona. "It was a Selfish Decision but I Never Regretted It." *The Guardian* (March 17, 2006).

About the Author: Fiona McIntosh was the editor of *Elle* magazine, a position she left to launch a British version of the Italian magazine *Grazia*. As of 2006, McIntosh splits her time between her career and caring for her children.

INTRODUCTION

For most of recorded history, women have been given few choices about how to spend their lives. Before the advent of effective contraception, women had little control over pregnancy and childbirth, consigning many of them to mothering roles whether they chose such work or not.

While equally intelligent, women were frequently prohibited from obtaining advanced education, further limiting their potential advancement in a career. Finally, social and cultural norms commonly dictated specific gender roles, restricting the avenues open to women and forbidding them to hold certain leadership roles in homes, commerce, and government. Together these factors created a presumption that a human being's gender, at least if that person was female, determined that individual's purpose in life.

Many women found these assigned roles fulfilling and eagerly took their places as mothers, wives, and homemakers. But throughout history, a small minority of women have chosen to pursue stereotypically masculine occupations, and during the twentieth century an incrasingly large number of women began seeking the same right that men generally have: the right to choose their own careers.

The study of human beings and why they enjoy working is a relatively young science. In 1975, Hackman and Oldham developed a model which stated in specific terms what most people generally assume: some jobs are simply better than others. More specifically, this model said that any job can be measured on several criteria, and that these criteria will determine the overall satisfaction level of the job. For example, jobs requiring the use of a wide range of skills are generally more satisfying than jobs requiring the use of one single skill repeatedly. In addition, jobs that provide feedback on performance tend to be more satisfying than jobs in which no feedback is received. These findings helped managers and industrial engineers redesign many jobs so that they were more satisfying to workers than before.

Unfortunately, the job satisfaction model also raised new questions. In some cases researchers observed workers who were completely satisfied with their jobs, despite those jobs' abysmally low satisfaction scores. Even more perplexing, they also identified workers whose jobs appeared to be perfectly designed, but who remained unhappy in their work. Such observations prompted further research, leading to the conclusion that while certain tasks are generally more satisfying than others, a more important consideration is actually the congruence or fit between the worker and the job. A close fit between the job's demands and the worker's abilities and interests is actually more important to job satisfaction than the specific characteristics of the job. This finding helps explain why some workers find very repetitive work interesting, while others require a great deal of variety to stay motivated.

A working mother takes her daughter to school. © ROB & SAS/CORBIS.

The job fit perspective provides a basic understanding of why some women find motherhood a fascinating adventure while others find it frustrating and unfulfilling. When motherhood is viewed as simply one more career option, rather than a woman's preordained destiny, it seems reasonable to expect that not all women will be well-suited to it, just as all men are not well-suited to working as accountants or as landscapers. The feminist movement of the late twentieth century began as an effort to gain for women the same career and life choices which men had always enjoyed.

▉ PRIMARY SOURCE

It was at a drinks party at my daughter's school last week that I realised how deeply unfashionable I am. I was chatting to the father of one of my daughter's friends when he said: "Of course, it's difficult for you mothers being at home all day fretting about the girls."

"Er, I am not at home all day, because I work."

"Gosh! Really! Work! Do you? I had no idea."

It was as if I said I drove a Ford Fiesta or had just bought Westlife's Greatest Hits or something. I don't know who was more surprised—he by the fact I worked, or me by the way I practically apologised for having a job. How has it come to this?

Working mothers have had such a bashing lately. Every week we are ticked off in the press. We leave childbearing so late in life that we end up with two children instead of, say, five, we let career stress impinge on the unformed minds of our unborn children, and we allow other people to help care for our children. Why we bother to work at all is anyone's guess because the iniquitous pay gap means our salaries are much lower than men's.

Oh look, here comes another salvo. Darla Shine, author of the new polemic Happy Housewives, argues that the only way to female redemption is to scrub our own floors, look after our children 24/7 and have tea on the table for our husbands by 6pm.

What works for Shine may well work for thousands of other Happy Housewife acolytes, but will never work for me. I know this because when I did stay at home all day after the birth of my first daughter Ruby I turned into a fishwife. Shine says her marriage has never been better since giving up work, yet mine was never worse.

As much as I loved being with my daughter, I found it incredibly difficult to imagine a life without the stimulation of work. It wasn't the mothering bit I found hard to cope with, it was the feeling of being suffocated by domestic chores. So I nagged my husband to be home on time, complained about "having to do everything around the house and look after a baby, you know" and worried that I'd never be able to hold an adult conversation again. I don't know who was happier about me returning to my job as editor of Elle magazine: myself or my emotionally exhausted husband.

After the birth of my second daughter, Eadie, two-and-half years later, I was ready for a break from full-time work and desperate for a chance to spend more time with the girls. Like many women, I thought I'd go in search of that holy grail of work/life balance: the freelance career. When I wasn't worrying about having too little work, I was complaining about having too much, but most of the time it worked incredibly well.

It made me realise there are two kinds of women—those who thrive at home and those who, like me, need to work. What makes one happy, makes the other miserable. It's a personality thing, and it's no use feeling guilty about it.

Life would have continued like that, picking up either commissions or children from school. But then a year ago I was offered another back-to-the-coal-face job.

At the time, Ruby had just started school, Eadie was still in nappies, we had a partly renovated house that looked like Gaza and a nanny threatening to leave because her boyfriend was returning to Australia and she "couldn't live without him." The timing could not have been worse, but the job offer couldn't have been better. It was one of those career opportunities you might only get once in your life. As editor-in-chief of Grazia magazine, I was to head up the team launching Britain's first weekly glossy, with a budget of £16m and a staff of 43. It would mean sleepless nights fretting over circulation figures, evenings out schmoozing advertisers, early morning breakfast meetings and business trips to Milan. I could kiss goodbye to my family life as I knew it, because this job was hardcore 24/7.

Launching a magazine is a life-sucking experience but a totally exhilarating one too. Rather like that first flush of love, you think of nothing else. Taking the job was a totally selfish decision that meant putting my work before my family. It meant missing sports days, children's teas and the reception class poetry recital (this is London). At the school gates, I was the mother in Miu Miu heels and full makeup holding my child at arm's length in case she messed up my hair. Around me were freshly scrubbed stay-at-home mothers whose children played at their feet like puppies.

There were days when I felt like the World's Worst Mother, but I never once regretted the decision to take the job, and if the opportunity came up again I'd jump at it. My girls appear to have emerged unscathed and their mother is a much nicer person than the one who would have been simmering with resentment had she not taken up the offer.

But I want to be a bigger presence in my girls' lives, particularly now they are getting older and need help answering life's important questions, such as "Are God and Father Christmas the same thing?" and "Are our goldfish in the same Heaven as the whale what did die in the Thames?" So I have handed over the reins at Grazia and returned to a more balanced three-day working week.

I know I am very lucky to be working in an industry that values female minds. Publishers know that to reach women readers, you need female executives and if that means offering them more flexible hours to keep them in the workforce, then that's what makes best economic sense.

This surely has to be the way forward for other industries. There are too many clever women out there with wasted educations and redundant skills who have chosen not to return to work because of the all or nothing culture.

Maybe it's not about having it all, but having almost all. In the end it's about that basic feminist principle: freedom of choice. Choose whatever makes you happiest and don't do what I did and beat yourself up about it.

SIGNIFICANCE

As the feminist movement took shape it became somewhat antagonistic. Women who chose to remain at home with children were frequently looked down on by radical feminists, whose rhetoric equated motherhood with second-class citizenship and slavery; as a result women who might have welcomed additional life opportunities chose to remain outside the feminist cause.

As women began seeking greater workplace opportunities, companies began to recognize the vast potential resource women represented. During the 1980s, women were often relegated to the so-called Mommy Track by the assumption that a woman's expected absence from work to have children would prevent her from being a key player in the office. By the 1990s, many employers were launching innovative programs that supported women who chose to have both careers and families, an option long available to working men. On-site daycare, job-sharing, and a general recognition of the value of mothering all created an atmosphere in which a woman's choice to balance family and career was respected and in many cases encouraged. Though many women still chose traditional female roles, those who wished for other choices increasingly found such options open to them.

As of 2006, some of the early leaders in the feminist movement have moderated their once harsh tone; Gloria Steinem, who famously taunted that women need men as much as a fish needs a bicycle, ultimately decided to marry at age sixty-six. Other outspoken opponents of mothering have found that raising children is not the mindless drudgery they once believed it to be. In 2005, CNN reported that China, which has long encouraged mothers to work outside the home, was experiencing a noticeable rise in mothers choosing to remain at home with their children. U.S. Census Bureau statistics also confirm that stay-at-home mothers are far more common in upper-income families, suggesting that staying at home may now be seen as a status symbol.

For many women, the solution to this dilemma appears to be more complex than simply a choice between career and children; in many cases women have found that a blend of the two provides a satisfying mix of career and home life.

FURTHER RESOURCES

Books

Peters, Joan. *When Mothers Work: Loving Our Children Without Sacrificing Ourselves.* New York: Perseus Books, 1997.

Ramming, Cindy. *All Mothers Work: A Guilt-Free Guide for the Stay at Home Mom.* New York: Avon Books, 1996.

Venker, Suzanne and Laura Schlessinger . *7 Myths of Working Mothers: Why Children and (Most) Careers Just Don't Mix.* Dallas, Texas: Spence Publishing, 2004.

Periodicals

Adelman, Rebecca. "Have it All. And Less." *Maclean's* 119 (2006): 40.

Gottfried, Adele and Allen Gottfried. "A Long-term Investigation of the Role of Maternal and Dual-earner Employment in Children's Development." *American Behavioral Scientist* 49 (2006): 1310–1327.

Wolf-Wendel, Lisa and Kelly Ward. "Academic Life and Motherhood: Variations by Institutional Type." *Higher Education.* 52 (2006): 487–521.

Web sites

CNN. "The Stay-at-home Generation." May 25, 2005 <http://edition.cnn.com/2005/WORLD/asiapcf/05/17/eyeonchina.work/index.html> (accessed July 21, 2006).

Columbia University News Service. "Stay-At-Home Mothers Grow in Number." June 23, 2003. <http://www.jrn.columbia.edu/studentwork/cns/2003-06-22/316.asp> (accessed July 21, 2006).

Salary.com. "Dream Job: Stay-At-Home-Mom." <http://www.salary.com/careers/layoutscripts/> (accessed July 21, 2006).

Let's Celebrate. There's Never Been a Better Time for Mothers

Editorial

By: Mary Riddell

Date: March 26, 2006

Source: Riddell, Mary. *The Observer* "Let's Celebrate. There's Never Been a Better Time for Mothers." March 26, 2006. <http://observer.guardian.co.uk/comment/story/0,,1739788,00.html> (accessed July 22, 2006).

About the Author: Mary Riddell is an award-winning London-based journalist and a weekly columnist for *The Observer.* She is also known for her columns in the *Daily Mail* and the *New Statesman,* and is the author of a biography of Katharine Worsley entitled *The Duchess of Kent* (2000). Riddell's commentaries cover topics ranging from family policy, social reform, and foreign relations to the British monarchy.

INTRODUCTION

Mary Riddell's column, written for Mother's Day in 2006, is an engaging commentary on the current status of motherhood in the United Kingdom. Riddell also touches on how mothering is perceived in the United States and Europe, and how this has changed in the last decade. Books, articles, blogs, and Internet forums and discussions about the nature of motherhood, its history, the best way to mother, and the so-called mommy wars between stay-at-home mothers and working mothers, have multiplied exponentially in the twenty-first century. Not only has more ink (and bandwidth) been consumed on and by mothers than ever before, but much of the writing on these topics has become progressively more polarized and fervent. The decision to have children or to remain childfree, human nature and sexual differences, feminism, economics, parenting styles and techniques, and matters of class, race, and religion are all important components of the recent literature on motherhood, which includes both non-fiction and fictional works. Although mothers have been around as long as humans have, at no other time has this state been so thoroughly examined, debated, and discussed.

PRIMARY SOURCE

Think yourself lucky if you get daffodils this morning. In a cold March, the Mother's Day crop is late. So acute is the shortage that the Daily Mail, ever vigilant for new forms of delinquency, warns of 'the risk of daffodil-rustling, with youngsters raiding parks and gardens to get hold of the traditional floral gift.' The great daffodil crisis, product of a frosty climate and laced with social peril, seems emblematic of motherhood itself.

Has there ever been a worse time to be a mum? Having children is expensive and career-limiting. Last week's report by the Office for National Statistics confirmed that more and more women are working but that they earn, on average, 87 per cent of a man's hourly rate. It isn't just the money, though.

There is the Greek chorus of doomsayers warning of the dangers of bad schools and nurseries for babies.

There are the maternal stereotypes: the martyr, the boardroom zombie, and the Chelsea tractor Boudicca, fighting to the death to get her children into the right clarinet class. Motherhood has little upside and no icons, unless you count Sharon Osbourne, recently named celebrity mum of the year.

The paradox is that almost no one seems to want children, apart from those who cannot have them. Ask not for whom the clock ticks. A cohort of wealthy women is trying to squeeze children into the metronomic beat of time between career suicide and biological deadline.

Now flip this dirge around. There has never been a better time to be a mother. In an age of medical marvels, social liberalism and a modestly caring state, you don't have to be married, part of a couple, heterosexual, young, solvent or even fertile, although some of the above would be an asset. Equally, there is no better time not to have a baby. Your independence and freedom will be envied by harassed colleagues struggling to earn the £43,000 it costs to raise a child from infant to stay-at-home lodger.

Anyone mourning the death of the British housewife should look at Katja Behling's new biography of Martha Freud, who bore her husband six children in eight years and nurtured his genius as a turkey might incubate an egg. According to Freud's grandson, the Oedipus complex would never have been explored if he 'had had, say, to take his daughter to her dancing classes.'

The world moves on, but modern motherhood remains uncherished. British society, never child-friendly, has become positively hostile. Celebrating birth is for mums' chatrooms, where people announce new arrivals ('Nappies Galore has another gorgeous boy') with an effusion unechoed outside.

The latest jeremiad is in Prospect magazine, where Alison Wolf outlines the downsides of women's freedom. She cites the death of sisterhood, a decline in female altruism and growing disincentives to have children. But rich women have always exploited poorer ones. There never was a sorority of nappy-boilers, united by grim confinements and a dearth of tumble driers. Or, if there was, we are better off without it.

On statistics, Wolf is on surer ground. As she notes, financial penalties are tapered. A female graduate, born in 1970 and with two children, can expect lifetime earnings almost as high as her husband's. For less-educated women, that figure drops to 57 per cent of a male income, falling to 34 per cent for women with no formal qualifications, who are likely to work part-time and have longer career breaks. Yet, of these rich women, 40 per cent will enter their forties with no children, while poorer ones will keep on having babies.

Although UK women are having, on average, 1.74 children, well below the replacement figure of 2.1, the idea that the population will soon be made up of home-grown Methuselahs and Polish plumbers is wrong. More babies are being born each year. But, right-wing commentators assert, they are the wrong sort of babies. What we require, in a theory that flirts worryingly with eugenics, are the unborn children of rich women.

What we actually need is a population policy to plug the baby gap and nurture better citizens of all backgrounds. According to the Institute of Public Policy Research, the number of children wished for but never conceived now stands at 90,000. In France, the strong birth rate of 1.94 is down to pro-family measures that benefit all women, irrespective of wealth.

None of this wholly explains, though, why the British nanny-hiring classes are so reluctant to reproduce. They won't suffer much financially. Their good jobs cannot simply be whipped away. Yes, women bear more responsibility than men, but it is bizarre that workforce Amazons still play Martha Freud to partners who cannot pack a lunchbox. Obviously, the state should enable men to spend more time with their families, and force them to support their offspring, but in an age when men are uniquely disposed to be good parents, women also demand puzzlingly little of the fathers of their children.

That is partly down to guilt. Women are schooled to think of motherhood as hellish. Avid for the best for their children and terrified of failure, they are harangued like a doomed platoon by the drill sergeants of child nurture.

Judith Warner, an American mother who wrote of getting in 'three full hours of high-intensity parenting before I left for work,' is barely a caricature, and yummy mummies imply that you might as well not bother unless you have an elastic torso that enables you to morph from labour ward to Hello! shoot.

How did things get so bad? Partly because of the myth of maternal gloom, often spread by affluent commentators with flexible lives. But chiefly because children's value has been so downgraded. Why have a baby? Not out of social conscience, for no one is altruistic enough to offer up a newborn on the altar of the British economy. Some argue that, in a material age, children are the antidote to workaholism, consumption and introspection, but that is rubbish. Having a child means more of all of those.

Hardly anyone ever tells the truth, which is that children recalibrate adults' soured outlook and remake their world. They cost a bit, but so does any luxury. Richer women are disenchanted because having babies is seen, mistakenly, in terms of civic duty or biological imperative.

Some mothers are weighed down, by a child's illness or aberration. But for most, motherhood means pleasure, not drudgery. That is why, with or without daffodils, mothers should be celebrating today. Unless they champion their status, society never will.

SIGNIFICANCE

As Riddell notes, there has been a trend toward more complicated portrayals of motherhood in many recent memoirs (sometimes called "memoirs") and novels. Although few critics agree with Riddell's statement that women are currently taught that motherhood is hellish, many argue that recent authors dwell too much on the unsavory aspects of motherhood. Several authors have replied that they are attempting to counter the unrealistic, overwhelmingly joyful or humorous accounts of motherhood that predominated before the 1990s.

Riddell also mentions the inherent stresses of intensive parenting practices that have become prevalent amongst some upper socioeconomic classes in the U.S., and to some extent in the U.K., as described by Warner. The enormous proliferation of advice literature on mothering, many competing schools of thought on the best way to parent, and the idealization of motherhood in the media all contribute to what Riddell characterizes as the current neurosis.

Alison Wolf's 2006 article on feminism, social changes in the U.K., and related shifts in birth rates, which Riddell characterizes as a jeremiad, is just one example of recent examinations of motherhood and the changing role that mothers (both employed and those whose contribution is not figured into gross national profits) play in current theories relating economics, social change, population growth, and public policy. As Riddell describes from Wolf's work, women with children (particularly those with less education or who take a break from employment to do childcare) can, on average, expect to have lower wages than men. Riddell hints that pro-family policies can mitigate ensuing social changes and cites France as a better model. Although specific changes in employer and government regulation are not detailed here, Riddell lauded one such change—extending maternity leave from six to nine months in the U.K.—in her column for Mother's Day in 2005. Her conclusion—that unless mothers champion their own status, society never will—foreshadows recent activism by mothers in the U.S., where policies are generally much less family-friendly than in Europe and the U.K.

A baby asleep in a baby carrier on its mother's chest, London, England, 2005. © RUNE HELLESTAD/CORBIS.

FURTHER RESOURCES
Books
Blades, Joan and Kristin Rowe-Finkbeiner. *The Motherhood Manifesto: What America's Moms Want—and What To Do About It.* New York: Nation Books, 2006.

Douglas, Susan J. and Meredith W. Michaels. *The Mommy Myth: The Idealization of Motherhood and How It Has Undermined Women.* New York: Free Press, 2004.

Peskowitz, Miriam. *The Truth Behind the Mommy Wars: Who Decides What Makes a Good Mother?* Emeryville, Calif.: Seal Press, 2005.

Warner, Judith. *Perfect Madness: Motherhood in the Age of Anxiety.* New York: Riverhead Books, 2005.

Periodicals
Riddell, Mary. "Go Ahead, Make Mother's Day." *The Observer* (March 6, 2005).

Web sites
The Mothers Movement Online. "The Builders of New Myths: Friedan, Feminism and the Future, by Judith Stadtman

Tucker." March 2006. <http://www.mothersmovement. org/features/06/03/newmyths_1.html> (accessed July 22, 2006).

Wolf, Alison. *Prospect Magazine.* "Working Girls." April 2006. <http://www.prospect-magazine.co.uk/article_ details.php?id=7398> (accessed July 22, 2006).

They Can Go Home Again

Newspaper article

By: Valerie Cotsalas

Date: March 19, 2006

Source: Cotsalas, Valerie. "They Can Go Home Again." *New York Times.* (March 19, 2006).

About the Author: Valerie Cotsalas is a journalist employed by the *New York Times.* Cotsalas specializes in articles that examine issues pertaining to real estate and home ownership. The *New York Times* is a daily newspaper first published in 1851, and is among the nation's largest newspapers, with a daily circulation of over one million copies.

INTRODUCTION

The multigenerational family that is resident under one roof is not a recent American phenomenon so much as it is a more prevalent one. In the last 100 years, various immigrant cultures to the United States have functioned within a tradition of additional generations being resident in a family home, particularly elderly parents. The most prominent examples of such arrangements are found in Italian, Hispanic, Central European, and south east Asian immigrant populations.

In the agricultural communities of the United States, it was relatively common for a family farm to be concurrently operated as a business by multiple generations. For reasons of both the exigencies of farm labor and economy, it was common for farm families to live either under one roof or in very close proximity to one another on the farm property.

Home ownership in the form of a single family detached residence became a middle class American icon after the Second World War (1938–1945). The desirability of a home in the suburbs became a visible symbol of American success. The newspaper article identifies this symbol as an enduring one, even where

Masahiro Yamada, an associate professor of sociology at Tokyo Gakugei University, speaks about his bestseller on adult children who live with their parents, *The Age of Parasite Singles,* at his university office in Tokyo, Japan, February 3, 2000. AP IMAGES.

the rapid changes in both the demographics and the economics of American society have rendered single family home ownership more difficult for young adults in real terms than at any other time in American history.

The period since 1990 has seen the emergence of a dynamic that is both cultural and economic in origin—the young adult who is otherwise self supporting or capable of same who is resident in their parent's home on an indefinite basis. This dynamic has two distinct components. The first is the type described as the "boomerang kids." As the name implies, these are adult children who have previously left home on an intended permanent basis who suffered a reversal in their economic fortunes due to debt, loss of employment, divorce, or other unanticipated event. For the boomerang children, the parental home functions as a sanctuary and a temporary refuge while the adult son or daughter determines their next steps.

The second part of the dynamic are the young adults who have always planned to leave home and establish an independent residence, but who have been prevented from doing so as a result of economic factors, as opposed to social or culture limits. This second group of young adults often have significant college education debt that limits their financial ability to permanently move out of their parent's home.

As a measure of the demographic importance associated with multigenerational living, the United States Bureau of Census began the compilation of statistical data with respect to the various aspects of this issue in 2000. The Bureau of Census defines a young adult as those persons between the ages of eighteen and thirty-four years of age.

▉ PRIMARY SOURCE

A PERMANENTLY unfolded futon bed, piles of clothing and the smell of stale smoke make Sean Sciubba's cottage in Sea Cliff, N.Y., seem a lot like a college dorm room.

"They call it 'the Studio,'" Mr. Sciubba, 23, said of the friends who visit, weary of the childhood bedrooms they have returned to in their own parents' homes.

Mr. Sciubba's loftlike converted garage behind his mother's lavender Victorian affords him more privacy.

"The only time I see my mother is when I'm in the office," Mr. Sciubba said. Both work at Sherlock Holmes Realty in Sea Cliff on Long Island; he is the rental manager and she is a real estate agent.

It is hardly news that 20- and 30-somethings are living with their parents, camped in a back cottage or a childhood bedroom. The arrangement passes for entertainment, from the Fox sitcom "Free Ride,"about a college graduate who moves back in with his parents, to the comedy "Failure to Launch," starring Matthew McConaughey and Sarah Jessica Parker, about a 35-year-old man who never left home.

But the cost of real estate is making plenty of strange housefellows, with siblings, elderly parents and children, work mates, and friends doubling up to save on the mortgage or rent.

Some local governments are cracking down on cohabitants who are not related. In extreme cases, where day laborers and other immigrants are crowded into houses meant for single families, they are evicting.

Even the classic "mother-daughter" arrangement—a single-family home with an apartment added for a parent—is increasingly likely to be illegal, as the cost of

building such an apartment to conform to building and zoning codes can run up to $100,000.

And yet people all over the suburbs are making shared housing work, with some finding happiness and comfort in living with those they know and maybe even love.

"It doesn't feel that crowded since they're all family," said Ismama Joseph, 52, who lives in a four-bedroom duplex in Norwalk, Conn., with her husband, two adult daughters, their husbands, and the five grandchildren she cares for while the others are at work. "But it would be impossible with strangers."

In Fairfield County, Conn., many older people—"people who have lived their entire lives in Norwalk"—are selling and moving in with their children, according to Carol Ann Falasca, a broker at Coldwell Banker Real Estate in Norwalk. "their children went to the schools here and all of a sudden they're retired and they cannot afford to stay because of the taxes,"she said.

In New Jersey, Gordon Crawford, a real estate agent with Re/Max Properties Unlimited in Morristown, said about 10 percent of his buyers have been groups of family members buying together.

One such group included Suzanne Rosengold, a single mother, who was living last year with her daughter, Hanna, in a one-bedroom rental apartment in Parsippany in the same complex as her parents.

When Ms. Rosengold's grandfather died last year, the family inherited a Florida condominium that they sold, planning to use the proceeds for a down payment on a house.

After looking at dozens of houses, the Rosengolds found a four-bedroom ranch in Lake Hiawatha, a suburb of Parsippany. All three generations moved in last July—the first time any of them had owned a home.

The mortgage payment is the same as the combined rents the Rosengolds were paying before. "It has really changed our whole lives," Ms. Rosengold said. "my daughter has her own room now. Before, she had a converted dining room."

Her father, Edward Rosengold, 63, said: "I do things now that I've never done before. I have my own workshop. I build things, I repair things."

In another three-generation household, in Fairfield, Conn., Christina and Raul Diaz live in a three-bedroom 1,750-square-foot ranch with Mr. Diaz's 59-year-old mother, Leonor Martinez. Ms. Martinez takes care of the couple's 2-year-old daughter, while they work in nearby Stamford.

But the household will be growing, Ms. Diaz said. Her mother, Beth Bodnar, 70, who recently retired, is moving in soon, and the couple hope to have another baby next year. Ms. Diaz has been looking for about four months for a bigger house that the family can afford in Fairfield. They need about 2,500 square feet and, ideally, a ground-floor master bedroom, she said.

But pickings are slim.

"We're probably going to have to put it off another year to save more,"Ms. Diaz said.

The couple are assuming that the real estate market is not going to change at all, she added. "My big concern is how much equity we can get out of our existing house, because I feel like it's a buyer's market, not a seller's market,"she said.

Baby boomers reaching retirement age who want to move to a warmer climate are also increasingly helping their adult children expand their homes or buy a larger house.

They don't want to lose total contact with their lives here after moving to Florida or Arizona, said Elayne Jassey, a real estate agent with Prudential Connecticut Realty in Stamford.

Expanding one's living space to accommodate a relative may be a good investment, in spite of the cost of complying with zoning codes and the possibility of higher property taxes.

While "real estate prices have exploded," said Robert Campbell, professor of real estate finance at Hofstra University in Hempstead, N.Y., construction costs have risen more slowly with inflation. Under those conditions, he said, "building onto your own house is one of the best things that you can possibly do."

But where young people are concerned, multigenerational living is often seen as temporary. Matt Wolff, 31, has been living at his parents' home in White Plains, N.Y., for two years since friends with whom he shared an apartment in Bronxville, N.Y., went their separate ways.

Mr. Wolff is saving for a down payment on a co-op, "the last bastion of affordability" in the area, according to his father, Nick Wolff, who owns Century 21 Wolff, a six-office real estate agency based in White Plains.

"It's not a problem for us," the senior Mr. Wolff said of his son's situation, "but from his standpoint, he's a grown man and wants to be on his own and have privacy."

On Long Island, Sean Sciubba also says he won't stay in his mother's cottage forever. "I work in real estate," he said. "I've done the research. Hopefully, I'll be able to get out of there soon."

SIGNIFICANCE

The significant impact of multigenerational living arrangements in modern American society is underscored by the demographic and economic data derived from the Bureau of Census studies. The census determined that in 2005, an estimated eighteen million young adults (those between the ages of eighteen and thirty-four) were resident in the homes of their parents. Some of this segment would be composed of young adults who were finishing high school or college and preparing to leave the parental home in their early twenties. This group however is also comprised of persons such as Sean Scuibba, whose circumstances are outlined in the newspaper article, or the boomerang kids who have returned to the parental home after a period of independence that extended for a number of years.

The census data also confirms that as of 2006, 4.2 million American households were composed of three or more family generations. Within that segment of the population, 2.4 million American grandparents are the primary care givers to their grandchildren.

While the single family detached home remains a compelling symbol of financial success for many young Americans, the ability to obtain home ownership is becoming increasingly difficult for the young adult segment of the population. The historical income data gathered by the United States Census determined that the median real income for persons under age thirty-five fell by over 12% in the period between 1974 and 2004. Housing prices rose significantly in real terms (adjusted for inflation) during the same time span. It is this economic platform that provides a partial explanation for the fact that the number of young adults living at home rose by fifty percent during the same period. This statistical conclusion is determined in the face of greater than ever numbers of young adults graduating from college and presumably better equipped to earn greater income and achieve greater economic mobility than could previous generations.

The corollary to the economic and demographic data respecting young adults residing in the parental home is the perception that such persons have somehow failed; the boomerang kid and the yet-to-leave young adult are often viewed as unsuccessful persons, as opposed to being regarded as pragmatic. The young adults involved in such scenarios invariably regard the residence with their parents as a short term solution entirely dictated by their present finances and their inability to afford to purchase or rent their preferred accommodations.

The usual root causes of a boomerang kid returning to the parental home are a marital breakup or divorce in the child's family or varying kinds of economic setbacks. The single mother birth rate is an additional factor recently identified in the statistical and academic literature. In American society prior to 1980, the African-American population had a higher incidence of single mothers than any other American population segment. The marriage rate for this demographic was also significantly lower then for the Caucasian American population (as of 2005, forty-two percent of African-American women were unmarried, versus twenty percent of the white American population). Since 1990, the birth rate among white single women has increased by a factor of ten, creating greater opportunities for multi-generational living arrangements where the single mother returns to her parent's home with her child.

The day-to-day living arrangements agreed upon between a young adult and parents are also potential points of significant stress within these family relationships. The imposition of house rules for a boomerang kid who has lived independently for a period of time is often a divisive issue between the parent and the child. As young adults now study longer in post secondary school environments, marry later than at any previous time in American history, and tend to carry greater amounts of personal debt, the parent who has young adult offspring that re-establishes residence in their home must consider the personal consequences of this supportive action over a temporary period.

FURTHER RESOURCES

Books

Furman, Elina. *Boomerang Nation: How to Survive Living with Your Parents...The Second Time Around.* New York: Simon and Schuster, 2005.

Hayden, Dolores. *Building Suburbia.* New York: Vintage, 2004.

Riley, Terence. *Un-Private House.* New York: Museum of Modern Art, 2002.

Periodicals

Kenny, Judith. "The Rise of the Polish Flat." *University of Wisconsin-Milwaukee / Graduate School.* 19 (2005) 2.

Web sites

Washington Post. "Marriage is for White People." March 20, 2006 <http://www.washingtonpost.com/wp-dyn/content/article/2006/03/25/AR2006032500029_pf.html> (accessed July 28, 2006).

United States Bureau of the Census. "Historical Income Data." 2006 <http://www.census.gov/hhes/www/income/histinc/histinctb.html> (accessed July 28, 2006).

4 Family Life and Family Relationships

Family Life and Family Relationships

Some of the relationships within families are covered in depth elsewhere in this volume. The chapter "Marriage, Divorce, and Remarriage" features spousal relationships, while "Parenting and Children" discusses parents and children primarily in the context of the young nuclear family. This chapter features family relationships in a broader context, from caring for elder family members to communing with ancestors. Idealized family relationships and daily life portrayed in art ("Mother, Sara, and the Baby") contrast with the sensationalist news accounts of feuding mountain families ("Family Feud in the Mountains"). "My Family and Other Vehicles" discusses the tradition of the family vacation and the interesting relationship that many families have with the family vehicle.

One of the primary traditional roles of the family has been the care of the young, the old, and the infirm.

The responsibilities of individuals for the care of extended family members features prominently in this chapter. "The Young Carer" discusses young adults who provide care for ill parents and other family members. "As Parents Age, Baby Boomers and Business Struggle to Cope" and "From the Age of Aquarius To the Age of Responsibility" discuss older adults caring for elderly family members and changing trends in elder care over the past several decades.

Finally, religion is an important aspect of some families, influencing family structure, dynamics, traditions, and relationships. "Communion with Ancestors" discusses a religious ritual in which family members inquire about the deceased relatives. "Family Life Among the Mormons" offers a nineteenth-century defense of polygamist families in Utah.

Taking the Census

Illustration

By: Thomas Worth

Date: 1870

Source: Worth, Thomas. "Taking the Census." *Harper's Weekly*. November 16, 1870. © Corbis.

About the Artist: Thomas Worth (1834–1917), was a painter, illustrator, and lithographer who worked at the New York studios of Currier and Ives. Many of his pieces were published in *Harper's Weekly*, where he became known for the "Darktown" print series, then considered a humorous look at racial differences. He also created many sports-themed paintings and prints, concerned with bicycling, horse racing, hunting, and fishing. This image is now a part of the Corbis Corporation's collection.

INTRODUCTION

Although the first official census of the American population was taken in 1790 during George Washington's presidency, the concept of a population count was not a new one. The first recorded census in the territories that were to become the United States occurred in Virginia. Most of the colonies conducted some periodic type of inhabitant count.

The Constitution specifies the requirement and parameters for a national census:

"Representatives and direct taxes shall be apportioned among the several states which may be included within this union, according to their respective numbers, which shall be determined by adding to the whole number of free persons, including those bound to service for a term of years, and excluding Indians not taxed, three fifths of all other Persons. The actual Enumeration shall be made within three years after the first meeting of the Congress of the United States, and within every subsequent term of ten years, in such manner as they shall by law direct. The number of Representatives shall not exceed one for every thirty thousand, but each state shall have at least one Representative; and until such enumeration shall be made, the state of New Hampshire shall be entitled to chuse three, Massachusetts eight, Rhode Island and Providence Plantations one, Connecticut five, New York six, New Jersey four, Pennsylvania eight, Delaware one, Maryland six, Virginia ten, North Carolina five, South Carolina five, and Georgia three."

Today census results are used to determine government funding, the number of congressional seats for each state, electoral college votes, state and federal planning, and to create a statistical "snapshot" of the American population.

In the beginning, the census merely listed the names of the (primarily male) household heads and generally either counted or estimated the remaining numbers of household members. Beginning with the sixth decennial (occurring every ten years at the start of the decade) census in 1850, each household member's name was recorded. With each decade, the census became increasingly complex, progressively lengthening the amount of time it took to collect, tabulate, and publish the data.

PRIMARY SOURCE

TAKING THE CENSUS

See primary source image.

SIGNIFICANCE

The initial census data collection in 1790 was done by United States marshals under the supervision of Thomas Jefferson, then secretary of state. It is an interesting historical note that the data gatherers were required to utilize a specific format for information presentation, but had to wrangle their own paper on which to do so. The data gathering continued to be done by marshals through the sixth census in 1840.

It took eighteen months to gather all of the data for the first census, which asked several questions per household. They were:
Number of free white males aged 16 and older;
The number of free white males below the age of 16;
The number of free white females of any age;
The number of other free persons, listed by skin color—including those Native American Indians who paid taxes;
Number of slaves

Three million, nine hundred thousand people were counted in the first census, which is believed to be an underestimation. The data was posted publicly, although that no longer occurs. Raw census data is now completely confidential and is not released to the public until seventy-two years after collection. At present, the raw data from the first census through that conducted in 1930 are part of the public record and may be viewed either electronically on the Internet or via microfilm at the National Archives. Aggre-

PRIMARY SOURCE

Taking the Census: An illustration of census taking by Thomas Worth, featured in *Harper's Weekly,* 1870. © CORBIS.

gate information for each of the decennial censuses is available for research purposes.

By 1810, the census broadened its range and began to look at business data as well, gathering information on manufacturing plants and their products. More questions on production were added in 1840, with sections on mining, agriculture, and fisheries. In 1850, other types of demographic variables were added, concerning poverty (then called pauperism), churches and their membership, crime, and taxation. The 1860 census was the last to document slave status. Some names and counts of slaves were specifically gathered, in addition to listing the names of each household member and a description thereof (age, race, position in the family as child, spouse, other relative, occupation, date and place of birth, occupation, level of education, and so on). Other slaves were listed by age and race only and grouped by owner.

As the country spread westward, the census grew along with it to accommodate new states and territories, as well as areas under America's protection or jurisdiction. As the population and its census grew, it took progressively longer to gather and tabulate the data, pushing back the publication dates by several years. By the 1880 and 1890 censuses, it was taking nearly the entire intervening decade to process and publish the results. The federal government recognized that, while valuable information was being gathered, it was no longer an efficient or effective process. As a result, the questions were pared down for the 1900 census, which collected just population, manufacturing, agriculture, and birth/death data.

With twentieth-century technological advances, it became possible to gather data more efficiently and to process and distribute the results far more quickly. As a result, many of the questions and topic areas that had been eliminated were returned to the census. By the middle of the twentieth century, the United States Census Bureau had adopted the use of statistical sampling techniques that permitted them to identify specific population segments and survey sufficient members of each group to determine that a representative data sample had been gathered and could be generalized to the whole of the nation. After the 1996 Census, the Supreme Court ruled this broad approach unconstitutional and mandated an actual enumeration in the majority of population segments. With computer technology, it has become possible to draw ever-larger samples and to analyze and publish the data quite rapidly. Data is collected by mail, telephone, and in-person surveyors, to gather as representative a grouping as possible each decade.

FURTHER RESOURCES

Books

Darga, Kenneth. *Sampling and the Census: A Case Against the Proposed Adjustments for Undercount.* Washington, D.C.: American Enterprise Institute , 1999.

Goyer, Doreen S. and Gera E. Draaijer. *The Handbook of National Population Censuses—Europe.* New York, NY: Greenwood Press, 1992.

Kertzer David I., and Dominique Arel, eds.*Census and Identity: the Politics of Race, Ethnicity, and Language in National Census.* Cambridge, UK: Cambridge University Press, 2002.

United States Bureau of the Census. *Abstract of the Fourteenth Census of the United States: 1920.* Washington, D.C.: Washington Government Printing Office, 1923.

Periodicals

South Dakota Department of Labor. "From Inkwell to Internet: the History of the U.S. Census." *Labor Market Information Center: Labor Bulletin.* (May 2002): 1-4.

U.S. Census Bureau. "History and Organization." *Factfinder for the Nation.* (May 2000): 1–13.

Web sites

Ask Art—The American Artists' Bluebook. "Biography for Thomas Worth." <http://www.askart.com/AskART/artists/biography.aspx?artist=19206> (accessed June 26, 2006).

Cornell University Law School Legal Information Institute (LII). "United States Constitution, Article I Section 2." <http://www.law.cornell.edu/constitution/constitution.articlei.html#section2> (accessed June 26, 2006).

U.S. Census Bureau. "History." May 29, 2003 <http://www.census.gov/acsd/www/history.html> (accessed June 26, 2006).

We Invite Your Attention to Our Family Bible

Advertisement

By: Bradley, Garretson & Co.

Date: August 1874

Source: *Library of Congress.* "Emergence of Advertising in America 1850–1920." 2006 <http://jepoch.dth.jp/ww/scriptorium.lib.duke.edu/eaa/ephemera/A00/A0077/A0077-72dpi.html> (accessed June 27, 2006).

About the Author: Bradley, Garretson & Co. was a prominent publishing company based in Philadelphia in the latter part of the nineteenth century. The Library of Congress is the largest library in the world as well as being the oldest federal cultural institution in the United States.

INTRODUCTION

The family Bible has been an institution in the homes of many generations of Christian families since the arrival of the first significant numbers of English colonists in the early part of the seventeenth century. In early colonial times, newspapers were non-existent (the first regularly available colonial newspapers were not published until 1719) and books of any sort were a rare and treasured commodity that were only available if received from Europe. The family Bible was used in a number of ways in a colonial household—as a means of assisting in religious devotions, in the furtherance of Christian education, and as the only source of pleasure reading.

The family Bible acquired an additional status in Victorian times in the United States. In addition to its significance as the most important and the most sacred Christian text, the *Bible* became an important symbol of family strength and vitality. The *Bible* was commonly used as a chronicle where the important family events were recorded from generation to generation, including births, baptisms, marriages, and deaths. The entire genealogy of the family was often set out inside the front or back cover of the *Bible*. Important documents that related to the religious practices of the family, such as the temperance pledges that were common in Protestant households after 1850, were often inserted into the family Bible for posterity. In every respect, the family Bible was regarded and maintained as a symbol of God's presence and protection over the family.

Family Bibles were usually published in a format that gave the book an undeniable heft; by 1874, the family Bible was often the most prized heirloom among the personal possessions of an American family. This 1874 advertisement emphasizes the important distinction between a regular Bible and a family Bible.

Bible publishing became a significant growth industry after 1810 in the United States. The American Bible Society (ABS) was founded in 1816 in New York City to spread the word of God and the Christian faith throughout the world. By the time of the Civil War in 1861, the ABS was distributing its Bible throughout America; Bibles were provided to the soldiers of both the Union and the Confederate armies through the duration of the conflict.

The success of the ABS was an incentive to a number of commercial publishers to manufacture and market their particular style of Bible. There was a high level of religious observance associated with the traditional text, the King James Version, first published in England in 1611. Nineteenth-century commercial publishers such as Bradley, Garretson & Co. did not alter the biblical text but marketed many different physical styles of Bibles. In 1901, the American Standard Version of the Bible was first offered for sale, a version that represented the first attempt in American Bible publishing to market a Bible that utilized contemporary language.

PRIMARY SOURCE

WE INVITE YOUR ATTENTION TO OUR FAMILY BIBLE

See primary source image.

SIGNIFICANCE

The technique employed by the Philadelphia publishers Bradley, Garretson, & Co. in their 1874 advertising circular to attract sales agents to promote and market their new family Bible was reflective of both the times and the product. The modern concept of a "hard sell" would have been inconceivable with respect to almost any commercial goods in 1874, particularly the most revered of published Christian works.

The United States in 1874 was an overwhelmingly Christian nation. The commercial sale of a Bible did not relate to its content because it could not be marketed in any other format except the then standard King James Version. The marketing efforts of a sales agent would be directed to the outward appearance and style of the Bradley, Garretson, & Co. product.

Philadelphia, Pa. August, 1874.

DEAR SIR :—

We invite your attention to our FAMILY BIBLE.

Within a radius of 20 miles around you, there are *hundreds*, probably, entirely without a copy of the Bible—two or three times as many without a FAMILY BIBLE. Then think of the changes caused every year by removal; 'of the new families established; of the tens of thousands of such communities; and you will see a field—vast almost beyond comprehension—for such a work.

The need of the *Family* BIBLE, over an ordinary Bible, we have endeavored to show in the lower half of the middle column, 2d page, of the enclosed circular. We send out men filled with this idea; their work is to *awaken a desire* for a *Family* BIBLE in every home where there is not one already.

In getting up the work, we have spared neither time, pains nor expense, until it is a book that people of *taste,* everywhere, will appreciate; while the prices are so low as to invite investment by those in the *humblest circumstances.* And, believing the words of Dr. Robinson, (see descriptive circular, first page,) we shall push this work to the utmost.

In America, any good book, well gotten up, sold at a fair price, and in the hands of an honest, industrious Agent, can be sold profitably. But all over the land there are thousands of families *actually waiting for* a FAMILY BIBLE.

Thousands who have Family Bibles will buy this for the sake of the additional matter it contains.

The coming season promises to be a prosperous one; there is every prospect of an early revival of trade. The crops all over the country were never better. Good crops are *real value*—genuine wealth; and this year ever bountiful mother earth is pouring out her gifts upon her children, with *unusual liberality.*

Last fall we had the panic; this fall we can have none—there is nothing to make one out of. Money in all the great centres goes a-begging for borrowers. The country is not overstocked with goods as it was, and every thing is in a far *healthier condition* than for years before.

Now is just the time to enter upon the *fall campaign.* Autumn is the Agent's harvest time. A list for September or October delivery should now be started; then for the *great Holiday season.*

A Complete Outfit costs but $3. (It is *worth* $5.) SPECIAL TERMS makes Agents' profits average nearly $5. per copy. Territory everywhere: make selections of Townships.

Take hold yourself, if no more than to canvass your own neighborhood; also get us Agents, thus availing yourself of our *LIBERAL OFFER.* Take an interest in the matter, and it shall not be without reward.

Bradley, Garretson & Co.

PRIMARY SOURCE

We Invite Your Attention to Our Family Bible: An 1874 advertisement, selling family Bibles, also tries to convince people to buy Bible sales packages and resell them as sales agents. THE LIBRARY OF CONGRESS.

The advertisement has a measure of subtle evangelism in its words, a tone consistent with an era where the public battles over alcohol and temperance were being led with an evangelical zeal by the Women's Christian Temperance Union and other Protestant forces. Bradley, Garretson, & Co. was not simply seeking a sales agent for their publications, with the opportunity to earn significant commissions—the company sought someone who could awaken a desire for its product in places where a family Bible was not yet found.

The use of commission-based sales agents in the U.S. publishing industry became more common as the geographic extent of the potential market grew. In an era when the only means of communication was by letter or telegraph, publishers could efficiently distribute their products through the creation of agents, each with an assigned geographical territory. The element of trust that existed by necessity between the publishers and the sales agents during the late Victorian era is profound by modern standards: the publisher implicitly trusted the agent to provide an honest accounting of products sold and revenues collected by the agent. A review of the relevant literature and sales records from this period reveals that problems in relation to agent dishonesty rarely occurred. It was a common practice for Bradley, Garretson & Co. to operate with just a verbal agreement with the agents; it seems that there was an understanding by both parties that the agreements regarding the distribution of Bibles needed no further guarantees.

The 1874 advertisement is also significant in that the *Bible* is the best-selling book in the history of the United States. From a publisher's perspective, the *Bible* was an attractive publishing proposition because there were no questions regarding copyright and there were no costs associated with translation or other improvements to the text. A quality packaging of the *Bible* text could lead to significant profits, as the American culture of the period was such that a family that did not have a Bible in their home would be looked upon as almost irreligious.

The business operations of Bradley, Garretson & Co. are also of interest in their own right. The company had offices in various parts of the United States by 1870; it also established a Canadian presence in the Ontario cities of Toronto and Brantford by 1876. This manner of business was significant as a multinational publishing operation, even one that involved the generally neighborly division between the United States and Canada, was highly unusual. Bradley, Garretson & Co. anticipated the international scope of the American publishing industry by several decades.

FURTHER RESOURCES

Books

Brown, Candy Gunther. *The Word in the World: Evangelical Writing, Publishing, and Reading in America, 1789–1880*. Chapel Hill: University of North Carolina Press, 2004.

Gutjahr, Paul. *An American Bible: A History of the Good Book in the United States, 1777–1880*. Palo Alto, Calif.: Stanford University Press, 1999.

Nord, David. *Faith in Reading: Religious Publishing and the Birth of Mass Media in America*. New York: Oxford University Press, 2004.

Sivulka, Juliann. *Soap, Sex, and Cigarettes: A Cultural History of American Advertising*. Belmont, Calif.: Wadsworth, 1997.

Family Life Among the Mormons

Magazine article

By: Lloyd Bryce

Date: 1890

Source: Bryce, Lloyd. "Family Life Among the Mormons." *North American Review*. 150 (1890):339-351.

About the Author: The *North American Review* is one of America's oldest literary magazines, published from 1815 until 1940 and from 1968 to present. In the early 1800's, the journal was considered the country's leading literary publication. Lloyd Bryce was it's editor from 1889 until 1896.

INTRODUCTION

In the late nineteenth century, as the territory of Utah, populated largely by members of the Church of Jesus Christ of Latter Day Saints (or Mormons) worked toward joining the United States in statehood, one fundamental issue stood in the way: Mormons of that era preached and practiced polygamy, the practice of men marrying multiple wives simultaneously.

The practice of polygamy is not unknown in world history or even in Judeo-Christian philosophy: Abraham, the man claimed as the spiritual father of Islam, Judaism, and Christianity, took multiple wives, as did King David, King Solomon, and many other prominent characters in the Old Testament. However mainstream Christian practice and teaching have consistently held that marriage is to be monogamous, and

SCENES IN AN AMERICAN HAREM.

BRIGHAM YOUNG AND HIS FAMILY ON THEIR WAY TO CHURCH.

An illustration of the family of Brigham Young on their way to church. © CORBIS.

in 1604, the British Parliament enacted a law making bigamy, or taking two wives, a crime.

When the American colonies left British rule, most of the newly formed states passed their own anti-polygamy laws; Virginia was the first to do so, voting in 1788 to prohibit polygamy, making the crime punishable by the death penalty. In 1862, the U.S. Congress enacted the Morrill Act, setting penalties up to a $500 fine and five years in prison for acts of bigamy committed in any U.S. territory. Later laws prohibited bigamists from voting or holding public office, and the final such law, passed in 1892, prohibited polygamists from immigrating to the U.S.

Utah's entry into the United States was delayed for several years by contention over polygamous marriage. From 1849 to 1887, the territory made six unsuccessful attempts to become a state. The final effort failed despite a proposed Utah law making polygamy a misdemeanor, which Congress held was not strict enough. In 1890, the church's president formally announced a change in church doctrine, and polygamy was made a felony in Utah. In 1896, the Utah territory was formally admitted to the United States.

While outsiders' images of polygamy often resemble a harem in which one man lives with numerous wives and dozens of children, the reality was much different. Polygamy was never practiced by the majority of Mormon men, even during the nineteenth century. Mormon polygamists generally took two wives, though some took many more. The practice of polygamy lasted as long as it did because Mormons believed their right to practice it was protected under the Constitution's guarantee of freedom of religion. However, federal courts held otherwise, repeatedly upholding laws prohibiting bigamy and polygamy.

As part of the Mormon church's efforts to improve its image in preparation for statehood, the church spent more than $140,000 on an extensive publicity campaign intended to improve non-Mormons' image of the church. During this period, a child of Brigham Young, the Mormon leader who led the exodus to Utah, shared his experience growing up in a polygamous family.

PRIMARY SOURCE

The common statement that plural marriage debases husbands, degrades wives, and brutalizes offspring, is false. It was not the case in ancient Israel; it is far less so in this enlightened age. If any one wishes to prove this, here in Utah are men, women, and, above all, children to speak for themselves.

My father, Brigham young, had fifty-six living children, all born healthy, bright, and without "spot or blemish" in body or mind. Thirty-one of the number were girls; twenty-five were boys. Seven died in infancy, three in childhood, seven more since reaching maturity. What bright memories we cherish of the happy times we spent beneath our father's tender watch-care, supplemented by the very sweetest mother-love ever given to mortals! Ever thinking of us and our welfare, father was particularly anxious about our education. Deprived of all advantages in his youth but the often-mentioned "thirteen-days' schooling," he determined we should have the opportunities he had missed....

In the year 1868, the University of Descret was organized. Those of us who were sufficiently advanced at once entered upon the year's course. The old council-house, where the school was first opened, saw a happy crowd of young people that first year, who accepted such innovations as departments, class-rooms, offices, and a faculty with cheerful adaptation. The young idea shot bravely toward the newly-risen sun of Progress, tipping the arrows with intelligence and perseverance, even when the feathers were quilled into such points as the rapid diagramming of sentences in place of the old "Mary's a noun because it's a name"; as concert reading, which sorely taxed unused tongues; as weekly compositions, which were a sad necessity; and as the order and regularity which marked the very tap of the bell.

In my papers is a relic of the sound university year in the shape of a modest printed paper, called the *College Lantern*, on whose editorial staff appear the names of two of Brigham Young's children, a son and daughter, among the weighty list of editors; six there were in all.

Let any one who wishes to know the mental calibre of polygamous children ask the genial and learned Dr. Park, who has stood at the head of this university for twenty years, who have been his brightest and keenest pupils. His unhesitating answer will be a convincing argument for my position....

Music was, from before my remembrance, the constant companion, bore, and comfort of father's family. Himself a natural musician and a fine bass singer, he early brought musical instruments—piano, organs, and a beautiful harp—and procured as competent musical teachers

for the children as the country afforded. We inherited, almost universally, his taste in this direction, and the old piano in the long parlor was rarely allowed to rest its weary keys, but was ever laughing under Phebe's nor Nettie's hands, sighing under Fannie's or Ellie's skilful touch, or groaning or rattling beneath the infliction of more juvenile learners.

How pleasant were the seasons of evening prayer when ten or twelve mothers with their broods of children, together with the various old ladies and orphans who dwelt under the sheltering care of this roof, came from every nook and corner of the quaint, old-fashioned, roomy house at the sound of the prayer-bell. Even the bell has a memory all its own, for no matter how faintly the sound came to our distant ears, we always knew whether father rang it or some of the others. He had a peculiar, measured, deliberate ting-tang that could not be successfully imitated....

To the clang of the familiar bell we crowded from upstairs and downstairs, each one taking his accustomed place, mothers surrounded by their children, while near father sat Aunt Eliza Snow, the honored plural wife of Joseph Smith, the prophet. A little merry or grave chat; questions asked and answered; then the quiet paternal request, "come now, let us have prayers," succeeded by a subdued rustle as every knee bowed and every tongue was stilled while the dear voice prayed for "the poor, the needy, the sick and the afflicted, the widow and the fatherless, that He might be a stay and a staff to the aged and a guide to the youth." The prayer was always a short, simple, earnest one, never too wearisome for the tiniest restless listener, while the sweetly solemn hush of the room held a calm over even the baby's laughing voice.

With the general amen, all resumed their seats and were at liberty to return to their rooms or to stay and hear the chat that usually followed. Sometimes, especially on Sunday evenings, the girls would be requested to sing and play, or we would all join in a hymn. Afterward father would kiss the children, dandle a baby on his knee with his own particular accompaniment of "link-e-toodle-ladle-iddle-oodle," surprising baby into round-eyed wonder by the odd noise; then a general good-night and we would all separate, father returning to his duties in the office. What a blessed time that regular, never-neglected prayer-time was! For every one complied with one of the few unwritten laws of the household that nothing but sickness was an excuse for absence.

In summer we were happy with our school, the frequent May walks, picnics, swimming in the "font," and all sorts of summer games and amusements. In winter, school for the days, varied by skating and sliding down hill; the evenings were very short to us, for they were filled with private theatricals, corn-parching and popping, munching apples and walnuts, or making molasses candy, for which a large hook was hung in one of the lower rooms to "pull" the candy into a creamy whiteness.

We had our troubles. We thought them very real in those days; but their chief cause lay in the violation of some necessary rule of discipline. Our meals were served promptly, and the unlucky wight who was an hour behind time was apt to go hungry till the next meal-time. This seemed severe, but it made us prompt and punctual. Sometimes, too, were apt to imagine that some were more favored than others, and that their supply of a dainty exceeded the strict measure of justice.

We were so numerous that we seldom went beyond our own home for amusement except to an occasional dancing party or theatre. Instead, we got up theatres and concerts, pantomimes and minstrel shows, with unwearied vigor and fun. Father was seldom so busy that he would not spend an hour or so witnessing the theatrical performance or aiding in the final rites of pulling candy and braiding it into creamy sticks of delicious sweetness....

As a physiological fact, of the fifty-six children born to Brigham Young, not one was halt, lame, or blind, all being perfect in body and of sound mind and intellect; no defects of mind or body save those general ones shared by humanity. The boys are a sound, healthy, industrious, and intelligent group of men, noted everywhere for their integrity and for the excellent care and attention bestowed upon their families. In short, the name Young is a synonym of a good, kind, faithful husband. Among them are lawyers, merchants, a railroad king, a banker, an architect, a civil engineer, and a manufacturer. One of them is a colonel in the United States army, while several have graduated from the Annapolis naval school and from the Ann Arbor law school.

The girls are finely developed physically, quick and bright in intellect, high-spirited, and often talented, especially in a musical way. A few of them were beautiful girls, and are still handsome women. All are nice girls, kind in disposition, generous and social in their natures. In short, outside of one or two of either sex, they are a family that any man might well be proud to call his own. This is given by way of argument, not boasting.

In describing the family of Brigham Young, I have in the main described the large polygamous families of Heber C. Kimball, Daniel H. Wells, Orson Pratt, and oth-

An illustration titled, "Brigham Young and His Wives." © BETTMANN/CORBIS.

ers, who are or have been our leading men, with the various differences of character and mind naturally inherited by the various children.

The women, or "wives," as they were affectionately termed, of these various families, undoubtedly saw heartaches and sad hours. Do they not suffer, let me ask, in monogamy? Our mothers were the pioneers in this new order of things, and they had no experiences of elders to guide them, no friendly voice to say, "Here did I stumble; take heed lest ye too fall." Yet they were sustained by the knowledge that their sorrows were such as broadened and deepened the channels of their beings, and their tears watered into existence the lovely flowers of unselfishness and charity.

SIGNIFICANCE

Polygamy is still practiced in the twenty-first century; by some estimates two percent of the population of Utah, or around 40,000 people were living in polygamous relationships in 1998. Critics of the practice, besides arguing that it is inherently wrong on moral and religious grounds, also raise concerns that polygamists may forcibly marry minor females. They also worry that property law in most states does not clearly define inheritance or paternity in cases involving multiple wives.

Proponents of polygamy point out that courts have consistently struck down state statutes restricting private sexual acts between consenting adults. They also note that cohabitation without marriage is legal, even if the arrangement involves one man and several women. Finally, they argue that the law allows multiple husbands or wives in quick succession, therefore it should not criminalize a person who wishes to permanently commit to two spouses.

In 2001, Tom Green, an admitted polygamist, was sentenced to five years in prison for having sex with a minor; the child in question was his wife, whom he married when she was thirteen years old. Green appealed the verdict to the Utah Supreme Court, which rejected his appeal. In 2004, a married couple and a proposed second wife sought a Utah marriage license, which they were denied. The three filed suit against the state, arguing that their rights had been violated. The judge hearing the case dismissed it, noting a long history of court decisions upholding the state's polygamy prohibition.

FURTHER RESOURCES

Books

Mackert, Mary. *The Sixth of Seven Wives: Escape from Modern Day Polygamy*. North Salt Lake, Utah: DMT Publishing, 2000.

Solomon, Dorothy. *Daughter of the Saints: Growing Up In Polygamy*. New York: W. W. Norton and Company, 2003.

van Wagoner, Richard S. *Mormon Polygamy: A History*. New York: Signature Books, 1992.

Periodicals

Frank, Robert H. "Polygamy and the Marriage Market: Who Would Have the Upper Hand?" *New York Times*. 155(2006):C3.

Knickerbocker, Brad. "Crackdown on Polygamy Group." *Christian Science Monitor*. 98(2006):2-4.

Murr, Andrew. "Polygamist on the Lam." *Newsweek*. 147(2006):37.

Web sites

Georgetown University Law School. "Royce Bernstein, Friend or Foe: Mormon Women's Suffrage as a Pawn in the Polygamy Debate, 1856–1896." 1999 <http://www.law.georgetown.edu/glh/rbernstein.htm (accessed June 28, 2006).

Public Broadcasting Service. "Brigham Young." <http://www.pbs.org/weta/thewest/people/s_z/young.htm> (accessed June 28, 2006).

USA Today. "Polygamy Laws Expose Our Own Hypocrisy." October 3, 2004 <http://www.usatoday.com/news/opinion/columnist/2004–10-03-turley_x.htm> (accessed June 28, 2006).

Family Feud in the Mountains

Magazine article

By: Anonymous

Date: January 1896

Source: "Family Feud in the Mountains." *American Missionary*. 50 [January 1896]: 92-93.

About the Author: Missionaries, such as those from the American Missionary Association, began to enter Appalachia from the North in great numbers after the Civil War in the late nineteenth century. Appalachians had a history of resisting evangelization and missionaries were not always welcomed.

INTRODUCTION

In the late nineteenth century popular imagination, Appalachia was often mentioned in the same breath with violence, social conflict, and lawlessness. Commentators of the day applied the term, "feuding," to sustained incidents of localized clan violence in Appalachia.

Sensationalistic writing helped shape the image of the region as a primitive, untamed place. Legends of mountain feuds worked to cement Appalachia's poor national image. With little evidence beyond anecdotes, vague impressions, and their own stereotypes of mountain life, writers depicted Appalachian families as prone to feuding.

National newspapers reported numerous examples of violent community conflicts throughout the Appalachian region of eastern Kentucky and Tennessee, and western North Carolina in the Reconstruction era. Family feuds were often the result of local property disputes or social conflicts. Rural communities cut off from access to law enforcement and courts often turned to extended families or community leaders for conflict resolution. It was not until 1885 that some of these clashes began to be identified as Appalachian family feuds. Contemporary journalists and novelists spun the myth of the family feud, relying on regional and ethnic stereotypes to sensationalize local stories.

■ PRIMARY SOURCE

I have recently witnessed the result of a Kentucky riot, the first since I came here. Two desperate factions met on the night of the 25th, at eleven o'clock. Four men and a woman were engaged in it. The leader of the first faction fired and shot the leader of the second faction in his own house, and another of the first faction fired at the leader of the second faction till he fell with two balls through his left arm, one ball broke his right leg, and two balls went into his back. The leader of the second faction shot the leader of the first faction in the right leg and he fell; both men lying within a few feet of each other. The wife of the leader of the second faction took one of his pistols and started to kill the first leader, but one of his men stepped up with two revolvers and told her not to fire, that he would kill her if she did. This ended the shooting. The first faction helped to carry the leader of the second faction in the house and then took the first leader away. They used thirty-two and forty-four calibers.

The first leader lives four miles from my house. When they told him he could not live he asked them to send for me. I went and helped dress his wounds and

sung and prayed with him. He said he had been a bad man, and asked me to pray for him. I heard to-day that some of his friends wanted him to send for some other minister, but he said no, he wanted no one but myself; and I expect to go and see him to-morrow if he is still living. I believe in the near future we will have a good hold in eastern Kentucky, if the American Missionary Association is successful in getting the right ministers. The minister's wife has a great deal to do with his success in this work....

SIGNIFICANCE

In the late nineteenth century, the idea of Social Darwinism gained the support of many influential Americans. In this theory, the poor were considered mired in poverty because they were too lazy, stupid, or criminal to compete effectively. Only the strong survived, as part of the natural order. Accordingly, Appalachia was considered the poorest part of the nation because of the actions of the Appalachians. It was acceptable for outsiders to take advantage of the many natural resources of the region because it was natural for the strong to exploit the weak. At the same time that popular accounts of feuding appeared in the press, timber and mineral corporations were scrambling to get a piece of the Appalachian bounty.

The popular portrayal of feuds fed the idea of Appalachia as a quaint and bizarre region that had little in common with the rest of the country. This idea has remained popular through succeeding decades. Appalachia remains one of the poorest regions in the United States, with illiteracy and unemployment rates higher than the national average. However, the region is also a culturally rich area with a diverse population. Reality does not match the old stereotype.

FURTHER RESOURCES
Books

Billings, Dwight B. and Kathleen M. Blee. *The Road to Poverty: The Making of Wealth and Hardship in Appalachia*. New York: Cambridge University Press, 2000.

Pudup, Mary Beth, Dwight B. Billings, and Altina L. Waller, eds. *Appalachia in the Making: The Mountain South in the Nineteenth Century*. Chapel Hill: University of North Carolina Press, 1995.

Waller, Altina L. *Feud: Hatfields, McCoys, and Social Change in Appalachia, 1860–1900*. Chapel Hill: University of North Carolina Press, 1988.

Mother, Sara, and the Baby

Drawing

By: Mary Cassatt

Date: 1901

Source: Corbis Corporation

About the Author: Mary Cassatt (1844–1926) was an American artist, printmaker, and painter. An Impressionist, she was strongly influenced by the French painters Edgar Degas and Gustave Courbet. In addition to the production of her own art, she supported other Impressionists, offering many young artists financial assistance as well as practical and promotional support. Among her more frequent artistic subjects were children and family scenes. She spent most of her life in France, living and working in Paris from the age of thirty until her death.

INTRODUCTION

Developmental psychologists and social science researchers know that sibling interactions affect a child's ability to form healthy and lasting relationships later in life. They are the first important social partnerships, involving shared parents, homes, play spaces, family members, and homes (sometimes sleeping areas as well). Children develop internal belief systems and layers of understanding about themselves and their place in the world based on the ways in which parents and other family members treat them. Siblings who are relatively close in age often form each other's first peer relationships, providing experience in conflict negotiation, property sharing, rule creation, and the natural consequences of behaviors.

Research indicates that there may be a significant relationship between the degree of affection and perceived cohesiveness of sibling relationships and later perceptions of personal adjustment and satisfaction with peer and partner relationships. There is also a positive correlation between very young children's perceptions of sibling bonds and parental and family dynamics: the greater the discord or unhappiness in parental or familial interactions reported by the parents or primary caregivers, the greater the stress between the siblings. Conversely, the greater the reported marital satisfaction, family social functioning, familial cohesiveness, and perceived closeness, the closer the sibling bonds. Developmental and social psychology research literature also suggests a correlation between self-assessments of sibling interactions and degree of bonding, and family assessments of within-family and extra-family social functioning.

The ways in which children create and develop their relationships with brothers and sisters of all types (biological, adopted, foster, other first-or second-degree live-in relatives, step- and extended family members), greatly influences their creation of future interactions, intimate (sexual and nonsexual) and otherwise. Research indicates that children use the degree of harmony (or disharmony) as a yardstick with which to assess their place in the family, as well as their general approach to interactions with the outside world. They use their experiences with conflict resolution and problem-solving with siblings to judge their place in the world: younger children subjected to physical or verbal aggression by older siblings are more likely to report anxiety and fearfulness, as well as submissiveness, in their interactions with other children than are those whose interactions involved either negotiation or lack of perceived significant conflicts.

PRIMARY SOURCE

MOTHER, SARA, AND THE BABY
See primary source image.

SIGNIFICANCE

Simply put, siblings experience their interactions from very different perspectives—colored somewhat by their age differences, places within the family, and individual temperaments and personalities. Extensive sibling group research conducted in many different countries shows that affection, support, friendship, and degree of interpersonal cooperation between sibling pairs and the outside world bears no significant relationship to the degree of argument or conflict between them. Among the most salient variables affected by age differences or birth order are degree of control or dominance, perceived power, degree of affection, and desire to be in the presence or to share time with the other. Others often mediated by birth order are jealousy, irritation, antagonism, competition, usually experienced by the elder in relation to the younger, and admiration, and keen interest in spending time together typically displayed by the younger. There is usually a degree of waxing and waning as the siblings mature: early closeness may give way to some distance and awkwardness in later childhood, only to be rekindled during the late adolescent and adult years.

PRIMARY SOURCE

Mother, Sara, and the Baby: American artist Mary Cassatt's painting, *Mother, Sara, and the Baby.* © CHRISTIE'S IMAGES/COR-BIS.

An 1886 illustration of children on a see-saw, from *From Gold to Grey.* © CORBIS.

In siblings of different ages (not twins) in which there are no major disparities caused by chronic or acute illness, physical, cognitive, or emotional disabilities, there are generally hierarchies of leadership, influence, ability to control the decision making process of the group, degree of dominance, and mentoring abilities across the sibling continuum—often, but not necessarily, mediated by chronological age, physical size, and birth order. Frequently, elder children take on the role, generally unasked, of teaching younger siblings essential life skills: letters and numbers, colors, facts about the world such as the names of the planets, days or the week, months of the year, and the like, simply as a rite of passage. In some households, the notion of family loyalty is emphasized until ingrained; in such families the siblings often champion one another and refuse to tolerate any negative behavior or bullying of younger—and sometimes older—siblings by "outsiders." They are supportive and kind to one another in public settings, such as school, places of worship, and other similar locales. That loyalty may or may not extend to household behavior.

In other families, sibling rivalry is keen, and kindness minimal. There may be considerable judgment and criticism, and frequent disagreements that may escalate into physical altercations, particularly when there are considerable differences in temperament, or one sibling is much more dominant and controlling than another. In such situations, there may be long-lasting rancor and eventual estrangement, or the siblings may eventually either settle or agree to let go of their differences and forge a healthy relationship after growing up.

The ways in which people experience themselves and others is affected considerably by the nature of sibling relationships. Not only is the nature of the everyday interactions important in each child's growing awareness of the workings of the world, but the self-comparison that goes on as a child watches the ways in which the outside world responds differently to each child in a family is pivotal in the development of each sibling's self-concept and sense of self-esteem. This may be especially so when there are clear-cut differences in abilities or talents, such as when one child is more artistic than another, or more academically or athletically skilled—the child whose talents are less obvious may acquire a feeling of being "less than" or may choose to strive to excel in other areas, depending on innate level of self-esteem.

Sibling relationships also set the stage for self-perceptions, developing coping skills, learning how to assert one's rights and defend those of another, in creating bonds of love and loyalty that will last for a lifetime, and aid in the healthy development and maintenance of future relationships with the outside world, as well as with significant others.

FURTHER RESOURCES

Books

Bank, Stephen P., and Michael D. Kahn. *The Sibling Bond.* New York, NY: Basic Books, 2003.

Barter, Judith, ed. *Mary Cassatt: Modern Woman.* New York: Harry N. Abrams, 1998.

Kelsh, Nick, and Anna Quindlen. *Siblings.* New York: Penguin Books, 1998.

Linn-Gust, Michelle. *Do They Have Bad Days in Heaven? Surviving the Suicide Loss of a Sibling.* Albuquerque, NM: Chellehead Works, 2001.

Sanders, Robert. *Sibling Relationships: Theory and Issues for Practice.* Hampshire, UK: Palgrave Macmillan, 2004.

Twerski, Abraham S., and Charles M. Schulz. *I Didn't Ask to Be in This Family: Sibling Relationships and How They Shape Adult Behavior and Relationships.* New York, NY : Henry Holt & Co., 1996.

Periodicals

Brody, G. H., Z. Stoneman, and M. Burke. "Child Temperaments, Maternal Differential Behavior, and Sibling Relationships." *Developmental Psychology.* 23, no. 3 (1987): 354–362.

Dunn, J. C. Stocker, and R. Plomin. "Assessing the Relationship between Young Siblings: A Research Note." *Journal of Child Psychology and Psychiatry.* 31 (September 1990): 983–991.

Martin, J. L., and H. S. Ross. "The Development of Aggression within Sibling Conflict." *Journal of Early Education and Development.* 6 (1995): 335–358.

Stocker, C. "Children's Perceptions of Relationships with Siblings, Friends, and Mothers: Compensatory Processes and Links with Adjustment." *Journal of Child Psychology and Psychiatry.* 35 (November 1994): 1447–1459.

The Family in Soviet Russia

Magazine article

By: Sidney Webb

Date: April 1933

Source: Webb, Sidney. "The Family in Soviet Russia." *Current History.* (April 1933): 52–60.

About the Author: Sidney Webb (1859–1947) was a British aristocrat who supported Socialism and the Soviet Union's shift from monarchy to a communist state. Webb served as a member of Parliament (MP) and was a member of the Fabian Society, which believed that capitalism had created an unjust and inefficient society. Other members included George Bernard Shaw (1856–1950) and Edward Carpenter (1844–1929).

INTRODUCTION

After the fall of the Russian monarchy in 1917, the Bolsheviks gained power with the aim of turning Russia into a collective society. In 1918 civil war broke out between Bolsheviks—"Reds"—who sought to turn Russia into an ideal communist society and monarchists, conservatives, and more moderate socialists—"Whites"—who resisted the Bolsheviks' extreme approach. By 1922 the Reds had won, but at the cost of more than fifteen million dead Russians. An additional one million fled the country; more than seven million children were orphaned or abandoned, many malnourished from famine and neglect, and the weakened Soviet government faced the question of how to manage the children while building a new society.

Upper class and aristocratic or royal women in pre-revolution Russia as well as peasant women experienced dramatic changes in their social roles. While many wealthy Russians fled the country in 1917 and 1918, those who stayed were subject to the new Bolshevik rules. The Soviet government worked to redefine gender roles; women were considered to be men's equals, and expected to be educated and to work in the same manner as men. To this end women from all classes were given greater opportunities to attend university and to work as doctors, engineers, and teachers; those not selected for university or professional positions worked as factory laborers, farm hands, and in government offices. Child care was managed by the state, with the *crèche* system, nurseries designed to watch infants and small children while mothers and fathers worked. The crèche system performed another crucial role: to educate mothers on their new role as

A breadline for mothers with babes-in-arms, in the Soviet Union, February 1, 1934. © BETTMANN/CORBIS.

workers for the state, and on how to raise their children to be productive members who followed the Soviet ideal.

As industrialization proceeded, and factory work was concentrated near cities, the old multi-generational family unit gave way to simple nuclear families in urban centers with a small number of children. Initially women were given broad reproductive rights; abortion was legalized in 1920 with strict parameters for safe abortions. According to Alice Withrow Field (1909–1960), in her 1932 book *Protection of Women and Children in Soviet Russia,*

> Out of every hundred pregnant women who come to the Moscow clinics, from eighteen to twenty ask for abortions. If the woman asking for the abortion is healthy, economically up to standard, living in good social conditions, is not burdened by a large family and is not mentally deficient (when she would probably not ask for the abortion), the doctors and social workers all try to prove to her that she does not need the abortion and that it would be a social crime if she did not bring her child into the

world, and that she would be endangering her own good health by such a step. If they cannot persuade her, the abortion is performed and it is considered important to do so, since a woman who will stand out against all such persuasion really does not want a child and is therefore unfit to have one.

Under the Tsar, abortion was illegal and a crime equal to murder.

The institution of marriage changed after the revolution. Religious marriage was replaced with civil marriage, and inheritance rights—removed in the early years after the revolution and civil war—were reinstated in part by the late 1920s. Marriage was stripped of its former economic meaning, according to Soviet ideology. By providing women with greater rights under communism, the Soviet government claimed, marriages could be based on mutual respect and affection rather than status or financial need.

This excerpt, written by Sidney Webb, British supporter of the Soviet state, gives a foreigner's perspective on the Soviet family.

...On no part of the life of Soviet Russia is there in other countries so much difference of assertion (if not of opinion) as on what is happening to the institution of the family. On no subject, perhaps, is it so difficult to make either an accurate or a convincing statement covering either all aspects of the inquiry or all parts of the U.S.S.R....

We must begin by realizing the nature and the magnitude of the changes that the revolution has wrought in the position, first of the women of Soviet Russia, and then of the children and adolescents....

How much Russia has lost, on the disappearance of practically all its upper and middle class women of leisure with their standards of value and their refinement of manners, it would be hard to estimate. Of educated women engaged in professional work (as doctors, scientists, teachers or writers, or in music, dancing or the drama) the number was formerly relatively small; and of such of these as have not emigrated with the wealthier classes, a considerable proportion seem to have accepted, more or less sympathetically, the new regime, under which they promptly found their feet and continued their careers amid the rapidly growing number of women professionals.

What we have to concentrate attention on is, none of these relatively small groups, but the great bulk of the adult women of pre-war Russia, at least nine-tenths of the whole, who were either the hard-working wives, daughters or widows of peasants, fishers or hunters or of independent handicraftsmen, or else domestic servants in superior households, or (in relatively small numbers) factory operatives, chiefly in textiles. There is little information available as to what that mystic entity "the family" in fact amounted to among these vast hordes of hard-working women, but pre-war native literature gives a dark picture. The great majority of them were illiterate and superstitious and in complete subjection to their husbands or fathers. It is not usually remembered that a large proportion of them, possible as many as one-fourth, were Mohammedans, and were habitually veiled, with the status and ignorance that this implies....

Now let us see what changes have occurred or are in progress. The first thing that the Bolshevik revolution brought to the women of Russia was their complete legal and constitutional emancipation; the second was their education on an equality with men; and the third was such a planning of the social and economic environment as could be devised to lighten, as far as practicable, the exceptional burdens of the maternal and domestic functions incident upon their sex. Thus women over 18 were at once given votes on the same conditions as men, with equal trade-union and co-operative membership, and equal eligibility for promotion. All occupations and all positions were thrown open to both sexes. No distinction is made between the sexes in wages or salaries, holidays or insurance benefits. No woman is deprived of her job on marriage, though she may, and often does, prefer to abandon it, perhaps only for a term of years, for child-bearing and motherhood. The laws relating to marriage and divorce, and their privileges and responsibilities, have been made the same for women as for men. It must be added that women working in industrial factories have been accorded certain special privileges and protection in the interests of the children no less than those of the mothers, such as sixteen weeks' continuous leave of absence on full pay round about their confinements, the right of taking time off without loss of pay to nurse their babies every few hours and the provision of a crèche at every industrial establishment, at which the young children may be safely left throughout the working day.

These changes, which few would object to characterizing as reforms, were, unlike so many that we have heard of, not merely enshrined in legislation. The visitor to the U.S.S.R. cannot fail to see them nearly everywhere in operation. In the various technical schools he will notice nearly as many girls as boys, learning to be engineers or carpenters, electricians or machinists. In every factory that he passes through—and not merely in the textile and clothing trades—he sees women working side by side with men, at the lathe, the bench or the forge, often sharing in the heaviest and most unpleasant tasks as well as in the skilled processes. Women work in and about the mines and the oil fields equally with the men. On board the Soviet mercantile marine there is a steadily increasing number of women sailors, engineers and wireless operators, usually dressed as men, as well as stewards and cooks and cleaners. A large majority of the school teachers and more than one-half of all the younger doctors are women. In all the offices women swarm not only as stenographers but also as translators, confidential secretaries and responsible executive assistants....

It is universally taken for granted that, so far as pay is concerned, not only is there no distinction of sex but also no inquiry as to whether a woman is or is not married or the mother of children. There is, accordingly, in Soviet Russia no such discouragement of matrimony as exists in Great Britain and some other countries, where the hundreds of thousands of women who are school teachers, civil servants and municipal employees are, in effect, forbidden to marry, under penalty of instantly losing their employment.

All this concerns, however, in the main, the women of the rapidly growing cities and other urban aggregations all over the U.S.S.R., together with such of the vocations, like teaching, doctoring and administration, as have to be exercised in town and country alike. The great majority of the women of Soviet Russia, as well as of the men, are connected with agriculture (together with hunting and fishing) or essentially with rural pursuits. What has happened to the wives and daughters in the 25,000,000 families of individual peasants, fishers and hunters? To them the revolution has brought the same legal and constitutional emancipation as to the women in industry and the professions. Even in the extensive areas in which Islam prevailed, the women have been set free, and many millions have abandoned the veil and are themselves learning to read and write, while rejoicing in being able to send their children, girls as well as boys, to the local school, and in an increasing number of cases to the technical college or the university.

The Soviet Government, in fact, is undoubtedly bringing to the country dwellers, year by year, a steadily increasing measure of the opportunities in education, medical attendance and social insurance now enjoyed by the cities, although in all these advantages the country necessarily lags behind the town. Thus, while in the cities there are varied educational opportunities for all the girls as well as for all the boys, and nearly every child is at school, this is naturally not yet the case throughout all the vast area from the Baltic to the Pacific, and from the Persian frontier to the Arctic Ocean, including much that is occupied by primitive tribes or nomads. A steady stream of additional doctors, largely women, is, year by year, sent into the villages; while the number of maternity and general hospitals, large or small, accessible to at least a proportion of the villages, increases annually....

The greatest change in the social circumstances of the peasant women began only five or six years ago with the concerted movement for the substitution of the collective farm for the individual small holding. This movement is still in progress, and reaches different heights in different places, both the number of collective farms and the degree of their collective organization showing a steady annual increase. Down to 1932 about 18,000,000 peasant holdings, with about 70,000,000 of population, had been more or less merged in about 226,000 collective farms, in some districts occupying the whole of the agricultural land. We need not consider here the vicissitudes of the movement, or the mistakes and failures that accompanied its progress, often, it is to be feared, with great cruelty to the recalcitrant kulaks (the relatively wealthy individual peasants). Nor can we critically scrutinize the measure of economic advantage, in the way of mechanization and increased production which has, in varying degree, already resulted from the change. The very low level of efficiency, alike among the workers and in the management, plainly brings down the produce to terribly poor rations wherever and whenever the weather

is unfavorable. Here we can deal only with its effect on the position of the women and children.

In a collective farm it is usual for the peasants to retain their own individual dwellings (or to erect new ones), each with its own garden ground, its own cow, and its own pigs and poultry. Only in a tiny proportion of cases does the collective farm take the form of a commune in which all the production is carried on in common and the whole proceeds are shared. Usually it is only the grain that is sown and harvested in common, the proceeds being divided between the government which has supplied the tractors (and often the seed and fertilizer), on the one hand, and the cooperating workers, male and female, each in proportion to the days or hours of labor actually contributed, on the other hand.

The collectivization does not usually stop at this point. The open meeting of adult residents, in conjunction with its elected committee, by which every collective farm is governed, presently begins to make such improvements as a modest grain store or a primitive silo, an improved dairy on modern lines, a new school building or a village hall, and presently a clubhouse, with its library, its dance floor and its cinema. Later there may be a crèche where the children can be safely left when the mother goes to work in the dairy or in the fields, a common kitchen and dining room in which such as choose may take their meals or purchase cooked food, and even a few bedrooms at a low rent for single men or widowers. Naturally, all this takes time, and the farms differ as much in the rate at which the collective amenities expand as in the order in which they are adopted. What delays progress is the sly skulking and neglect of work manifested by many of the sullen peasants, together with the inefficiency of the management, which naturally has to be overcome, very largely by painful "trial and error."

But almost from the start there beings, for the women, a social revolution. Life as lived in the old cluster of timber-framed mud-huts that used to be the peasant village and labor as spent in solitude on the scattered strips of each peasant's holding become alike transformed. No one can know by personal inspection what is happening on as many as 226,000 collective farms. But a significant confidential report was lately made, not by an transient visitor but by a well-qualified informant who had seen the farms repeatedly in many different provinces, to the effect that, whatever the degree of efficiency attained, while the old man peasant had only unwillingly come into the new organization and was still sullen about it, his wife and also his children almost invariably rejoiced in the change....

The resulting emancipation of the wife and mother, as well as of the children, cannot easily be estimated. This is what has been happening during the past seven years, in varying degrees and at very different grades of efficiency of collective administration, to two-thirds of all the village population of Soviet Russia....

In every form of propaganda, the main insistence is on respect for the emerging personality of the child and the utmost possible development of his or her individuality, having always in mind that the child is the future citizen and producer, whose individual capacity must be raised to the utmost. In the home, as in the school, there must be only the most sparing use of mere prohibitions. The child should always be induced to choose the more excellent way. To strike a child is, by Soviet law, a criminal offense. Parents are taught that punishment of any kind is felt by the child as an insult, and should as far as possible be avoided. Self-government must be aimed at in home and school, even to the discomfort of the elders, and even if there has to be some discreet "weighting of the alternatives" by parent or teacher in order to steer the choice.

To the child, even from tender years, in infancy as in adolescence, the incessant lesson is its obligation to serve, according to its powers, successively in the household, in the school, in the factory and in the State. To this end the children's needs are ceaselessly attended to. So far as government administration can insure it in so vast a country, whoever else goes short the child always has a full ration of milk, of clothing, and of schooling, together with hospital and other medical attendance. Making every allowance for the imperfection of vital statistics, all the evidence points to a great and continuous decrease in the infantile and child death rates.

There are toys and games in every institution and on sale within reach of every parent, with ample provision for play and recreation out of doors as well as indoors. But the toys are as deliberately planned as the curriculum or the books—no tin soldiers and few dolls, but abundance of bricks for building, miniature tools for actual use, and working models of locomotives, airplanes and automobiles, through which it is intended and hoped that the whole population may in time acquire "machine sense." The visitor may see, as the slogan on the gay poster decorating an infant crèche: "Games are not mere play, but preparation for creative labor." When the elder children go into camp in the Summer they are shown that it is immense fun not to "play at Indians," but to help the peasants in their agricultural work; one party of twenty was proud to be told that they were ranked, in the aggregate, as four grown men. The Pioneers find their joy largely in the voluntary "social work" that they undertake in groups, helping the younger or more backward children in their lessons, "liquidating illiteracy" among the adults of their neighborhood, clearing away accumulations of dirt or debris, forming "shock brigades" to reinforce the

workers where production is falling behind the plan or when some special task has to be got through with a minimum of delay.

And these children stick at nothing! The Moscow Pioneers took it into their heads the year before last to wait upon many of the directors of the theatres and cinemas in order to give their own views upon the current productions, and to expostulate on their shortcomings and defects. In a small urban district some 200 miles from Leningrad the Pioneers undertook to "liquidate" the excessive consumption of vodka that prevailed. They got put up in every workshop the following appeal on posters manufactured by themselves:

> We, your children, call on you to give up drinking, to help us to shut drink shops and to use them as cultural institutions, pioneer clubs, reading rooms...

The children whose parents drink are always backward at school

> Remember that every bottle you drink would buy a textbook or exercise book for your child. Respond to our call and give us the chance of being well-developed, healthy and cultured human beings. We must have healthier home surroundings. (Signed) Your Children, the Pioneers of [the district.]

The school band then led a gaily decorated procession of children round the workers' quarters. They booed the men as they came out. A public meeting was held in which the children took the leading part. As an immediate result hundreds of workmen are reported to have promised to give up vodka.

This emancipation of children and adolescents, together with the constant encouragement of their utmost participation in social work of every kind, makes of course for a "priggishness" among the young and an attitude of criticism of their lax and slovenly elders which is not altogether pleasing to the bulk of their fellow citizens of mature age. Thus the new cult of hygienic living among the Pioneers may be excellent, but their irritating habit of "opening windows in other people's houses" is frequently complained of by elderly relatives. But as an instrument of lifting the people of Russia out of the dirt, disease, illiteracy, thieving and brutishness of pre-revolutionary days the self-governing democracy of Communist youth appears to be extraordinarily well devised.

There arises the interesting question: "What is the sexual morality that is being evolved among the 5,000,000 or 6,000,000 Pioneers and Comsomols?" For this widespread organization of the Soviet youth involves intimate social intercourse between boys and girls. They are constantly together. They meet continually, not only in school or college but also in the hierarchy of meetings, committees, representative conferences and executives that constitute the League of Communist Youth. They associate in sports and games, in "social inspections" and "shock brigades" and in all sorts of voluntary social work. Hygienic self-control seems to be the dominant note, together with full responsibility for any offspring, a responsibility enforced by the strictly administered law as to parental maintenance of children by father and mother alike, according to their economic capacity. Subject to this emphasis on personal hygiene and parental responsibility, there is undoubtedly considerable freedom in sex relationships according to choice, without any sense of sin, but with the constant reminder that efficiency in study or production must not be impaired. You must not waste time or strength on sex. To do so is like indulgence in betting and gambling, alcoholic drink and even the smoking of cigarettes—"bad form" among the Comsomols.

Now these great and far-reaching changes among the women, children and adolescents of Soviet Russia, paralleled, of course, by no less important changes among the men, must inevitably have caused changes of like importance in the institution of the family. These changes require analysis. We may note, to begin with, that there is no sign of any decay of the family group which mankind has derived from its vertebrate ancestors, and which doubtless owes its great survival value to the advantage to the offspring of maternal devotion and prolonged personal care. Not even the most hostile critic reports any deliberate abandonment of children by their parents. Mother-love seems to be the same in Soviet Russia as elsewhere, and Soviet fathers appear to be just as much interested in their children as British or American. The children form just as much a part of the family circle as with the American or British wage-earning class. The crèche, the school and the college take the young people out of the home just about as much as the same institutions, within comparable income grades and similar household resources, do elsewhere. Whether children and adolescents are less obedient to their parents or more than contemporary British or Americans, it seems impossible to compute. The answer to any such criticism is that the young people in all countries in the twentieth century are much less under their parent's thumbs, perhaps even less under their parents' influence, than was the case in the nineteenth century. There seems available no specific evidence that this particular emancipation has gone further in one country than in another....

There is undoubtedly in Soviet Russia a greater freedom than in many other countries in sexual intercourse, based on mutual attraction and friendship, among the unmarried of both sexes and all ages. Such unions, which are utterly without sense of sin, are condemned neither by law nor by public opinion, and they often turn into suc-cessful permanent marriages. Divorce is at the will of either party, but there is a strict enforcement of the legal responsibility of both parents for the maintenance of any offspring, according to their respective economic capacities. Anything like promiscuity, with or without marriage, is now seriously reprobated by opinion. "I do not want to inquire into your private affairs," Stalin is reported to have said to an important party member who was leading a scandalous life, "but if there is any more nonsense about women you will go to a place where there are no women."

We may perhaps sum up by saying that the great increase in personal freedom brought about by the revolution, together with the almost universal falling away of religious and conventional inhibitions, undoubtedly led, for the first decade or so, to greater instability of family life and to looser relations between the sexes based on mutual friendship....

During the past few years public opinion seems to have been moving strongly in favor of—to use a native expression—"stabilization," and any tendency to prompt, reckless or repeated divorce meets with condemnation. No general or centralized statistics permit of comparison between the number of divorces and those of marriages. Such figures as have been published for particular cities and years appear to show totals (and local variations) in Soviet Russia not markedly unlike those of parts of Scandinavia and different States of the United States.

SIGNIFICANCE

As Webb notes, every facet of family life was changed by the Soviet regime: mothers, wives, fathers, husbands, and children alike were given new roles in society and even in the home as the new ideals were backed up with action.

The Young Pioneer Organization of the Soviet Union, founded in 1922 and in place through 1990 when the Soviet Union began to disband, was an after-school organization similar to the Boy Scouts; in the USSR its mission shifted to support the state; as Webb observes, "a 'priggishness' among the young and an attitude of criticism of their lax and slovenly elders which is not altogether pleasing to the bulk of their fellow citizens of mature age." By using preteen and teenage children to monitor social rules and to pressure those who violated new norms, the Soviet government shifted the balance of power in family and neighborhood relationships.

Men under the new Soviet government were expected to absorb a great deal of change in gender roles; the Soviets characterized pre-revolution families as patriarchal, with too much power centered in the man. Alexandra Kollantai, the U.S.S.R.'s first Minister of Social Welfare, stated that once the new Soviet mores became part of society, "Family households will inevitably die a natural death with the growth in number of communal houses of different types to suit different tastes. Once it has ceased to be a unit of consumption, the family will be unable to exist in its present form; it will fall asunder and be liquidated." Fredrich Engels viewed the family as an agent of capitalism; private property and inheritance laws turned the family into an economic, rather than emotional, unit. By abolishing private property and placing children in the hands of the state as their mothers worked alongside men as equals, Engels, Lenin, Stalin, and other political thinkers and leaders believed that the revolution would continue on.

By 1936, reproductive rights began to change; Stalin's government offered stipends to families with many children, and by the late 1930s the government began to restrict abortion. In the early 1940s single persons and childless couples were given an additional tax, and the state supported illegitimate children; the crèche system was intact though less pervasive, as more mothers were permitted to stay at home with children on a limited basis. The goal, in Stalin's view, was to produce more children to become workers in the system.

By the early 1980s, an article in *New Internationalist*, from December 1982, noted that "There are women cosmonauts, women street sweepers and women scientists in the Soviet Union today. In fact, two thirds of all Russian women work outside the home, though they are still only 45 per cent of the labour force. But because power relationships within the family have remained largely unchallenged women remain second class citizens." The gender role changes promoted in the early years of the U.S.S.R. incorporated the state's role in assuming child care, maternity care, and other functions to support the family and women's work; as the costs of such programs became overbearing, the USSR dropped or cut funding for such designs, leaving women with a double burden: child care and job. The revolution designed to free women from oppression gave women greater work opportunities but did not shift the classic gender role paradigm found in many societies.

FURTHER RESOURCES
Books

Clements, Barbara Evans. *Bolshevik Women*. Cambridge, U.K., and New York: Cambridge University Press, 1997.

Engels, Fredrich. *The Origin of the Family, Private Property and the State*. Hottzingen-Zurich, Germany: 1884.

Field, Withrow Alice. *Protection of Women and Children in Soviet Russia*. New York: E.P. Dutton, 1932.

Goldman, Wendy Z. *Women, the State and Revolution: Soviet Family Policy and Social Life, 1917–1936*. New York: Cambridge University Press, 1993.

Heywood, Colin. *A History of Childhood: Children and Childhood in the West from Medieval to Modern Times*. Cambridge, U.K.: Polity Press, 2001.

Wood, Elizabeth A. *The Baba and the Comrade: Gender and Politics in Revolutionary Russia*. Bloomington: Indiana University Press, 2001.

Zelizer, Viviana. *Pricing the Priceless Child: The Changing Social Value of Children*. Princeton, N.J.: Princeton University Press, 1994.

Web site
New Internationalist. "Two Steps Forward, One Step Back." December 1982 <http://www.newint.org/issue118/two.htm> (accessed July 10, 2006).

Not Mine, But Ours

Magazine article

By: Elmo Stoll

Date: November 1977

Source: Stoll, Elmo. "Not Mine, But Ours." *Family Life Magazine* (November 1977).

About the Author: Elmo Stoll was the pastor and founder of the Christian Community in Tennessee. An Old Order Amish by birth from Ontario, Canada, Stoll created an intentional Christian community that brought together people from different Christian denominations to work together as a diverse community in the 1970s, opening Anabaptist communities to outsiders.

INTRODUCTION

The Old Order Amish originated in Switzerland during the 1520s. Believing in the separation of church and state, and rejecting infant baptism, the Amish—also known as Anabaptists—were considered heretics in the sixteenth century. Called the "Plain People" or "Amish" in the United States, they trace their origins in the U.S. to William Penn, who provided the Amish with a safe haven in Penn's Woods, or what

An Amish family in a horse-drawn wagon. © THOMAS B. HOLLYMAN. SCIENCE SOURCE/PHOTO RESEARCHERS. REPRODUCED BY PERMIS-
SION.

came to be known as Pennsylvania. More than eighty percent of all Amish are in Pennsylvania, Ohio, and Indiana, though they have established communities in nineteen states and in Canada and parts of Central America.

The word "Amish" comes from Jacob Amman, a Bishop within the Anabaptist church who promoted the basic tenets of Old Order Amish life: plain clothing, non-violence, rejection of technology and higher education, and a focus on the Bible as a guide for daily life.

Numbering more than 80,000 worldwide, the Amish have steadily come into conflict with modern society. As compulsory education laws were passed in the U.S. between the 1850s and 1920s and high school attendance became mandatory for all children through the age of sixteen in most states, the Amish tradition of stopping education at eighth grade to focus on the community and to build a nuclear family of one's own clashed with public policy. Amish people do not vaccinate their children and reject some aspects of modern medicine, leading to clashes with public health offi-

cials and mandatory vaccination laws for school entry. In addition, the Amish reject all electricity, telephones, cars, and airplane travel; communities rarely number more than two hundred; and members who choose to break rules are banished or shunned.

In 1990, Elmo Stoll, then in his mid-40s, broke away from the Old Order Amish community in Ontario and developed a new vision for diverse Christians to live together. Throughout the 1970s and 1980s, Stoll was a frequent contributor to *Family Life*, one of the rare magazines for "plain people." In this essay, written thirteen years before Stoll broke with his church, he articulates a concern for the changes in modern American family life.

■ PRIMARY SOURCE

Somehow the family should be such a close-knit unit that sharing is the most natural thing in the world. Sharing cannot be difficult where there is a strong feeling of love and appreciation for each other. Learning to share our toys and childhood belongings should be the foundation for easy sharing on a wider scale in the adult world.

However, families are not only for sharing material possessions. More important yet is the sharing of feelings, of problems, and of joys. In the shelter of the home, we should be able to discuss with frankness our hopes and disappointments, knowing that we are speaking to those we can trust.

Another thing that should be shared within the family is work. No home is without work, and it is fortunate that this is so. Any child who doesn't grow up helping with dishes, or doing chores, or running errands—has been cheated out of a good start in life. The family should be the place to learn to work cheerfully and well, even eagerly. Work should be shared by everyone willingly chipping in, and not by a legalistic insistence that each does an earmarked portion.

A happy family life requires giving of ourselves. We must learn to sacrifice, learn to give up our will for the other.

Some families are just so many individuals with the same last name, living in the same house. They seem to lead separate lives, go their own ways, each independent of the other. If you ask where another member of the family is, they rarely know. Apparently, they don't know where the rest of the family is, or what they are doing. Each is busy living their own life. They lack the essential elements of a joyful family life—love, togetherness, loyalty, sharing.

These sad little groups of lonely individuals are not families at all. They are failures. They are missing out on one of the greatest challenges on this earth—building a meaningful family relationship where work, possessions, and even feelings can be shared in love and trust.

SIGNIFICANCE

Stoll's critique of the modern family in the late 1970s became even more relevant as technologies such as email, the Internet, cell phones, and other personal devices helped to separate people from community and from social dependence in real life, rather than virtual life online. Social forces affecting the family in 1977 included the dramatic increase in mothers entering the workforce, divorce rates that were on the rise, increased crime rates, and juvenile delinquency and teenage pregnancy rates that painted a picture of families in crisis.

While stereotypes of Amish life include the belief that the plain people reinforce a repressive culture that forces children into the flock, in fact all adolescent Amish boys and girls experience *rumspringa*, a term

that translates roughly as "running around." During *rumspringa* the Amish teenager has an opportunity to experience worldly life; many choose to smoke, drink alcohol, or use street drugs, and use modern technology such as cars, telephones, and computers. In Amish life the children are granted a time to experiment, and then to decide whether to be baptized as full adults and to remain a part of their community by choice, not coercion. Eighty-five to ninety percent of all Amish teens return to their communities after *rumspringa*; the foundations of community and cooperation are most often cited as reasons for this choice. Stoll, in his article, champions this connection and points to the lack of such meaning and cooperation in worldly families.

Stoll sought to create a community that would welcome non-Anabaptists into a slower, community-rich life that could bridge the Amish tradition and the more worldly life, to blend both into a diverse community of Christians living together with similar goals. The Christian Communities started with the Cookville, Tennessee project, which incorporated Old Order Amish, German Anabaptists, and Mennonites, as well as "seekers," those who were not from plain people background but sought that life. In time, four more communities developed, all between 1990 and 1998; Stoll died of a heart attack in 1998 at the age of fifty-four. By 2004, the five communities had disbanded to be absorbed by nearby plain people communities.

As technology increased at a rapid pace, online chat rooms, message boards, and networking websites gave people the tools to connect virtually. While families are pulled in more directions physically between school, work, sports, and other responsibilities, Stoll's commentary and vision speaks to a different option, one that 80,000 people have been living for nearly five centuries.

FURTHER RESOURCES
Books

Hostetler, John A. *Amish Society*. Baltimore, MD: Johns Hopkins University Press, 1993.

Schactman, Tom. *Rumspringa: To Be or Not to Be Amish*. New York: North Point Press, 2006.

Stoll, Elmo. *The Midnight Test*. Aylmer, Ontario: Pathway Publishers, 1990.

Stoll, James, David Luthy, and Elmo Stoll. *Seeking True Values*. Aylmer, Ontario: Pathway Publishers, 1968.

I Knew It! I'm Really a Nubian Princess (…Well, in a Previous Life)

Magazine article

By: Angella Johnson

Date: March 2, 2003

Source: Johnson, Angella. "I Knew It! I'm Really a Nubian Princess (…Well, in a Previous Life)." *The Mail on Sunday (London)*, March 2, 2003.

About the Author: Angella Johnson has written for numerous British publications including *The Times, London Daily News,* and *The Guardian.* She is also a popular speaker.

INTRODUCTION

Men and women throughout history have been judged and evaluated based on the identity of their parents. Monarchies thrived based on the assumption that royalty was an inherited trait and that only certain individuals, descended from royalty, were fit to sit on the throne. The caste system of India dictated certain life roles depending on one's family, and birth into certain classes doomed one to a life of poverty and social rejection. Families frequently passed occupations from generation to generation, gradually developing a surname associated with their trade, such as Carpenter (woodworker), Cooper (barrel maker), and Ferrier (horse shoer).

In some cases men and women of mixed ethnic heritage have been required to prove their membership in a certain group based on their ancestry; individuals wishing to prove their membership in a Native American tribe can do so by demonstrating that they had a Native American ancestor within several previous generations. Hawaii's famous private Kamehameha School has long given preference to applicants of Hawaiian descent, even in cases where an applicant can claim only a tiny degree of Hawaiian ancestry. Recent court cases have challenged the policy as being discriminatory.

Southern states attempting to stop blacks from voting in the years after the Civil War frequently employed Grandfather Clauses, which stated that the descendents of any man who voted prior to 1867 could vote in current elections; because no blacks could vote prior to 1867, this policy effectively allowed voting by otherwise ineligible whites but no blacks. In some states residents of mixed ancestry were considered white only if they had a certain percentage of white ancestors, otherwise they were labeled black.

In attempting to advance the so-called Aryan race and exterminate the Jews, Hitler and the Nazis needed a clear definition of exactly who was Jewish. The standard they chose defined a Jew as any person with three or four Jewish grandparents, or who was married to a Jew. Those with one or two Jewish grandparents were considered inferior to non-Jews but not to the degree of an actual Jew. In order to be accepted as a true Aryan, a member of Hitler's so-called superior race, one had to prove his Aryan bloodline back to at least the year 1750.

The discovery of DNA in 1953 and subsequent advances in genetic research have vastly broadened the understanding of individuality and how human characteristics are passed from generation to generation. DNA, short for deoxyribonucleic acid, is the material within human cells which contains the genetic blueprint for growth and life. DNA is found in all human cells, making it particularly useful to criminologists who might use the DNA from a strand of human hair to identify a criminal. In one of its most significant applications DNA evidence has exonerated numerous men from serving time for rape and other crimes. On July 11, 2006, James Tillman was released from a Connecticut prison after serving eighteen years of a forty-four-year sentence after DNA tests proved that Tillman could not have committed the rape which led to his imprisonment.

DNA tests are also helpful for mothers wishing to identify the father of a child. For about $100, numerous labs will analyze DNA samples from a man and a child, then determine whether the man is the child's father. DNA testing is also commercially available for partners wishing to determine whether a spouse or partner has been sexually active with another person.

In the early years of the twenty-first century several companies began offering DNA analysis to determine a person's historic anthropological group. While not always specific in its findings this test allows an individual to determine where her ancestors originated, providing potential clues to her racial background.

■ PRIMARY SOURCE

I always thought I knew exactly who I was and where I came from. I was born on the Caribbean island of Jamaica, so were my parents and their parents before them. But having come to Britain at the age of seven and

Schoolchildren process samples of their own DNA in a Human Genome learning lab in New York City. © GEORGE STEIN-METZ/CORBIS.

spent virtually all of my life since then in this country, I have always considered myself to be British-Jamaican.

Last week I learned differently. After sending a sample of my DNA to a laboratory in Oxfordshire, a geneticist informed me that I am, in fact, an L3F Lalamika. This revelation meant nothing to me, but after further investigation it seems I belong to a rare and precise genetic group. Lalamika is found in only one million of the planet's six billion people—which makes me pretty special.

But even more remarkable was the analysis of my DNA which showed that I share genetic material with people from Nubia, Egypt, Somalia, Iraq, the nomadic Tuaregs of West Africa and the Islamic Fulbe tribe of Nigeria.

That is a fascinating geographical cocktail whose ingredients tell an extraordinary story of slavery, kidnap and rape spanning thousands of years.

The test I took to discover this could not have been simpler. I took a swab of skin tissue, delicately extracted from inside my cheeks with a toothbrush (taking care to avoid the teeth, otherwise there was a danger of discov-

ering the DNA of what I ate for lunch), put it in an envelope and sent it off to the laboratory.

Just two weeks later, I had before me a map of my DNA, a document that told me not just what I was now but where I had come from over thousands of years. The test, by a company called Oxford Ancestors, based in Kidlington, Oxfordshire used my mitochondrial DNA (mtDNA) – genetic information passed exclusively through the female line. This gives, in effect, a clearer picture than tracing the DNA through the paternal line, which contains more mutations.

The analysis begins from the premise that about 150,000 years ago there was a single human female, "Eve," from whom we are all directly descended. As human DNA diversified and the population grew, particular strains of DNA developed and these have been identified by scientists and divided into 36 clans. My Lalamika clan is an offshoot from Lara, the dominant clan of Africa and west Eurasia.

As it happens, relatively little is known about Lalamika because of its rarity. But DNA samples appear to show that the type never strayed far from Africa, unlike other descendants of Eve who went on to populate the rest of the world. For example, Helena—another clan—accounts for 47 per cent of native Europeans. She is the most common of European clan mothers and can be traced all over the world.

But my roots are a good deal more complicated and surprising.

About 20,000 years ago my ancestors were, according to my DNA, from Nubia, one of Africa's first developed black cultures whose history was charted from 3,100 BC onwards by written records, from Egypt and Rome. Geographically, it covered a 500-mile stretch of land along the river Nile, which on today's map is one-third in southern Egypt and the rest in northern Sudan, It was once a land boasting great, natural wealth in the form of gold, ebony, ivory and incense.

Evidence suggests that around 900 BC, a Nubian monarchy began to emerge with an unusually high number of ruling queens and princesses.

Their physical characteristics of darker skin colour, Mediterranean facial features and frizzy hair meant they stood out from neighbouring Arabs to the north.

The Egyptian Pharaohs coveted Nubia's wealth and colonised the area at various times in its history—and they weren't the only ones. During the slave trade, between the 15th and 19th Centuries, Nubians often became victims of raiding parties of Abyssinians who attacked their villages at night and kidnapped young men and women.

The young women were frequently raped. They would be taken north and sold to the Arabic slave traders of northern Africa and the Middle East lands that are now part of Iraq. There they were kept in bondage, and again young women were sexually abused by both the traders and owners.

Historians have found that the darker-skinned slaves were less popular among the lighter-skinned Arabs and were often sold to the Tuareg tribesmen of northern Africa and the Sahara, who were nomadic stockbreeders. Their roving existence took them westwards across the vast expanse of the Sahara, where they would trade animals and slaves in the markets of the West African coast.

In the 400 years from 1450 to 1850 about 21 million Africans were enslaved. Traders made fabulous profits and slavery was accepted as the norm in most African societies long before Europeans arrived.

But once they began arriving in the 16th Century, the trade in slaves boomed. Millions—among them my ancestors—were marched across the desert, often forced to carry ivory and copper. When they reached a port they were inspected like animals, sold and crammed into ships and transported to the New World—America and the Caribbean.

By the late 19th Century, 12 million Africans, about a third of them women, had made that voyage. Up to two million slaves died on the Atlantic crossings, which took from one to nine months on trading ships owned by white men. Probably as many again perished before they even made it on to the ships.

I now know that my ancestors must have made the long, forced march across the desert to reach Nigeria because my DNA, which shows strong influences from Eastern Africa, also shares key similarities with the DNA of the Fulbe people, the dominant tribe of Nigeria.

The next journey of my forebears would have been across the Atlantic to Jamaica. My mother knows that she was born in Jamaica and so were her parents, but before that she knows no more about our family history. The problem is that as slaves, many Africans were forced to abandon their languages, their cultures and their identities.

Families were separated and scattered, never to meet again. Few written records were kept and many of them have been destroyed over time. The result is that 400 years on, descendants have very little detailed knowledge of where they originally came from.

Now the study of DNA is changing all that. It is revolutionising our understanding of history and revealing many surprises. A recent BBC study which sampled 200 volunteers established that around 13 per cent of the DNA inherited by black Britons did not originate from Africa. In fact, it found that one in four black men had a white father in his family tree.

Mark Anderson, a 23 year old Londoner, took part in the study. He was shocked to find out that his paternal line did not lead back to the Caribbean but to Germany.

He said: "I wasn't expecting to hear that at all. I just thought, 'How on Earth is that possible?' In hindsight it makes perfect sense. European slavers had sex with African women. So, of course, many of us would have European blood. But at the time it was a massive shock."

So am I equally shocked by what I have discovered about myself? Absolutely, I had expected to find some white blood in me, especially as my mother is quite light in complexion. But never in my wildest dreams had I expected to find such strong Arabic and Islamic connections. I'm hoping that my father, whose paternal line apparently goes back to Ghana, will get his DNA tested to see if I can discover more.

But not everyone can get a precise account of their own development through their DNA. The scientific process is not simple. Most of our chromosomes become jumbled up as they are passed on but the mitochondrial (female) and Y (male) chromosomes continue through the generations unchanged, providing stable havens where distinctive DNA sequences and markers can settle and take root, first within families, then, as those families expand, within clans and ethnic groups. This provides rich material for reconstructing the major migrations and dispersals of our past, but using it to trace the ancestral origins of individuals is less precise.

Only about a tenth of people of African-Caribbean origin have mtDNA sequences that are sufficiently distinctive to be linked to particular areas. In the case of black people displaced through slavery, the overwhelming majority can expect to receive answers no more precise than that they originated in West Africa.

Given the history of the slave trade and the fact that Africa has hundreds of ethnic groups whose land boundaries were introduced only with the arrival of Europeans, it is perhaps not telling them very much.

Even a reliable DNA match traces the ethnic or regional origins of just one ancestor out of many. Going back just ten generations, each of us has about 1,000 ancestors; go back further and the figure is soon in the millions. Yet with ancestral pride on the increase—genealogy is the second most popular subject (after pornography) on the Internet—more and more people, white and black, are turning to genetics hoping to fill in the blanks of their ancestral backgrounds.

Several firms already offer 'dNA genealogy' tests, but behind the scenes geneticists are divided over just how meaningful and reliable the tests are. I was lucky—my DNA sequence was unusual enough to give a better picture of my past.

But Dr. David Ashworth, director of Oxford Ancestors, warns: "You can get some sense of where your roots lie, but it is not everything that you are.

While this process offers a fascinating insight into the human condition; it's only a tiny component. This is a very crude measurement because it follows only a single ancestral line. It must always be kept in perspective that this is just a little part of what you are.

There are 3.5 billion base pairs of DNA passed from your parents. We look at just 400 of them."

Dr. Peter Forster, geneticist at the McDonald Institute at Oxford University, says: "most people are curious about where they come from. They want answers to bolster their sense of identity. No one likes the feeling of not knowing how they match up with the past. It's a psychological need similar to those feelings expressed by adopted children. What we are now able to do is clear up uncertainty and give peace of mind."

Peace of mind? Perhaps. For me it has opened up a whole new perspective on life, a fascinating insight into my own genetic make-up. It has answered many questions—but left me wanting to know even more.

SIGNIFICANCE

The science of DNA continues to advance at a rapid pace. Among the more profound findings was the discovery that the individual differences known as race have little to do with genes. Differences in skin color and other physical differences between different races are actually no larger than many differences found within specific racial groups, meaning that two white women may be less genetically similar than a white woman and a black woman from the same region. The Nazi goal of keeping Aryans racially pure was based on the false assumption that white Germans had only white ancestors, a possibility now considered virtually impossible. Ironically many Germans in the Nazi regime probably shared more genetic similarities with the Jews they were persecuting than with each other.

DNA evidence received its most public exposure during the 1995 murder trial of former football star O.J. Simpson. Blood and other evidence collected during the investigation appeared to place Simpson at the crime scene and blood from both victims was also found in Simpson's automobile. Despite what appeared to be an airtight DNA case, prosecutors attempting to interpret the DNA findings for the jury struggled to explain the process's complexity, and Simpson was ultimately acquitted despite the seemingly conclusive forensic results. Later trials have used DNA evidence more successfully.

2003 witnessed the conclusion of a thirteen year project to decode the structure of human DNA. Called the Human Genome Project, this massive undertaking sought to identify and map all 20-25,000 genes in human DNA. The completion of this international research project was expected to set the stage for significant advances in disease diagnosis and treatment.

FURTHER RESOURCES
Books

Smolenyak, Megan, and Ann Turner. *Trace Your Roots with DNA: Using Genetic Tests to Explore Your Family Tree.* New York: Rodale Press, 2004.

Stebbins, Michael. *Sex, Drugs, and DNA: Science's Taboos Confronted.* New York: Macmillan, 2006.

Watson, James, and Andrew Berry. *DNA: The Secret of Life.* New York: Knopf, 2004.

Periodicals

Kalb, Claudia, et al. "In Our Blood." *Newsweek*. (February 6, 2006): 46–55.

Lemonick, Michael D., et al. "Who Were the First Americans?" *Time* (March 13, 2006):44–52.

Wade, Nicholas. "In the Body of an Accounting Professor: A Little Bit of the Mongol Hordes." *New York Times* (June 6, 2006): 95–97.

Web sites

Forbes. "DNA Evidence Clears Wrongly Convicted Man." July 11, 2006 <http://www.forbes.com/business/commerce/feeds/ap/2006/07/11/ap2872434.html> (accessed July 13, 2006).

Nature. "Double-Helix: 50 Years of DNA." 2003 <http://www.nature.com/nature/dna50/index.html> (accessed July 12, 2006).

Two Heads Are Better Than Three

Book excerpt

By: Mary Roach

Date: 2005

Source: Moses, Kate and Camille Peri, ed. *Because I Said So.* New York: Harper Collins, 2005.

About the Author: Mary Roach is a San Francisco based journalist and author who has made frequent contributions to various American magazines and periodicals.

INTRODUCTION

There is little question that the popular connotations associated with the position of stepmother in the modern American family are often negative ones. Literature, beginning with fairy tales such as *Snow white* and *Cinderella* serve to reinforce the stereotypical stepmother as mean, evil, cruel, or wicked.

The etymology of the term is not so malicious. The prefix 'step' is derived from Old English, and referred to a child who was bereaved due to being orphaned; a stepparent was thus, one who became the parent to an orphaned child. It was only at the beginning of the twentieth century that the concept of stepparentage moved beyond a relationship through marriage with an orphaned child. In contemporary language, a stepparent relationship is said to be cre-

ated through any second marriage where one or both of the new spouses has a biological or adopted child that will be a part of the new family unit. Given the increased incidence of common law relationships in modern American society, a child previously born to a common law spouse entering into a new common law union is also referred to as a stepchild.

The statistical evidence with respect to the creation of various kinds of steprelations in the United States underscores the broadening application of the 'step' designation. It is estimated that as of 2006, approximately one third of all American families included a stepfamily component. The English lexicographer Samuel Johnson observed in 1770 that a second marriage was the triumph of hope over experience; modern American attitudes to re-marriage echo Johnson's sentiments, as seventy-five percent of all divorced Americans will re-marry, usually within five years of their initial divorce. In 2005, over forty percent of all marriage licenses issued in the United States related to a re-marriage of at least one of the new spouses.

The ability of a stepparent generally to assert parental influence within a new family structure is one that is dependent more upon the manner in which the new spouses agree that their home and the relationships with the children shall be organized, than it does based upon the law. Stepparents often inherit pre-existing child custody, access, and support agreements or court orders that influence the ability of the stepparent to assume a truly parental role with a stepchild. Where a stepparent commences family life in circumstances where the former spouse to their new partner is resident in the same geographic area and the former spouse asserts ongoing parental control over the new stepchild or children, the ability of the stepparent to become a meaningful, parent like part of the stepchildren's life is often very difficult. In such cases, the stepparent is cast in the role of the usurper as described in the following book excerpt.

■ PRIMARY SOURCE

In the early days of transplant science, a horribly enthusiastic surgeon named Vladimir Demikhov grafted the head of a puppy onto the neck of a full-grown dog—a dog that already had a head, thank you very much. In the files for my last book, I have a photograph of the aftermath of this ill-advised undertaking. The severed head is sewn into the front of the neck of the intact dog, nose up, so that the two canines are face-to-face, constantly reminded of each other's presence. You can almost see the Wellbutrin bottle in the background.

Bear with me, I'm working on a metaphor here.

Seven years ago, I met a man and fell in love. He had been married before and had two young daughters. Because I was in love, and because at that time his children lived with their mother in another state and our visits with them went well, I did not give the complexities of the situation all that much thought. I did not read even one of the dozen or so books out there about "blended families." (I love the term "blended." I love the ridiculous optimism of it. It suggests an outcome that is smooth and delightful and effortless to attain. "I'll be the mango!" "I'll be bananas!" "Dad, you push frappe!")

After a couple years the man's family moved back to our city. Do you see what I wrote? "The man's family." They were his family, and I was his second wife. His parents are her kids' grandparents, which gives his ex-wife a permanent slot there between the generations on the family tree. I don't know if there's even a protocol for adding second wives to family trees. I'm imagining a faint dotted line of the sort used by mapmakers to delineate unpaved roads or proposed subway extensions that have been in the works since the Eisenhower administration. There is an inalterable solidity to the ties of matrilineage. These are people attached to one another by the uncorrodable bonds of blood and ancestry and family photo albums. A second wife is a flimsy, sewn-on thing.

This became clear to me shortly after their return. My husband's ex-wife gave me a present and a card that said, "Welcome to the family." This was an extraordinarily nice gesture, for she is an extraordinarily nice and generous person, but for some reason it did not sit right with me. When you first fall in love with someone, you have a sense of the two of you as a complete and perfect universe. Like any new couple, you want to feel like the core of a family unit. It was naïve and self-centered, but such is the nature of new love. Reading that card was my Demikhov moment. You are the stitched-on dog head, it might as well have said. No, I thought You are. No, you are!

Then I forgot about it, because things were going well. My husband's kids like me, and when the four of us were together, I permitted myself to think of us as a family. The transplant, it seemed, had taken. Of course, this probably made my husband's ex-wife—"my ex-wife," as I sometimes slip up and call her—feel like the unwanted dog head. (With stepfamilies, it seems, some one always has to be holding the "big fat loser alone at recess" card. I once saw a book entitled *How to Win as a Stepfamily*. I imagined opening it up and finding 213 blank pages with the last page saying, "Ha, ha, ha, ha, ha, ha, you can't!!!!")

As it turned out, the ex-wife did not have to feel this way for long. Soon it was my turn. Like transplanted appendages, stepparents are allowed to thrive and feel good for a short while before the rejection stage begins.

Family counselors call this the "honeymoon period." Inevitably and all too soon, the honeymoon ends. Someone starts to have issues.

Often this coincides with someone hitting puberty. Up until puberty, you can pretty much get a kid to go along with anything. All kids have issues with a parent's remarriage, but the issues remain more or less subcutaneous until adolescence. As long as the equilibrium holds, stepparents—provided they are not abusive, overbearing boors—are treated like any other adult in the child's universe: one more person to play Chinese checkers or spring for lip gloss. Not the greatest thing in the world, but not the worst.

Then comes puberty. Now the issues demand to be heard. They unionize. They organize demonstrations and carry signs. This is a period when everything is annoying, and a stepmother, especially to a girl, can top the list. A stepmother is a random extraneous adult thrown into a girl's life, day in and day out, taking up her dad's time and attention, which she doesn't want anyway these days but she's going to resent its absence nonetheless. The child who just last year was walking hand-in-hand with you to the corner store is now refusing to laugh at your jokes or look you in the eye.

I was no longer me; I had become the things I represented: someone standing in the way of Mom and Dad's remarriage, someone who usurps dad's love. When I look at the situation from a stepchild's perspective, I can understand the resentment. Of course they have issues. I would too. That doesn't mean I enjoy it or handle it well. Issues breed issues. It is not easy to enjoy the company of someone who makes it clear, however subtly, that she wishes you'd go away. Not surprisingly, the odds are not in favor of the stepfamily living happily ever after. I read somewhere that sixty percent of marriages involving "blended" families end in divorce. Rocks in the Osterizer.

Part of the problem is this loaded and mostly outmoded word *stepparent*. It's a holdover from the days when divorce was uncommon and stepparents were mainly people married to widows and widowers. Unless an actual parent has died and the stepparent functions as an ersatz actual parent, the word just makes everyone uncomfortable. It sets up confusing expectations. (Under the heading "relationship" on my older stepdaughter's high school emergency contact form, it says, for me, "Dad's wife.") If people are referring to you as a stepparent, you imagine you will be occupying some sort of vaguely parent-like post, and that even if you don't behave like a parent and mete out discipline or pick them up at school, there will be some sort of familial bond. But why should there be? A child who has two loving parents does not need or want a third. Especially a bogus one who didn't give birth to you and who can't be relied on to send letters while you're at summer camp and who doesn't know the songs you all sang in the car together when you were growing up. Who is this woman? What is she doing at parents' night? How did she get into a book about mothers?

While I'm not wild about my status as stitched-on appendage, I view it as just. No one owes me otherwise. And there have been times—there *are* times—when I feel genuinely loved and appreciated by one or another of my stepkids. To feel the affection or love of someone who has cause and cultural rubber-stamp to resent you is a uniquely precious thing. Unlike the love between parent and child, this love you don't take for granted. It's an Indian summer kind of love—maybe it'll show up this week, maybe it won't. But when it does, it's a gift, and you run out and bask in it.

We're an odd, ungainly thing, this three-headed family of ours, but we seem to have adapted to our condition. All families have some sort of metaphorical deformity. There are ripped-out hearts and overactive spleens, forked tongues and wandering loins. Relatively speaking, we're as normal and healthy as the next dog.

SIGNIFICANCE

A significant feature of the perception of the modern stepmother is the fact that the law has not generally kept pace with societal trends concerning the importance of the stepfamily in American society. While the applicable legal definitions vary from state to state, it is a generally accepted principle of American family law that a parent may be defined first as a legal parent, a person who has a relationship with a child either through birth or by adoption. The second class of parent is found in both the legal academic literature as well as through inclusion in many definitions of the term that have evolved in recent American case law. In particular, the extended definition of parent may include those persons who have stood in the place of a parent in relation to a child, providing support or care to a child for a period of time without the benefit of a biological relationship or court order. A stepparent does not necessarily fall within either definition, a fact that tends to make their assertion of a parental role in the stepfamily structure more difficult.

Conversely, the absence of a concrete legally defined role for the stepmother in the modern American family creates significant grey areas if the marriage or cohabitation that created the step-relationship is terminated. A stepparent upon such a termination has no *prima facie* obligation to provide support for the stepchild or children; the ability of a stepparent to secure custody or to exercise access to a stepchild is an emerging legal issue that has not yet been definitively

resolved. It is clear that in all American jurisdictions, a step-parent who had fulfilled a parental role towards her stepchildren for many years would likely be unsuccessful in any custody contest involving a biological parent, no matter how strong her relationship was with the stepchildren.

It is clear that the negative connotations associated with stepfamily status are far more frequently associated with a stepmother than with a stepfather or a stepchild. The author of the primary source uses the expression 'matrilineage' in this context. In its strict sense, matrilineage is the tracing of one's line of descent through the maternal side of the family. In the context of the primary source, there is an undoubted weight to the argument that mothers are the more respected parent in a typical family setting; the fact that mothers are the custodial parents for the children of a marriage in over seventy-five percent of all cases on marital breakup supports this view.

A number of theories have been advanced in the academic literature as to why the stepmother has been frequently vilified; a common conclusion is the perception that the new stepmother is regarded as a barrier to a child obtaining the fundamental nurturing that is only obtainable from a biological mother. In support of this notion is the considerable research data that suggests that stepfamilies formed after the death of a previous spouse are far more harmonious and stable entities than those created in the wake of a divorce.

When the current legal framework with respect to stepparents is combined with the common perceptions of the stepmother in American society, the result is the creation of new obligations within the stepfamily structure for the stepmother, with lesser rights, privileges, and degree of acceptance than that afforded the biological mother of the stepchild.

Where the stepmother perceives themselves as a biological entity that has been transplanted by marriage into an existing family, as opposed to being a component of a new family order, the stepmother will often correspondingly expect the new family to operate as though it were a traditional biological family. To be successful, stepfamilies must be treated as unique structures and not equated to the biological variety, to avoid the undue influence of the prior history of the partners and any turmoil or tension associated with the prior biological family.

It is an enduring irony of the regard in which various members of the extended American family are viewed that the only other family member that attracts an equally negative stereotype to that of the stepmother is the mother-in-law.

FURTHER RESOURCES

Books

Marquardt, Elizabeth. *Between Two Worlds: The Inner Lives of Children of Divorce*. New York: Crown Books, 2005.

Waterman, Barbara. *Birth of an Adoptive, Foster or Stepmother: Beyond Biological Mothering Attachments*. London: Jessica Kingsley, 2004.

Periodicals

Laythe, Joseph. "The Wicked Stepmother?: The Edna Mumbulo Case of 1930." *Journal of Criminal Justice and Popular Culture*, University of Albany. 9 (2) (2002): 33-54.

Ramsey, Sarah H. "Constructing Parenthood for Step-Parents." *Duke University Journal of Gender Law and Policy*. 8 (2002):285-295.

From the Age of Aquarius To the Age of Responsibility

Report

By: Pew Research Center

Date: December 8, 2005

Source: *Pew Research Center*. "From the Age of Aquarius To the Age of Responsibility." December 8, 2005 <http://pewresearch.org/assets/social/pdf/socialtrends-boomers120805.pdf> (accessed June 28, 2006).

About the Author: The Pew Research Center conducts research on issues, attitudes, and trends. It conducts extensive public opinion polls and scientific research, delivering its findings in reports and briefings.

INTRODUCTION

World War II (1938–1945) was the bloodiest conflict in human history, with a death toll in the hundreds of millions and a financial toll in the hundreds of billions. By the war's end, life throughout the United States had been significantly disrupted, as husbands and fathers went off to battle, factories stopped producing cars and began building bombers, and women's participation in the civilian workforce climbed by 50 percent. Many aspects of ordinary life had been put on hold and basic commodities such as coffee and car tires had been strictly rationed. With numerous young men overseas, marriages were frequently postponed, and birth rates declined.

Following the war's end, American G.I.s returned home ready to get on with their lives. This sudden influx of labor severely taxed the economy, and some returning soldiers faced difficulty finding work while companies labored to shift from wartime to peacetime production. Many of the soldiers arrived home ready to begin or expand their families, and the years following the war became a period of skyrocketing birth rates. This enormous post-war generation, larger than any before it, included 75 million men and women born between 1946 and 1964, and was christened the Baby Boom.

The Baby Boom generation has moved through United States history like an earthquake, straining basic services at each stage of life. As the baby boomers began reaching school age, public education was stretched to the limit and school systems built numerous new campuses trying to keep up. Boomers also played a key role in the massive expansion of the economy, swelling the work force as they took jobs. Boomer investment in the stock market played a role in the stock run-up of the 1980's and 1990's, and as Boomers retire they are expected to stress the retirement infrastructure.

The 1960's were difficult years for the nation, as the largest cohort in history reached the traditionally tumultuous teenage and young adult years. The rise of teenage culture and the hippie counterculture played a significant role in the schisms which developed between Baby Boomers and their parents' generation, a division aptly summed up in the advice "never trust anyone over age 30." As young men and women, the Baby Boomers railed against everything they disliked about their parents' generation, including their perceived obsession with work and upward mobility; ironically upon reaching adulthood many Boomers seemed to imitate and at times exceed their parents' economic aspirations. By the late twentieth century the Boomers were raising teenage children of their own, and many found that the parent-child relationship feels quite different when viewed from the other side.

■ PRIMARY SOURCE

Baby Boomers Approach Age 60

From the Age of Aquarius To the Age of Responsibility

1. Introduction and Overview

As they advance toward the threshold of old age, the nation's 75 million baby boomers are in an extended "sandwich" phase of their family life cycle, with many either raising minor children or providing financial and other forms of support to adult children or to aging parents.

In the past year, 50% of all boomers were raising one or more young children and/or providing primary financial support to one or more adult children.

Another 17% whose only children are ages 18 and older were providing some financial assistance to at least one such child, according to a Pew Research Center survey that explores intergenerational relationships within families.

In addition, two-in-ten boomers were providing some financial assistance to a parent.

The boomers currently range in age from 41 through 59—meaning that, like middle-aged generations before them, they are in a stage of life when it is natural to give more than to take when it comes to relationships with both parents and children.

However, changing demographics within families have prolonged this sandwich period for boomers. At a time in life when many are looking ahead to their own retirement, boomers are likely either to have parents who are still living, children who are still young or adult children who are still in need of financial support.

To be sure, few boomers bear all of these responsibilities simultaneously. For example, only about 13% of boomers are providing some financial support to an elderly parent at the same time they are also either raising a minor child or supporting an adult child. Still, most boomers are playing at least one of these roles, meaning that, at a relatively advanced stage of their own life cycle, they have a relatively full plate of family responsibilities.

Boomers are more likely to have living parents.

Thanks to advances in life expectancy, 71 percent of today's boomers have at least one living parent, whereas in 1989, just 60 percent of people who were ages 41–59 reported that they had at least one living parent, according to a Gallup survey. Even though today's elderly are more likely than the elderly of previous generations to enjoy higher income levels and better health, many still rely on their boomer children for assistance of one kind or another, be it caregiving or help with household errands.

But this reliance is not onesided—as with most kin to kin relationships, support flows in both directions. When asked who relies more on whom—you or your parents, 25% of boomers say their parents rely more on them, 10% say they rely more on their parents, and 11% volunteer that they rely on one another equally. A majority (53%) say neither parent nor child relies on the other. Boomers' reports of their financial exchanges with parents generally mirror this two-way pattern of felt reliance. Some 29% of boomers who have a parent say they gave financial support to a parent in the past year and 19% of

boomers with a parent report receiving financial support from a parent.

Boomers are likely to have grown children in financial need.

When it comes to providing financial support for children, the parental role now typically extends beyond the time when a child is a minor. Some 63% of all boomers have at least one child ages 18 and older, and of this group of boomer parents, about two thirds (68%) are supporting an adult child financially, either as the primary (33%) or secondary (35%) source of support.

Today's young adults are more likely than young adults in previous generations to be burdened by heavy expenses or debt, and it is possible that the pattern of financial support by parents to adult children reflects the steadily rising cost of "big ticket" coming-into-adulthood expenses such as college tuition or the purchase of a home. In the past twenty years the cost of both college tuition and buying a first home has roughly doubled in inflation-adjusted dollars, and in the past 10 years the number of young adults with a federal student loan has also nearly doubled.

What's a family responsibility?

When boomer parents provide financial support for their children's college costs, they are fulfilling what they and most other Americans view as a basic responsibility of parenthood. Of five different kinds of intrafamily, multi-generational exchanges tested in this survey, paying for college is the one that the greatest number of Americans of all ages and backgrounds view as a responsibility. Some 62% of the adult population—and 66% of all boomers—describe it that way.

A small majority of boomers also say it is a parent's responsibility to take into one's home an elderly parent who wishes to move in. On the other hand, a solid majority of boomers, along with the rest of the adult population, do not view it as a parent's responsibility to take an adult child into one's home or to save for a child's inheritance, nor do they view it as grandparent's responsibility to help out with child care.

Satisfaction with family life

Nine-in-ten boomers say they are very (72%) or somewhat (18%) satisfied with their family life, and in these assessments, they are in sync with adults who are younger and older than they are.

There is virtually no difference in these assessments of family life between boomers who are providing financial assistance to parents or adult children and those who are not. However, among the 13% of boomers who have an elderly parent needing help to care for himself or herself there is less overall contentment with family life. Just 65% of boomers who have a parent in that sort of need say they are very satisfied with their family life; by contrast, 75% of boomers who have a parent able to handle these things on his or her own say they are very satisfied with their family life.

Looking Ahead

As boomers look ahead toward their own old age, their crystal ball is a bit cloudy but there is no widespread sense of foreboding. The generation whose iconic youthful rallying cry was to "never trust anyone over 30" apparently doesn't feel so bad about approaching a chronological milestone twice that number. The oldest boomers will turn 60 in January.

Asked which generation will enjoy old age the most, a slight plurality of boomers (33%) say that theirs will. The remainder say either that their parents' generation (26%) or their children's generation (31%) will. Older boomers (ages 51–59) are more optimistic than younger boomers (ages 41–50) about their prospects in old age, with 38% of older boomers saying their generation will enjoy old age the most but only 29% of younger boomers expressing that view.

And despite gloomy assessments from many economists and politicians about the fiscal crunch that society will face once this famously outsized generation hits retirement age, boomers are cautiously optimistic when they contemplate their own financial situation in retirement.

About a quarter (26%) of boomers say they expect to "live very comfortably" once they retire; another 29% say they will be able to "meet expenses with a little left over"; and another 24% say they will be able to "just meet basic living expenses." Some 17 percent, however, say they will "not have enough for the basics" and this level of apprehension is slightly higher among boomers than it is among current retirees (12% feel this way) or among adults ages 18 to 40 (10% feel this way).

These findings are from a telephone survey of a nationally representative, randomly-selected sample of 3,014 adults, including 1,117 boomers, that was conducted from Oct. 5 through Nov. 6, 2005.

SIGNIFICANCE

For aging Baby Boomers retirement and old age may well become just the latest aspect of life to be shaken up and restructured. In many aspects old age today is far less certain than it was for the Boomers' parents: few companies today offer guaranteed retirement pensions, meaning the days of a gold watch and guaranteed medical care at age sixty-five are gone. Long life expectancies also mean that many Boomers may choose to change jobs or begin working part-time

at sixty-five rather than retiring entirely. With the typical Boomer living twenty years or more after age sixty-five, demographers expect to see a growing number of healthy, active senior citizens participating in numerous aspects of work and leisure life.

While previous generations generally expected aging parents to move in with them near the end of their lives, Boomers today are far more likely to expect aging parents to live elsewhere, just as they expect to live away from their children's homes when they become elderly. Such changes in attitude are already fueling a building boom in the retirement care industry.

As the Baby Boom generation reaches the later years of life it is once again expected to impact the entire nation with its passing. The Congressional Budget Office (CBO) projects that as Boomers begin retiring and receiving federal retirement payments the number of retirees will soon overwhelm the number of active workers, straining and potentially bankrupting the nation's Social Security system. Some economists also fear that as Boomers retire and begin selling the stocks held in their retirement accounts the markets as a whole may experience stagnation or decline. Finally, current projections suggest that many Boomers have not accumulated adequate savings, despite higher lifetime earnings than any previous generation.

The passage of the post World War II generation has brought enormous changes to many aspects of American life. Though the specifics remain impossible to predict, it appears inevitable that their retirement and senior years will alter the U.S. economy and culture in significant and unexpected ways.

FURTHER RESOURCES

Books

Harris, Leslie M. *After Fifty: How the Baby Boom Will Redefine the Mature Market*. Ithaca, NY: Paramount Books, 2003.

Macunovich, Diane J. *Birth Quake: The Baby Boom and Its Aftershocks*. Chicago: The University of Chicago Press, 2002.

Zal, H. Michael. *The Sandwich Generation: Caught between Growing Children and Aging Parents*. Philadelphia, PA: Perseus Publishing, 1992.

Periodicals

Kadlec, Dan. "Grandpa Goes to College." *Time* (July 3, 2006): 94.

MacMillan, Amanda. "Relief for the Sandwich Generation." *Prevention* 57 (2005): 94.

Park, Andrew. "Between a Rocker and a High Chair." *Business Week* (Feb 21, 2005): 86–88.

Web sites

American Institute of Certified Public Accountants. "Financial Tips for the Sandwich Generation." <http://www.aicpa.org/download/financialliteracy/Sandwich_Generation_Toolkit/Financial_Tips.pdf> (accessed July 16, 2006).

Ohio State University. "Aging Families—The Sandwich Generation." <http://hec.osu.edu/famlife/aging/PDFs/Sandwich%20Generation.final.pdf> (accessed July 16, 2006).

Case Study: The Young Carer

News article

By: Liza Ramrayka

Date: April 5, 2006

Source: *Guardian Online.* "Case Study: The Young Carer." April 5, 2006 <http://society.guardian.co.uk/macmillansupplement/story/0,,1747462,00.html> (accessed June 8, 2006).

About the Author: Liza Ramrayka has written two books about fundraising, volunteerism, and working at non-profit organizations—*Working in Fundraising* and *The Good Trustee Guide.* She also writes for the United Kingdom's *Guardian* and *Guardian Online,* as well as *VSmagazine,* the news and informational publication for the United Kingdom's National Council for Voluntary Organizations. Ms. Ramrayka wrote a series of articles for the *Guardian* about carers (caregivers) in the United Kingdom and the challenges they face.

INTRODUCTION

Young carers are children and youth below the age of eighteen in the United Kingdom who devote significant time to service as volunteer caregivers for a parent, sibling, or other relative in the household. The person being cared for must be significantly hampered in their ability to conduct activities of daily living by chronic physical or mental illness or disability. Much young carer data is based on statistics from survey research involving more than 6,100 young carers. It is quite difficult to quantify the number of youthful caregivers accurately, as families are often unwilling to discuss these roles for fear of intervention by child welfare agencies (out of concern that a young carer may be removed from the home if there are allegations of neglect or parental inability).

Across the United Kingdom, there are slightly more young female caregivers than male (56% v. 44%), and their average age is twelve years. Considerably nearly two-thirds come from single-parent families. Of those in single-parent homes, most provide care for their mother. In two-parent families, the youth most often cares for a sibling. Adults who need care may have a disability or chronic physical health concern, or may have a mental illness or substance abuse–related impairment. Among those responding to that section of the survey (96%), almost none of the parents who needed care were working. This could limit finances to pay for outside caregivers (beyond what would be available through third-party payer or government-sponsored programs without cost), increasing the need for the youthful caregiver's assistance.

Most commonly, the person needing care has a physical health condition or disability; less frequently, a mental illness or a substance abuse/addiction issue is involved. In any case, the caregiving may involve household maintenance—such as cooking, cleaning, grocery shopping, and laundry, among other chores. General and personal care may also be needed, such as administering medication, changing dressings, transfer from bed to wheelchair or other mobility assistance, and help with feeding, washing, dressing, and toileting. It is also common for young carers to help care for younger siblings, and to be a source of emotional support for the person in need of care, as well as other family members. As the frequency with which young people have taken on caregiving roles has become more widely known (particularly so in the more developed nations), support and assistance projects have been created and implemented for them.

■ PRIMARY SOURCE

Case Study: The Young Carer

Liza Ramrayka

Wednesday April 5, 2006

After Newcastle United, 14-year-old Jayde Guy's main loves are badminton and hanging out with friends at the Metro Centre near her hometown of Birtley in Gateshead. Nothing unusual there except that when Jayde comes home from school, she takes on the role of sole carer for her mum Joyce who was diagnosed with lung cancer last year.

Unlike her friends who can play sports after school, Jayde has quickly become used to her new role as a young carer in a single-parent household. Currently studying for her GSCEs next year, Jayde discusses her mum's operation last October and current chemotherapy in a matter-of-fact way that belies her age.

"Since the operation, mum gets out of breath easily. So when she's not feeling well, I do the dishes and the other housework. When you see her out of breath it looks exhausting. I tell her to sit down but she's very independent."

Since last year, Jayde has had regular visits from Karen, a support worker from the Gateshead Crossroads (Carers for Carers) scheme [program] in Tyne and Wear. The support is the result of a partnership between Crossroads and Macmillan to provide help to young carers (aged 6–19) looking after a parent or sibling with cancer.

"When I first met Karen, she asked me about what I liked and didn't like doing. I said I liked going to the Metro Centre, and sports like football and badminton. She takes me out to places to give me a break. We go to the sports complex or go shopping, have some food and drink. She took me Christmas shopping at Fenwicks and got free tickets for the Newcastle match the other week. "

Jayde likes the fact that Karen is sensitive to the family's needs. "Karen is friendly and really understands what's happening with mum. I can talk to her and it's really useful to have someone to talk to outside the family," she says.

Lynne Readman is the Macmillan young carers manager for the scheme.

"Young carers often don't get the opportunities to mix with other people their own age. So we take them out in groups to do the fun things they want to do—theme parks, horseriding, things that other young people would normally get to do. We give one-to-one support for young people who might not want to go out in groups. Some also email us questions and we send them information, advice and support."

For Jayde, the scheme brings some normality to her life. "It gives you a break and someone to talk to, which is brilliant."

SIGNIFICANCE

Young carers almost never choose their roles—they are simply faced with the need to take on (sometimes unexpected) responsibilities due to family circumstances and, according to the information compiled by Dearden and others, generally do so with little hesitation. The tasks they engage in are defined by the nature of the illness or disability, but can vary with time and changing condition of the person(s) they care for. Young carers can miss school due to the exigencies of their roles, although the most recent UK research indi-

cates that this has lessened by several percentage points since the first survey was completed in the mid–1990s.

Case-specific information presented by Aldridge and Becker suggests that young carers experience anger, frustration, fear, anxiety, isolation from peers and others, and considerable confusion about their roles and responsibilities. They are rarely given useful information by medical professionals about the nature and severity of the illness or medical needs of the person for whom they are responsible, and are often socially isolated from peers because of the nature and extent of their responsibilities—survey data indicates that most carers spend an average of ten to twenty hours per week performing their duties. They are frequently unable—and sometimes unwilling—to take part in social activities with peers. Becker and Aldridge refer to a "caring curfew," which is the time limit—generally brief—that young carers feel comfortable leaving their charges alone and going out to spend time for themselves.

As awareness of both the presence and the needs of young caregivers has grown, so too have the resources with which to support them. In the United Kingdom, the number of projects designed specifically to assist and support young carers has more than quadrupled since 1995—growing from fewer than forty to more than 200 in just over ten years. In addition, the education and training of health care and helping professionals, such as medical social workers, family and primary care practitioners, and nurses, has been updated to include young carers. School personnel such as teachers, social workers, and guidance personnel are also being given tools with which to identify and support them.

Young carers' projects have been implemented in Great Britain, Scotland, Northern Ireland, the United States, Australia, New Zealand, Wales, Malta, Canada, and Zimbabwe, among other countries. Key functions include increasing young carers' visibility and highlighting their needs and concerns. The projects give them a forum in which to voice their needs and concerns, to interact with peers who share their circumstances, to be afforded respite care and opportunities to socialize with other youth, and to garner understandable and realistic information about the disability or illness of the person for whom they give care. Such projects also frequently offer counseling and emotional support services, as well as recreational and community activities. In addition, many create an important referral and communications link between school systems, social welfare and other social service agencies, community networks, medical and other health care practitioners, and service providers who can offer assistance to the young carers and their families.

FURTHER RESOURCES

Books

Aldridge, J., and S. Becker. *Children Caring for Parents with Mental Illness: Perspectives of Young Carers, Parents and Professionals.* Bristol, United Kingdom: Policy Press, 2003.

———. *The National Handbook of Young Carers Projects.* London: Carers National Association and Young Carers Research Group, 1998.

Becker, S., J. Aldridge, and C. Dearden. *Young Carers and their Families.* Oxford, United Kingdom: Blackwell Science, 1998.

Dearden, C., and S. Becker. *Growing Up Caring: Vulnerability and Transition to Adulthood—Young Carers' Experiences.* Leicester, United Kingdom: Youth Work Press, 2000.

———. *Young Carers in the UK: The 2004 Report.* London: Carers UK, 2004.

Frank, J. *Couldn't Care More: A Study of Young Carers and their Needs.* London: The Children's Society, 1995.

Frank, J., C. Tatum, and S. Tucker. *On Small Shoulders: Learning from the Experiences of Former Young Carers.* London, United Kingdom: The Children's Society, 1999.

Franklin, Bob, ed. *The New Handbook of Children's Rights: Comparative Policy and Practice.* London: Routledge, 2001.

National Alliance for Caregiving and United Hospital Fund. *Young Caregivers in the U.S.: Report of Findings.* Bethesda, MD: National Alliance for Caregiving, 2005.

Web sites

Alzheimer Society, Niagara Region. "Young Carers Initiative Niagara." <http://www.alzheimerniagara.ca/YCIN.htm> (accessed June 12, 2006).

Department of Family and Community Services. "Young Carers Research Project: Final Report." September 2001 <http://www.carersaustralia.com.au/documents/young_carersfinal_report.pdf> (accessed June 12, 2006).

As Parents Age, Baby Boomers Struggle to Cope

Newspaper article

By: Jane Gross

Date: March 25, 2006

Source: Gross, Jane. "As Parents Age, Baby Boomers Struggle to Cope." *New York Times* (March 25, 2006).

About the Author: Jane Gross is a staff writer with the *New York Times.* The *New York Times* is one of the nation's largest daily newspapers, with a circulation of over one million copies.

INTRODUCTION

The period of population growth in the Unites States known as the Baby Boom commenced in 1946 with the return of millions of military personnel to the U.S. from their service during the Second World War. Social scientists generally regard the end of the Baby Boom as occurring in 1964, the year that represents the beginning of a sharp decline in the American birth rate that continued for over twenty years. The year 2006 is significant as it represents the year in which the first year of the Baby Boom demographic reaches age sixty. This particular segment of the post war generation is a part of the most multi-layered family dynamic ever observed in America history, as the sixty-year-old "boomer" is often a part of an extended family structure that includes their own parent or parents who are over eighty years of age, their children ranging in age from teenagers to young adults, and possibly grandchildren. Divorce and remarriage have created the potential for further family extensions and blendings for these first Baby Boomers, circumstances that often impose care responsibilities in every direction.

The familial responsibilities faced by the Baby Boom generation to contribute to the care of their own parents often creates significant pressure on these persons in their work environment. This class of employee is faced with the challenge of balancing their employment responsibilities with elder care obligations. Elder care can manifest itself in a broad spectrum of demands upon an employee's time, ranging from the taking of personal telephone calls during the work day, to the need for flexible work hours in order to deliver care to the parent. Elder care can also involve responding to emergencies that may take an employee away from their work on short notice.

It was the Baby Boom generation that served to legitimize child care arrangements as an appropriate extension of how parents organized their family lives in relation to their daily employment obligations. Elder care is not so established or respected in the culture of corporate America.

Presenteeism is a concept that has evolved in the context of the issues created by elder care and the obligation faced by many American employees to assist an older parent during what is ostensibly the regular work day. Where absenteeism is defined as a frequent or chronic inability of an employee to attend their work on a regular basis, presenteeism has two distinct connotations. The first is as an antonym to absenteeism; where an employee puts in 'face time' at their place of employment, no matter whether they are sick, injured, or otherwise limited in their productivity. The second meaning of presenteeism is where the employee is physically present at their workplace, but is either distracted by their external responsibilities, such as elder care, or where the employee takes unsanctioned and unreported time out of the work day to attend to their parent's needs, such as shopping, domestic chores, or transporting the parent to appointments.

▌ PRIMARY SOURCE

Nancy Goodman's employer, a telecommunications company in Boston, offers benefits to help employees care for elderly parents. But she found them nearly useless during four years of caring for her mother, who has Parkinson's disease, and her father, who died of kidney failure last year.

"They say they want to do the right thing," Ms. Goodman, 58, said of her employer, which she would not identify for fear of losing her job. "But when it comes down to it, they're not seeing the true picture."

Ms. Goodman's lament is common, as corporate America scrambles to help the soaring number of baby boomers, mostly working women, whose obligation to frail, elderly parents results in absenteeism, workday distractions, or stress-related health problems.

Companies are responding, but experts say they often use child care benefits as a model when they do not suit the different and unpredictable needs of the elderly. In addition, at a time of cutbacks in expensive health insurance and pensions, the most commonly offered benefits are those that cost a company little or nothing, like referral services and unpaid leaves.

Ms. Goodman, for instance, tried her company's referral service to supplement inadequate staffing when her parents lived at an assisted living center in Connecticut. It was "like going to the yellow pages," she said, since it did not relieve her of the time-consuming tasks of arranging for and supervising the services from afar. Ms. Goodman was also entitled to a year's leave of absence, a benefit a new mother might appreciate. But if she took a leave now, what happened if her mother lingered?

Employees with ailing parents, more than 20 million nationwide, cite other benefits that would allow them to focus more on their jobs, like geriatric case managers to guide them through the mysteries of Medicaid and Medicare, or backup care for emergencies like a last-minute business trip. Companies that offer this kind of hands-on assistance generally pay for at least part of the service.

But they are rare. According to the Society for Human Resource Management, which represents more than 200,000 human resource and other corporate officials, 39 percent of its members said in 2003 that elder care benefits were "too costly to be feasible." Only 1 percent of their companies subsidized any elder care benefits last year. And only 3 percent offered the emergency backup care—subsidized or otherwise—that experts say saves money by keeping workers at work.

"The perception among companies is that they can't afford elder care benefits," said Frank Scanlan, a spokesman for the society.

It is the largest companies that are the most generous, but even those often subscribe to the mistaken notion that the Mommy Track and the Daughter Track are the same, said Chris Gatti, president of the Work Options Group in Superior, Colo. Work Options, whose clients employ 400,000 people nationwide, provides in-home care for children and the elderly.

"These benefits fall under the same umbrella but are fundamentally different," Mr. Gatti said. "Child care programs are relatively straight-forward and easy to administer compared to elder care, which is a maze with lots of sharp corners and dark secluded places."

An individual supervisor can ease an employee's burden but still leave them vulnerable to management changes. Just 6 percent of employers have written policies about elder care, according to surveys by the Society for Human Resource Management, while 76 percent say they help employees on a case-by-case basis.

For Ms. Goodman, the one godsend since her father died and her mother moved into her Boston apartment has been permission to work at home. But that is likely to change with a new boss. "I'm walking on eggs right now," Ms. Goodman said.

The distinctions between child care and elder care have become apparent as the first of the 77 million baby boomers turn 60 and their parents live past 85, joining the fastest-growing segment of the population.

The most obvious is that children's schedules are predictable —a school holiday next Monday —while elderly parents' needs —a trip to the emergency room —are crisis-driven. Also, children are raised at home; an elderly parent often lives far away.

Guiding the decisions of an elderly parent also requires mastery of arcane legal, financial and medical matters.

"It's a new and very confusing skill set," said Maureen Corcoran, a vice president at Prudential Financial. "You don't just give people a list; you lead them there. Otherwise they spend hours upon hours figuring it out themselves."

For both employees and employers, the costs of elder care are enormous, according to studies by the MetLife Mature Market Institute, which is in the midst of updated analysis to reflect rapidly changing demographics.

The price tag for employers in 1997 ranged from $11.5 billion to $29 billion a year. Most expensive were the replacement of lost workers (at least $4.9 billion a year), workday interruptions ($3.7 billion) and absenteeism ($885 million). The employees lose salary, Social Security and pension benefits as a result of refusing promotions, switching to part-time work or retiring early.

Certain benefits mitigate these costs, and certain companies have learned there is a clear return on investment. At Prudential, for instance, subsidized emergency backup care prevents absenteeism and workday interruptions. Prudential's 21,000 employees, with one phone call to Work Options Group, can get help for parents by the next morning, for a co-payment of $4 an hour.

A $20-an-hour aide, on an eight-hour shift, would otherwise cost a Prudential employee $160, rather than $32. Yet the company says it will save $650,000 during a three-year contract with Work Options, Ms. Corcoran said, because "if our employees needs are taken care of, they can focus on work."

Diane Yankencheck, a Prudential employee in Newark, said the service kept her working during a crisis. Her father has a degenerative neurological disease and round-the-clock care. Her mother manages the household, or did until she broke her wrist. Now an aide from Work Options cooks, cleans, and helps her bathe and dress.

Kent Burtis, a Verizon technician in Bayville, N.J., uses similar backup care for his father, who is paralyzed and incontinent. For a while, Mr. Burtis spent hours before work feeding, diapering, and dressing him. Now an aide does the morning shift. "It's kept me from slitting my throat," Mr. Burtis said.

Elder care benefits most often seem a luxury at small companies and nonprofits. So even at AARP, dedicated to the needs of older Americans, Deborah Russell, the director of work force issues, was daunted by coordinating long-distance care for her mother and then missing weeks of work to be at her bedside when death neared.

Ms. Russell and her two sisters, grateful for AARP's excellent referral service, still spent "an inordinate amount of time on the telephone" during working hours, distracted and unproductive. As their mother's condition deteriorated, and the siblings rotated weeks in Florida, Ms. Russell used paid vacation time rather than the 12 weeks of unpaid leave guaranteed by the federal Family Medical Leave Act or AARP's more generous 16-week program, also unpaid.

Another benefit assumed to be useful is the flexible spending account, governed by the Internal Revenue Service and widely offered by companies. It permits the use of pretax dollars for dependent care, as long as the dependent meets the I.R.S. definition. Virtually all children do, but most aged parents do not. That means tax breaks for baby sitters but not companions for the elderly.

Experts disagree about whether women will push employers for help with their parents, as they did 30 years ago when child care was their pressing issue.

Ellen Galinsky, 63, president of the Family and Work Institute, led the charge for a day care center at Bank Street College when she was a researcher there in 1969. After "huge resistance," the center opened in 1974. Ms. Galinsky predicts a similar awakening to elder care issues because "demographics are destiny."

"Everyone I know is dealing with this," said Ms. Galinsky, who recently stayed at the bedside of her 98-year-old mother for the last two months of her life. The institute allows unlimited sick leave for such family emergencies. But even with that leeway, Ms. Galinsky said: "I was on another planet. It's like no other experience. I barely have words for how hard it is."

Todd Groves, founder of LTC Financial Partners in Seattle, who advises human resource managers on long term care, is not convinced that women like Ms. Galinsky will have the same galvanizing effect this time around, regardless of their numbers or their passion.

"Back then you still had a paternal business culture," Mr. Groves said. "Now people feel out on their own. They are fearful about their careers and don't feel they can ask for help."

SIGNIFICANCE

The article highlights an emerging problem rooted in the widely held attitude of American employers regarding employee involvement in the daily care of their children in contrast with the efforts made by many employees to assist their own aging parents. In most of the world's cultures, including the United States, there exists both a legal and moral duty to support a dependent, whether the dependent is a child or an aging parent. In the current American corporate culture, child care is a well established aspect of employment; taking time from one's work to attend to an educational, medical or social need of one's child is an accepted part of the modern American workplace.

There is a significant irony in the fact that the Baby Boom generation was the force instrumental in making child care a prominent feature of modern employment, a trend that began amidst much controversy in the late 1960s and early 1970s. As women began to both enter the workforce in record numbers as well as to maintain a career path after giving birth to their children, child care, both in-home and that provided by third party organizations, became an accepted part of the daily workday routine of millions of American workers. The Baby Boom generation is now faced with both the cost and the strain upon workplace environments created by elder care requirements.

The cost of presenteeism in all of its forms is a significant one. In one 2004 study published in the *Journal of Occupational and Environmental Medicine*, presenteeism, including undocumented absences by employees to assist a family member, was estimated to cost business 255 dollars per employee per year, a figure that represents sixty percent of the total cost attributable to the lost productivity caused by illness.

Presenteeism and the often hidden impact upon corporate productivity caused by absence from work and distractions while physically present at work pose more significant problems than does simple absenteeism. It is estimated that approximately fifty-nine million American workers do not have any form of paid sick leave; thirty percent of the American workforce enjoy the benefits of employment where they may attend to a sick child without consequence. There are no significant corresponding offerings of coverage for elder care, a circumstance that sometimes drives employees to not disclose the nature of their time away from the workplace to attend to such duties.

United States Census data confirms the demographic shift to an older American society where there are an ever increasing number of persons who are most likely to require the assistance of their children with their ongoing needs. The persons providing such elder care themselves are also likely to be older. By the year 2010, the Census estimates that for the first time in its history, fifty-one percent of the American workforce will be over the age of forty. By the year 2020, twenty percent of the American workforce will be over the age of fifty-five, compared to thirteen percent of that demographic in the year 2000.

Elder care insurance programs are generally in their infancy. Unlike traditional child daycare, where the costs are relatively fixed and predictable year to year, elder care is variable due to the unpredictable nature of the elder person's needs. Corporations have been resistant to providing such programs as an employment benefit due to their cost.

Proponents of elder care as a formal aspect of the American employment benefits landscape point to the greater honesty and less stress that would result if employees were able to deal with elder care issues in a direct fashion, avoiding the presenteeism identified in the study noted above. Advocates of elder care as an insurable aspect of an employee's relationship to an employer point to the long term financial savings of reduced presenteeism. As with the child care tax credits available to working parents in many jurisdictions, the pronounced shift in American demographics to an older society may drive a similar form of tax relief for those providing elder care.

FURTHER RESOURCES
Books
Cassidy, Thomas. *Elder Care*. Sacramento, California: Citadel, 2004.

Dychtwald, Ken. *Age Power: How the 21st Century will be Ruled by the New Old*. New York: Penguin USA, 2000.

Marosy, Jean Paul. *A Manager's Guide to Elder Care and Work*. Westport, Connecticut: Greenwood, 1999.

Periodicals
Goetzel, Ron Z., et al. "Health, Absence, Disability, and Presenteeism Cost Estimates." *Journal of Occupational and Environmental Medicine*. 46 (2004) 4:398–412.

Web sites
Institute for Women's Policy Research. "Fact Sheet." 205 <http://www.iwpr.org/pdf/B250.pdf> (accessed July 27, 2006).

Cornell Chronicle. "Economists coin the term 'presenteeism'-for on the job health slowdowns." April 22, 2004. <http://www.news.cornell.edu/Chronicle/04/4.22.04/presenteeism.html> (accessed July 26, 2006).

My Family and Other Vehicles

News Article

By: Anna Melville-James

Date: April 8, 2006

Source: Melville-James, Anna. *Guardian Unlimited*. "My Family and Other Vehicles." <http://www.guardian.

co.uk/family/story/0,,1748639,00.html> (accessed July 21, 2006).

About the Author: Anna Melville-James is a freelance writer specializing in travel, the environment, and family life. Her work has appeared in numerous British publications.

INTRODUCTION

The automobile has played a central role in the development of modern American life. Fueled by cheap petroleum and inspired by an enormously profitable auto industry, Americans are known throughout the world for their dependence on, and their love for, their family cars. With most families now owning multiple cars, suburban homes often devote a substantial portion of their floor space to storing automobiles.

Given their love of cars and driving, as well as the expense of buying airplane tickets for several children, many Americans choose to drive on their summer vacations. The advent of oversized family vehicles with air conditioning and in-car video players in the 1990s made lengthy trips even less daunting to undertake, but long before cross-country travel was comfortable, numerous families loaded up and left home seeking adventure.

Americans, despite their claimed love of leisure, actually take far less vacation time than citizens in most other advanced nations. In 2005, the World Tourism Organization reported that the average American takes only thirteen vacation days per year, far behind workers in Canada (twenty-six), Japan (twenty-five) and Germany (thirty-five). Despite this and other differences, a handful of American and European vacationers share a common passion: their love of the Volkswagen Tent Camper.

Ferdinand Porsche's name is synonymous with expensive performance cars. But in 1931, the German car designer's thoughts were on a different kind of automobile, one that could be mass-produced and afforded by virtually everyone. While the major German automakers were not interested in such a project, Porsche's ideas soon gained the attention of Adolf Hitler, whose dream of a "people's car" led him to fund Porsche's work. The result was the Volkswagen Beetle. Production was set to start just as World War II began and the factory was quickly converted for wartime use, which included military vehicles built on a VW chassis.

Following the war, the British found themselves in possession of the VW factory; unsure what else to do, they began assembling vehicles from leftover parts. The British converted some Beetles to truck-

A Volkswagen camper van. © SAM DIEPHUIS/ZEFA/CORBIS.

like carriers in order to move parts around the factory, and a foreign customer suggested they create a simple cargo van. In the years that followed, that van evolved into more than ninety different customized designs, including delivery wagons, ice cream trucks, fire engines, and beer haulers. The utilitarian vehicles were prized mainly for their reliability.

Along the way, Volkswagen designed a rudimentary camper van, with a pop-up roof, a sink, and a primitive stove. Like the other vans it was little more than a box on wheels, but it soon found a home in the United States, whose car-crazed residents purchased more than 150,000 of the camper vans in the years leading up to 1963. Despite some minor refinements, the camper van, also known as the VW Type 2, remained spartan and functional throughout its lifetime. The vehicle's low cost and ease of maintenance made it a hit and more than five million were eventually produced.

■ PRIMARY SOURCE

MY FAMILY AND OTHER VEHICLES

FOR THREE FAMILIES WHO HAVE CARED FOR AND TRAVELLED IN THEM, THEIR VW CAMPER VAN IS A

WELL-LOVED MEMBER OF THEIR TRIBE, SAYS ANNA MELVILLE-JAMES

The Polleys

The family Brian and Mary Polley, daughters April, 16, and Jo, 19, and Edd the cairn terrier

The van A 1965 split-screen VW campervan with Dormobile elevating roof, called Sonny. They have done 10,000 miles in her and she has broken down just once, at Boscastle in Cornwall.

"We'd been to VW rallies out of interest, but we found Sonny on a website," says Mary. "Brian drove it back from Wales with me following in the car, watching him having to lunge across to shut the passenger door every time he went round a corner! From the beginning, April and Jo loved the van's 'skater-surfer' effect and told me I had to use it on the school run, even though—as Brian says—it's like steering a Christmas pudding.

"These vans do have a personality—Sonny is definitely a 'she,' and like the Tardis. You'd think it would be a squash, but get the awning up and everything packs away nicely. Friends of mine think I'm crazy to go camping in this cold van, and when it rains I wonder, why are we doing this? But it's usually too far away to come home so you just get on with it."

That hardy spirit was tested to the full when the Polley family visited Cornwall in 2004.

"We were on holiday in St Austell and decided to visit Boscastle to see if it was having better weather. It was raining badly en route. As we pootled down the valley to the town you could see the stream had turned into a fast-flowing river, but we didn't think anything of it at the time. April went to the museum and we sat outside. Within a short time the water was up to the banks and in the time it took to shout for April and walk back to the car park 700 yards away, it was knee deep and cars had started to float and hit the wall.

"After 10 minutes we saw water coming down the road, so we stood on a picnic table before heading for a pub, until water built up there and we had to leave. By then, cars were steadily floating down the high street.

"It seemed like we spent all day getting to safety, but also like minutes. We'd had to go through gardens and shelter in someone's garage at one point as the water came past us. We were scared but we just kept telling each other we loved each other."

Stranded residents and visitors were eventually evacuated, and the Polleys resigned themselves to having lost Sonny, until they realised their beleaguered van had become an overnight celebrity. "While we were in the centre I got a call from the school where I work to ask what was going on. Nobody knew we were in Boscastle,

and it turned out they'd seen our van in the evening paper. TV crews had been taking aerial flood shots and our van was in them. Friends watching the national news had also seen it floating in the car park, probably because it was bright and stuck out." Sonny was rescued by the police and the RAC and the Polleys returned to the road last June.

"Once we got it back we were determined to keep it, even though to other people it looked finished," says Brian. "I love the van, but you have to have patience. I took bin bags of twigs out of it, and put in new brakes, doors and second-hand windows. Only the engine didn't need replacing—it was still working once the mud had been cleared out! With all the work I've done since it got damaged, it's probably more my van now that it was before."

Last August, undeterred by their experience, the Polleys took Sonny back to Boscastle. "We wanted to see what it looked like. I don't think it erased all the bad memories but it was nice to see how much had been done in such a short period of time. And we even saw a billboard with a picture of the van on it while we were there. I think we may just go to Cornwall again this summer. We really did enjoy it last year—the weather was lovely."

The Childs family

The family Terry Childs and children Amanda, 22, Trevor, 20, Matthew, 8

The van A 1967 split-screen four-berth Canterbury Pitt conversion van with a pop top, called Rosie. She has 95,000 miles on the clock and has required six breakdown call-outs.

Rosie had been put out to pasture after failing her MOT, but when Terry Childs and her family first saw her they couldn't resist getting her back on the road.

"We had a two-berth, 1973 Bay VW van in 1985 when we were expecting Trevor. Two years later, we heard of this van that was being scrapped. It had spent months in a field and the owner offered its elevated roof to put on ours so we could have bunks. When we arrived, it was three foot deep in nettles, but had character and we fell in love.

"We joined the Split-Screen Van Club because we needed advice and rare parts—and had her on the road within a year. The first time we camped was in north Wales and we took my mother. We'd taken a tent, but it was raining heavily so we all slept in the van. As the gale blew, my husband, Steve, wriggled round in his sleeping bag on a bunk, but because it was original canvas he fell through it and ended up on top of my mother.

"It was July, wet and horrible, we had our first breakdown but it was a great holiday and cemented our love affair with the van. You get such a buzz driving it. I'm only five foot but [in it] I can see over walls and hedges. The children loved the van from the word go, but Rosie filled a lot of time—and that would be their news at school, which everyone thought was a bit odd. As far as a lot of people were concerned it was a 'hippy van.' Now, though, it's 'vintage' and Matthew, born in 1998, accepts it as really cool."

In 2002, Steve was diagnosed with motor neurone disease, but Rosie continued to be a focal point for them. "In 2003 we went to the Lake District and Scotland with my sister and her husband, who own a 1971 VW Bay, her son, my mother and my other sister's daughter. That trip is a milestone in our family's memory. My husband had given up work and he couldn't drive the van or lift a spanner by this stage. But on this trip he climbed to the top of Ben Nevis. This was a year before he died, almost to the day.

"The following day, after returning home, we caught the ferry to visit our daughter in Germany and spent two weeks travelling down the Rhine and through the Austrian Alps. As Matthew enjoys telling people, that was where I drove up a mountain in first gear with the handbrake on. In four weeks, we drove 3,400 miles.

"Steve's health continued to decline, and in February 2004, a chest infection started to affect his breathing. We continued to camp, and went to a rally in May. That was the weekend my little boy learned to ride his bike with Steve looking on. The last VW event we went to together was in August. Steve was using breathing apparatus and we planned to get electricity for it at the next meeting in September.

"Steve died on August 31. I asked myself what would he have wanted us to do. He had spent so many years and all his spare time on Rosie. It was a big part of our lives. We felt that we weren't going to give up on our van and VW connections. So we faced the meeting bravely, hoping, not unkindly, that it would also make people face us.

"After our big trip, Steve and I talked about the van needing restoration. Once he died I agonised over its future and decided work had to be done. I spent £12,000 on it and by June 2005 it was looking fantastic. When I picked it up I said: 'Wow, it's no different, it's my van!'—which probably didn't please the restoration guy! But there is a lifetime of memories still in it. I didn't want it to be restored to concourse condition, just to extend its life so we could carry on having holidays. I left the hubcap dents in, and the VW symbol at the front just as it was—with a bit of rust. People ask: 'Aren't you going to spray it?'and I say, 'No, it makes the van.' It sums up my husband's attitude—he just wanted to be out there enjoying it."

The Emmetts

The family Brian and Sue Emmett, son Paul and wife Fiona, grandchildren Daniel, 5, and Heather, 11, daughter Lisa, husband Mark and grandchildren Katie, 2, and Luke, 5, and Molly the golden retriever

The van 1963 split-screen VW campervan, four-berth Devon conversion with fixed roof, named Sally. She has done 55,000 miles. No breakdowns so far.

Brian and Sue Emmett and their children, Lisa and Paul, had happy memories of family camping holidays. So when Paul bought a split-screen VW van it wasn't long before they had all caught the camper van bug. "I bought Paul the first of his many Beetles 16 years ago, and six years ago he decided he wanted a VW van," says Brian. "His first van was Barney, which he sold to Lisa when he bought Charlie, a split-screen Samba.

"We didn't want it purely as a show vehicle, but to have weekends away in as a family. We all live within six miles of each other and my son works with me in the family business. We're all very close and that's rolled out into our holidays—you want to spend as much time as you can with your kids.

"We've had some quite luxurious motor caravans over the years and now we've gone back to something basic. But it's more fun. We lie there and laugh—it's lovely. Having the van now is another lease of life—we can still enjoy going out with the children and grandchildren, but it's still our thing as well.

"When we got Sally, Sue made a bib for the front of the van with her name on it, and we see people mouth the name as we go past. VW vans always put a smile on people's faces."

Paul and his wife, Fiona, and Lisa and her husband, Mark, have recently sold their split-screens to buy larger 1980s Type 25 VW vans to accommodate their families. For Brian, though, there can only be one van: "We can't imagine life without Sally. She's always cleaned and polished." His wife, Sue, is equally smitten—to her, Sally is "family." "I don't think there's enough space in her to go on long holidays. If I were 20 years younger then maybe. But really she's a short-holiday girl."

"When we're in the van, the children never ask, 'Are we there yet?'" says Lisa. "And it's just really nice for the kids to have holidays with Nanny and Pappy, and the dog as well!"

But are the next generation going to be as keen on carrying on the tradition?

"My five-year-old son, Luke, is obsessed by VWs and will identify them as we drive along," says Lisa. "It wouldn't surprise me if they bought their own vans when they grow up and I can see a day when we all go on holiday together with them as well."

SIGNIFICANCE

Because of their somewhat unconventional appearance, as well as their ability to transport and house numerous people inexpensively, the VW camper became exceptionally popular with the flower children of the 1960s. Painted in psychedelic colors and decorated with oversized flowers and peace symbols, VW campers became the transportation of choice for hippies traveling the country.

The Volkswagen Type 2 remained in production until 1979, when the decades-old design was replaced with a more up-to-date model bearing little resemblance to the original. Although VW campers have not been produced for more than two decades, many of them remain in service—some updated and lavishly furnished—and numerous fan clubs around the world meet to swap stories and trade parts. Several agencies also rent VW campers so anyone can experience the rugged thrill of driving one of these legendary vehicles.

During the 1990s, Volkswagen engineers created a concept car that resembled the Volkswagen Beetle. Intended only for exhibition at the Detroit Auto Show, the car created such a furor that the company decided to produce a new Beetle. The model appeared in dealerships in 1997 and was an instant hit. A similar future appears possible for the venerable VW van. After showing a concept van, VW announced in early 2006 that it would begin production of a new van based on a Chrysler platform. Given the new van's stately appointments and high price, it appears unlikely to attract the same type of buyers as the original.

FURTHER RESOURCES

Books

Eccles, David. *VW Camper—The Inside Story: A Guide to VW Camping Conversions and Interiors 1951–2005*. Ramsbury, Wiltshire, U.K.: Crowood Press, 2005.

Mintz, Steven. *Domestic Revolutions: A Social History of American Family Life*. New York: The Free Press, 1988.

Seume, Keith. *VW Beetle: A Comprehensive Illustrated History of the World's Most Popular Car*. Osceola, Wisc.: Motorbooks International, 1997.

Periodicals

Brooke, Jill. "Fun for the Entire Family, But Not All at Once." *New York Times* 155 (2006): 2.

Sansone, Arrica. "You Can Afford a Family Vacation." *Good Housekeeping* 242 (2006): 136–142.

Taras, Jeffrey. "A Magic Bus for a Weekend or for a Long Strange Trip." *New York Times* 144 (1995): 11.

Web sites

British Broadcasting Company. "A Brief History of the VW Type II Bus." <http://www.bbc.co.uk/dna/h2g2/A649181> (accessed July 21, 2006).

Westminster College. "VW History." <http://people.westminstercollege.edu/staff/bknorr/html/history.htm> (accessed July 21, 2006).

Siblings of Disabled Have Their Own Troubles

News article

By: Gretchen Cook

Date: April 4, 2006

Source: Cook, Gretchen. "Siblings of Disabled Have Their Own Troubles." *New York Times*. (4 April 2006).

About the Author: Gretchen Cook writes on topics related to health and disabilities for the *New York Times*.

INTRODUCTION

Until the 1960s, most physically and developmentally disabled children were placed in institutions or segregated educationally in special schools or separate classrooms. Private schools for the disabled, such as the Perkins School for the Blind, were founded in the nineteenth century and continue to operate for children with physical and developmental handicaps. By the late 1960s, parents of disabled children fought for greater education and medical rights for their children; the 1975 Education for All Handicapped Children Act was a piece of federal legislation that provided sweeping education rights for such students.

As a result, more children with disabilities became part of the social and educational environment in neighborhood schools. By the late 1970s and early 1980s, a new educational theory for special education students—mainstreaming—sought to place special education students into regular classes for as much of the day as possible, to help students acclimate to the academic and social atmosphere of classrooms where students did not have disabilities. The siblings of students with disabilities, therefore, spent more time in contact with their disabled brothers and sisters, either

A nine-year-old girl with serious birth defects plays catch with her sister using velcro paddles and a ball. © LAURA DWIGHT/CORBIS.

at home or in school. In the 1980s, 1990s, and into the twenty-first century, more children were diagnosed with special needs than at any previous time in public education history. As diagnoses of autism spectrum disorders reached a rate of 1 in 166 in 2005, and as better detection and diagnosis of conditions such as dyslexia, attention deficit disorder, early-onset bipolar disorder, and other conditions led to greater numbers of children in special education, more than seven million children in the U.S. have come to be identified as the sibling of a disabled child.

Research on the attitudes and outcomes of siblings of disabled children is scant; because their numbers are growing, researchers and psychology professionals are beginning to examine the impact their siblings' disability has on these children. Siblings of disabled children are often expected by parents to

be more mature, to handle more household tasks, and later in life to be the assumed caretakers for disabled siblings once the parents die or become too incapacitated to provide direct or indirect care to the child with a disability, while in the past a disabled brother or sister might have been placed in an institution or a halfway house. The following article notes the increasing trend and examines how siblings cope.

■ PRIMARY SOURCE

When he was growing up in Oregon, Graham Seaton found it virtually impossible to bring children home from school to play.

"I knew there was something wrong with my place," he recalled. "But I didn't know how to explain what that was."

He knew that he would have to tell his friends why they could play only in his bedroom—and only with the door locked. And that, ultimately, he would have to explain what was "wrong" with his older brother Burleigh, who is profoundly autistic.

"I just didn't have the words," he said.

Now 30, Mr. Seaton said he realized that as a child, he felt he could not ask his parents for those words.

"I was so aware I couldn't make a big deal with my family," he said. "My parents already had enough on their hands."

An estimated seven million "typically developing" American children have siblings with disabilities, according to the Arc of the United States, a leading advocacy group for the mentally retarded. Those children face many of the same challenges—and joys—as their parents, but they also face other problems. Some resent the extra demands placed on them at an early age by their disabled siblings, and many feel neglected by their often overburdened parents.

Some children say they fear "catching" their siblings' disabilities. Others may wish that they, too, were disabled, so that they could get all the attention their siblings do. And many suffer embarrassment about their siblings' inappropriate behavior or abnormal appearance, and then feel guilty about it.

These are difficult emotions for children to struggle with, and Don Meyer, director of the Arc's sibling support project, says the needs of siblings like Mr. Seaton are often overlooked. Most assistance organizations and support groups are intended for disabled children themselves or for their parents.

"These brothers and sisters will likely have the longest-lasting relationships of anyone, relationships easily in excess of 65 years," Mr. Meyer said. "They should be remembered at every turn."

Still, many siblings welcome the early maturity and responsibility that come with having a disabled brother or sister. They are often well versed in the details of their siblings' disabilities, and they take pride in being able to explain them in sophisticated ways. For example, Hannah, 16, of Dearborn, Mich., who did not want her last name used out of concerns for her privacy, said she related better to adults than to children her age because of having to cope with her brother Ian's autism.

But that maturity does not inoculate her from embarrassment about Ian's outbursts, particularly during church services.

"Sometimes he'll kind of start making noises, and then sometimes he'll kick and flail his arms, or he'll start rocking and crying," Hannah said. "My mother will take him outside, but it's still, like, okayyyyy."

Suzanne Ripley, who has two sons with cerebral palsy, says that a child's disability can embarrass parents, too, but that embarrassment can be more acute for siblings, especially those in the throes of adolescent conformity. Young siblings are also prone to teasing from other children, who do not have the social inhibitions of adults. But Ms. Ripley, the director of the National Dissemination Center for Children With Disabilities, based in Washington, notes that adults can often be just as rude.

"People tend to be uncomfortable with anyone who's different, so they look for a second and then look away," Ms. Ripley said. "Imagine how that would make you feel" as a child.

Parents like Ms. Ripley are likely to seek comfort through talking with others about their conflicting emotions. But children may not have the sophistication to do so or they may feel guilty about acknowledging any negative feelings they have.

Hannah, for example, says she loves her 13-year-old brother and feels terrible about her reactions to his outbursts.

"I know it's not his fault and that's the way he is, and so I shouldn't really be embarrassed, but sometimes I am," she said.

But she said she did not discuss those feelings with her parents.

"They'd get that, 'Oh well, you can deal with it' kind of attitude," she said. "I know they would listen, but they would get defensive."

Ally Cirelli, a 9-year-old in Towson, Md., whose sister is developmentally disabled, says the biggest complaint she hears from her peers is that the disabled siblings get all the attention.

Some are so jealous of their siblings that they wish they had their own disability, and the special treatment that comes with it, she said. But Ally, too, avoids talking to her parents about her feelings. And she is quick to backpedal when she does talk about it, insisting that her sister, Katie, 8, does not embarrass her "all that often," and that she is "really fun" to play with.

Mr. Meyer, of the Arc, says children need a place where they can openly discuss these concerns and emotions. To fill this gap, he started the sibling support project, which is based in Seattle and provides information and holds discussion groups for children around the country. In 2005, Mr. Meyer also published "The Sibling Slam Book: What It's Really Like to Have a Brother or Sister With Special Needs," a collection of candid remarks by 80 children.

Mr. Meyer said that when asked about the most embarrassing moment of their lives, few of the children cited anything having to do with their disabled siblings. Instead, most recounted the usual teenage humiliations: problems in romantic relationships or dealing with parents.

And that, Mr. Meyer says, underscores an important point: "When I talk to parents about embarrassment (about disabled siblings), I ask them to keep in mind that it's an age-related condition," he said. "That's the good news, that a lot of that seems to be resolved by even their late teens."

The work of disability advocates and the main-streaming of children with special needs in schools and in the wider society has fostered more awareness of—and less discomfort with—disabilities.

Ms. Ripley, for her part, says she has noticed a change in public attitudes, especially when she is struggling to maneuver with her sons in public places.

"I'm finding that people are more and more helpful," she said. "That didn't used to happen."

SIGNIFICANCE

As of the year 2004, 8.6 percent of all children ages three through twenty-one in the United States were classified as being served by the Individuals with Disabilities Education Act (IDEA), the revised version of the 1975 Education for All Handicapped Children Act. Between 1994 and 2004, the rate of increase for children falling under the umbrella of IDEA was 9.25 percent; as these rates increase, the number of siblings of children with disabilities continues to increase as well.

As this article notes, siblings of children with disabilities face unique challenges. Some children express a secret wish for their own disability, to receive the extra attention their siblings receive, while others act out or play the role of perfect child, all while dealing with peer pressure regarding their sibling's status.

At the same time, research as of 2006 suggests that siblings of disabled children are emotionally well-adjusted, and in some research studies demonstrate more compassion, empathy, and appreciation of their own non-disabled status. While some studies show that the first year after diagnosis leads to some adjustment problems, siblings of disabled children demonstrate long-term emotional and psychological health in spite of—or perhaps because of—their experience in a family with a disabled child.

While researchers have studied the siblings of mentally ill persons for years, the siblings of disabled children represent a relatively new facet for research and study as disability in the childhood population—

most notably developmental disabilities—have a greater impact on American educational and social institutions.

FURTHER RESOURCES

Books

Connors, Claire and Kirsten Stalker. *The Experiences and Views of Disabled Children and their Siblings: Implications for Practice and Policy.* London: Jessica Kingsley Publishers, 2003.

Growing Up With Disability, edited by Carol Robinson and Kirsten Stalker. London: Jessica Kingsley Publishers, 1998.

Mayer, Don. *The Sibling Slam Book: What It's Really Like To Have A Brother Or Sister With Special Needs.* Bethesda, Md.: Woodbine House, 2005.

Periodicals

Epkins, C. "An Initial Look at Sibling Reports on Children's Behavior: Comparisons with Children's Self-reports and Relations with Siblings' Self-reports and Sibling Relationships." *Journal of Abnormal Child Psychology* 27 (October 1999): 371–381.

Muchnick, Jeanne. "Giving a Voice to Siblings of the Disabled." *New York Times* (19 March 2000).

Father Figures

News article

By: Polly Curtis

Date: April 8, 2006

Source: Curtis, Polly. *The Guardian.* "Father Figures." April 8, 2006. <http://money.guardian.co.uk/worklifebalance/story/0,,1749367,00.html> (accessed July 23, 2006).

About the Author: Polly Curtis is a reporter for the print and online versions of *The Guardian* in the United Kingdom, writing on topics related to education and society.

INTRODUCTION

Gender roles and division of labor in families have changed dramatically in the United States and Western Europe over the past fifty years. Women gained the right to vote in most western nations by 1950 and entered the workforce in greater numbers for a wide range of reasons, from personal fulfillment to financial

A father and daughter read together on the front porch, 1996. © ARIEL SKELLEY/CORBIS.

need. By the 1960s and 1970s, the modern family had trimmed down; families with four or five children were replaced with those with two or three offspring, and because women were sharing the burden of earning income, they began to expect men to share some of the burden of household management and childcare.

As the divorce rate in the United States and England climbed in the 1970s, reaching fourteen divorces per one thousand in England in 2004 and 4.2 divorces per one thousand in 1999 in the United States, the number of non-custodial fathers climbed. Combined with an increase in the number of children born to women out of wedlock—thirty-five percent of all births in the United States in 2004 and forty-two percent in England—cultural critics, psychologists, and researchers began to examine the impact of the father on family life and child development.

A great deal of research into fatherhood and the role of a father's involvement—or lack of involvement—cites the obvious: having a loving father involved in a child's life helps the child to be emotionally secure. A 1997 U.S. study shows that children with fathers who participate in educational activities have higher grades and higher participation rates in

school activities and sports, while a 1996 poll by the National Center for Fathering shows that more than fifty-seven percent of fathers believe that their workplaces do not recognize the need for fathers to have more flexibility to attend such events and to have more flex-time for family issues.

■ PRIMARY SOURCE

My dad used to drop my siblings and me off at school each morning on the way to work. We'd listen to the radio and chat about our day and I was oblivious to the fact that this was the 1980s and for a man to say to his office that he wouldn't be in before 10am because he was doing the school run was very unusual. He got a lot of stick for it, but that's the way it worked in my house.

Fast forward 20 years and things are changing slowly. A mum's struggle makes daily headlines. Having a baby will cost me hundreds of thousands over my lifetime, according to one report. Parenthood is seen as a mum's dilemma. But new government research suggests that now dads are speaking up too.

The survey of 2,504 mothers of 17-month old babies and 1,512 of the children's fathers revealed that dads are now deeply involved in their kids' upbringing. The proportion of fathers working flexible hours to fit around childcare arrangements rose from 11% to 31% between 2002 and 2005. The number working from home doubled from 14% to 29%. It's all part, say fathers' campaigning groups, of a real change in the home and workplace.

"This is evidence that there is a social revolution going on, with fathers not just talking about being more involved with their children but renegotiating their lives to allow for it," says Jack O'Sullivan of information charity Fathers Direct. "It's really good for children, families and fathers themselves who get the benefit of being a dad."

The renegotiating of dads' roles includes working shorter hours (18% said they did), moving their working day backward or forward to fit around their families (14%), changing hours to fit with their partners' work (27%) and changing jobs altogether (22%).

It's just what my dad did—bar the change of job. But back in the 80s when the yuppy working culture meant 7.30 am board meetings and 14-hour days, my dad's logic—that he was working to 7pm most days so a 10 am start was fair—did not go down well.

Some believe little has changed. "We need to modernise the laws to keep up to track with the speed of this social change, to let fathers play the part they want to play in their children's lives," says O'sullivan.

One of the government's proposals on this front is that parents should be able to share their parental leave allowance, so that parents could decide how to share out the year's leave when a new child is born. This will be a popular option for some parents—but could also cause some rows. A quarter of mums said they would consider sharing some of their 12 months of parental leave with their partner. But a third of new fathers would like the option to spend longer with their small children.

Announcing the research conducted by the Policy Study Institute, trade and industry secretary Alan Johnson said there had been a "positive culture change in the home and workplace. Mothers are taking more time off when their child is born, the majority of fathers are taking up their new entitlement to paternity leave, and the number of new dads now working flexibly has tripled."

He claimed the findings in the 146-page report were evidence that the government's policy is working. After maternity leave was extended from 18 to 26 weeks and unpaid additional leave from 29 to 52 weeks last year, half of mothers took 26 weeks leave compared with 9% in 2002 and a further 14% took the full 52 weeks, compared with just 5% three years previously.

But while the government is trumpeting the improved take-up of maternity and paternity leave and the evidence that dads are getting more involved, women who have children are still counting the cost to their careers. Some 17 months after the birth of their child, one in four mothers were not working; some had attempted a return to work only to give it up later. But fewer mothers switched jobs when they returned—something the report's authors suggested showed employers were taking their commitments to working mothers more seriously.

Three quarters of women who were not working said that they wanted to spend more time with their children. But 16% said they couldn't afford childcare, 13% said their job didn't provide suitable hours and 12% could not find the right childcare. The most likely to return to work were those in "higher level" jobs with better flexible working opportunities, or those with heavy mortgage commitments.

The government's report did not ask the same questions of the fathers. Why? Simply because so few are providing the principal care for their children. Dads might be more involved, but shifting their working day is not the same as shifting their entire careers.

Carena Rogers, policy officer at the National Family and Parenting Institute, says: "Mothers are still much more pressured to give up their careers and it can be very difficult to get back into work."

My dad might have been a trailblazer, but there's still a way to go.

SIGNIFICANCE

The English maternity leave system, unlike the United States system, provides up to twenty-six weeks paid leave for new mothers, but both countries give no paternity leave. In 2002, Iceland began a program that gave fathers three months leave with eighty percent pay, with virtually one hundred percent of fathers taking the paternity leave after the birth of a child. Iceland's birth rate is the second highest in Europe; in addition to the three months for fathers, mothers receive three months and the couple receives three more months to split between them. Paternity policies such as Iceland's, or paternity leave policies in Sweden and Denmark, have led to marked increases in fathers' participation in their children's early years.

As the author notes, her father was an anomaly, but a trailblazer; the percentages of fathers willing to change their work life for the sake of children is steadily increasing. In Sweden, fathers who take less than two months' paternity leave are looked down upon, while in the United States, where paternity leave policies are scarce and provided by private employers, fathers wishing to take more than their set vacation days for a new birth are considered to be less committed to their career. Although the United States has the Family Medical Leave Act, which guarantees twelve weeks of unpaid leave and bars employers from firing employees who take the leave, the law applies only to businesses with fifty employees or more, and because the time is unpaid most fathers cannot afford to take time off using FMLA.

Single fathers, like single mothers, have been on the rise as well; in the United States in 1970 there were 400,000 single fathers; in 2005 there were 2.3 million. While *Time* magazine analyzed the twenty-two percent of women with graduate and professional degrees who choose to stay at home with their children, the 157,000 men who identified themselves as stay-at-home dads in 2005 receive little attention; viewed not as a trend but a fluke, stay-at-home fathers are viewed as men between full-time jobs or starting a new business, though mothers who choose to stay at home are rarely viewed the same way.

In the United States, only six percent of fathers provide the majority of child care for their school-aged children as of 2005, yet thirty-two percent of fathers who work night or midnight shifts provide child care for their preschool-age children while their wives work. Between 1981 and 2006, the amount of time full-time employed fathers spent with their children each day rose from 1.8 hours to 2.7 hours. The changes, though slow, steadily increase the amount of time and involvement fathers have in their children's daily lives.

FURTHER RESOURCES
Books
Fatherhood: Research, Interventions, and Policies, edited by H. Elizabeth Peters and Gary W. Peterson. Binghamton, N.Y.: Haworth Press, 2000.

Periodicals
Atkinson, Maxine and Stephen Blackwelder. "Fathering in the 20th Century." *Journal of Marriage and the Family* 55 (1993): 975–986.

Cocks, Jay. "How Long Till Equality?" *Time* (July 12, 1982).

National Center for Education Statistics. "Fathers' Involvement in Schools." *Government Printing Office* (1997).

Web sites
At Home Dad. <http://www.athomedad.com> (accessed July 22, 2006).

National Center for Fathering. <http://www.fathers.com> (accessed July 22, 2006).

National Fatherhood Initiative. <http://www.fatherhood.org> (accessed July 22, 2006).

Time.com. "Bring on the Daddy Wars." <http://www.time.com/time/nation/article/0,8599,1168125,00.html> (accessed July 22, 2006).

5 Work and Gender Roles

Work and Gender Roles

A family is a functioning economic unit. Throughout history, families have operated farms or businesses, pooling financial resources and dividing labor among family members. Similarly, resources and labor are divided for tasks within the family. One person may look after children; another may prepare meals or clean the home. Some members may work outside of the home to provide the family with income. For generations, many of these tasks have been divided according to gender. In Western society, women looked after children and tended the home, while men worked outside of the home to provide income. While this arrangement is often described as traditional, many traditional families had wives that produced goods and garnered income in addition to raising children. Farming families often divided hard labor among all of the family members.

While children have long provided labor in the household or on family farms, urban working-class families often sent children to work in the same factories as their parents. Some industries, such as textile, depended on semi-skilled child laborers to operate complex machinery or do rapid, fine needlework. Child labor helped support families, but it came at a heavy cost. Children in factories could not attend school. They worked long hours, at dangerous jobs, and were often exploited. Children were typically paid less than adults for the same day's work. "Testimony of Ann and Elizabeth Eggley, Child Mine Workers," and "Homework Destroys Family Life" discuss the effects of child labor on the family and society, and also discuss the impacts of child labor reform on families.

Women working outside the home is also not a new phenomenon, but for much of the nineteenth and twentieth centuries, female industrial workers were predominantly young, poor, and single or married without children. Many were recent immigrants. Many women worked as governesses or domestic servants, with a greater variation in their ages, ethnicities, marital status, and socio-economic class. "A Young Lady, of Good Family and Education, Desires an Engagement as Governess" features classified advertisements for employment within a family home.

For middle- and upper-class women who predominantly stayed in the home, the end of the era of abundant and affordable servant labor meant an increasing amount of time spent doing menial household chores. "Twenty-six Hours a Day" provided the housewife with helpful hints on time and household management. Advertisements for home appliances, like "Washing Day Reform," promised greater leisure time for housewives and domestic servants, but mounting duties and expectations created the infamous "housewives paradox" where some assert that technology has not freed the in-home worker as promised.

With the rise of feminism, the family structure again changed. Many women chose to leave the home and enter college or the workforce. "For the Benefit of the Girl About to Graduate," "With Puck's Apologies to the Coming Woman," and "Election Day!" all warn of the perils of women leaving the domestic sphere. Women participating in college, the workforce, or civil life were portrayed as masculine, uncaring, poor mothers, and usually unattractive. For generations, many women have sought to separate their professional and family identities, desiring equity to men in marriage, partnership, parenting, the workforce, and society.

Household Work

Book excerpt

By: Dimitri Ivanovich Rostislavov

Date: c. 1820

Source: Rostislavov, Dimitri Ivanovich. "Household Work." In *Provincial Russia in the Age of Enlightenment*, edited by Alexander M. Martin. Chicago: Northern Illinois University Press, 2002.

About the Author: Alexander M. Martin is Professor of Russian and European History at Oglethorpe University in Atlanta, Georgia.

INTRODUCTION

The selection of a career is among the most challenging decisions foisted upon modern young people. College freshmen are often asked to select a major field of study, a choice that will determine how they spend their college years and may well define their career options, all at the age of eighteen. While occupations today are largely a matter of personal or family choice, vocational choices were once made at the moment of birth and were often based largely on the person's gender.

Throughout history, certain occupations have been considered appropriate for men, while other work was reserved primarily for women. Although women have frequently distinguished themselves in combat situations, the armed forces have traditionally been a male domain. Conversely, while many men have excelled as primary school educators, these teaching positions continue to be held largely by women. The terms "nurse" and "flight attendant" typically produce images of a woman, while the terms "doctor" and "mayor" generally conjure up male imagery.

These gender-occupational stereotypes have deep roots; for many centuries, male and female work roles were largely prescribed by society. Even in farm settings where both husband and wife worked at home, specific tasks were automatically under the oversight of the man, while others belonged to the woman. In some cases certain roles are better suited to one gender: the heavy work of plowing or baling hay tends to be accomplished more easily by men, due to their larger muscle mass. In contrast, the work of knitting and sewing may be better suited to women, who generally exhibit better fine motor skills. These are of course generalizations and in many families do

A musician entertains a family as they gather for refreshments outside their cabin in Russia, 1852. © HULTON-DEUTSCH COLLECTION/CORBIS.

not apply, yet for generations these expectations remained the norm.

Other aspects of home life were also determined by tradition. With several generations of a family often sharing the same dwelling, decision-making and financial choices had the potential to become convoluted. The role of elderly parents in particular offered the potential for conflict, as families wrestled with whether senior family members should be treated as equals, subordinates, or superiors. Once again, cultural norms generally dictated this decision, with elders perceived quite differently depending on which culture they lived in.

Russia at the dawn of the twentieth century was an enormous country, larger than the United States, India, and China combined. The country had been ruled for three centuries by a single family, the Romanovs, and the nation remained deeply traditional, with elderly parents heading households even if the home was owned by grandchildren, and men and women filling distinctly defined work roles. In these ways, nineteenth-century Russia was quite similar to numerous other nations around the globe.

PRIMARY SOURCE

When we moved to Tuma, my father became the senior priest and district superintendent there, and he was already around thirty years old, yet neither he nor my mother at once became the full masters in the house they owned. Among the clergy at that time, or at least among many of its members, the same custom prevailed that survives to the present in peasant families. Here, the old man and old woman—the father or grandfather, and the mother or grandmother—rule until the day they die, unless they voluntarily step down, even if their children are the actual householders, hold honored positions [as elected community leaders] such as foreman (*starshin*) or elder (*starostay*), support the family entirely by their own labor, and so on. I knew Ivan Maksimovich, the bailiff of the hamlet of Korobovskaia in the parish of Dmitrovskii Pogost, a sprightly, intelligent man who was the despot of his estate. Yet this very despot occupied only second place at home, where his father, a man over seventy, would not let him take charge of anything. "In the estate office or the communal assembly, you're the bailiff," the old man would say, "but here I'm the head of the family, and you'll do as I tell you." Something of that sort also went on in our family: in managing the household, Father and Mother had elders over them, whom they had to obey.

Village households divide their work into two parts, called the women's household and the men's household. Women's work includes taking care of those domestic animals whose meat or other products are used for food (cows, sheep, swine, chickens, geese, and so on) as well as preparing and storing cheese, butter and milk, and—the most important thing—managing the kitchen. In this department, so to speak, the mistress of the house is the commander. Men's work includes looking after the horses and all the fieldwork; here the master is the one giving the orders.

In our home in Tuma the mistress at first was my great-grandmother, Grandfather's mother Avdot'ia Mikhailovna, who already had over seventy years "on her shoulders." Even so, she was a tireless worker who would get up earlier than almost anyone else, make sure the cows were milked and sometimes milk them herself, in the summer she would often drive out livestock out to graze with the other livestock of the village, and she would decide what food should be prepared that day. She would not leave the stove once it was lit; some foods she would prepare by herself, others she would assign to someone else, and both Grandmother and Mother were admitted only as helpers and advisers. During lunch and dinner, she almost never sat down at the table, instead pouring cabbage soup into the pot, cutting up the beef, preparing the porridge, and so on, and sometimes she would even serve up the food. Don't think that anyone forced her to do this—no, my late great-grandmother was not one who could take orders from someone else. She was a woman of extremely tough, unbending character who kept all her direct descendants under her thumb; even Grandfather was a little scared of her and did what she said. On the other hand, both Mother and Grandmother would have been happy if the old woman had transferred control over the household to them, because she did not much like to take advice from any one, paid no heed to any needs that were new to her, and kept everything in her hands the old-fashioned way. She was in charge because she was accustomed to it and considered it both her duty and her right. I am amazed even now when I think of how she would walk across the muddy courtyard, barefoot and slightly stooped, and shout at the workwomen or the workman. Here, she would drive the sheep into the shed. There, she would milk the cow or check whether it was being done right. Almost every evening, she would count the sheep, lambs, chickens, and so on. She would strain the milk and crawl into the outdoor cellar to set up the milk jugs or have someone else do it in front of her, and so on. She was always busy, allowing herself to rest only after lunch and at night, and she almost always slept on the stove without ever spreading anything under herself.

She even, as the Russian saying has it, "died in midstride." [Following a popular custom] she would, as a very old woman, go to confession and receive communion every six weeks and, so to speak, permanently prepare to die. On the eve, or actually the very day of her death, she was active as was her habit; she had merely been saying for two or three days that she was growing tired quickly, but still she was running the entire household. After dinner, she stayed with Mother, the bought girls, and my oldest sister in the cabin, where they were spinning. Great-grandmother climbed onto the stove and apparently went to sleep. Suddenly, she began to snort strangely, which the girls found funny, so they started laughing. But Mother made them stop and, when the same snorting recurred several times, she decided to examine the old woman with a light. When she looked at her and saw with horror that a deathly pallor was spreading across her face, she began rubbing the dying woman's temples and gave orders for Grandfather and Father, who were sleeping in the annex, to be awakened at once. They came running, and when they lifted her from the stove she was still alive but unconscious. Following custom, they laid her down in the icon corner and placed a burning wax candle in her hands; she was still breathing, but after a few minutes she died. I was sleeping in the annex that night when I awoke and saw Father looking very grave. "You've slept long enough," he told me, "our grandmother has died." I was puzzled by these words, and could not figure out which of our grandmothers—his or mine—had passed away, since I had seen both of them in good health just the evening before. How could one of them have died? When I reached the cabin, I saw the deceased who had already been properly arranged. The Psalter was being read over her, and a few strangers were already standing about who had come to gaze upon the deceased and mourn her death. They made me kiss her. For the first time in my life, I kissed a dead person, and touching the cold lips seemed somehow strange and terrifying to me. I was sorry that she had died. Although she had been querulous, for some reason she had loved me and often indulged me, giving me some milk to drink separately from the others, or a bone with some meat still on it, or discreetly slipping some goodies into my hand. Altogether, her funeral was an important event for me. For the first time, I saw a death in my own home, and, both at home and in church, I watched with curiosity the various rites and traditions with which it is our custom to see off the deceased on their final voyage.

[After Great-grandmother's death, and with Grandmother Fekla Akimovna being sickly and losing her eyesight, Mother became the head of the women's part of the household. This meant that she alone had to spin, weave, and sew the clothing for the entire household. She also directed the home schooling of their six children, though Rostislavov, by the time he was seven or eight, was expected to help his younger siblings learn to read and to babysit the youngest.]

My sisters, however, spent little time on scholarship and reading, and that mostly between the ages of five and seven. At that time they were learning to read, that is, they would read through and learn the alphabet, the Book of Hours and the Psalter. Later, they would also learn to write, little by little, to while away the time, on holidays, sometimes by teaching themselves. For that reason you could not expect them to be like the girls of the urban clergy and show much intellectual curiosity when they were young. Only my oldest sister liked reading books in the civil print even before she got married. Once they were married, however, hardly any of my sisters were averse to listening to a book or reading it themselves, and not only saints' lives. Talking with their brothers, getting to know noble landowners, the ideas that were spreading about the vital importance of education, their own sons who returned from school and talked about what they had learned, and so on—all of that awakened their curiosity. My sister Mar'ia was even quite familiar with European geography and all of them knew biblical history quite well, a knowledge that my sister Aleksandra very ably passed on to her own children.

At the age of seven and sometimes even six, my sisters were put to work on women's tasks or handicrafts, especially spinning, and that is where I will begin. For the purposes of the household tasks of my sisters, and indeed almost all village women and girls, the year was divided into two parts: the "working season," when the field work and other agricultural activities took place, and the "nonworking season," when there was little or no such work to be done. When the nonworking season began, in September, or October, they would usually sit down on their *donets* by their distaff to spin.[1]. Initially, as it always is with children, my sisters themselves wanted to start spinning, especially once they grew tired of learning to read. At first they were taught little by little how to spin, but by age seven or eight each of them had become a pretty good spinner. It may be that they sometimes became tired of spending entire days sitting on the donets, but by then getting away was difficult. Each one usually received lessons and was held accountable if she was careless. But by age ten or eleven they were already becoming very competitive in their work—each wanted to spin as much and as well as possible, and they were prepared to sit up all night. When that occurred, Mother sometimes had to force them to go to bed to protect their health.

I have to admit that I also enjoyed being there when they were at work. At the time when I was finishing my seminary education, it would happen that my four sisters, Mother, the two bought girls, the old woman Praskov'ia, and sometimes even Grandmother before she lost her eyesight, would all be sitting at their distaffs. It was fun to watch the seven or eight spinners, spread across all the benches, pinching the flax on the distaffs with their left hand and drawing it out into a thread, while their right hand turned the spindle around which the finished spun thread was wound. They usually did not sit in silence, but instead talked, joked, and above all sang songs. The latter especially happened in the evenings. I already mentioned that my sisters had very good voices. Both bought girls, especially Tat'iana, sang masterfully, and even Mother, when she was younger, did not refuse to add her excellent voice to the general chorus. And so, it would happen that six or more of them would start singing soulful Russian songs, with harmony, dignity, and emotion, and you would listen spellbound. No wonder that almost all of us would gather by torchlight in the cabin in the evenings to listen to them—that is how I first discovered my love for Russian songs, which has not left me even in my old age. Sometimes they grew tired of songs, or they were not permitted to sing them, for example during fasts. Then someone would tell Russian tales, of which my mother knew many. Grandfather also sometimes told about life in the olden days. However, I was not always an idle spectator and listener. My sisters like it very much when I wound the thread they had spun into skeins; for the Christmas season, when I came home from the seminary, they would ready their cops, that is, the thread that had been wound around the spindle during spinning, and I rarely refused to wind the thread into a skein.

Spinning ended at the beginning of spring, around or after Easter, and they would prepare their looms to weave linen. From Easter until St. Peter's Day(2) and almost until September there was weaving in our house, on not just one, but even two or three looms.[…]

Even those persons of the female sex who were not sitting at the loom did not remain idle. Some unwound the skeins onto "drums" (cylinders made from tree bark), some wound the thread from these drums onto a thin rod, that is, wound them onto spools that were used for the filling in weaving linen fabric. But most were occupied with sewing linens (bel'e) and also with plaiting lace and making designs with all sorts of needlework. Another handicraft that was considered indispensable for unmarried girls was knitting stockings with five needles and with one [needle]. I, too, knew how to knit with five needles and sometime knitted mittens for my hands when I was at the church school.

Nor were my sisters excused from washing linens and even floors. In the annex, the floor was usually washed on Saturdays, though not every week, but in the kitchen it was done only before Easter, the Christmas holidays, the patronal festivals and any particularly festive occasion. Hunched over and barefoot, with rags and brooms in their hands, my sisters and the bought girls would wash the floors. As for the linens, almost the entire female part of the family was involved in washing them at home and especially by the little river. As long as she was in good health, even Mother would go with them the two versts from the village to the river Narma, past the hamlet of Kabanovo, where she would wash clothes by hand and pound them with a washboard(3) just like the others. Truth be told, none of us lived like lords.

The dress of the female half of our family was not poor, but neither was it very rich. [Grandmother would wear traditional village clothes, particularly the Kokoshnik (a tiaralike female headdress) and suknia (a colorful, sleeveless dress that was made of coarse sloth and buttoned in the front), but never cotton print dresses. Mother, on the other hand, apparently never wore the kokoshniki that were part of her trousseau, and in Palishchi and initially in Tuma she wore a suknia only for everyday use around the house but printed cotton dresses for special occasions. Later on, she abandoned these old-fashioned clothes completely and wore only cotton, woolen, and even silk dresses. On her head she never wore a cap or hat, but always a kerchief. The sisters dressed in the same way as their mother.]

I might as well also tell you what sort of dandy I was. I must say that I never was, nor did I even know how to be, a dandy. My parents were burdened with a huge family—they had to prepare trousseaus for five daughters and provide for the school and seminary education of four sons—so expecting them to dress us "like lords' would have been absurd.

[Except for special occasions, Rostislavov wore typical village garb—long, tuniclike shirts (rubakhi) and long johns, both made from homespun linen, as well as traditional peasant coats. He was already a seminary student when he received his first nankeen cotton pantaloons (more elegant, close-fitting trousers) and his first frock coat made from store-bought, factory-made cloth.]

(1) A donets is a wooden board, several feet in length and a few inches wide, that lies flat on the ground. One end curves upward and supports the distaff, a wooden staff whose cleft end holds the flax from which the thread is drawn.

(2) June 29.

(3) The wash was wrapped around a cylindrical roller (skalka) and then cleaned by pressing the roller against a flat, corrugated washboard (valeh).

SIGNIFICANCE

In the spring of 1917, with citizens rioting in the streets, the Romanovs abdicated the Russian throne, leaving a provisional government in charge of the financially struggling nation. In November the Communist Party, led by Vladimir Lenin, took control of St. Petersburg and arrested the members of the provisional government and the Czar's family. The quiet, relatively bloodless revolution produced the first communist government in the world, and led to a reevaluation of centuries-old customs in Russia.

The communists advocated land ownership by the people, as well as broad rights for the working class. Because the revolution to reach its full potential required equality for all individuals, the new government declared women and men constitutionally equal. Women were encouraged to work outside their homes and to pursue advanced education. Working women were also given government-funded maternity leave, a practice uncommon in the West until decades later. On paper, the new regime's gender policy was among the most progressive on earth.

As the Soviet Union expanded its territory and its influence, it appeared to offer women much broader rights than many other nations. During World War II, the United States eventually began recruiting women to fill defense plant jobs, while the Soviet workforce had been integrated for many years. And as the space age dawned, the Soviet space program scored two firsts, sending both the first man and the first woman into space. Not until two decades later, in 1983, did an American woman reach outer space.

Despite women's equal legal status in the Soviet empire, the passage of time revealed discrepancies between policy and practice. While the Soviets sent one woman into orbit early in their space program, the cosmonaut corps was overwhelmingly male, and only a handful of women number among the hundreds of space travelers from the Soviet Union. In the terrestrial workplace, women were encouraged to work but few were able to climb the ranks of management, while most held lower level posts. The leadership and upper ranks of the Communist Party remained almost entirely male in makeup, a situation largely identical to that in modern communist China. In 1987, Soviet leader Gorbachev wrote that women in the nation had the same rights, pay, and opportunities as men. Gorbachev's policy of openness would soon reveal that this claim was somewhat exaggerated.

While the Soviet Union's leaders clearly stated the case for women's equality in the workplace, their numerous declarations of women's rights in the early years of the U.S.S.R. apparently failed to undo centuries of tradition and cultural expectations. Ironically, women in the West ultimately made much greater economic gains under capitalism than those made under the far more rigid system of communism.

As of 2003, female workers in the United States earned approximately 77 cents for each dollar earned by men. The cause of this difference remains the subject of ongoing debate and research.

FURTHER RESOURCES

Books

Delafield, E. M. *The Provincial Lady in Russia: I Visit the Soviets.* Chicago: Academy Chicago Publishers, 1985.

Goldman, Wendy Z. *Women, the State and Revolution: Soviet Family Policy and Social Life, 1917–1936.* New York: Cambridge University Press, 1993.

Politics and Society in Provincial Russia: Saratov, 1590–1917, edited by Rex Wade and Scott Seregny. Columbus, Ohio: Ohio State University Press, 1989.

Periodicals

Evtuhov, Catherine. "Voices from the Provinces: Living and Writing in Nizhnii Novgorod, 1870–1905." *Journal of Popular Culture* 31 (1998):33–48.

White, Anne. "Social Change in Provincial Russia: The Intelligentsia in a Raion Centre." *Europe Asia Studies.* 44 (2002): 677–694.

Web sites

The Jamestown Foundation. "Russian National Unity: A Political Challenge for Provincial Russia." March 26, 1999. <http://www.jamestown.org/publications_details.php?volume_id=6&issue_id=350&article_id=3643> (accessed July 19, 2006).

Public Broadcasting Service. "A Romanov Album." <http://www.pbs.org/redfiles/rao/gallery/romanoff/hist.html> (accessed July 19, 2006).

Certificate of Indenture for Henry Barr

Legal document

By: Anonymous

Date: May 8, 1837

Source: *Jewish Women's Archive.* "Certificate of Indenture for Henry Barr." <http://www.jwa.org/teach/primarysources/artifacts_01.pdf //> (accessed July 22, 2006).

About the Author: Founded in 1995, the Jewish Women's Archive exists to locate and disseminate stories about Jewish women and their accomplishments.

INTRODUCTION

While formal schooling is required by law in most countries today, the need for education and training has existed since before recorded history. Although much of today's primary education curriculum focuses on academic subjects such as history and literature, the earliest forms of education focused on vocational skills, and in many cultures the most common manner in which to learn a skill was by working for several years with an expert in that field. Such an arrangement was known as an indenture.

Indentures were legally binding contracts. Though the form varied throughout the centuries and between cultures, an indenture commonly consisted of a contract specifying how long the learner would work for the master, what his compensation would be, and how he would behave during the term of the contract. The contract was normally written in multiple copies; small matching tears, or indentures, were made in the sides of the pages to signify that the copies were legally binding and making any forgery easier to detect.

In practice, indentured servanthood resembled a modern-day adoption. The student, often a young man in his early teens, generally agreed to live in the household of the master during his indenture. While training he received little or no pay and agreed to follow certain behavioral requirements; indentured servants were frequently forbidden to marry during their period of training. In exchange, the master craftsman was generally responsible for providing food, shelter, and clothing for the student during his years of training. The student also typically received some small compensation upon his graduation, in an amount specified by the original contract. Masters of indentured servants had many of the same legal rights as parents.

Upon completing his indenture, the student was not recognized as a master of the craft until he had been examined by other members of his craft guild. This process frequently took the form of a test piece, sometimes called a masterpiece, which the student would create and submit for evaluation. Following the acceptance of this work, the craftsman would be recognized as a master in his field. Many early Americans, including Benjamin Franklin, learned their crafts through the process of indentured servanthood.

PRIMARY SOURCE

This Indenture witnesseth, that Henry Barr—with the consent of the Manager of the Orphan Society, by their Binding Committee, Eliza, Otto Sullagard Leitman—hath put himself, and by these present, and for other good causes, doth voluntarily, and of his own free will and accord, put himself apprentice to Alexander Harper—to learn the art, trade and mystery of a Druggist and after the manner of an apprentice, to serve the said Alexander Harper from the day of the date hereof, for and during, and to the full end and term of nine years, three monthes and four days—next ensuing. During all which term, the said apprentice doth covenent and promise his said master faithfully to service, his secrets to keep, and his lawful commands every where readily to obey. He shall not waste his said master's goods, nor lend them unlawfully to any. He shall not contract matrimony within the said term. At cards, dice, or any other unlawful game he shall not play, whereby his said master may have damage. With his own goods nor the goods of others, without lisence from his said master, he shall neither buy nor sell. He shall not absent himself, day nor night, from his said master's service, without his leave; nor haunt ale-houses, taverns or play-houses; but in all things behave himself as a faithful apprentice ought to do, during the said terms. And the said master on his part doth covenant and prom-

ise to use the utmost endeavors to teach, or cause to be taught or instructed the said apprentice, in the trade or mystery of a Druggist and produce and provide for him sufficient meat, drink, clothing—lodging and washing, fitting for an apprentice, during the said term; and give him nine quarters half-day schooling; and when free, give him two complete suits of clothes, one of which to be new and shall, at the expiration of this child's time, come forward and satisfy the said Managers, that the terms of this Indenture have been complied with. And for the true performance of all and singular covenants and agreements aforesaid, the said parties bind themselves, each unto the other, firmly by these presents.

In witness whereof, the said parties have interchangeabley set their hands and seals hereunto. Dated the Eight day of May Anno Domini one thousand eight hundred and thirty seven.

Sealed, delivered and acknowledged before me,

R. Colustron
Alex Harper
Eliza Otto
Mary Loitman
Henry Barr

It is earnestly recommend to Masters and Mistresses, to give every opportunity to their Apprentices, to attend Public Worship and Sabbath School.

SIGNIFICANCE

The indenture system worked well in many cases but also created the opportunity for abuse. In the American colonies, poor parents sometimes indentured children younger than ten to a craftsman so that the child might learn a trade. Such practices relieved the family of the cost of the child's support and could potentially provide the child with the skills to earn a living, though in return the parents largely surrendered their role as parents. In other cases, impoverished Europeans seeking passage to North America signed indentures requiring them to work for many years on plantations. Such arrangements, which provided no skill training, were actually just a form of exploitation, providing little benefit to the servant. Such abuses gave the entire practice of indentured servanthood a checkered reputation, and eventually led to legal protections for workers.

As industrialization changed the nature of production, craftsmen no longer needed to be skilled in all aspects of a craft; consequently training a student no longer required many years of education. In many fields, experienced workers began training beginners in a period known as an apprenticeship. While some apprenticeship arrangements were virtually identical to indentured servanthood, most were far less encompassing, dealing with workplace training and little else. Whereas the indentured servant moved in with the master's family and was supported by him, the apprentice normally came to work and returned to his home each day, often earning a reduced wage during his period of training. During the 1800s, most skilled laborers learned their crafts by serving apprenticeships.

While some employers dealt fairly with apprentices, others exploited their lack of experience, forcing them to work long hours for little or no pay. In 1911, the state of Wisconsin passed the first laws regulating apprenticeships, placing them under the oversight of a state-appointed commission and requiring that all apprentices attend a minimum amount of school each week. Similar laws were soon passed in other states, and in 1934 the U.S. Secretary of Labor appointed a commission to set and enforce fair labor practices for employers with apprentices.

In 1937, Congress passed the Fitzgerald Act, creating the Bureau of Apprenticeship and Training within the Department of Labor. This board, which included representatives of labor, industry, and education, regulates apprenticeships in the United States; it currently oversees more than eight hundred licensed apprenticeship programs concentrated primarily in the construction, manufacturing, and service industries. Apprenticeships today are often funded and administered by labor unions in order to ensure that union members are fully trained and competent to carry out their trade.

FURTHER RESOURCES
Books
Alderman, Clifford. *Colonists for Sale: The Story of Indentured Servants in America.* New York: Macmillan, 1975.

Klepp, Susan, et al. *The Infortunate: The Voyage and Adventures of William Moraley, An Indentured Servant.* University Park, Penn.: Pennsylvania State University Press, 2005.

Salinger, Sharon V. *'To Serve Well and Faithfully': Labor and Indentured Servants in Pennsylvania, 1682–1800.* New York: Cambridge University Press, 1987.

Periodicals
"The Institution of Slavery in New York." *New York Amsterdam News* 96 (2005): 11.

Silverman, David J. "The Impact of Indentured Servitude on the Society and Culture of Southern New England Indians." *New England Quarterly* 74 (2001): 622–666.

Teicher, Stacy A. "Door-to-door Sales Crews or Indentured Servants?" *Christian Science Monitor.* 91 (1999): 89–90.

Web sites
National Joint Apprenticeship and Training Committee. "Apprenticeship Training." <http://www.njatc.org/apprentice.htm> (accessed July 22, 2006).

Robert E. Lee Memorial Association. "Indentured Servants and Transported Convicts." <http://www.stratfordhall.org/ed-servants.html> (accessed July 22, 2006).

U.S. Department of Labor. "Apprenticeship." <http://www.dol.gov/dol/topic/training/apprenticeship.htm> (accessed July 22, 2006).

The Influence of Women

Book excerpt

By: Sarah Stickney Ellis

Date: 1839

Source: Ellis, Sarah Stickney. "The Influence of Women." In *The Women of England: Their Social Duties and Domestic Habits.* London: Fisher, Son, & Co., 1839.

About the Author: Sarah Stickney Ellis was a wife and mother of the middle class in England. Ellis published more than thirty poems, histories, and other documents during her lifetime to contribute to her family's income.

INTRODUCTION

In the late 1820s and early 1830s, as industrialization increased in both England and the northern United States, new opportunities for middle-class families emerged. A "living wage" for middle managers and supervisors in some factory settings, as well as those men who worked as lawyers, physicians, government clerks, merchants, and teachers, allowed middle-class families to have a father who worked full time while the mother tended to the home and children. Such an arrangement had always been possible for the upper classes, with servants assisting the mother, and for rural women who wove childcare into the ebb and flow of the day's work on farms. This new sector of the middle class, however, gave rise to the modern notion of a "stay at home mother," or a woman whose sole responsibility was the management of the home and children.

In the United States, this trend emerged during President Andrew Jackson's administration; the "Era of the Common Man" had ushered in a new sense of common good, and the voting populace had tripled in just four years as property requirements dropped and new states were added to the nation. The middle-class woman who ruled the home, the so-called "Republican" motherhood ideal, was responsible for a wide range of personal and social tasks. In addition to managing housework and cooking, either on her own or with her servant or children's help, the ideal middle-class mother and wife, according to Catharine Beecher, the author of the 1842 book *A Treatise on Domestic Economy*, was a "woman, who is rearing a family of children; the woman, who labors in the schoolroom; the woman, who, in her retired chamber, earns, with her needle, the mite, which contributes to the intellectual and moral elevation of her Country; even the humble domestic, whose example and influence may be moulding and forming young minds, while her faithful services sustain a prosperous domestic state—each and all may be animated by the consciousness that they are agents in accomplishing the greatest work that ever was committed to human responsibility." By controlling the home and hearth, and training young male minds for work and politics, the ideal mother and wife filled her role in society in complement to that of the males in her life.

Writers on both sides of the Atlantic spoke of the merits of what came to be called the "cult of domesticity." By divorcing women from the workplace, or even the need to bring in an income to help support the family, this change in women's roles separated them from the world of work, politics, and society. Many women focused on children, church, and the house; by the late 1830s and early 1840s, magazines such as Godey's Lady's Book reinforced the primacy of women in the home. Sarah Stickney Ellis, a middle-class mother from England, wrote about the ideal of "true womanhood" in her book *The Women of England: Their Social Duties and Domestic Habits*. Ellis and other such writers argued that women did not need education beyond moral, religious, and domestic teachings; the ideal wife and mother would be a shepherd for her family, leading them down a moral path, keeping a clean and industrious home, and teaching her children proper moral and social lessons. This excerpt from her book discusses her view of the inherent differences between men and women, and the impact of these differences on gender roles.

■ PRIMARY SOURCE

It is not to be presumed that women possess more power than men; but happily for them, such are their

A Victorian woman sits reading with a young girl in this mid-nineteenth century photograph. © HULTON-DEUTSCH COLLECTION/CORBIS.

early impressions, associations, and general position in the world, that their moral feelings are less liable to be impaired by pecuniary objects which too often constitute the chief end of man, and which, even under the limitations of better principle, necessarily engage a large portion of his thoughts. There are many humble-minded women, not remarkable for any particular intellectual endowments, who yet possess so clear a sense of the right and wrong of individual actions, as to be of essential service in aiding the judgments of their husbands, brothers, or sons, in those intricate affairs in which it is sometimes difficult to dissever worldly wisdom from religious duty.

And surely they now need more than ever all the assistance which Providence has kindly provided, to win them away from this warfare, to remind them that they hare hastening on towards a world into which none of the treasures they are amassing can be admitted; and next to those holier influences which operate through the medium of revelation, or through the mysterious instrumentality of Divine love, I have little hesitation in saying, that the society of woman in her highest moral capacity, is best calculated to effect this purpose.

How often has man returned to his home with a mind confused by the many voices, which in the mart, the exchange, or the public assembly, have addressed themselves to his inborn selfishness, or his worldly pride; and while his integrity was shaken, and his resolution gave way beneath the pressure of apparent necessity, or the insidious pretences of expediency, he has stood corrected before the clear eye of woman, as it looked directly to the naked truth, and detected the lurking evil of the specious act he was about to commit. Nay, so potent may have become this secret influence, that he may have borne it about with him like a kind of second conscience, for mental reference, and spiritual counsel, in moments of trial; and when the snares of the world were around him, and temptations from within and without have bribed over the witness in his own bosom, he has thought of the humble monitress who sat alone, guarding the fireside comforts of his distant home; and the remembrance of her character, clothed in moral beauty, has scattered the clouds before his mental vision, and sent him back to that beloved home, a wiser and a better man.

SIGNIFICANCE

A "pure" woman exhibited four key traits: piety, purity, submissiveness, and domesticity. As Ellis notes, the world outside the home was viewed as a source of temptation. The emergence of the cult of domesticity coincided with the Moral Reform or Purity Movement, an effort to abolish prostitution and to encourage abstinence for all sexual relations aside from procreation. Syphilis and other sexually transmitted diseases were on the rise, brought home by straying husbands; the focus on purity was not an entirely selfless act on the part of the Republican mother. Through the Purity Movement women gained some political experience; the paradox that women were uniquely suited to campaign against vice using public lectures, protests, and publications helped to foster future political involvement in issues outside of moral questions.

A pure woman was, under this philosophy, to embody piety, purity, submissiveness, and domesticity to such a degree that when her husband faced vice directly, he would immediately think of "the humble monitress … clothed in moral beauty." This placed the burden of the husband's vice on the wife; if only she were pure enough, he would not seek out prostitutes or the company of drinkers or gamblers, according to articles and books preaching domesticity as an answer to venereal disease, alcoholism, and other social problems.

A vocal opposition to the cult of domesticity emerged in the mid–1840s and early 1850s. Women who had learned to organize politically during purity crusades used those skills to argue for greater rights for women in the United States and England. The 1848 Seneca Falls Convention for women's rights and the formation of the National Woman Suffrage Association by Lucretia Mott, Elizabeth Cady Stanton, and Susan B. Anthony set the stage for the next seventy-two years, as social norms changed regarding gender identity, women's intellectual abilities, and women's civil rights. On the cusp of the passage of the 19th Amendment, which granted women the right to vote in 1920, supporters of the more traditional ideal of pure womanhood argued against the amendment on the grounds that husbands represented wives' interests with their vote; politics would morally corrupt women.

In the late twentieth century echoes of the cult of domesticity could be found in the book *Fascinating Womanhood*, by Helen Andelin. The book focuses on the "submissive wife," who hands over all decisions to her husband. According to Andelin, "It is the woman's role to stay home to care for the needs of the household and among other things to nurture, train, teach and discipline the children. When the man is gone all day earning the living, in a very challenging world, he needs and deserves to have peace, rest, quiet and well-behaved children." Like the cult of domesticity in the middle of the nineteenth century, this concept of women acting as a moral compass, deferential to the husband, retains a role in some sectors of modern U.S. society.

FURTHER RESOURCES
Books

Andelin, Helen. *Fascinating Womanhood*. New York: Bantam, 1992.

Beecher, Catharine. *A Treatise on Domestic Economy*. Boston: T.H. Webb, 1842.

Dubois, Ellen Carol. *Feminism and Suffrage: The Emergence of an Independent Women's Movement in America, 1848–1869*. Ithaca, N.Y.: Cornell University Press, 1999.

Matthews, Glenna. *"Just a Housewife": The Rise and Fall of Domesticity in America*. New York: Oxford University Press USA, 1989.

Robertson, Una A. *The Illustrated History of the Housewife, 1650–1950*. London: Palgrave MacMillan, 1999.

Testimony of Ann and Elizabeth Eggley, Child Mine Workers

News article

By: Ann and Elizabeth Eggley

Date: c. 1842

Source: *The Longman Anthology of British Literature*, edited by David Damrosch. New York: Pearson/Longman, 2004.

About the Author: Ann and Elizabeth Eggley, ages eighteen and sixteen respectively, were child workers called to testify before Parliament as part of the investigations into the 1842 Factory Acts.

INTRODUCTION

Child labor has been an integral part of families in most societies, whether the child worked on farms, tended to younger siblings, managed household tasks, or worked in family businesses. As the industrial revolution changed the nature of labor and economics in Great Britain and the United States, however, the structure of children's work changed as well.

Children began to work as wage earners, earning one half to one fourth the wages of a grown man, and often even less. For lower-income families, families that lost farming rights or land, or those in search of jobs in general, the acceptance of child wage earners in settings such as factories and mines made the difference between starvation and subsistence living. In mining communities in Wales and in the Appalachian Mountain region in the United States, children as young as three worked in the mines as runners, gathered coal by

A group of Pennsylvania Coal Company mine workers, including many child laborers, pose for a photo in 1911. NATIONAL ARCHIVES AND RECORDS ADMINISTRATION.

hand, or dragged loads of coal through small shafts that required a child-sized body for passage. Mary Barrett, age fourteen, described her experience working as a "hurrier," one who pushed bundles or trams full of coal: "I hurry for my brother John, and come down at seven o'clock about; I go up at six, sometimes seven; I do not like working in pit, but I am obliged to get a living; I work always without stockings, or shoes, or trousers; I wear nothing but my chemise; I have to go up to the headings with the men; they are all naked there; I am got well used to that, and don't care now much about it; I was afraid at first, and did not like it; they never behave rudely to me; I cannot read or write."

Initial objections to child labor came from adult male workers, who claimed that the employment of children took away jobs from grown men who needed to support their families. Mining companies and textile mill owners claimed that the children did work that no one else could or would, and at wages that helped keep the entire company running and profitable. Other objections to the mine work included fears of vice; grown men often worked naked in the mines, to combat the heat, and young girls worked with chemises or very little clothing, side by side with the men. As J.C. Symons, a Sub-Commissioner investigating the mines, referred to such conditions as "the picture of a nursery for juvenile vice."

The third objection, that children so young were working fourteen hour days, six and seven days per week, and were sent into the mines at the age of four or five and dying by their mid–20s, came to the forefront of British society by the early 1840s. Demand for coal skyrocketed with industrialization; coal-powered factories, railroads, and steamships fed the need, and labor in the mines was backbreaking and deadly. New workers were constantly needed, but reformers began to argue that children were being abused not only by fellow workers but by an economic system that deprived them of their education, their health, and their childhoods.

In addition, the Victorian view of the child changed; childhood innocence and emotional and spiritual significance became a popular Victorian ideal. The contradiction between such an ideal for children of the upper and middle classes and the working conditions for poor children in the mines led to calls for reform.

The following testimonies by two teenage girls paints a dramatic picture of life in the mines.

■ PRIMARY SOURCE

Ann Eggley, eighteen years old.—I'm sure I don't know how to spell my name. We go at four in the morning, and sometimes at half-past four. We begin to work as soon as we get down. We get out after four, sometimes at five, in the evening. We work the whole time except an hour for dinner, and sometimes we haven't time to eat. I hurry by myself, and have done so for long. I know the corves are very heavy they are the biggest corves anywhere about. The work is far too hard for me; the sweat runs off me all over sometimes. I am very tired at night. Sometimes when we get home at night we have not power to wash us, and then we go to bed. Sometimes we fall asleep in the chair. Father said last night it was both a shame and disgrace for girls to work as we do, but there was nought else for us to do. I have tried to get winding to do, but could not. I begun to hurry when I was seven and I have been hurrying ever since. I have been 11 years in the pit. The girls are always tired. I was poorly twice this winter; it was with headache. I hurry for Robert Wiggins; he is not akin to me. I riddle for him. We all riddle for them except the littlest when there is two. We don't always get enough to eat and drink, but we get a good supper. I have known my father go at two in the morning to work when we worked at Twibell's, where there is a day-hole to the pit, and he didn't come out till four. I am quite sure that we work constantly 12 hours except on Saturdays. We wear trousers and our shifts in the pit, and great big shoes clinkered and nailed. The girls never work naked to the waist in our pit. The men don't insult us in the pit. The conduct of the girls in the pit is good enough sometimes and sometimes bad enough. I never went to a day-school. I went a little to a Sunday-school, but I soon gave it over. I thought it too bad to be confined both Sundays and weekdays. I walk about and get the fresh air on Sundays. I have not learnt to read. I don't know my letters. I have never learnt nought. I never go to church or chapel; there is no church or chapel at Gawber, there is none nearer than a mile. If I was married I would not go to the pits, but I know some married women that do. The men do not insult the girls with us, but I think they do in some. I have never heard that a good man came into the world who was God's Son to save sinners. I never heard of Christ at all. Nobody has ever told me about him, nor have my father and mother ever taught me to pray. I know no prayer; I never pray. I have been taught nothing about such things.

Elizabeth Eggley, sixteen years old.—I am sister to the last witness. I hurry in the same pit, and work for my father. I find my work very much too hard for me. I hurry alone. It tries me in my arms and back most. We go to work between four and five in the morning. If we are not there by half past five we are not allowed to go down at all. We come out at four, five, or six at night as it happens. We stop in generally 12 hours, and sometimes longer. We have to hurry only from the bank-face down to the horse-gate and back. I am sure it is very hard work and tires us very much; it is too hard for girls to do. We sometimes go to sleep before we get to bed. We haven't a very good house: we have but two rooms for all the family. I have never been to school except four times, and then I gave over because I could not get things to go in. I cannot read; I do not know my letters. I don't know who Jesus Christ was. I never heard of Adam either. I never heard about them at all. I have often been obliged to stop in bed all Sunday to rest myself. I never go to church or chapel.

SIGNIFICANCE

The testimony from Ann and Elizabeth Eggley, and from other children working in the mines, shocked Victorian sensibilities. In this testimony, the girls' ignorance regarding basic Christianity was startling for investigators; not only were children working in mines deprived of a basic elementary education, but many were also denied the time or freedom to attend Sunday school and receive rudimentary Christian education, a condition Victorian reformers used in their crusade to change child labor laws.

When possible, fathers and other male relatives attempted to have their daughters and sisters "hurry" for them, to supervise their children and relatives from unwanted sexual advances; while Ann and Elizabeth Eggley testify that there were no sexual harassment issues for them in the mines, many reports indicate that men working in mines sexually assaulted young girls and women. As Ann Eggley notes, her father stated that it was a "shame and a disgrace" that his girls worked such long hours and under such harsh conditions, but for large, poor families, the children's income was a requirement for survival.

Most married women did not work in the pits, instead staying at home to manage children and household, though Ann Eggley's testimony is telling. Some families were so poor as to require the mother's mine work for survival. From a social status standpoint, marriage for young girls such as Ann and Elizabeth could mean relief from heavy mine work; domestic management, even as the wife of a low-paid mine worker, was far preferable to the life of a teenage girl working eighty to ninety hours a week in the pits.

Though Parliament had attempted to limit child labor as early as 1809, and the 1842 Mining Act prohibits women and children from working in the mines, the first act that had any strength came in 1847, when the working day was limited to ten hours for men,

women, and children. Later legislation limited the ages for work, and compulsory education laws helped to provide basic education for all children. In the United States, where children and families experienced similar working and social conditions, the Keating-Owen Act of 1916 attempted to protect child workers, but it was not until the 1938 Fair Labor Standards Act was passed that children gained legal protections from child labor abuses.

FURTHER RESOURCES
Books

Dubofsky, Melvyn. *Hard Work: The Making of Labor History.* Champaign, IL: University of Illinois Press, 2000.

Hindman, Hugh D. *Child Labor: An American History.* Armonk, NY: M.E. Sharpe, 2002.

Zelizer, Viviana. *Pricing the Priceless Child: The Changing Social Value of Children.* Princeton, NJ: Princeton University Press, 1994.

Web sites

Human Rights Watch. "Child Labor." <http://www.hrw.org/children/labor.htm> (accessed July 21, 2006).

OurDocuments.gov. "Keating-Owen Child Labor Act of 1916." <http://www.ourdocuments.gov/> (accessed July 21, 2006).

Married Women's Property Act of 1848

Legislation

By: Senate and Assembly of the State of New York

Date: April 7, 1848

Source: *Library of Congress. American Memory Project.* "Married Women's Property Laws" 2006 <http://memory.loc.gov/ammem/awhhtml/awlaw3/property_law.html> (accessed June 19, 2006).

About the Author: Legislative power in the State of New York is vested in two elected houses, the Assembly and the Senate, subject to veto by the governor. The process by which laws are enacted in New York today is essentially unchanged from 1848.

INTRODUCTION

Prior to the enactment of various women's property laws in the United States in the mid-nineteenth

Emmeline Pankhurst (1858-1928) pauses in her reading for a portrait. Pankhurst wrote the first bill for Women's Suffrage in Great Britain in the late 1860s and the Married Women's Property Acts of 1870 and 1882. © BETTMANN/CORBIS.

century, most legislation with respect to a woman's dealings with both land and income were settled by a number of well established common law principles. The most important doctrine that operated with regard to women and property was the distinction between a woman as a chattel and a woman as an individual person with freestanding rights to property ownership and decision making.

In many cultures, the act of marriage either ended a woman's independent existence or transferred control of her life from her father to her husband; a dowry paid to a husband on marriage—a feature of marriage in many cultures—represents the subsuming of the woman's property rights into those of her husband.

In 1848, dower rights, broadly defined as the life estate to which every married woman was entitled if her husband died without leaving a will, were the only property rights to which a woman in the United States was entitled as a consequence of marriage. Where a

woman disputed the will or otherwise believed that it was not adequate provision for her needs, she could claim a one-third share of the value of all property in which the husband had an interest at his death. Dower created a life estate only; the woman cold not control these assets by sale or through a bequest of her own.

Women's limited property rights at the time of the 1848 New York enactment were consistent with the general legal status of women in North America and all other jurisdictions where English legal traditions were in place. Women were assumed to take a subordinate role in family matters, were not permitted to vote, and could not purchase or hold property.

The evolution of property law that permitted a married woman to hold property and deal with it independent of her husband was a lengthy process. The first American law that permitted a woman any control over land was an 1808 Connecticut law that allowed women to leave a will and effect transfers through her bequests. When the New York State legislation was enacted in 1848, the forerunner to the modern American feminism movement began to take shape in the northeastern United States. The leaders of this movement, including Susan B. Anthony (1820–1906), called for the general advancement of women's rights, including those in relation to property, voting, and employment.

PRIMARY SOURCE

AN ACT for the effectual protection of the property of married women.

Passed April 7, 1848.

The People of the State of New York, represented in Senate and Assembly do enact as follows:

Sec. 1. The real and personal property of any female who may hereafter marry, and which she shall own at the time of marriage, and the rents issues and profits thereof shall not be subject to the disposal of her husband, nor be liable for his debts, and shall continue her sole and separate property, as if she were a single female.

Sec. 2 The real and personal property, and the rents issues and profits thereof of any female now married shall not be subject to the disposal of her husband; but shall be her sole and separate property as if she were a single female except so far as the same may be liable for the debts of her husband heretofore contracted.

Sec. 3. It shall be lawful for any married female to receive, by gift, grant devise or bequest, from any person other than her husband and hold to her sole and separate use, as if she were a single female, real and personal property, and the rents, issues and profits thereof, and the same shall not be subject to the disposal of her husband, nor be liable for his debts.

Sec. 4. All contracts made between persons in contemplation of marriage shall remain in full force after such marriage takes place.

SIGNIFICANCE

The Married Women's Property Act of 1848 is one of the most important property law enactments in American history. It became the template for the laws passed in other states that allowed women to own and control property. Interestingly, while English law is the root of much American law, the British Parliament did not pass a similar statute until 1882.

Before the passage of the New York legislation and the subsequent enactments in other states, women could not sue or be sued with respect to property

because they were not legal entities. The right to own and control property created a collateral right to initiate or defend legal actions in relation to property.

The New York legislation carved out a place for married women in the otherwise restrictive common law rules that were tied to the notions of a marriage as a single legal unit between a man and a woman, and the limited protection provided to a woman through her dower rights. The first important aspect of the New York law was the express approval of the concept that a woman's land or personal property that she brought into a marriage remained her own. Such property was protected from seizure or any other action by any creditor of her husband. This provision alone represented an exception to the rule that marriage created a single economic unit.

Similar protection was extended to a woman who obtained property through a gift or bequest during marriage. Prior to the enactment of the New York law, if a woman's father left property to a married daughter, it fell into her husband's control. For this reason, many women's marriageability was assessed by how likely they were to inherit significant property from their fathers.

The 1848 New York legislation was truly seminal. All other matrimonial property laws passed in the state of New York, including those that have governed estate planning, marital separation, and rules concerning the calculation of the distribution of the property acquired by spouses during the course of marriage can be traced to this enactment.

The legislation's immediate influence, in addition to its use as a model by other states, is reflected in the Homestead Act of 1862, a federal statute that governed how land could be acquired in the western territories of the United States. Consistent with the notion that married women could hold property independently, the Homestead Act gave title to new land to the head of a household, with no limitations on gender.

In July 1848 the first Women's Rights convention was organized in Seneca Falls, New York—a state seen as an enlightened environment. Wishing to advance women's rights further still, a key platform in the convention's declaration noted that even where a woman owned land, she paid taxes to a government that did not allow her to vote.

While the right of women to hold property became entrenched in most jurisdictions by 1900, the laws were not consistent across the United States. In areas where the English legal tradition was second to that of Spain or Mexico, as in the Southwestern border states of California, Texas and New Mexico, women's property rights evolved in a somewhat different fashion. In these states a community of property regime was prescribed, meaning a woman's property was held communally with that of her husband; such property could only be managed by the wife in the event of her husband's death. Married women's property laws in these jurisdictions were not brought into line with those in other American states until the twentieth century.

FURTHER RESOURCES

Books

Dickenson, Donna. *Property, Women and Politics: Subjects or Objects*. New Brunswick, NJ: Rutgers University Press, 1997.

Hoff, Joan. *Law, Gender and Injustice: A Legal History of U.S. Women*. New York: New York University Press, 1991.

Periodicals

Chused, Richard H. "The Married Women's Property Law 1800–1850." *Georgetown Law Journal*. 71 (1983): 1359–1425.

Web sites

University of Virginia. "Mid-Century Women's Rights Movement: Selected Texts." 2004 <http://etext.lib.virginia.edu/railton/uncletom/womanmov.html> (accessed June 20, 2006).

The Book of Household Management

Book excerpt

By: Mrs. Isabella Beeton

Date: 1861

Source: Beeton, Isabella. *The Book of Household Management*. London: S.O. Beeton, 1861.

About the Author: Isabella Mary Mayson was born in London in 1836, and married Samuel O. Beeton, a publisher, in 1856. Soon after this, she began writing cooking articles for one of her husband's magazines, the *Englishwoman's Domestic Magazine*, taking over editorial responsibilities in the following years. In 1861 Isabella Beeton's monthly articles were collected and published in the *Book of Household Management*, which was a great success, selling over 60,000 copies in its first year, and about two million copies by 1868.

Isabella Beeton, however, died of puerperal [childbed] fever in 1865, about a week after the birth of her fourth child, and a little more than a month before her twenty-ninth birthday. Her book was reprinted and adapted numerous times over the next century and a half, until Mrs. Beeton and her book had become synonymous with old-fashioned British cooking and the well-managed Victorian household.

INTRODUCTION

Mrs. Beeton's Book of Household Management was the most widely owned household book in nineteenth-century England. According to Nicola Humble, editor of an Oxford World's Classics 2000 reprint, *Household Management* was "massive in its scope as well as its influence" and "the most famous English cookery book ever published." Humble also noted, however, that it "must rank as one of the great unread classics.... Everyone has heard of it, a number of people own a copy ... but it is rarely considered as anything other than a culinary curiosity."

With over 1,100 pages, including 900 pages of recipes, *Household Management* also contains such Victorian miscellany as a recipe for the common black draught (a laxative), advice on how much to pay the butler, how to bathe and feed a baby, and the history of the onion. Mrs. Beeton was only 22 when she wrote most of its sections and 25 when her compendium was published. Her biographers note that although many of the recipes were copied from other works, such as Eliza Acton's 1845 *Modern Cookery for Private Families*, Beeton never took personal credit for this part of her book. She is said to have carefully tested each recipe before changing its format and arrangement, and often wrote supplementary essays on particular foods.

▮ PRIMARY SOURCE

THE BOOK OF HOUSEHOLD MANAGEMENT

Comprising Information for the Mistress, Housekeeper, Cook, Kitchen-Maid, Butler, Footman, Coachman, Valet, Upper and Under House-Maids, Lady's-Maid, Maid-of-all-Work, Laundry-Maid, Nurse and Nurse-Maid, Monthly Wet and Sick Nurses, etc. etc.—also Sanitary, Medical, & Legal Memoranda: With a History of the Origin, Properties, and Uses of All Things Connected with Home Life and Comfort

PREFACE.

I must frankly own, that if I had known, beforehand, that this book would have cost me the labour which it has, I should never have been courageous enough to commence it. What moved me, in the first instance, to

"Hanging the Washing, a Beautiful Spring Morning," by Helen Allingham, 1899. © FINE ART PHOTOGRAPHIC LIBRARY/CORBIS.

attempt a work like this, was the discomfort and suffering which I had seen brought upon men and women by household management. I have always thought that there is no more fruitful source of family discontent than a housewife's badly-cooked dinners and untidy ways. Men are now so well served out of doors,—at their clubs, well-ordered taverns, and dining-houses, that in order to compete with the attractions of these places, a mistress must be thoroughly acquainted with the theory and practice of cookery, as well as be perfectly conversant with all the other arts of making and keeping a comfortable home....

CHAPTER I.

THE MISTRESS.

"Strength, and honour are her clothing; and she shall rejoice in time to come. She openeth her mouth with wisdom; and in her tongue is the law of kindness. She looketh well to the ways of her household; and eateth not the bread of idleness. Her children arise up, and call her blessed; her husband also, and he praiseth her."—Proverbs, xxxi. 25–28.

1. AS WITH THE COMMANDER OF AN ARMY, or the leader of any enterprise, so it is with the mistress of a house. Her spirit will be seen through the whole establishment; and just in proportion as she performs her duties intelligently and thoroughly, so will her domestics follow in her path. Of all those acquirements, which more particularly belong to the feminine character, there are none which take a higher rank, in our estimation, than such as enter into a knowledge of household duties; for on these are perpetually dependent the happiness, comfort, and well-being of a family....

3. EARLY RISING IS ONE OF THE MOST ESSENTIAL QUALITIES which enter into good Household Management, as it is not only the parent of health, but of innumerable other advantages. Indeed, when a mistress is an early riser, it is almost certain that her house will be orderly and well-managed. On the contrary, if she remain in bed till a late hour, then the domestics, who, as we have before observed, invariably partake somewhat of their mistress's character, will surely become sluggards....

7. FRIENDSHIPS SHOULD NOT BE HASTILY FORMED, nor the heart given, at once, to every new-comer. There are ladies who uniformly smile at, and approve everything and everybody, and who possess neither the courage to reprehend vice, nor the generous warmth to defend virtue. The friendship of such persons is without attachment, and their love without affection or even preference....

8. HOSPITALITY IS A MOST EXCELLENT VIRTUE; but care must be taken that the love of company, for its own sake, does not become a prevailing passion; for then the habit is no longer hospitality, but dissipation.... With respect to the continuance of friendships it may be found necessary, in some cases, for a mistress to relinquish, on assuming the responsibility of a household, many of those commenced in the earlier parts of her life....

9. IN CONVERSATION, TRIFLING OCCURRENCES, such as small disappointments, petty annoyances, and other every-day incidents, should never be mentioned to your friends. The extreme injudiciousness of repeating these will be at once apparent, when we reflect on the unsatisfactory discussions which they to frequently occasion, and on the load of advice which they are the cause of being tendered, and which his, too often, of a kind neither to be useful nor agreeable.... If the mistress be a wife, never let an account of her husband's failings pass her lips....

24. AFTER BREAKFAST IS OVER, it will be well for the mistress to make a round of the kitchen and other offices, to see that all are in order, and that the morning's work has been properly performed by the various domestics. The orders for the day should then be given, and any questions which the domestics desire to ask, respecting their several departments, should be answered, and any special articles they may require, handed to them from the store-closet....

25. AFTER THIS GENERAL SUPERINTENDENCE of her servants, the mistress, if a mother of a young family, may devote herself to the instruction of some of its younger members, or to the examination of the state of their wardrobe, leaving the later portion of the morning for reading, or for some amusing recreation....

27. AFTER LUNCHEON, MORNING CALLS AND VISITS may be made and received. These may be divided under three heads: those of ceremony, friendship, and congratulation or condolence. Visits of ceremony, or courtesy, which occasionally merge into those of friendship, are to be paid under various circumstances. Thus, they are uniformly required after dining at a friend's house, or after a ball, picnic, or any other party. These visits should be short, a stay of from fifteen to twenty minutes being quite sufficient. A lady paying a visit may remove her boa or neckerchief; but neither her shawl nor bonnet....

When other visitors are announced, it is well to retire as soon as possible, taking care to let it appear that their arrival is not the cause. When they are quietly seated, and the bustle of their entrance is over, rise from your chair, taking a kind leave of the hostess, and bowing politely to the guests. Should you call at an inconvenient time, not having ascertained the luncheon hour, or from any other inadvertence, retire as soon as possible, without, however, showing that you feel yourself an intruder. It is not difficult for any well-bred or even good-tempered person, to know what to say on such an occasion, and, on politely withdrawing, a promise can be made to call again, if the lady you have called on, appear really disappointed.

28. IN PAYING VISITS OF FRIENDSHIP, it will not be so necessary to be guided by etiquette as in paying visits of ceremony; and if a lady be pressed by her friend to remove her shawl and bonnet, it can be done if it will not interfere with her subsequent arrangements.... During these visits, the manners should be easy and cheerful, and the subjects of conversation such as may be readily terminated. Serious discussions or arguments are to be altogether avoided....

SIGNIFICANCE

Isabella Beeton's all-encompassing work became queen of the British advice books for women (also known as prescriptive literature) soon after its publication in 1861. This type of literature flourished in the second half of the nineteenth century, as the new more mobile and ambitious middle class—with more literate women—emerged. Many reprints, revisions, and related works, such as *Mrs. Beeton's Book of Baking, Beeton's Book of Needlework*, etc., continued to guide aspiring or uncertain housewives throughout the twentieth century. New editions of Beeton are still popular, for both their nostalgic and historic value, and as an introduction to basic cooking. Although recipes constitute the bulk of *Household Management*, it is the other advice—on everything that a woman needs to know and do to create the perfect Victorian home—that makes Beeton's book so interesting to historians and so quaint for modern readers.

Beeton's work is often used to demonstrate the ideology of separate spheres in England. In this construct, women were thought to work and wield influence mainly in the domestic sphere, or the home, while men inhabited the larger public sphere, which included business and politics. According to Lynn Abrams on the BBC website, Mrs. Beeton was "the very embodiment of the Victorian ideology of a woman's place being in the home," and her work demonstrates the complexity, the rituals, and the limits of the domestic sphere. *Household Management* is also a quintessential piece of nineteenth-century classification and promotion, with its assiduously organized particulars of the ideal middle-class wife's (and mother's) temperament, activities, and etiquette. Mrs. Beeton makes it clear that the mistress of the house bears the awesome responsibility of improving the world by improving the lives of those in her household—and that her encyclopedic book holds the keys to this crucial undertaking.

It should be noted that the circumspect, hardworking, and knowledgeable wife and mother, and the elaborate yet comfortable household portrayed in Beeton's book represent ideals that were difficult if not impossible for most Victorian women to attain. Like the other Victorian stereotypes, Mrs. Beeton and her book idealize a past that was undoubtedly messier and more complicated than the well-ordered life that Mrs. Beeton promised.

FURTHER RESOURCES

Books

Gordon, Eleanor, and Gwyneth Nair. *Public Lives: Women, Family and Society in Victorian Britain*. New Haven, CT: Yale University Press, 2003.

Hughes, Kathryn. *The Short Life and Long Times of Mrs. Beeton*. New York: Alfred A. Knopf, 2006.

Periodicals

Kerber, Linda K. "Separate Spheres, Female Worlds, Woman's Place: The Rhetoric of Women's History." *Journal of American History*. 75 (1988):9–39.

Web sites

Abrams, Lynn. *British Broadcasting Corporation*. "Ideals of Womanhood in Victorian Britain." January 1, 2001 <http://www.bbc.co.uk/history/society_culture/welfare/idealwomen_01.shtml> (accessed June 11, 2006).

Oxford World's Classics: The Magazine. "A Place for Everything and Everything in Its Place, by Nicola Humble." 2000 <http://www.oup.co.uk/worldsclassics/magarchive/mag1/article01/> (accessed June 19, 2006).

A Young Lady, of Good Family and Education, Desires an Engagement as Governess

Advertisement

By: Anonymous

Date: May 15, 1866

Source: Anonymous. "A Young Lady, of Good Family and Education, Desires an Engagement as Governess." *Times* (London) (May 15, 1866).

About the Author: These "positions desired" and "positions offered" advertisements were placed in the *Times*, England's main newspaper, which has been published daily since 1785.

INTRODUCTION

The role of the governess in English society, and particularly during the Victorian Era, was that of a substitute mother and tutor. While children of the wealthy had nannies or nurses who attended to the child's bathing, health, and general physical and emotional well-being, the governess taught young boys academic subjects to prepare them to enter school, and tutored young women through their teenage years in some academic subjects as well. For both boys and girls the governess also served as a female role model of comportment, morality, and social behavior; while she did not replace their mother, in wealthy families the governess guided the children in social graces, manners, and the art of being a proper member of upper-class Victorian society.

While some governesses lived with the family that employed her, others came to the house each day. Those who "lived in" were treated better than the nanny or nurse and other servants in the home, but was still a quasi-servant. Nannies, nurses, kitchen staff, and domestic servants referred to the children as "Miss" and "Master," the governess called them by their first names. In turn, governesses themselves were referred to as "Miss." In the Charlotte Brontë classic *Jane Eyre*, for example, the main character, a governess, is referred to as "Miss Eyre"; nannies were simply called "Nanny." The governess' ambiguous social status within the family—neither household servant, guest, social peer, nor family member—created strife in some households.

The governess and the lady of the house could develop strained relationships. The only acceptable

The Governess, by Richard Redgrave. © STAPLETON COLLECTION/CORBIS.

women for governess positions were those of the middle- and upper-middle classes who were well educated but, for various reasons, found themselves in need of an income. Therefore, in terms of social experience and upbringing, governesses had once been equal or nearly equal to the mothers who employed them, and yet were now beneath them. Typical governesses were poor widows or orphaned daughters left with no option but to find employment as a governess.

The following advertisements, from the London *Times* in 1866, provide insight into the types of governess positions women sought and those offered. The emphasis on languages and music in these advertisements reflects social and educational expectations for women in this era.

■ PRIMARY SOURCE

A young lady, of good family and education, desires an engagement as governess in a gentleman's family. Acquirements—English, French, good drawing. Address Beta, Gumbleton's post-office, Chapham road.

A foreign protestant governess required, for a family of position, for young children. English, French, and music. 40 upwards. Apply, personally, Lad Superintendent, Governess Institute, Hanover-street, Hanover-square.

A young lady, with seven years' experience, wishes a re-engagement as governess to young children. She teaches thorough English and good music. Address B.B., No. 115, Sloane-street, Chelsea.

A lady desires to recommend her German protestant governess to teach her own language in a family or school.

Salary 25. Good needlewoman. Can teach music to beginners.—B.B. Hughes' library, Park-street, Regent's-park.

A nursery governess wanted, to take charge of four little girls, and assist with their wardrobe. Music the only accomplishment required. Address, stating full particulars, to B. T., Newport, Mon.

A young German protestant lady is desirous of an engagement as governess. She teaches, besides her own language, music and the rudiments of French. A gentleman's family preferred. Terms moderate. Address to B. B., 13, Trinity-street, Cambridge.

An experienced governess desires a Re-engagement, in a gentleman's family. Qualifications are English, French and music. Also an earnest and conscientious desire to be faithful and kind to the charge committed to her. Address A. D., care of Mrs. Braumpton, 26, Newland-street, Kensington.

A young lady desires a re-engagement as governess in a family or school. She is thoroughly competent to instruct in English, French, and good music, having held a situation as musical. Highest references. Address B.D., post-office, Camberwell, new-road.

A young lady, just returned from the continent, wishes an engagement as a resident governess. She feels quite competent to impart an English education, with good French and music. Address A. B., Robert's library, Arabella-row, Pinkco.

SIGNIFICANCE

A typical governess received a small room in the family's home, her meals, and a small stipend, enough to keep her in decent clothes and shoes but not enough to support herself outside the family. Governesses who lived in the family home ate with the children unless invited by the parents to join them or to attend dinner parties; such events could be either pleasant and a refreshing experience, a reminder of her past status in society, or could be awkward and difficult.

In the 1860s more than 20,000 governesses were employed, but far more women sought such positions than could be hired. Governesses were a tradition in France and Germany as well; in the late 1800s Marie Curie, the future Nobel prize winner, worked as a governess, using her wages to support her sister through medical school, who in turn supported Curie as she studied at the Sorbonne. For families of the middle and upper classes who fell on hard times, the governess position was crucial; it enabled women to live in a manner to which they were accustomed, and to use their education to earn a respectable wage to help themselves or their families.

The role of governess exists in modern society; recruiting agencies train and screen candidates for positions as in-home teachers. Some agencies emphasize the English skills of British governesses; families wishing to teach their children English often employee them as language teachers while providing childcare and tutoring in other subjects. Other governesses are full-time teachers for students who home-school.

Twenty-first century governesses are often university students or graduates who view such work as a well paid stepping-stone to a teaching career. Unlike their 1866 counterparts, they have a wide array of employment options and come to governess work by choice rather than by circumstance, and the relationship to their students is defined by employment, not social class.

FURTHER RESOURCES
Books

Beecher, Catharine. *A Treatise on Domestic Economy*. Boston: T.H. Webb, 1842.

Broughton, Trev, and Ruth Symes, eds. *The Governess: An Anthology*. Palgrave Macmillan, 1998.

Ellis, Sarah Stickney. *The Women of England: Their Social Duties and Domestic Habits*. London: Fisher, Son, & Co., 1839.

Hughes, Kathryn. *The Victorian Governess*. London: Rio Grande, 2002.

Zelizer, Viviana. *Pricing the Priceless Child: The Changing Social Value of Children*. Princeton, NJ: Princeton University Press, 1994.

Reynolds v. United States

Utah Polygamy Prosecution, 1888

Judicial decision

By: Morrison R. Waite

Date: October 1878

Source: Morrison R. Waite. *"Reynolds v. United States."* *United States Reports*. 95 (1878): 145.

About the Author: Morrison R. Waite (1816–1888) served as the Chief Justice of the Supreme Court of the United States from 1874 until his death in 1888. The Supreme Court is the nation's highest appellate court, composed of eight associate justices and a chief justice.

Polygamist Alex Joseph stands with his numerous wives and children, May 1979. © CORBIS.

INTRODUCTION

George Reynolds, a member of the early Church of Jesus Christ of Latter Day Saints, known as the Mormons, was prosecuted for bigamy in the Utah Territory in 1877. The federal authorities and the Mormon church had been at odds over the practice of polygamy since the sect's founding in 1830 by Joseph Smith, Jr. In 1844, Joseph Smith, Jr. himself was arrested and jailed for inciting a riot in Illinois after attempting to destroy a newspaper that exposed the Mormon practice of polygamy. He was murdered shortly afterward by a mob who broke into his jail cell. In 1846, after Smith's murder and fearful of more violence against Smith's followers, the Mormon leadership determined that its adherents would relocate to the then-remote Utah territory. The church established its headquarters in Salt Lake City, where Mormon leader Brigham Young was shortly thereafter established as the territorial governor.

The Mormons made a number of efforts to declare themselves free of English common law, the basis of the American legal system. Young believed that only statutes passed by an elected assembly could be binding upon its citizens. Polygamy had once been a capital offense in England, where common law had grown from Christian roots where marriage was an institution between one man and one woman.

Many Mormons who settled in the Utah territory after 1847 believed that polygamy was not merely permitted, but ordained by God, citing passages in the Old Testament to buttress their position. In 1857, after tensions with federal authorities over Young's insistence that common law was not applicable in Utah became sufficiently heated, troops were dispatched to Salt Lake City, starting the "Utah War." Despite this, a segment of the territorial population who practiced polygamy remained, with the tacit encouragement of the Mormon church.

George Reynolds was prosecuted on the basis of a federal law that rendered polygamy illegal; the first such statute was passed by Congress in 1862. While a number of procedural issues were raised by Reynolds in his appeal, most notably the manner in which jury selection occurred as well as the admissibility of prior sworn testimony in his trial, the heart of Reynolds's defense was his assertion that he was bound by a religious duty to practice polygamy.

PRIMARY SOURCE

U.S. Supreme Court

REYNOLDS v. U.S., 98 U.S. 145 (1878)

98 U.S. 145

REYNOLDS v. UNITED STATES.

October Term, 1878

This is an indictment found in the District Court for the third judicial district of the Territory of Utah, charging George Reynolds with bigamy, in violation of sect. 5352 of the Revised Statutes, which, omitting its exceptions, is as follows:—"Every person having a husband or wife living, who marries another, whether married or single, in a Territory, or other place over which the United States have exclusive jurisdiction, is guilty of bigamy, and shall be punished by a fine of not more than $500, and by imprisonment for a term of not more than five years." ...

MR. CHIEF JUSTICE WAITE delivered the opinion of the court. ...

As to the defence of religious belief or duty.

On the trial, the plaintiff in error, the accused, proved that at the time of his alleged second marriage he was, and for many years before had been, a member of the Church of Jesus Christ of Latter-Day Saints, commonly called the Mormon Church, and a believer in its doctrines; that it was an accepted doctrine of that church "that it was the duty of male members of said church, circumstances permitting, to practise polygamy; ... that this duty was enjoined by different books which the members of said church believed to be of divine origin, and among others the Holy Bible, and also that the members of the church believed that the practice of polygamy was directly enjoined upon the male members thereof by the Almighty God, in a revelation to Joseph Smith, the founder and prophet of said church; that the failing or refusing to practise polygamy by such male members of said church, when circumstances would admit, would be punished, and that the penalty for such failure and refusal would be damnation in the life to come." He also proved "that he had received permission from the recognized authorities in said church to enter into polygamous marriage;...that Daniel H. Wells, one having authority in said church to perform the marriage ceremony, married the said defendant on or about the time the crime is alleged to have been committed, to some woman by the name of Schofield,

and that such marriage ceremony was performed under and pursuant to the doctrines of said church."

Upon this proof he asked the court to instruct the jury that if they found from the evidence that he "was married as charged-if he was married-in pursuance of and in conformity with what he believed at the time to be a religious duty, that the verdict must be 'not guilty.'" This request was refused, and the court did charge "that there must have been a criminal intent, but that if the defendant, under the influence of a religious belief that it was right,—under an inspiration, if you please, that it was right,—deliberately married a second time, having a first wife living, the want of consciousness of evil intent—the want of understanding on his part that he was committing a crime—did not excuse him; but the law inexorably in such case implies the criminal intent."

Upon this charge and refusal to charge the question is raised, whether religious belief can be accepted as a justification of an overt act made criminal by the law of the land. The inquiry is not as to the power of Congress to prescribe criminal laws for the Territories, but as to the guilt of one who knowingly violates a law which has been properly enacted, if he entertains a religious belief that the law is wrong.

Congress cannot pass a law for the government of the Territories which shall prohibit the free exercise of religion. The first amendment to the Constitution expressly forbids such legislation. Religious freedom is guaranteed everywhere throughout the United States, so far as congressional interference is concerned. The question to be determined is, whether the law now under consideration comes within this prohibition. The word "religion" is not defined in the Constitution. We must go elsewhere, therefore, to ascertain its meaning, and nowhere more appropriately, we think, than to the history of the times in the midst of which the provision was adopted....

Five of the States, while adopting the Constitution, proposed amendments. Three—New Hampshire, New York, and Virginia—included in one form or another a declaration of religious freedom in the changes they desired to have made, as did also North Carolina, where the convention at first declined to ratify the Constitution until the proposed amendments were acted upon. Accordingly, at the first session of the first Congress the amendment now under consideration was proposed with others by Mr. Madison. It met the views of the advocates of religious freedom, and was adopted. Mr. Jefferson afterwards, in reply to an address to him by a committee of the Danbury Baptist Association (8 id. 113), took occasion to say: "Believing with you that religion is a matter which lies solely between man and his God; that he owes account to none other for his faith or his worship; that the legislative powers of the government reach actions only, and not opinions,—I contemplate with sovereign reverence that act of the whole American people which declared that their legislature should 'make no law respecting an establishment of religion or prohibiting the free exercise thereof,' thus building a wall of separation between church and State. Adhering to this expression of the supreme will of the nation in behalf of the rights of conscience, I shall see with sincere satisfaction the progress of those sentiments which tend to restore man to all his natural rights, convinced he has no natural right in opposition to his social duties." Coming as this does from an acknowledged leader of the advocates of the measure, it may be accepted almost as an authoritative declaration of the scope and effect of the amendment thus secured. Congress was deprived of all legislative power over mere opinion, but was left free to reach actions which were in violation of social duties or subversive of good order.

Polygamy has always been odious among the northern and western nations of Europe, and, until the establishment of the Mormon Church, was almost exclusively a feature of the life of Asiatic and of African people. At common law, the second marriage was always void (2 Kent, Com. 79), and from the earliest history of England polygamy has been treated as an offence against society....

In connection with the case we are now considering, it is a significant fact that on the 8th of December, 1788, after the passage of the act establishing religious freedom, and after the convention of Virginia had recommended as an amendment to the Constitution of the United States the declaration in a bill of rights that "all men have an equal, natural, and unalienable right to the free exercise of religion, according to the dictates of conscience," the legislature of that State substantially enacted the statute of James I., death penalty included, because, as recited in the preamble, "it hath been doubted whether bigamy or poligamy be punishable by the laws of this Commonwealth." ... From that day to this we think it may safely be said there never has been a time in any State of the Union when polygamy has not been an offence against society, cognizable by the civil courts and punishable with more or less severity. In the face of all this evidence, it is impossible to believe that the constitutional guaranty of religious freedom was intended to prohibit legislation in respect to this most important feature of social life. Marriage, while from its very nature a sacred obligation, is nevertheless, in most civilized nations, a civil contract, and usually regulated by law. Upon it society may be said to be built, and out of its fruits spring social relations and social obligations and duties, with which government is necessarily required to deal. In fact, according as monogamous or polygamous marriages are allowed, do we find the principles on which

the government of the people, to a greater or less extent, rests.... An exceptional colony of polygamists under an exceptional leadership may sometimes exist for a time without appearing to disturb the social condition of the people who surround it; but there cannot be a doubt that, unless restricted by some form of constitution, it is within the legitimate scope of the power of every civil government to determine whether polygamy or monogamy shall be the law of social life under its dominion.

In our opinion, the statute immediately under consideration is within the legislative power of Congress. It is constitutional and valid as prescribing a rule of action for all those residing in the Territories, and in places over which the United States have exclusive control. This being so, the only question which remains is, whether those who make polygamy a part of their religion are excepted from the operation of the statute. If they are, then those who do not make polygamy a part of their religious belief may be found guilty and punished, while those who do, must be acquitted and go free. This would be introducing a new element into criminal law. Laws are made for the government of actions, and while they cannot interfere with mere religious belief and opinions, they may with practices. Suppose one believed that human sacrifices were a necessary part of religious worship, would it be seriously contended that the civil government under which he lived could not interfere to prevent a sacrifice? Or if a wife religiously believed it was her duty to burn herself upon the funeral pile [sic] of her dead husband, would it be beyond the power of the civil government to prevent her carrying her belief into practice?

So here, as a law of the organization of society under the exclusive dominion of the United States, it is provided that plural marriages shall not be allowed. Can a man excuse his practices to the contrary because of his religious belief? To permit this would be to make the professed doctrines of religious belief superior to the law of the land, and in effect to permit every citizen to become a law unto himself. Government could exist only in name under such circumstances.

A criminal intent is generally an element of crime, but every man is presumed to intend the necessary and legitimate consequences of what he knowingly does. Here the accused knew he had been once married, and that his first wife was living. He also knew that his second marriage was forbidden by law. When, therefore, he married the second time, he is presumed to have intended to break the law. And the breaking of the law is the crime. Every act necessary to constitute the crime was knowingly done, and the crime was therefore knowingly committed. Ignorance of a fact may sometimes be taken as evidence of a want of criminal intent, but not ignorance of the law. The only defence of the accused in this case is his belief that the law ought not to have been enacted. It matters not that his belief was a part of his professed religion: it was still belief, and belief only....

SIGNIFICANCE

In this opinion, Chief Justice Waite endeavored to address the issue of whether a person may deliberately violate the law on the strength of a religious belief. He was careful to specify the history of the Mormon tenets concerning polygamy, and included the additional visions attributed to its founder Joseph Smith in 1830.

The central constitutional question was the protection claimed by the First Amendment right to freedom of religion. Chief Justice Waite was careful not to suggest, either directly or indirectly, that the Mormon faith was bizarre or un-Christian, as many then viewed it, nor were Reynolds' First Amendment rights influenced by Mormonism's position outside the American mainstream. It is clear, however, that no religious practice or belief, accepted or fringe, could be protected if its practices violated the law of the land. Waite also emphasized the longstanding legal principle that everyone is presumed to intend the natural consequences of their own actions, such as deliberately entering into a second marriage while bound by a first.

The principles enunciated in *Reynolds* have been applied in modern times, including prosecutions for the consumption of peyote (an illegal hallucinogen), that is part of Hopi Indian religious ceremonies, as well as proceedings involving Rastafarians, a Jamaica-based religious sect who regard marijuana as a sacrament of their faith.

A series of federal polygamy convictions followed the *Reynolds* decision, and the issue became an impediment to Utah's desire for statehood. As a result, in 1890 Mormon leadership under Wilson Woodruff issued an official decree that polygamy was no longer a part of Mormon practice, as it was contrary to the laws of the land. Utah was admitted to the Union in 1896, but there is considerable evidence, that Woodruff himself entered into a polygamous marriage in 1897, as did Mormon leader Joseph F. Smith, who was convicted and fined for polygamy in 1906.

Despite the official edict against polygamy, a number of Mormons did not accept the ruling. These adherents, who became known as Mormon 'fundamentalists,' continued to practice polygamy. Many decided to leave Utah even before Woodruff's dictum; as early as 1885 fundamentalists had migrated to Mexico and Canada. Another group of fundamentalists established a colony in Short Creek, Arizona, in 1928. In 1953, law enforcement officials raided the settlement and arrested thirty-one men for polygamy, taking into custody over 200 women and children who formed extended polygamous families. Fundamentalists also settled in Bountiful, a town in British Columbia, Canada, in 1947. Although the group's polygamist practices were known to Canadian police, they were not prosecuted. Canadian authorities believed that the protections provided in the Canadian Charter of Rights and Freedoms would afford a defense to any charge of polygamy.

The fundamentalist Mormons in Bountiful are, in a sense, philosophical descendants of George Reynolds and the original Mormon settlers who went to Utah in 1847. Canada's federal Justice Department commissioned a study in 2005, which argued for the legalization of polygamy. The study stated, among other points, that there was little difference between the criminalization of polygamy and the criminalization of adultery. Conservative Christians argued that if polygamists were granted de facto immunity from prosecution on the basis of their religious beliefs, same-sex marriages, a contentious issue in both Canada and the United States, could not be prohibited.

The Bountiful polygamy allegations stirred renewed interest about similar groups in both Utah and Arizona. In 1998, the Mormon church reiterated its long-standing opposition to polygamy, indicating that any Mormon engaged in the practice would be excommunicated. In 2003, Utah passed a specific child bigamy law, providing lengthy jail terms for anyone who took a child under age eighteen as a second wife.

In 2006, Warren Jeffs, the leader of a Utah-based fundamentalist polygamist sect, the Fundamentalist Latter Day Saints (FLDS), was placed on the Federal Bureau of Investigation's (FBI's) Ten Most Wanted List, which lists among his crimes sexual assault on a minor and conspiracy to commit sexual misconduct with a minor. The federal government is offering $100,000 for information that leads to his arrest.

FURTHER RESOURCES
Books

Gordon, Sarah Barringer. *The Mormon Question: Polygamy and Constitutional Conflict in Nineteenth Century America.* Chapel Hill, NC: University of North Carolina Press, 2001.

Van Wagoner, Richard S. *Mormon Polygamy: A History.* Salt Lake City: Signature Books, 2004.

Web sites

University of Utah. "Polygamy." 2006 <http://www.media. utah.edu/UHE/p/POLYGAMY.html> (accessed June 20, 2006).

Economist. "Polygamy in Canada: Hunting Bountiful." June 8, 2004 <http://www.economist.com/world/na/display Story.cfm?story_id=2907136> (accessed June 20, 2006).

Twenty-Six Hours a Day

Magazine article

By: Mary Blake

Date: February 1878

Source: Blake, Mary. "Twenty-Six Hours a Day." *Scribner's Monthly.* 15 (1878): 554-555.

About the Author: Mary Elizabeth McGrath was born in Ireland in 1840, and emigrated to Boston with her family around 1850, where she first attended Emerson's Private School and then the Academy of the Sacred Heart in Manhattanville, New York. In 1865, she married John G. Blake, with whom she had eleven children. She was a prolific poet and columnist whose work was published in several newspapers and magazines, including the *Boston Journal*, *Catholic World*, and *Scribner's Monthly*. Blake also wrote two books of children's poetry, three travel books, and had three volumes of poems published, including *Poems* (1882), *Verses along the Way* (1890), and *In the Harbour of Hope* (1907), before her death in 1907. Although Mary McGrath Blake was quite popular in the late nineteenth century, her work is not well-known today.

INTRODUCTION

Mary Blake's description of desperate late nineteenth century housewives probably sounds familiar to modern mothers (and some fathers) who never seem to be able to catch up with the many household tasks associated with family life, whether they stay home with children or are employed outside the house. Blake's advice to mothers—to prioritize their work, relax some housekeeping standards, and simplify their houses and social lives in order to find some time for themselves—while keeping children's welfare paramount—is also quite recognizable. Strikingly similar suggestions are still found in twenty-first century women's magazines, and in recent self-help and organizational books aimed mainly at women, especially mothers. Although discussions of sewing and mending have been dropped from most of these recent works, the attention that mothers are urged to pay to their children's safety, education, and wellbeing has greatly increased. Other household

jobs have not greatly decreased in importance or in the amount of time spent on them, despite the adoption of modern labor-saving appliances, as Cowan demonstrated in *More Work for Mother* in 1983, or with more recent male contributions to household work.

■ PRIMARY SOURCE

"Well," exclaimed tired Mrs. Motherly, "if anybody needs twenty-six hours a day, I am sure I do, and ten days a week into the bargain. The days are not half long enough, and when night comes, the thought of the things I ought to have done but couldn't, tires me more than all I have done. This very day, when I expected to do so much sewing, has slipped away, while I have trotted around after the children, washing faces, brushing tangled hair, putting on rubber boots and taking them off again in fifteen minutes, and picking up blocks and playthings, scarves and mittens over and over again. I have mended unexpected tears in jackets and dresses, put court-plaster on 'skatched finders,' settled twenty quarrels between the baby and the next older, threaded needles for 'make-believe sewings,' and all the time been trying to sew, or dust, or sweep, or make gingerbread, till I feel as if I were in a dozen pieces, and every piece trying to do something different. At night I am so tired that all I ask for is a place to crawl into and sleep if I can, and even that must be with one eye open to see that the baby doesn't get uncovered. Yet there *are* people so unfeeling as to say I ought to try to get time to read and all that!"

Not so fast, my little mother. It is all true, every word of it, but let us see if it isn't possible to save a little time out of even these busy, wearying days for something higher than mere physical needs.

In order to find out how to save it, let us see what we do with it. Suppose we sort over work as we do our work-baskets, and see if we cannot make a little time by saving it.

The first and most important of our duties is the care of the children, including, of course, their physical, moral and intellectual training.

Next comes the housekeeping, *i.e.*, the literal keeping the house in order, looking after its cleanliness and general pleasantness.

Then, cooking or preparing and serving the food, including the care of the table and all that pertains to it. This is really another part of the housekeeping, and perhaps ought to be included in it, except that in some households the details are given over entirely to servants, while in others they are in greater or less degree the work of the lady of the house.

And lastly, the sewing.

Entitled "Household Druge and Slave," this Charles Stanley Reinhart woodcut shows the hard work women are expected to do in the home. © BETTMANN/CORBIS.

As regards the care the children it is almost impossible that there can be any superfluities. To every true mother, their welfare is first and foremost. Better that cobwebs festoon our parlor wall, and dust lie inch deep

on our books, than that we neglect our children for anything, no matter how good that thing in itself may be. Missionary meetings at one end of the scale, and balls and fashionable society at the other, are all blameworthy, if on account of them the children suffer. When "culture" turns them over to the tender mercies of servants, it becomes only a refined form of selfishness.

SIGNIFICANCE

Twenty-Six Hours a Day is an example of the women's advice literature (also known as prescriptive literature) that proliferated throughout the nineteenth century. Such magazine articles, newspaper columns, and books, like those described by Leavitt (2002), greatly increased in number and popularity in Europe and America in the late 1800s. It is a particularly rich source of data for research on attitudes about gender, changing gender roles, childrearing techniques, and evolving ideologies.

The growth of this literature was closely related to other changes in domestic life. Women were increasingly literate, and families were more mobile. As more Nineteenth century men became involved in the new industrial economy, women became more exclusively identified with the domestic sphere. Historian Barbara Welter first portrayed this as the "Cult of True Womanhood" (1976). Also called the "Cult of Domesticity" or "real womanhood," this ideal was characterized by pious, pure, submissive, and domestic women. Above all else, however, these women were devoted to their children. Lewis describes the construction and emotional underpinnings of self-sacrifice in her work on *Mother's Love*. Blake herself stresses the importance and perceived naturalness of this form of motherhood with her use of the terms "true mother" and "children's birthright," emphasizing near the end of her article that "The popular verdict is right, so far as this, that a mother's first duty is to her family, and nothing which conflicts with and forces her to neglect that, is either womanly or proper" (p. 560).

More recent researchers have added depth and complexity to Welter's work by focusing on the structure of "true womanhood" in different times and places, by exploring "how it helped to maintain class- and race-based hierarchies of power; and how it justified women's exclusion from participatory democracy" (Roberts 2002: 150), and noting how women challenged or negotiated the ideal. Interestingly, despite Blake's affirmation of the primacy of motherhood, *Twenty-Six Hours a Day* also displays the seeds of early feminist attitudes about women's work. Blake acknowledges the difficulty of childcare and housework, and suggests that there are ways to simplify it. Furthermore, her assertion that "Women are singularly slow to comprehend that their time is worth anything in dollars and cents" (p. 560) and her firm

declaration that women need an intellectual life outside the home, were ideas that were championed more fully in the twentieth century.

FURTHER RESOURCES

Books

Cowan, Ruth Schwartz. *More Work for Mother: The Ironies of Household Technology from the Open Hearth to the Microwave*. New York: Basic Books, 1983.

Leavitt, Sarah A. *From Catharine Beecher to Martha Stewart: A Cultural History of Domestic Advice*. Chapel Hill, N.C.: University of North Carolina Press, 2002.

Welter, Barbara. *Dimity Convictions: The American Woman in the Nineteenth Century*. Athens, Ohio: Ohio University Press, 1976.

Periodicals

Roberts, Mary Louise. "True Womanhood Revisited." *Journal of Women's History*. 14 (1) (2002):150–155.

For the Benefit of the Girl About to Graduate

Editorial cartoon

By: Charles Howard Johnson

Date: May 22, 1890

Source: *Library of Congress*. "For the Benefit of the Girl About to Graduate." 1890.

About the Author: Charles Howard Johnson (?–1896) was a well-known magazine illustrator based in New York City. His work frequently appeared in the leading magazines of the day, including *Life* magazine.

INTRODUCTION

When the English colonists first began arriving in North America in significant numbers after 1620, the formal education of the young people of the colony was of secondary importance to the manual labor that they represented. Such labor was required to make a success of the agricultural work that was at the heart of the early colonial establishment.

The first elementary school was established in 1635 in Massachusetts, with a colony-wide policy of schooling or apprenticeships in place by 1642. Harvard College was established in 1636 in Cambridge, Massachusetts, a time when there was no significant demand for advanced education given the nature of the colonial structure. The next prominent colleges to be established were Yale (1701) and Princeton (1746). These schools had significant connections to the Protestant church and each played an important role in the education of the colonial clergy.

The University of Pennsylvania was established in 1751; Benjamin Franklin and other colonial leaders in Philadelphia sought to establish an institution that was not directed to the training of clergy or religious studies, but one that would prepare its students for a career in business or commerce. After the Revolutionary War, there was a growth in the establishment of universities across the United States.

Relative to modern college and university enrollments in the United States, the American institutions after 1800 educated a very small fraction of the population. Women were prohibited from admission to any of the established universities; the prevailing societal values were such that women were expected to work exclusively in the home and there was no perceived need for women to have access to higher education.

It was the expansion of the United States westward across the continent in the early 1800s that indirectly served as a stimulus to the establishment of women's higher education. As new territories and states west of the Appalachian Mountains solidified their social and governmental structures, the desire to establish school systems led to a need for teachers. Women had become a part of various local school systems after 1800 without the benefit of extensive training as they were not permitted access to the male institutions. The "normal" schools, a name derived from the French term *ecole normale*, meaning instruction in the education norms, were established to provide a two-year instructional program for teachers. The first normal school was founded in Massachusetts in 1823; the schools proved a very popular means to provide teachers with a base level of instructional education. The normal schools represented the primary access point for American women to any form of higher education until the latter part of the nineteenth century.

In response to the prohibitions in place at the university level in the country, a small number of institutions catering exclusively to female students were founded. Most were located in the northeastern states, and the most prominent of these colleges were those that were later known as the "Seven Sisters," founded between 1837 (Mount Holyoke Seminary) and 1889 (Barnard College). The other Seven Sisters institutions included Bryn Mawr, Radcliffe, Smith, Vassar, and Wellesley colleges.

At the time of this editorial cartoon in 1890, teaching remained a primary career for a young woman who sought an education. Education was generally out of the question for the poor; the expectation of both typical middle-class young women and society at large was that teaching or a similar career might be pursued for a period prior to marriage and the raising of a family. The university-educated career woman contributing income to a two-income family was a concept that remained many decades in the future.

PRIMARY SOURCE

FOR THE BENEFIT OF THE GIRL ABOUT TO GRADUATE
See primary source image.

SIGNIFICANCE

By 1890, the pursuit of an education and a career outside of the home had moved from the status of novelty to a more common, if not accepted, fact of American life. Through the combined availability of the normal schools for teachers and the four-year women's colleges, a significant number of middle- and upper-class women with the means to pay for university education were able to pursue careers—teaching, nursing, library science, and social work were the most common courses of study.

For many women, the Victorian attitudes respecting the proper place of a woman and the desire for education came into significant conflict. The Charles Howard Johnson cartoon is of particular interest in this regard as it neatly illustrates the pressures that educated women experienced to conform to the societal norm of marriage and family.

A number of modern analyses of the history of women's education in the United States refer to the university graduates of this era (1890 to 1920) as the first beneficiaries of expanding women's education. More than 30 percent of these graduates did not marry by age fifty, a fact that suggests that education and a subsequent career were circumstances that propelled many women out of the societal mainstream.

The Howard cartoon contains a mixture of blunt and subtle messages for the viewer. The dreaming female on the eve of her graduation appears to have conjured up an animated army of pots, pans, utensils, and other domestic tools. The placards carried by the animated figures challenge the student and her education: "Are you with us?"; "Can you use me?"; and "Have you any idea who I am?" These phrases suggest that the female's education is of little value when com-

■ PRIMARY SOURCE

For the Benefit of the Girl About to Graduate: An editorial cartoon from 1890 illustrating the societal expectations of the time for a woman, including running a traditional household, clashing with the desire for university education and career outside the home. THE LIBRARY OF CONGRESS.

pared with the domestic virtue of housekeeping and cooking.

The books arrayed on the shelves and on the desk of the student are also significant. "Goethe's Cookbook" is a mocking reference to the work of the influential German philosopher Johann Wolfgang von Goethe (1749–1832). "The Care of Lamps" serves to trivialize the subjects a woman might study in university.

There is no question that the views represented by the animated domestic figures in the cartoon reflect a significant percentage of public opinion concerning the relevance of women's higher education in 1890. At the time of this cartoon's publication, women did not have the right to vote anywhere in the United States and discrimination on the basis of gender was ingrained in every aspect of society.

From the perspective of modern society, the scene depicted in this cartoon is far removed from current attitudes regarding the status of women in America.

The university-going American female ceased to be a novelty after World War II. As university education became increasingly accessible into the 1960s, approximately 35 percent of all American university entrants were female. The 1972 passage of Title IX, part of the Educational Amendments to the 1964 Civil Rights Act, served to accentuate the principles of equal educational opportunity for men and women, as institutions were now mandated by law to ensure that there was gender equality in the programs offered.

In 2006, for every 100 male students entering university, there were 135 female students. Female applicants tended to achieve higher scores on the Scholastic Aptitude Test (SAT) administered to most prospective university entrants in the United States. In many professional and graduate schools, including the former male bastion of law, it is common for female students to constitute a majority of the graduates.

In 1890, the average age at marriage of a single American woman who had never previously been married was 24.7 years. In 2006, the comparable age was 27.7 years. While the greater availability of a university education is not the predominate factor in this increase of three years, the related ability of women to seek career employment is a contributing factor.

FURTHER RESOURCES

Books

Martin, Jane. *Women and Education 1800–1980*. New York: Palgrave MacMillan, 2004.

Palmieri, Patricia Ann. *In Adamless Eden: The Community of Women Faculty at Wellesley*. New Haven, Conn.: Yale University Press, 1995.

Periodicals

Goldin, Claudia. "Working Paper 10331/Long Road to the Fast Track." *National Bureau of Economic Research* 3 (2004).

Web sites

Harvard University. "The Quiet Revolution That Transformed Women: Employment, Education and Family." June 2006 <http://www.aeaweb.org/annual_mtg_papers?2006/0106_1645_0101pdf> (accessed June 28, 2006).

Stanford University. "Why the U.S. Led in Education Lessons from Economic History." June 2006 <http://comparativepolitics.stanford.edu/Papers.205-06/Elis_12_June_2006.pdf> (accessed June 29, 2006).

Washing Day Reform

Advertisement

By: Anonymous

Date: 1890

Source: Photo by Hulton Archive/Getty Images.

About the Photographer: Getty Images provides photographs, film footage, and digital content, including current and historical photographs, moving images, and political cartoons. The photographer is unknown.

INTRODUCTION

The term "women's work" has little meaning in an era when most jobs can be held by both men and women, and equality in hiring, pay, and promotion is guaranteed by federal law. Historically the term included a pejorative implication, a suggestion that men and women were genetically suited for specific types of labor, and the work allocated to women was generally beneath the dignity of a man to perform. Women's work frequently included childcare, cooking meals, and cleaning the home; in many cultures the true definition of woman's work amounted to completing the tasks assigned by her husband. Despite television hostess Martha Stewart's ability to make basic household tasks appear fascinating and entertaining, the term "housework" implies drudgery and boredom to most women today.

Housework in the nineteenth century was time-consuming and physically demanding. Cooking took place on a wood or coal stove that required continuous fueling and that continually heated the kitchen, even during the summer. Historians estimate the daily fuel usage of a coal stove at around fifty pounds, some of which had to be removed as ashes after being burned. Food preparation typically involved numerous preliminary steps: live chickens had to be killed, plucked, and cleaned; flour had to be sifted before use; and nuts had to be shelled. In many homes water was carried inside one bucket at a time as needed, and was slowly heated on the stove before use.

Between the numerous tasks required to prepare meals, women of the 1800s were also expected to clean the house. Nineteenth century houses were filled with sources of soot and ash, including the previously mentioned stove, along with fireplaces and kerosene lamps, all of which created a constant film on walls and curtains. Lamps also had to be fueled and trimmed daily. Most homes had wooden floors, which required sweeping, and large rugs that were periodically taken outside and beaten with a large metal tool to loosen accumulated dust.

Of all the tasks required in the home, washing clothes was one of the more demanding. The process began with carrying water, an average of fifty gallons per load. Clothes were normally soaked overnight in tubs, then rubbed across rough washboards with lye soap to remove stains. Once scrubbed the clothes were transferred to fresh tubs in which they were boiled while being stirred with a stick. The clothes were then rinsed—white clothes were rinsed a second time in laundry bluing—and the garments were carried outside to line dry. Ironing and starching were optional steps.

The coming of the Industrial Revolution and the twentieth century brought the promise of relief for overworked housewives. In quick succession enterprising inventors developed practical electric irons, vacuum cleaners, and toasters. As more homes installed plumbing, the task of carrying water disappeared, and by the 1920s many middle class wives

WASHING-DAY REFORM.

HARPER TWELVETREES'

UNRIVALLED LABOUR-SAVING

VILLA WASHER,

Wringer and Mangler combined, £5 5s. (Cash Price, £4 15s.), or without **Wringer and Mangler**, £2 15s. (Cash Price, £2 10s.)

Does the Fortnight's Family Wash in Four Hours, without RUBBING or BOILING, as certified by thousands of delighted purchasers.

The Rev. J. ROBINSON, Great Sampford, Braintree, writes—" With the aid of the servant, aged 14, the Fortnight's Family Washing for six in family is done in four hours."

Mrs. CHARLES PAMMENT, St. Saviour's Villa, Bury St. Edmunds—" Our Fortnight's Family Wash, which formerly occupied from 8 A.M. till 8 P.M., is now done in three hours, and the copper fire is out five hours sooner than it used to be."

Carriage paid; free trial; easy instalment payments, or ten per cent. cash discount.

New Illustrated Catalogue, 48 pages, post free, from

HARPER TWELVETREES, *Laundry Machinist,*

80, FINSBURY PAVEMENT, LONDON, E.C.

PRIMARY SOURCE

Washing Day Reform: An advertisement for an early-model washing machine claims that the device can finish two weeks worth of laundry for a family of six in four hours, January 1, 1890. PHOTO BY HULTON ARCHIVE/GETTY IMAGES.

A 1949 appliance sales demonstration. On the left a model demonstrates a 1906 Thor washing machine, in contrast with her 1949 counterpart on the right, demonstrating a new model Thor machine that washes clothes and dishes. © BETTMANN/CORBIS.

could eagerly anticipate the arrival of a modern electric washing machine in their homes.

PRIMARY SOURCE

WASHING DAY REFORM

See primary source image.

SIGNIFICANCE

The modern home is far cleaner, more comfortable, and safer than homes of the nineteenth century.

Many home cleaning and meal preparation tasks have become automated, freeing women (and in some cases, men) for other tasks. Despite numerous technological advances and the development of countless labor saving devices, a strange irony exists in the fact that full-time housewives today work approximately the same number of hours caring for their homes as their grandmothers did in the 1920's.

Several factors play a role in this unexpected outcome. While modern housewives spend no time carrying water, they do spend large blocks of time traveling to the supermarket and the discount store to purchase cleaning products and groceries. Modern housewives enjoy the convenience of electric dishwashers; however they also load and unload several times as many dishes as their grandmothers owned, reducing the time savings somewhat. And whereas home cleaning has become far less labor intensive, standards of cleanliness are far higher and homes are several times larger, making the task less physically demanding but in many cases just as time-consuming. Finally, labor-saving devices must be purchased, maintained, and repaired, raising their total cost of ownership and in some cases reducing the actual amount of time they save.

Like most other inventions, home labor-saving devices invariably produce unexpected outcomes for their owners, in some cases actually increasing the amount of time required to complete the task. Despite such experiences the market for labor-saving cleaning tools and products remains vibrant. In the 1990s the first home robotic vacuums became available, promising to keep floors clean automatically; by the turn of the century more than 1 million Roombas had been sold.

FURTHER RESOURCES

Books

Brewer, Priscilla. *From Fireplace to Cookstove: Technology and the Domestic Ideal in America*. New York: Syracuse University Press, 2000.

Cowan, Ruth Schwartz. *More Work for Mother: The Ironies of Household Technology from the Open Hearth to the Microwave*. New York: Basic Books, 1983.

Stanley, Autumn. *Mothers and Daughters of Invention: Notes for a Revised History of Technology*. Metuchen, N.J.: Scarecrow Press, 1993.

Periodicals

Fox, Bonnie J. "Selling the Mechanized Household: 70 Years of Ads in Ladies Home Journal." *Gender & Society*. 4 (1990):25–40.

Santiago, Chiori. "It All Comes Out in the Wash." *Smithsonian*. 28(1997):84–92.

Web sites

CBS News. "The History of Housework." April 5, 1999 <http://www.cbsnews.com/stories/1999/04/02/broadcasts/main41492.shtml> (accessed July 7, 2006).

Smithsonian Institution Libraries. "The Making of a Homemaker." <http://www.sil.si.edu/ondisplay/making-home maker/> (accessed July 18, 2006).

U.S. Library of Congress. "The History of Household Technology with Constance Carter." <http://www.loc.gov/rr/program/journey/household.html> (accessed July 1, 2006).

The Degraded Status of Woman in the *Bible*

Book excerpt

By: Elizabeth Cady Stanton

Date: 1895

Source: *Library of Congress*. "Votes for Women: Selections from the National American Woman Suffrage Association Collection, 1848–1921." 2006 <http://memory.loc.gov/cgi-bin/query/gt; (accessed June 20, 2006).

About the Author: Elizabeth Cady Stanton (1815–1902) was one of the most influential women's rights proponents in America during the nineteenth century. Stanton was a prolific writer on women's issues and she worked as an organizer on a broad range of women's issues, including female suffrage, property rights, temperance, and the liberalization of existing divorce laws.

INTRODUCTION

Elizabeth Cady Stanton advanced a number of causes in the course of her life, all of which were tied to the advancement of the position of women in American society. In the early portion of her career as an activist, her chief pursuit was securing the abolition of slavery; Stanton's husband, Henry Stanton, was a noted anti-slavery orator at the time of their marriage in 1840. It is a feature of Stanton's later work in the women's rights movements that she could draw upon the experience of raising her seven children when advancing arguments for the improvement of the status of women in America.

Stanton's first significant organizational success for the women's movement was the first national women's rights convention held in Seneca Falls, New York, in July, 1848. In April of that year, the state of New York had passed its first *Married Women's Property Act*, a law that granted married woman distinct legal control over property that they either brought into a marriage or inherited during the course of a marriage. The *Declaration of Sentiments* that was published as a confirmation of the position of the Seneca Falls convention delegates regarding the demanded changes in the place of women in American society was authored by Stanton. The first broad articulation of the goals of the American women rights movement, the Declaration called for wholesale reform of property, voting, and divorce laws.

The Foolish Virgins, a painting from a series of Bible illustrations by James Tissot. © BROOKLYN MUSEUM OF ART/CORBIS.

In 1851, Stanton met Susan B. Anthony (1820–1906), who shared Stanton's passions for suffrage and property law reform. Stanton and Anthony remained influential at the head of the women's rights movement in the United States until their respective deaths. Stanton was a vigorous debater of women's issues in many venues throughout the United States from the end of the Civil War to the 1880s. Stanton's writings were a fundamental component of the philosophy underlying the American women's movement well into the twentieth century.

Stanton was a well-educated woman for the times and her various writings reflect a considerable understanding of Christian theology. Like many leaders of the feminist movements that grew throughout North America in the 1960s and 1970s, Stanton did not profess a conventional faith in God and Christian worship. Organized religion was an institution that she viewed as one that limited the ability of women to find their true place in society. The chief target of attack in her 1895 work, the *Woman's Bible,* was the relationship between the expressions of Christian faith and the subordination of women through church practices.

PRIMARY SOURCE

The Pentateuch makes woman a mere afterthought in creation; the author of sin; cursed in her maternity; a subject in marriage; and claims divine authority for this four-fold bondage, this wholesale desecration of the mothers of the race. While some admit that this invidious language of the Old Testament is disparaging to woman, they claim that the New Testament honors her. But the letters of the apostles to the churches, giving directions for the discipline of women, are equally invidious, as the following texts prove:

"Wives, obey your husbands. If you would know anything, ask your husbands at home. Let your women keep silence in the churches, with their heads covered. Let not your women usurp authority over the man, for as Christ is the head of the church so is the man the head of the woman. Man was prior in creation, the woman was of the man, therefore shall be in subjection to him."

No symbols or metaphors can twist honor or dignity out of such sentiments. Here, in plain English, woman's position is as degraded as in the Old Testament.

As the *Bible* is in every woman's hands, and she is trained to believe it "the word of God," it is impossible to describe her feelings of doubt and distrust, as she awakes to her status in the scale of being; the helpless, hopeless position assigned her by the Creator, according to the Scriptures.

Men can never understand the fear of everlasting punishment that fills the souls of women and children. The orthodox religion, as drawn from the *Bible* and expounded by the church, is enough to drive the most imaginative and sensitive natures to despair and death. Having conversed with many young women in sanatoriums, insane asylums, and in the ordinary walks of life, suffering with religious melancholia; having witnessed the agony of young mothers in childbirth, believing they were cursed of God in their maternity; and with painful memories of my own fears and bewilderment in girlhood, I have endeavored to dissipate these religious superstitions from the minds of women, and base their faith on science and reason, where I found for myself at last that peace and comfort I could never find in the *Bible* and the church. I saw the first step to this end was to convince them that the *Bible* was neither written nor inspired by the Creator of the Universe, the Infinite Intelligence, the soul and center of Life, Love and Light; but that the *Bible* emanated, in common with all church literature, from the brain of man. Seeing that just in proportion as women are devout believers in the dogmas of the church their lives are shadowed with fears of the unknown, the less they believe, the better for their own happiness and development. It was the religious devotee that threw her child under the car of Juggernaut, that gave her body a living sacrifice on the funeral pyre of her husband, to please God and save souls; for the same reason the devotees of our day build churches and parsonages, educate young men for the ministry, endow theological seminaries, make surplices and embroider slippers for the priesthood.

It may not be amiss for man to accept the *Bible*, as it honors and exalts him. It is a title deed for him to inherit the earth. According to the Pentateuch he communes with the gods, in performing miracles he is equal in power and glory with his Creator, can command the sun and moon to stand still to lengthen the day and lighten the night, if need be, to finish his battles. He can stand in the most holy places in the temples, where woman may never enter; he can eat the consecrated bread and meat, denied her; in fact, there is a suspicion of unworthiness and uncleanness seductively infused into the books of

Moses against the whole female sex, in animal as well as human life. *The first born male* kid is the only fit burnt offering to the Lord; if preceded by a female it is unfit.

As the *Bible* gives us two opposite accounts of the creation of woman and her true position, so the church gives two opposite interpretations of the will of the God concerning her true sphere of action. When ecclesiastics wish to rouse woman's enthusiasm to lift a church debt or raise a pastor's salary, then they try to show her that she owes all she is and all the liberty she enjoys to the *Bible* and Christian religion; they dwell on the great honor God conferred on the sex in choosing a woman to be the mother of his only begotten son.

But when woman asks for equal rights and privileges in the church, to fill the office of pastor, elder, deacon or trustee, to be admitted as a delegate to the synods, general assemblies or conferences, then the bishops quote texts to show that all these positions are forbidden by the *Bible*. And so completely have these clerical tergiversations perverted the religious element in woman's nature, and blinded her to her individual interests, that she does not see that her religious bondage is the source of her degradation.

The honor and worship accorded the ideal mother, of the ideal man, has done naught to elevate the real mother, of the real man. So far from woman owing what liberty she does enjoy, to the *Bible* and the church, they have been the greatest block in the way of her development. The vantage ground woman holds to-day is due to all the forces of civilization, to science, discovery, invention, rationalism, the religion of humanity chanted in the golden rule round the globe centuries before the Christian religion was known. It is not to *Bible*s, prayer books, catechisms, liturgies, the canon law and church creeds and organizations, that woman owes one step in her progress, for all these alike have been hostile, and still are, to her freedom and development.

Canon Charles Kingsley well said, long ago: "This will never be a good world for woman, until the last remnant of the canon law is swept from the face of the earth." It is the insidious influence of this law that degrades woman to-day in social life and the state as well as in the church; giving us one moral code for man, another for woman, endowing him with political freedom, with all the rights that belong to a citizen of a republic, while she is a slave, a subject, a mere pariah in the state.

When the canon law with its icy fingers touched the old Roman civil law it robbed woman of many privileges she before enjoyed. The old English common law, too, reflects many of its hideous features and has infused its deadly poison into the statute laws of every state in this new republic. For fifty years the women of this nation have tried to dam up this deadly stream that poisons all their lives, but thus far they have lacked the insight or courage to follow it back to its source and there strike the blow at the fountain of all tyranny, religious superstition, priestly power and the canon law. We may learn the effect of the canon on the civil law from the opinion of Lord Brougham. He says the English common law for woman is a disgrace to the civilization and Christianity of the nineteenth century....The simple story of the Scotch peasant's wife shows how the Book impresses a thoughtful woman, not blinded by fear, to express her real opinions.

Sitting in her cottage door at the twilight hour reading her *Bible*, the bishop passing by, said, "My good woman, do you enjoy that book?" "Nay, nay, Reverend Sir, as I read of all the misery woman brought into the world, and for which there is no remedy, I am ashamed that I was born a woman. I am sorry that the good Lord ever wrote the Book, and told the men all he has concerning us; it gives them an excuse for the contempt and cruelty with which they treat us." Yea, verily, here is the source and center of woman's degradation; out of these ideas grew witchcraft and celibacy, that made woman for ages the helpless victim of man's lust and power; out of these ideas grew the monstrous delusion of the curse and uncleanness of motherhood, that required all women at one time to stand up before the whole congregation "to be churched" as it was called, after the birth of a child, returning thanks to the Lord for her safety. As if peril and suffering were part of the eternal law, and not the result of its violation through our own ignorance and folly, and our artificial habits of life. However, there are some considerations and characters in the Book that can give woman a few crumbs of comfort. The first chapter of Genesis has several valuable suggestions. "God said, Let us make man in our own image. Male and female made he *them*, and gave *them* dominion over the earth, and all that dwells therein." "Let us," shows plurality in the Godhead, a heavenly mother as well as a heavenly father, the feminine as well as the masculine element. Without these two forces in equilibrium, there could have been no perpetuation of life in the mineral, vegetable and animal kingdoms; as necessary in the material world as the positive and negative electricity, the centripetal and centrifugal forces. "He gave them dominion over everything." Here the equality of the sexes is recognized, and this idea is echoed back from the New Testament. "There is neither Jew nor Greek, male nor female, bond nor free, for ye are all one in Christ Jesus." We not only have this broad principle of equality enunciated, but we have some grand types of women presented for our admiration. Deborah for her courage and military prowess. Huldah for her learning, prophetic insight, and statesmanship, seated in the college in Jerusalem, where Josiah the king sends his cabinet ministers to consult her

as to the policy of his government. Esther, who ruled as well as reigned with Ahasuerus the king, and Vashti, who scorned the apostle's command, "Wives, obey your husbands." She refused the king's command to grace with her presence his reveling court. Tennyson pays this tribute to her virtue and dignity:

"O Vashti! noble Vashti,

Summoned forth, she kept her state

And left the drunken king to brawl

In Shushan underneath his palms."

These characters and principles would furnish good texts for sermons and examples for aspiring young women in the churches, but the sons of Levi shy round all these interesting facts, and maintain a discreet silence, but they should awake woman to her true position as an equal factor in the scale of being. We never have any sermons to inspire woman with self-respect and a desire for her own higher development. The cardinal virtue for her to cultivate is self-sacrifice and an humble submission to the discipline of the church. As a badge of her subjection she is always required to appear in church with her head covered....

SIGNIFICANCE

At the time Elizabeth Cady Stanton wrote these words, she was eighty years of age and nearing the end of her long career as a women's rights advocate. Her blunt critique of the *Bible* as, among other observations, the product of self-serving men and not God is an approach that in 1895 was nothing short of heretical. Organized religion, whether Protestant, Catholic, or Jewish, was then the most established institution in American society.

The primary significance of the *Woman's Bible* has two separate but related aspects. The first is that the work was published at all, given the prominent position of organized religion in American society. The second was that the attacks directed by Stanton against both Christian religion and the *Bible* neatly parallel the broader arguments made by the women's rights movements against other societal institutions in this period, in particular marriage and restrictive divorce laws, the right to vote, and the right of women to freely deal with property. In this second aspect, the struggles of women against the inflexible institutions of the Church are a metaphor for the broader women's rights battles.

Stanton's reference to the Pentateuch is often referred to in Christian faiths as the law of Moses as represented in the first five Books of the Old Testament. Mirroring many issues advanced by the women's movement in the latter part of the nineteenth century, the Old Testament has numerous references to women as chattels of men. Stanton's analysis of the restrictions placed upon women in these ancient texts is at the root of her argument that such restrictions could not have been the wish of the Creator, but were instead the creation of men.

Stanton also challenges the argument that the New Testament essentially balanced the more troubling laws of the Old Testament through specific passages that honored women. Stanton described such arguments as ones intended to placate women, not enlighten them. Stanton characterizes the portrayal of women in the *Bible* as akin to props for the male oriented narratives, as there are in her reckoning no true female role models in the *Bible* to illustrate the strength and the character of women on their own terms. Stanton's reference to the practice of 'churching' and the notion that child birth renders a woman unclean underscores her disdain for the attitudes of organized religion to women.

The Women's Bible represents a culmination of the propositions first advanced by Stanton in the *Declaration of Sentiments* published after the first women's rights convention in 1848, and reiterated by her colleague Matilda Joselyn Gage and others in the 1876 *Declaration of Rights*, a later milestone of the women's rights movement. Stanton, Anthony and Gage co-authored the *History of Women's Suffrage* between 1881 and 1889, which also developed similar arguments. Stanton and her fellow women's rights leaders were effective in marshalling sympathetic publishers to print their works and to ensure a significant degree of circulation throughout the United States.

Many social commentators have noted that the influence of organized religion has declined in modern American society if influence is assessed by the indicators of church attendance and declared religious affiliation. In a converse relationship to that known at the time of the publication of the *Woman's Bible*, women have a greater role today in the traditional Protestant faiths than they have ever had in church history. In 1895, a female minister was unheard of in most mainstream churches; only the Quakers (Society of Friends) and the Salvation Army regularly permitted women to minister to their adherents. By 1980, both the United Methodist and the Episcopal Churches were examples of denominations with significant numbers of female priests.

What Stanton and her contemporaries called the women's rights movement is now equated to the modern feminist movement. Feminist concepts engaged significant public interest from the 1960s onward through the writings and public statements of persons such as Betty Friedan (1921–2006) and Gloria Steinem (b. 1934). In contrast to Stanton, modern feminism has centered significant attention on issues related to sexuality and gender, such as the availability of abortion on demand.

FURTHER RESOURCES

Books

Frymer-Kensky, Tikva. *Reading the Women of the Bible: A New Interpretation of their Stories.* New York: Schocken Books, 2004.

Malone, Mary T. *Women and Christianity: From the Reformation to the 21st Century.* Maryknoll, N.Y.: Orbis, 2003.

Stanton, Elizabeth Cady. *The Woman's Bible.* Boston: Northeastern University Press, 1993.

Web sites

Rutgers University. "Stanton and Anthony Paper Project Online." July, 2001 <http://ecssba.rutgers.edu/studies/ecsbio.html> (accessed June 21, 2006).

Wall Street Journal. "Church Ladies." October 21, 2005 <http://www.opinionjournal.com/taste/?id=110007439> (accessed June 18, 2006).

A.D. 1915, With Puck's Apologies to the "Coming Woman"

Editorial cartoon

By: Fredrick Burr Opper

Date: 1895

Source: Opper, Frederick Burr. A.D. 1915, With Puck's Apologies to the "Coming Woman." © Corbis.

About the Artist: Fredrick Burr Opper (1857–1937) was a cartoonist for *Puck*, America's first successful humor magazine. Published from 1877 to 1918, it was known for its colorful cartoons that satirized the political and social issues of the day. Opper left *Puck* in 1899 to draw weekly cartoons for William Randolph Hearst's *New York Journal*. Vision problems forced him into semiretirement in 1932.

INTRODUCTION

American women began formally agitating for the right to vote in 1848 at the Seneca Falls Convention. Seventy-two years later, the passage of the Nineteenth Amendment to the Constitution gave women the ballot. The fight had been long and bitter.

Almost as soon as the woman's rights movement got underway in the mid-nineteenth century, negative visual images of women activists began to appear in the popular press. Such images typically showed suffrage activists as aggressive, cigar-smoking, pants-wearing shrews who neglected their children and forced their men into domestic drudgery. Men who supported woman suffrage were portrayed as being forced to baby-sit, cook, or wield a mop, usually making a mess of all these tasks. By conveying the message that women seeking to change traditional gender roles would harm society's moral and political structure, this pictorial rhetoric slowed down the political advance of women.

Until the suffrage battle, women were generally excluded from the world of cartooning. Visual satire was created by men and focused on the world of men. In the U.S., humor magazines, such as *Puck*, did not become popular until the last years of the decade. They used humor as social commentary to guide their readers to a particular point of view.

PRIMARY SOURCE

A.D. 1915, WITH PUCK'S APOLOGIES TO THE "COMING WOMAN"

See primary source image.

SIGNIFICANCE

By the start of the twentieth century, the campaign for woman suffrage had won a few victories, but only in the West. The majority of Americans were either indifferent to the idea or openly hostile to it. In response, women activists decided to turn the tables and use cartoons for their own advantage. They began to harness the power of images to work for their side of the suffrage argument.

Pro-suffrage cartoons used two persuasive techniques. Some of the cartoons presented the vote as a means to end the historical oppression of women. Most of the images pointed out that civilization lost ground by excluding women from active citizenship. The cartoonists contended that women voters, given the chance, would improve humanity. To a Progressive era audience eager to use the power of government to

PRIMARY SOURCE

A.D. 1915, With Puck's Apologies to the "Coming Woman": The cover of this 1895 edition of *Puck* paints a mocking picture of a future where woman suffrage has thrown traditional household roles into confusion. © CORBIS.

fix society's ills, it was a powerful argument. This message combined with women's contributions during World War I to persuade men to grant women the ballot in 1920.

FURTHER RESOURCES
Books

DuBois, Ellen Carol. *Feminism and Suffrage: The Emergence of an Independent Women's Movement in America, 1848–1869.* Ithaca, NY: Cornell University Press , 1978.

Sheppard, Alice. *Cartooning for Suffrage.* Albuquerque: University of New Mexico Press, 1994.

Wheeler, Marjorie Spruill, ed. *One Woman, One Vote: Rediscovering the Woman Suffrage Movement.* Troutdale, OR: New Sage Press, 1995.

Homework Destroys Family Life

Poster

By: Anonymous

Date: c. 1900

Source: Corbis Corporation

About the Author: This photograph is part of the collection of the Corbis Corporation, headquartered in Seattle, with a worldwide archive of over seventy million images.

INTRODUCTION

When modern children complain about homework, they are typically lamenting school-related assignments. But at the beginning of the twentieth century, the term homework had a far different meaning. In that era, homework referred to labor done for pay in one's home, and in particular to sewing and other manual work which filled the afternoons and evenings of many young children in large cities. Many of these children were forced to spend most of their non-school hours working.

Throughout history, children have been expected to work. Agricultural life often required the efforts of the entire family, and schools often closed during harvest time, as many rural children helped harvest crops

A woman and four young girls busily string flowers into wreaths for a living in their New York tenement apartment. © CORBIS.

and drive livestock to market. With the coming of the Industrial Age, rural American families migrated to cities where the parents took jobs in factories or offices and the children had the opportunity to attend school. Public education was compulsory, but attendance was poorly policed.

In 1906, an extensive study of child labor in New York City was commissioned. Child labor laws existed at that time, prohibiting youth under the age of fourteen from working in factories or stores. But throughout the densely crowded tenements of the city, the report's authors repeatedly observed young children carrying boxes containing partially finished clothing or pieces of artificial flowers. Investigating the situation further they found that while state law prohibited school-aged children from working in their homes during school hours, it did not regulate after-hours work. As a result many school children labored in their homes from the end of school until well into the night. The law also provided no regulation of younger children, meaning preschoolers could legally work at home all day.

This system of home labor was loosely regulated; state law prohibited the manufacture of forty-one specific items in homes, though all others could be legally produced. The home labor system actually simplified the lives of factory owners, who sent out unfinished goods and paid a piece-rate for finished products, simplifying compliance with New York labor laws.

The report concluded that numerous poor children were being denied the basic rights of children, specifically the chance to receive an education, the opportunity to enjoy playing, and, in the case of many immigrants, the chance to learn the English language. The problem was widespread: in 1901 the city of New York legally licensed more than 16,000 home workrooms, while the number of unlicensed workrooms was impossible to determine.

PRIMARY SOURCE

HOMEWORK DESTROYS FAMILY LIFE

See primary source image.

SIGNIFICANCE

School attendance and child labor laws in the United States today are much more rigorously enforced. The federal Fair Labor Standards Act (FLSA) regulates labor by minors, prohibiting most children under age fourteen from being employed by a business. During the school year fourteen and fifteen

PRIMARY SOURCE

Homework Destroys Family Life: An anti-child labor poster from the early 1900s entitled "Homework Destroys Family Life" shows problems associated with tenement labor. CORBIS

year olds may be employed, but their labor is limited to eighteen hours per week and they may not work before 7 A.M. or after 7 P.M. Sixteen and seventeen year olds may work unlimited hours, but are prohibited from holding potentially hazardous jobs such as mining, logging, or operating metal-forming machinery. Youths as young as ten may work in some farm-related positions with parental consent.

Youth workers are guaranteed the federal minimum wage, and hours over forty per week must be paid at a rate of time and a half. Employees under twenty years of age may be paid a slightly lower wage their first ninety days of employment; however federal law prohibits firing a current employee in order to hire another at the lower starting wage.

Child labor today is currently defined as any work which exploits children or keeps them from attending school. Poverty in many countries motivates child labor, often in hazardous environments and for low wages. In some countries children are conscripted and forced to join military units. Employers frequently prefer child laborers since they are energetic and rarely protest poor treatment.

While child labor has been largely eradicated in the United States, American companies now conduct a growing share of their business overseas. Clothing firms in particular now manufacture the vast majority of their products in other countries, many of which provide little legal protection for employees. In the 1990's several large companies came under fire for allegedly contracting with factories employing children. Nike Apparel was one of the targeted firms, and in 1998 the company ordered all its contract manufacturers to set a minimum age of sixteen for workers; companies violating this policy are required to remove the underage workers, continue paying their wages, place them in school, and rehire them when they are old enough. Critics of Nike's policies accuse them of covering up violations in their factories.

As of 2006, the United Nations agency UNICEF estimated that 246 million children worldwide were employed in child labor and that 171 million of those positions were hazardous. More than two-thirds of child labor at that time took place in agriculture-related and fishing/hunting industries; approximately sixty percent of child labor occurred in Asia.

FURTHER RESOURCES

Books

Orr, Deborah. *Slave Chocolate?* New York: McFarland and Company, 2005.

Periodicals

Kambhampati, Umas. And Raji Rajan. "Economic Growth: A panacea for child labor?" *World Development.* 34(2006):426-445.

Togunde, Dimeji and Arielle Carter. "Socioeconomic causes of child labor in urban Nigeria." *Journal of Children and Poverty.* 12(2006):73-89.

Web sites

Charities and the Commons. "Child Labor in New York City Tenements." <http://www.tenant.net/Community/LES/kleeck9.html> (accessed June 21, 2006).

Child Labor Coalition. "An Overview of Federal Child Labor Laws." <http://www.stopchildlabor.org/USchildlabor/fact1.htm> (accessed June 21, 2006).

Nike Apparel. "Workers and Factories Code of Conduct." March, 2005 <http://www.nike.com/nikebiz/> (accessed June 21, 2006).

Election Day!

Editorial cartoon

By: E.W. Gustin

Date: c. 1909

Source: *Library of Congress.* "By Popular Demand: Votes for Women Suffrage Pictures 1850–1920." October 19, 1998 <http://memory.loc.gov/service/pnp/cph/> (accessed July 3, 2006).

About the Artist: E.W. Gustin was a noted political and editorial cartoonist in the United States in the early twentieth century. A number of Gustin's cartoons that pertain to women's issues are maintained in the collections of the Library of Congress.

INTRODUCTION

At the time of the publication of the political cartoon *Election Day*, the political lobby that had become known as the suffragette movement in both the United States and in England had been a feature of the national politics in each country since the 1840s. In that period the first pamphlets were circulated in both countries urging the reform of election laws to permit women to vote. The first American women's rights convention was held in 1848, organized by advocates that included Elizabeth Cady Stanton (1815–1902); the right of women to vote was a center piece of the *Declaration of Sentiments* published after the convention was concluded.

"Suffragette" was a term coined in the latter part of the nineteenth century to describe a female supporter of the extension of the vote to women in political elections. A "suffragist" was a unisexual term describing such supporters irrespective of their gender.

In the early days of agitation for voting reform, the right to vote tended to be advanced by women's groups along with a broad range of issues that included women's property rights, more equitable divorce laws, better access to higher education, and employment equity. Two distinct events, one in the United States and another in Great Britain, propelled the formation of distinct suffragette movements in each country. The English legislation known as the *Second Great Reform Act* in 1867 attracted significant debate regarding women's voting rights; one of the notable champions of the cause was the English philosopher and political commentator John Stuart Mill (1806–1873). When the efforts to include women's voting rights in the legislation failed, the suffrage movement had its first formal organization, the National Society for Women's Suffrage.

In 1893, the former British colony of New Zealand became the first nation to permit women to vote. This further development led to the more forceful agitation by suffrage groups in England until the beginning of World War I in 1914.

In the United States, voting rights were extended to the emancipated black population and recently emigrated foreign men after the conclusion of the Civil War in 1865. The exclusion of women in the face of these developments was a powerful spur to the women's movement. A notable early example of public attention called to the issue was the attempt by women's leader Susan B. Anthony (1820–1906), co-founder of the national Women's Suffrage Association in 1869, to vote in the presidential elections in Rochester, New York in 1872, actions that lead to her prosecution and a favorable public reaction.

The later American suffragette leadership, including Lucy Burns (1879–1966) and Alice Paul (1885–1977), had ongoing contact with their British counterparts in the suffragette movement. In the United States, the suffragettes tended to organize generally peaceful political protests; the English suffragette campaign in the early 1900s was marked by a number of examples of violence, including arson.

A number of American states moved to permit women to vote prior to 1920; Jeanette Rankin of Montana was elected to the House of Representatives in 1916. The Nineteenth Amendment to the United States Constitution securing the right of women to vote was ratified on August 26, 1920. The British House of Parliament enacted legislation in 1918 that permitted women aged thirty or older to vote; full voting rights to adult women were extended in 1928.

PRIMARY SOURCE

ELECTION DAY!

See primary source image.

PRIMARY SOURCE

Election Day!: An editorial cartoon from 1909 depicting a woman going to vote on Election Day. It implies that giving women the vote will cause them to abandon their traditional work in the home. THE LIBRARY OF CONGRESS.

SIGNIFICANCE

When the cartoon was published in 1909, the entrenchment of voting rights for women in the United States was eleven years away. The domestic scene depicted in the E.W. Gustin work is a subtle depiction of what the artist anticipates will be the ultimate outcome of the suffragette movement.

The cartoon contrasts two figures. At the door is a rather formidable appearing woman preparing to go out and cast her vote. Her bewildered looking husband with two unhappy twin babies on his lap remains behind, a figure of confusion. The broken plate on the kitchen floor and the washing visible through the window enhance the artist's suggestion that the husband has significant domestic responsibility in his wife's absence, and that the husband seems ill-equipped to discharge those duties.

My wife's joined the Suffrage Movement.
(I've suffered ever since!)

This 1910 postcard plays on fears about the effect womens suffrage might have on family life. © LAKE COUNTY MUSEUM/CORBIS.

In the bottom right corner of the cartoon is a leaflet for the Hen Party. "Hen" was a well established and somewhat dismissive slang term often used in this period to describe a woman, and a "hen party" is an expression that refers to a social gathering of women. In the political context of the women's vote and an election day, hen party represents a clever play on words by the cartoonist. His usage of the expression in this context is significant because any political party described as the Hen Party could readily be taken as a ridiculing of the forces behind the suffragette movement in 1909.

In 1909, the relationship between the suffragette movement and the various groups that advocated the broader reform of the status of women in American society can be summarized by the aphorism, "all feminists are suffragettes, but not all suffragettes are fem-

inists." Feminism as a term used by those favoring the advancement of women's rights dates from approximately 1890 in the United States.

At the time of the 1909 cartoon, there were three distinct aspects to the feminist movement in the United States, with the beginnings of each component of the movement dating to approximately 1870. The first was the suffrage movement; towards the end of the nineteenth century, this group emphasized that the Victorian ideal of the woman as being a purer and better person than a man was a sound basis as to why women should be voting. This group urged reform on the basis that women would not be corruptible in political matters and therefore better voters than men. These suffragettes restricted their public advocacy to the right of women to vote.

The second aspect was a group that may be described as the social feminists. One of their prominent leaders was Carrie Chapman Catt (1859–1947), the founder of the National American Women Suffrage Association in 1895. After the passage of the Nineteenth Amendment, Catt organized the League of Women Voters in 1920. The social feminists directed their political efforts to the use of the vote to achieve social change.

Radical feminism comprised the third part of the movement; this constituency launched comprehensive attacks on the structure of American society as it related to women. Radical feminism is very much an expression to be taken in its context, as arguments that were radical in the early 1900s are today a part of the mainstream, particularly those respecting employment equality for women and the freedom of women to work outside of the home environment.

While the domestic scene depicted in the 1909 cartoon was a humorous forecast of what might occur upon the extension of the franchise to women in America, the final significant impetus to the securing of the vote was World War I. As men were dispatched overseas in the conflict, American women entered the workforce in then non-traditional jobs. As it became apparent that women could capably carry out work that had been the preserve of men until the war, the arguments in favor of women's suffrage became more widely accepted.

FURTHER RESOURCES
Books

Baker, Jean H. *Sisters: The Lives of American Suffragists.* New York: Hill and Wang, 2005.

Clift, Eleanor. *Founding Sisters and the Nineteenth Amendment.* New York: Wiley and Son, 2003.

Web sites

Gilder Lehman Institute of American History. "Woman's Suffrage Broadsides." 2006 <http://gilderlehman.org/collection/docs_archive_WomensSuffrage_Broadsides.html> (accessed June 23, 2006).

University of Wisconsin. "Women, Feminism, and Sex in Progressive America." 2003 <http://us.history.wisc.edu/hist102/lectures/lecture14.html> (accessed June 23, 2006).

To Mothers—Our Duty

Magazine article

By: Margaret H. Sanger

Date: March 26, 1911

Source: Sanger, Margaret H. "To Mothers—Our Duty." *The New York Call* (March 26, 1911): 15

About the Author: Margaret Sanger (1879–1966) was a nurse who fought for public access to information on contraception in the early part of the twentieth century. Her efforts to disseminate birth control information led to her repeated arrests for violating the Comstock Law in the United States. She helped to found Planned Parenthood, an organization that helps provide health and gynecological care for women in the U.S.

INTRODUCTION

Margaret Sanger's opinions and actions reached into many sectors of American society in the first two decades of the twentieth century. As the daughter of a woman who bore eleven children and died by fifty, partly a result of repeated pregnancies and childbirth, Sanger saw firsthand the results of uncontrollable reproduction. Trained as a nurse, Sanger began to work in New York City's Lower East side as industrialization and urbanization, combined with intense immigration as Jewish people from Eastern Europe fled repressive pogroms and discrimination in Europe, led to squalid conditions and public health crises in tenements and slums.

Sanger was approached, repeatedly, by poor and middle-class men and women alike, desperately seeking some form of contraception. Dissemination of information or supplies related to contraception was illegal under federal law in the United States; the 1873 Comstock Law made it a crime to distribute information, literature, or supplies designed to aid in birth control. By 1912, Sanger realized that unfettered capitalism combined with unchecked reproduction was creating an underclass of poor children who were sent into the factories at young ages to help their families avoid starvation and eviction. In Sanger's opinion, as stated in her 1915 essay "Comstockery in America," "I saw that it is the working class children who fill the mills, factories, sweatshops, orphan asylums and reformatories, because through ignorance they were brought into the world, and this ignorance continues to be perpetuated." Sanger sought to end the "ignorance" concerning birth control by offering families the needed information to control the size and timing of their families.

Sanger became a strong supporter of the Socialist Party as well, and in this essay, printed in 1911, before her work in the first birth control clinic in the U.S. and before her 1916 arrest for violating the Comstock Law, we see the formation of her thoughts on the impact of capitalism, child labor, and unchecked reproduction on the family.

PRIMARY SOURCE

In this day and age, when women are striving to their utmost to compete with their sisters in matters of dress, fashion, in "bridge," or anything which offers amusement or diversion from the old routine of our mothers' day, we hear a great deal from the male element about "Woman's Duty." This question of "duty" seems to be a stickler, and seems to confine itself to woman only.

This "duty," so called, means that women should remain at home, not necessarily to drudge—not at all—for among those women referred to above, the servant question forms a large part of their conversation; but "duty" means the care of the home, of the children—the problem of feeding them carefully (even scientifically), of making their little bodies strong and robust, in fact, of giving them a good foundation mentally and physically—for life.

Most men think a woman's duty is done when she attends to these needs of her children, but to me she has but begun to do her duty.

Let us take a young woman in the most ideal conditions of this life; she has given much thought and consideration to the life of her boy long before he was born, her every thought for almost a year was this child. He now comes into the world a rosy, healthy being, and she feels proud her work is so well begun; and she may well be proud.

Then follow the years of care. Every conceivable attention, mental and moral, she gives him; his childhood, his boyhood, is one joyous song of the pleasures of living, and after years of these joys he emerges into manhood. He is now ready for the great battle of life.

This mother has done her duty, and she sends him forth, clean, honest, moral, to get his living, but has she ever given the manner in which he is to obtain that living a thought? That is considered outside woman's "duty."

We women can build them up, these bodies and minds, build them up to our highest expectations and then push them out upon a world whose system is greed, exploitation, graft and scientific robbery.

Can we expect these morals to stay built up in these corrupt surroundings? As this case is an ideal one, so it is an exceptional one; let us turn, then, to one which is no exception.

This is the case of the most abused, most dejected, most imposed upon class of mothers which our social system presents to us, and their number is legion.

Here we find the little mothers at 8, 9 and 10 years of age; here we see them already at work carrying responsibilities of the home, factory or mill; education is a thing apart from this child, childhood yearnings are crushed, childish joys are barred here, there is time for but one thing—work. Work through childhood, through girlhood and womanhood.

We follow this child-mother up to the marriage day and find she has given her childhood, girlhood, womanhood, her strength, her very life to the factory or mill for an existence, an existence which the owner of the factory would not allow his horse or dog. Her face is pale and pinched with that hunting look of poverty; it never changes—she is born, lives and dies with that look. She is married at night after the day's work, that she lose not one day's time.

On, on in the same monotonous way; on, on, waiting for the end. There's no time for her to think of the little one's coming; she must work only the harder because of its coming.

After months of worry, toil, privation and physical exhaustion this child, too, is born. Let us see what this woman gives to society. Her child is undersized, underfed, weak, sickly and ofttimes deformed. It, too, has paid the price of birth; it has given its little strength with every heartbeat, that it may be born, and now it is here, cheated and swindled of its birthright.

Women, women, arouse yourselves! If you are not so unfortunately placed, it is but a trick of circumstances.

If you are well clothed, well fed, today it is these women who have helped you to do so. And are you doing anything for these women? Ministers of the Gospel, what are you doing for these women and unborn babies? You reformers, conservatives, call yourselves what you wish,

what are you doing for this condition of society which demands of its unborn such an awful price of birth? Do you think your duty is done if you have clothed or fed one or fifty of these victims for a day, a week, a year, perhaps? Oh, mothers, sisters, women of this land, awake! How can you slumber when these conditions exist?

The day is passed when we can selfishly protect our own. In order to protect our own, in matters of disease, in conditions where milk, water, food or drugs are unsafe for our own loved ones, we cannot hesitate to fight for all, for we realize we can only save our own by so doing.

Again I say: Women, awake, awake to this system and help these downtrodden women back to their homes, back to their little ones, back to that which belongs to every mother—the care and love of her offspring.

By the way, do we ever hear the male element, who so strongly advocate "home duty" for the "bridge" mother, advocate home duty for these women? It is only the "bridge" women's children who need the care and attention of the mother, evidently.

Let us turn to the mother we have just beheld with her new-born infant. What is to be done with this subnormal piece of humanity? Does it not need even more care and attention than a normal child? But what does it get? Dire poverty drives this mother back again to the factory (no intelligent person will say she goes willingly). It is the fear of the loss of a job, debts and another mouth to feed that compels her to leave this newborn infant in the care of any one who has the room to keep it. Any friend or neighbor who works at home can take care of this little waif.

We all know the type—hard working, ignorant, with scarcely time to attend to the actual needs of her own.

The little one is placed here among the filth and debris of the workshop. It grows through babyhood and childhood motherless, fatherless and moral-less.

Of course, there are other alternatives, such as the charity kindergartens, but always the mother on the industrial field is cheated of love and care of her offspring.

In this age of Christianity, in this advanced twentieth century, when science has discovered the methods of breeding the finest horses and dogs, when science has turned its searchlight upon every form of plant life; upon the different parasites which tend to destroy plant life, what has it done toward extricating the parasite poverty, which destroys humanity? Senator Owen, of Oklahoma, said recently:

"We spend $500,000 to exterminate the insect that eats the cotton plant.... We have millions for conservation of the forests. Our Senators and Representatives jump to their feet the minute one mentions raising the tariff on wool or on steel, but we can get no such interest when it comes to saving human lives...."

If man would do his duty to Human Beings, as well as he does to Things, we [would] have no need of leaving the little ones to the care of strangers all day. We would have no need of giving our babies' lives to the factory before they are born. We would have no need of seeing our little ones grow up in mental, moral, and physical starvation. We would have no need of suffering the awful pangs, of seeing them go out of the world, so soon, pangs which are so much keener than those which bring them here. All these and a thousand other sufferings and evils could be stamped out if man would do his duty.

There are two steps toward progress in this universe—organization and specialization. Mothers, let us not consider we are progressing. Let us not consider we have done our duty, until we have first organized. Then let us specialize in attacking and stamping out this social system.

We must organize—all women who have one vestige of love in our hearts, for children; all women who have interest in the progress of humanity; all should organize, but not alone.

We should organize under a banner which advocates our cause. We should join the party (there is but one, the Socialist party) which solves the problems of each and every grievance of these working women and children.

First, we should demand through this party absolute equality of the sexes.

Second, to put back the mothers or the prospective mothers, into the homes, and give her a pension sufficient to keep herself and child. I can hear wails of protest concerning this last demand, on the ground that it will make vagrants of the fathers or will give them more time and money for saloons. All I can ask is that you look into this, find out what has been done, and the results you will find will remove that argument completely. It has been the experience of those interested in this, that when a man feels his burdens partly lifted, he is mentally and physically better fitted for life's work.

Third, to support and educate the children, and by support we mean clearly to feed and clothe them, until they are at least 16 years of age.

Fourth, to keep every child, regardless of race, color, or creed, in this United States out of all factories, mills and all industrial fields which tend to dwarf the physical or mental development of the children.

Last, to pull down completely this system, which mangles and stunts the minds, morals and bodies of our boys and men; to fight this awful viper, which undoes all our life's work, to crush and stamp it out forever. This, mothers, is a duty which must go hand in hand with our every day duties, or our life's work will be all for nothing.

SIGNIFICANCE

Sanger's essay fights against stereotypes about the role of women; nineteenth-century writers such as Sarah Stickney Ellis in England and Catharine Beecher in the United States had championed the cult of domesticity and true womanhood—the idea that a woman's place is in the home, with no political or economic power, her primary functions as mother, wife, and housekeeper. In working with poor women and middle-class women who had no control over reproduction and in taking into account the toll on their bodies and the divided attention and money needed to support large families, Sanger developed a viewpoint that stressed the need to examine family conditions as they were—not the ideal—and to give families the power to make changes to improve the health of the mothers and children within families.

In blending her viewpoint with Socialism, however, Sanger simultaneously appealed to some immigrants who were members of the Socialist party while alienating middle-class reformers who agreed with her positions on birth control, but were firmly anti-Socialist and viewed Socialism as a threat to American security. Sanger allied herself with the labor movement and pushed for women's equality. Her personal dealings with mothers who experienced health problems from repeat pregnancies and childbirth, and with children who died from simple childhood diseases and malnutrition, led her to the conviction that capitalism caused such inequalities in society and that Socialism needed to prevail, for the good of the family and society as a whole.

Sanger's appeal spoke to educated middle-class women; by speaking to them as fellow mothers, she urged these women to view poor and immigrant women as mothers, trying desperately to raise healthy sons. In pointing to the inevitable fate that children of the poor faced—destructive factory work at young ages—Sanger attempted to show how child labor laws were crucial in helping all families. The Keating-Owen Child Labor Act would not be passed for another five years after Sanger wrote this essay, and it would be ruled unconstitutional; not until 1938 did the Fair Labor Standards Act help to prevent the "little mothers" Sanger discusses.

Sanger's final five points, a manifesto of sorts, includes issues of relevance in modern society. Women's equality, economic recognition of stay-at-home parent work, child subsidy payments such as those seen in Canada or Scandinavian countries, child labor protections, and regulation and control of capitalism are themes subject to debate and consideration in the first decade of the twenty-first century; the impact of each on the family is significant. While advances have been made toward women's equality and child labor regulation, Sanger's key points continue to stimulate policy discussions. Economic support for families and children from federal agencies, such as Temporary Aid to Needy Families, and nutrition programs for women and children and childcare subsidies did not exist in Sanger's time—these programs came about in part as a result of progressive reformers such as Sanger. As she continued to write and to work on making birth control accessible for all families, Sanger set the stage for a reshaping of the size of American families, women's control over their bodies, and a change in gender roles.

FURTHER RESOURCES

Books

Beecher, Catharine. *A Treatise on Domestic Economy*. Boston: T.H. Webb, 1842.

Ellis, Sarah Stickney. *The Women of England: Their Social Duties and Domestic Habits*. London: Fisher, Son, & Co., 1839.

Hindman, Hugh D. *Child Labor: An American History*. Armonk, N.Y.: M.E. Sharpe, 2002.

Matthews, Glenna. *"Just a Housewife": The Rise and Fall of Domesticity in America*. New York: Oxford University Press, USA, 1989.

Sanger, Margaret. *The Autobiography of Margaret Sanger*. Mineola, N.Y.: Dover Publications, 2004.

———. *The Selected Papers of Margaret Sanger*. Champaign, Ill.: University of Illinois Press, 2002.

Zelizer, Viviana. *Pricing the Priceless Child: The Changing Social Value of Children*. Princeton, N.J.: Princeton University Press, 1994.

Nursery for Field Working Mothers

Photograph

By: Underwood & Underwood

Date: c. 1919–1930

Source: © Underwood & Underwood/Corbis.

About the Photographer: Underwood & Underwood was a stereograph company, producing high-quality images from 1882 through 1920. The stereograph technique involved taking photographs using two cameras positioned slightly apart; the resulting images, when viewed correctly, took on a three-dimensional aspect. The photograph is now a part of the Corbis Corporation's collection.

INTRODUCTION

By the end of 1917 in Russia, the former monarchy was abolished and the Bolshevik Party came into power. The Russian Revolution led to a complete overhaul in Russian government and society. A civil war between "Reds"—Bolsheviks who advocated strong Marxist ideals in reshaping society—and "Whites"—more moderate socialists, monarchists, and conservatives who disagreed vigorously with the rigid changes desired by the Bolsheviks—ended by 1922. The Reds won, and immediately set forthwith a plan to restructure Russian society with Communist ideals in mind.

The civil war had devastated Russia, with more than 15 million killed and the economy gutted. With the civil war so close on the heels of World War I, the Bolsheviks faced a country that had spent nearly a decade at war, and famines as well as peasant work stoppages caused severe disruptions in the food supply.

The communist ideal for the Russian family focused on the mother and the father as workers for the state; with the weight of personal economic responsibility lifted, according to the communist ideal, the family could be bonded to one another via common affection, rather than as an economic unit. Mothers as well as fathers were expected to work in factories, farms, and offices. To meet this end, a nationwide network of children's nurseries—*creches*, were formed by the Soviet Government's Institute for the Protection of Women and Children to manage the child care of infants and small children.

The creches were widespread. Each creche held approximately one hundred children, and parents were not guaranteed a spot in the creche for their children; in the early years after the revolution and civil war there were waiting lists for children to enter the creche. The creche was located on the farm where parents worked or close to factories, in part so that breastfeeding mothers could take breaks to nurse their children.

When a mother entered the creche with her child, she undressed the child, then handed him or her to a nurse—the child's "home clothes" were not permitted in the creche. The nurse, specially trained to work with children in the nursery, then took the child,

Nursery for Field Working Mothers: A woman tends to babies in a collective nursery for the children of field workers while the children's mothers and other farm workers march past them on their way to work, in the Soviet Union, 1920s.
© UNDERWOOD & UNDERWOOD/CORBIS.

dressed it in approved clothes, and started the day's schedule. Ill children who were contagious were not permitted in the creche, and, if a mother brought a child with fleas or bugs, the mother and child were sent home, an official inspected the home, and the family was reprimanded until the home was clean and the child was free of bugs.

Children were separated by age, bathed, dressed, and fed immediately after being surrendered by their mothers, and kept to a strict schedule each day. As this photograph shows, in many instances nursery workers maintained the creche outdoors, to give the babies as much fresh air as possible.

NURSERY FOR FIELD WORKING MOTHERS
See primary source image.

SIGNIFICANCE

Creches were instruments of the state. In Soviet Russia the government slowly assumed many functions previously performed by the family, such as child care, eldercare, maternity care, and child socialization. In addition, Soviet reorganization led to the breakdown of the traditional, patriarchal, multi-generation house-

Nursery workers serve tea to a group of Southwark toddlers at a day nursery for the children of working mothers. Borough, Southwark, London, England, United Kingdom, 1928. © HULTON-DEUTSCH COLLECTION/CORBIS.

hold. As urbanization increased, and the government focused on rapid industrialization, the new family that emerged was a small, two-parent family of creation, without older relatives living in close proximity.

The creche workers focused not only on caring for the children, but also counseled mothers on proper child care at home and worked to indoctrinate mothers with Soviet ideals. Equality for men and women was an important tenet in Soviet Russia, and mothers who expressed extreme attachment to their children were counseled on their role as a worker in society, and the contribution they made for the glory of communism and Soviet progress. In addition, creche workers taught mothers that the creche was better than home life: The children received proper nutrition; were made to exercise vigorously for muscle development; were taught to live on a strict schedule in such a way as to foster good factory, military, or farm work habits; and were provided with medical care by the doctors and nurses on staff at creches who caught illness before it became too severe. With this counsel, the creche served to spread Soviet propaganda, reduce child mortality, and help with the transition from family life under the old monarchical system to the ideal Soviet society, with

women, men, and children serving the interests of the state through conformity, hard work, and equality.

By freeing women from the tasks of motherhood so that they could work for the state, the Soviet ideal of the family conformed to Frederich Engels's ideal in his 1884 book *The Origin of the Family, Private Property and the State*: private household and child care functions would become a societal, rather than personal, responsibility, allowing the state to manage and raise the children. Each Soviet infant was assigned to a creche ideally, though shortages of slots for children was a problem in the early Bolshevik years. By raising children as members of the state rather than as private citizens under parental supervision, and by training mothers to relinquish control over their child's basic child care and to follow creche guidelines for care at home, the emerging Soviet state sought to break the pre-Soviet family pattern and establish a new paradigm for family and societal relations.

FURTHER RESOURCES
Books

Clements, Barbara Evans. *Bolshevik Women*. Cambridge, U.K.: Cambridge University Press, 1997.

Engels, Fredrich. *The Origin of the Family, Private Property and the State*. Hottzingen-Zurich, Germany, 1884.

Goldman, Wendy Z. *Women, the State and Revolution: Soviet Family Policy and Social Life, 1917–1936*. New York: Cambridge University Press, 1993.

Heywood, Colin. *A History of Childhood: Children and Childhood in the West from Medieval to Modern Times*. Oxford and Cambridge, U.K.: Polity Press, 2001.

Withrow, Alice. *Protection of Women and Children in Soviet Russia*. New York: E.P. Dutton, 1932.

Wood, Elizabeth A. *The Baba and the Comrade: Gender and Politics in Revolutionary Russia*. Bloomington: Indiana University Press, 2001.

Zelizer, Viviana. *Pricing the Priceless Child: The Changing Social Value of Children*. Princenton, N.J.: Princeton University Press, 1994.

Unfair to Babies!

Advertisement

By: Erik Hans Krause

Date: November 8, 1938

Source: Krause, Erik Hans. *Unfair to Babies!: A Helpless Infant Can't Go on Strike: It Depends on Your Care.* Rochester, NY: WPA Federal Art Project, 1938. Courtesy of the Library of Congress.

About the Author: Illustrator Erik Hans Krause was born in Germany in 1899 and moved to New York City. Unable to find work during the Great Depression, he joined the Works Progress Administration as a graphic artist.

INTRODUCTION

Until the twentieth century, most governments did not get involved with child care. In the 1930s, as parents suffered under the financial stresses of the Great Depression, the U.S. government broke from tradition to promote good child care habits and to offer day care to working parents. Artists from the Works Progress Administration, such as Erik Hans Krause, created posters to further government goals.

Formal child care was rarely needed in preindustrial societies. In these agrarian societies, adults placed their offspring nearby while they worked and used various devices such as cradleboards to keep very young children out of harm's way. In general, child care was not seen as the exclusive task of mothers, but was shared with fathers, older siblings, servants, and neighbors.

These arrangements became strained as market-based demands sped up the pace of production and factories drew workers out of homes and fields. It became difficult for family members to blend child care with paying work. Reformers deplored situations in which children were either left alone or in the care of sisters only slightly older than their charges. In response, the first nurseries were established in the 1890s. However, not all reformers believed that the nurseries and day care were best for children. The U.S. Children's Bureau, founded in 1912 as a branch of the federal government, called for a policy that would support mothers so they could stay at home with their children. By 1930, nearly every state had passed some form of mother's pension law but the pensions were not enough to support low-income mothers. The coming of the Great Depression forced more mothers into the work force and led to increased government efforts to protect the health and safety of children.

PRIMARY SOURCE

UNFAIR TO BABIES!

See primary source image.

PRIMARY SOURCE

Unfair to Babies!: A Works Progress Administration poster promoting proper baby care. THE LIBRARY OF CONGRESS.

SIGNIFICANCE

Public opinion in the United States has been slow to accept the ideas of maternal employment and child care. Although the popular media frequently reported on the spread of "latchkey children," such stories typically blamed working mothers, not a lack of affordable child care. Day care centers set up by the federal government during the Great Depression and World War II lost funding shortly after the war ended. In 1946, Congress refused to pass the Maternal and Child Welfare Act that would have continued federal funding for child care. During the Korean War, Congress approved a public child-care program as a way of enabling women to take the place of military-age men in the workforce but then refused to appropriate funds

Farmer John Barnett and his family, who struggled to survive during the Great Depression on their farm in Woodward, USA, 1935. PHOTO BY KEYSTONE/GETTY IMAGES.

for it. Finally, in 1954, Congress found a non-controversial approach to child care when it approved the child-care tax deduction. This legislation enabled low to moderate income families to deduct some child care costs from their income taxes provided that the child care services were needed to permit the taxpayer to hold gainful employment.

By the late 1960s, Congress began urging poor and low income women to enter the workforce. It did so to reduce the number of Americans receiving welfare in the form of Aid to Families with Dependent Children (AFDC). In 1996, the Personal Responsibility and Work Opportunity Act replaced AFDC. Though more public funds for child care became available than ever before, problems of supply and quality continue to limit access to child care for welfare recipients who are compelled to take employment. Moderate income families must cope with ever-rising cost for child care. For all families, the quality of child care is compromised by the high rate of turnover in the field as the result of low pay and poor benefits.

FURTHER RESOURCES

Books

McKinzie, Richard D. *The New Deal for Artists*. Princeton, NJ: Princeton University Press, 1973.

Michel, Sonya. *Children's Interests/Mother's Rights: The Shaping of America's Child Care Policy*. New Haven, CT: Yale University Press, 1999.

Rose, Elizabeth. *A Mother's Job: The History of Day Care, 1890–1960*. New York: Oxford University Press, 1998.

Come to Denver

The Chance of Your Lifetime

Advertisement

By: Anonymous

Date: 1953

Source: Photo by MPI/Getty Images.

About the Author: Getty Images is a provider of photographs, film footage, and digital content, including current and historical photographs and political cartoons. The photographer is unknown.

INTRODUCTION

The arrival of European explorers and settlers in North America set the stage for numerous conflicts, none more significant than the clash fueled by the two cultures' differing views on property ownership. To the Europeans, real estate was an asset to be owned, bought, sold, and exploited for profit, while the Native Americans viewed land as a public asset. This fundamental difference in understanding led to numerous conflicts as explorers attempted to buy, and in some cases take, land from the natives, who failed to grasp the significance of the transactions they were being offered.

As the open ranges of North America were carved into farms, ranches, and estates, the indigenous people found themselves being gradually confined to small sections of their previous migratory ranges. In some cases they attacked settlers in an attempt to regain the use of their lands, while in others they pursued legal action against the government. Beginning in 1786, Indian tribes ceding land to the U.S. government kept or "reserved" a portion of the land for their own use. These "reservations" were intended to become the

COME TO DENVER.

THE CHANCE OF YOUR LIFETIME !

Good Jobs

Retail Trade
Manufacturing
Government-Federal, State, Local
Wholesale Trade
Construction of Buildings, Etc.

Happy Homes

Beautiful Houses
Many Churches
Exciting Community Life
Over Half of Homes Owned by Residents
Convenient Stores-Shopping Centers

Training

Vocational Training
Auto Mech., Beauty Shop, Drafting,
Nursing, Office Work, Watchmaking
Adult Education
Evening High School, Arts and Crafts
Job Improvement, Home-making

Beautiful Colorado

"Tallest" State, 48 Mt. Peaks Over 14,000 Ft.
350 Days Sunshine, Mild Winters
Zoos, Museums, Mountain Parks, Drives
Picnic Areas, Lakes, Amusement Parks
Big Game Hunting, Trout Fishing, Camping

PRIMARY SOURCE

Come to Denver: This 1953 advertisement is intended to encourage Native Americans to leave their reservations and move to urban areas where there would be more opportunities for education and employment. PHOTO BY MPI/GETTY IMAGES.

Indians' new homes as they transitioned from a nomadic life to a fixed agricultural existence.

During the 1800's the federal government took greater liberties in confiscating Indian land and relocating the residents, sometimes by force. A report prepared in 1908 by the Commissioner of Indian Affairs listed 161 separate reservations in the United States, covering a total land area of 52 million acres. Life on these reservations was starkly different than Indian life before. With no experience as farmers many Indians found the new lifestyle frustrating and distasteful, and in time the reservations became centers of poverty and illiteracy. Numerous solutions were tried and numerous initiatives launched but despite federal financial support the reservations remained poverty-stricken and backward.

Through the decades numerous efforts were made to improve the lives of Native Americans, some urging them to remain on the reservations, others encouraging them to move. Some cities, recognizing the limited opportunity on the reservations and needing laborers to fuel their growing economies, began recruiting Indians to leave the reservations and relocate.

PRIMARY SOURCE

COME TO DENVER

See primary source image.

Princess O-Me-Me, a Chippewa, Sun Road, a Pueblo, and Chief Whirling Thunder, a Winnebago, look over Chicago's skyline from the roof of the hotel Sherman. © UNDERWOOD & UNDERWOOD/CORBIS.

SIGNIFICANCE

Despite decades of effort, Indian reservations in the early twenty-first century remain among the poorest and least healthy regions in the United States. The 1990 census found almost two million Native Americans and native Alaskans living in the United States; of that total almost 400,000 live on reservations. Across the country Native Americans have the highest rates of unemployment, poverty, and health problems of any ethnic group. A study conducted from 1991 to 2000 found that Native American residents of the Warm Springs Reservation in Oregon were living an average of only 47 years, significantly less than the Oregon average of 74 years. While the leading cause of death for all Americans is heart disease, a study of 5,000 Native Americans in Oregon found that the leading cause of death was automobile accidents, seventy-two percent of which involved alcohol. Researchers continue probing the reasons for native Americans' lower life expectancies.

Shannon County, South Dakota, has the unpleasant distinction of being the poorest county in the nation. In 1997 the county, populated mostly by Native Americans, had an unemployment rate of 80 percent and a per capita income of less than $3,500. Many of the residents live in surplus army housing moved to the reservation in the 1960s. While many of the houses should be condemned, tribal leaders are reluctant to do so, because such a decision would leave the residents homeless. In some houses residents without electricity run extension cords from neighboring homes to provide winter heat.

American Indian reservations share many of the social and economic problems faced in most inner city areas, including high crime rates, poor health, and deteriorating infrastructure. While the United States provides ongoing financial assistance to Indian tribes, these programs lack strong political backing, and in recent years have experienced funding cuts. The large number of Native Americans on reservations makes most potential solutions extremely expensive, and decades of failure have created skepticism that the problems can be solved at all.

Despite numerous failures, efforts to improve Native Americans' lives continue. In 2005, the American Indian College Fund launched an unlikely ad campaign encouraging young Native Americans to remain on reservations and complete their education at tribal colleges. These institutions, offering tribal cultural education along with traditional academic subjects, provide an unexpected benefit: Statistics show that students who attend these colleges are several times more likely to graduate than those who leave the reservation to attend a university.

FURTHER RESOURCES

Books

Dandekar, Vinayak Mahadev. *The Indian Economy, 1947–92: Population, Poverty and Employment.* New York: Sage, 1996.

Frantz, Klaus. *Indian Reservations in the United States: Territory, Sovereignty, and Socioeconomic Change.* Chicago: University of Chicago Press, 1999.

Tiller, Veronica E. Velarde, ed. *Tiller's Guide to Indian Country: Economic Profiles of American Indian Reservations.* Albuquerque, N.Mex.: BowArrow Publishing, 2006.

Periodicals

Rivera, Hector, and Roland Tharp. "A Native American Community's Involvement and Empowerment to Guide Their Children's Development in the School Setting." *Journal of Community Psychology* 34 (2006): 435–451.

Staba, David. "State to Forgo Cigarette Tax to Keep Peace with Indians." *New York Times* (March 21, 2006): B5.

Steakley, Lia. "Washington State Offers Mea Culpa for Hood Canal Delay." *Engineering News Record* 256 (June 12, 2006): 16.

Web sites

National Park Service. "Indian Reservations in the Continental United States." <http://www.cr.nps.gov/nagpra/DOCUMENTS/ResMAP.HTM> (accessed July 16, 2006).

U.S. Department of Justice. "Policing on Indian Reservations." July 2001 <http://www.ncjrs.gov/pdffiles1/nij/188095.pdf> (accessed July 16, 2006).

If Union Families Don't Look for the Union Label, Who Will?

Union advertising campaign, 1975

Advertisement

By: International Ladies' Garment Workers Union

Date: c. 1975

Source: *Library of Congress.* "American Memory Project." 2006 <http://memory.loc.gov/ammem/awhhtml/awpnp6/d15.html> (accessed July 3, 2006).

About the Author: The International Ladies' Garment Worker Union (ILGWU) was founded in 1900. Throughout much of its history the ILGWU was one of America's largest and most influential unions. In the face of a decline in production by domestic garment manufacturers, the ILGWU ceased independent operations after its merger with a larger textile workers union in 1995.

INTRODUCTION

The American union movement can trace its roots to the mid-nineteenth century, when small groups of workers began to associate into larger federations. The most prominent of the early trade unions was the Knights of Labor, founded in 1869. It was surpassed in national influence by the American Federation of Labor, founded by Samuel Gompers (1850–1924) in 1886. The early unions were engaged in ongoing conflicts with the manufacturing concerns of the time, and there was little legislative protection for the advancement of union interests; bitter and often violent confrontations were the norm during labor disputes in this period.

The ILGWU was founded in New York city in 1900 to advance the interest of the overwhelmingly female constituency among the employees in the American garment trades. In particular, the ILGWU had a large percentage of Jewish and foreign workers in its membership. A terrible fire at the Triangle Shirtwaist Company in New York in 1911 caused the deaths of more than 140 employees, most of whom were young female immigrants. A subsequent inquiry revealed that these deaths were attributable to the workers becoming trapped in the factory as the fire spread; the workers could not escape because the factory doors were kept locked by management during working hours. This evidence of corporate disregard for the safety of the workers was a significant spur to the growth of the ILGWU membership.

The ILGWU leadership became engaged in a series of ideological battles after 1920, as socialist, communist, anarchist and other radical elements endeavored to gain control of the union. David Dubinsky (1892–1982) became the ILGWU president in 1932, a post he held until 1965. Dubinsky charted a moderate political course that stressed conciliation over conflict with the garment industry owners. The ILGWU was also known for its progressive approach to issues such as education and the securing of extended health benefits for its membership. By 1940, the ILGWU was one of the most powerful American unions, with more than 300,000 members. Eleanor Roosevelt, wife of President Franklin Roosevelt was one of a number of influential supporters of the ILGWU.

The ILGWU reached its membership peak in 1969, when it had more than 450,000 members. In the 1970s, the influence of the ILGWU declined as the

If union families don't look for the union label, who will?

(Anything without it is either non-union or non-American.)

Made in U.S.A.

International Ladies' Garment Workers' Union

■ **PRIMARY SOURCE**

If Union Families Don't Look for the Union Label, Who Will?: An advertisement encouraging union workers to purchase only union-made clothes for their families. The picture illustrates several generations of women checking for the "union-made" label. THE LIBRARY OF CONGRESS.

American garment industry began to suffer the combined adverse effects of lower cost foreign imported clothing and the relocation of American owned garment factories to countries that could supply cheaper labor. In 1995 the ILGWU was reduced to a membership of 125,000, and it merged with a larger textile union to create UNITE, the Union of Needletrades, Industrial and Textile Workers. In 2004, UNITE was itself amalgamated into a larger entity, partnered with a hotel workers union.

■ **PRIMARY SOURCE**

IF UNION FAMILIES DON'T LOOK FOR THE UNION LABEL, WHO WILL?

See primary source image.

A late nineteenth century label for union workers cigar box, 1898. © MUSEUM OF THE CITY OF NEW YORK/CORBIS.

SIGNIFICANCE

The growth in the stature of American labor unions occurred against a remarkable backdrop of worker–management confrontation that began in earnest with the Haymarket Square riots in Chicago in 1886. In the years that followed, violent strikes were common in the United States, from the battles between the miners' unions and mine owners in the western United States, to the coal mining, textiles and silk workers strikes in the East. The prominence achieved by the ILGWU after 1900 is notable for the lack of violence involved in any of its disputes with the individual factory owners in the garment industry.

Throughout its history, and most prominently during the tenure of David Dubinsky as its president, the ILGWU had a membership comprised of more than 75 percent women; its executive leadership positions remained occupied almost exclusively by men.

However, the ILGWU was regarded as a union that was a strong advocate of women's interests, particularly in its efforts to advance programs such as pay equity and employee health benefits. Prior to the entry of the United States into World War II, the ILGWU and Dubinsky established the Jewish Labor Committee (JLC), an organization that assisted Jewish interests in occupied Europe both during and after the war. Many Jews, primarily women and children, were rescued from the consequences of the German occupation through the efforts of the JLC.

The ILGWU's 1975 advertisement is a significant public pronouncement in a number of respects. The photograph emphasizes the connection between the predominately female garment makers and the female influence and interest in the purchase of the garments produced. The four generations of women pictured symbolize the history of American garment manufacture represented by this physical time line that spans the entire period of the ILGWU's existence.

There is an irony implicit in the advertisement in that the four generations of white women depicted were not representative of the composition of the union membership in 1975. In the early days of the ILGWU , its membership was largely composed of female Jews and Italians; by 1975, the membership demographic had shifted to a mixture predominately made up of persons of black, Hispanic, and Asian heritages.

At the time of the advertisement's publication in 1975, the ILGWU was beginning to feel the pressure from lower priced offshore clothing imports that compelled the union to seek a merger in 1995. In 1975, the union attempted to counter the pressure on the industry posed by lower offshore garment prices with the statement that appears in the lower left corner of the photograph, where in reference to the importance of the union label, the reader is told that anything without the label is either non-union or un-American. The reference to un-American products is an interesting appeal to American patriotism; the ILGWU message is clearly articulated—patriotism is worth more than the simple sticker price. This argument was a central feature of the American domestic automobile manufacturing sector advertising campaigns after 1980, when that industry faced similar foreign pressures.

The rise and the decline of the influence of the ILGWU mirrored the progress of the American economy over its lifetime. The ILGWU prospered during the Great Depression as the Roosevelt New Deal legislation known as the *National Industrial Recovery Act* provided significantly greater guarantees regarding the right to organize a labor union than had its predecessors. Under the most union friendly regime to that time in American history, the ILGWU grew to exceed 300,000 members by 1940.

The decline of the ILGWU reflected the overall state of American organized labor into the 1990s. In 1953, more than 35 percent of all private sector workers belonged to a union. When the United States Bureau of Labor Statistics began tracking national union membership in 1983, 20.1 percent of all American workers belonged to unions. By 2005, the number had fallen to 12.5 percent. The 2005 statistics confirmed that New York state had the highest percentage of union workers at 26 percent of its workforce; in North Carolina and South Carolina, less than 3 percent of all labor is union based.

The American trend is reflected to a lesser degree in the economies of Britain and Canada, both traditionally union-friendly nations. Union membership in Britain has declined from 31 percent to 26 percent since 1995; in Canada during the same period, the decline in union membership has been measured at more than 3 percent.

FURTHER RESOURCES
Books

Parmet, Robert. *The Master of Seventh Avenue: David Dubinsky and America's Labor Movement.* New York: New York University Press, 2005.

Tyler, Gus. *Look for the Union Label: A History of the International Ladies' Garment Workers Union.* Armonk, New York: M.E. Sharpe, 1995.

Web sites

Syracuse University. "Fannia Mae Cohen—Education Leader in Labor and Workers Education." 2006 <http://www-distance.syr.edu/long.html> (accessed July 3, 2006).

Washington Post. "Labor's Divisions Widen as Membership Declines." March 7, 2005 <http://www.washingtonpost.com/ap-dyn/articles/A11958–2005Mar6.html> (accessed June 25, 2006).

Carmen Carter Remembers Turkey Farming

Essay

By: Carmen Carter

Date: January 1, 1982

Source: Zaslow, Jeffrey. "Carmen Carter Remembers Turkey Farming." *Michigan History Magazine.* 66 (1982).

Fred Schmeeckle, a Farm Security Administration borrower and dryland farmer, with his family in Weld County, Colorado, October 1939. © CORBIS.

About the Author: Carmen Carter was a wife and mother during the Great Depression of the 1930s. She and her family survived by bartering, buying and selling, and making do with less.

INTRODUCTION

The Great Depression of the 1930s marked the lowest point for the American economy. While an open market economy invariably expands and contracts over time, no recession before or after the Great Depression has approached the scale of this painful era in American life. From 1929 to 1932, the average American's income fell by forty percent, and families that had been contemplating a bright future were suddenly facing potential disaster. Banks failed, wiping out family savings, and unemployment soared to twenty-five percent, leaving many homes without an income. In an era before most government aid programs or bank insurance, many families found themselves facing the real possibility of starvation.

The causes of the Depression are fairly well understood, and most economists assume the massive crash resulted from a series of poorly timed events that converged to decimate the U.S. economy. The stage for the collapse was set in the 1920s, which brought a massive economic boom in the United States. The soaring stock market in particular was a source of fascination to Americans of all walks of life, who found that they could borrow money "on margin" to invest in stocks. In this way, a small investment could quickly multiply, and stock prices soon reached levels which defied any realistic assessment of what the underlying companies were worth.

With so many Americans borrowing to invest in the markets, the Federal Reserve foresaw a potential recession if stocks declined. To prevent this possibility the agency began raising interest rates in 1928, but in 1929 the stock market crashed, cutting the market value of American business by 10% in a single day. In response many firms and individuals cut back on spending plans, setting the stage for a rapid decline in the size and prosperity of the U.S. economy.

The following years brought more bad news, as more banks failed and the economy continued to contract. As prices plummeted, businesses continued to cut back, firing workers and shutting down production. Soon the decline entered a vicious cycle which would continue for much of the decade.

■ PRIMARY SOURCE

In 1929 Orlo and I had been married two years and had a year old son, Douglas. We were just nicely getting started in the turkey raising business on his parents' farm near Bridgeton. We had about a thousand young turkeys that spring and we bought feed on credit during the growing season and paid for it when we sold the turkeys at Thanksgiving time.

But that year was different. The newspapers were full of news about bank closing, businesses failing, and people out of work. There was just no money and we could not sell the turkeys. So we were in debt with no way out.

But when we read about the bread lines and soup kitchens in the cities, we felt we were lucky because we raised our own food. Our house was rent free, just keep it in repair. Our fuel, which was wood, was free for the cutting. Then our second child, Iris, was born and our biggest expense was doctor bills. However, this too was solved when our doctor agreed to take turkeys and garden produce for pay.

About that time my husband and a friend started operating a crate and box factory near Maple Island. After expenses they were each making about a dollar a day. Food was cheap. Coffee was 19 cents a pound, butter 20 cents, bacon the same, with a five pound bag of sugar or flour about 25 cents.

Gasoline was five gallons for a dollar so for recreation we would get into our 1926 Overland Whippet and go for long rides. We also had an Atwater Kent radio we could listen to when we could buy batteries for it.

I had always liked to write poetry so I decided to submit some to Grit, a weekly newspaper. I was delighted when they accepted them and paid me $2 each for them. That money bought a large bag of groceries at that time. I continued to write for Grit for several years.

Orlo finally got a job as a mechanic at a garage in Grant. He earned $15 a week and for us the Depression was over. But it taught us to really appreciate what we had.

SIGNIFICANCE

Families in the Great Depression often found themselves pulling together to survive. Fathers took whatever work they could find, and businessmen frequently found themselves grateful for low-paying work as manual laborers. Mothers also took in odd jobs when they could, though with so little cash in the economy few people could afford to pay for anything. The children of the era grew up in a world of need, and many of them grew up to be habitual savers.

Family entertainment during the Depression typically consisted of whatever diversion could be found. The Depression coincided closely with the popularization of the radio; by 1935 two-thirds of American homes had a radio in the house, and many Depression-era families spent their evenings at home listening to free entertainment. Serials such as Little Orphan Annie and The Shadow brought listeners back week after week, and as the economic slump lingered President Roosevelt took to the airwaves, addressing the nation in a series of Fireside Chats that lasted through World War II.

Americans had little recovery time after the depression ended; World War II followed close on the heels of the downturn, simultaneously reviving the U.S. economy and throwing America into the bloodiest conflict in history. By the time the war ended the economy was booming and the United States had emerged as the world's most powerful nation.

In the years since the Depression, numerous safeguards have been created to prevent a repeat of the economic tumble of 1929. Banking regulations have been tightened, and bank deposits are now federally insured, protecting depositors in the event of bank failure. Stock purchases are also more tightly regulated, and buyers must invest a minimum of 50%, rather than borrowing up to 90% as they once could. The Federal Reserve also acts much more quickly now to guarantee liquidity in the money supply during crises, such as in the days following the 2001 terrorist attacks. The vastly increased size of the U.S. economy also helps provide economic stability, making another catastrophic depression far less likely.

FURTHER RESOURCES
Books

Freedman, Russell. *Children of the Great Depression*. New York: Clarion Books, 2005.

Kyvig, David E. *Daily Life in the United States, 1920–1940: How Americans Lived during the Roaring Twenties and the Great Depression*. Chicago: Ivan Dee Publisher, 2004.

McElvaine, Robert S. *The Great Depression: America 1929–1941*. New York: Three Rivers Press, 1993.

Periodicals

Gillett, Rachel. "Music of the Great Depression." *Journal of Popular Culture* 39 (2006): 501–503.

Kimball, Richard. "The March of Spare Time: The Problem and Promise of Leisure in the Great Depression." *Journal of American History* 9 (2006): 268–269.

Web sites

Herbert Hoover Presidential Library and Museum. "Gallery Six: The Great Depression." <http://hoover.archives.gov/exhibits/Hooverstory/gallery06/gallery06.html> (accessed July 11, 2006).

Public Broadcasting Service. "The Great Depression." <http://www.pbs.org/wgbh/amex/dustbowl/peopleevents/pandeAMEX05.html> (accessed July 11, 2006).

University of Wisconsin. "Crashing Hopes: The Great Depression." <http://us.history.wisc.edu/hist102/lectures/lecture18.html !view July 11, 2006).

Mother Superior

Book review

By: Pamela Paul

Date: April 16, 2006

Source: Paul, Pamela. "Mother Superior." *The New York Times*, (April 16, 2006).

About the Author: Pamela Paul is an author and journalist. Her most recent book, *Pornified: How the Culture of Pornography is Transforming Our Lives, Our Relationships and Our Families* (2005), was named one of the Best Books of the Year by *The San Francisco Chronicle*. She is also the author of *The Starter Marriage and the Future of Matrimony*, (2002); her next book, on the parenting business, is expected to be published in 2008.

INTRODUCTION

Most three and four year olds are convinced that their parents are super-human. Fathers are often seen as exceptionally strong, with professional sports potential, while mothers are viewed as the source of the world's very best cookies and medical care, the latter often provided in the form of a kiss. As they grow, children normally come to recognize their parents'

limitations and weaknesses, sometimes short-changing their parents for the work they did. And once they become parents themselves many children find a new respect for their own parents and the tremendous effort required to raise children and keep a home functioning.

While toddlers mistakenly see their mommies as able to accomplish anything and everything, a raging debate continues over whether women are actually capable of doing everything; more specifically the question asks whether one woman can simultaneously fill the often competing roles of mother, wife, homemaker and professional. A related debate continues over which of these roles is even appropriate for women.

The feminist agenda of the 1960s and 1970s was based on a fairly straightforward contention: Women had been relegated to a single career path (homemaking) and that had to change. To these feminist crusaders, women were owed the same set of career choices which men had always enjoyed, and in the feminist framework the choice facing women should be a simple one: homemaking or career. Convinced that most women would immediately flee the chores of domestic oversight if given the chance, feminists focused their efforts on giving women that option.

The reality of this effort has turned out quite differently than expected. Women today enjoy more opportunities in the workplace than ever before; women have served at the highest levels of state and federal government and political commentators now discuss the possibility of a female president without a second thought. For the strongly career-minded women, the feminist revolution has opened up numerous new opportunities.

But not all women have benefited equally. In one sense feminism achieved its goal: The percentage of America women in the labor force doubled in the last half century, rising from thirty percent in 1950 to sixty percent in 2002. Women now make up almost half the paid workforce, and though some pay disparities remain, women's progress has been rapid.

In 1989, Arlie Hochschild published an extensive survey of male and female roles in the home. She concluded that women, despite taking jobs outside the home, remained largely responsible for domestic tasks as well. Her book, entitled *The Second Shift*, made the case that women, despite their economic contributions and employment freedom, were still expected to shoulder the lion's share of work in the home. From her perspective, women had gained new jobs, but had been forced to continue doing the old as well, making

Mrs. Krantz of Minneapolis beams at her apple pie baking in the oven, 1951. © BETTMANN/CORBIS.

their new situation actually more difficult than many women of previous generations.

As to the question of whether women are able to be both mothers and professionals, the statistics remain relatively constant for women with small children. Depending on the age of the children involved, from fifty-eight percent to seventy-two percent of mothers work outside the home, suggesting that due to necessity or desire, many women are choosing to do it all.

■ PRIMARY SOURCE

The subjects of matrimony, housewifery, child rearing and Martha may seem mundane, but for many women, they arouse fierce emotions—bitterness, contempt, envy, nostalgia, desire—depending on one's domestic arrangements and level of dissatisfaction. We are still waging war and wagging fingers over diapers and bed

sheets. Caitlin Flanagan, a staff writer for *The New Yorker*, is right out there on the front line—and feeling the fire. Among a certain clique of mothers-in-the-know (media feminists, mommy bloggers, Urban Baby posters), Flanagan isn't just disliked—she's reviled.

The Internet bristles with animosity toward Flanagan's written opinions and personal choices. Familiar charges of elitism hound the well-heeled, former stay-at-home mom for judging others' household decisions. Holes in her arguments are pried open to ridicule. She is called an amateur, a know-it-all and a nobody unjustly handed perches at both *The Atlantic Monthly* and *The New Yorker*.

But here's what I think really bothers Flanagan's critics: No matter how vociferously they disagree with her on some things, they find themselves agreeing with much of what she writes. One suspects that were such readers to open Flanagan's essay collection, "To Hell With All That," without knowing its provenance, they would page through it eagerly, nodding and sighing and chuckling to themselves. Flanagan writes with intelligence, wit and brio. She's likable.

It turns out Flanagan is an equal-opportunity satirist, neither the feminist turncoat nor nouveau Phyllis Schlafly that her detractors presume her to be. (Flanagan calls herself a liberal who is "not entirely incapable of good old-fashioned feminist rage.") Her résumé—former teacher and failed novelist—is hardly that of an ideological crusader. So while she mocks the radical feminist Alix Kates Shulman, author of a 1970 marriage contract that called for absolute equality at home, as someone who has "earned herself a spot on almost any short list of very silly people," she goes on to explain: "I am reluctant to make too much sport of her document.... I am a wife and mother of young children in a very different time from Shulman's, a time that is in many respects more brutal and more brutalizing … a time that has made hypocrites of many contemporary feminists in ways that Shulman and her sisters in arms were not hypocrites." What's more: "You have to give those old libbers their due: they spent a lot of time thinking about the unpleasantness of housework and the unfairness of its age-old tendency to fall upon women."

Flanagan's major points—that most women hate housework but want to be good at it anyway, that women say they want men to contribute an equal share in the domestic arena but don't want to sleep with the kind of men who do, that married people should have sex—are hardly revolutionary (or counterrevolutionary, for that matter). What makes Flanagan's book original and vital is that she is a realist, willing to acknowledge the essential gray areas in too often polarized positions. As it stands, sensitivities are so attuned to the slightest insult of any one of women's myriad work-life choices that Flanagan's simplest observations—for example, when a woman works something is lost—are taken as an indictment of working women. Yet any working mother can see the truth in such a statement: time spent working = less time with children = something lost. What's appalling is that pointing this out raises such ire.

Not that Flanagan doesn't deserve some censure. Though she is less feisty in the book than in her magazine articles (here she dismisses a controversial creed she wrote for *The Atlantic* on working women and nannies as "convoluted and slightly insane" and herself at the time as "a fanatic with a nut cause"), she commits some of the same mistakes. She surrounds kernels of truth with cavalier half-truths; calls assumptions into question, but doesn't always provide convincing answers. Take dinnertime. In order to resurrect that font of nostalgia, the postwar family dinner, she writes, "we would need to revive the cultural traditions that created it: the one-income fam-

ily, the middle-class tendency toward frugality, and the understanding that one's children's prospects won't include elite private colleges and stratospheric professional success, both of which may hinge on tremendous achievements in the world of extracurricular activities." It's not so much what Flanagan says, but what she fails to mention. No faulting an economy that demands overwork and skimps on child-care benefits. No questioning that Mom's the one who cooks. No challenging the idea that kids must be scheduled to the max in order to make the Ivies.

To all this, Flanagan might say, "I was being ironic!" But she's also trying to make important points. These are undermined by a feckless urge to poke fun. It's easy to seize on one of her throwaway lines, however amusing, as evidence of insensitivity or ignorance. She can come across as a self-satisfied classroom prankster, grinning at her own impolitic gibes and daring her targets to cry.

Even as Flanagan's detractors can take her too seriously, Flanagan doesn't always take herself seriously enough. The book is somewhat repetitive, as if she assumes readers won't bother to read straight through, surprising because the previously published material has been substantially reworked. More distressing are Flanagan's contradictions, which make it easy to dismiss her. Like many contrarians, she spends too much time arguing against everyone else and not enough time considering her own opinions. She rails against doctrinaire feminists, yuppie parents, stay-at-home moms, political correctites and wives who won't put out. But she's often as guilty as her targets. She mocks boomers who pal around with their kids, then takes vacations at family-friendly resorts where she splashes about with her children. She laments her generation's failures at household maintenance, then admits she's "far too educated and uppity to have knuckled down and learned anything about stain removal" herself. Self-deprecating, yes. But also hypocritical.

Yet even dyed-in-the-wool Flanagan haters might enjoy reading her make fun of herself. Mocking her own stint as a listless stay-at-home mom with nanny, she writes: "I would switch on MSNBC, feed and change the babies, and put on the teakettle. At last, the 'Today' show would begin. I would watch straight through and with an intensity of which the producers could only have dreamed." When she leaves her "oppressive apartment," she is frantic, lurching around with pent-up frustration. Loathing the inner housewife, indeed.

The love in the book's subtitle seems to refer to Flanagan's mother. At heart, "To Hell With All That" is an attempt to understand, commemorate and legitimize her mother's life as a housewife and nurse, two underappreciated female vocations. She opens her book in the emptiness of her recently dead and dearly loved mother's home and closes with the difficulty she has facing cancer without the comfort of a mother's presence. If it seems as if Flanagan wants to turn back the clock to an era of capable and solicitous homemakers, you can understand why.

SIGNIFICANCE

Hochschild's book, which portrayed women as overworked household servants putting in far more hours each week than their husbands, helped revive the feminist arguments of the 1970s. Once again women appeared to be carrying the load for men who were unwilling to do their fair share.

Astute observers correctly noted several flaws in Hochschild's reasoning, including the fact that she chose to count only certain tasks as housework, largely ignoring household tasks usually done by men. They also critiqued her assumption that men and women each work 40 hours per week outside the home, despite the fact that studies show the average full-time employed man working eight hours more per week than his female counterpart.

In 2006, the University of Michigan Institute for Social Research (ISR) released a study addressing the shortcomings of Hochschilds work. This new study found that when the noted differences are factored into the comparison, men actually contribute slightly more hours each week to supporting the family. The ISR study concluded that men have actually been doing their fair share of work at home, when adjusted for hours worked outside the home, for the past four decades.

Women today face a tyranny of choice. While their grandmothers were generally content to limit their education, marry, and start a family, today's women must make numerous decisions about education, home, and career. These choices are further complicated by the mixed messages women receive, some praising them for their career success and others commending them for their child raising efforts. Whereas women of the past faced no options, today's women frequently find themselves struggling with too many options, unsure how to accomplish them all and unwilling to give any of them up.

Despite extensive academic research on the topic, the question of whether men do their fair share of housework or not remains a subject of intense disagreement in many homes.

FURTHER RESOURCES

Books

Edelman, Hope. *Motherless Mothers: How Mother Loss Shapes the Parents We Become*. New York: Harper Collins, 2006.

Hoff, Christina. *Who Stole Feminism? How Women Have Betrayed Women*. New York: Touchstone, 1994.

Lukas, Carrie. *The Politically Incorrect Guide to Women, Sex and Feminism*. Washington, D.C.: Regnery Publishing, 2006.

Periodicals

De Pasquale, Lisa. "Exploding the Antiquated Feminist Agenda." *Human Events* 15 (2006): 96–98.

Pollitt, Katha. "Mommy Wars, Round 587." *Nation* 283 (3) (2006): 10.

Ruderman, Ellen G. "Discussion of "Nuturance and Self-Sabotage: Psychoanalytic Serspectives on Women's Fear of Success." *International Forum of Psychoanalysis* 15 (2006): 96–98.

Web sites

University of California, Santa Barbara. "Black American Feminism." April 6, 2006 <http://www.library.ucsb.edu/subjects/blackfeminism/> (accessed July 10, 2006).

University of Michigan News Service. "U.S. Husbands are Doing More Housework While Wives are Doing Less." <http://www.umich.edu/news/index.html?Releases/2002/Mar02/chr031202a> (accessed July 10, 2006).

Virginia Tech University: Center for Digital Discourse and Culture. "Feminist Theory." 1999 <http://www.cddc.vt.edu/feminism/> (accessed July 10, 2006).

Health, Housing, and Family Planning

Health, Housing, and Family Planning

While concerns of health, housing, and family planning may now seem like unrelated concerns, to social reformers in the United States and Britain at the turn of the twentieth century, these were inseparable issues. Reformers championed the removal of slums and tenements, as they linked poor housing to poor public health. Some promoted family planning and birth control methods as a solution to urban crowding and poverty. While some of these reform crusades may have been motivated by ethnic prejudice (especially against recent immigrant populations) and eugenics, their basic ideas on suitable housing, family planning rights, and family health revolutionized both the family and society in the modern era.

Reformers viewed the family as a valuable agent of positive social change. The temperance movement advocated family abstention from alcohol as a means of promoting general health, religious ideals, and protecting women and children by reducing incidences of domestic violence. "The Fruits of Intemperance," "Family Temperance Pledge," and the "Shadow of Danger" all feature images associated with anti-alcohol campaigns directed at family participation or family safety.

Much like temperance crusaders, public health officials and the medical community also targeted the family. Beginning in the 1890s, major U.S. cities began to replace tenement slums with specially designed apartment blocks with indoor plumbing, clean water, more ample ventilation, and working windows—all features that were considered to improve the health of families living in the developments. The trend of family-centered housing boomed after World War II (1938–1945). The explosion of the suburbs removed affluent and middle-class families from densely populated urban areas. Advertisements billed suburban developments as clean, safe, and family-oriented. However, after the birth of the suburbs, many low-income and minority families remained in urban neighborhoods that had seen scant improvements since the turn-of-the century reforms.

Finally, the birth control revolution fundamentally transformed the modern family. Family planning permitted couples to have fewer children. Advances in medicine and disease control reduced childhood mortality, making the once-common loss of a child an increasingly scarce event as the twentieth century progressed. Early family planning advocates targeted low-income and minority (often immigrant) populations, but use of birth control rapidly spread among women of all socio-economic classes.

Today, family planning and medicine once again intersect. China instituted a controversial one child per family policy to limit population growth. In developed nations, family planning has gained a new meaning—planning and attempting to have children. "A Few Good Sperm" and "Babies on Ice" describe new and sometimes contentious options for having children and forming families.

The Fruits of Intemperance

Photograph

By: Nathaniel Currier and James Merritt Ives

Date: 1870

Source: Corbis Corporation

About the Author: This image was first published in 1870 by the famous New York lithographers Nathaniel Currier (1813–1888) and James Merritt Ives (1824–1895), the most famous lithographers in American history. Lithography, the first efficient method of mass producing color images, was discovered in 1798 and introduced to the United States in 1830. It is a form of printing in which a flat stone *(lithos)* or metal plate is specially treated to transfer ink to paper pressed against it. Currier and Ives became famous through the publication of hundreds of evocative landscapes and scenes of American life.

INTRODUCTION

The manufacture and consumption of alcohol was a prominent feature of American society from its earliest colonial times. In an age when water was frequently unsafe to drink, the predominantly English colonists brought their affinity for beer to the New World, and the beverage was consumed by all ages and classes of persons.

Distilled spirits were a later addition to the colonies. Rum imported from the West Indies proved so popular that a distillery was established in Boston in 1700. With the arrival of settlers of Scotch and Irish descent, grain whiskeys were produced in homemade stills. Whiskey also had the advantage of being easier to store than beer.

Alcohol consumption in America increased in popularity after Independence; the period between 1790 and 1830 was the era of the heaviest drinking in American history. Alcohol was consumed at all hours of the day and in every setting. Modern studies suggest that the average adult per capita consumption of pure alcohol during this period was over 7 gallons (27

The Fruits of Intemperance: A Currier & Ives lithograph depicts a happy and prosperous family. © MUSEUM OF THE CITY OF NEW YORK/CORBIS.

liters) per year; in 2005 average consumption was 2.3 gallons (8.5 liters). Alcohol was widely believed to be a healthy and stimulating beverage in any form.

The first significant opposition to the widespread consumption of alcohol was found in the publications of Dr. Benjamin Rush of Philadelphia, who launched a series of pointed attacks on hard liquor consumption in 1792; as with other early temperance advocates, Rush favored beer and wine instead. The only religious opposition came from the Methodist and Quaker denominations.

The next significant challenge to the prevailing American attitude towards alcohol came as a result of the massive wave of German immigration that occurred between 1830 and 1860. Almost 900,000 Germans settled in the United States during this period, bringing with them their affinity for lager beer; names such as Coors, Schlitz, Budweiser, and Busch are a part of this brewing legacy today. The popularity of German brews served as a point of emphasis for the temperance (moderation in alcohol)

proponents. The concept of temperance as alcohol in moderation slowly gave way to a movement advocating total abstinence.

Temperance moved from the margins of American society into a mainstream conflict with the founding of the American Temperance Society in 1826, which became an early leader in the ever-widening war. In the popular illustration *Tree of Intemperance*, published by A.D. Fillmore in 1855, the biblical images of the serpent, tree, and temptation are interwoven with the progressive growth of alcohol into an assortment of vices.

The Fruits of Intemperance is an illustration that is significant both as artwork and in its relationship to the temperance forces that were beginning to assert their influence over American society in 1870. It portrays an intemperate father, the putative head of the household, who has wholly failed his lost and defenseless family by leading them down a dark and barren roadway. This theme of failure and destitution is a recurring one in the temperance artwork of this period.

■ PRIMARY SOURCE

A Currier & Ives lithograph showing the alledged effects of alcohol on family life, used as propaganda by the temperance movement. © MUSEUM OF THE CITY OF NEW YORK/CORBIS.

PRIMARY SOURCE

FRUITS OF INTEMPERANCE

See primary source image.

SIGNIFICANCE

The Fruits of Intemperance was produced not to advance the interests of the temperance movement, but because Currier and Ives had identified a market for works that appealed to temperance supporters. The image's publication is evidence that this market was significant, or Currier and Ives would not have printed it—in fact, they described themselves as publishers of popular images.

The most powerful arguments advanced by the temperance movement were those that attacked alcohol as a destroyer of the family unit, both in terms of relationships and the ability of a father to support his family. This argument was not built upon scientific studies or empirical evidence, but the immorality of alcohol and the resulting exposure of all family members to sinful behavior. In contrast, modern arguments against excessive alcohol consumption focus on the physiological effects; morality is seen as a private, not societal issue. Modern medicine defines alcoholism as a disease, which would not fit the 1870 temperance supporters' moral template.

The state of Maine first banned the sale of alcohol in 1851; by 1860 there were 12 "dry" states The progress of the temperance movements was slowed by the Civil War (1861–1865). By 1870, temperance forces were well established in every state of the Union, and the movement had abandoned the notion that moderate alcohol consumption was acceptable—alcohol was characterized as a poison in any amount. This was not built upon medical theories, just as there was no science to support alcohol's health benefits, as had been the accepted basis for its widespread consumption in the early 1800s.

The strength gained by the temperance movement across America by 1870 was not founded entirely upon the connection that it advanced between alcohol and sin. In many respects the temperance movement was beginning to be accepted by people who saw temperance as promising something entirely positive—a better, happier, and more productive society. Unlike the other important social causes of the era, including the extension of full citizenship rights to blacks, the agitation for women's rights, and the political battles that arose following the Civil War, temperance bred an optimistic outlook and it was accordingly a less bitter and divisive issue.

The social issues captured by *The Fruits of Intemperance* are those that would be advanced more aggressively in the years following 1874 with the formation of the Women's Christian Temperance Movement (WCTU).

FURTHER RESOURCES

Books

Frick, John. *Theatre, Culture and Temperance Reform in Nineteenth Century America*. New York: Cambridge University Press, 2003.

Pegram, Thomas R. *Battling Demon Rum: The Struggle for a Dry America 1800–1933*. Chicago: Ivan R. Dee, 1998.

Lender, Mark Edward, and James Kirby Martin. *Drinking in America: A History*. New York: The Free Press, 1983.

Web sites

Wisconsin Historical Society. "Brewing and Prohibition." <Brewing and Prohibition.>http://www.wisconsinhistory.org/turningpoints/tp-051/?action=more_essay> (accessed June 19, 2006).

Family Temperance Pledge

Pledge

By: Anonymous

Date: c. 1887

Source: *Library of Congress*. "An American Time Capsule: Three Centuries of Broadsides and Other Printed Ephemera." 2004. <http://memory.loc.gov/cgi-bin/query> (accessed June 27, 2006).

About the Author: The Library of Congress is the oldest federal cultural institution in the United States. The Library of Congress, through its American Memory project, maintains numerous collections of historical material stored in a variety of media, all of which are accessible to the public.

INTRODUCTION

The formation of the American Temperance Society in 1826 was the first significant mass organizational effort by the various forces favoring either a restriction or an outright prohibition on the manufacture, consumption, and sale of alcohol in the United States. The temperance movement at that time had a strong moral and Christian outlook, as the connection

FAMILY TEMPERANCE PLEDGE

TEMPERANCE LEADS TO VIRTUE & HAPPINESS

INTEMPERANCE TENDS TO POVERTY AND RUIN.

"WINE IS A MOCKER, STRONG DRINK IS RAGING: AND WHOSOEVER IS DECEIVED THEREBY IS NOT WISE".

We the undersigned Family of _____ Agree with each other that we will not Buy, Sell or Use intoxicating Liquors as a beverage and will use our Best Endeavors to Curtail and Prevent the Sale and use of the Same by others.

Signatures.　　　Signatures.　　　Signatures.

PRIMARY SOURCE

Family Temperance Pledge: A Family Temperance Pledge form, with blank lines for family members to sign promising not to buy or drink intoxicating liquors, 1885. THE LIBRARY OF CONGRESS.

was ceaselessly drawn by these advocates between excessive alcohol consumption and sin.

The Washingtonians, a temperance organization based in Washington, D.C., between 1840 and 1850, are a testament to the popular temperance trends of the time. The Washingtonians advocated a more individual and reflective approach to the temperance question; their philosophical views had many similarities to the modern Alcoholics Anonymous programs. The influence of the Washingtonians waned after 1850 as the broader notions of alcohol as a vice and a destroyer of Christian families was the ascendant temperance philosophy.

A number of very active temperance societies were formed in the 1850s, a development concurrent with the statutory prohibition of all alcohol in twelve American states by 1855. At the end of the Civil War in 1865,

the temperance movement resumed its drive to rid America of alcohol. The zeal of the temperance forces was heightened by the formation of the Women's Christian Temperance Union (WCTU) in 1874. The WCTU professed a desire to work toward the elimination of alcohol with "a mother's love", an outlook that was reflected by the powerful grassroots nature of the efforts of the WCTU. From early in its history, the WCTU asserted significant influence in the political arena concerning the temperance question.

The Family Temperance Pledge was a device encouraged by the WCTU and other Christian temperance reformers; it is likely that hundreds of thousands of these documents were signed by individuals and families committing themselves to abstention from alcohol in the period between 1870 and the enactment of the Volstead Act, which created nationwide Prohibition in 1919. The expression "to take the pledge" became a part of the American lexicon during this period.

The Family Temperance Pledge was intended not only to secure a promise by the taker of the pledge that they would abstain absolutely from the consumption of any alcoholic beverage; the pledge was also commonly linked to broader moral principles through a connection to the family Bible. The family Bible was often the most important possession in a Christian home, as in addition to its religious content and sacred words, the Bible was the record of all of the important dates and events in a family history. When the Family Temperance Pledge was inserted into a family Bible, it was presumed to be a promise made to God that the pledge would be honored.

PRIMARY SOURCE

FAMILY TEMPERANCE PLEDGE

See primary source image.

SIGNIFICANCE

The Family Temperance Pledge as depicted here is significant in that it dates from 1887, a midway point between the 1874 founding of the powerful WCTU, a body that successfully waged a grassroots campaign for the elimination of alcohol across America, and 1893, the year in which the politically influential Anti-Saloon League was formed. The pledge was a most effective reinforcement of the temperance message in hundreds of thousands of American homes during this period.

The "taking of the pledge" was the reinforcement relied upon by temperance advocates to convert the words of a supporter into a concrete action. It was assumed by all parties involved in the temperance campaigns that a person who executed the pledge, often in the presence of family with the family Bible near at hand, would be subject to strong moral influence to maintain the pledge. The family Bible had an iconic status in all Christian households of the period.

The pledge was an approach consistent with the other means used by the WCTU, led by Frances Willard (1838–1898), to promote its cause. A common promotional tactic was the assembly of local WCTU members for a prayer, after which the group would then enter a saloon and forcefully request that the saloon be closed. This assertive but nonviolent technique was very popular throughout the entire temperance campaign as waged by the WCTU.

The Family Temperance Pledge depicted here is significant in the manner in which the moral issues related to both abstinence and alcohol consumption are portrayed. The taking of the pledge on one hand is connected to virtue, happiness, and obvious prosperity. Alcohol is portrayed on the opposite side of the document as the root cause of a dilapidated neighborhood and a sordid lifestyle; poverty and ruin are pictured as the inevitable result of drink. It is notable that the scenes illustrated on the pledge are consistent with American temperance in this period—there are two stark choices offered, with no shades of grey and no room for compromise or a middle ground.

Consistent with the concept of becoming a part of a movement or a common cause, the pledge taker also assumed the additional obligation to use his best efforts to either curtail or prevent the use of alcohol by others. The pledge taker was making a commitment to seek out other drinkers and assist them in undergoing a conversion to the temperance movement. This obligation parallels the approach taken by Christian evangelists in both the 1880s and in modern times—the temperance advocate was expected to be not only a believer, but also a missionary for the movement.

Although it has adopted a much lower public profile in recent history, the WCTU continues today as the oldest women's association in North America. The WCTU still advocates abstinence from the consumption of alcohol.

The Anti-Saloon League, directed by Wayne Wheeler (1869–1927), was another organization that grew from the broader temperance movement. It was able to become the most powerful political lobby in the United States due to the grassroots commitment of a large segment of the American population to the temperance cause, furthered through the proliferation of the Family Temperance Pledge.

In addition to the implementation of Prohibition through the passage of the Volstead Act in 1919 and the Eighteenth Amendment, after 1900 a number of prominent Americans, including John D. Rockefeller, William Randolph Hearst, and Henry Ford, made public their support for Prohibition, elevating a grassroots movement to one with the endorsement of a segment of the elite of American society.

The moral temperance crusade in 1880s America is unlikely to be successfully replicated today. While the American constitutional freedoms of expression and association permit temperance to be advanced as a modern national cause, the alcohol industry and its prominent place in the American economy have rendered alcohol manufacturing a sizable contributor to the tax revenues received by the federal and state governments.

The final significance of the Family Temperance Pledge is in its implicit characterization of alcohol abuse. Alcohol was regarded by the temperance followers as a personal vice and an example of immorality. This view is in contrast to the modern medically based definition of alcohol abuse as a disease that requires treatment and ongoing support for the alcoholic.

FURTHER RESOURCES

Books

Mattingly, Carol. *Well Tempered Women*. Carbondale, Ill.: Southern Illinois Press, 1998.

Szymanski, Anne-Marie. *Pathways to Prohibition: Radicals, Moderates and Social Movement Outcomes*. Raleigh, N.C.: Duke University Press, 2003.

Web sites

George Mason University. "P.T. Barnum As a Temperance Speaker." 2006 <http://chrm.gmu.edu/lostmuseum/lm/48> (accessed June 27, 2006).

State University of New York at Potsdam. "History of Anti-Alcohol Movements in the U.S." 2006 <http://www2.potsdam.edu.hansondj/controversies/1124913901.html> (accessed June 27, 2006).

Buying the Family a Home

Newspaper article

By: Anonymous

Date: August 3, 1907

Source: "Buying the Family a Home." *Cleveland Journal*. 5 (August 3, 1907): 4.

About the Author: The *Cleveland Journal* was a weekly newspaper published in Cleveland, Ohio, from 1903–1913. The paper focused primarily on news and issues of interest to African-American readers.

INTRODUCTION

Owning a home brings numerous advantages not available to those who rent their residence. While rents typically increase each year (and can be increased at whatever rate the landlord chooses) mortgage payments are often fixed for the life of the loan; in most cases wages continue to rise, making the mortgage payment a gradually decreasing portion of the homeowner's income. In addition, real estate usually appreciates in value, meaning that a home often becomes an increasingly valuable asset and often serves as the cornerstone of financial security.

Real estate owners also benefit at retirement: A paid-off house provides rent-free living during a phase of life when income typically decreases, as well as providing a durable asset that can be left to one's heirs. Home owners also receive federal income tax deductions, reducing the actual cost of ownership; in practice this difference means that a $900 rent payment actually costs more for many Americans than a $900 mortgage payment, which may be offset by several hundred dollars in tax savings.

Beyond the purely financial advantages, home ownership also brings numerous social and psychological benefits. For many Americans, buying their first home is a milestone of independence, and owning a home is considered by many to be the defining element of what has figuratively been called the American Dream.

Home ownership is not enjoyed equally by all ethnic groups in America. In 1900 home ownership was less common than it is today, although it was becoming more widespread. At that time 46% of white men owned their own homes; among African-American men the rate was much lower—only 20%. Recognizing the many economic and social problems associated with renting, some black writers began urging their readers to take the necessary steps to become home owners.

PRIMARY SOURCE

Buying a Home for the Family

What is a family without a home? Where is home? Dryden tells us that "Home is the sacred refuge of our life." If we are to judge by the place some people live, there is very little sacredness about it.

Home, like wine, grows better with age. The memories of years help to make home sacred. To go back to the spot where one's childhood was spent, and there to look upon familiar scenes, every fence post has a meaning. Can life offer richer blessings? Such privileges are made possible by wise parents saving of their means and buying an abiding place. Then the rains may come, the winds blow and beat upon that house, but it will still stand in father or mother's name.

Not so with the rented house. From month to month every family living in a rented house is taking a chance of being in the street the succeeding month. Especially is this true in cities, as Cleveland, where extensive building is always in progress.

A family poses for a photo in front of their newly purchased home. © ROYALTY-FREE/CORBIS.

The best way to keep a roof overhead is to own the roof.

More people in Cleveland should own homes. Thousands and thousands of dollars are spent for rent that should go towards buying homes. People who own real estate are always considered more substantial citizens than those who merely own a single van of household goods. Why not? The best time to start to buy a home is NOW.

SIGNIFICANCE

The twentieth century was a period of increasing home ownership among virtually all racial groups, as more Americans shifted from renting homes to buying them. However the gap between white and black home ownership remained largely static during the first forty years of the century. Among the many causes of this discrepancy was rampant housing discrimination. Blacks were often turned away when attempting to rent in white neighborhoods, and new housing developments often included language in their advertising making it clear that blacks could not build there; such restrictions tended to keep blacks from enjoying better neighborhoods and more rapid property appreciation.

Blacks also frequently encountered difficulties when applying for a mortgage to build or purchase a home. In many cities banks would refuse to make business or home loans in certain lower-income neighborhoods, a then-legal practice known as *redlining*. Banks that employed this practice argued that these less-affluent neighborhoods were more dangerous, hence loans in these neighborhoods carried a higher level of risk. However such claims were rarely substantiated and the policies typically resulted in black homeowners facing added difficulty in buying a home. The practice also meant that segregated neighborhoods tended to stay segregated.

Redlining and other discriminatory housing practices were common until the 1960s, but despite these barriers black home ownership rates inched up. In 1968, shortly after the death of civil rights leader Martin Luther King, Jr., Congress passed the Fair Housing Act, explicitly prohibiting discrimination in housing rentals, sales, and all other real estate–related activities. As a result, black home ownership rates climbed sharply.

By 1990 black home ownership rates had risen dramatically, reaching 52%. The ownership gap of 26 percentage points in 1900 had fallen to fewer than 20. Other studies have found slightly lower rates of home ownership, though all available data suggests that as of 2005 the black ownership rate remains approximately 50%.

In the twenty-first century, home ownership remains a common goal for Americans; in 2004 the Census Bureau reported ownership rates in America at an all-time high of 69%, although the gap between white and black home ownership rates remained greater than 20%.

FURTHER RESOURCES
Books

Ong, Paul M. *The Effects of Race and Life-Cycle on Home Ownership: A Study of Blacks and Whites in Los Angeles 1970 to 1980*. Los Angeles: Graduate School of Architecture and Urban Planning, University of California, Los Angeles, 1986.

Stacey, William. *Black Home Ownership: A Sociological Case Study of Metropolitan Jacksonville*. New York: Praeger, 1972.

Struyk, Raymond J. *Determinants of the Rate of Home Ownership of Black Relative to White Households*. Washington, D. C.: Urban Institute, 1977.

Periodicals

Bajaj, Vikas, and Ron Nixon. "For Minorities, Signs of Trouble in Foreclosures." *New York Times*. 155 (February 22, 2006): A1, C8.

Collins, William, and Robert Margo. "Race and Home Ownership: A Century-Long View." *Explorations in Economic History*. 38, no. 1 (January 2001): 68–92.

Anonymous. "Single Black Female, in Her Own House Women on the World Stage." *The Economist*. 373 (November 18, 2004): 35.

Web sites

Harvard University: Joint Center for Housing Studies. "Publications: Home Ownership." <http://www.jchs.harvard.edu/publications/homeownership/index.html> (accessed July 3, 2006).

U.S. Census Bureau: Housing Vacancies and Homeownership. "Annual Statistics:2004." February 17, 2005 <http://www.census.gov/hhes/www/housing/hvs/annual04/ann04t20.html> (accessed July 3, 2006).

Upjohn Institute for Employment Research. "Black-White Segregation, Discrimination, and Home-Ownership." August, 2001 <http://www.upjohninst.org/publications/wp/01-71.pdf> (accessed July 3, 2006).

The Shadow of Danger

Poster

By: Strengthen America Campaign

Date: c. 1925

Source: Strengthen America Campaign. "The Shadow of Danger." Corbis, 1925.

About the Author: The New-York-based Strengthen America Campaign included a number of organizations devoted to the merits of Prohibition. This Prohibition advertisement poster is a part of a collection of images maintained in the archives of Corbis Corporation, a worldwide provider of visual content materials to such communications groups as advertisers, broadcasters, designers, magazines, media organizations, newspapers, and producers. The creator of the advertisement is unknown.

INTRODUCTION

The legal prohibition against the manufacture, possession, sale, or consumption of alcohol or related products was created with the passage of the National Prohibition Act of 1919, more commonly known as the Volstead Act. Prohibition was enshrined as an amendment to the United States Constitution in 1920 by way of the 18th Amendment.

The Volstead Act was the culmination of a fierce political and social battle waged for the capture of American public opinion that had lasted almost one hundred years. The consumption of alcoholic beverages had been a significant part of American daily life since the earliest colonial times. In the English

The Shadow of Danger

If you believe that the traffic in Alcohol does more harm than good *help stop it!*

Strengthen America Campaign

Strengthen America Campaign - 105 East Twenty Second Street, New York City, N.Y.

■ PRIMARY SOURCE

The Shadow of Danger: A Prohibition-era poster shows a whiskey bottle casting a "shadow of danger" over a mother and child, suggesting the harm that alcohol can do to families. © CORBIS. REPRODUCED BY PERMISSION.

colonies, the brewing and the drinking of beer was an accepted social custom in all classes of society. American statesman Benjamin Franklin once observed that for him, beer was proof of God's love for his human creatures.

Drunkenness and its associated disruptions to both family life and the maintenance of gainful employment was known to be a pressing social concern throughout the United States in the early 1800s. Temperance groups were formed to promote the moderate consumption of alcohol, with the popular argument favoring temperance being the protection of families. Various Protestant and evangelical religious groups soon embraced the notion that abstinence, and not mere moderation, was the only viable means to rid society of the evil of alcohol abuse. The melding of religious forces and social opposition to alcohol led to

the creation of the Women's Christian Temperance Union (WCTU) in 1879; the WCTU soon had a membership in the hundreds of thousands across the United States.

After 1900, the increasing influence of the WCTU was buttressed by organizations such as the Anti-Saloon League, founded in Ohio in 1893 and led by the influential Wayne Wheeler (1869–1927). The evangelist William Ashley (Billy) Sunday (1862–1935) was a popular preacher who attracted a large national following while he campaigned forcefully for Prohibition in his revival meeting style.

Prohibition had gained ground well before the passage of the Volstead Act, as three states and a number of local municipalities had banned alcohol prior to 1910.

The national campaign for Prohibition turned in favor of the temperance/abolitionist forces when Wheeler and the Anti-Saloon League adopted the tactic of using its significant church membership base to assert pressure on both local and national political candidates; Wheeler directed the prohibition supporters to vote solely regarding the candidate's stand on Prohibition. By the time that the Volstead Act was before Congress in 1919, Wheeler was widely regarded as one of the most influential persons in American politics.

The forces favoring American Prohibition were so significant in 1919 that even a veto of the legislation by President Woodrow Wilson could not deflect the path to the desired constitutional amendment ratified on January 16, 1920.

■ PRIMARY SOURCE

THE SHADOW OF DANGER

See primary source image.

■

SIGNIFICANCE

The image depicted on the Prohibition advertisement is an extension of the primary argument advanced in favor of the extension of Prohibition after the passage of the Volstead Act—the protection of innocent family members from the consequences of the abuse of alcohol by another family member, most often the father and husband. As in the advertisement, alcohol is portrayed as a form of poison, not a controllable or social beverage.

The advertisement is aimed at one of the significant constituencies of the movement that had led to the enactment of Prohibition. Unlike most political causes in the modern age, Prohibition was achieved exclusively through intensive regional grassroots campaigns that attracted little, if any, significant corporate support.

It may be said that with Prohibition, American society traded one set of compelling social problems associated with alcohol for an entirely different but equally vexing group. The first was the fact that Prohibition did not eliminate alcohol abuse in the United States. Clandestine and illegal alcohol consumption using products produced by bootleggers led to thousands of incidences of death or serious injury caused by the consumption of poisonous homemade alcohol mixtures.

The most visible and notorious issue arising from the introduction of Prohibition was the blatant disregard for the law itself across America. It is estimated that for every 260 arrests for violations of the Volstead Act, a single conviction resulted. The use of homemade stills and other private manufacturing of alcohol was a significant cottage industry in America after 1920. The rise of illegal drinking establishments, known variously as clip joints, blind pigs, and speakeasies, became a part of the folklore of the period.

The combined effect of off-shore liquor smuggling, particularly from Canada, and the entry of organized criminals into the liquor industry created significant gaps in law enforcement through bribery and other forms of corruption. Throughout the 1920s, a public perception existed that many law, police, and political officials were complicit in the work of the liquor smuggling industry. Underworld leaders such as Al Capone acquired both wealth and international notoriety during the Prohibition period.

As powerful as the forces favoring Prohibition had grown prior to 1920, public support for Prohibition declined dramatically as the 1920s advanced. Influential and articulate social commentators, such as Baltimore newspaper columnist H.L. Mencken, repeatedly painted Prohibition as a folly and a waste of government resources that encouraged crime. Mencken, who coined the phrase *The Bible Belt* as a derogatory reference to American religion, praised the virtues of alcohol in his daily columns as vigorously as he attacked the Anti-Saloon League. By 1932, seventy-four percent of Americans favored a repeal of the 18th Amendment. With the election of President Franklin Roosevelt in 1932, a known "wet" or person who opposed Prohibition, the repeal forces achieved their victory in 1933.

A poster urging people to vote in favor of the prohibition of alcohol. DAVID J. & JANICE L. FRENT COLLECTION/CORBIS.

The enduring significance of the Prohibition campaign can be found in the limitations to alcohol sale and consumption that persisted in many American jurisdictions long after the repeal of the 18th Amendment. Eighteen states maintained either complete or partial prohibitions against alcohol until 1966. As of 2006, sixteen states have retained centralized control over the sale and distribution of alcohol from government-authorized outlets.

The modern attitude of the American public at large toward alcohol also reflects a number of concepts at the heart of the institution of Prohibition in 1920. One example is the greater severity of the criminal consequences for alcohol-related misconduct. Every American state and the federal government devotes public funds to combat offenses such as drinking and driving as well as to educate the public concerning the risks of alcohol excess. Drinking and driving has been elevated from the status of a social indiscretion in the period prior to the Second World War to fully criminal conduct that attracts significant legal sanctions in every American state. In a sense, these measures are reminiscent of a true temperance movement, as opposed to outright abstinence from alcohol.

While there are elements of American society, such as the marketing of professional sports, that tend to promote alcohol as a lifestyle choice, a Bloomberg Institute study conducted in 2005 indicated that forty-two percent of all Americans consumed little or no alcohol in the course of a year. While a return to Prohibition is doubtful, it seems equally unlikely that America will ever accept alcohol in the unconditional fashion of early America.

FURTHER RESOURCES

Books

Behr, Edward. *Prohibition: Thirteen Years that Changed America*. New York: Arcade Publishing, 1997.

Hirshfield, Al and Gordon Kahn. *The Speakeasies of 1932.* New York: Applause Books, 2003.

Rogers, Mary Elizabeth . *Mencken: The American Iconoclast*. New York: Oxford University Press, 2005.

Web sites

State University of New York/Potsdam. "National Prohibition of Alcohol in the United States." <http://www2.potsdam.edu/hansondj/Controversies/1091124904.html> (accessed July 22, 2006).

PRIMARY SOURCE

Your Family Needs Protection Against Syphilis A poster encouraging examination and treatment for syphilis. THE LIBRARY OF CONGRESS.

Your Family Needs Protection Against Syphilis

Poster

By: Anonymous

Date: c. 1936

Source: *American Memory Project, Library of Congress.* "Your Family Needs Protection Against Syphilis." <http://memory.loc.gov/ammem/wpaposters/wpahome.html> (accessed July 15, 2006).

About the Artist: The United States Library of Congress is the nation's official library, responsible for collecting and organizing historically significant documents, photographs, and digital media.

INTRODUCTION

Syphilis is a sexually transmitted bacterial disease. It has few symptoms during its initial stage, and in many cases individuals who are unaware of their infection pass the disease to others. The disease's second stage includes symptoms such as a rash, headaches, fatigue, and patchy hair loss. In many cases the symptoms are similar to other conditions, complicating the diagnosis.

In its final stage, syphilis may produce few outward symptoms but attacks internal organs including the brain, heart, and nervous system, resulting in paralysis, numbness, dementia, and blindness. In some cases the disease can be fatal. Syphilis can also be passed from a pregnant mother to an unborn child.

Prior to 1906, syphilis could not be conclusively diagnosed. That year, the first reliable test was developed, though it yielded a high rate of false positive results. Improved methods soon followed, and by the 1930s, syphilis testing was simple and reliable.

Efforts to prevent syphillis transmission, mainly through education of how it is contracted and spread, were especially acute during both World War I (1915–1918) and World War II (1938–1945), when mass movements of troops across continents brought perfect conditions for the bacteria to take hold in uninfected populations.

■ PRIMARY SOURCE

YOUR FAMILY NEEDS PROTECTION AGAINST SYPHILIS
  See primary source image.

■

SIGNIFICANCE

Before the nature of syphilis was understood, numerous remedies were tried, most of them worthless. From the fifteenth to the nineteenth century, treatment with mercury or arsenic compounds were the most common treatment, with the substances either rubbed on the lesions, administered in vaporous form, or taken by mouth. The advent of antibiotics following World War II closed the circle, rendering the disease both detectable and treatable. The arrival of antibiotics such as penicillin, which was first widely used to treat wounds and infections including syphillis among American troops, eventually was expected to signal the end of many infectious diseases. While prudent use of antibiotics has produced a dramatic reduction in deaths from many diseases, misuse of antibiotics has also created problems. Ear infections are among the more painful health conditions experienced by children, and for many years doctors commonly prescribed antibiotics for ear infections. It is now known that ear infections are often caused by viral infections, making antibiotics useless. However the overuse of antibiotics is blamed for the increase in antibiotic-resistant strains of bacteria, making some common conditions much harder to treat.

In 1999, the U.S. Centers for Disease Control (CDC) announced an initiative to end syphilis in the United States. By 2001, syphilis rates were down overall, however they soon began to rise again, prompting a renewed emphasis on the problem. In 2006, the CDC announced new measures designed to target

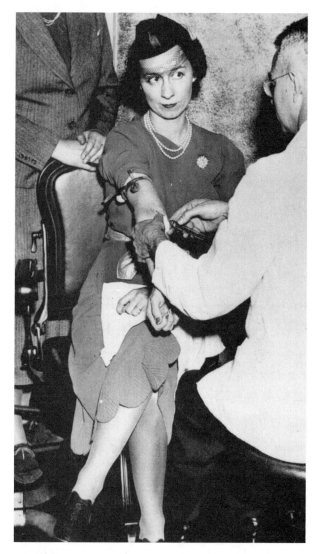

Mrs. Wright MacMillan, the Chairman of the Hygiene Committee of the League of Women Voters, takes a Wasserman test for syphillis, October 10, 1937. By doing so she is hoping to set an example for other women and encourage them to be tested and help stamp out syphilis. © BETTMANN/CORBIS.

specific at-risk populations and create rapid-response measures to contain outbreaks before they could spread. In 2004, approximately 7300 new cases of syphilis were diagnosed in the United States.

FURTHER RESOURCES
Books

Holmes, King K., et al., eds. *Sexually Transmitted Diseases.* New York: McGraw Hill, 1999.

Jones, James H. *Bad Blood: The Tuskegee Syphilis Experiment.* New York: The Free Press, 1993.

Periodicals

Krebs, Brian. "How a Lowly Fungus Saves Human Lives." *Washington Post* (March 11, 1998): H01.

U.S. Centers for Disease Control and Prevention. "Syphilis Elimination Accomplishments to Date." *Together We Can: The National Plan to Eliminate Syphilis from the United States.* May 8, 2006.

Web sites

American Social Health Association. "Sexually Transmitted Diseases." <http://www.ashastd.org> (accessed July 16, 2006).

Public Broadcasting Service. "Ehrlich finds cure for syphilis: 1909." 1998 <http://www.pbs.org/wgbh/aso/databank/entries/dm09sy.html> (accessed July 16, 2006).

Tuberculosis: Don't Kiss Me!

Poster

By: Anonymous

Date: c. 1936

Source: *Library of Congress.* "By the People, For the People: Posters from the WPA, 1936–1943." <http://memory.loc.gov/ammem/wpaposters/wpahome.html> (accessed July 23, 2006).

About the Author: The United States Library of Congress is the nation's official library, with responsibility for collecting and organizing historically significant documents, photographs, and digital media.

INTRODUCTION

In the late 1800s and early 1900s, tuberculosis was the leading cause of death in the United States. The disease, first isolated and named in the late 1830s, is caused by a bacterium that attacks the lungs but can also affect the central nervous system, joints, and circulatory system. Tuberculosis (TB) became a feared condition. With no known cure and a high contagion rate, the disease soon became the primary public health concern for doctors and later government officials who monitored and controlled disease in urban areas.

Tuberculosis is highly contagious, spread by droplets when infected persons cough or sneeze. Known by a variety of names such as "consumption," "white plague," "lung sickness," and known to the ancient Greeks as "pthisis," a single infected person can transmit the disease to twenty people within one year. Crowded living conditions, such as those experienced in cities and in poor tenements and slums, create systems of transmission that breed tuberculosis epidemics. Such epidemics were rampant in the early 1900s in the United States as immigrants and rural citizens clustered in densely-populated sectors of cities, migrating to the city for job opportunities as manufacturing expanded at the turn of the century.

Tuberculosis treatment consisted largely of quarantining and, if the patient had the means, sending the patient to a sanatorium, a quasi-hospital in the countryside or the mountains, designed to provide the patient with fresh air to help heal infected lungs. Hermann Bremer, a German physician who contracted TB, traveled to the Himalayas and found himself cured of his symptoms. Convinced that fresh air at high altitudes combined with healthy food was the key to curing TB, Bremer wrote about his theories, and some sanatoriums changed their procedures. Another doctor, Edward Trudeau, conducted a series of experiments with rabbits, finding that a diet of healthy vegetables in the Adirondack mountains helped to cure or slow down the progression of TB. People from the upper classes frequented sanatoriums for long periods to regain health; middle-class patients struggled to afford the sanatoriums, often using precious resources to send an ill father or mother. The poor, however, could not take time off work, be away from household responsibilities, or afford the fees required of such treatment.

Public health campaigns at the turn of the century focused on the prevention of public spitting, and encouraged people to eat well, get plenty of fresh air, and to exercise. For poor, urban workers who spent fourteen hours a day, six or seven days a week, in poorly ventilated factories with few breaks, this advice was impossible to follow. In the 1920s, a TB vaccine became popular, but it was ineffective against adults with pulmonary TB and lost popularity as other treatments became available.

The following poster was designed in approximately 1936 as part of a public health campaign supported by the Works Progress Administration, a "workfare" program designed under Franklin D. Roosevelt's presidency as the country worked to pull itself out of the Great Depression.

■ PRIMARY SOURCE

TUBERCULOSIS: DON'T KISS ME!

See primary source image.

PRIMARY SOURCE

Tuberculosis: Don't Kiss Me! A poster warning of the infectious nature of tuberculosis. THE LIBRARY OF CONGRESS.

Children eating a meal at a tuberculosis health camp, September 15, 1938. © BETTMANN/CORBIS.

SIGNIFICANCE

Shortly before the end of World War II, antibiotics such as streptomycin became the treatment of choice for TB, but until then, controlling the agents of infection was the only major tool public health officials had in controlling TB. While infection rates had dropped from the high rates at the turn of the century, by 1936 TB was still a major source of mortality and morbidity worldwide.

Lung x-rays could help doctors to diagnose and monitor TB. On VE Day after World War II, residents of Harlem received free chest x-rays, one of many such campaigns designed to help detect and control tuberculosis. By the time streptomycin and other drugs became common treatments, researchers found that the drugs could halt the progress of the disease in children, preventing it from reaching the brain. Stopping the disease from spreading, though, was as important as treating existing cases. Public education campaigns focused on families of small children, to preserve their health and prevent children from becoming carriers.

As of 2005, nearly one third of the population worldwide has TB, either an active case or an asymptomatic version. Five to ten percent of all TB carriers will develop a full-blown case of the disease. The incidence rate is lowest in the Americas and highest in Southeast Asia, with Africa a close second. More than fifteen million people die each year worldwide from TB.

Before the use of antibiotics in the 1940s, family members of an infected TB patient had a twenty-two percent infection rate. Children were at further risk, given the nature of feeding, toileting, and domestic care of children. The quote "your kiss of affection: the germ of infection" was designed to make adults think twice about common practices such as kissing babies on cheeks and mouths. This poster, part of a widespread campaign to educate the public, helped families to manage TB, reduce transmission, and help keep children safer.

FURTHER RESOURCES

Books

Rothman, Sheila M. *Living in the Shadow of Death: Tuberculosis and the Social Experience of Illness in American History*. Baltimore, MD: Johns Hopkins University Press, 1995.

Smith, Jason Scott. *Building New Deal Liberalism: The Political Economy of Public Works, 1933–1956*. Cambridge, UK: Cambridge University Press, 2005.

Watkins, T.H. *The Hungry Years: A Narrative History of the Great Depression in America*. New York: Owl Books, 2000.

Web sites

World Health Organization. "Tuberculosis." <http://www.who.int/topics/tuberculosis/en> (accessed July 22, 2006).

Low Rent Homes for Low Income Families

Poster

By: Anonymous

Date: c. 1940

Source: *Library of Congress*. "By the People, For the People: Posters from the WPA, 1936–1943." <http://memory.loc.gov/ammem/wpaposters/wpahome.html> (accessed July 23, 2006).

About the Author: The United States Library of Congress is the nation's official library, with responsibility for collecting and organizing historically significant documents, photographs, and digital media.

INTRODUCTION

The Great Depression was one of the most trying eras in American history. Widespread unemployment, thousands of bank failures, and the collapse of the economy meant that even Americans desperate for work faced bleak prospects of finding employment. In a fundamental shift in government policy and citizen attitudes, President Roosevelt embarked on a massive social relief effort, making the federal government for the first time the insurer of last resort for American citizens. The Social Security System was among the major programs begun during the New Deal, and it went on to become the largest legacy of this massive

■ **PRIMARY SOURCE**

Low Rent Homes for Low Income Families: A poster advertises low rent homes for families. THE LIBRARY OF CONGRESS.

effort to restart the economy and guarantee sustenance for citizens.

Roosevelt's first term had focused on creating a massive social safety net. Despite the scope of these efforts, however, the new programs failed to substantially improve economic conditions. In launching his second term, Roosevelt feared that continuing to simply distribute money to unemployed workers would keep them fed but would also demoralize them. To address this concern the Roosevelt Administration established the Works Progress Administration (WPA) in 1935, which was renamed the Works Projects Administration in 1939.

The WPA was tasked with hiring and coordinating labor to complete "small useful projects" throughout the nation. These projects encompassed a surprisingly diverse range of occupations, from manual labor and construction to art and writing. Federal Project Number One, a massive cultural development project sponsored by the WPA, included five separate efforts: the Federal Art Project, the Federal Music Project, the Federal Theatre Project, the Federal Writers Project, and the Historical Records Survey.

Federal One, as the project was nicknamed, would become the largest single federal initiative ever devoted solely to arts and culture, and within one year of its launch employed more than 40,000 artists and other employees. In addition to producing works of art, these employees also conducted thousands of art and music classes for other citizens and presented an average of 4,000 musical performances each month.

The WPA is most commonly remembered for its enormous construction projects. In a 1939 brochure the agency's director listed some of its accomplishments up to that date: 279,000 miles of roads built or improved, 29,000 new bridges constructed, 15,000 parks and athletic fields built or improved, 544 sewage treatment plants constructed, and 250,000 homes hooked into sanitary sewer systems. In addition, the

WPA built more than 17,000 public buildings such as schools, post offices, and hospitals. Consistent with its underlying purpose of supporting poor families, the WPA limited its hiring almost entirely to heads of households, while single men received aid through other programs.

In 1939, the WPA began construction of a low-income housing project in Cleveland, Ohio. Valleyview Homes Estate included more than five hundred brick and concrete homes built at a total cost of $3.5 million. The neighborhood, designed as temporary housing for families displaced by the Depression, included a community center and offices, and featured murals and sculptures created by WPA artists.

■ **PRIMARY SOURCE**

LOW RENT HOMES FOR LOW INCOME FAMILIES
See primary source image.

Steel cabins for migrant worker families at a labor camp in Visalia, California, March, 1940. © CORBIS.

SIGNIFICANCE

As the Works Projects Administration expanded, it continued to spend the vast majority of its funds on salaries and other direct payments to workers, putting the bulk of its funding directly into beneficiaries' hands. In addition, with the WPA charged to invest in publicly beneficial projects that would not compete with private firms, its efforts frequently stimulated private sector spending as well, multiplying the local economic impact of WPA investment. By 1936, the agency employed approximately one-fourth of the nation's unemployed workers, and its immense popularity helped sweep President Roosevelt to a landslide reelection.

Critics of the WPA claimed that it was bureaucratic and inefficient in its operations, and they took steps to shrink it in the following years, limiting the length of time an individual could work for WPA and cutting wages. In response to the proposed wage cuts, several thousand WPA construction workers went on strike, though their efforts were unsuccessful. A 1939 Senate report harshly criticized the WPA and further bolstered the claims of the agency's critics. In the years leading up to and during World War II, the U.S. economy recovered and unemployment largely disappeared. In 1943, the Works Projects Administration was officially dissolved. During its lifetime the agency spent about $11 billion and employed a total of 8.5 million workers.

In the years since Valleyview Homes Estate opened in 1940, about half the houses were torn down due to disrepair or to make way for a highway project. In 2005, the remaining 240 homes in the neighborhood were demolished to make way for a new housing development funded by a $19.5 million federal housing grant. Several of the depression-era murals and other artistic creations remaining in Valleyview were salvaged prior to its demolition.

FURTHER RESOURCES

Books

Becker, Heather, et al. *Art for the People: The Rediscovery and Preservation of Progressive and WPA-Era Murals in the Chicago Public Schools, 1904–1943.* San Francisco: Chronicle Books, 2002.

Denoon, Christopher. *Posters of the WPA.* Seattle: University of Washington Press, 1987.

Hiler, Megan, et al. *An Ornery Bunch: Tales and Anecdotes Collected by the WPA Montana Writers Project.* New York: Falcon, 1999.

Periodicals

Taylor, Zanthe. "Singing for Their Supper: The Negro Units of the Federal Theater Project and Their Plays." *Theater* 27 (1997): 42–59.

Thompson, Rachel Yarnell. "A North Dakota New Deal." *Social Education* 60 (1996): 292–294.

Westbrook, Robert. "A Nice WPA Job." *Dissent* 53 (2006): 124–127.

Web sites

Indiana University Lilly Library. "The Works Projects Administration in Indiana." 1996. <http://www.indiana.edu/~liblilly/wpa/wpa.html> (accessed July 22, 2006).

National New Deal Preservation Association. "New Deal/WPA Art in Cleveland, Ohio." 2006. <http://www.wpamurals.com/cleveland.html> (accessed July 22, 2006).

University of Texas: THSA Online. "Works Project Administration." 2001. <http://www.tsha.utexas.edu/handbook/online/articles/WW/ncw1.html> (accessed July 22, 2006).

New York Suburb of Levittown

Photograph

By: Arthur Green

Date: April 13, 1949

Source: Corbis Corporation

About the Author: This photograph is part of the collection of the Corbis Corporation, headquartered in Seattle, with a worldwide archive of over seventy million images.

INTRODUCTION

In the decades prior to World War II (1939–1945), many people in the United States lived in cramped apartments in the cities and border towns to the cities. In the 1920s, the home building industry was dominated by a few builders who completed, on average, four to five homes per year. The Great Depression and World War II, however, would mark a shift in the attitudes toward home buying. Following the depression, the federal government enacted legislation under Franklin Roosevelt's New Deal policies to reconstruct the mortgage system. The introduction of a system of mortgage insurance took the risk out of speculative development. This enabled developers

PRIMARY SOURCE

The New York Suburb of Levittown: An aerial view of Levittown, New York, during construction in 1949. © UPI/CORBIS-BETTMANN. REPRODUCED BY PERMISSION.

such as the Levitts to begin large scale operations of development.

Abraham Levitt, a real estate attorney, also dabbled in real estate investing in the 1930s. During the depression, Levitt held an investment on a Rockville Centre property that was about to be defaulted on by the developer. In order to protect his investment, Abraham Levitt and his sons, Alfred and William, created Levitt and Sons, a construction company. As a result of the successful completion of the Rockville Centre development, called Strathmore, Levitt and Sons sought to create more efficient methods of constructing. The company began purchasing land and building homes throughout the Great Depression.

In 1941, Levitt and Sons was awarded a contract from the federal government to build 2,350 homes for shipyard defense workers in Norfolk, Virginia. Fol-

lowing the completion of this project, William enlisted in the U.S. Navy. The experience of building large-scale numbers of units, in addition to his time in the service and a study of assembly line techniques employed by the auto industry, led William Levitt to propose the building of low-cost, mass-produced homes for war veterans.

As World War II came to a close, the federal government continued to enact programs that would allow for the housing boom that followed the war. The Federal Housing Administration guaranteed the loans that were made to builders, which lessened the risk involved in speculative building. Federal highway building programs offered access to cities to those who lived outside. In addition, the veterans returning from the war front were faced with a housing shortage and as a provision of the G.I. Bill were offered low-interest mortgages.

During the depression, the region in the Hempstead Plains in Nassau County, NY called the Island of Trees was largely agricultural. However, the golden nematode blight began to affect the potato farms in the area. Farmers were forced to sell off their lands for survival. In 1946, Levitt and Sons purchased a 1,000 acre potato farm that would later be developed into Levittown.

PRIMARY SOURCE

THE NEW YORK SUBURB OF LEVITTOWN
See primary source image.

SIGNIFICANCE

The first suburbs in the United States were in Levittown, New York, approximately twenty-five miles east of Manhattan. In 1946, Levitt and Sons purchased a 1,000-acre potato farm and the next year announced the plan to build 2,000 rental homes earmarked for service members returning from the war. Within days, newspapers reported that the 2,000 homes had been rented. The production of homes had become so efficient that by 1948, the company was completing thirty homes per day. In 1949, Levitt and Sons began to sell their "ranch" homes which sat on 1/7-acre lots. Prospective buyers could choose from five different models that varied only in their exterior color, roof line, and window placements. The 750-square foot homes had two bedrooms, a living room, kitchen, and unfinished attic. There was no garage. The homes were outfitted with General Electric stoves and refrigerators and stainless steel sinks and cabinets. In order to purchase or rent these homes, individuals were required to sign a covenant that promised not to allow blacks to use or occupy the property.

William Levitt modeled the assembly line techniques seen in the automobile industry to create the low-cost homes. Dividing the home building process into twenty-seven operations, Levitt used his workers, often non-union and unskilled, as the moveable part of the assembly line. Teams would move from site to site completing their operations. This revolutionary change to home building resulted in William Levitt's appearance on *Time* magazine's front cover. From 1947 to 1951, Levitt and Sons built 17,447 homes.

By revolutionizing the mass production of homes, Levitt made home buying a possibility to many. As

builders began to replicate his mass production of homes, suburbs quickly began to develop across the nation.

FURTHER RESOURCES
Periodicals

Guido, Daniel Walker. "Pioneers of Production Home Building." *Builder*, May 1, 2001.

Gutis, Philip, S. "Levittown, L.I. at 40: Once a Solution, Now a Problem." *New York Times*, September 21, 1987.

Lacayo, Richard. "Time 100: Suburban Legend William Levitt" *Time*, December 7, 1998.

Leopold, Ellen. "The Levittown Legacy." *Monthly Review* 56 (6) (November 1, 2000).

Web site

Levittown Historical Society "Levittown History." <http://www.levittownhistoricalsociety.org/index2.htm> (accessed June 15, 2006).

Please Stop at Two

Singapore Family Planning Poster, 1972

Poster

By: Anonymous

Date: c. 1972

Source: Corbis Corporation

About the Artist: This family planning poster is a part of the Bettmann Collection of images maintained by the Corbis Corporation, a worldwide provider of visual content to advertisers, broadcasters, designers, magazines, media organizations, newspapers, and producers. The creator of the poster is unknown.

INTRODUCTION

The Republic of Singapore underwent a remarkable social and economic transformation after the end of the Second World War. The Southeast Asian island nation, a struggling Third World economy in the immediate postwar period, had a rapidly growing population with one of the highest birthrates in the world per capita, coupled with a poor standard of living. Even today Singapore, comprised of the city and the surrounding islands, is one of the most densely populated nations in the world.

included abortion, which was legalized in 1970 and encouraged as a population-control method. Between 1969 and 1972, the government also imposed significant disincentives for families who chose to have more than two children, including income tax consequences and the elimination of paid maternity leave for government employees. The government offered rewards to those Singaporeans who underwent voluntary sterilization, and promoted the use and the understanding of various forms of contraception.

After 1975, the Singapore birth rate had been reduced to a level that would maintain the then current population level of almost three million persons. Government analysts saw the desired rise in economic performance, with an accompanying higher standard of living, better education, and a higher rate of female employment (with children being born later in their mother's lives).

New demographic concerns appeared in 1985, however, when the birth rate fell below the point at which the population was being sustained. In 1986, the "Stop at Two" campaign was replaced by "Have Three or More, If You Can Afford It" campaign. The government created incentives to have larger families, including a 1989 provision in which a fourth child earned its parents a $20,000 tax rebate.

In 1990, Singapore remained a boom economy, nicknamed one of the Asian "tigers" whose economic growth was rivaled only by Hong Kong, South Korea, and Taiwan. In 2006, Singapore enacted a further child subsidy program, dubbed a "baby bonus", in the government's ongoing efforts to manage the growth of its population.

PRIMARY SOURCE

Please Stop at Two: A poster at a Singapore family planning clinic encourages families to have no more than two children. © UPI/CORBIS-BETTMANN. REPRODUCED BY PERMISSION.

The government supported the formation of the Singapore Family Planning Association in 1949, a private organization that represented one of the earliest government-sanctioned popular efforts to reduce fertility. The country's birth rate peaked in 1957, leading to fears that unchecked population growth would destroy its economy and create the future economic burden of a larger and older population.

When Lee Kuan Yew became president in 1959, the nation began to reform virtually every social and political institution. Lee was determined that Singapore would become a First World economy; a cornerstone of that ambition was reduction in the national birthrate.

The policies enacted by Singapore were comprehensive. "Stop at Two," the national campaign,

PRIMARY SOURCE

Please Stop at Two
   See primary source image.

SIGNIFICANCE
   This 1972 photograph of a Singapore family planning poster was taken at the height of one of the most aggressive and comprehensive population control campaigns ever undertaken in any country. The poster uses the image of a stork—a symbol associated with birth and parenthood—to further the government message. The sign hanging from the stork that references a work stoppage cleverly underscores the aggressive nature of the campaign.

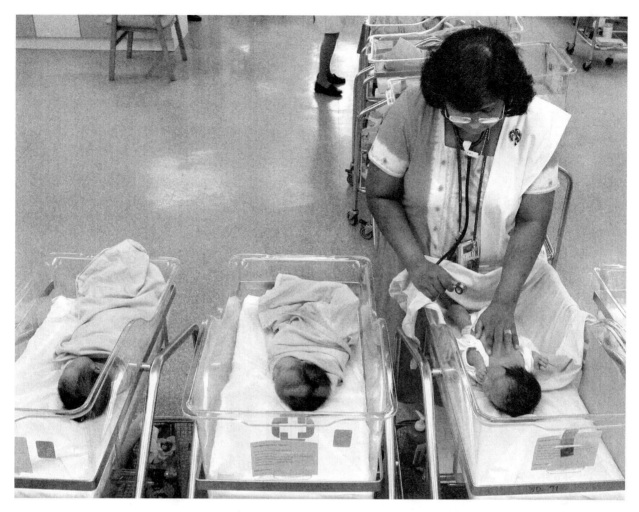

A neonatologist checks a newborn baby at a maternity ward at KK Women's and Children's Hospital in Singapore. © JONATHAN DRAKE/EPA/CORBIS.

Other countries created different types of incentives—and disincentives—for the creation of larger families. The "baby bonus" was popular in countries such as Canada throughout the post-World War II period. These monthly government subsidies were a minor incentive that encouraged families to have more children. China, the world's most populous nation, enacted a one-child policy to curb population growth in 1979. It has been a permanent feature of Chinese domestic policy since then, with mixed results; the population has continued to grow, but at a slower rate.

The Singapore population control initiatives were remarkable on a number of levels, beginning with the legalization of abortion in 1970. In contrast with the protracted battles over the procedure in many countries, Singapore treated abortion as only

one of a number of tools to achieve its goals in population control. The availability and legality of abortion in Singapore remained unaffected by the reversal in government policy to encourage population growth in 1986.

Without eliminating complete freedom of choice in family planning, the government of Singapore has been more actively involved in the influence of the family decision-making process than any government in the world, with the exception of China. Western nations of comparable economic and social stability have never seriously proposed such comprehensive measures. Modern Singapore is a sophisticated, buoyant economy; a 2006 Mercer Consulting survey gave Singapore the thirty-fourth-highest quality of living standard among world cities. The current population of approximately 4.5 million persons is racially, culturally and religiously diverse.

It is equally significant that Singapore has directed its attention to fertility as the primary tool of encouraging a population increase, as opposed to other methods, such as increasing immigration. Implicit in the government policies is the recognition that the encouragement of greater immigration carries with it a range of other social factors. Singapore is not a homogeneous nation, but it has a dominant ethnic group (Chinese), and a number of smaller ethnic populations who live in relative social harmony. Assimilating immigrants into the unique demographic mixture that is Singapore would present challenges; to permit immigrant cultures to live in a fashion inconsistent with Singapore culture might provoke disharmony. Aggressive policy making in family planning matters exchanged some individual family freedom of choice for a national objective.

A significant political outcome of Singapore's family planning policies was the long political career of Lee Kuan Yew, who served as president from 1965 to 1990, the time frame in which the family planning policies were implemented and executed. Yew believed that the "Stop at Two" campaign helped increase understanding of the importance of proper family planning to Singapore's viability. In his book, *From Third World to First: The Singapore Story*, Yew concluded that the nation's economic success in the 1990s would not have occurred without the population-management policies.

FURTHER RESOURCES

Books

Yew, Lee Kuan. *From Third World to First: The Singapore Story 1965–2000*. New York: Harper Collins, 2000.

Periodicals

Pyle, Jean l. "Women, the Family and Economic Restructuring: The Singapore Model." *Review of Social Economics*. 2 (1997): 215–223.

Web sites

RAND. "Family Planning in Developing Countries." 1999 <http://www.rand.org/pubs/issue_paper/IP176?index2.html> (accessed June 26, 2006).

Republic of Singapore. "Changing Contraceptive Choices of Singapore Women." 2000 <http://www.singstat.gov.sg/ssn/feat/2Q99/featapr991.pdf> (accessed June 26, 2006).

So Lucky to Give Birth in England

News article

By: Randi Hutter-Epstein

Date: December 4, 2001

Source: Hutter-Epstein, Randi. "So Lucky to Give Birth in England." *New York Times*. (December 4, 2001).

About the Author: Randi Hutter-Epstein is a mother and author who has written extensively on the experience of raising children.

INTRODUCTION

Childbirth is one of the most significant and life-changing events of human existence. Throughout history, cultural expectations and superstition have played significant roles in the way it is experienced. In particular, young mothers-to-be frequently find themselves receiving an overwhelming amount of advice and instruction, further complicating an already challenging phase of life.

Ancient Europeans presented mothers-to-be with a lengthy list of behaviors to avoid during pregnancy to avoid harming their unborn child. For example, pregnant women were cautioned that wearing a rope in place of a belt would result in their child ultimately being hanged. Pregnant women were also warned not to visit a place where cloth was being bleached, otherwise their children would be born with pale skin.

After giving birth, new mothers faced a veritable minefield of dangerous behaviors, any one of which would supposedly result in pain or misfortune. Newly delivered mothers who walked through a field or garden would supposedly make that piece of land infertile for several years, and the woman who stuck pins or needles into curtains in the six weeks after childbirth would give her child bad teeth.

Child care and parenting were also the subject of numerous superstitions and taboos. Upon the appearance of a child's first tooth, parents were admonished to slap the child across the face, as this was claimed to make the rest of the teething process easier. When putting a newborn to bed care was required, since laying the child first on its left side would cause the child to grow up to be clumsy.

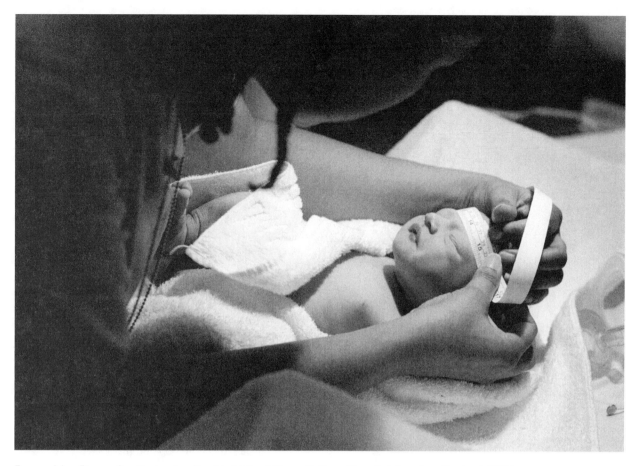

Fergus Max Regan-Quail, shortly after his birth at Kings College Hospital, London, England, 2004. © LOUIS QUAIL/CORBIS.

While these gems of parenting wisdom appear ridiculous in light of modern medical knowledge, modern parents often receive even more advice, some of it contradictory. For many years, mothers were encouraged to put their babies to bed face-down; this position was believed to be safer in the event a baby spat up during sleep, since it might not be able to clear its mouth of vomit sleeping face-up.

In later years, further research concluded that babies have no difficulty turning their head if they vomit, and that choking is not a major threat. Numerous studies also support a relationship between sleeping face-down and the occurrence of sudden infant death syndrome (SIDS), in which an otherwise healthy baby dies while sleeping. In response to this new understanding, health agencies launched a campaign called "Back to Sleep," which offered extensive advice on how to make cribs safer and why babies should sleep on their backs. Not surprisingly this new advice was received with skepticism by some older women who raised their children the old way.

In addition to creating enormous change in the life of a family, childbirth is also a major financial event. As of 2006, a typical hospital delivery in the United States cost $6,000 to $10,000; complications or a premature birth can raise these costs by a factor of ten, giving insurers a significant interest in the health of mothers and babies. Many developed nations outside the United States provide government-funded health care for all their citizens and these governments frequently take additional steps to reduce long-term complications and costs. For this reason, giving birth in a foreign country can be a very different experience than giving birth in the United States.

■ **PRIMARY SOURCE**

So Lucky to Give Birth in England

I gave birth to one child in England and three more in the United States. And when friends ask me about my overseas birthing experience, I tell them I was lucky to be in London the first time around.

I am not referring to medical expertise. I am talking about attitudes toward pregnancy and the much-needed help mothers get after their babies are born.

Of course, there are exceptions, but I found British doctors, nurses and expectant mothers a lot more relaxed about pregnancy than Americans.

In England, for instance, my doctor condoned my daily glass of wine.

Back then, I was shocked when I returned to the United States for a visit and my pregnant friends had what-to-eat and what-to-avoid lists. If worrying had any effect on the growing fetus, I figured, at least my nine months were carefree. (Maybe I was rationalizing my daily ice cream binges and my 15-pound weight gain in the first trimester.)

During my most recent pregnancy, about two years ago in New York, other expectant mothers still eyed my glass of wine disapprovingly.

The best part of having babies British-style was the aftercare. Every woman who gives birth in Britain, rich or poor, gets a house call by a midwife every day for at least 10 days. The midwives check on the mother's recuperation and monitor the baby's development.

I must admit, when I first heard about the home care system, I cringed. I imagined a snippy old English nanny in a starched uniform telling me exactly how I should nurse my newborn and setting sleeping schedules with military precision.

But it wasn't like that at all. The midwives were young, earthy women who would sit with me, have a cup of tea and provide reassurance.

"The intention is not to take over the care of the baby from the woman, but to support her caring for her own baby," Melanie Every, a midwife and the Royal College of Midwives' regional manager for the south of England, told me recently.

The visiting midwife program is financed by Britain's National Health Service. If midwives detect a medical problem in the baby or the mother, they can channel the woman into proper medical care. They are also on call 24 hours a day, every day.

There are no statistics to prove that house calls by midwives save lives. There have not been any studies. But it seems logical that if a mother is not feeding her baby well, or does not know how to nurse a newborn, a midwife can offer help before the problem worsens into a life-threatening condition.

My midwife checked to make sure my uterus was going back to its normal size and my stitches were heal-

ing properly. She ensured that breast-feeding was going well and that I was taking care of myself. She also checked my baby's weight every day and made sure he was urinating and moving his bowels normally.

Weighing the baby during home visits was the most amusing part of all. The English, not ones to buy into modern technology quickly, still used a century-old technique for weighing a newborn. The scales look like the cloths that hang from the legendary stork's mouth. They are actually old-fashioned fishmongers' scales. The Royal College of Midwives is considering going digital but hasn't yet.

Besides the medical checks, the best part for me and most mothers I spoke with is the emotional support these visitors provide. They answer all sorts of questions, even seemingly silly ones about where to shop for newborn clothes.

I was discharged from the service after 10 days because my baby and I were doing well. Six weeks later, a community health visitor came to call, with a psychological test about postpartum depression.

Again, I was skeptical about the government's prying into my private life. And again, I wound up feeling grateful for the visit. My visitor and I sat on the floor and discussed my feelings about motherhood and how I was coping. Just knowing that someone recognized the enormous changes in my life boosted my spirits.

Contrast all this to my next pregnancy in New York City. I gave birth to twins, was discharged within 48 hours and sent home to fend for myself.

Sure, I was an experienced mother, but I really missed my English midwives. I missed my afternoon teas, my dollop of emotional reassurance—much, much needed in those first few days.

Best of all was that in England, where I was the foreigner, I felt connected to a community, one that cared for its new babies and new mothers.

SIGNIFICANCE

Childbirth practices and their associated costs have become the subject of a tug-of-war in the United States. During the early 1990's major insurers began limiting post-delivery hospital stays to reduce costs; in many cases mothers were discharged from the hospital twenty-four hours after delivery, while in a few extreme cases the stay was limited to as little as eight. While such policies reduce short-term costs by shortening hospital stays, research suggests that children discharged this quickly are at a greater risk of complications, potentially offsetting these savings with higher costs later.

In the face of such policies, several states enacted provisions requiring a minimum hospital stay after delivery. In 1996, Congress passed the Newborns' and Mothers' Health Protection Act. This law requires health insurers to pay for a forty-eight-hour hospital stay following vaginal delivery and a ninety-six-hour stay following a caesarian birth. Doctors are allowed to discharge mothers and babies sooner, but insurers cannot pay incentives to doctors who choose to do so. As hospital costs climb, some women choose to deliver their babies at home, a practice that seems out of place in the twenty-first century, but which generally provides good outcomes at a far lower cost.

FURTHER RESOURCES

Books

Goer, Henci, and Rhonda Wheeler. *The Thinking Woman's Guide to a Better Birth*. New York: Perigee Trade, 1999.

Nichols, Francine, and Sharron Smith Humenick. *Childbirth Education: Practice, Research and Theory*. New York: Saunders, 2000.

Simkin, Penny, et al. *Pregnancy, Childbirth, and the Newborn, Revised and Updated: The Complete Guide*. New York: Meadowbrook Press, 2001.

Periodicals

Glass, Jennifer and Leda Nath. "Religious Conservatism and Women's Market Behavior Following Marriage and Childbirth." *Journal of Marriage and Family*. 68, no. 3(2006): 611–629.

McCool, W.F. and S.A. Simeone. "Birth in the United States: An overview of Trends Past and Present." *Nursing Clinics of North America*. 37, no. 4(2002): 735–746.

Web sites

University of Pittsburgh. "Superstitions: Pregnancy, Childbirth, and Postnatal Care." <http://www.pitt.edu/ dash/superstition.html> (accessed July 10, 2006).

U.S. Department of Labor. "Frequently Asked Questions about Newborns' and Mothers' Health Protection" <http://www.dol.gov/ebsa/faqs/faq_consumer_newborns.html> (accessed July 10, 2006).

Washington Post Online. "More Stress on Moms: When Babies Come in Twos or Threes, the Pressure More Than Doubles." February 23, 1999 <http://www.washingtonpost.com/wp-srv/national/health/multiples/mothersofmult022298.htm> (accessed July 10, 2006).

Orphaned by AIDS

Photograph

By: Gideon Mendel

Date: June 16, 2004

Source: Corbis

About the Photographer: Gideon Mendel is a South African–born freelance photographer who has been published in most international magazines. He has won World Press Photo awards and received the prestigious Eugene Smith grant for his work on AIDS in Africa. This photograph is part of the collection at Corbis, a worldwide provider of visual content materials to advertisers, broadcasters, designers, magazines, new media organizations, newspapers, and producers.

INTRODUCTION

Millions of children have been orphaned in Africa as a result of the HIV/AIDS epidemic. When parents and other family members succumb to the disease, grandparents, older siblings, foster families, or orphanages raise the children. In some cases, however, AIDS orphans are left to fend for themselves, living on the streets. The children hawk sandals, bars of soap, rolls of tissue, and other items on street corners, often offering their labor if they have no goods to sell. AIDS orphans are found throughout the world, but eight out of ten of these children live in sub-Saharan Africa.

HIV stands for human immunodeficiency virus, and typically develops into acquired immune deficiency syndrome (AIDS), a disease that destroys the immune system and ultimately kills the patient. Approximately 2.7 million people in sub-Saharan Africa acquire HIV each year. The disease is sexually transmitted, but can also be spread through blood-to-blood contact. In Swaziland, a small country in the southern part of Africa, 33.4 percent of the adult (age eighteen to forty-nine) population has HIV/AIDS, the highest rate in Africa. In the mid–1990s, the life expectancy for people born in Swaziland was fifty-one years. AIDS had reduced it to 39.4 years by the beginning of the twenty-first century. Most of those who die are young adults between the ages of fifteen and forty-nine, the segment of society that typically provides the labor force.

With no family safety net, AIDS orphans often suffer from poor health, psychological distress, and are vulnerable to abuse and exploitation. Many have

HIV/AIDS themselves. Because there are so many of them, community care is often their only option. A variety of charities and international agencies such as World Vision and the Joint United Nations Programme on HIV/AIDS (UNAIDS), care for AIDS orphans, as do many African churches. Despite such assistance, however, there are not enough funds to fight the HIV/AIDS epidemic and provide the care that both patients and orphans need.

A small number of adoption agencies in the United States, Europe, Australia, and other countries work with African governments to arrange for healthy AIDS orphans (those who do not have HIV/AIDS) to be adopted by families in industrialized countries. These children are often put in special orphanages to await placement. Although some do end up in new families overseas, the number is not large enough to curb the social problems facing AIDS orphans.

PRIMARY SOURCE

ORPHANED BY AIDS

See primary source image.

SIGNIFICANCE

The HIV/AIDS epidemic is increasing already high poverty levels throughout sub-Saharan Africa. The United Nations Development Program (UNDP) reports that households caring for orphans earn thirty-one percent less income than others. The number of deaths from HIV/AIDS has depleted human resources, weakening the education system as teachers die, reducing agricultural productivity, and straining industrial sectors.

Over fifty-five percent of HIV/AIDS victims are female, putting rural households headed by women at

PRIMARY SOURCE

Orphaned by AIDS: Nosipho Ndlangamandla, an eleven-year-old orphaned by the AIDS epidemic in southern Africa, combs her hair for school. She lives with her grandmother in Bhanganoma, Swaziland. June 16, 2004. © GIDEON MENDEL FOR THE GLOBAL FUND/CORBIS.

An orphaned Thai tolder. Her parents were killed by the AIDS epidemic. © JEREMY HORNER/CORBIS. REPRODUCED BY PERMISSION.

an even higher risk of poverty, as women often have less access to treatment, less education, and fewer opportunities to find work. These social challenges are expected to become more severe as the rate of HIV/AIDS rises.

Many international organizations and other bilateral initiatives, such as George W. Bush's President's Emergency Plan for AIDS Relief (PEPFAR), work with African governments, communities, and families to help reduce the prevalence of HIV/AIDS and mitigate the epidemic's medical, social, and economic effects. These organizations teach people how to avoid HIV through the proper use of birth control, staying faithful to one partner, and abstaining from sexual activity. In addition, groups such as the Global Fund make retroviral drugs, which are widely available to HIV/AIDS patients in developed countries, accessible to people in sub-Saharan Africa.

FURTHER RESOURCES

Books

Foster, Geoff, Carol Levine, and John G. Williamson, eds. *A Generation at Risk: The Global Impact of HIV/AIDS on Orphans and Vulnerable Children*. New York: Cambridge University Press, 2005.

Guest, Emma. *Children of AIDS: Africa's Orphan Crisis*. London: Pluto Press, 2003.

Hunter, Susan S. *Black Death: AIDS in Africa*. New York: Palgrave Macmillan, 2003.

Subbarao, Kalanidhi, and Dian Coury. *Reaching Out to Africa's Orphans: A Framework for Public Action (Africa Region Human Development Series)*. Washington, D.C.: World Bank, 2004.

Periodicals

Karon, Tony. "AIDS Orphan's Preventable Death Challenges Those Left Behind." *Time*. (June 1, 2001).

Kristof, Nicholas, D. "A Plague of Orphans and Lonely Grandmothers." *New York Times*. (May 30 2006): A19.

Web sites

UNAIDS: Joint United Nations Programme on HIV/AIDS <http://www.unaids.org/en/> (accessed June 24, 2006).

Use of Contraception and Use of Family Planning Services in the United States: 1982–2002

Report

By: William D. Mosher, et al.

Date: 2004

Source: Mosher, William D., et al. "Use of Contraception and Use of Family Planning Services in the United States: 1982–2002." *Advance Data from Vital and Health Statistics*. Centers for Desease Control and Prevention, December 10, 2004.

About the Author: William D. Mosher is a researcher at the National Center for Health Statistics in Hyattsville, Maryland. The Centers for Disease Control and Prevention funds research into disease causes, prevention, and treatment.

INTRODUCTION

For most of human history, pregnancy and childbirth have been impossible to reliably prevent or plan, although numerous methods have been tried. Some,

A women uses a dispensing machine to obtain free condoms or contraceptive pills. The dispenser was placed in a Bejing suburb as part of a pilot project for family planning and AIDS prevention. Residents have a chip card to operate the machine at any time of day. © REINHARD KRAUSE/REUTERS/CORBIS.

such as walking over the graves of deceased female ancestors, have no effect; others, such as male withdrawal before ejaculation, are relatively effective but fail often. Without a basic understanding of human physiology and reproductive anatomy, family planning advice throughout history ranged from absolutely useless to surprisingly effective. For most families, consistent family planning remained difficult or impossible.

While numerous methods of contraception have been devised, information about them was not always readily available. Because of the moral dilemmas often associated with sexual activity, some critics believed that public discussion of contraception should be forbidden, and in 1874 the U.S. Congress passed legislation defining contraception information as obscene. Despite the ban, primitive contraceptives continued to be manufactured and sold, and in 1880 the production of animal-skin condoms began. Condoms were legal-

ized in the United States in 1918 after U.S. troops began bringing them home from World War I.

The 1920s marked the first decade in which birth control methods appear to have significantly impacted birth rates; despite the low reliability of available methods, families frequently employed multiple techniques, resulting in a measurable drop in pregnancies, which continued through the 1940s. Speeding the adoption of birth control were activists such as Margaret Sanger, who worked to extend birth control access to poor and working-class women. Sanger, who was frequently arrested for publicly discussing birth control, continued her efforts on behalf of women throughout her life. Despite her work, birth control of any kind remained illegal in some states, even for married couples; a prohibitive statute in Connecticut remained on the books until 1965 when the U.S. Supreme Court struck it down.

With the spread of AIDS during the 1980s, massive educational campaigns were launched in order to educate Americans about disease prevention. As a result, condoms for the first time entered the public vocabulary, and today they are widely advertised and sold in a variety of styles. Female birth control is also readily available in numerous forms and at little or no cost, allowing women to choose their preferred method of contraception.

■ PRIMARY SOURCE

Contraceptive use in the United States is virtually universal among women of reproductive age:

98 percent of all women who had ever had intercourse had used at least one contraceptive method. In 2002, 90 percent had ever had a partner who used the male condom.

82 percent had ever used the oral contraceptive pill, and 56 percent had ever had a partner who used withdrawal.

The leading method of contraception in the United States in 2002 was the oral contraceptive pill. It was being used by 11.6 million women 15–44 years of age; it had ever been used by 44.5 million women 15–44 years of age. The second leading method was female sterilization have been the two leading methods in the United States since 1982.

Between 1982 and 2002, the percentage of women who had ever had a partner using the male condom rose from 52 percent in 1982 to 90 percent in 2002. The percent whose partner had ever used withdrawal increased from 25 to 56 between 1982 and 2002. In contrast, the percentage who had ever used the Today sponge, intrauterine device (the IUD), the Diaphragm, calendar rhythm, and spermicidal foam decreased between 1995 and 2002.

Non-Hispanic Black or African American women and Hispanic or Latina women were somewhat less likely to have ever used the oral contraceptive pill than non-Hispanic white women, but these groups were more likely than white women to have used the 3-month injectable contraceptive called Depo-Provera.

The percentage of women who used a method of contraception at their first premarital intercourse increased from 43 percent in the 1970s to 79 percent in 1999–2002. Most of this increase was due to an increase in use of the male condom at first premarital intercourse, from 22 percent in the 1970s to 67 percent in 1999–2002, although use of the pill also increased.

About 62 percent of the 61.6 million women 15–44 years of age—5 out of 8—were currently using contraception in 2002. Most of those who were not using contraception were currently pregnant, trying to become pregnant, sterile for medical (noncontraceptive) reasons, unable to conceive, or had not had intercourse recently (or ever).

The percentage of all women 15–44 who were sexually active and not using contraception increased from 5.4 percent in 1995 to 7.4 percent in 2002. This represents an apparent increase of 1.43 million women between 1995 and 2002, and could raise the rate of unintended pregnancy, particularly among women 20 years of age and over, and black women.

Non-Hispanic Black and Hispanic women were more likely to use female sterilization as a method of contraception than Non-Hispanic white women, but white women were more likely to rely on male sterilization.

The percentage of contraceptors 22–44 years of age who chose female sterilization as a method of birth control varied sharply by education. Female sterilization accounts for 55 percent of users without a high school degree in 2002 compared with just 13 percent of contraceptors with a 4-year college degree.

While contraceptors with less education tend to rely on female sterilization, contraceptors with more education tend to rely on the oral contraceptive pill: just 11 percent of contraceptors without a high school degree used the pill in 2002, compared with 42 percent of contraceptors with a 4-year college degree.

This report also shows the extent of use of the condom with other methods of birth control. About 10 percent of never married women had a partner who was using male condoms as their most effective method of contraception in 2002, but another 7 percent were using condoms along with a more effective method—such as the pill or Depo-Provera—so a total of 17 percent were using the condom. Among married women, however, this kind of combination use was much less common.

About 42 percent of women 15–44 years of age received one or more family planning-related medical services from a medical care provider in the 12 months before the 2002 survey. The pattern of use of these services by age closely coincides with the pattern of oral contraceptive use by age: 63 percent of women 20–24 years of age and 20 percent of women 40–44 used such services in the year before the survey.

The percentage of women 15–44 years of age who used family planning services in the last 12 months increased from 33 percent in 1995 to 42 percent in 2002. About 29 percent of females 15–19 years of age received some family planning services in 1995 compared with 40 percent in 2002. Increases also occurred in other age groups.

SIGNIFICANCE

When this report was published in 2004, birth control had become an accepted and widely used option. Most significantly, the study found that the vast majority of sexually active women, with the exception of those for whom pregnancy was desired or impossible, were choosing to use birth control. The type of birth control varied widely across demographic groups, with college educated women more likely to use oral contraceptives than high school dropouts, and less likely to opt for female sterilization.

Minority women were also more likely to use Depo Provera, a hormone injection which prevented pregnancy for three months. A significant number of women also reported having received family planning services in the previous twelve months, suggesting that family planning and birth control advice and services had become widely available.

Some women's rights advocates claim that female sexual issues frequently receive inferior support compared to male sexual issues. Following the introduction of Viagra and other drugs designed to enhance male sexual performance in the late 1990s, insurance companies appeared to be following a double standard, paying up to $10.00 per pill for the male drugs but often refusing to pay the monthly costs of female birth control pills. States quickly began passing legislation requiring insurers to pay for birth control pills, which cost about $30.00 per month.

As of 2006, female birth control was available in multiple methods, including permanent sterilization, implanted hormone capsules good for five years, monthly injections, and a variety of barrier methods. In 2001, Johnson and Johnson introduced a weekly birth control patch that prevented pregnancy by providing a steady dose of hormones through the skin. In some cases federal and private programs pay some or all of the cost of birth control supplies, making family planning an option for lower income women.

Male birth control remained limited to two options: condoms and sterilization. Pharmaceutical companies continued their efforts to develop an oral or injectable male contraceptive, and several drugs were in the testing phase. While development of the female birth control pill was relatively trouble-free, drug makers found the male alternative far harder to create. In particular, scientists struggled to synthesize drugs effective at stopping sperm production without inhibiting other aspects of male sexual performance.

Easy access to contraception has had a marked impact on birth rates in the United States. Despite far better health care and longer life expectancies, which would tend to raise birth rates, U.S. birth rates in 2000 had fallen to 14.7 per 1,000, or less than half their 1910 rate of 30.1

FURTHER RESOURCES
Books

Hatcher, Robert A., et al. *Contraceptive Technology*, 18th Revised Edition. New York: Ardent Media, 2004.

Marks, Lara V. *Sexual Chemistry: A History of the Contraceptive Pill*. New Haven, Conn.: Yale University Press, 2001.

Watkins, Elizabeth S. *On the Pill: A Social History of Oral Contraceptives, 1950–1970*. Baltimore, Md.: Johns Hopkins University Press, 1998.

Periodicals

"Anthony Comstock and His Adversaries: The Mixed Legacy of the Battle for Free Speech." *Communication Law & Policy* 11 (2006): 317–366.

Friedman, Lawrence M. "Griswold v. Connecticut: Birth Control and the Constitutional Right of Privacy." *Journal of Interdisciplinary History* 37 (2006): 161–163.

Tanne, Janice Hopkins. "Gap in Contraceptive Use Between Rich and Poor is Growing in U.S." *British Medical Journal* 332 (2006): 1170.

Web sites

ABC News. "Erections Get Insurance; Why Not the Pill?" June 19, 2002. <http://abcnews.go.com/US/story?id=91538> (accessed July 22, 2006).

Michigan State University. "Margaret Sanger and the 1920s Birth Control Movement." 2000. <http://www.msu.edu/course/mc/112/1920s/Sanger/index.html> (accessed July 22, 2006).

U.S. Food and Drug Administration. "Birth Control Guide." December 2003. <http://www.fda.gov/fdac/features/1997/babytabl.html> (accessed July 22, 2006).

One-Child Policy in China

Congressional testimony

By: Arthur E. Dewey

Date: December 14, 2004

A Chinese family with one child, in line with government policy. © LIU LIQUN/CORBIS.

Source: Dewey, Arthur E. "One-Child Policy in China." *House International Relations Committee Hearing, U.S. State Department*. (14 December 2004).

About the Author: Arthur E. Dewey was the assistant secretary for the Bureau of Population, Refugees, and Migration within the State Department in the George W. Bush administration as of 2006.

INTRODUCTION

China's one-child policy has been the source of political and social controversy since Deng Xiaoping implemented it in 1979 as part of the country's "birth-planning" program. Created as part of an effort to control China's population growth, which had dropped from 2% to 1.5% in the previous thirty years, the new law limited married couples to one child, with some exceptions. If both members of a married couple are only children, then the couple may have a second child; tradition in China dictates that the son must support his parents and grandparents, leaving one man to support up to six elders, and one woman (as an only child) to support her parents and grandparents as well.

Two children in such a family would help to alleviate the pressure.

Other exceptions permit couples in rural areas to have a second child if the first is a girl; the ratio of boys to girls for second children is 152 to 100, reflecting the intense pressure and desire to have a male child, and the use of technology to abort female fetuses, especially second children.

Unmarried women were not permitted to have children under the new law; given the choice to give the child up for adoption or to abort, women made both choices, and the abortions—viewed as coercive by U.S. critics of the policy—became an issue for U.S. foreign policy officials. Contraception is widely available in China, and official statistics place contraception use at approximately 83%, more than double the consistent rate of contraception use in the U.S. by women of childbearing age. More than 38% of all Chinese women have been sterilized, and nearly 8% of Chinese men have been sterilized as well.

The 1985 Kemp–Kasten Amendment, passed by Congress and signed by President Ronald Reagan, prohibits the use of tax dollars for any organization or program that involves "coercive abortion or involuntary sterilization." As news of China's abortion rate became known, coupled with stories of pressure to abort second fetuses and allegations of involuntary sterilization for families that reached the two-child mark, U.S. policy makers, largely Republican conservatives, pressed foreign policy officials to apply Kemp–Kasten to diplomatic and humanitarian concerns in China.

In 2002 the U.S., under President George W. Bush, withheld more than $34 million in funding for United National Family Planning Administration (UNFPA) programs on this basis, declaring that China's one-child policy led to coercive abortions and involuntary sterilizations. In 2004 the assistant secretary for the Bureau of Population, Refugees, and Migration, Arthur E. Dewey, testified before Congress on this matter.

■ PRIMARY SOURCE

Thank you Chairman Smith and Members of the Committee for providing us with an opportunity to appear before you today to discuss the one-child policy in China.

The Bush Administration is deeply committed to advancing human rights issues, in China and around the globe. The Administration is also deeply committed to upholding liberty and the dignity of human life, and we strongly and absolutely oppose the practice of coercive abortions and sterilizations wherever they occur.

I'm here today to tell you how we are ground-truthing population matters in China, and recount what we've done to advance respect for the value of human life in that country. In my testimony, I will describe our findings and the challenges that remain ahead.

When I came to this post 3 years ago, I had conflicting reports concerning China's population practices. Some said that there was no coercion that would trigger the Kemp–Kasten prohibition of U.S. funding to the UN Population Fund, UNFPA. Others said that there was. So the State Department dispatched a Blue Ribbon Team in May 2002 to get the facts.

On its return from a week in China, the team recommended continuation of funding of UNFPA. But it also suggested doing what it lacked time to do during its brief mission, that is to translate the legislation governing birth planning policies in the counties where UNFPA worked, and also to find out how these policies were implemented and enforced.

The evidence drawn from these follow-on steps clearly showed us that the large fees and penalties for out-of-plan births assessed in implementing China's regulations are tantamount to coercion that leads to abortion. UNFPA support of, and participation in, China's population-planning activities allows the Chinese government to implement more effectively its program of coercive abortion, thus triggering the Kemp–Kasten prohibition on support to any organization that supports or participates in the management of a program of coercive abortion or involuntary sterilization.

These findings were based on an application of the law to the facts on the ground, leading the Secretary of State to determine that Kemp–Kasten applies, and as a result we have been prohibited from funding UNFPA during the past 3 years.

In 2002, I began a dialogue with China regarding its birth planning law. We have had six rounds of discussions on this important issue, the most recent in early November when I traveled to Beijing to meet with senior Chinese officials to press for reforms. In all of our conversations with our Chinese counterparts, we laid out our understanding, based on the Universal Declaration of Human Rights, as well as the 1994 Cairo Declaration on Population and Development, that there should be no coercion, in any form, in any nation's population policies.

We made measurable progress in these negotiations, but fell short in getting the coercive measures lifted, which would have permitted resumption of UNFPA funding. We believe China's population policies, including the so-called "one-child" policy, are undergoing an assessment and evaluation with the Chinese leadership. The Chinese Government, in our view, may be beginning to understand that its coercive birth planning regime has had extremely negative social, economic, and human rights consequences for the nation.

In our 2 years of negotiations, we have seen encouraging movement in China's approach to population issues, and the reduction of coercion in birth planning programs. For example, provincial legislation in 25 of China's 31 provinces, municipalities, and autonomous regions, has been amended to eliminate the requirement that married couples must obtain government permission ("birth permits") before the woman becomes pregnant.

This may prove to be an important change. Without birth permits there may be no effective overall mechanism for systematically enforcing birth targets and quotas in each county. We hope that the elimination of this repressive mechanism of control and interference in family life will be extended throughout all of China, and, as I have said, we will be monitoring this issue very closely.

The Chinese Government has also started a new government public information pilot project to highlight the status of the girl child. This could be an important step for human rights in eliminating discrimination against women and girls in China. Such an effort responds to the continuing reports of sex selective abortions in China and abandonment of girl babies, horrific behaviors that result from the devastating combination of the one-child policy and traditional son preference. Respect for the inherent worth and human dignity of the girl child, from conception through adulthood, is an essential element of a just society. This initiative is only a small step forward, but it does indicate some acknowledgement that the birth planning regime has resulted in very negative outcomes.

The one-child policy has certainly contributed to the stark gender imbalance in China, which, according to the 2000 census, was about 117 males to 100 females. For second births, the national ratio was about 152 to 100. Moreover, China's aging population and rising ratio of dependent to wage-earning adults pose tremendous challenges for the country. The lack of effective pension and social welfare systems for senior citizens results in a growing burden on China's working age population. Many Chinese "one-child" couples, lacking siblings, are hard-pressed to support two sets of aging parents.

Also of note, under the national birth planning law, Chinese citizens—in theory—have the ability under the Administrative Procedures Law to sue officials who violate their "family planning rights." The government has established a "hotline" for citizens to report abusive family planning practices to the federal authorities. We are gathering information on use of this hotline, and its effectiveness in dealing with alleged abuses. I want to emphasize that it is the practical implementation of these measures that matters, not public pronouncements.

In addition, the Chinese authorities I met with last month emphatically declared the end of any health and education penalties for "out-of-plan" children, such as higher school tuition fees. These children are no longer to be treated as second-class citizens. We will be watching closely to see if this is implemented, and to the extent that it is, this would be a very welcome development indeed.

Yet, let me be clear. China's birth planning law and policies retain harshly coercive elements in law and practice. Forced abortion and sterilization are egregious violations of human rights, and should be of concern to the global human rights community, as well as to the Chinese themselves. Unfortunately, we have not seen willingness in other parts of the international community to stand with us on these human rights issues.

In our discussions with the Chinese Government, we have urged them to implement fully the principle recog-

nized in the Program of Action of the International Conference on Population and Development, the ICPD, that couples, not governments, should decide the number and spacing of their children. On many occasions, the Chinese authorities have professed great commitment to the ICPD. Such statements, no matter how fervent or how frequent, will ring hollow and will be little more than empty rhetoric until that day when Chinese birth planning programs become Chinese family planning programs, fully voluntary and free of all forms of coercion.

A national Law on Population and Birth Planning went into effect on September 1, 2002. The law provides that the state shall employ measures to place population growth under control, improve the quality of the population, and conduct birth planning. The law requires married couples to employ birth control measures. While provinces have some latitude in how they implement certain aspects of the law, it also requires counties to use specific measures to limit the total number of births in each county.

The law grants married couples the right to have a single child and allows eligible couples to apply for permission to have a second child if they meet conditions stipulated in local and provincial regulations. Many provincial regulations require women to wait four years or more after their first birth before making such an application. These regulations also prohibit single women who become pregnant from giving birth, but enforcement of this prohibition reportedly varies widely throughout China.

The law specifies a number of birth limitation measures by the government that amount to coercion. Party members and civil servants who parent an "out-of-plan" child are very likely to face administrative sanction, including job loss or demotion. Couples who give birth to an unapproved child are likely to be assessed a social compensation fee, which can range from one-half the local average annual household income to as much as ten times that level.

As social compensation fee policies are set at the provincial level, and implemented locally, we understand enforcement varies greatly, with some areas waiving or greatly reducing the fees, and others imposing them at a high level. The Chinese have changed the national law so that any fees collected now go to national, not local authorities. We are told that this step has been taken to reduce the extensive corruption that had been associated with the collection of these fees. Some Chinese authorities would like to see an end to the social compensation fees, recognizing their coercive nature, and witnessing that they are especially burdensome on the poor, while more affluent citizens simply pay the fee and have additional children.

Nonetheless, as we have noted in our Human Rights Report, the social compensation fees remain a harsh and effective enforcement tool. During "unauthorized pregnancies," women are sometimes visited by birth planning workers who use the threat of the social compensation fees to pressure women to terminate their pregnancies. In many cases, these penalties and the level of harassment from officials leave women little practical alternative but to undergo abortion and therefore these fees, and related punitive measures, amount to a program of coercive abortion.

And in circumstances when social compensation fees and intense psychological and social pressure are not sufficient to compel women to have an abortion, there are reports, albeit declining, of instances where the authorities have physically forced a woman to terminate a pregnancy.

Finally, I would also like to raise the problem of forced and coerced sterilization. Forced sterilizations continue to occur, most frequently when couples have more children than the allowable number. Women may be allowed to carry the "excess" child to term, but then one member of a couple is strongly pressured to be sterilized. In some cases, they may be asked to go to a hospital under other pretenses, or sterilized without consent. Additionally, if doctors find that a couple is at risk of transmitting disabling congenital defects to their children, the couple may marry only if they agree to use birth control or undergo sterilization.

I want to assure Members that we will continue to seek engagement with the Chinese authorities on these difficult and important issues. Our embassy in Beijing and our consulates throughout China track developments in this area very closely. We will continue to urge China to move to a human rights based approach to population issues.

Thank you, and I would be happy to answer any questions that Committee members may have.

SIGNIFICANCE

Dewey's testimony highlighted the current one-child policy in China, both its codified version and in practice. Parents who choose to limit their families to one child receive a "one-child certificate" and are frequently given preferred jobs, housing, and maternity leaves, while those who have more than one child are charged higher tuition for school for the second child, higher day care rates, higher tax penalties, and in some cases discrimination from local government officials.

China's orphanages exploded in the 1990s, filled with baby girls abandoned under the one-child policy.

Highlighted by a 1995 BBC documentary called "The Dying Rooms," orphaned baby girls were tied to chairs, left to dehydrate or starve, given little if any medical care, and in some instances actively murdered in orphanages. International adoption agencies responded to higher demand for Chinese girls from adoptive parents in the U.S. and Europe, though poor publicity from the documentary led to a temporary shutdown of the adoption system, as the Chinese government responded to the documentary with outrage. Over 95% of all children adopted from China are female.

Critics of the U.S. decision to withhold UNFPA funding point to the harm this brings to beneficiaries of other UNFPA programs funded by U.S. dues; others charge that alienating the Chinese government with accusations of coercive abortion and involuntary sterilization policies does not help those families in China seeking solutions; access to Chinese citizens through international humanitarian organizations is the best approach to creating change from within.

While many Chinese women benefit from the one-child policy, which gives them greater maternity rights, more earning power, and better education opportunities, others circumvent the policy by studying abroad with spouses and conceiving and delivering while outside China, coming back with two or more children without coercion or harassment. Higher-income families simply pay the penalties as part of the price of having more than one child; in fact, among the upper classes families of two or three children have become a status symbol, a sign of wealth and prosperity, in stark contrast to those families experiencing coercion.

FURTHER RESOURCES

Books

Fong, Vanessa. *Only Hope: Coming of Age Under China's One-Child Policy*. Palo Alto, Calif.: Stanford University Press, 2004.

United States. One Hundred Eighth Congress. *China: Human Rights Violations and Coercion in One-Child Policy Enforcement: Hearing before the Committee on International Relations, House of Representatives*. Washington, D.C.: U. S. Government Printing Office, 2005.

Periodicals

Greenhalgh, Susan. "Science, Modernity, and the Making of China's One-Child Policy." *Population and Development Review* 29, no. 2 (June 2003): 163–196.

Web sites

BBC News. "China Steps up 'One Child' Policy." September 25, 2000 <http://news.bbc.co.uk/2/hi/asia-pacific/941511.stm> (accessed June 11, 2006).

United Nations. "International Conference on Population and Development." <http://www.un.org/popin/icpd2.htm> (accessed June 11, 2006).

A Surrogate Dries Her Tears

News article

By: Lisa Baker

Date: December 11, 2005

Source: Baker, Lisa. *NewYorkTimes.com.* "A Surrogate Dries Her Tears." December 11, 2005. <http://www.nytimes.com> (accessed July 22, 2006).

About the Author: Lisa Baker is a teacher and writer who lives in Westchester County, New York, with her husband and son.

INTRODUCTION

Modern surrogacy began in the United States in the late 1970s, when a Michigan lawyer, Noel Keane, drew up the first contract for surrogacy in 1976. In the early years of surrogacy, many relationships were between family members; a sister carried a baby for her siblings, or a cousin carried a baby for a cousin. There are two forms of surrogacy: traditional and gestational. Traditional surrogacy involves the surrogate's egg and the adoptive father's sperm; the surrogate legally gives the baby, who is genetically linked to the surrogate, to the adoptive parents. Until the advent of in vitro fertilization, all surrogate relationships were traditional surrogacy; in vitro fertilization allows gestational surrogacy, in which an egg that is not the surrogate's is fertilized by the adoptive father's sperm, then the fertilized egg is implanted in the surrogate.

Since the late 1970s, more than 35,000 babies have been born in the United States as part of surrogacy arrangements. As surrogacy gained in popularity, state laws were implemented and rules about medical coverage, surrogate fees, surrogate contact with the baby, and other legal matters became legal issues for courts and legislatures to consider, while social acceptance of surrogacy came slowly.

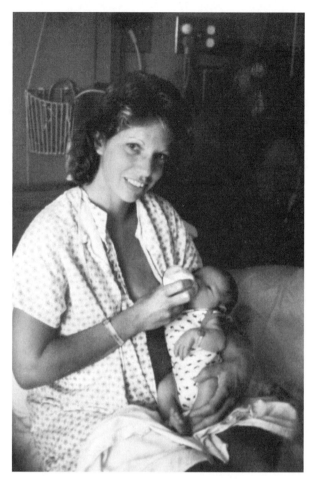

Surrogate mother Nancy Barras feeds a baby. © WAGNER GARY/CORBIS SYGMA.

Unlike traditional adoption, surrogacy allows one or both adoptive parents to have a genetic link to the baby. At the same time, traditional surrogacy carried risks for adoptive parents, in that the surrogate, biologically, was the child's mother. The 1986 case involving "Baby M" gained national attention when Mary Beth Whitehead, a traditional surrogate, sued for custody of Baby M rather than giving her over to the contracted adoptive parents, William and Elizabeth Stern. The case tested the boundaries of the law; reproductive technology and surrogate contracts created complex family and custody issues for the court's consideration. While a lower court awarded custody to the Sterns in 1987, in 1988 the Supreme Court of New Jersey overturned the ruling, giving William Stern custody, while Mary Beth Whitehead received visitation rights. In this instance, with no biological link to the child, Elizabeth Stern was not considered for custody initially, though Mary Beth Whitehead's parental rights were terminated, and Elizabeth Stern was free to adopt Baby M.

As in vitro fertilization became more consistent and implantations more successful, gestational surrogacy gained in popularity for parents wishing to build a family via surrogacy. Because the surrogate did not need to use her own egg, the question of biological motherhood did not play into any legal issues that may arise in the future. In the following essay Lisa Baker, a teacher in New York, details her experience as a traditional surrogate, contracted with a gay couple from California seeking to raise a baby. Baker explores the emotional side of surrogacy and its impact on her family.

PRIMARY SOURCE

In the bright California sunshine I'm watching a little girl run around the playground. Her wispy blond hair escapes once again from the ponytail one of her fathers carefully formed for her. She is adorable in her pink, black and white dress with matching shoes.

This is the fourth time I've visited since I gave birth to her two years ago. When I first arrive at her home, she hardly registers my presence. But eventually she figures out ways to engage me: pointing at light switches, so I can turn them on; bringing my shoes to me; taking my hand and pulling me to the playground slide.

She doesn't call me by name or call me Mommy. There are photographs of me and my family in her home, but I don't know whether she connects them to me, or whether that matters.

Her fathers tell me stories about her life: how she adores her nanny, a beautiful young Mexican-born woman, and how she sometimes plays with the nanny's nieces and nephews in their neighborhood. When she's there, she calls the nanny's mother Mom.

My heart lurches when I hear this.

I didn't expect to care so much about how I fit into this child's life. When I first got the idea to be a surrogate, I just wanted to help a married couple, our relatives, become parents. My husband's cousin Laura was married months after we were. She and Allen were eager to start a big family. But while Jerry and I got pregnant the first time we tried, and I carried my healthy baby to term, Laura was never able to maintain a pregnancy.

This misfortune gnawed at me. At the time I was finishing graduate school and already had exactly what I'd hoped and planned for my life: husband, child and Ph.D. by the age of 30. I wanted to do something tangible to help the world instead of just cloistering myself as another narrowly focused academic. But as a working mother I felt constrained.

I had a 6-year-old son, so I could hardly run off and join the Peace Corps. And my husband and I were too overwhelmed raising one child to contemplate taking in multiple foster children.

But my body was healthy and strong. My pregnancy had been easy. I felt I had leftover reproductive capacity, yet we didn't want more children ourselves.

Jerry and I discussed telling Laura and Allen that I'd carry a baby for them. But by the time we broached the subject with them over dinner one night, they were already in the process of adopting.

I was surprised to feel so disappointed.

At my university and through the Unitarian Universalist church, I was becoming friends with many gay couples. It occurred to me I could take my offer one stop further by extending it to a gay male couple who wanted to have children. I would be providing an egg as well as a uterus, but I could do that, couldn't I?

I began my research. In the university library I found law journal articles portraying surrogacy as the exploitation of lower-class women as well as analyses of the infamous "Baby M" case, in which the surrogate went to court to request custody of the baby. I didn't recognize myself in those articles. I knew I could make my own decisions and fulfill my own commitments.

To my surprise I felt more kinship when I visited online surrogacy sites. At first I was bewildered by the world of "IP's" (intended parents) and "surrobabies." (Surrobabies?) But I could see that the surrogates were deeply proud of what they were doing. They valued their families and wanted to give other couples the same chance. Even more selflessly, they risked the disapproval of family and friends to do so.

I thought, If these women can do this, I can too. So, rather impulsively—I didn't expect anyone to respond and hadn't even discussed it with Jerry—I posted an ad on surromomsonline.com.

The process was not unlike online dating, but instead of selling yourself, you're selling your genes and your fertility: details like SAT scores, Ivy League degrees and physical health and appearance get more prominent play than one's fetishes and measurements. In my ad I said I was specifically seeking a gay couple, and within days I got a promising response from California.

These guys had been together for 10 years: one was in entertainment, the other a nurse. They explained they had investigated adoption but found it difficult for gay men. They had been at this for a while and already had screened many potential surrogates.

I took a deep breath and went to discuss it with Jerry. He had been enthusiastic about my offer of surrogacy to his cousin, but this was something else entirely, and it scared him. "What if the couple walks when the baby is born?" he wanted to know. "What are the risks?" He didn't dismiss the idea out of hand, but he wanted to protect his family, as did I. It took months of research and talking, but finally we decided to do it. Our developing trust in the would-be fathers made our decision easier.

Early on I told them I would take the customary surrogate's fee they had offered—$15,000—and put it in my son's college account. But later, when it became clear that New York State's antisurrogacy laws would cause problems, even though the insemination and birth would be in California, I said I'd forgo the fee. This had never been about money.

I flew to California for inseminations. Despite my research I was still surprised that it only required five minutes with my feet in stirrups to make me pregnant. At the amniocentesis in New York a few months later, the future fathers held my hands and stared rapt at the monitor as they saw their child for the first time.

When the due date approached, we scheduled a C-section in California. I flew out weeks ahead to await the birth. My husband and son (plane tickets generously provided by the new fathers) arrived a few days before she was to be born.

As I lay in recovery, her fathers brought her to see me. I held her in my arms, feeling so proud of what I had done. The baby's grandfather sat next to my hospital bed, warmly clasped my hands and thanked me for the gift I had given his family.

During the next week, as I held the baby close in her fathers' home, I made a promise that I would always be there for her: I would answer her questions and build a relationship with her, if she wanted one.

When it was time to return to my hotel and prepare to fly home, I held her in my arms one last time and wept. I couldn't bear to let go. Her fathers were quick to reassure me.

"This isn't an end," one said. "It's only the beginning."

The other added, "You can visit any time you want."

But I couldn't stop crying. Later at the hotel I pulled myself together and e-mailed them an explanation: "I know she is where she belongs. But I will never again hold her as a baby. When I see her next, she'll be a big girl. She'll be your project, not mine."

At home I tried to settle back into the rhythms of my old life. I taught my students, debriefed my third-grade son after school, did household chores.

But in my quiet home office, when everyone was gone, my attention wandered from the lecture notes on my desk. I checked my e-mail constantly, ravenous for pictures of the baby. I lived for phone updates from her fathers.

One day I couldn't hold it together any longer and broke down in tears. I had never wept like that, without any sense of how or when the pain might stop. I called my therapist and said, "I just want to be holding that baby."

I hadn't expected it to be so hard. Which made me feel stupid. Why wouldn't it be hard for a mother to give up a baby she had carried, a baby that was part her? Even though I knew she wasn't mine—had never been mine—she and I were one organism. Despite all my mental preparation I felt as if she had been ripped out of my body, ripped out of my arms.

One of the fathers became my lifeline. He called every day; he let me cry. At his urging I booked a flight to visit and then counted the weeks. She would be 3 months old.

When I held her, I still felt that she was part of me, that she could have been my child. But I didn't cry. She was so clearly in the right place.

Now, two years later, I watch her run around with her friends on the playground. I search for the right words to describe how I feel about her. She feels like a niece to me, but more than a niece. I feel I have a special responsibility toward her, but what is it?

My son, who visits her with me, thinks it's obvious I am her mother. I gave birth to her; she looks like me; there's nobody else to point to. Will the day come when she sees me as her mother too?

During the pregnancy I knew some people disapproved of what I was doing. Painfully (for me and for them), my parents thought it was a terrible idea. They wondered: If this child is not well taken care of, how could you not feel responsible for her?

I had made my own peace with this. But what about her feelings?

Will she one day disapprove of me as well? Will she wonder how I could choose to bring her into the world and not raise her? Or will she think of me at all?

On the playground her father minds the diaper bag and asks her if she wants a snack. I stand to the side and watch, feeling useless. But then she takes my hand and leads me to the slide, and I am reminded that I need to leave it to her. She keeps finding ways to bring me into her world, and for this I am grateful.

SIGNIFICANCE

Surrogacy originally developed for couples in which the woman was infertile, or too old to conceive; by the 1990s it had become a method for gay couples to adopt a child of their own, either using a donor egg or traditional surrogacy with one of the fathers' sperm. Lisa Baker fits the mold for the "typical" surrogate in the U.S.: in her thirties, married, in a professional career, and with one or more children.

Many surrogates choose surrogacy because their own pregnancies were smooth, out of a desire to give a child to someone who cannot conceive or achieve a full-term pregnancy, or, in rare cases, for the fee, which can range from nothing to $50,000. Surrogate contracts since the Baby M incident have become complex and detailed, with sections on abortion, selective reduction should multiple eggs implant, medical procedures, and in some cases restrictions on the mother's activities while pregnant. Custody issues are spelled out in such contracts as well; traditional surrogacy is considered to be riskier for adoptive parents, as many states—like New Jersey—now prohibit traditional surrogates from receiving a fee for their service and grant traditional surrogates the right to change their mind and to assert parental rights.

High-profile celebrities, such as television show host Joan Lunden and soap opera actress Dierdre Hall, have publicized their experiences using surrogate mothers to carry their later-in-life children; Lunden has two sets of twins via surrogate, both born after she turned 50. While some surrogacy agencies exist in which professionals perform physical and psychological tests to screen potential surrogates, the Internet has revolutionized the process, with Web sites designed to help connect potential surrogates with couples wishing to enter into contracts.

As a relatively new social and familial phenomenon, researchers are beginning to delve into questions about the impact of gestational vs. traditional surrogacy on the surrogate, her partner, and her biological children, who spend the entire pregnancy going through its ups and downs, experience the birth, but do not go home with a baby. In Baker's case, as she ponders how her son feels about his half-sibling being raised by a couple he does not know, her traditional surrogacy complicates the question.

Reproductive technology continues to advance. From the first baby conceived via artificial insemination in 1978 to modern advances in artificial wombs, such change challenges notions of motherhood, families, and custodial rights while granting potential parents new opportunities for building families.

FURTHER RESOURCES

Books

Shanley, Mary L. *Making Babies, Making Families: What Matters Most in an Age of Reproductive Technologies, Surrogacy, Adoption, and Same-Sex and Unwed Parents' Rights.* Boston: Beacon Press, 2002.

Periodicals

Levine, Hal B. "Gestational Surrogacy: Nature and Culture in Kinship." *Ethnology* 42 (2003).

Spar, Debora L. "For Love and Money: The Political Economy of Commercial Surrogacy." *Review of International Political Economy* 12 (May 2005): 287–309.

Stacey, Judith. "Gay Parenthood and the Decline of Paternity as We Knew It." *Sexualities* 9 (2006): 27–55.

Why Stop?

News article

By: Sarah Ebner

Date: February 4, 2006

Source: *The Guardian Limited.* "Why stop?." February 4, 2006 <http://www.guardian.co.uk/family/story/0,,1701474,00.html> (accessed June 24, 2006).

About the Author: Sarah Ebner is a journalist who contributes regularly to the *London Times* and to the Guardian series of newspapers and online media, headquartered in the United Kingdom. She has also written for the *London Daily Post* and the *Liverpool Echo.*

INTRODUCTION

Family size is determined by a number of factors, among which are financial and childcare resources, dwelling size, parental age, marital status, job or occupational demands, and medical and fertility factors (ability to carry pregnancies to term, physical and other potential gestational complications, and the like). The appearance of the family has changed during the past several generations in America, as the economy has shifted away from agrarian pursuits, rural populations—although those certainly continue to exist in America, just to a significantly lesser degree than they did when the population was much smaller—and subsistence living, to more urban and suburban population concentrations, with their attendant grouped and smaller housing arrangements, diminished available land for construction, and increased cost of living.

The number of large families, like the one pictured here, has decreased significantly over the last thirty years. © KEVIN DODGE/CORBIS.

Before the growth of technology, there was economic benefit in having a larger family, as it contributed to available labor and resource. As demographic and socioeconomic shifts occur in which occupations have shifted to more industry and technology and less family farming types of pursuits, it has become progressively less feasible for a middle class family to support a large number of children.

In most of the developed countries of the world, the trend has been for people to marry later, to discourage (or outlaw) child labor, to emphasize education, and to embrace lifestyle choices and creature comforts that are not financially accessible if all available resources are being directed at childrearing. As a result of these and a complex interaction of cultural and sociodemographic factors, the number of children per family has been gradually declining since the middle of the twentieth century. Decisions about family size are made with an eye toward the ever-increasing costs associated with the raising of each individual child through maturity.

According to data published by the US Census Bureau (from year 2000 data), the average household size has decreased steadily, with five or more person homes diminishing from twenty-one to about ten per cent between 1970 and 2003. The average number of people making up a household in the United States stood at about 2.5 in 2003. Overall, fertility rates have declined, and average number of children per family has decreased during the past thirty plus years, despite changes in the demographics of family make-up—more single women are giving birth than in the past, and more single parent families with household heads of either gender exist, but there are fewer children per family than there were in previous generations.

◾ PRIMARY SOURCE

For the Bakers, one is a handful. For the Alis, six was their destiny. Sarah Ebner asks half a dozen families how many children they have—and why

One

Jennifer and Simon Baker have one son, Alex, four

Jennifer, 42, says: "Before having Alex, I had my mind set on more children—I am one of four children myself. But I had no idea how hard it was going to be in the first year. Motherhood was a big shock—I didn't even get to brush my teeth for the first few months and the sleepless nights took me by surprise.

"When I went back to my old job full-time, it was really difficult. I was working in sales and travelling a lot, so I was away up to three nights a week. With no family nearby, my relationship with Simon came under strain, and I felt terribly guilty about not seeing enough of Alex. I wasn't there the first time he crawled.

"I decided to change my career in order to not just be a weekend mum. Now I'm a business and personal development coach I seriously couldn't be happier, but we've made a clear decision not to have any more children. I have the energy to give Alex the time he needs, but if we had more that would be very difficult.

By having one child, I have the best of both worlds. I'm a mum, which is what I've always wanted, and I have a career that I'm passionate about. I take my hat off to working mothers with more than one child. I admire and respect how they cope."

Simon, 45, says: "We get comments from people about having one child—things such as, 'What a shame.'

"We don't want Alex to suffer because of a decision that we've made. We know that we have to get him out and about so he's at nursery in the week and with friends at weekends. We have lots of friends with children who we see a lot and go away with. Yes, it's different having one child, but I'm convinced that Alex will only miss out if we give him cause to.

"The best thing about having one is that you do have time to give, that you wouldn't physically have if you had more children. There is a risk that you could be overbearing, but we're aware of that, so hopefully it won't happen."

Two

Neela Mistry-Bradshaw and her husband, Clinton Bradshaw, have two girls: Amber, three, and Keira, one

Neela, 33, says: "I originally wanted five children, because I thought it would be fun, but I ended up having two because it's much easier. I'm the oldest of three myself, and I wouldn't have wanted to stop at one because I think they'd be lonely. If you have two they can play with each other and look after each other. I think one always gets left out if there is an odd number, so I wouldn't want three.

"I feel very lucky that we have been able to choose the size of our family. I think we've got a wonderful age gap and we've made a lot of friends through having children. It was difficult having a baby and toddler when Keira was just born. But the life-saver was the support of other mummies.

"I'm quite career-minded and I always wanted to have stopped having children by now. I think people with three or more are mad, and brave too. I want to get on with my life now."

Clinton, 33, says: "Once we had our two children we realised that more kids would make things harder. We'd have to get a larger car and a bigger house. So there were financial and practical reasons for sticking with two. But that wasn't the only reason. When we had Amber, our first, it changed our life, so it didn't seem as if there was much upheaval going from one to two. But three? When you have two, each parent can look after one at a time. What do people do with a third one? I think another child may have put a strain on things. We would be more stressed and that would filter through to the children."

Three

Mewe and Petrus Mechese have two girls—Shola, 10, and Tuoyo, two—and a boy, Tosan, 11

Mewe, 42, says: "When I was a teenager, I went to see a fortune teller and she told me I'd have three children. It wasn't exactly planned like that, but that's what's happened.

"It didn't seem fair to have only one child, but although Tosan was planned, I then got pregnant very quickly with Shola. They've got a very small gap between them and sometimes it was like having twins. My son was jealous when Shola was born—I've got a video clip where I'm trying to feed her and he's t—" After I had Tosan I went back to work full-time. With two I was more tired and financially it got harder because I cut my hours to three days a week. With three, there are even more financial and practical pressures. A lot of things are aimed at two parents and two children so we have to make sure we're always very well organised.

"I do think it's manageable, but if I did have four, I'd have to be a full-time mother. I don't think I'd be able to balance working and looking after them, my husband and the house."

Petrus says: "I am very happy with my three children, but I don't want four! I had thought we would stop at two and having three children is hard work.

"I grew up in a very big family—I am one of six-but that was in Nigeria. I knew that it would be harder here, so I said to my wife we should plan to just have two children. Things don't always work out to plan.

"It's not easy financially, but I do think it's good for the children. The older two are very happy with their little sister and it's made them more independent. The older ones do their own thing, while the younger one comes to me to play. I enjoy spending time with her, but I wouldn't be able to cope with another one."

Four

Jane and Alon Domb have four kids: Arielle, nine, Guy, seven, Aiden, four, and Jed, 20 months

Jane, 41, says: "Both Alon and I come from families with four children, and we always said that we wanted three or four children ourselves. Two seemed too neat, tidy and symmetrical for us.

"Going from one to two was the hardest. It was really full-on. I simply couldn't work out when you could factor in the sleep and rest that people tell you to get when you have one baby. But going from two to three was a breeze. Aiden was a summer baby and I would go out every day of the school holidays with the three children. It was very enjoyable.

"Jed was a lovely surprise, but it was a bit relentless for the first six months. The minute one child stopped wanting me, another one started. But then it all turned a corner and became a delight. Life is never boring, but I'm still not convinced that all the children get enough one-to-one attention.

"When I was having our third, people asked if it was an accident, which it wasn't. Then when I had a fourth, people asked me if I was planning the next one. I'm not. Five was never on the agenda."

Alon, 43, says: "I liked growing up as one of four—there was always someone to play with—and I always wanted at least three. It's clearly a longer period before you can resume normal life without feeling tired most of the time, but it's fun. It's like having your own little clan.

"I didn't notice any particular jump in going from one number to another. For me, going from nought to one was the biggest jump. Coming to terms with being a father was so vast that everything was marginal after that.

"There are financial pressures, but you don't spend four times as much on food or heating, so there are economies of scale.

"I don't think we'll be having any more. I like the dynamic of four and I want to get my life back. I'm hoping that will happen when the youngest is about four—only another two years to go!"

Five

Sheila and David Long have five children: Eric, 11, Micah, nine, Rebecca, seven, Timmy, four, and Ruth, 22 months

Sheila, 42, says: "I really enjoyed being one of four children myself, and that made me keen to have my own big brood. If you fell out with one sibling, there were always

others to play with. I think as far as the children are concerned, the more siblings the better. When we were having Ruthie, the other kids were so excited.

"Obviously they can't all get sole attention and if anybody misses out right now, it's probably Timmy. The kids are home-educated, so I do school in the mornings with the older three, while he plays and draws. But after lunch I try to spend time with him and the other children read to him too.

"Having five children is labour-intensive, but they've all brought us so much joy. The only downside is the laundry. Our bedroom is like a utility room with a bed in it.

"The only pressure to stop having children comes from my mother, who thinks that an easy life is a great life. I'd rather be busy with the children."

David, 34, says: "When I was a teenager I was renowned for saying that I would never have kids. It seemed too daunting. But I then met my lovely wife Sheila and everything changed.

"It was really cool when we had Eric. We immediately wanted more. Mind you, I'm glad they come one at a time because you really are learning with the first child.

"The biggest jump was from two to three. When we had Micah, there were two parents and two kids, but with Rebecca, suddenly if all three were crying, something had to give. We had to learn to prioritise.

"I can't imagine life without any of my kids. When I get home from work, they line up and jump into my arms. That's the most exciting thing for me."

Six

Nasreen and Sharafat Ali have six children: Sheraz, 15, Ambreen, 14, Anees, 12, Danyaal, seven, Faara, six, and Haris, nine months

Nasreen, 38, says: "My mum died when I was 15 and, as the oldest girl in a family of eight children, I had a lot of looking after to do. It wasn't easy, which is why I don't find my own big family particularly hard work. It's normal to me.

"Financially it is hard, though, and it was a real strain when I was studying to become a social worker and we were both on income support. We've never been on holiday as a family, and I would love to do that. But I don't think the children miss out—they've got uncles and aunts who help, and I've always got time for them.

"I'm a very committed person, not the sort who stays at home. I work from 9 to 5 each day. Then I come home and cook tea—I don't believe in takeaways. After 8pm, the children vanish to their rooms and my husband puts Haris to bed. Then we're able to spend a bit of time together, although I hope that when the children are older, there will be more time for us as a couple.

"The best thing about having such a big family is that I never get lonely. All my children are completely different and I'd be lost without them. I do think that it's sometimes too hard supporting and rearing them, so I would say that if you're not working, it might be more sensible to stick to four."

Sharafat, 40, says: "I think six children was our destiny and I love them all. I'm very content and don't think I could ask for anything more. I'm happy with what I've got.

"I'm sure it's good for the children to have each other too. There's nothing I don't like about it, except that Nasreen and I don't have enough time together. Most of our time revolves around the children.

"The only thing I would say is that we're definitely not going to have any more! We only want the children we can look after and care for. That means drawing a line at six."

SIGNIFICANCE

In addition to a slowly growing subpopulation of "natalists" who endeavor to have families that are as large as possible, believing that their central mission in adult life is parenthood and the rearing of the next generation, there remains a group of individuals in the United States who are committed to having very large families. They are often a self-described "underground subculture," existing in a society—and, indeed, in a global culture, that discourages the considerable use of resources inherent in the raising of families that contain significantly greater numbers of children than are the norm for their demographic area.

According to the 2000 Census, the average American family has (just under) two children; so few have more than six children that the Census Bureau has eliminated that as a demographic category. There is evidence that families with considerably more than the average number of children may be subject to bias and negative communication from peers and strangers alike. As a result, they sometimes express a belief that they must resort to elaborate explanations to justify their family size to others and to themselves, and that they sometimes either isolate socially in order to avoid criticism, or seek out communities or organizations that encourage large family size.

Mueller and Yoder coined the term "supernormative mothers" to describe mothers who bear, adopt, or otherwise raise four or more children. Their research results support the hypothesis that families with more children may be subject to criticism from other adult members of the dominant culture. Indeed, there is some suggestion in their research population that "outsiders" make a variety of negative value judgments about parents of large families: that they may be neglectful or even abusive to their offspring, that they are diminishing financial and natural resources that belong to the entire population, that they are living in poverty or tapping into governmental or local resources that ought to be given to other, "more deserving" (smaller) families simply because of their size, and that they are unable to adequately parent or otherwise attend to the needs of their children. The same research data suggests that children growing up in large families may also experience a lack of social support or approval. Perceived social support affords several protective functions: It insulates from negative circumstances (such as financial stresses, illness, and the like), increases ability to cope with the pressures and demands of daily life, increases feelings of self-efficacy, personal empowerment, and parenting satisfaction. There is considerable evidence, published by Moore and Chase-Lansdale, as well as by Rosenfeld and Richman, that a feeling of social support or approval can have long-lasing positive impacts on children's future successes.

In a progressively more technologically advanced society, in which citizens are potentially isolated either by life circumstances or perceptions of social stigma, a sense of "virtual community" can sometimes be gained by participating in Internet "chat groups" or information boards populated by other people with similar issues or values, or by attending in-person support groups for parents of large families. Because there may be a lack of community support for large families, considerable satisfaction and relief may be found by being able to turn to others with similar experiences for advice and support, and for answers to questions specific to extra-large families—such as the best spacing of siblings, how to decide when the family is big enough, how to provide for larger numbers of children on limited income, how to buy an appropriately sized vehicle, how to shop for clothing and shoes, how to travel with a group of small children, and how to manage natural family planning.

FURTHER RESOURCES
Books

Bock, Gisela, and Pat Thane, eds. *Maternity and Gender Policies: Women and the Rise of the European Welfare States.* London: Routledge, 1991.

Cheal, David. *New Poverty: Families in Postmodern Society.* Westport, Conn.: Praeger Publishers, 1996.

Cutrona, Carolyn E. *Social Support in Couples.* Thousand Oaks, Calif.: Sage, 1996.

Folbre, Nancy. *Who Pays for the Kids?* New York: Routledge, 1994 .

Gauthier, Anne Helene. *The State and the Family: A Comparative Analysis of Family Policies in Industrialized Countries.* Oxford: Clarendon Press, 1998.

Periodicals

Clyde, A. "Is Big Beautiful?" *Family Life* (March/April 1997): 46–47.

Erdwins, C. J. "The Relationship of Women's Role Strain to Social Support, Role Satisfaction, and self-Efficacy." *Family Relations.* 50(3) (2001): 230–238.

Finfgeld, D.L. "Therapeutic Groups Online: The Good, the Bad, and the Unknown." *Issues in Mental Health Nursing* 21 (2000): 241–255.

Godfrey, A. W. "Crowd Control." *Commonweal* 128(3) (2001): 31.

Ko, M. "Why Large Families Face Insults." *Alberta Report Newsmagazine* 26(8) (1999): 30–31.

Web sites

The Christian Science Monitor. "Life with a Supersized Family." September 19, 2001 <http://www.csmonitor.com/2001/0919/p15s1-lifp.html> (accessed June 23, 2006).

United States Census Bureau. "U. S. Census 2000." March 17, 2006 <http://www.census.gov/main/www/cen2000.html> (accessed June 23, 2006).

The Weekly Standard. "David Brooks." 2006 <http://www.weeklystandard.com/aboutus/bio_brooks.asp> (accessed June 22, 2006).

Babies on Ice

Newspaper Article

By: Viv Groskop

Date: March 4, 2006

Source: Groskop, Vic. *Guardian Newspapers Limited.* "Babies on Ice." (March 4, 2006).

About the Author: Viv Groskop is a journalist who writes for the *Guardian* newspapers in the United Kingdom. She contributes regularly to the *New Statesman*, a British publication that was started in 1913. She has also written for the (London) *Independent* and *Times*, among others.

INTRODUCTION

As women have become progressively more involved in the workforce, the age at which they begin to have children has risen steadily. Often they choose to put off childbearing until well into their thirties, and sometimes beyond. In addition to career aspirations, women often cite the lack of a stable relationship and/or second income among the reasons for not having babies when they're at their most fertile.

Females are born with a finite supply of eggs that begin to "age out" of fertility as they pass their middle and late twenties. Fertility decreases annually after thirty, the number of viable eggs diminishes, and the odds of miscarriage or pregnancy complications increase, although it's important to remember that the relative fertility of each individual is determined by a complex amalgam of genetics, personal history, and other health factors. Complications such as kidney disease, high blood pressure, and diabetes all affect an individual's chances of successful pregnancy and uncomplicated delivery, as do lifestyle factors such as diet, drug or alcohol use, exercise, and the like. While the viability of individual eggs inevitably erodes over time, the ability of a woman's uterus to sustain a pregnancy is far less age limited: it is physically possible to carry a pregnancy to term even when well beyond menopause.

It has been possible to harvest and preserve human sperm for decades, and cryopreservation (freezing) techniques have improved to the point where it is possible to maintain its viability for ten or more years. The same technology has evolved over the past two to three decades to allow human embryos and eggs to be frozen for later use by either the original donor or for another, infertile woman. Embryos (at the stage of several cell divisions after fertilization) have been successfully frozen and thawed more often than have unfertilized eggs.

PRIMARY SOURCE

Until last year, only one "ice baby"—conceived from a frozen egg as part of the IVF [in vitro fertilization] process—had been born in the UK. The past 12 months have seen another three: twins born in September 2005, and a fourth baby due to be born earlier this year. Egg freezing—once a near-impossible technique with a negligible success rate—is becoming a reality.

The Holy Grail of the world of assisted reproduction, egg freezing is the ultimate in fertility control for women. Originally pioneered as a technique for those about to undergo fertility-threatening chemotherapy, its universal

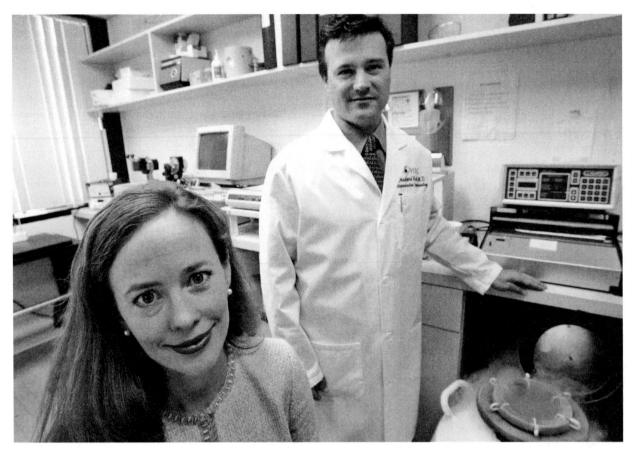

Christy Jones, president and founder of Extend Fertility, and Dr. Bradford Kolb in Pasadena, California, August 16, 2004. Extended Fertility charges $15,000 to freeze eggs for women 40 and under as a kind of biological insurance policy. AP IMAGES.

potential—were there no moral objections—is extraordinary. Christy Jones, founder of one of the US's first egg freezing clinics, describes it as "on a par with the introduction of the pill." If it were ever to catch on, it would in fact be far bigger than that.

Egg freezing allows women to choose a conception date by freezing eggs in their 20s for use as late as their 50s. It is fertility intervention for women who don't necessarily have fertility problems, a sort of precautionary IVF. And, because a healthy woman can carry a baby in her womb long after menopause, in theory it gives her (almost) the same reproductive window as a man.

The procedure is the same as IVF. The ovaries are stimulated to produce a batch of eggs, which are then removed with a needle under a mild sedative or general anaesthetic. The eggs are then drained of fluid, injected with a sort of antifreeze, frozen and stored at −196C in liquid nitrogen. They can be stored indefinitely.

Until last year, the technique remained relatively obscure due to its low success rates. But in June 2005,

Dr. Eleonora Porcu, Europe's leading authority on egg freezing, announced amazing new figures: 80% of eggs were surviving the freeze-thaw process in trials, and pregnancy rates were up to 20%, close to the success rate of regular IVF. So far, around 150 frozen-egg babies have been born worldwide, to patients who needed the technique for medical or ethical reasons—either because they had their eggs harvested prior to chemotherapy or because they had moral objections to the freezing of embryos.

Earlier this year, the London-based Science Media Centre organised a briefing session with a panel of fertility experts which concluded that "putting fertility on ice" could become commonplace in the UK within 10 years. New techniques, it concluded, mean that women in their 20s and 30s would be able to store their eggs for future use as a matter of routine.

In the US, it is predicted that by 2007 we will see the results of "lifestyle egg freezing": the birth of the first ice baby born by choice to a career woman, using eggs she had harvested a few years back. Around two dozen US clinics offer the service for $5,000. Here in the UK, half a dozen clinics can help you out for around £2,000.

It is the commercial potential for egg freezing that makes it particularly contentious. Some supporters of the technique—including Porcu—are opposed to using it expressly to delay fertility. Porcu is keen to advertise its successes in medical and ethical cases, but counsels strongly against widespread use—especially for what she considers the "wrong" (ie, non-essential) reasons. Others—such as Dr Gillian Lockwood, of Midland Fertility Services in Birmingham, who assisted in the conception of all four UK ice babies (all "ethical" cases)—believe the technique should be open to anyone who wants it, without judging their reasons.

Many in the infertility business are simply resigned to the onward march of market forces. Geoffrey Trew, consultant in reproductive medicine and surgery at IVF Hammersmith, undertakes egg freezing for cancer and leukaemia patients, but draws the line at patients who want to pay their way for personal reasons. He thinks that when egg freezing is not the only medical option, it offers a false insurance policy: "If a patient is 31 or 32, it is far better to discuss smoking, obesity and diet, and to advise her that she is better off not freezing her eggs but thinking a bit more about her fertility."…

Dr. Porcu, speaking from her clinic in Bologna, Italy, is adamant that ethical and medical reasons should be at the heart of decisions to use egg freezing. The technology, she says, was not designed as a form of DIY reproductive delay. She argues the very idea is anti-women because it allows society to maintain the pretence that having a family is a hindrance to a career. She argues that it is taking birth control too far: "You have to take pills. You have to induce superovulation. All this, not because you have a disease but for some hypothetical pregnancy after the age of 40? I think it is risky. And the idea of postponing a pregnancy because it is not accepted in your workplace when you are 30? This is something really violent towards women."

Dr Lockwood at Midland Fertility Services argues the opposite. Egg freezing is, as she puts it, "the ultimate in family planning." At her clinic in Walsall, on the outskirts of Birmingham, the atmosphere is cheery and unclinical. Lockwood has treated hundreds of IVF couples and dozens of candidates for egg freezing, a significant minority for "lifestyle reasons."…

Lockwood, 50, is the sort of physician you trust immediately: bright, thoughtful, sensitive, an easy manner. She believes women should have access to technology to help them combine career and motherhood. She decided to specialise in fertility issues early: "When I was in my 20s, a consultant told me, '[M]y dear, you will have

to choose whether you want to be a mother or a doctor.' I thought, 'We'll see about that.'" A mother of three, she had her first child at 26. You are inclined to believe her when she talks about how easy it would be to get your eggs frozen—and the benefits for women who currently have no chance of having a child in addition to the adult life and career they want. She is passionate about the freedom this would give women.…

Lockwood says that, in her experience, the women who choose to freeze their eggs for social reasons are more likely to be in their late 30s or early 40s. "Often they've been in a relationship that they assumed was going to lead to marriage and motherhood—possibly for 10 years. Then at 37, 38, the boyfriend says, 'I don't think fatherhood is for me.' Or he meets someone else. This woman—who has always assumed that eventually a baby or two would come along—finds herself single with her biological clock running down quite fast."

Lockwood becomes quite emotional when talking about this. She has obviously been faced with the grief of dozens of women in this situation. She has to tell some of these potential patients that it really is too late for them: "I need to know that they know that by the time they're in their late 30s the chance of any of those eggs turning into a live birth is very low." Lockwood consents to freeze their eggs only if she is convinced that "they know this is not an insurance policy, that it is just a possibility."

The clinic has so far had few approaches from women in their late 20s and early 30s. Lockwood regrets this: "If only they knew that, from the age of 35, it takes twice as long to get pregnant as under 35. That from the age of 40, the miscarriage rate is 40%, and from the age of 45, the miscarriage rate is 70%." Whatever your age or situation, she says, egg freezing can buy you time: "Eggs can be stored indefinitely. It's not like fish fingers in your freezer where you need to eat them within three months."

One of Lockwood's "lifestyle" egg freezing patients, "Lucy" (not her real name) agrees—with some reluctance—to talk anonymously over the phone. Not, she says, because she is ashamed of what she has done, but because she is a "private person." Lucy, 40, a worker in the IT industry in the Midlands, is one of an estimated 100 British women who have had their eggs frozen because they eventually want a child but are not in a relationship.

Her scenario is straight out of Dr Lockwood's casebook. At 28 she met the man with whom she thought she would have children. They never quite got round to it, and when she was 35 the relationship broke up unexpectedly. She decided to have her eggs frozen two years ago, at 38, after seeing television coverage of the Perry family. Now 12 of Lucy's eggs are stored at the Midland clinic. She admits that she does not know if they will ever be fertilised. "There is no guarantee I am going to meet somebody," she says, "I just think that if there are options available that can put you in a position where you have a choice, I'm all for it. I wanted the pressure taken off me because time was running out."

The procedure was harmless, she says, although her views on it seem mixed: "I can't even remember it now. It must be like childbirth—you forget about it as soon as you've got your baby. People are scared of the pain of giving birth, but it's something you just do. You put yourself in that position because the end result is what you want. I remember being at home for a couple of days, feeling uncomfortable and quite weak. But it was nothing, really."

The likelihood of Lucy's efforts resulting in a live birth is small: "I can't remember the percentage they gave me, but I know it wasn't very high. It didn't bother me because I had no other choice." There are other issues, questions she can't answer. Will she meet a man within the 10-year storage limit? (Although she could apply for an extension past the age of 48, and even give birth after the menopause.) If not, does she go down the sperm donor route? Until what age is she prepared to wait? She just doesn't know.

In the meantime, it seems egg freezing is being recommended by health professionals in the U.S. as an insurance policy for women in their mid–20s. Kristina Cashion, 27, a law student from Houston, Texas, popped up on one of hundreds of U.S. internet fertility forums. We spoke over the phone. She went for a routine checkup at her doctor's last year: "As I'm lying back on the exam table, the nurse says, 'I want to talk to you about possibly harvesting some of your eggs and getting them frozen. Because with the career you've chosen, it could be many years before you have time to have a child and your fertility will cut in half by the time you're 30.'"

Cashion, who is getting married this year and plans a family eventually, was horrified. Worse, one of her law professors told her the nurse's concerns were legitimate and that she, too, wanted to let her students know they "cannot put off having children indefinitely." At a later check-up, another doctor reassured Cashion it was "nothing to be concerned about at this point in life." Still, it has become a hot topic on campus. Cashion says half her friends have investigated the cost of egg freezing (although she doesn't know anyone who has gone through with it)....

Dr. Gillian Lockwood, however, has a powerful argument in favour of the technique. As IVF use increases anyway, surely it makes more sense to plan for what's really going on in women's lives, rather than bury our heads in the sand? "As a doctor, I would much rather try to help a 40-year-old get pregnant with her own eggs that she had frozen when she was 30. You have a statistically much better chance using a 30-year-old's eggs; a 40-year-old's eggs don't implant well. It's the age of the egg that determines the quality—it's nothing to do with the age of the uterus."

Dr. Porcu, of course, disagrees. She finds this kind of family planning depressing: "To say when you are 30, 'Probably in 10 years I will need IVF so I'll freeze my eggs.'" Her voice trails off. She is rendered speechless by the idea. "I don't think women should trust this. Not—and I want to be precise—because of the technique itself. It works. But to trust this technique for the planning of your reproductive life. Well, I am a bit perplexed by the idea." Suddenly she realises the one application it does have. She laughs. "Hmm, I think this is a way for doctors to earn money."

SIGNIFICANCE

Cryopreservation for unfertilized eggs was originally intended for women who were either about to undergo medical procedures that could interfere with fertility or that had potential implications for DNA alteration in unfertilized eggs. The use of egg freezing to delay healthy or lower-risk childbearing, or to donate eggs—analogous to the way in which men donate sperm to banks—evolved only within the past several years, because it is far more difficult to freeze a human egg than it is human sperm. This is mainly because the oocyte (egg) is the largest cell in the human body, and it contains a significant amount of water. When frozen, the water turns to ice, which can damage the cell's membranes. Freezing technology had to be developed that could eliminate the water and freeze the egg and its cellular contents without damaging either the cell structure or its genetic contents.

Unlike thawed sperm, which is often simply placed inside the uterus or at the cervix of the woman seeking insemination, thawed eggs cannot simply be put back into a woman's body to be fertilized—They must be fertilized by means of assisted reproductive technology (ART), outside the body. As technology advances, however, it will become progressively easier and less costly to harvest, thaw, and fertilize human eggs, whether for the woman from whom they were harvested or for donation to another.

Because egg production is fixed, meaning that a female is born with all of the egg follicles she will ever have, eggs age over time and become less viable—less easily fertilized and carried through a successful full-term pregnancy. With each month after the onset of menses, the quality of the eggs released can vary, with significantly reduced potential fertility after the age of 35. By harvesting eggs and freezing them in her 20s or early 30s, a woman may be able to postpone a healthy and viable pregnancy for a decade or more.

Scientists hope to develop a freezing technology that will give unfertilized eggs the same potential viability as frozen embryos. During the first decade of the twenty-first century, Japanese scientists developed an effective method that eliminated the formation of cell-wall damaging ice crystals. This advance may boost the potential fertility rates of thawed eggs from 1:100 to 10:100, making it far more cost-effective. This may make it progressively more possible for women to use egg freezing to postpone child-bearing until they are ready to do so, rather than feeling that their "biological clock" is running down.

Several fertility clinics specializing in the harvesting and freezing of human eggs have been opened, primarily in larger cities in the United States. For varying fees, unfertilized eggs are harvested, frozen, and banked for later use. At present, fertility and viability rates for the thawed eggs remain considerably lower than thawed sperm—in part because eggs are generally fertilized singly, with the addition of several million sperm. As technology improves and fertilization rates for thawed eggs increase, it will become more and more affordable for women who wish to delay child-bearing to avail themselves of this possibility.

FURTHER RESOURCES

Books

Bauer, M.W., and G. Gaskell, eds. *Biotechnology: The Making of a Global Controversy*. Cambridge, UK: Cambridge University Press, 2002.

Blank, R.H., and J. Merrick. *Human Reproduction, Emerging Technologies, and Conflicting Rights*. Washington, DC: CQ Press, 1995.

Gaskell, G., and M. W. Bauer, eds. *Biotechnology 1996–2000: The Years of Controversy*. London, UK: Science Museum, 2001.

Harris. J., and Søren Holm, eds. *The Future of Reproduction: Ethics, Choice, and Regulation*. Oxford, UK: Oxford University Press, 1998.

Saetnam, A.R., N. Oudshoorn, and M. Kirejczyk, eds. *Bodies of Technology: Women's Involvement with Reproductive Medicine*. Columbus, OH: Ohio State University Press, 2000.

United States Department of Health and Human Services. *2003 Assisted Reproductive Technology Success Rates: National Summary and Fertility Clinic Reports*. Atlanta, GA: Centers for Disease Control and Prevention, December 2005.

Periodicals

Abdalla, H. I. "A National Oocyte Donation Society Is Needed." *Human Reproduction*. 11, no. 11 (November 1996): 1255–1356.

Abdalla, H., and J. W. Studd. "Egg Donation and Medical Ethics." *British Medical Journal*. 299 (1989): 120.

Gosden, R.C. "Maternal Age: A Major Factor Affecting the Prospects and Outcome of Pregnancy." *Annals of the New York Academy of Science*. 442 (1985): 45–57.

Hansen, J. "Older Maternal Age and Pregnancy Outcome: A Review of the Literature." *Obstetrics and Gynaecology Survey*. 41 (1986): 726–734.

Salter, B. "Medicine, Civil Society and the State: Continuities in Biopolitics?" *Swiss Political Science Review*. 9, no. 2 (2003): 135–142.

Salter, B. "Who Rules? The New Politics of Medical Regulation." *Social Science and Medicine*. 52, no. 6 (March 2001): 871–873.

Web sites

International Assisted Reproduction Center. "Fertility Options." 2006 <http://www.fertilityhelp.com/CM/AboutAssisted Reproduction/Fertility_Options.asp> (accessed June 21, 2006).

Reuters. "Japan Experts Devise New Human Egg Freezing Method." June 19, 2006 <http://www.alertnet.org/ thenews/newsdesk/L1994843.htm> (accessed June 22, 2006).

American Surrogacy Center (TASC). "TASC Articles: Medical." <http://www.surrogacy.com/Articles/> (accessed June 21, 2006).

San Diego Union-Tribune. "Commercial Freezing of Human Eggs Has Backers, Opponents." September 29, 2004 <http://www.signonsandiego.com/uniontrib/ 20040929/news_1c29eggs.html> (accessed June 22, 2006).

Wanted: A Few Good Sperm

News article

By: Jennifer Egan

Date: March 19, 2006

Source: Egan, Jennifer. "Wanted: A Few Good Sperm." *The New York Times*. (19 March 2006)

About the Author: Jennifer Egan has published three books and writes for such publications as the *New York Times Magazine, Zoetrope, The New Yorker*, and

Harper's. Her book *Look at Me* was a finalist for the National Book Award.

INTRODUCTION

Single motherhood by choice, rather than circumstance, emerged as a trend in the United States in the early 1980s. In 1981, Jane Mattes founded the organization Single Mothers By Choice, in response to a lack of support for mothers like her, who had chosen single motherhood, rather than fallen into it by circumstance. As career choices opened up for women in the 1970s and 1980s, greater numbers of women found themselves in their late thirties and early forties unmarried, yet wanting to have biological or adopted children, but outside of marriage. Mattes' organization focuses on support; part of its philosophy includes "support and information to single mothers by choice and to single women considering motherhood, to provide a peer group for our children, and to clarify the public's understanding of single mothers by choice." Though no statistics are kept to determine how many women in the United States are single mothers by choice, the number of women seeking membership in organizations such as Single Mothers By Choice and the National Organization of Single Mothers is on the rise.

In 1981, there were 19.1 births per one thousand women to single mothers; in 2001 that figure had increased to 35.5. Births to women over the age of thirty-five have nearly doubled in the past two decades. Many professional women devote their twenties to their graduate degrees and first jobs, their thirties to professional advancement, and find themselves at the end of their thirties ready for a child—but without a suitable partner. As Sylvia Ann Hewlett notes in her controversial 2002 book *Creating a Life: What Every Woman Needs to Know About Having a Baby and a Career*, reproductive technologies can help women to become pregnant without male partners, but they cannot stop the advance of natural fertility reduction. When only ten percent of women over the age of forty-two are able to conceive naturally, but the majority of women in polls do not know that fertility begins to decline at age twenty-seven, Hewlett's book connected the "man shortage" for professional women touted by the media for years with the expectation that babies could wait until after a career was established.

Sperm and egg banks have experienced dramatic rises in business over the past twenty years, selling sperm and more recently, eggs, to married heterosexual couples, single heterosexual women, lesbian couples, couples hiring surrogates, and a wide range of other couples making choices using these banks. More than one hundred sperm banks operate in the United

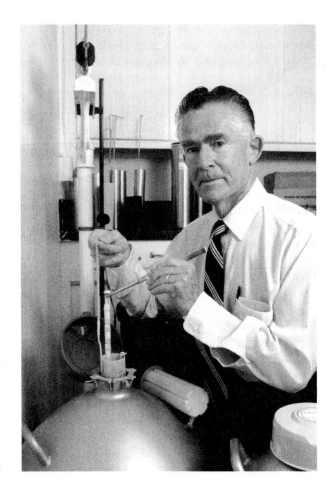

Dr. Robert Graham founder of the Genius Sperm Bank in San Diego, is photographed with a vial of sperm, July 1982. Dr. Graham provided the sperm to Dr. Aftom Blake who gave birth to Doron Blake. PHOTO PAUL HARRIS/LIAISON.

States, and women can select characteristics ranging from hair color to shoe size to IQ from donors.

Meanwhile, single, well-educated, professional women like Karyn in the article below find themselves shopping for sperm donors online as they make their decision to be a single mother by choice.

◼ PRIMARY SOURCE

One day last October, Karyn, a thirty-nine-year-old executive, pulled her online dating profile off *Jdate* and *Match.com*, two sites she had been using, along with an endless series of leads, tips and blind dates arranged by friends and colleagues, to search for a man she wanted to marry and raise a family with. At long last, after something like one hundred dates in the past ten years and several serious relationships, she had found the man she refers to, tongue only slightly in cheek, as "the one." It all began last summer, when she broke off a relationship with a younger man who wasn't ready for children and got serious about the idea of conceiving on her own. She gathered information about fertility doctors and sperm banks. "Then a childhood friend of mine was over," she told me. "I pulled up the Web site of the only sperm bank that I know of that has adult photos. There happened to be one Jewish person. I pulled up the photo, and I looked at my friend, and I looked at his picture, and I said, 'Oh, my God.' I can't say love at first sight, because, you know. But he was the one."

Sperm donors, like online daters, answer myriad questions about heroes, hobbies and favorite things. Karyn read her donor's profile and liked what she saw. "You can tell he comes from a warm family, some very educated," she said. He had worked as a chef. He had "proven fertility," meaning that at least one woman conceived using his sperm. Like all sperm donors, he was free from any sexually transmitted diseases or testable genetic disorders. "People in New York change sex partners quicker than the crosstown bus," Karyn said. "I'd be a lot more concerned about my date next week." But she especially liked the fact that he was an identity-release donor (also called an "open donor" or a "yes donor")—a growing and extremely popular category of sperm donors who are willing to be contacted by any offspring who reach the age of eighteen.

The next morning, Karyn called the bank and spoke with a woman who worked there. "She said: 'I have to be honest. He's very popular, and I only have eight units in store right now. I'm not sure how much longer he might be in the program,' Karyn told me. "Most women in New York impulse-buy Manolo Blahniks, and I said, 'I'll take the eight units.' It was $3,100." The price included six months of storage.

That hefty purchase, and the strong sense of connection she felt to the donor, galvanized Karyn: she made an appointment with a reproductive endocrinologist and gave up alcohol and caffeine. At work, she took on a position of greater responsibility and longer hours—with a higher salary—to save money. She went on a wait list to buy more of the donor's sperm when it became available. (All donor sperm must be quarantined for six months—the maximum incubation period for H.I.V.—so that the donor can be retested for the disease before it is released.) She told her parents and married sister what was going on, e-mailing the donor's picture to her father with an invitation that he meet his son-in-law. She also printed the donor's picture and kept it on the coffee table of her Manhattan studio apartment, where she sleeps in a Murphy bed. "I kind of glance at it as I pass," she said of the picture. "It's almost like when you date someone,

and you keep looking at them, and you're, like, Are they cute? But every time I pass, I'm, like, Oh, he's really cute. It's a comforting feeling."

When I suggested that she must be a type who is prone to love at first sight, she just laughed. "With online dating, friends used to say: 'What about him? What about him?' I'd say: 'don't like the nose. Ah, the eyes are a little buggy. He really likes to golf, and you know I don't like golfing.' There was always something. If I said this about everyone," she concluded, "I would have married someone about seventy-five dates ago."

Karyn said she hoped to join a population of women that everyone agrees is expanding, although by how much is hard to pin down because single mothers by choice (or choice mothers), as they are sometimes called, aren't separated statistically from, say, babies born to unwed teenagers. Between 1999 and 2003 there was an almost seventeen percent jump in the number of babies born to unmarried women between ages thirty and forty-four in America, according to the National Center for Human Statistics, while the number born to unmarried women between fifteen and twenty-four actually decreased by nearly six percent. Single Mothers by Choice, a twenty-five-year-old support group, took in nearly double the number of new members in 2005 as it did ten years ago, and its roughly 4,000 current members include women in Israel, Australia and Switzerland. The California Cryobank, the largest sperm bank in the country, owed a third of its business to single women in 2005, shipping them 9,600 vials of sperm, each good for one insemination.

As recently as the early 60's, a "respectable" woman needed to be married just to have sex, not to speak of children; a child born out of wedlock was a source of deepest shame. Yet this radical social change feels strangely inevitable; nearly a third of American households are headed by women alone, many of whom not only raise their children on their own but also support them. All that remains is conception, and it is small wonder that women have begun chipping away at needing a man for that—especially after Sylvia Ann Hewlett's controversial 2002 book, "Creating a Life: Professional Women and the Quest for Children," sounded alarms about declining fertility rates in women over thirty-five. The Internet is also a factor; as well as holding meetings through local chapters around the country, Single Mothers by Choice hosts eleven Listservs, each addressing a different aspect of single motherhood. Women around the world pore over these lists, exchanging tips and information, selling one another leftover vials of sperm. (Once sperm has shipped, it can't be returned to the bank.) Karyn found both her sperm bank and reproductive endocrinologist on these Listservs. Three-quarters of the members of Single Mothers by Choice choose to conceive with donor sperm, as lesbian couples have been doing for many years—adoption is costly, slow-moving and often biased against single people. Buying sperm over the Internet, on the other hand, is not much different from buying shoes.

SIGNIFICANCE

In 2005 and 2006, Republican lawmakers in Indiana and Virginia crafted laws that would prohibit single women from using reproductive technologies such as artificial insemination, intrauterine insemination, or in vitro fertilization; though the laws were struck down in committee in both states, the message was clear. Women who choose single motherhood, outside of marriage, are viewed by religious conservatives as aberrations.

Vice President Dan Quayle, in 1992, famously pointed to fictional television character Murphy Brown as an example of highly paid professional mothers who, in his words, were "mocking the importance of fathers, by bearing a child alone, and calling it just another 'lifestyle choice'." The television character Murphy Brown was not a single mother by choice—her character had become pregnant by accident, and she chose to keep the baby—while Qualye's choice to use a fictional character to make a social point was derided by late night television comedians and policy experts alike. His message, though, was embraced by cultural conservatives such as James Dobson, founder of Focus on the Family, who stated that "virtually every poll taken during the firestorm revealed that the majority of the people agreed with Mr. Quayle." However, when Sex and the City's fictional character Miranda gave birth as a single mother just ten years later, the episode triggered barely a ripple or comment from the media or cultural critics.

More than thirty percent of all children born in the United States are born to unmarried mothers; single mothers by choice represent a small percentage of these births. Although their numbers are small, the women who join Single Mothers By Choice are organized, having created a sibling registry using donor numbers from sperm banks; single mothers who used the same donor for conception can connect with other single mothers by choice to meet and know their child's half-sibling. This non-traditional approach to building a family has become part of the milieu of choices in modern parenting, a sea change since 1978, when the world welcomed Louise Brown as the first test tube baby; in vitro fertilization now assists thousands of single mothers by choice to fulfill their family dreams.

FURTHER RESOURCES

Books

Warner, Judith. *Perfect Madness: Motherhood in the Age of Anxiety*. New York: Riverhead Hardcover, 2005.

Wattes, Jane. *Single Mothers by Choice: A Guidebook for Single Women Who Are Considering or Have Chosen Motherhood*. New York: Three Rivers Press, 1994.

Wolf, Naomi. *Misconceptions: Truth, Lies, and the Unexpected on the Journey to Motherhood*. New York: Anchor, 2003.

Periodicals

Bock, Jane D. "Doing the Right Thing? Single Mothers by Choice and the Struggle for Legitimacy." *Gender and Society*. 14 (February 2000): 62-86.

Gibbs, Nancy. "Making Time for a Baby." *Time Magazine*. (15 April 2002).

By Surmounting a Few Production Humps, Camel Milk Could Bring in Billions

News article

By: Anonymous

Date: April 19, 2006

Source: *United Nations News Centre*. "By Surmounting a Few Production Humps, Camel Milk Could Bring in Billions." April 19, 2006 <http://www.un.org/apps/news/> (accessed July 12, 2006).

About the Author: Founded in 1946, the United Nations is an international mediation and aid agency. Its various divisions help mediate political disputes, police militarily unstable regions, and work to improve living conditions throughout the world.

INTRODUCTION

The nomadic lifestyle, in which people regularly relocate from place to place with all their possessions, has existed for centuries. Prior to the development of agriculture and the need to remain near crops, many families subsisted by moving from place to place. In some cultures, these moves were undertaken to follow game animals such as the buffalo of North America. Desert regions, which provided little opportunity for

A nomad boy drinks camel milk in the desert of Somalia, 2003. © LIBA TAYLOR/CORBIS.

agriculture or extensive grazing in a single location often gave rise to nomadic lifestyles, as herders moved their animals to find new food sources.

In most developed countries, nomadic lifestyles are the exception today, because modern life often revolves around a fixed home, schools, employment, and other immobile elements of industrialized life. Nomadic life in the early twenty-first century is limited primarily to less developed areas of the world, and even in these regions political and economic changes are forcing nomads to adjust their lifestyles.

In Saudi Arabia, where nomadic herders have traveled the desert for centuries, around 100,000 remain. However, nomadic life has become more difficult in recent years. Camels, the traditional workhorse of the dessert, have become much more expensive to maintain. Previously extensive rangeland has been severely curtailed by urban growth, limiting the nomads to a sharply reduced range. International competition has also changed the nomadic way of life, as imported sheep and goats reduce the price nomadic herders receive for their livestock.

Some nomads today practice a hybrid lifestyle, choosing to remain within a limited area so their children may attend school. In other cases, nomads take part-time jobs on game hunting ranches to earn the cash they now require to buy water and feed for their livestock. Because of range restrictions, many of the traditional pasture areas have been overgrazed, forcing ever increasing investments in feed and water. In some ways, the new lifestyle of many nomads has come to more closely resemble ranching. As a result of these changes, nomads are being gradually drawn into the mainstream community, at least economically and in many cases geographically.

PRIMARY SOURCE

By surmounting a few production humps, camel milk could bring in billions—UN

19 April 2006— Developing camel dairy products such as milk can not only provide more food to people in arid and semi-arid areas but also give nomadic herders a rich source of income, with a $10 billion world market entirely within the realm of possibility, according to the United Nations Food and Agriculture Organization (FAO).

"The potential is massive. Milk is money," FAO's Dairy and Meat expert Anthony Bennett said in a review of camel milk potential, noting that the agency is hoping donors and investors will come forward to develop the sector not only at the local level but helping it move into lucrative markets in the Middle East and the West.

"No one's suggesting intensive camel dairy farming, but just with improved feed, husbandry and veterinary care daily yields could rise to 20 litres," he added, noting that at present production is a low-tech business with a meagre five litres a day considered a decent yield. Since fresh camel milk fetches roughly $1 a litre on African markets, that would mean serious money for nomad herders who now have few other sources of revenue.

From the Western Sahara to Mongolia demand is booming for camel milk, but there just isn't enough to go round. State-of the art camel rearing is rudimentary, and much of the 5.4 million tonnes of milk currently produced every year by the world population of some 20 million camels is guzzled by young camels themselves. To devotees, camel milk is pure nectar. While slightly saltier than cows' milk, it is three times as rich in Vitamin C as its bovine equivalent. But tapping the market involves surmounting a series of humps in production, manufacturing and marketing.

One problem lies in the milk itself, which has so far not proved to be compatible with the UHT (Ultra High Temperature) treatment needed to make it long-lasting. But the main challenge stems from the fact that the producers involved are, overwhelmingly, nomads, a situation similar to a tomato cannery depending on suppliers who regularly disappear, taking their tomatoes with them.

Another problem is that nomad camel herders are often reluctant to sell their spare milk, which tradition reserves for honoured guests and the poor. It has been noted, however, that such reluctance can be dispelled by the offer of a good price.

Jumping on the camel train, Vienna-based chocolatier Johann Georg Hochleitner intends to launch this autumn a low-fat, camel milk chocolate with funding from the Abu Dhabi royal family, making it in Austria from powdered milk produced at Al Ain in the United Arab Emirates, then shipping 50 tons back to the Gulf each month.

"It sounds crazy but it's a huge project. There's a potential market of 200 million in the Arab world," Mr. Hochleitner says.

SIGNIFICANCE

China's Xinjiang province is home to more than one million residents, most of them historically nomadic. In 2004 the Chinese government began a massive project to relocate these residents into more permanent government-funded communities with modern housing and schools. The result was a generational shift as a traditionally nomadic population adopted a fixed lifestyle. In the newly settled communities, livestock survival rates have climbed in the initial years following the change, however only time will tell how well the human residents adapt to their new surroundings and lifestyle.

Modern technology has enabled some previously fixed workers to adopt a more nomadic existence. While many creative undertakings such as writing and publishing have long depended on the ability to easily transport or mail paper documents, the advent of widespread e-mail access has allowed many such workers to labor in virtually any location. As an example, this book was created by authors and editors who are geographically separated on multiple continents and in some cases have never met in person. For such workers, technology has eliminated the need for a fixed work location.

For many years, seniors in northern climates have followed an annual migratory path to Florida each year, living in rented housing there to avoid the harsh winters at home. Some retirees are taking this practice one step further by selling their primary residences and living entirely in a motor home or other recreational vehicle as they travel. In some cases, they fill part-time jobs at national parks and other tourist locations, while others simply travel and sightsee. These modern nomads are known in Australia as Grey Nomads and are found on virtually every continent.

While senior nomads appear likely to proliferate, the future of the traditional nomadic life appears cloudy. Some nomads have already accepted the need to do business with the outside world and are experiencing both the benefits and the costs of such an arrangement. Some nomadic people will undoubtedly choose to maintain their existing lifestyle; however, increasing communication with the outside world may lead some of their offspring to abandon their traditional lifestyle for a more modern existence. The exit of the young, combined with increasing economic pressure can be expected to put tremendous pressure on nomads in the coming years.

FURTHER RESOURCES

Books

Gelman, Rita. *Tales of a Female Nomad: Living at Large in the World*. New York: Three Rivers Press, 2001.

Grant, Richard. *American Nomads: Travels with Lost Conquistadors, Mountain Men, Cowboys, Indians, Hoboes, Truckers, and Bullriders*. New York: Grove Press, 2003.

Khazanov, Anatoly. *Nomads and the Outside World*. Milwaukee: University of Wisconsin Press, 1994.

Periodicals

Abraham, Curtis. "Unsettled Existence." *New Scientist*. 189 (2006): 18.

Garcea, Elena. "Semi-Permanent Foragers in Semi-Arid Environments of North Africa." *World Archeology*. 38 (2006): 197–219.

Ward, Christopher J. "Mongols, Turks, and Others: Eurasian Nomads and the Sedentary World." *New York Times*. 17 (2006): 95–97.

Web sites

Academy of Natural Sciences. "Horsemen of the Mongolian Steppes: Nomadic Life Beyond the Great Wall." <http://www.acnatsci.org/museum/traveling/horsemen.html> (accessed July 12, 2006).

China Daily. "1 Million Xinjiang Herdsmen Say Goodbye to Nomadic Life." August 8, 2005 <http://www.chinadaily.com.cn/english/doc/2005-08/08/content_467256.htm> (accessed July 12, 2006).

Our Flesh and Blood

News article

By: Emma Cook

Date: March 25, 2006

Source: Cook, Emma. *The Guardian Newspapers Limited*. "Our Flesh and Blood." (March 25, 2006).

About the Author: Emma Cook is a journalist and writer who contributes regularly to the *Guardian* newspapers in the United Kingdom. She has also written for the *London Independent*. In addition, she is a broadcast journalist for BBC Wales and is well known for her in-depth interview style, both in print and broadcast.

INTRODUCTION

Living donor transplantation surgery first occurred in the United States in 1954, between iden-tical twins. Ronal Herrick's healthy kidney was given to his brother Richard, who suffered from chronic kidney failure. The operation, which took place at the hospital now known as Brigham and Women's (then called Peter Bent Brigham), was a success.

There is a perpetual shortage of available donor organs from cadavers, and it is not uncommon to wait many years for the availability of suitable donor organs. Often, those in need of new organs for survival die without ever having reached the top of their particular waiting list. Living donors may be a viable option for some persons for whom there is a friend or relative who is an appropriate tissue match. Several different organs may be acquired from living donors; the most successfully transplanted to date are lung, liver, intestine, pancreas, heart, and kidney.

Kidney transplants occur with greater frequency than do any other type of living organ donor (LOD) surgeries. The risks are relatively low, as a person can live a (basically) normal life with a single kidney—which will expand and take on the workload of the missing organ. In an LOD liver transplant, a small segment of the liver is removed and transplanted into the recipient. In both individuals, the liver may fully regenerate and regain its original level of functionality. A lobe of one lung can be resected and transplanted to another individual; the lung does not regenerate. A portion of the pancreas can be resected and transplanted with no danger to either individual. Small segments of the intestine can be removed form one person and transplanted into another, although this is an infrequent operation. Among the rarest LOD transplants involves the heart: Very infrequently, a person with pulmonary disease will receive a "bloc" transplant involving heart and lungs from a cadaver donor; their healthy heart can be transplanted into another person.

The National Organ Transplant Act (NOTA), which was legislated in 1984, outlaws the exchange of money for donor organs; it is legal for the recipient to pay for the donor's transportation, lodging, lost wages, and the cost of the transplant procedure.

■ PRIMARY SOURCE

Bill has always been close to his daughter Laura. Thirty-eight years ago, he held her minutes after she was born, and marvelled at her vulnerability; her back barely bigger than the palm of his hand. "Now I can't believe that things have come full circle," he says. "Who'd have thought that that tiny baby would have saved my life?"

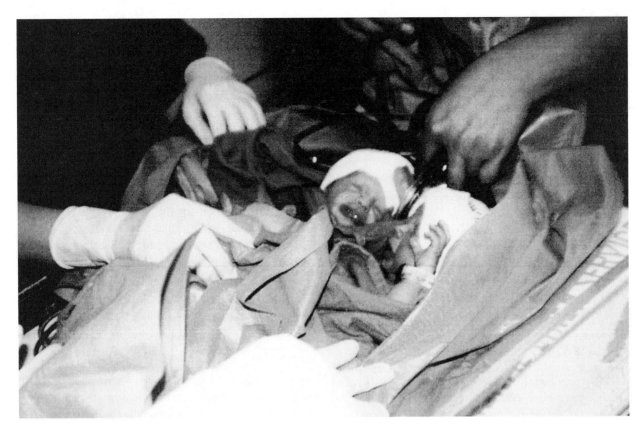

Twins Sydney and Morgan Reed, at Covenant Hospital in Lubbock, Texas, February 29, 2004. The twins were carried to term by their grandmother, Marianne Thoms, who volunteered to be a surrogate mother after her son and daughter-in-law Shawn and Traci Reed learned that Traci could not carry a child. AP IMAGES.

Last October, Laura donated her kidney to Bill, now 63, after he was diagnosed with polycystic kidney disease (PKD), a genetic disorder leading to kidney failure. "My dad kept saying he didn't want my kidney, he didn't want me to go through any heartache and pain. I was adamant I wanted to do it; I'm a mother of two and I wanted my dad to watch them growing up. Deep down I knew he felt it was his only chance." Laura had two sisters, but they both had young babies, while her brother also suffered from PKD. So Laura was the obvious donor.

Then the bombshell dropped. After a series of blood and tissue tests, the hospital told them that Bill wasn't actually Laura's biological father. It was a secret her mother, now divorced from Bill, had kept from both of them. "Neither of us had any idea. I was gutted," says Laura. "I challenged my mum but she just wouldn't talk about it. If anything, it made me more determined than ever. I wanted to be part of him; to have a real part of me existing in him."

Bill no longer tried to dissuade her, now that he knew how much it meant to her. "I felt such a mix of emotions knowing what she was about to do; gratitude, love, worry

if anything should happen to her. I didn't want her to think my feelings towards her as a father had changed. I'll always be her Dad; the rest is history. It still seems a little unreal that part of her is ticking away inside of me happily and healthily."

Laura and Bill have no regrets about their decision, but there have been emotional consequences. Laura found her mother's deceit difficult to reconcile and hasn't told her other siblings about the discovery for fear it would break the family apart.

Family sacrifice of this kind isn't unusual and neither are the emotional complexities that follow. "Often when relations make the decision to donate, it is an instant response that can be uninformed. They don't always take on board the psychological effects," says Celia Eggeling, renal counsellor for the South West Thames Renal and Transplantation Unit. Understandably, it is difficult to be rational here; a loved one falls ill and the desire to help is overwhelming. Beyond the health concerns, other considerations seem trivial.

In terms of related organ donation, these instincts are being encouraged. More than 5,000 people are waiting for a kidney transplant, yet fewer than 2,000 can be carried out each year. Transplants from living donors are highly successful and already account for one in four of all kidney transplants in the UK. When living donors and patients are close relatives, the chance of a successful transplant are improved.

Of course, there is relief when an operation is successful and a loved one has a new lease of life but there can be more uncomfortable emotions, too. Apprehension, doubt and anxiety are all likely to creep in before and after a donation. What is crucial in any physical family sacrifice is the strength of the relationship between giver and recipient. After Emma Wellesley, 35, was diagnosed with a rare lung complaint at the age of 19, she knew she wouldn't be able to have children naturally—her lungs and heart would be too weak to sustain a pregnancy. So when Emma wanted children, her mother, Annie Casserley, 53, offered to act as a surrogate mother, carrying an embryo from her daughter and son-in-law.

"Mum was the only person in the world I would have trusted. I don't think it's changed anything between us, except now we see each other more. When it comes to telling [my daughter] Annie Trinity, I'm not bothered. She'll know she was surrounded by people who loved her," says Emma. Her mother had a healthy pregnancy and gave birth by caesarean last September. Despite the extraordinary conditions, she felt surprisingly detached and single-minded about her undertaking. "I couldn't bear to see Emma heartbroken. When I was pregnant, I was taking care of Emma's baby in my womb, looking after her for a while—in the same way I'd look after my other two grandchildren."

However the motivation behind some family sacrifices are less clear-cut to those involved. Last year, Greg Sanukonanu, 34, donated a kidney to his sister Celestina Lepcha, 29, with the help of St George's Hospital in south London. Greg took six months' unpaid leave from his job at a boarding school in India, and stayed in London, leaving behind his wife and five-year-old son. It was an enormous commitment but Greg was happy to make it: "I was ready to do something for her because, as a family, we are close." Initially Celestina felt uncomfortable with his offer. "I felt if anything had gone wrong, what would I say to his family?" Fortunately, all went well. "After the operation I was in tears, I was so thankful to him. I couldn't explain to him how grateful I felt."

Yet, deep down, Celestina also felt puzzled. She hadn't been close to Greg when they were growing up. "We didn't get along. He used to have a short-temper and we would fight." Celestina hopes they will be closer since the operation, even though Greg is back in India. "One thing is clear: although he doesn't show it, I know he loves me."

There are numerous reasons why relatives step forward to donate and the dynamics of every family's history will have a bearing. "There can be rivalry and competitiveness," explains Eggeling. "One parent or sibling can feel they should donate as a way of getting back into a family if they've been estranged. There is also a weeding-out process; a pecking order about who is the most suitable depending on if they're married, with children or single."

What one tends to assume is that the instinct to prolong or improve the life of a child, sibling, parent and partner is all-powerful. But there are situations where relatives feel unable to donate. This is most likely to happen when family pressure to go ahead has been too great to bear. Jean Mitchell, a counsellor at a hospital in Surrey, recalls a case where a brother had agreed to give his sister a kidney but refused a few days before the operation. Scared at the prospect of losing an organ, he was overwhelmed by family expectation. "He felt he had to give in to her and hadn't been given enough choice," recalls Jean.

In another case, she says, an only son with three younger siblings was the perfect kidney match for his father. "He felt unable to proceed and it was such a slap in the face to his parents. He had always felt that his wishes had been ignored; that he was always bowing to his father's wishes."

Two years later, the family are still searching for an outside donor. "We had to tell him how courageous he was being," says Jean. "Our role is to protect the potential donor, even if it means the rest of the family vent their anger and disappointment on us." She has also come across parents who refuse to donate to a child. "One mother said, 'my daughter's been ill since she was a child, now it's my son's turn to have some of me.' Her daughter is still on dialysis."

One dynamic is clear. Relatives, especially children, are more happy to give when they feel they have control and less likely to when they feel they are relatively powerless within their family. "Young children usually want to do what their parents tell them but as they get older they have different views. They need to know they can say 'No,'" explains Diane Melvin, a consultant clinical psychologist at Great Ormond Street hospital for children.

When children aren't old enough to make an informed decision, different emotional and ethical issues have to be resolved. Last year Ethan Barnes, now six, donated bone marrow cells to his sister Willow, three, who suffers from Hurler's syndrome, a rare genetic condition where excess sugars build up in the heart, liver and kidneys.

Willow was diagnosed at 21 months, and the search for a donor began. "When they told us Ethan was a match it was scary," says their mother, Charlotte. "He wanted to help Willow but we did think, what are we doing to him?

"I wondered if I was using Ethan, exploiting him to help Willow." Since the operation last October any doubts have passed; Ethan recovered almost immediately and Willow is now healthy and active. "Yet if it had gone wrong, we didn't have a clue how to explain it to Ethan, how to stop him feeling guilty if she hadn't survived."

"It's tough on families," says Diane. "A transplant will have an effect on everyone—immediately and in the long term." Particularly if the donation is unsuccessful. "People may feel; my cells or my organ wasn't good enough," she says. But where there is a healthy amount of emotional independence and understanding, family relationships can be enriched.

Certainly, Laura doesn't regret her decision to donate to Bill. "My father is a changed man. It makes me feel so satisfied, watching him go from strength to strength. But our relationship hasn't changed at all; in light of everything, he'll always be my dad."

Jean Mitchell and Laura and Bill are pseudonyms.

SIGNIFICANCE

The most common form of LOD transplantation occurs between people who are genetic relatives, followed by unrelated but requested donors. Requested donation is when the potential recipient, or that person's representative, asks a specific healthy person to donate an organ to him or her. In those cases, it is imperative that the potential donor become thoroughly educated about the process, and be thoroughly apprised of the potential physical and emotional impacts of either decision (to donate an organ or to choose to refuse to do so). Among the major issues for family members can be the sense of guilt, or of feeling pressured to donate an organ to someone else when they may not feel comfortable doing so. For women of childbearing age, there may be realistic concerns about the implications for future pregnancies. For person of either gender, there may be concerns about potential health risks, complications or length of the surgical procedure and the recovery period.

There are myriad emotional concerns to be considered for a requested or related living organ donor: First, there is the question of whether there is a single potential donor, or more than one to choose from. In the former case, there are possible pressures inherent if the recipient cannot survive without the transplanted organ. Both donor and recipient must communicate about the chance that the surgery, or refusal, will impact their future relationship. An added emotional piece is the chance that the donor will be found unsuitable for the surgery, or that unexpected medical or historical information will be discovered as a result of the pre-transplant screening processes. If the donor is accepted and the surgery occurs uneventfully, there is still the ongoing concern of rejection of the transplanted organ, and the emotional strain of donating an organ that causes illness, or even death, for the requesting or related recipient. It is essential that both donor and recipient be as fully informed as possible of all potential exigencies before the transplant proceeds. The donor must also be made aware of future implications for obtaining life, health, disability or long-term care insurance, and the possibility that medical or psychological complications arising from the organ donation (for the donor) might not be covered by personal medical insurance (as the transplant was paid for by the recipient) or might be considered a pre-existing condition that could possibly preclude the individual from obtaining future coverage.

In an effort to minimize the potential psychological, social, and economic ramifications for both donor and recipient, many transplant centers are now requiring thorough psychological assessments as part of the intake and evaluation process. Many people find it quite difficult to make a decision regarding whether or not to donate an organ to a relative or a known recipient while they are alive, but are able to easily opt for designation as an organ donor after death. There are normal and natural grief and loss issues (often, but not always) associated with the possibility of giving away a body part, no matter how strongly the donor feels about offering to improve the health of the recipient. Some people have religious or spiritual concerns about donation of a body part as well. Despite the potential complications on myriad levels, many individuals willingly donate organs to family members or friends, and some choose to donate organs altruistically, when no known recipient is involved, but the need is known to exist.

FURTHER RESOURCES
Books

Edwards, Jeanette, et al. *Technologies of Procreation: Kinship in the Age of Assisted Conception.* New York: Routledge, 1999.

Fox, Renee C., and Judith P. Swazey. *Spare Parts.* New York: Oxford University Press, 1992.

Gold, Richard E. *Body Parts*. Washington, D.C.: Georgetown University Press, 1997.

Levinson, Ralph, and Michael J. Reiss. *Key Issues in Bioethics: A Guide for Teachers*. New York: RoutledgeFalmer, 2003 .

Youngner, Stuart J., Renee C. Fox, and Laurence J. O'Connell, eds. *Organ Transplantation: Meanings and Realities*. Madison: University of Wisconsin Press, 1996.

Periodicals

Levey, A.S., S. Hou, and B.L. Bush . "Kidney Transplantation from Unrelated Living Donors: Time to Reclaim a Discarded Opportunity." *New England Journal of Medicine* 314 (1986): 914–916.

Nelson, James L. "Transplantation through a Glass Darkly." *Hastings Center Report* 27(1) (January–February 1997): 29–37.

Radcliffe-Richards, Janet, et al. "The Case for Allowing Kidney Sales." *Lancet* 352 (June 27, 1998): 1950–1952.

Strong, R.W., and S. V. Lynch. "Ethical Issues in Living Related Donor Liver Transplantation (review)." *Transplantation Proceedings* 28(4) (August 1996): 2366–2369.

Veatch, Robert M., and J. B. Pitt. "The myth of presumed consent: Ethical problems in new organ procurement strategies." *Transplantation Proceedings*. 27(2) (April 1995): 1888–1892.

7 The Family in Literature and Media

The Family in Literature and Media

Many of today's established myths about family life have been created and popularized by television and movies. Early television fostered the perfected image of the traditional middle-class family: a stay-at-home mother, a gainfully employed father, well-behaved children, and an orderly suburban home. "Family portrait of Ozzie and Harriet" presents a look at the stylized families of 1950s and 1960s television.

For years, television in the United States showed few minority families, low-income families, or portrayed little family conflict. Beginning in the 1970s, shows began to regularly feature more diverse themes and characters. Single women and minorities became title characters of popular, primetime shows. Series focused on once-taboo family issues such a pregnancy, divorce, sex, remarriage, and family conflict. As television and movies presented more adult themes, some lawmakers and members of the public called for increasing regulation or restriction of content, claiming that limiting certain TV programs to late-night or giving movies ratings would help shield children from inappropriate content. Others decried the content of popular media as a mark of declining social esteem for the family. In 1992, U.S. Vice President Dan Quayle famously denounced the television comedy *Murphy Brown* because the show's title character was an unwed mother.

In recent years, shows such as the *The Simpsons* have centered on families with realistic—if not exaggerated—foibles. African-American families, immigrant families, interracial and interethnic families, single parent, and same-sex parent families have all been featured in prominent media releases.

Questions about the appropriateness of various programs and movies for family viewing have also garnered public attention. Media is no longer limited to the silver screen or television. Internet content is also the focus of child protection advocates. Several entries discuss the roles of parents and government regulation in protecting children from potentially unsuitable media content and online predators.

Finally, just as popular media today both creates and reflects the changing concepts of the family in society, so too has literature. Literary portrayals of the family featured in this chapter range from polished to gritty. Their subjects grapple with marriage, family relations, and death. An excerpt from "Pride and Prejudice" discusses problems of an early nineteenth-century family with no male heir, dependent on their daughters' marriages for economic security. The somber mood of a family dealing with death in "A Death in the Family" contrasts vividly to the boisterous family conflict from an excerpt of "A Portrait of the Artist as a Young Man."

Pride and Prejudice

Book excerpt

By: Jane Austen

Date: 1813

Source: Signet Classic Books

About the Author: English novelist Jane Austen (1775–1817) wrote novels that depicted domestic life in early nineteenth century England, focusing in particular on comedies of manners that showed the intricate courting rites of the day and the pitfalls inherent in being a young, single woman of little means.

INTRODUCTION

Jane Austen's beloved novel *Pride and Prejudice* follows the fortunes of the Bennet sisters, five girls who, through no fault of their own, find themselves in the position of needing to marry well, yet have very little to offer a prospective husband beyond their own individual charms. At a time when property in England traditionally went to the eldest son, with little or no chance of any inheritance for the daughters in a family, a good dowry was imperative in the search for a husband. Likewise, younger brothers who were forced to join the military or the church as they could not expect an inheritance, frequently sought out brides with money or property in their own right in order to supplement their incomes. The idea of marriage for the sake of affection alone was frequently set aside in order to secure the comfort and prosperity of the couple in question, and in many cases other family members as well.

PRIMARY SOURCE

Chapter Seven

Mr. Bennet's property consisted almost entirely in an estate of two thousand a year, which, unfortunately for his daughters, was entailed in default of heirs male, on a distant relation; and their mother's fortune, though ample for her situation in life, could but ill supply the deficiency of his. Her father had been an attorney in Meryton, and had left her four thousand pounds.

She had a sister married to a Mr. Philips, who had been a clerk to their father, and succeeded him in the business, and a brother settled in London in a respectable line of trade.

The village of Longbourn was only one mile from Meryton; a most convenient distance for the young ladies, who were usually tempted thither three or four times a week to pay their duty to their aunt and to a milliner's shop just over the way. The two youngest of the family, Catherine and Lydia, were particularly frequent in these attentions; their minds were more vacant than their sisters', and when nothing better offered, a walk to Meryton was necessary to amuse their morning hours and furnish conversation for the evening; and however bare of news the country in general might be, they always contrived to learn some from their aunt. At present, indeed, they were well supplied both with news and happiness by the recent arrival of a militia regiment in the neighbourhood; it was to remain the whole winter, and Meryton was the headquarters.

Their visits to Mrs. Philips were now productive of the most interesting intelligence. Everyday added something to their knowledge of the officers' names and connections. Their lodgings were not long a secret, and at length they began to know the officers themselves. Mr. Philips visited them all, and this opened to his nieces a source of felicity unknown before. They could talk of nothing but officers; and Mr. Bingley's large fortune, the mention of which gave animation to their mother, was worthless in their eyes when opposed to the regimentals of an ensign.

SIGNIFICANCE

Pride and Prejudice begins with Mrs. Bennet's discovery that a young man has newly moved into the neighborhood, renting one of the more regal houses and thereby indicating that he has some measure of wealth, a fact that, along with his single status, is confirmed by local gossip. As the mother of five single daughters, Mrs. Bennet is intent on making the young man's acquaintance as soon as possible and preferably before the other young ladies in the neighborhood catch his attention. The reason for her anxiety and her overbearing matchmaking tendencies throughout Austen's novel, is that Mr. Bennet's house and fortune are under an entailment, which means that at some point a legal document was prepared to insure that the estate should never be subdivided among heirs, and that it was required to go to the next male relative in line of succession. In Mr. Bennet's case, because he has no sons, his male cousin will inherit his property. This leaves him with very little money to provide his daughters with dowries, and he will be unable to leave them anything upon his death. The Bennet girls must therefore rely on their looks and personality to win husbands. It is

Jane Austen. PUBLIC DOMAIN.

down socially and could not hope to recover their previous standing. Family members were expected to help each other to prevent such measures, and orphans or other women without family commonly went into some form of service.

The inheritance system was based in the laws of primogeniture, which originated with the royal family. Under primogeniture, the crown passed to the monarch's eldest son, with each son after him next in line for the throne, until the first son had a son of his own. Should the monarch fail to produce a male heir, the crown would pass to his next closest male relative, such as a brother or nephew. Property was passed down in this same manner, the idea being to maintain the size and authority of the estates, and not to divide them among a number of heirs, which would lessen the power of the owners. Titled individuals would pass their title along with the estates that accompanied them, and by law these properties could not be seized for any reason as long as the title was passed to the heir. Where large fortunes were at stake, feuding within a family could result in attempt to alter the line of succession by eliminating the heir to a property. First sons were also considered to be the best matches when young women sought a husband, as they stood to inherit the majority of their family's wealth.

their mother's hope that a wealthy young man will take an interest in one of the older daughters and, because of his own financial status, agree to marry despite the lack of monetary enticements. If one daughter marries sufficiently well, she will be able to help her sisters to make suitable marriages as well, or, at the very least, help support any single sisters following their father's death.

Situations such as this were common in England around the Regency period and were particularly difficult for people considered ladies and gentlemen, ranking above the working class, but not so high as the peerage. Individuals falling into this middle class had enough money for a modest lifestyle, with servants and entertainments, but could face financial difficulties if an estate passed out of the family. Ladies, in particular, were at a disadvantage, as Austen points out in one of her other novels, *Sense and Sensibility*, for while younger sons who failed to inherit had the option of joining the church or the military and supporting themselves in that way, women of a certain class could not work. Should they become desperate, they might take a post as a governess, but in doing so they were accepting a step

FURTHER RESOURCES

Books

Auerback, Emily. *Searching for Jane Austen.* Madison: University of Wisconsin Press, 2006.

Austen, Jane. *Jane Austen's Letters.* Philadelphia: Pavilion Press, 2003.

Austen, Jane. *Sense and Sensibility.* New York: Penguin Books, 1999.

Pool, Daniel. *What Jane Austen Ate and Charles Dickens Knew: From Fox Hunting to Whist: The Facts of Daily Life in Nineteenth-Century England.* Carmichael, Calif.: Touchstone, 1994.

Shields, Carol. *Jane Austen.* New York: Penguin, 2005.

Web sites

Jane Austen Centre. "Jane Austen Centre in Bath, Somerset , England <http://www.janeausten.co.uk/centre/index. html> (accessed June 27, 2006).

Jane Austen Society of North America. "Jane Austen Society of North America." June 26, 2006 <http://www.jasna. org/> (accessed June 27, 2006).

In the Garret

Poem

By: Louisa May Alcott

Date: 1869

Source: Alcott, Louisa May. *Little Women*. Mahwah, N.J.: Watermill Press, 1869.

About the Author: Louisa May Alcott (1832–1888) was raised in the Boston area. Her family owned a farm in Concord, Massachusetts and her father was Amos Bronson Alcott, a Transcendentalist. For a time, the Alcott family worked in Harvard, Massachusetts, to establish a utopian community called Fruitlands; Alcott was a strong progressive, an abolitionist, and a supporter of women's rights.

INTRODUCTION

Louisa May Alcott, a popular female writer whose work was published from the 1840s to the 1890s, began her life as the daughter of a Transcendentalist farmer, Amos Bronson Alcott. Her mother, Abigail May, was from an old New England family, and Louisa grew up schooled at home by her parents, older siblings, or occasional governesses. Her parents moved the family to Harvard, Massachusetts in 1843, to Fruitlands, a utopian community in which no animal labor, nor any male labor, would be used; the entire farm and community would be run by women. The men would be free to contemplate philosophy and progress. The Alcott family was progressive, agreeing with the abolitionist movement and firmly pro-women's rights. The Fruitlands experience lasted less than a year; the family moved to Concord, Massachusetts.

Alcott published her first short story in 1852, though she'd written four years before, at the age of sixteen. Over time, Alcott became a well-published writer, writing romance novels and thrillers in her time. Her books, published under the pseudonym A. M. Barnard, were passionate and earned her a steady audience as well as an income as a writer of popular fiction.

Alcott wrote *Little Women* at the request of her publisher; the book was an immediate success. Few stories accessible to child readers had female protagonists. Alcott's girls—Meg, Jo, Amy, and Beth—had distinct personalities that represented different facets of Alcott's own personality, and the story line struck a chord with readers. Mr. March is off to war and the family, headed by Marmee (Mrs. March) is struggling financially. Jo, the second daughter, is a hopeful writer.

In this poem, Jo's suitor, Fredrich, gives her a poem she once submitted for publication.

■ PRIMARY SOURCE

Four little chests all in a row,
Dim with dust, and won by time,
All fashioned and filled, long ago,
By children now in their prime.
Four little keys hung side by side,
With faded ribbons, brae and gay
When fastened there, with childish pride
Long ago, on a rainy day.

Four little names, one on each lid,
Carved out by a boyish hand,
And underneath there lieth hid
Histories of a happy band,
Once playing here, and pausing oft
To hear the sweet refrain,
That came and went on the roof aloft,
In the falling summer rain.

"Meg" on the first lid, smooth and fair.
I look in with loving eyes,
For folded here, with well-known care,
A goodly gathering lies,
The record of a peaceful life—
Gifts to gentle child and girl,
A bridal gown, lines to a wife,
A tiny shoe, a baby curl.
No toys in this first chest remain,
For all are carried away,
In their old age, to join again
In another small Meg's play.

Ah, happy mother! Well I know
You hear, like a sweet refrain,
Lullabies ever soft and lo,
In the falling summer rain.

"Jo" on the next lid, scratched and worn,
And within a motley store
Of headless dolls, of schoolbooks torn,
Birds and beasts that speak no more;
Spoils brought home from the fairy ground
Only trod by youthful feet,
Dreams of a future never found,
Memories of a past still sweet;
Half-writ poems, stories wild,
April letters, warm and cold,
Diaries of a willful child,
Hints of a woman early old;

A woman in a lonely home,
Hearing, like a sad refrain—
"Be worthy love, and love will come,"
In the falling summer rain.

My Beth! The dust is always swept
From the lid that bears your name,
As if by loving eyes that wept,
By careful hands that often came.
Death canonized for us one saint,
Ever less human than divine,
And still we lay, with tender plaint,
Relics in this household shrine—
The silver bell, so seldom rung,
The little cap which last she wore,
The fair, dead Catherine that hung
By angels borne above her door;
The songs she sang, without lament,
In her prison house of pain,
Forever are they sweetly blunt
With the falling summer rain.

Upon the last lid's polished field—
Legend now both fair and true—
A gallant knight bears on his shield,
"my," in letters gold and blue.

Within lie snoods that bound her hair,
Slippers that have danced their last,
Faded flowers laid by with care,
Fans whose airy toils are past;
Gay valentines, all ardent flames,
Trifles that have borne their part
In girlish hopes and fears and shames,
The record of a maiden heart
Now learning fairer, truer spells,
Hearing, like a blithe refrain,
The silver sound of bridal bells
In falling summer rain.

Four little chests all in a row,
Dim with dust, and worn by time,
Four women, taught by weal and woe
To love and labor in their prime.
Four sisters, parted for an hour
None lost, one only gone before,
Made by loves immortal power,
Nearest and dearest evermore.

A family portrait of the television family the Ingalls, stars of the series *Little House on the Prairie*. From left to right: Michael Landon, Karen Grassle, Melissa Sue Anderson, Sidney Greenbush, and Melissa Gilbert. © BETTMANN/CORBIS.

Oh, when these hidden stores of ours
Lie open to the Father's sight,
May they be rich in golden hours,
Deeds that show fairer for the light
Lives whose brave music long shall ring,
Like a spirit-stirring strain,
Souls that shall gladly soar and sing
In the long sunshine after rain.

SIGNIFICANCE

The poem is sentimental in tone, and Jo herself dismisses the verse: "'It's very bad poetry, but I felt it when I wrote it, one day when I was very lonely, and had a good cry on a rag bag. I never thought it would go where it could tell tales,' said Jo." Alcott once described *Little Women* as "moral paper for children"; though the book was based on her own childhood, the writing includes a wide range of morality lessons that were standard for the time, in spite of Alcott's less conventional upbringing.

Little Women created a model for post-Civil War families and inspired young girls who wished to be like Jo, who cast off ideals concerning femininity in favor of the writer's life—until she fell in love. Alcott wrote a succession of books on the March family—*Good Wives* (1869), *Little Men* (1871), and *Jo's Boys* (1886)—that brought her money and fame. The books set a tone for how families should act, and although the books dealt with dark themes—war, child death, deceit—the eternal optimism of the characters and story lines remain popular into the twenty-first century.

In *Little Women*, Alcott created four archetypes for women: Meg, prim and proper; Jo, feisty and independent; Beth, fragile and innocent; and Amy, spoiled and eager for attention and love. The poem *In the Garret* uses imagery to capture each girls' spirit. As girls read these stories in the late 1800s, they found their personality match in one of the four girls and used the stories as guides for proper comportment and for problem solving in the social and personal arena. In addition, Marmee, the strong mother figure, assumes the role of single parent in the book; the girls were expected to listen to Marmee while Mr. March was off at war, and cooperation was stressed in the book as the solution to a wide range of problems. By reinforcing family as the central force for problem-solving and support, *Little Women* gave readers moral lessons within the context of lively, interesting stories that readers enjoyed and demanded.

FURTHER RESOURCES

Books

Beecher, Catharine. *A Treatise on Domestic Economy*. Boston: T.H. Webb, 1842.

Dubois, Ellen Carol. *Feminism and Suffrage: The Emergence of an Independent Women's Movement in America, 1848–1869*. Ithaca, N.Y.: Cornell University Press, 1999.

Kelly, Mary C. *Private Woman, Public Stage: Literary Domesticity in Nineteenth-Century America*. Chapel Hill: University of North Carolina Press, 2001.

Stern, Madeline. *Louisa May Alcott: A Biography*. Boston: Northeastern University Press, 1999.

Zelizer, Viviana. *Pricing the Priceless Child: The Changing Social Value of Children*. Princeton, N.J.: Princeton University Press, 1994.

A Portrait of the Artist as a Young Man

Book excerpt

By: James Joyce

Date: 1916

Source: Joyce, James. *A Portrait of the Artist as a Young Man*. New York: Penguin, 2003. The book was first published in the United States in 1916.

About the Author: James Joyce (1882–1941), a twentieth century Irish expatriate writer and poet, wrote such masterpieces as *The Dubliners*, *A Portrait of the Artist as a Young Man*, and *Ulysses*.

INTRODUCTION

James Joyce's *A Portrait of the Artist as a Young Man* is a largely autobiographical *kunstlerroman* (a novel about an artist coming of age). The book portrays the early life of Stephen Dedalus, a partial reflection of Joyce, through his philosophical awakening.

The novel's milieu (setting) spans from Stephen's entrance into university to his self-exile from Ireland and journey to Paris. The Dedalus family is portrayed against the backdrop of late-nineteenth century Dublin, in an Ireland fraught with religious and political turmoil.

In circa 1890, the Irish nationalist and Member of Parliament Charles Stewart Parnell became a face

James Joyce and his family in their Paris home, February 7, 1934. Mr. Joyce and his wife are standing. Seated are Mr. And Mrs. George Joyce, the author's son and daughter-in-law, with their child, Stephen James Joyce, between them. © BETTMANN/CORBIS.

of controversy that captured newspaper headlines and provoked fiery discussions in public houses. These historical events are imported into Joyce's novel as Parnell becomes the subject of Dedalus family discussion. Parnell, champion of home rule for Ireland, the elimination of landlords, and protection of tenants' rights, was at first effective in his arguments in Parliament. His affair with the married Katherine O'Shea, however, gave the Catholic Church the excuse to abandon him. Without the backing of the national religion it was difficult to promote nationalism. Thus, Parnell's political influence waned, and many of his supporters, deemed Parnalites, mourned his political decay.

After refusing the British Liberal Party's demand that he resign as leader of the Irish Parliamentary Party, Parnell published a rebuttal, *Manifesto of the*

Irish People, but was soon thereafter voted off his position. Parnell blamed his own party, the Irish Catholic clergy, and the Gladstonian Liberals (A reference to William Gladstone, leader of the Liberal Party, who became England's Prime Minister in 1870). Parnell died of a heart attack on October 6, 1891. His death provides the historical backdrop for the beginning of Joyce's novel.

In his novel, Joyce's characters explore and debate key topics derived from the Parnell scandal, including whether preaching politics from the altar is in the interest of the priest's flock, guiding it to morality and away from such "sins" as an adulterous leader, or if the scandal is the cause of Ireland's political paralysis, through the use of God's name and the payment of favors between the Catholic hierarchy and the British crown.

PRIMARY SOURCE

He was for Ireland and Parnell and so was his father: and so was Dante too for one night at the band on the esplanade she had hit a gentleman on the head with her umbrella because he had taken off his hat when the band played *God Save the Queen* at the end.

Mr Dedalus gave a snort of contempt.

"Ah, John," he said. "It is true for them. We are an unfortunate priestridden race and always were and always will be till the end of the chapter."

Uncle Charles shook his head, saying:

"A bad business! A bad business!"

Mr Dedalus repeated:

A priestridden Godforsaken race!"

He pointed to the portrait of his grandfather on the wall to his right.

"Do you see that old chap up there, John? He said. He was a good Irishman when there was no money in the job. He was condemned to death as a whiteboy. But he had a saying about our clerical friends, that he would never let one of them put his two feet under his mahogany."

Dante broke in angrily:

"If we are a priestridden race we ought to be proud of it! They are the apple of God's eye. *Touch the not, says Christ, for they are the apple of My eye.*

"And can we not love our country then?"asked Mr Casey. "Are we not to follow the man that was born to lead us?"

"A traitor to his country! replied Dante. A traitor, an adulterer! The priests were right to abandon him. The priests were always the true friends of Ireland."

"Were they, faith?" said Mr Casey.

He threw his fist on the table and, frowning angrily, protruded one finger after another.

"Didn't the bishops of Ireland betray us in the time of the union when bishop Lanigan presented an address of loyalty to the Marquess Cornwallis? Didn't the bishops and priests sell the aspirations of their country in 1829 in return for catholic emancipation? Didn't they denounce the fenian movement from the pulpit and in the confessionbox? And didn't they dishonor the ashes of Terence Bellew MacManus?"

His face was glowing with anger and Stephen felt the glow rise in his own cheek as the spoken words thrilled him. Mr Dedalus uttered a guffaw of coarse scorn.

"O, by God, he cried, I forgot little old Paul Cullen! Another apple of God's eye!"

Dante bent across the table and cried to Mr Casey:

"Right! Right! They were always right! God and morality and religion come first."

Mrs Dedalus, seeing her excitement, said to her:

"Mrs Riordan, don't excite yourself answering them."

"God and religion before everything! Dante cried. God and religion before the world!"

Mr Casey raised his clenched fist and brought it down on the table with a crash.

"Very well, then," he shouted hoarsely, "if it comes to that, no God for Ireland!"

"John! John!" cried Mr Dedalus, seizing his guest by the coat sleeve.

Dante stared across the table, her cheeks shaking. Mr Casey struggled up from his chair and bent across the table towards her, scraping the air from before his eyes with one hand as if he were tearing aside a cobweb.

"No God for Ireland!" he cried. "We have had too much God in Ireland. Away with God!"

"Blasphemer! Devil!" screamed Dante, starting to her feet and almost spitting in his face.

Uncle Charles and Mr Dedalus pulled Mr Casey back into his chair again, talking to him from both sides reasonably. He stared before them with his dark flaming eyes, repeating:

"Away with God, I say!"

Dante shoved her chair violently aside and left the table, upsetting her napkinring which rolled slowly along the carpet and came to rest against the foot of an easychair. Mrs Dedalus rose quickly and followed her towards the door. At the door Dante turned round violently and shouted down the room, her cheeks flushed and quivering with rage:

"Devil out of hell! We won! We crushed him to death! Fiend!"

The door slammed behind her.

Mr Casey, freeing his arms from his holders, suddenly bowed his head on his hands with a sob of pain.

"Poor Parnell!" he cried loudly. "My dead king!"

He sobbed loudly and bitterly.

Stephen, raising his terrorstricken face, saw that his father's eyes were full of tears.

Mourners stand around the grave at the funeral of Irish politician and nationalist Charles Stewart Parnell in Glasnevin, Ireland. © SEAN SEXTON COLLECTION/CORBIS.

SIGNIFICANCE

This excerpt from Joyce's novel highlighted the Christmas dinner table of an 1890s Irish family that was embroiled in internal conflict over the issues of politics and religion in a country where the two were often cogs in the same machine. Such societal issues were arguably the cause of family accord as well as ruin. A legacy of fervid Catholicism within an Irish family could have easily been threatened by an allegiant nationalist member—be it brother, aunt, or cousin. Similar viewpoints to those displayed by Mr. Dedalus and Mr. Casey during Christmas dinner would have easily been observed by conservative Catholics as disloyal to the Church as well as the Catholic family.

Young Stephen Dedalus' first Christmas dinner at the adult table is also his first encounter with the emotionally charged subjects of Ireland's social unrest: religion and politics. His inadvertent political lesson—

one that his mother attempts to muffle—results from the argument between Mr. Dedalus, Mr. Casey (Mr. Dedalus' friend) and Dante, or Mrs. Riordan, the Dedalus children's governess. Dante is a conservative Catholic who believes that priests inform politics because they must "direct their flocks" and proclaims "God and religion before everything!" Mr. Dedalus is a Parnalite and staunch Irish nationalist who refers to his family's history and that of Ireland's in defense of his position on the Catholic Church's interference in Panell's, and therefore Ireland's, progression. Mr. Casey, the more extreme Parnalite of the two, is also a Fenien and defiantly cries, "No God for Ireland! We have had too much God in Ireland. Away with God!"—a statement so strong that even Mr. Dedalus tries to calm him.

However, the two philosophies reared their heads too strongly for this family to forget. Parnell had recently died of a heart attack and a thick tension hovered over Ireland. For some, their king was dead, while others rejoiced that their souls were intact, although the British still held their land and oversaw their laws.

Passions divided both Irish politics and families. The same rivaling that occurs at the Dedalus Christmas dinner disrupts relationships to the point of tears and upset napkin rings, builds confusion in the young mind of Stephen Dedalus. Confusion, yet a want for indifference in the place of the stifling consequence of the two social enemies, a very autonomous view in Ireland at the dawn of the twentieth century.

The reader, knowing Stephen's fondness towards his mother, can recognize that he seems to mentally mimic the peace that she tries to incorporate during dinner. However, this relationship is later thinned due to her strong Catholic faith and Stephen's abandonment of it. Stephen's desire for an autonomous, artistic progression does not include Ireland, religion, or his family. He eventually resolves, "to express myself in some mode of life or art as freely as I can and as wholly as I can, using for my defense the only arms I allow myself to use—silence, exile, and cunning." Thus, this family, this episode in Irish literature, is unique and important in terms of displaying the social unrest found on the streets as well as in the homes of Ireland, though was not inescapable in the name of art and autonomy for the young Stephen Dedalus, nor his creator James Joyce.

In the novel, Stephen Dedalus achieves independence from his family as a young man and an artist. In reality, Ireland achieved independence from England in 1921 (although in a divided state, as Northern Ireland remained loyal to the Crown). The Catholic Church also remains a driving force in Ireland, as over sixty percent of the population is baptized in the Catholic Church, and over eighty percent of schools are under church control.

FURTHER RESOURCES

Web sites

Clare County Library. "Charles Stewart Parnell." <http://www.clarelibrary.ie/eolas/coclare/people/parnell.htm> (accessed July 22, 2006).

James Joyce Centre. <http://www.jamesjoyce.ie/home/> (accessed July 22, 2006).

Roots Web. "A Timeline of Irish History." <http://www.rootsweb.com/~fianna/history/> (accessed July 22, 2006).

Family Listening to News on the Radio

Photograph

By: Anonymous

Date: October 8, 1939

Source: *Bettmann/Corbis*. "Family Listening to News on the Radio." <http://www.corbis.com> (accessed June 16, 2006).

About the Photographer: This photograph resides in the Bettmann Archives of Corbis Corporation, an image group headquartered in Seattle, with a worldwide archive of over seventy million images.

INTRODUCTION

As the United States expanded from thirteen small colonies to a broad expanse of states, communication technology struggled to keep pace. The need for quick communication spawned numerous schemes to bridge the distances. In 1860 and 1861, the short-lived Pony Express employed a series of riders and fresh horses every ten miles to travel a 2000-mile route in ten to sixteen days, depending on the weather. The Pony Express briefly provided the fastest route for cross-country news delivery, but it became outmoded with the completion of the first transcontinental telegraph line in 1861.

Although the telegraph allowed news to traverse the country at the speed of electricity, information was often stuck in a bottleneck once it arrived. Americans still received most of their news from daily newspapers, meaning that most developments were not widely reported until the following morning. The holdup at this final leg of news delivery remained in place for many years.

In the late 1800s, researchers exploring the properties of electricity noticed that an electric spark produced waves that could be detected remotely, suggesting that it might be possible to send telegraph messages without wires. Several years of further research and experimentation followed, and in 1896 Italian inventor Guglielmo Marconi (1874–1937) filed for a British patent on the first practical radio transmitter and receiver.

In 1919, the Radio Corporation of America, known today as RCA, was created to promote the radio market, and radio quickly spread throughout the United States. By 1935, two-thirds of American families owned a radio; four national networks, along with numerous regional services, broadcast around the clock. Newspapers found themselves fighting to keep advertising dollars, which were slowly trickling away to broadcasters. As the Great Depression (1929–1939) lingered, many Americans turned to radio for free news and entertainment.

The 1930s witnessed the debut of several immensely successful radio programs. In 1931, radio dramas were becoming increasingly popular and the *Little Orphan Annie* show premiered, telling the serialized tale of Annie's adventures punctuated with plugs for the show's sponsors. Other radio hits of the 1930s included *The Shadow* and *Amos 'n' Andy*. Producers

supplied variety, musical, and quiz shows to meet the growing demand. Most of these programs aired in the evening, making a family night around the radio a common event.

President Franklin Roosevelt (1882–1945) frequently spoke to the nation via radio, and a 1934 editorial noted that this new medium enabled the president to instantly respond to attacks on himself or his policies, a capability enjoyed by no previous president. From 1933 to 1944, as the nation moved from the Great Depression into World War II (1939–1945), the president broadcast a series of thirty "Fireside Chats" in which he spoke directly to the American

PRIMARY SOURCE

Family Listening to News on the Radio: A family gathers in front of the radio to listen to a news report on October 8, 1939. Prior to the development of television the family radio was a focal point for information and entertainment. © BETTMANN/CORBIS.

people about the banking crisis, the New Deal, and the progress of the war effort.

PRIMARY SOURCE

FAMILY LISTENING TO NEWS ON THE RADIO
See primary source image.

SIGNIFICANCE

The arrival of commercial radio changed the national culture in many ways. For the first time, Americans could receive breaking news as it was happening, and enormous news-gathering organizations evolved to meet the hunger for up-to-the-minute news. Politicians, formerly forced to rely on some-times hostile newspaper editors to communicate their messages, could now bypass the press entirely, speaking directly to voters. Workplace conversations began to focus on the previous night's episode of a favorite show, as the country's individual entertainment tastes converged around radio programs. Radio began producing new celebrities, including dramatic performers, musicians, news reporters, and even disc jockeys, like the pioneering Wolfman Jack.

The development of television signaled the end of radio's golden age, and numerous shows, including *Gunsmoke*, made the leap from radio to television, in some cases airing on both simultaneously. The post-war economic boom also spawned new entertainment choices, producing an increasingly fragmented marketplace and ensuring that radio would never again

Martha Beyer and her children sit near a radio, awaiting news about the U.S.S. *Squalus,* a submarine that suffered a valve failure and sank on May 23, 1939. She would later hear that her brother, a crewman on the submarine, survived the accident. © BETTMANN/CORBIS.

play the central role it had played in American family life during the 1930s and 1940s.

A century after radio's development, the medium remains strong. News and talk formats dominate the original AM band, while music predominates on FM. Satellite radio offers multiple formats, and online streaming audio and podcasting have created new ways to enjoy the traditional listening experience offered by radio. While television has taken radio's place as today's primary entertainment delivery vehicle, radio remains a popular entertainment choice. Arbitron, the agency that measures radio listening rates in the United States, identifies forty-seven distinct programming formats available today. A 2004 study found that during a given day, eighty-three percent of Americans listen to the radio.

FURTHER RESOURCES

Books

Maltin, Leonard. *The Great American Broadcast: A Celebration of Radio's Golden Age.* New York: Penguin Putnam, 1997.

Oriard, Michael. *King Football: Sport and Spectacle in the Golden Age of Radio and Newsreels, Movies and Magazines, the Weekly and the Daily Press.* Charlotte: University of North Carolina Press, 2001.

Siegel, Susan and David S. Siegel. *A Resource Guide to the Golden Age of Radio: Special Collections, Bibliography, and the Internet.* Yorktown Heights, N.Y.: Book Hunter Press, 2006.

Periodicals

Absher, Frank. "Revealing an Innocent Age." *St. Louis Journalism Review* 33 (2003): 13.

Schuchat, Dan. "Early Radio in the United States." *Social Education* Supplement (May/June 2005): M4–M8.

Zaslow, Jeffrey. "At Festivals, Fans of Radio, Silent Film Pine for Old-Timers." *Wall Street Journal* 246 (October 21, 2005): A1–A9.

Web sites

Radio and Television Museum. "Welcome to the Radio and Television Museum." <http://www.radiohistory.org/> (accessed June 20, 2006).

University of Maryland. "National Public Broadcasting Archives." <http://www.lib.umd.edu/NPBA/index.html> (accessed June 19, 2006).

University of San Diego. "Golden Age of Radio, 1935–1950." <http://history.sandiego.edu/gen/recording/radio2.html> (accessed June 20, 2006).

New Jersey Seashore

Poster

By: Anonymous

Date: 1953

Source: Corbis

About the Author: This photograph is part of the collection of the Corbis Corporation, headquartered in Seattle. Corbis maintains a worldwide archive of more than 70 million images.

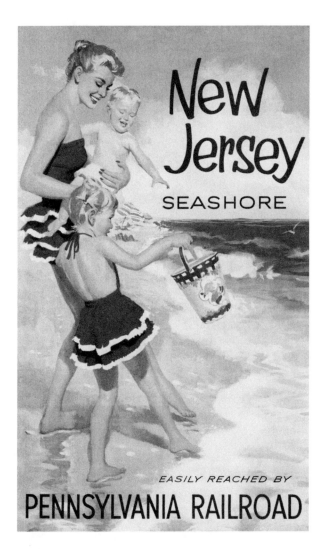

PRIMARY SOURCE

New Jersey Seashore: A poster advertising family vacations on the Jersey Shore. © SWIM INK 2, LLC/CORBIS.

INTRODUCTION

As Americans earned more money and enjoyed more free time, vacation travel became more popular. Once a pastime reserved for the wealthy, families of every income level took to the roads and rails in the twentieth century. The family vacation became a staple of American life.

Vacations were not always common. Throughout history, most travelers have typically been religious pilgrims or men on business. Travel was uncomfortable and often dangerous. For ages, travelers had worried about being attacked by bandits. By the nineteenth century, travelers on stagecoaches typically arrived at their destinations bruised and battered from being slammed around the inside of the coach as it bounced on rutted dirt roads. Early steam locomotives sprayed their passengers with burning cinders, occasionally setting clothing on fire.

Advances in transportation made travel easier and faster. Working class families, in particular, were able to take trips to nearby sites, such as the New Jersey seashore, because mass transit systems had made such travel quick, comfortable, and affordable. As more families bought cars, railroad travel lost popularity. In response, railroads used romanticized images of tourist destinations to boost business.

PRIMARY SOURCE

NEW JERSEY SEASHORE

See primary source image.

SIGNIFICANCE

Family vacations have become a cherished part of life but the concept of such a vacation is new to the modern age. In the late nineteenth century, Americans began to copy the social travel habits of elite Europeans. Wealthy young adults, mostly men, took the grand tour of Europe as a rite of passage. Along with seeing the most notable examples of art and architecture, they made lifetime business contacts during a trip that lasted from one month to two years abroad.

B.F. Keith's Theater on Garden Pier, overlooking the Atlantic City, New Jersey, coastline. © CORBIS.

When Americans turned their attention toward their own country at the start of the twentieth century, vacation destinations changed as well. Spurred on by the new conservation movement and the formation of the national park system, Americans took their families across the United States to experience its beauty. They went to Yosemite National Park, Florida, California and the seashore.

While such natural sites have never lost popularity, other travel destinations have emerged. Amusement parks, largely post-World War II creations that capitalized on the baby boom and greater discretionary income, have become synonymous with family vacations. Often described as tourist factories, places such as Walt Disney World and Six Flags have become meccas for families with children. As the tourist factories recognize, most family vacations center on notions of family togetherness. The high mobility of Americans in the post-war era has led to a new type of family vacation that focuses on reuniting with relatives whether in a park, private home, or resort area.

FURTHER RESOURCES
Books

Braden, Donna R., and Judith E. Endelman. *Americans on Vacation*. Dearborn, MI: Henry Ford Museum and Greenfield Village, 1990.

Jakle, John. *The Tourist: Travel in Twentieth-Century North America*. Lincoln: University of Nebraska Press, 1985.

Rothman, Hal K. *Devil's Bargains: Tourism in the Twentieth-Century American West*. Lawrence: University Press of Kansas, 1998.

Family Portrait of Ozzie and Harriet

Photograph

By: Anonymous

Date: April 19, 1956

Source: Bettmann/Corbis

About the Photographer: This photograph resides in the Bettmann Archives of Corbis Corporation, an image group headquartered in Seattle, with a worldwide archive of over seventy million images.

INTRODUCTION

Television has always provided a window into the American consciousness, in some cases reflecting reality and in others portraying a vision of possible reality. Television series like *M*A*S*H*, which blatantly poked fun at U.S. military involvement in Asia, and the original Superman, who fought for "truth, justice, and the American way", both reflected the concerns of their day in a world uneasy at the saber-rattling of the Cold War. Shows like *Lassie* celebrated classic themes of growing up, while adventures like *Star Trek* stirred the imaginations of multiple generations, depicting a future still filled with adventure but no longer facing the mundane worries of today.

While television today is seen as simply a delivery medium, the pioneers of television foresaw it as far more than an entertainment device—they believed it was a revolutionary tool to bring education and enlightenment to the world. For this reason, the content of early television programs was closely regulated, both by the broadcast industry itself and by the Federal Communications Commission (FCC), which oversaw broadcasting and was empowered to fine broadcasters for vulgar or profane content.

Given these limitations, the television programs of the 1950s and 1960s appear laughably benign by modern standards. Characters rarely became angry, violated the law, or faced problems that couldn't be resolved by the end of the episode. Oddly, television characters also never seemed to use the restroom, and even married couples frequently slept in separate beds to avoid the implication that they might be having physical relations. Of the many famous television families, none blurred the line with real life more completely than the popular series *The Adventures of Ozzie and Harriet*.

From 1952 to 1966, America looked on as the Nelsons, a traditional nuclear family with two sons, dealt with the challenges of being a family. Foreshadowing the reality television shows of a half-century later, Ozzie and Harriet Nelson played themselves, living with their two sons in a television house modeled after their actual residence. Events in their sons' lives, including their marriages, were woven into episodes of the show, and when son Rick began a real-life singing career, his character on the show did likewise, further blurring the line between reality and fantasy. For more than a decade, the family lived out a sanitized version of real life in prime time, and millions of Americans enjoyed visiting the Nelson home each week.

Family Portrait of Ozzie and Harriet: The Nelson family, stars of *The Adventures of Ozzie and Harriet,* April 19, 1956. Clockwise from top: Ozzie, David, Harriet, and Rickey. © BETTMANN/CORBIS.

Family Portrait of Ozzie and Harriet

See primary source image.

SIGNIFICANCE

With the success of the Nelsons, television quickly generated a slew of copycat programs depicting families. These families, including Ward and June Cleaver and Rob and Laura Petrie, closely followed the Nelson model, filling each episode with clean humor, minor crises, and satisfying conclusions. Even *The Honeymooners*, whose characters could be far more abrasive, seemed to live in a world with few real problems. While Americans undoubtedly knew these families were too perfect to be real, they quickly came to see the characters as friends.

As television matured, audiences became bored with the imaginary world in which everyone was polite and conflict never occurred; in response, 1970s television portrayed a diverse array of families, many of them confronting serious difficulties. *The Waltons*, which ran from 1972–1981, depicted a poor rural family living in Depression-era America. This impoverished family faced conflict on a weekly basis, including concerns about starvation, struggles with alcoholism, and the reality of illness and death. At times sappy, the series retained the charm of the 1960s television families while injecting a dose of real-world drama.

Archie Bunker, the central character in the sitcom *All in the Family*, demonstrated that television families could be just as unpleasant as real ones. Bigoted and boorish, Bunker called his wife "dingbat" and his son-in-law "meathead," ruling his house with sarcasm and political incorrectness. Ironically, despite his obnoxious behavior, Bunker was generally considered a good husband and provider. *All in the Family* opened the door for dysfunctional television families. The show ran from 1971–1979.

Television frequently succeeds by recycling previous concepts. In 2002, fifty years after *Ozzie and Harriet* premiered, MTV launched a new series entitled *The Osbournes*. Like its forebear, the new series focused on the day-to-day life of a musician named Ozzie, this time featuring former heavy-metal star Ozzy Osbourne. Like the older series, the new one included the musician's wife and two children in episodes revolving around the family's experiences. Unlike the original, however, the new series was not edited for content; it also portrayed problems including a child's drug addiction, alcoholism, a near-fatal car accident,

Ozzie Nelson with Harriet and family on the *The Adventures of Ozzie and Harriet,* October 1, 1958. PHOTO BY RALPH CRANE//TIME LIFE PICTURES/GETTY IMAGES.

and the news that Osbourne's wife had been diagnosed with cancer. The show ran for four seasons.

Aided by singing appearances on his family's show, Ozzie and Harriet Nelson's son Rick went on to a successful musical career and was later inducted into the Rock and Roll Hall of Fame. In 2006, Ozzy Osbourne's daughter Kelly, who was also pursuing a singing career, announced that her next reality show would take place in a brothel.

FURTHER RESOURCES
Books

Brooks, Marla. *The American Family on Television: A Chronology of 121 Shows, 1948–2004.* New York: McFarland and Company, 2005.

Douglas, William. *Television Families: Is Something Wrong in Suburbia?* Mahwah, NJ: Lawrence Erlbaum Associates, 2003.

Spigel, Lynn. *Make Room for TV: Television and the Family Ideal in Postwar America*. Chicago: University of Chicago Press, 1992.

Periodicals

Anonymous. "Family Fare Proponents Push a la Carte Cable." *Christian Century*. 123 (January 24, 2006): 11.

Atkinson, Claire. "At Last, the Whole Family Can Watch Sex on TV." *Advertising Age*. 76 (September 19, 2005):3–5.

Kipnis, Jill. "Family Shows Are Serious Business." *Billboard*. 117 (2005): 26.

Web sites

American Academy of Child and Adolescent Psychiatry: Facts for Families.. "Children and Watching TV." February 2005 <http://www.aacap.org/publications/factsfam/tv.htm> (accessed June 16, 2006).

American Academy of Pediatrics. "Television and the Family." <http://www.aap.org/family/tv1.htm> (accessed June 16, 2006).

Black, Brown, and Beige

Magazine article

By: Terry Teachout

Date: July 18, 1986

Source: Teachout, Terry. "Black, Brown, and Beige." *National Review* (July 18, 1986).

About the Author: Terry Teachout has written for several top journals, magazines and other publications such as the *Wall Street Journal*, *National Review*, and the *New York Times*. He was previously an editor of *Harper's* magazine and an editorial columnist for the *New York Daily News*. Also a music commentator and critic, he is a member of the National Council on the Arts based in Washington, D.C. Teachout has also written several books and biographical works, including his latest *All in the Dances: A Brief Life of George Balanchine*.

INTRODUCTION

The Cosby Show was a surprise hit of the late 1980s. The main cast featured comedian Bill Cosby as Heathcliff Huxtable, the father of five children along with his wife, Claire, portrayed by Phylicia Rashad. The children's characters were Sondra (Sabrina Le Beauf), Denise (Lisa Bonet), Theo (Malcolm Jamal

Warner), Vanessa (Tempestt Bledsoe), and Rudy (Keisha Knight Pulliam). This African-American family was to represent an upper middle-class household; Cliff Huxtable was an obstetrician and gynecologist and Claire was an attorney, and they lived in a white neighborhood of Brooklyn, New York.

There is some controversy as to how the show was portrayed. Some felt that racial attachments or lack thereof were an unrealistic depiction of African-American middle-class living. Terry Teachout also considers this puzzling since Bill Cosby's character continually appears more typically Black American than the other family members, including the two elder daughters, who attend schools such as Princeton and spend time traveling abroad. The son and younger daughters have been integrated into what is typically seen as traditional white middle class as they share similar dilemmas as other sitcom episodes of the time.

Teachout both critiques and praises this program, which brought NBC television to the top of the ratings for nearly eight years. *The Cosby Show* won numerous awards, including three Golden Globes, the NAACP Image Award, and six Emmy awards.

Though Teachout sees the family scenes to be inventive, entertaining, and masterfully developed by Cosby and the producers, they appear to lack plausibility. The decision to ignore mainstream issues of the times such as AIDS, sex, and poverty led white viewers to believe that black Americans were more like themselves, representing the adult baby-boomer generation. They can relate to successful parents rearing families and working mothers. Whereas, for the black viewers, the show appears to represent or advocate an ideal to which black middle-class families should conform.

■ PRIMARY SOURCE

Situation comedies are the stock exchange of American desire. When breadwinning and housewifery were up, television gave us Leave It to Beaver and My Three Sons. As Americans gradually abandoned the crumbling ideal of the nuclear family and began to look for emotional satisfaction in the surrogate womb of the workplace, new shows like Barney Miller and M*A*S*H began to dominate the sitcom scene. Even Mary Tyler Moore, who cheerfully kept house for Dick Van Dyke in the forgotten days of the New Frontier, worked for a Minneapolis TV station and discreetly slept with handsome young men throughout the reign of Richard Nixon. It wasn't Mary's fault. It wasn't even Nixon's fault. The Nielsens made her do it.

Now that the toddlers of the Eisenhower era have finally grasped the levers of demographic power, what are

Bill Cosby talks over a scene with Tempestt Bledsoe on the set of *The Cosby Show.* © JACQUES M. CHENET/CORBIS.

today's sitcoms telling us about their desires and priorities? Not quite what you'd expect. No one, for example, ever makes jokes about power breakfasts on television. (Ambition is no laughing matter for baby-boomers.) And Hometown, CBS's attempt to cash in on the Big Chill mystique, was a major disaster. Who cares about aging revolutionaries in search of an extended family? What people really want to see on television these days are attractive young couples who have figured out how to make two jobs and three kids a viable proposition. That's why the most successful program on television today is NBC's The Cosby Show, a traditional family sitcom whose plots are straight out of Father Knows Best by Julia.

For white middle-class viewers, The Cosby Show is an exercise in face value. The dilemmas are more or less universal ones, the emotional tone generally convincing. The appeal of the program derives in large part from the strong baby-boomer orientation of the scripts. Cliff is a doctor, Clair a lawyer. Parental authority is tactfully exercised with warmth and wit. Sexism is a dirty word. Regular viewers with an eye for the implausible, though, quickly begin to develop a long list of unanswered questions. One assumes that the Huxtables employ domestic help, but we

never see a cleaning lady, just as we rarely see Clair at work. Who took care of the youngest daughter before she started kindergarten? What kind of sex lives do the older daughters have? And what kind of middle-class family can drop $10,000 on a painting at Sotheby's?

Seen from this angle, The Cosby Show is a hip pipedream, a pristine vision of a successful nuclear family in the age of the working mother. But the black middle-class viewer, despite the fact that The Cosby Show systematically avoids racially oriented thematic material, is getting a very different message. For him The Cosby Show is surely a parable of ambition, a golden vision of upward mobility with a poorly hidden agenda. Each episode frankly advocates the kind of assimilation that Eldridge Cleaver and Stokely Carmichael were supposed to have put the torch to long ago. The Huxtables live in what is obviously a white neighborhood. Their children will go to Ivy League colleges. The two oldest daughters are deracinated to an astonishing, even eerie, degree. (Indeed, one is already going to Princeton and summering in Paris; the other is a beige Valley Girl.) Racist slurs are never heard, racist behavior never encountered, by the Huxtable family.

Bill Cosby's authentic "blackness" confuses the issue to some degree, but the point is that there is an issue to be confused. One sign of this confusion is the new credit sequence filmed for The Cosby Show's current season, in which all of the cast members are shown dancing. This sequence is obviously designed to provide conclusive evidence that Cliff, Clair, and the kids are really and truly black. Hugh Beaumont and Barbara Billingsley, we are surely meant to think, were never that cool.

One might explain all of this away were it not for the fact the producers of The Cosby Show are known to exercise deliberate and conscious control over every aspect of the program from the hairstyles worn by Clair and the girls to the posters on the wall of Theo's bedroom. Psychologist Alvin Poussaint is regularly consulted on how each new production wrinkle will be interpreted by the black community. Cosby himself has a doctorate (of sorts) in education, a fact that is announced to the world every week when the credits of The Cosby Show roll. The Cosby Show is, to use a hideously canting phrase, "politically correct." Is the long-repressed dream of black assimilation now politically correct as well? The New York Times tells us that a majority of American blacks approve of the way Ronald Reagan is doing his job. The Cosby Show is the hottest ticket on television among black professionals in New York. Something interesting is definitely going on here, but Bill Cosby is only telling us part of the story. Fans of The Cosby Show will find some of this criticism churlish, and they have a point. No one has any business complaining about the fact that The Cosby Show is not set in Harlem. That's as fatuous as it is racist. No, the real problem with The Cosby Show is that is fails to dramatize its vision of black assimilation in the context of the world outside the four walls of the Huxtable household. Not only are the answers too easy, the questions never even get asked.

Such candor, of course, may not be possible in a half-hour situation comedy, even one as charming and intelligent as The Cosby Show. Most television programs that attempt to deal with "problems" usually do so in a remorselessly schematic way, skipping from child abuse to marijuana to incest to AIDS with all the verve of a well-oiled metronome. The Cosby Show has consistently avoided this kind of childish treatment of "problems," but it has done so at the expense of authenticity. There was more social nuance in a single episode of The Honeymooners than in the entire first season of The Cosby Show. One feels in the end that Bill Cosby and his writers are too gifted to be aiming so low, too smart to be telling us so little about the way we live now.

SIGNIFICANCE

Television sitcoms or situation comedies represent the heart of American inclinations. In its early years, role models and daily living were represented by shows such as *Leave It to Beaver*. When the notion of family in America begin to fracture from this ideal, perceptibly it transformed its footing to the workplace, says Teachout. The job was where all expressions of gratification and self-worth were asserted. At that time, *Barney Miller* and *M*A*S*H* came to the forefront on television.

In 1986, what was popular for "white middle-class" viewers to watch were good-looking parents that know how to successfully juggle family life with two working adults, says Teachout. During this time *The Cosby Show* became hugely favorable as it fit this description perfectly. Airing on NBC, the show depicted the conventional family "whose plots are straight out of *Father Knows Best*."

According to Teachout, the lightly veiled message for other blacks was to rise to this social position and act like the Huxtables. Send your children to the best colleges, disregard your ethnicity, fit or "assimilate," says Teachout, into white society.

FURTHER RESOURCES
Web sites

National Review. "The Cosby Show." July 18, 1986. <http://www.findarticles.com/p/articles/mi_m1282/is_v38/ai_4307692/print> (accessed July 22, 2006).

TV.com. "The Cosby Show." Septermber 20, 1984. <http://www.tv.com/the-cosby-show/show/481/summary.html?full_summary=1&tag=showspace_links;full_summary> (accessed July 22, 2006).

WritersReps.com. "Terry Teachout." <http://writersreps.com/author.cfm?AuthorID=185> (accessed July 22, 2006).

In Today's TV Families, Who Knows Best?

Newspaper article

By: Elizabeth Stone

Date: May 13, 1990

Source: Stone, Elizabeth. "In Today's TV Families, Who's Right?" *New York Times*, May 13, 1990.

The cast of the television series *Father Know's Best*. Clockwise from lower left: Lauren Chapin, Elinor Donahue, Robert Young, Jane Wyatt, and Billy Gray. AP/WIDE WORLD PHOTOS. REPRODUCED BY PERMISSION.

About the Author: Elizabeth Stone is a writer and educator in English and media studies, and the author of a number of books, including *Black Sheep and Kissing Cousins: How Our Family Stories Shape Us*.

INTRODUCTION

Television programming has changed steadily over the decades, reflecting political, economic, and social shifts in the viewing population, as well as the desire of television executives to provide audiences with something new. Programs meant for a family audience, in particular, have morphed according to the alterations in American family structure.

In the 1950s, popular shows such as *The Adventures of Ozzie and Harriet* and *Father Knows Best* reflected a traditional family structure, with two parents in traditional roles of paternal provider and maternal caregiver. By the 1960s and 1970s, television families began to reflect changes in the demographics, with programs such as *The Partridge Family* and *The Brady Bunch*.

In the 1980s, many television shows, including *Growing Pains* and *Full House*, reversed the standard parent/child role, with television children outpacing their parents in intelligence and wit. Rather than influencing the way viewers look at the family structure, however, these programs are often a result of changes in real-life American families and are designed to appeal to their target audiences.

■ PRIMARY SOURCE

In Today's TV Families, Who Knows Best?

Recently, on ABC's *Growing Pains*, Mike (Kirk Cameron) got what he thought was his big break—a walk-on part in a TV series as a nameless cop dying of gunshot wounds. Mike's sister, Carol (Tracey Gold), recognized the part for the inconsequential bit of body spasm it was and offered only the most measured of congratulations. But Dad (Alan Thicke), a psychologist who's supposed to know better, was mostly interested in having Mike get the autograph of the buxom series star. Who was the center of moral authority in this TV family moment? Certainly not Dad. Almost as recently on *Roseanne* also on ABC, the eponymous heroine's adolescent daughter, Darlene, wrote a poem good enough for her to read aloud before a nighttime parent assembly. But Darlene balked, saying she wasn't going to go because she didn't want to look like a nerd. Conflict ensued between her and Roseanne (Roseanne Barr), who herself had written a notebook full of poetry as an adolescent. Roseanne prevailed. Darlene read. Both these instances illustrate where the center of authority lies in two different families; though opposite, each is becoming predictable on nighttime TV series. When the TV family in question is working class, or minority, the heavy-duty moral considerations, when they need to be made, are typically made by the parents. Not infallibly, but reflectively, with hands on.

These working-class characters are direct descendants of a previous generation of middle-class TV parents, such as Ozzie and Harriet Nelson, Danny Thomas or Robert Young, all of whom, after struggling and groping, did come to know best. And today, there are an increasing number of such struggling parents (though now almost all working class) on TV—NBC's *Grand* and *227*, ABC's *Family Matters* and *Life Goes On*—to choose from. It's as if the working-class or minority parents are compensated for the heft they may lack in the real world by having it at home with their children (except for Homer Simpson of *The Simpsons*, the animated cartoon series on Fox, who rues, with Kafkaesque angst, his lack of puissance anywhere in the world—at home with his wife and three children, at the company picnic, and certainly at the nuclear power plant where he works). Or perhaps on a more cynical level, the programs are self-consciously designed opiates for working-class audiences, soothingly enhancing their image even as they satirically skewer the image of those with more money.

When the parents are middle-class or better, they, like Dad in *Growing Pains*, seem to lack any real authority within the family at all—the sole exception to this is NBC's *Cosby*, where the parents are just as smart as if they were blue collar. (Is this because, as upper-middle-class minorities, they can have it both ways?) As for other white-collar prime-time examples—for instance, ABC's *Full House*, NBC's *My Two Dads* or even ABC's *Who's the Boss?*, which is bi-collar—the adults are vacuous or worse. The most pressing dilemma facing the father (played by Dan Lauria) on ABC's *Wonder Years* in recent episodes is whether or not the family should trade in its old car for a new one.

As for the youngsters, none of them—working or middle-class—is bad. But the working-class kids are generally kid-kids, with not a whit of wisdom beyond their years. Eddie (Darius McCrary) on *Family Matters* thinks the world revolves around a new pair of Nikes; Roseanne's offspring live for the malls, and Edda (Sara Rue) on *Grand* is preoccupied with her weight.

If we want to find a TV child wise beyond his or her years, the place to look these days is in the upper-middle-class family, especially the one where both parents are professionals. The wisest child of all is the teenager Doogie Howser, M.D., featured on the show of the same name on ABC. Doogie (Neil Patrick Harris) does get by with a bit of help from his parents, now and then. But, as a recent episode demonstrated, his father has his own professional problems that Doogie finds a solution for. It is Doogie alone who must consider the life-and-death medical ethics of performing an appendectomy on his girlfriend, or search his own soul for signs of unexamined racism.

Meanwhile, in *the Wonder Years*, though some of the moral subtlety of Kevin Arnold (Fred Savage) comes from the voiceover presence of his adult self looking back (just like Pip in Dickens's *Great Expectations*), it also clearly lies in the child himself, if his bemused quizzicality is any index to the life within. What should he do about retrieving a valentine for Winnie (Danica McKellar) from an old girlfriend's locker, where it has been mistakenly placed? What about when his best friend, Paul (Josh Saviano), and Winnie seem to like one another? Where should his loyalties lie? The answers, of course, roll in rather patly at the end of 30 minutes, but Kevin, to his credit, notices the questions and struggles with them with never so much as a glance in his parents' direction. They do not seem likely sources of wisdom, frankly.

How is it that parents who are apparently so smart in the world are so stupid at home? Why are they such inadequate resources for their children? Maybe part of the point is that they're too busy being smart in the world to be at home much or to be well informed about the pressing intricacies of home life. Perhaps the wisdom of upper-middle-class children can be seen as a precocity forced on them, a measure of the parents' abdication of the family for the world.

Children of whatever class are likely to be their parents' successors, at home or in the world. The tacit vindication of the middle-class parents' way, ironically enough, is all too evident in the wisdom of their children, who—if wisdom counts for anything—will surely inherit the world and comfortable futures, their parents legacy to them. As to the children of the working class, their parents don't have the world to leave to them—but maybe they'll grow up to inherit the home.

SIGNIFICANCE

Television sitcoms may resemble real life, but the situations and the characters remain fictional, and though life does occasionally emulate art, the reverse is far more typical. In the 1950s, families enjoyed the prosperity that followed World War II, and the idealized picture of parents and children enjoying a night in front of the television together was often a reality. Television shows reflected that audience, where women were mothers and housewives and men came home from a day at work to enjoy dinner with their families. Parents worked hard and children either listened to authority figures or got into harmless mischief in programs such as *Leave It to Beaver* and *Dennis the Menace*.

In the decades that followed, however, the American family began to change. Divorce became more common, increasing the number of single-parent households and combined families due to remarriage. Women started working outside the home on a more regular basis, sometimes as the sole support of their family. As a result, television programmers began to appeal to these less-than-traditional households, airing shows about single mothers like Shirley Partridge, raising children on her own, and parents like Mike and Carol Brady, who encouraged their children from previous marriages to consider each other siblings. These idealized outlooks were meant to entertain people who were already familiar with the difficulties inherent in their situations.

By the 1980s, fewer and fewer families were able to sit down and watch television together as a unit. Two-income homes were becoming the norm, and children were becoming steadily more independent. As a result, the viewing audience shifted. Many television programs that traditionally targeted families began to gear themselves to a younger viewing audience overall, as advertisers became aware of the spending power of teenagers. While the shows still appealed on some level to adults, they also began to depict teens as more independent and capable, in some cases allowing them to overshadow their television parents. Children frequently became the focus of the shows, with parents' storylines fading into the background. In programs such as *Growing Pains*, *My Two Dads*, and *Family Ties*, the children are smart, capable, and sometimes outwit the adults. However, in other instances, those same children still get into trouble and require their parents to rescue them. The balance allowed for a more well-rounded viewing audience and a broader range of advertising.

The discrepancies between characters in family shows with upper- and upper-middle class characters versus working class characters can be explained in a number of ways. In previous decades, middle-class and blue-collar families appeared on a disproportionately small number of television shows. As programmers worked to adjust this ratio, introducing shows that represented working-class and minority families, they also worked to balance the family dynamics within those programs, and to avoid including too many clichés. Programs such as *The Jeffersons*, *Married with Children*, and *Roseanne* each focused on a specific characteristic of the family on which they based their humor, rather than depicting a standard family dynamic or a reversal of the parent/child relationship. Because of this, parents often came across as still in control of their children, rather than the opposite.

Meanwhile, upper- and upper-middle-class families depicted on television could be objects of humor because they were successful and driven and needed a flaw to humanize them and make them interesting to the viewing audience. Television shows need to resolve conflict week after week, and so even in an idealized television family, there must be something wrong to drive the story forward and keep viewers turning on the television.

FURTHER RESOURCES
Books

Hammamoto, Darrell Y. *Nervous Laughter: Television Situation Comedy and Liberal Democratic Ideology*. New York: Praeger, 1989.

Taylor, Ella. *Prime-Time Families: Television Culture in Postwar America*. Berkeley: University of California Press, 1989.

William, Douglas. *Television Families: Is Something Wrong in Suburbia?* Mahwah, NJ: Lawrence Erlbaum Associates, 2003.

Web sites

Museum of Broadcast Communications. "Family on Television <http://www.museum.tv/archives/etv/F/htmlF/family-ontel/familyontel.htm> (accessed June 28, 2006).

———. "Social Class and Television <http://www.museum.tv/archives/etv/S/htmlS/socialclass/socialclass.htm> (accessed June 28, 2006).

University of Virginia. "We Are the MTV Generation" <http://forums.itc.virginia.edu/q-folio/fall2002/edis542/UserItemDetail.cfm?IDUserItem=489> (accessed June 28, 2006).

Address to the Commonwealth Club of California

On Family Values

Speech

By: Dan Quayle

Date: May 19, 1992

Source: *Dan Quayle: Speeches: Address to the Commonwealth Club of California.* "On Family Values." May 19, 1992 <http://www.vicepresidentdanquayle.com/speeches_StandingFirm_CCC_1.html> (accessed June 19, 2006).

About the Author: Vice President James Danforth Quayle (b. 1947) served the United States from 1989 to 1993 under former President George H.W. Bush. Born in Indiana, Quayle received his law degree from the Indianapolis University School of Law. He began his career in public service in 1971, working in the Attorney General's office. Quayle also practiced law with his wife and worked as publisher of the family newspaper *The Huntington Herald-Press*. Entering the Republican political arena as a Congressman in 1976 and serving in the House of Representatives, he represented Indiana for two terms. Quayle entered the Senate race of 1980, which he won and was re-elected in 1986. He was called upon by George H.W. Bush to run for the Vice Presidency, attaining this office in 1988 at the age of forty-one. He has published a book of his memoirs, *Standing Firm, A Vice Presidential Memoir* (1994), which was a *New York Times* bestseller; and has also authored *The American Family* (1996) and *Worth Fighting For* (1999). Since 2000, Quayle has been chairman of Cerberus Global Investments, a

Murphy Brown, played by Candice Bergen, holds her newborn son on the TV show *Murphy Brown.* The story generated controversy when Vice President Dan Quayle commented on the show as being contrary to traditional family values because Brown was a single mother. © BETTMANN/CORBIS.

major investment company in the United States with international offices in Japan, Germany, and Korea.

Introduction

This topic of family values was initiated by the Los Angeles riots that occurred in 1992. The riots were sparked by a verdict of a predominantly white jury that acquitted four policemen who were video-taped beating Rodney King, a black man who had been apprehended after fleeing the police. The rioting resulted in mass looting, injuries, and several deaths. Former Vice President Dan Quayle was asked about these domestic events by Japanese leaders while in Japan meeting on international affairs.

In relating the riots to the breakdown of values within society among inner city residents, there were comments suggested by some of the Japanese officials that diversity was to blame. They also argued that racial differences create problems that weaken a society. Quayle refuted these remarks noting that because of diverse backgrounds and cultures in America, they have enjoyed tremendous success economically as a nation. He also refuted those in the United States that explained away the riots as justifiable or pardonable behavior. However, the underlying question—what transpired that provoked the riots in Los Angeles— still required an explanation.

In this 1992 speech to the Commonwealth Club of California, Quayle remarks on how the decline of family values in American society contributed to this tragedy. He discusses how fathers are necessary components of the family, despite how it was portrayed by television personas of the time (Murphy Brown, for instance); how two parents are essentially and statistically necessary to prevent poverty from being transferred from one generation to the next; and how governmental programs should find strategies that support the family structure rather than promote its breakup.

■ PRIMARY SOURCE

I was born in 1947, so I'm considered one of those "Baby Boomers" we keep reading about. But let's look at one unfortunate legacy of the "Boomer" generation. When we were young, it was fashionable to declare war against traditional values. Indulgence and self-gratification seemed to have no consequences. Many of our generation glamorized casual sex and drug use, evaded responsibility and trashed authority.

Today the "Boomers" are middle-aged and middle class. The responsibility of having families has helped many recover traditional values. And, of course, the great majority of those in the middle class survived the turbulent legacy of the 60s and 70s. But many of the poor, with less to fall back on, did not.

The intergenerational poverty that troubles us so much today is predominantly a poverty of values. Our inner cities are filled with children having children; with people who have not been able to take advantage of educational opportunities; with people who are dependent on drugs or the narcotic of welfare. To be sure, many people in the ghettos struggle very hard against these tides— and sometimes win. But too many feel they have no hope and nothing to lose. This poverty is, again, fundamentally a poverty of values.

Unless we change the basic rules of society in our inner cities, we cannot expect anything else to change. We will simply get more of what we saw three weeks ago. New thinking, new ideas, new strategies are needed.

For the government, transforming underclass culture means that our policies and programs must create a different incentive system. Our policies must be premised on, and must reinforce, values such as: family, hard work, integrity and personal responsibility.

I think we can all agree that government's first obligation is to maintain order. We are a nation of laws, not looting. It has become clear that the riots were fueled by the vicious gangs that terrorize the inner cities. We are committed to breaking those gangs and restoring law and order. As James Q. Wilson has written, "Programs of economic restructuring will not work so long as gangs control the streets."

Some people say "law and order" are code words. Well, they are code words. Code words for safety, getting control of the streets, and freedom from fear. And let's not forget that, in 1990, 84 percent of the crimes committed by blacks were committed against blacks.

We are for law and order. If a single mother raising her children in the ghetto has to worry about drive-by shootings, drug deals, or whether her children will join gangs and die violently, her difficult task becomes impossible. We're for law and order because we can't expect children to learn in dangerous schools. We're for law and order because if property isn't protected, who will build businesses?

As one step on behalf of law and order—and on behalf of opportunity as well—the President has initiated the "Weed and Seed" program—to "weed out" criminals and "seed" neighborhoods with programs that address root causes of crime. And we have encouraged community based policing, which gets the police on the street so they interact with citizens.

Safety is absolutely necessary. But it's not sufficient. Our urban strategy is to empower the poor by giving them control over their lives. To do that, our urban agenda includes:

- Fully funding the Home-ownership and Opportunity for People Everywhere program. HOPE—as we call it—will help public housing residents become homeowners. Subsidized housing all too often merely made rich investors richer. Home ownership will give the poor a stake in their neighborhoods, and a chance to build equity.
- Creating enterprise zones by slashing taxes in targeted areas, including a zero capital gains tax, to spur entrepreneurship, economic development, and job creation in inner cities.

- Instituting our education strategy, AMERICA 2000, to raise academic standards and to give the poor the same choices about how and where to educate their children that rich people have.
- Promoting welfare reform to remove the penalties for marriage, create incentives for saving, and give communities greater control over how the programs are administered.

These programs are empowerment programs. They are based on the same principles as the Job Training Partnership Act, which aimed to help disadvantaged young people and dislocated workers to develop their skills to give them an opportunity to get ahead. Empowering the poor will strengthen families. And right now, the failure of our families is hurting America deeply. When families fail, society fails. The anarchy and lack of structure in our inner cities are testament to how quickly civilization falls apart when the family foundation cracks. Children need love and discipline. They need mothers and fathers. A welfare check is not a husband. The state is not a father. It is from parents that children learn how to behave in society; it is from parents above all that children come to understand values and themselves as men and women, mothers and fathers.

And for those concerned about children growing up in poverty, we should know this: marriage is probably the best anti-poverty program of all. Among families headed by married couples today, there is a poverty rate of 5.7 percent. But 33.4 percent of families headed by a single mother are in poverty today.

Nature abhors a vacuum. Where there are no mature, responsible men around to teach boys how to be good men, gangs serve in their place. In fact; gangs have become a surrogate family for much of a generation of inner-city boys. I recently visited with some former gang members in Albuquerque, New Mexico. In a private meeting, they told me why they had joined gangs. These teenage boys said that gangs gave them a sense of security. They made them feel wanted, and useful. They got support from their friends. And, they said, "It was like having a family." "Like family"—unfortunately, that says it all.

The system perpetuates itself as these young men father children whom they have no intention of caring for, by women whose welfare checks support them. Teenage girls, mired in the same hopelessness, lack sufficient motive to say no to this trap.

Answers to our problems won't be easy.

We can start by dismantling a welfare system that encourages dependency and subsidizes broken families. We can attach conditions—such as school attendance, or work—to welfare. We can limit the time a recipient gets benefits. We can stop penalizing marriage for welfare mothers. We can enforce child support payments.

Ultimately however, marriage is a moral issue that requires cultural consensus, and the use of social sanctions. Bearing babies irresponsibly is, simply, wrong. Failing to support children one has fathered is wrong. We must be unequivocal about this.

It doesn't help matters when prime time TV has Murphy Brown—a character who supposedly epitomizes today's intelligent, highly paid, professional woman;—mocking the importance of fathers, by bearing a child alone, and calling it just another "lifestyle choice."

I know it is not fashionable to talk about moral values, but we need to do it. Even though our cultural leaders in Hollywood, network TV, the national newspapers routinely jeer at them, I think that most of us in this room know that some things are good, and other things are wrong. Now it's time to make the discussion public.

It's time to talk again about family, hard work, integrity and personal responsibility. We cannot be embarrassed out of our belief that two parents, married to each other, are better in most cases for children than one. That honest work is better than hand-outs—or crime. That we are our brothers' keepers. That it's worth making an effort, even when the rewards aren't immediate. So I think the time has come to renew our public commitment to our Judeo-Christian values-in our churches and synagogues, our civic organizations and our schools. We are, as our children recite each morning, "one nation under God." That's a useful framework for acknowledging a duty and an authority higher than our own pleasures and personal ambitions.

If we lived more thoroughly by these values, we would live in a better society. For the poor, renewing these values will give people the strength to help themselves by acquiring the tools to achieve self-sufficiency, a good education, job training, and property. Then they will move from permanent dependence to dignified independence.

Shelby Steele, in his great book, *The Content of Our Character*, writes, "Personal responsibility is the brick and mortar of power. The responsible person knows that the quality of his life is something that he will have to make inside the limits of his fate.... The quality of his life will pretty much reflect his efforts." I believe that the Bush administration's empowerment agenda will help the poor gain that power, by creating opportunity, and letting people make the choices that free citizens must make.

Though our hearts have been pained by the events in Los Angeles, we should take this tragedy as an opportunity for self-examination and progress. So let the national debate roar on. I, for one, will join it. The President will lead it. The American people will participate in it. And as a result, we will become an even stronger nation.

SIGNIFICANCE

Quayle's reference to the Murphy Brown persona caused this speech to garner far more publicity than would otherwise have been the case. The producers of the television sitcom promptly used reference as the basis for a double-length episode, widely watched, that featured Ms. Brown viewing the speech on television, being assured by her friends that it was of no importance ("It's DAN QUAYLE!—FORGET it!"), and then discovering, in the onslaught of reporters and publicity, that when the Vice President makes a statement about someone, it can't be taken lightly.

In the years immediately following Quayle's speech, the raised consciousness of the importance of fathers in the family—whether or not the speech was a factor—was evident in the founding of the National Fatherhood Initiative, established in 1993 to improve the well-being of children by increasing the proportion of children growing up with involved, responsible, and committed fathers; and in the 1995 Million Man March in Washington, D.C., to demonstrate commitment of African American men to be better fathers and husbands.

Two of the four officers acquitted of beating Rodney King were later convicted on federal charges of violating his civil rights. King sued the city of Los Angeles and settled for $3.8 million; he later had other conflicts with the law and entered a substance abuse rehabilitation program. The South Central neighborhood, where the riots originated, became the recipient of $1.4 billion through an initiative called Rebuild Los Angeles, spearheaded by a coalition of city officials and businesses. Nevertheless, the neighborhood remains one of Los Angeles' poorest, with high unemployment. The Reverend Cecil Murray, pastor of the AME church in South Central, remarked cautiously in an interview on CNN ten years after the event that though the "wounds had not healed,"…"there are isolated moments where you can note progress here."

FURTHER RESOURCES
Book
Quayle, Dan. *Standing Firm*. Harpercollins, 1995.

Web site
Cnn.com/U.S. "Los Angeles Riot Still Echoes a Decade Later" April 29, 2002 <http://archives.cnn.com/2002/US/04/28/la.riot.anniversary/index.html> (accessed June 29, 2006).

Dan Quayle Was Right

Journal article

By: Barbara Dafoe Whitehead

Date: April, 1993

Source: Whitehead, Barbara Dafoe. "Dan Quayle was Right." *The Atlantic.* 4 (1993): 47.

About the Author: Barbara Dafoe Whitehead is an American social scientist and author who specializes in the research and analysis of family issues, including the impact of separation and divorce upon family structures. She has written a number of books, including *The Divorce Culture.*

INTRODUCTION

During the 1991–1992 American television season, the popular situation comedy *Murphy Brown* featured on ongoing story line that explored a number of issues regarding the pregnancy of the program's lead character, the successful and unmarried career woman Murphy Brown, as portrayed by actress Candice Bergen. The final episode of the season culminated in Brown giving birth to her child.

In 1992, American Vice-President Dan Quayle touched off a firestorm of media commentary when he stated that the Murphy Brown character set a poor example for the people of America. Quayle remarked that while he had not personally watched the program, the decision of Murphy Brown to deliberately choose to have a child out of wedlock was an indication of how the liberal forces of the entertainment industry in general and those of television in particular had eroded traditional American family values. Quayle particularly criticized the characterization given to Murphy Brown's decision to become a single mother as one representing a lifestyle choice.

The public comments regarding the observations of Quayle were representative of the different fissures in American public opinion at the time concerning the concept of single motherhood. Quayle was roundly attacked by both the entertainment industry and various women's groups. The entertainment industry to a large degree responded by stating that programs such as *Murphy Brown* simply reflected the reality of modern American society, and that *Murphy Brown* was a mirror and not a political statement, nor did the production particularly advocate one approach to parenting and family structure over another. Women's groups saw the Quayle statements about a television

character as indicative of the true attitudes held by the Republican Reagan administration and conservatives generally regarding the position of women in the workplace. These commentators observed that the fictional Murphy Brown clearly embraced motherhood as an important concept, a fact of importance to society as a whole.

Quayle attracted considerable support for his views from religious conservative groups across America. The expression 'family values' was commonly employed by conservatives to encompass a wide range of principles as being the most desirable and American basis for the family; the traditional two parent family structure was at the heart of this definition.

The four part essay *Dan Quayle was Right*, of which the excerpted primary source below is the fourth part, was published in April 1993, approximately one year after the furor concerning Murphy Brown had first arisen. The contest between the portrayal of unwed motherhood on Murphy Brown and the conservative views of Vice President Quayle continued into the next television season, as the producers of the program wove the Quayle comments and their controversy into the storyline of the program.

▌ PRIMARY SOURCE

The Two Parent Advantage

… Though far from perfect as a social institution, the intact family offers children greater security and better outcomes than its fast-growing alternatives: single-parent and stepparent families. Not only does the intact family protect the child from poverty and economic insecurity; it also provides greater noneconomic investments of parental time, attention, and emotional support over the entire life course. This does not mean that all two-parent families are better for children than all single-parent families. But in the face of the evidence it becomes increasingly difficult to sustain the proposition that all family structures produce equally good outcomes for children.

Curiously, many in the research community are hesitant to say that two-parent families generally promote better outcomes for children than single-parent families. Some argue that we need finer measures of the extent of the family-structure effect. As one scholar has noted, it is possible, by disaggregating the data in certain ways, to make family structure "go away" as an independent variable. Other researchers point to studies that show that children suffer psychological effects as a result of family conflict preceding family breakup. Consequently, they reason, it is the conflict rather than the structure of the family that is responsible for many of the problems associated with family disruption. Others, including Judith Wallerstein, caution against treating children in divorced families and children in intact families as separate populations, because doing so tends to exaggerate the differences between the two groups. "We have to take this family by family," Wallerstein says.

Some of the caution among researchers can also be attributed to ideological pressures. Privately, social scientists worry that their research may serve ideological causes that they themselves do not support, or that their work may be misinterpreted as an attempt to "tell people what to do." Some are fearful that they will be attacked by feminist colleagues, or, more generally, that their comments will be regarded as an effort to turn back the clock to the 1950s—a goal that has almost no constituency in the academy. Even more fundamental, it has become risky for anyone—scholar, politician, religious leader—to make normative statements today. This reflects not only the persistent drive toward "value neutrality" in the professions but also a deep confusion about the purposes of public discourse. The dominant view appears to be that social criticism, like criticism of individuals, is psychologically damaging. The worst thing you can do is to make people feel guilty or bad about themselves.

When one sets aside these constraints, however, the case against the two-parent family is remarkably weak. It is true that disaggregating data can make family structure less significant as a factor, just as disaggregating Hurricane Andrew into wind, rain, and tides can make it disappear as a meteorological phenomenon. Nonetheless, research opinion as well as common sense suggests that the effects of changes in family structure are great enough to cause concern. Nicholas Zill argues that many of the risk factors for children are doubled or more than doubled as the result of family disruption. "In epidemiological terms," he writes, "the doubling of a hazard is a substantial increase. The increase in risk that dietary cholesterol poses for cardiovascular disease, for example, is far less than double, yet millions of Americans have altered their diets because of the perceived hazard."

The argument that family conflict, rather than the breakup of parents, is the cause of children's psychological distress is persuasive on its face. Children who grow up in high-conflict families, whether the families stay together or eventually split up, are undoubtedly at great psychological risk. And surely no one would dispute that there must be societal measures available, including divorce, to remove children from families where they are in danger. Yet only a minority of divorces grows out of pathological situations; much more common are divorces in families unscarred by physical assault. Moreover, an equally compelling hypothesis is that family breakup generates its own conflict. Certainly, many families exhibit

more conflictual and even violent behavior as a consequence of divorce than they did before divorce.

Finally, it is important to note that clinical insights are different from sociological findings. Clinicians work with individual families, who cannot and should not be defined by statistical aggregates. Appropriate to a clinical approach, moreover, is a focus on the internal dynamics of family functioning and on the immense variability in human behavior. Nevertheless, there is enough empirical evidence to justify sociological statements about the causes of declining child well-being and to demonstrate that despite the plasticity of human response, there are some useful rules of thumb to guide our thinking about and policies affecting the family.

For example, Sara McLanahan says, three structural constants are commonly associated with intact families, even intact families who would not win any "Family of the Year" awards. The first is economic. In intact families, children share in the income of two adults. Indeed, as a number of analysts have pointed out, the two-parent family is becoming more rather than less necessary, because more and more families need two incomes to sustain a middle-class standard of living.

McLanahan believes that most intact families also provide a stable authority structure. Family breakup commonly upsets the established boundaries of authority in a family. Children are often required to make decisions or accept responsibilities once considered the province of parents. Moreover, children, even very young children, are often expected to behave like mature adults, so that the grown-ups in the family can be free to deal with the emotional fallout of the failed relationship. In some instances family disruption creates a complete vacuum in authority; everyone invents his or her own rules. With lines of authority disrupted or absent, children find it much more difficult to engage in the normal kinds of testing behavior, the trial and error, the failing and succeeding, that define the developmental pathway toward character and competence. McLanahan says, "Children need to be the ones to challenge the rules. The parents need to set the boundaries and let the kids push the boundaries. The children shouldn't have to walk the straight and narrow at all times."

Finally, McLanahan holds that children in intact families benefit from stability in what she neutrally terms "household personnel." Family disruption frequently brings new adults into the family, including stepparents, live-in boyfriends or girlfriends, and casual sexual partners. Like stepfathers, boyfriends can present a real threat to children's, particularly to daughters', security and well-being. But physical or sexual abuse represents only the most extreme such threat. Even the very best of boyfriends can disrupt and undermine a child's sense of peace and security, McLanahan says. "It's not as though you're going from an unhappy marriage to peacefulness. There can be a constant changing until the mother finds a suitable partner."

McLanahan's argument helps explain why children of widows tend to do better than children of divorced or unmarried mothers. Widows differ from other single mothers in all three respects. They are economically more secure, because they receive more public assistance through Survivors Insurance, and possibly private insurance or other kinds of support from family members. Thus widows are less likely to leave the neighborhood in search of a new or better job and a cheaper house or apartment. Moreover, the death of a father is not likely to disrupt the authority structure radically. When a father dies, he is no longer physically present, but his death does not dethrone him as an authority figure in the child's life. On the contrary, his authority may be magnified through death. The mother can draw on the powerful memory of the departed father as a way of intensifying her parental authority: "Your father would have wanted it this way." Finally, since widows tend to be older than divorced mothers, their love life may be less distracting.

Regarding the two-parent family, the sociologist David Popenoe, who has devoted much of his career to the study of families, both in the United States and in Scandinavia, makes this straightforward assertion: Social science research is almost never conclusive. There are always methodological difficulties and stones left unturned. Yet in three decades of work as a social scientist, I know of few other bodies of data in which the weight of evidence is so decisively on one side of the issue: on the whole, for children, two-parent families are preferable to single-parent and stepfamilies.

SIGNIFICANCE

The right of women to make their own choices concerning education, career, family, and motherhood has been a central aspect of the broad range of the issues that have stimulated international debates on women's issues since the work of American reformers Elizabeth Cady Stanton and Susan B. Anthony in the nineteenth century.

The 1993 conclusions of Barbara Dafoe Whitehead were advanced against an ongoing debate in American society about the viability of all types of family structures. It is apparent from a careful reading of Whitehead's conclusions concerning the traditional two parent family that hers is not an ideologically based case, but rather an analysis that is as empirical as social science research and its inherent variability can ever be.

An important aspect of Whitehead's analysis is the absence of any consideration of the element of 'lifestyle choice' of single motherhood and resultant family structure that sparked the controversy surrounding the comments of Vice President Dan Quayle. The Whitehead analysis does not attach a value to the concept of whether a woman may derive any personal fulfillment in her execution of a family choice. Whitehead sees the advantages of the traditional two parent family structure from the perspective of the best possible outcomes for its family members. Economic benefits, the usual lines of authority between parents and children, and inherent stability for children in being a part of a fixed family grouping are all factors that are unrelated to any consideration of personal fulfillment through the exercise of a personal choice, in the manner of the fictional Murphy Brown.

It is significant that while marriage and cohabitation are the result of a choice, as often is single motherhood, Whitehead perceives there to be significantly better stability and positive outcomes in families where a father has died to create a family led by a single parent than ones formed through choice.

Whitehead also develops the notion that simply having a second parental figure present, whether through casual domestic partnerships, or by longer term cohabitation, does not generate the same level of stability to the family unit as does the traditional two biological parent model. Numerical data provided through the 2000 American census suggests that children age twelve to seventeen who resided in a blended family unit were significantly more likely to experience emotional difficulties, a lower level of engagement with their schoolwork, and criminal law involvement than those children who were resident in a family with two biological parents.

An ironic aspect of the furor generated by the remarks of Dan Quayle is that his target, the concept that having a child beyond the traditional two parent structure is an erosion of family values, is perhaps not the most compelling social issue raised by the fictional Murphy Brown. In deciding to have her child as a single mother, Brown, an archetypal successful career woman, clearly exercised her choice to not terminate her pregnancy and have an abortion. Abortion is among the most profound battleground issues in America over the past forty years. The 1973 United States Supreme Court decision in *Roe v. Wade*, where the Court legalized the concept of abortion on demand, is one of the most influential and controversial decisions in American legal history.

The decision of Murphy Brown to have her child is the type of decision that would otherwise be applauded by conservative women's groups of the type that supported Dan Quayle's views about single motherhood. In this respect, Quayle criticized one choice made by Murphy Brown that implicitly involved a moral decision that he and his constituency would otherwise support.

FURTHER RESOURCES

Books

Atwood, Joan D. and Frank Genovese. *Therapy with Single Parents*. Binghamton, New York: Haworth Press, 2006.

McLanahan, Sarah and Gary Sandefur. *Growing Up with a Single Parent*. Cambridge, Massachusetts: Harvard University Press, 1994.

Web sites

Urban Institute. "Beyond the Two Parent Family." May 2001 <http://www.urban.org/url.cfm?ID=310339> (accessed June 21, 2006).

Simpsons Creator on Poking Fun

Magazine article

By: M. S. Mason

Date: April 17, 1998

Source: Mason, M. S. "Simpsons' Creator on Poking Fun." *Christian Science Monitor*. April 17, 1998: B1.

About the Author: M. S. Mason is a staff writer for the *Christian Science Monitor*. He writes on television and popular culture.

INTRODUCTION

Early television programming was tightly regulated. Convinced that television had the potential to improve human life, the medium's pioneers insisted that programming conform to a rigid set of guidelines for content and taste. Networks employed their own censors to ensure that profane or vulgar material did not air, protecting the networks from potential fines and other penalties. The Federal Communication Commission (FCC), established in 1934 to regulate interstate communication, set and enforced broadcast standards.

As a result of this self-censorship, many early television programs were quite idealistic in their portrayal of American life, depicting homes as cheery, congenial places in a world free of war, hunger, and conflict. Programs such as *The Adventures of Ozzie and Harriet* and *Leave it to Beaver* told the stories of model American families headed by industrious working fathers and held together by loving stay-at-home mothers. In many ways, these television families reflected an idealized vision of a nineteenth-century family unit living with twentieth-century conveniences.

Despite their unrealistic portrayal of American life, the shows faced little competition and soon became hits, running for hundreds of episodes apiece. As television became a staple of American family life, its portrayal of American families was absorbed by children, many of whom eventually realized the fallacy of what they watched. Some of these children grew up to produce their own television shows about American families; in at least one case, a show produced in the 1980s was conceived as a parody of the fairy-tale family shows of the 1950s and 1960s.

PRIMARY SOURCE

Simpsons Creator on Poking Fun

There's a little bit of Matt Groening in Bart Simpson. The man who created the diminutive provocateur for *The Simpsons* says he grew up watching too much television and fantasized what he would do if he got his own TV show.

"Well this is what I would have done, and I did it," he says, adding wryly, "At an early age I was most strongly affected by *Leave It to Beaver* and *Ozzie and Harriet*. [*The Simpsons*] is my skewed reaction to those shows."

Mr. Groening's baby is the longest-running prime-time animated series in television history. It has won a Peabody Award, 12 Emmys, and a shelf-load of assorted others. About to hatch its 200th episode, *Trash of the Titans* (Fox, April 26, 8–8:30 p.m.), the "plausible impossible" family long ago achieved pop-icon status.

In the best tradition of TV families, the Simpsons love one another, no matter what. The show has all the elements of its live-action family-oriented prototypes, with a twist: an involved community; assorted villains; a sweet, annoying next-door neighbor; and the family itself—a goofy dad whose frailties get him into trouble; a loving, sensible mom who usually gets him out again; two adorable little girls; and one 10-year-old trickster.

Bart is Dennis the Menace with self-awareness—a kid so abused by the public school system that when he

Matt Groening poses with cutouts of the characters from his famous creation: *The Simpsons*. © DOUGLAS KIRKLAND/COR-BIS.

was labeled a failure in kindergarten, he found his self-esteem as the class stand-up comic. But Bart's pranks can be obnoxious, and he has worried many parents and teachers who fret publicly about his bad influence—his cheeky back talk, his enthusiastic naughtiness, and his inattention at school. He's no role model.

"Bart isn't a good example," agrees Groening. "He isn't a good role model. But I used to get letters saying, *Homer isn't wearing a seat belt; he's a bad example.* But you can laugh at him because you don't want to be like him."

The nature of Bart's abrasive commentary is satirical. And the nature of the best satire is, of course, to poke fun at human foibles. When it's good, satire makes you think, and *The Simpsons* skewers everything from nuclear waste to alien abductions, the movies, TV, and official hypocrisy.

"For me, it's hard to approach satire directly. I don't think we sit down and say, 'How do we satirize this subject?' We are trying to make a solid half-hour of entertainment—cram as many jokes in there as we can. But everybody [on the writing staff], Republicans and Democrats, has a strong point of view. And we share a vision that our leaders aren't always telling us the truth, that our institutions sometimes fail us, and that people in media don't necessarily have any corner on wisdom—because we're in media ourselves and we know what idiots we are," he laughs.

"So we just have fun with it." Satire, says Groening, is about "not taking ourselves too seriously. Solemnity is always used by authority to stop critical thinking. 'You can't make a joke about that' is a way of shutting people up. It's a cartoon: [Making jokes] is what we're supposed to do."

Mining his own experience, Groening based his characters on people he knew and named many of them after people he loves. "Homer is not like my father, also named Homer, except that my father did get mad sometimes. But he wasn't stupid, fat, or bald. My father was a cartoonist and filmmaker, so he's not like Homer.

"There is a little bit of my mother in Marge. My mom is long-suffering like Marge, and she did have tall hair when I was a kid. She always denied it, but we have photos. My sisters, Lisa and Maggie, aren't really like Lisa and Maggie [in the show]—although Lisa claims she always was the unrecognized talent, and [she thinks] it's great the way I captured that."

But, he emphasizes, the characters aren't designed to inflict vengeance on people in real life. "Over the course of the show, some of them have taken on doltish characteristics, and now I'm afraid to call up some of these people," he laughs.

"Overall," says Groening, "I've always said it is a celebration of the American family at its wildest."

SIGNIFICANCE

The Simpsons got its start in 1987 as a series of short sketches on the short-lived *Tracey Ullman Show*. By 1990, the Fox Network had ordered an entire season of the shows, which went on to become one of the upstart broadcaster's first prime-time hits.

During its first few seasons, the popular show stirred frequent controversy. Bart's smart mouth and penchant for causing trouble drew criticism from schoolteachers who claimed to be seeing imitations in their own classrooms; partly in response to this criticism, later seasons focused more on Homer and his adventures. In 1992, President Bush criticized the fictional family, complaining in a major speech that America needed to become more like the family portrayed in the series *The Waltons* and less like Homer and the Simpsons. Following Dan Quayle's widely publicized spelling gaffe during a visit to an elementary school in 1992, Bart Simpson, who appears in the show's opening credits writing a single phrase repeatedly, began one episode by writing, "It's potato, not potatoe."

In 2006, *The Simpsons* entered its eighteenth season, having run longer than any of the 1960s family shows it parodied. A feature film version was slated for 2007 release. Much of the success of *The Simpsons* can be attributed to exceptionally good writing, but the show also demonstrates the lasting appeal of stories that revolve around families. According to writer Marla Brooks, American television has averaged two new shows focusing on families each year since the late 1940s, suggesting that the tried-and-true formula retains much of its appeal. While Homer and Marge are clearly not Ozzie and Harriet, their experiences in some ways better mirror their viewers' lives than the earlier show did. The show's willingness to make fun of anybody and anything, regardless of political affiliation or viewpoint has also endeared it to an educated audience that appreciates its sharp satire.

A retrospective of television families finds that they differ in virtually every imaginable way, but one common thread seems to unite them—particularly those that remain on the air for many years: the family members genuinely care about one another. From blustery Archie Bunker to clueless Homer Simpson and congenial Mike Brady, the fathers appear genuinely concerned about their families, despite frequent confusion about how to express that concern. While the forms and the norms of behavior may change, the image of a cohesive loving family unit remains deeply appealing. And if the characters can make an audience laugh as well, all the better.

FURTHER RESOURCES
Books

Brooks, Marla. *The American Family on Television: A Chronology of 121 Shows, 1948–2004*. New York: McFarland and Company, 2005.

Brown, Alan, and Chris Logan. *The Psychology of the Simpsons: D'oh!* Dallas: BenBella Books, 2006.

Spigel, Lynn. *Make Room for TV: Television and the Family Ideal in Postwar America*. Chicago: University of Chicago Press, 1992.

Periodicals

Goodale, Gloria. "Ozzy and Ozzie: TV family guys, one tattooed." *Christian Science Monitor*. 94 (April 19, 2002): 1.

Kachka, Boris. "Building a Better TV Family." *New York Magazine*. 35 (September 8, 2002): 94.

Kipnis, Jill. "Family Shows Are Serious Business." *Billboard*. 117 (2005): 26.

Web sites

Syracuse University Library: Media Services. "Television History Archive." 2005 <http://libwww.syr.edu/information/media/archive/main.htm> (accessed June 16, 2006).

University of North Texas: Department of Radio, Television and Film. "Radio and Television History Sites." <http://www.rtvf.unt.edu/links/histsites.htm> (accessed June 16, 2006).

University of San Diego: History Department. "Television's Golden Age." <http://history.sandiego.edu/gen/recording/television6.html> (accessed June 16, 2006).

MediaQuotient: National Survey of Family Media Habits, Knowledge, and Attitudes

Report

By: Douglas A. Gentile and David A. Walsh

Date: 1999

Source: *National Institute on Media and the Family.* "MediaQuotient: National Survey of Family Media Habits, Knowledge, and Attitudes." 1999 <http://www.mediafamily.org/research/report_mqexecsum.shtml> (accessed June 29, 2006).

About the Author: Douglas A. Gentile is the director of the media research laboratory at Iowa State University. David A. Walsh founded the National Institute on Media and the Family in 1996. Each author has written extensively on the issues associated with media influences and the family.

INTRODUCTION

The media habits of the American family have been affected by two separate forces—the expansion of the technologies that support various media, and the fundamental changes in the structure of the American family, particularly with regard to the control asserted by parents over the nature and the extent of the exposure of their children to all media.

The singular term 'medium' originally meant the form in which information was achieved; print, radio, and television were distinct media, separate entities from the information that was being transmitted or conveyed. In modern usage, the plural "media" is employed interchangeably as a definition of both the content and the mechanism to deliver it; this broader concept was popularized by social commentator Marshall McLuhan (1911–1980), whose 1967 book, *The Medium Is the Message: An Inventory of Effects* is the seminal work on the importance of media in modern society. McLuhan forecast both the rise and the desirability of electronic mass media.

Prior to 1920, the only media that influenced the American family was print. By 1900, the newspaper had become a feature of daily American life. Publishers were effectively self-regulating, avoiding any offensive or inappropriate content that might provoke a negative reaction from their readership. The use of bad language or the portrayal of sexually explicit situations was unheard of, and the likelihood that a child would be exposed to age-inappropriate written material during this period was negligible.

The radio became a central feature in many American homes after 1920 and it soon rivaled the newspaper as an influential force in society. The ability of a child or adolescent to access radio programming that might be seen as a negative influence remained nonexistent, however, as radio programming was an entirely family-oriented source of entertainment and news.

The introduction of the television to the American home, a process that began in the late 1940s, was the most important development in the media habits of the American family until that time. Television networks began to produce programming that was tailored to young people, and advertisers used these programs to target the youth audience. By 1970, American television was a sophisticated medium that expanded the envelope of available programming to include adult language and situations. This occurred as the rising divorce rate also created a greater number of single-parent households, where supervision and control of a child's television viewing was less rigid than in the past. The emergence of the two-income family, where both parents worked outside of the home left more children at home and unsupervised than at any previous time in history.

The use of personal computers in American homes eclipsed even the impact of television. The Internet represented a limitless broadening of media choices for American family members; unlike television, radio, and print formats, the control over the content of Internet communication rested primarily with the user.

■ PRIMARY SOURCE

MediaQuotient: National Survey of Family Media Habits, Knowledge, and Attitudes

Executive Summary

This study provides a detailed picture of family media habits, including the use of television, movies, videos, computer and video games, the Internet, music, and print media.

Some Key Findings

Media Habits and Attitudes

Over half of parents of 2- to 17-year-olds have seen effects of violent video games, television, and movies on their children.

- 51 percent "agree" or "strongly agree" that their children are affected by the violence they see in video games
- 57 percent of parents "agree" or "strongly agree" that their children are affected by the violence they see in movies or on TV

Parents have expressed their concerns about the amount of sexual and violent content their children see in many surveys. While both sexual and violent content concern parents, the amount of sexual content has routinely been of slightly greater concern to parents. For the first time, this study shows that more parents are concerned about the amount of violent content their children see:

- 81 percent of parents of 2- to 17-year-olds "agree" or "strongly agree" that they are concerned about the amount of violent content their children see in movies or on TV
- 77 percent of parents "agree" or "strongly agree" that they are concerned about the amount of sexual content their children see in movies or on TV

The average American child:

- Watches 25 hours of television each week
- Plays computer or video games for 7 hours each week
- Accesses the Internet from home for 4 hours each week (among those who have Internet access)

20 percent of 2- to 7-year-olds, 46 percent of 8- to 12-year-olds, and 56 percent of 13- to 17-year-olds have televisions in their bedrooms. Children who have television sets in their bedrooms watch more television than children who do not have television sets in their bedrooms (5 hours per week more, on average).

Although parents are concerned, and children are using media for many hours each day:

- Only 58 percent of parents have rules about how much TV may be watched
- Only 34 percent of parents "always" or "often" use the TV rating
- Only 40 percent of parents "always" or "often" look at the industry ratings before renting or buying computer or video games
- One-quarter (26%) of parents with Internet access use a blocking device for their children's Internet use

Perhaps this pattern is due to the fact that 36 percent of parents think that media have less influence on their children compared to most children, whereas only six percent think that media have more influence on their children compared to most children....

The Connection between Media Habits and School Performance

Family media habits can affect children's school performance. While it has been known for many years that the amount of television children watch is related to school performance (e.g., Huston et al., 1992), this study gives insight into many specific facets of media use that were not known previously. Furthermore, this study measured many types of electronic media as well as alternatives to electronic media, thus giving a more complete picture of family media habits.

Some key predictors of school performance include:

- Families that use electronic media less and read more have children who do better in school
- Parents who report that their children's behavior is less affected by media do **better** in school
- Children who participate in more alternatives to electronic media with their parents' support perform **better** in school
- Families that have the TV on during meals more frequently have children who do **more poorly** in school
- Families that report having the TV on more often even if no one is watching have children who do **more poorly** in school
- The average American child watches 25 hours of television a week. Children who watch less television do **better** in school. (The American Academy of Pediatrics recommends that children watch television "no more than 1 to 2 hours per day.")
- Parents who report that their children copy characters they have seen on TV more often have children who do **more poorly** in school
- Parents who report that their children more often watch TV before bed have children who do **more poorly** in school
- Families that play games or do activities together more frequently have children who do **better** in school
- Parents who read to their children more have children who like to read more. Children who like to read more do **better** in school
- Parents who agree more strongly that they are comfortable with the types of music their children listen to have children who do **better** in school
- Parents who report that they know what movie their child is going to see more often have children who do **better** in school
- Parents who report that their children play video or computer games less often have children who do **better** in school

The Connection between Media Habits and Media Effects

This study shows that one result of being influenced by the media (such as copying characters seen on TV, wanting to dress like sports or media stars, wanting to buy products seen on TV, parents seeing media have a negative effect, etc.) is a drop in school performance. However, the amount that media influence children is important in its own right. When asked how much their children are influenced by media compared to other children, parents are likely to report that their children are influenced less than other children (parents are six times more likely to say that their children are influenced less than they are to say that their children are influenced more). Yet, most families score lower on the Media Effects category of MediaQuotient than on any other category.

Some key predictors of how much children are influenced by media include:

- Parents who report that their children like to read more are also **more likely** to report having seen media have a **positive effect** on their children (as defined by parents)
- Parents who talk to their children about television programs more often are also **more likely** to report having seen media have a **positive effect** on their children.
- Parents who report that their children "always" or "often" watch educational television are less likely to report having seen media have a **negative effect** on their children

Implications

The various forms of electronic media that we have developed during the 20th century are very powerful. Because they are so powerful, they can benefit or harm children and communities dependent on how they are used. Wise use of media can help develop knowledge and skills, as well as provide engaging entertainment. However, unwise use can be harmful. The MediaQuotient research clearly shows how family media habits affect children in a variety of ways. Parents with more knowledge are better able to maximize the benefits and minimize the harm of these technologies. MediaQuotient can provide that knowledge and, in addition, offer suggestions for creating a healthier media diet.

Methodology

A national random sample of 527 parents of two to seventeen-year-olds completed MediaQuotient questionnaires. The study was conducted by mail with telephone follow-up. The data collection was conducted by the independent research firm Anderson, Niebuhr & Associates, Inc. All data collection occurred between July 30 and November 4, 1998. The data reflect responses from all socioeconomic statuses. The data are weighted by income level to reflect national income distributions appropriately. The overall response rate for the study was 55 percent. The data are accurate to ±4% with a 95% confidence level.

SIGNIFICANCE

The primary source draws a significant parallel between media habits and media effect, particularly with respect to the academic performance of children. Parents are clearly identified as people who can channel the media influences that ought to be experienced by the child.

The MediaQuotient study begins with the established premise that there exists a clear relationship between television viewing by children and school performance. There are many learned analyses of the question dating to the 1970s; wherever television has been employed as a de facto nanny, children tend to spend significant amounts of time watching television, and they tend to perform poorly in school in relation to children who watch less. The effect of the time spent by children on the Internet is now being evaluated in a similar fashion.

In modern American society, the media influences to which young people are exposed can rarely be isolated into distinct streams. Communication technologies have converged; Print, television, Internet, video games (often linked to their own web sites), interactive wireless telephones, and instant messaging are media sources that are often accessed simultaneously by a user. To understand how these modern media forces can influence a child, a parent must understand the nature and the extent of these technologies.

The MediaQuotient study also shows that turning off or simply blocking out the various media sources available to a modern American child is not a sensible strategy to limit negative media influences. Broad-based computer literacy is essential to virtually any position in the modern American workforce. College and university education has mandated the laptop computer as a necessary tool. High schools have made computer-based learning increasingly important.

One conclusion that can be drawn from the study is that a simple and ongoing dialogue is the best way to help a child understand media influences. This approach is not widespread, however, as numerous studies have shown that most American parents do not know what their children are doing on the Internet.

The study also suggests that where parents avoid making the television set the surrogate parent or babysitter, the child performs better in school. The twenty-five hours of weekly television viewing mentioned in the primary source has already been amended; a typical American child now spends 35 hours per week watching television, playing video or computer games, or accessing the Internet.

The relative freedom enjoyed by American children to use the Internet in their homes without interference is illustrated by statistical data that confirms that over fifty percent of American homes with Internet access have no rules about information viewed on the web, by instant messaging, or in e-mail. This profile is consistent with similar studies conducted in both Canada and Great Britain; over seventy percent of children aged 14 to 15 in Great Britain reported that their home computer usage was never supervised. In Canada, over seventy percent of parents surveyed stated that they had little or no discussion with their children regarding Internet access.

In 1990, phenomena such as identity theft, predatory stalking, and similar types of Internet crime did not exist. The interactive nature of electronic technology has introduced corresponding threats to family security that were unimaginable a generation ago. The extensive use of computers by children in an unsupervised or an uneducated fashion creates opportunities for exploitation. The family may be exposed to the risk of economic compromise and identity theft if a child unwittingly reveals confidential financial information. If parents do not educate themselves about children's Internet habits, or if the family operates without Internet/computer usage rules, the risk of falling victim to an unscrupulous influence is significant.

FURTHER RESOURCES

Books

Baker, Leigh. *Protecting Your Children from Sexual Predators.* New York: St. Martin's Press, 2002.

Sullivan, Mike. *Safety Monitor: How to Protect Your Kids Online.* Chicago: Bonus Press, 2002.

Periodicals

Gentile, Douglas A., and David A. Walsh. "A Normative Study of Family Media Habits." *Applied Developmental Psychology.* 23, no. 2 (202):157–158.

Hancox, Robert J., Barry J. Milne, and Richie Poult. "Association between Child-Adolescent Television Viewing and Adult Health: A Longitudinal Birth Cohort Study." *Lancet.* 364 (2004): 257–262.

Web sites

Brody, Jane. *New York Times.* "Children, Media and Sex: A Big Book of Blank Pages." January 31, 2006 <http://www.nytimes.com/2006/01/31/health/> (accessed June 28, 2006).

American Association of Child and Adolescent Psychiatry. "Children and Watching T.V." February 2005 <http://www.aacap.org/page/> (accessed June 29, 2006).

My Family Will Swoosh for Nike

Commercialism and the Family

Newspaper article

By: Jamie Linton

Date: March 31, 1999

Source: Linton, Jamie. "My Family Will Swoosh for Nike." *Ottawa Citizen* (March 31, 1999).

About the Author: Jamie Linton is a freelance journalist based in Ontario, Canada. The *Ottawa Citizen* is a daily newspaper founded in 1845 and owned by the media consortium CanWest Global.

INTRODUCTION

The use of a particular logo, emblem, or other corporate brand to publicize a consumer product is a venerable and proven marketing technique. While the traditional notions of product utility, reliability, and value remain important factors in the ability of a manufacturer or service provider to successfully promote a consumer product, the product image as conveyed by its brand has become an essential aspect of modern marketing.

'Branding' is the conversion of a corporate name, slogan, or logo into a distinct and freestanding entity. The corporate brand is often marketed to the consumer in a fashion that renders it distinct from the product itself.

Many of the oldest known corporate brands have endured through generations of consumers and a variety of shifts in consumer tastes and attitudes. The Michelin Man, also known as Bibendum, has been a cornerstone of the Michelin Tire manufacturing empire since it was first unveiled at a Lyon exhibition in 1894. The Converse All Star running shoes, featuring the distinctive ankle patch and the signature of

Six Nike sports shoes rest on a table at the company headquarters in Portland, Oregon, for the unveiling of the 1982 Air-Force line of basketball shoes. © BETTMANN/CORBIS. REPRODUCED BY PERMISSION.

basketball player Chuck Taylor, the long time Converse ambassador, have displayed this logo since the early 1920s. Products such as Rolex watches and Cartier jewelry rely upon the cachet established through association with their name to achieve a similar effect.

Among the most successful examples of corporate branding in the history of marketing is that of Nike shoes and the company's use of basketball star Michael Jordan as its chief advertising symbol. After Jordan became the featured Nike representative in 1985, Nike sales grew dramatically, both in its home American markets as well as on a global basis. Jordan, both as embodied in the stylized logo of his basketball dunking form, and through marketing slogans such as 'Be Like Mike', became one of the most recognizable humans on the planet. The Nike symbols themselves became the icons of American, and later global, culture. The power of the Nike logo and its marketing

was such that Jordan became one of the first athletes to earn more money from his participation in the process of corporate brand development than he earned from playing his chosen sport.

Unlike traditional sporting goods advertising campaigns, where the manufacturer tended to focus upon the ability of the product to assist the athlete in the improvement of their overall performance, the ground breaking Nike approach with its focus upon Michael Jordan devoted proportionately little time to the physical characteristics of the equipment. Nike enjoyed tremendous success through its cause and effect type association with Jordan.

The enduring success of the Nike branding campaign is evidenced by the fact that Jordan continues to be a feature in Nike advertisements, and notwithstanding his retirement from professional basketball in 2001, Jordan's name is synonymous with Nike in a way that Chuck Taylor was the personification of Converse in an earlier and less complicated consumer era. Michael Jordan is unquestionably one of the most famous Americans who has ever lived.

In the modern world, it is virtually impossible for consumers to avoid the marketing strategy that may be summarized as brand first, product second.

◼ PRIMARY SOURCE

My wife and I have decided to develop a new business strategy for our family. As of now, we are officially looking for a suitable corporate sponsor. Forget working like dogs and trying to make ends meet. That old-fashioned stuff is for losers. We're aiming to be the world's first Nike Family. Failing that, we will accept Disney, RJR Nabisco, Tommy Hilfiger, Liz Claiborne, Roots, Loblaw, Microsoft, Ford, or the Bank of Montreal.

This was my idea, but I admit that it didn't just come out of the blue. The University of Ottawa football program inspired me. Recently, it was announced that the football Gee Gees have cut a deal with Nike U.S.A. According to newspaper reports, nearly half of their program costs are to be covered by Nike. They get new uniforms, shoes and practice jerseys and will even be able to tuck away a portion of the profits from the Nike products they sell. All for merely displaying the "swoosh" logo on their jerseys.

Now that's a deal.

This happy state of affairs contrast sharply with the fate of the other university football program in the nation's capital. The poor Carleton Ravens squad was forced into extinction because it was costing the university too much. Too bad they didn't get a suitable corporate sponsor in time.

With the decline of virtually every publicly funded program in existence, the ever-increasing cost of living and growing sovereignty of those kind and generous corporations, the strategy of getting yourself a suitable corporate sponsor only makes sense. And judging from the swash of corporate logos all over the uniforms, hats, vest, cars, boats, kit bags, tackle boxes and accessories of more and more athletes, teams, entertainers, and personage of various kinds, I'm not the only one who thinks this way.

Of course, generous as they are, corporations like Nike don't sponsor just anybody. You have to be good. In fact, you have to be the best. Nike doesn't want its swoosh appearing on the shoulders of losers. That's why my family is in training to become the best damn little family in the western world.

I'll let you in on our secret training regimen: We wake at 05:00 and watch Disney movies together until 06:00. This gives our family a strong moral foundation. Thanks to Dis-

ney, we know our roles and we develop the perfect North American idiom. From 06:00 to 07:00 we exercise our bodies. Nothing but Nike products touches our flesh.

We then eat a healthy breakfast of products manufactured in various parts of the world by RJR Nabisco. (In the interests of luring RJR Nabisco as a corporate sponsor, my wife and I were prepared to smoke a token cigarette each Sunday evening. Fortunately, they sold their tobacco division to a Japanese company last month.)

During the working-school hours of the day, we are trained not to think, say or do anything that could be construed as offensive to anyone. We are very bullish about what we wear, however: Tommy Hilfiger for me, Liz Claiborne for my wife, and Roots all around for the kids.

At suppertime, we consume as many processed foods as possible, as these conveniently come in boxes with the brand names clearly displayed. In any case, it all originates from Loblaw. (The whole family shops there every Thursday evening. The kids actually think the food comes from machines in the back, behind the deli section.)

The evenings are ours to enjoy as a family. This is our own, special time, for which we assiduously guard our privacy. I am proud to divulge, however, that we relax with Microsoft computer products and take care not to let the kids surf the net alone.

On weekends, we tend to shop. Our Ford Mountain Master practically knows it own way to all the respectable malls. We avoid the inner city and the countryside, as it wouldn't do to have that gorgeous machine get dented or muddied. (One never knows when the Ford people might come calling.)

We have been in training for some time now and everything is going swimmingly. We need a corporate sponsor soon, though, as it costs a fortune for a family to compete at this level. That's where the Bank of Montreal comes in. Let me tell you, the kind people there have been only too happy to help us in our effort to become the perfect North American family.

If there are any corporate executives out there who happen to read this little article and like what you hear, please get in touch with me through the *Citizen*. Oh God! I nearly forgot to mention that we read nothing but *Southam News* products.

◼ SIGNIFICANCE

Media and communications expert Marshall McLuhan famously forecast in the 1960s that the medium of communication had become the substantive message. In a collateral fashion, corporate brands, logos, and other marketing devices are now so pervasive in modern culture that they have become as important and as valuable as the product to which they are affixed.

The commercial and marketing issue that is not yet resolved is whether a successful branding of a product by a corporation results in a permanent capture of a share of the market, or whether such branding represents a transient success. The branding process requires a significant investment in both time and resources on the part of a corporation; Nike's utilization of Michael Jordan made a successful company even more so, but it is doubtful a small company could afford the start up costs of such a significant branding effort.

Branding (or re-branding in the case of corporations seeking to change consumer attitudes concerning their products) is not a guarantee of profitability. The merger of Chrysler with the German automobile manufacturer Daimler is a vivid example. Since the 1998 merger of these two large companies, and in the face of a determined advertising campaign to advance the new Daimler Chrysler brand, the company has continued to lose both money and market share world wide.

The primary source article makes reference to the salvation of the University of Ottawa football program in 1999 through the intervention of Nike, who became the primary sponsor of the team and thus provided the financial support required to keep the team viable. This type of corporate involvement in a university sports program was noteworthy because it was rare for such corporations to participate in this fashion in Canadian university sports; it was a practice that had been commonplace in the American college and university athletic systems for many years prior to 1999. All major American college football and basketball programs were and continue to be the subject of generous corporate sponsorships. Athletic equipment manufacturers were not involved in Canadian university sports because there was little prospect of a meaningful return upon this advertising and branding investment, as Canadian university sport lacks the commercial appeal of its American counterpart. Companies generally only advance their brand in those environments where they are certain to obtain a positive financial return. This inherent aspect of corporate behavior would eliminate the whimsical suggestion of a family corporate sponsorship as advanced in the primary source article.

Like other aspects of marketing, branding is a subset of applied psychology, where positive identification with the brand by the consumer is the ultimate objective of the marketer. In recent years, branding has grown to include activities with no direct relation-

ship to the target product. Examples of this trend include the purchasing of naming rights to sports stadiums by corporations; Fed Ex Field in Washington, D.C. and AT & T Park in San Francisco are two of many examples.

The attraction of the brands for the typical consumer, a variation of the classic debate of style versus substance, has sometimes manifested itself in bizarre ways. A noteworthy example occurred in July 2005, in what was humorously referred to in contemporary newspaper headlines as the unacceptable face of capitalism, a Utah woman agreed to have the name of an on line casino tattooed on her forehead in return for a payment of $15,000. The casino explained its strategy as an attempt to put its brand and its name forward in a novel way that was guaranteed to generate a public reaction.

FURTHER RESOURCES

Books

Antorini, Yun Mi, Fabian Csaba, and Majken Schultz, ed. *Corporate Branding*. Copenhagen: Copenhagen Business School Press, 2005.

Balmer, John M.T. *Revealing the Corporation: Perspectives on Identity, Image, Reputation and Corporate Branding*. London: Routledge, 2003.

Gregory, James R. and Jack R. Weichmann. *Branding Across Borders: A Guide to Global Branding Marketing*. New York: McGraw-Hill, 2001.

Web sites

Manchester Guardian. "Look, No Brands..." 2000 <http://observer.guardian.co.uk/review/story/0,6903,396082,06.html> (accessed June 30, 2006).

A Family Affair

Book review

By: David Herbert Donald

Date: January 16, 2000

Source: The *New York Times*, June 16, 2000. <http://query.nytimes.com/gst/> (accessed June 6, 2006).

About the Author: Two-time Pulizer-Prize winner David Herbert Donald (b. 1920) is one of the nation's most respected presidential scholars and a leading historian. In addition to several books on Abraham Lincoln, he has written extensively on the Civil War and Reconstruction, along with books about Thomas Wolfe, Charles Sumner, and Andrew Johnson. He reviewed *Polk's Folly*, for The *New York Times*.

INTRODUCTION

In addition to a remarkable heritage, whose lineage is depicted in his book *Polk's Folly*, William R. Polk (b. 1929) is an accomplished historian and foreign policy expert. A sought-after lecturer, he has spoken on topics such as the Iraq war, terrorism and guerilla warfare. He has written a number of books on the Middle East.

Polk grew up in Fort Worth, Texas. During World War II, he attended the New Mexico Military Institute and was involved in cavalry training. Prior to attending college, he studied in Latin America and worked for a newspaper in Rome. Then he went on to attend Harvard University and Oxford University. In addition, he studied at Universities in Mexico, Chile, and Cairo. While teaching at Harvard from 1958 to 1961, President John F. Kennedy (1917–1963) appointed Polk as a member of the Policy Council of the U.S. Department of State.

After retiring from the government in 1965, Polk became the Professor of History at the University of Chicago. He founded the Center for Middle Eastern Studies, and in 1967 became the president of the Adlai Stevenson Institute of International Affairs. In addition to planning the United Nations Environmental Program and other accomplishments, the Institute contributed to events that set the foundation for the European Union.

Polk is well traveled and has visited Africa, Asia, Europe and Latin America. He currently resides in France. His most recent book is *Birth of America*.

■ PRIMARY SOURCE

POLK's FOLLY

An American Family History.
By William R. Polk.
Illustrated. 512 pp. New York:
Doubleday. $29.95.

"Who is James K. Polk?" cynics jeered when the Democrats nominated the first dark-horse candidate for the presidency in 1844. In fact, "Little Jimmie" was a man with a track record as speaker of the House of Representatives and as governor of Tennessee. He proved to be one of the ablest and—if success is measured by achievement of one's goals—most successful American presidents of the 19th century, responsible for waging the Mexican War and for annexing the vast southwestern part of the United States. Yet even today his name is hardly a household word.

Polk's Folly, by William R. Polk, demonstrates that the Polks are an underestimated clan, whose members have been involved in nearly every stage of American development and have participated with bravery and determination in every one of the country's wars. The story begins with Robert Polk, who migrated from Scotland and then Ireland to the Chesapeake Bay region around 1680 and settled on some of the worst land in Maryland, "'too swampy to farm" and "a perfect breeding ground for mosquitoes."No wonder it was called *Polk's Folly*. His children and grandchildren moved west for better land, but there they faced hostile Indians, who kidnapped Delilah, one of the Polk daughters-in-law, and compelled her to march from Kentucky to the fort that later became Detroit.

In the next generation Polks pushed down the eastern side of the Appalachian Mountains to North Carolina, where Thomas Polk, who had somehow learned how to be a surveyor, became a man of wealth and prominence. He was one of the signers of the so-called Mecklenburg Resolves, declaring independence from the English crown, in 1775. During the American Revolution, one of his sons was killed in battle with the British and another was desperately wounded. Both father and surviving son endured the grim winter of 1777 at Valley Forge.

In the early years of the Republic, Will Polk, who as a surveyor had the advantage of being able to pick out the best plots of land in the newly opened West, moved with most of his family to central Tennessee. There they became great slaveholders and built some of the most beautiful antebellum mansions. One of Will's sons, who had acquired thousands of acres of rich Tennessee land, could literally claim to be father of his county, because "he fathered at least 14 children," who in turn "produced 92 children, who gave him 307 great-grandchildren." One of these was the future president of the United States.

During the Civil War, Leonidas Polk, who was a bishop of the Episcopal Church but had been educated at West Point, reluctantly suspended his plan to create the new University of the South at Sewanee in order to accept appointment in the Confederate Army, where he rose to the rank of lieutenant general. When he was killed by Union gunfire in 1864, one Confederate soldier lamented his loss as "the greatest the South ever sustained."

In the bitter post-Civil War years the Polks struggled to survive. One member of the family fled to Switzerland, where his daughter married a French nobleman. Another emigrated to Brazil. Others moved to Texas. Migrating north, William Mecklenburg Polk became head of the medical department at Cornell University. Of the Polks who stayed at home, Leonidas Lafayette became a leader in the Farmers' Alliance and, had he not died prematurely, might well have become the presidential nominee of the Populist Party in 1892.

During the administration of Woodrow Wilson, Frank L. Polk was counselor of the Department of State and, much of the time, acting secretary of state. Polks fought bravely in both the World Wars. Afterward, George Polk became a famous, and controversial journalist, who was murdered in Greece in 1948, and James H. Polk was United States commander in Berlin when President Kennedy made his "Ich bin ein Berliner" speech. In a different but hardly less dangerous role, Lucius Burch emerged as a prominent civil rights attorney in Tennessee, chosen by Dr. Martin Luther King Jr. just before his assassination to represent the striking sanitation workers in their fight against the local racist political machine.

It is reasonable to ask why, with this distinguished record of public service, the Polks have not been widely recognized as one of this country's notable families, like the Adamses and the Kennedys, the Rockefellers and the Roosevelts. Part of the answer is the lack of documentary records for so much of the story. The first three generations of Polks in America left almost no written records. This is not because they were illiterate; even Magdalen, wife of the founder, Robert, was able to write her own will at a time when few women could read or write. But war and fire destroyed many records, and the Polks were so constantly on the move that nobody could preserve papers and letters. For later generations, beginning about 1830, documentation is voluminous and includes the day-by-day diary that James K. Polk kept throughout his presidency. But, except perhaps in the most recent generation, Polks have not been introspective or speculative; they were men and women of action.

William R. Polk, a former history professor at the University of Chicago and himself a member of the clan, has attempted to handle these problems by resorting to what he calls "astronomy"—attempting to reconstruct what a particular member of the family must have thought and felt by asking, "What was happening around him, what was his 'position' and what would a person in that position probably have done?" This admittedly speculative procedure allows him to include entertaining descriptions of the Scotch-Irish immigrants, of conditions aboard the tiny ship on which they sailed to America, of life on the vast slave plantations of the Old South, of vigilante violence in the riotous West. No matter that it is impossible to prove that any particular member of the Polk clan had these specific experiences, and no matter either that Pro-

fessor Polk, an expert on the history of the Arab world, does not always get the nuances of American history exactly right. His method has enabled him to produce a spirited, broad-scale saga of an American family we ought to remember. Perhaps someone will see that the Polk story, covering the whole range of American history, has all the ingredients for a superb television documentary series.

David Herbert Donald's most recent books are *Lincoln* and *Lincoln at Home*.

SIGNIFICANCE

America's eleventh president, John Knox Polk, is a controversial figure. According to many historians, he is a great president—one of the most successful since Washington in accomplishing his goals. Polk succeeded in acquiring Oregon, California, and New Mexico; settled the border dispute between Texas and Mexico; created a new federal depository process; reduced tariffs; and gave the executive office more power and influence. However, critics assert that Polk missed the mark by failing to address key issues of the time. He chose to focus on expanding U.S. territories and waging war and did not use his considerable influence to address the issue of slavery and its social and political ramifications. In any event, at the end of his term, Polk was a celebrated figure. Keeping his word to serve only one term, and aided by a quick American victory in the war, his reputation remained unscathed.

Stories of important families in U.S. history are an influential part of American cultural mythology. From immigration to the American colonies to participation in the American Revolution, frontiersmen to President of the United States, the story of the Polk family—like many others—is a personal account of the history of the United States. Thus, the story of the Polk family captures the public imagination as the story of an American dynasty.

FURTHER RESOURCES
Books

McCormac, Eugene I. *James K. Polk: A Political Biography.* New York: Russell & Russell, Inc., 1965.

Periodicals

Wilentz, Sean. "The Worst President in History?: One of America's Leading Historians Assesses George W. Bush." *Rolling Stone.* May 4, 2006.

Web sites

American President. "President James Knox Polk." <http://www.americanpresident.org/history/jamespolk/biography> (accessed June 19, 2006).

The Internet and the Family 2000: The View from Parents—The View from Kids

Report

By: Joseph Turow and Lilach Nir

Date: May 2000

Source: Turow, Joseph, and Lilach Nir. *Annenberg Public Policy Center, University of Pennsylvania Report Series.* "The Internet and the Family 2000: The View from Parents, the View from Kids." Report 33. May 2000 <http://www.annenbergpublicpolicycenter.org/04_inf o_society/family/finalrepor_fam.pdf> (accessed June 29, 2006).

About the Author: The Annenberg Public Policy Center was established at the University of Pennsylvania in 1994. It conducts research and it promotes public discussion regarding media, communication, and public policy. Joseph Turow, a professor at the Annenberg School of Communications, has authored over fifty articles and eight books dealing with various aspects of mass communications. Lilach Nir is a professor at the Hebrew University of Jerusalem.

INTRODUCTION

The Internet and the Family 2000 highlights the historic tension that exists between parents, who are responsible for their family's moral integrity and leadership, and children, who as adolescents often seek experiences independent of their family, with or without parental consent. The Internet is the most profound example of this parent/child dynamic in the history of the American family. The speed, immediacy, and relative ease with which it can be accessed by an adolescent have fundamentally changed the definition of parental control over media.

In the 1950s and 1960s, when television was the dominant external social influence in most American homes, parents could control what their children watched. Most sets were in a relatively open and accessible portion of the home, rendering any televi-

A family together at their computer. © ROB LEWINE/CORBIS.

sion watching a quasi-public event. If a parent did not wish a child to watch television, the set could simply be turned off. In addition, programming was crafted for a conservative audience, and there was rarely any impropriety in language or the situations portrayed. When Elvis Presley appeared on television in 1957, for example, the *Ed Sullivan Show* refused to show his suggestive hip gyrations. Ten years later, the show insisted that the lyrics of the Rolling Stones song "Let's Spend the Night Together" undergo a revision before the band could perform it.

The technological advances that propelled the home computer and its related technologies to a lead position among media influences altered the parent/child dynamic in two key respects. The first was the speed of the technological change: it was not uncommon for children in the family to know much more about the family computer than the adult who bought it and paid the monthly Internet access account. In homes where the parent was absent for large portions of the day, or did not monitor their children's computer habits, the computer-savvy child could gain a level of technical superiority in the home.

The second aspect was the interactive nature of the computer. Children, through personal e-mail accounts, instant-messenger systems, and chat rooms, had a means to interact with a host of persons entirely beyond their parents' control, unless they supervised their child's computer use.

▆ PRIMARY SOURCE

THE INTERNET AND THE FAMILY 2000: THE VIEW FROM PARENTS—THE VIEW FROM KIDS

CONCLUDING REMARKS

If there is one point that our study highlights it is that many—in fact, probably most—American families are filled with contradictions when it comes to the Internet. Parents fear that it can harm their kids but feel that their kids need it. Parents and kids individually say they have talked to each other about giving out information over the Web, but parents and kids in the same family don't remember doing it. Kids agree that parents should have a say on the information they give out over the Web but nevertheless find it acceptable to give out sensitive personal and family information to Web sites in exchange for a valuable free gift.

It should not be surprising that these sorts of contradictions lead to tensions. This year's Annenberg report on the Internet and the Family has focused on the contradictions and tensions surrounding the release of family information. We have found that three out of four parents say

they are concerned that their children "give out personal information about themselves when visiting Web sites or chat rooms." Smaller, though still quite substantial, proportions of parents and youngsters report having experienced at least some incidents of disagreement, worry or anger in the family over kids' release of information to the Web. The proportions of families feeling such tensions will likely grow in coming years as new technologies for learning about individuals proliferate on the Internet. For media and marketers, information about teens is an increasingly valuable commodity. For logical business reasons they will pursue knowledge about youngsters and their families as aggressively as possible.

The task for civic society is to set up a counterbalance to their efforts that establishes norms about what is ethically and legally correct for media and marketers to do. We might note here that Federal and university research guidelines require academic investigators to get parents' permission to interview tweens and teens about something as benign as their general attitudes toward the Web. It is ironic that marketers can track, aggregate and store far more personal responses to questions by individuals in these age groups without getting any permission from parents at all.

Nevertheless, while one can agree (as almost all parents do) that teenagers should get permission from parents before giving information to sites, legislation that forces Web sites to get that permission raises complex issues. A clear drawback is that mandating Web sites to get parental permission from youngsters age 10 to 17 is impractical in an era when youngsters can discover ways to get around such requirements or forge their parents' permission.

Even if it becomes possible for a site to verify whether a visitor is or is not a teen, we have to question whether this sort of verification is socially desirable. What might be the consequences of the "electronic carding" of tweens and teens? Would many Web sites simply prohibit teens from entering rather than go to the trouble to turn off their tracking and profiling software for them? More controversially, would it mean that teens could not participate in chat rooms or listservs where information about users is systematically collected? If so, would that be infringing on the right of the youngsters to express their opinions in open forums?

Clearly, the new digital technologies are creating circumstances where society's interest in encouraging parents to supervise their youngsters is colliding with society's interest in encouraging youngsters' to speak out and participate in public discussions. We hesitate to suggest that the FTC rules that guide Web sites regarding children under 13 should be applied to youngsters 13 and over. At the same time, we reject the notion that teens should be approachable by Web sites as if they are fully responsible and independent adults in need of no parental supervision. We believe that the best policy in this area lies in aggressively encouraging family discussions of privacy norms along with limited Federal regulation.

- Our study points to the importance of urging parents and their children to talk in detail about how to approach requests by Web sites for personal and family data. Parents should not take for granted that traditional cautions such as "don't give out your name" or "don't talk to strangers" will be enough for the Web. Family members need to understand how all sorts of information about their interests can be tracked through cookies and related software without their even knowing it.
- Many parents cannot develop norms about family privacy alone. Our study and others have found that parents simply do not know enough about the Web to be aware of the way Web sites gather information and what to do about it. Here is a terrific opportunity for community groups, libraries, schools, and state and Federal agencies to work together on campaigns aimed at making information privacy a hot family topic and bringing community members together to learn about it.
- One way to get family members talking about these issues when children are relatively young (say, aged 6 through 12) is to convince parents and kids to surf the Web together. Encouraging family Web surfing, and family discussions about Web surfing, ought to be a priority of government and nonprofit organizations that care about enriching Americans' Internet experiences.
- Logically connected to encouraging community and family discussions of information privacy is the need for individuals to know what Web sites know about them. Our research shows that virtually all parents believe that they should have a legal right to that information. A Web Freedom of Information Act should be passed that allows every person access to all data, including clickstream data, that a Web site connects to his or her individual computer or name. Whether parents should have the right to access their youngsters' data should be a matter of public discussion.
- Our finding that youngsters are substantially more likely than parents to give up personal information to a Web site when increasing values are associated with a free gift supports suggestions for another Federal regulation: Web sites aimed at tweens and teens should be prohibited from offering free gifts, including prizes through sweepstakes, if those gifts

are tied in direct or indirect ways to the youngsters' disclosure of information.

We fully expect that some of these suggestions will be more controversial than others. All of them will take a lot of work. But then, it will take a lot of work from many quarters of society to help maximize the benefits of the Internet for the family.

SIGNIFICANCE

Many parents have a love/hate relationship with their children's computer and Internet access. They fear the possibly unhealthy or dangerous aspects of Internet access in all of its guises and are equally certain of the crucial role that computer literacy will play in their children's education and vocational futures.

This is especially true with respect to the safeguarding of confidential information. The authors identify concerns about Internet marketing efforts and the ability of a commercial web site to track those persons who access their sites. Parents don't want their family to be targeted by companies contacted by a child through the Internet. Many say that they have implemented rules about sharing any family information over the Internet.

A number of studies published since 2000 suggest that parents' intentions to regulate Internet use to protect personal information are honored more in the breach than in the observance. A series of studies conducted in the United States and Canada are instructive. (Canada is a useful statistical comparison because of the shared mass media influences with the United States coupled with a similar level of home computer usage.) A United States Department of Justice study published in 2005 revealed that fifty percent of all adolescents used their home computers without any adult supervision; twenty percent of females under the age of eighteen surveyed had been sexually solicited online, as had ten percent of the males in that age group. The American computer technology magazine *CNET* published a 2005 poll that suggested that over fifty percent of American families did not use software on their home computers to monitor or to filter undesirable web content; in the same poll, forty-two percent of parents did not review any of their children's instant messaging records to determine whether their children were engaged in any risky contacts through this means.

The Canadian organization Media Awareness Network determined in 2004 that seventy-one percent of all adolescent computer users maintained a free web-based e-mail account, such as Hotmail®; eighty-six percent of these users revealed their gender, sixty-eight percent used their real name, thirty percent provided their address, and twenty percent gave their telephone number as part of their account registration. This apparently careless attitude toward the dissemination of personal information creates significant risks, given that the information is posted on an Internet accessible forum.

A variety of available programs can either shield the identity of the computer contacting a particular web site or remove "cookies"—the cyberspace trail created by a user. In addition, sophisticated popup-blocking, spyware, and adware programs are a simple solution to website marketing.

The most critical issue now facing parents and children regarding home computer and Internet usage is privacy. MySpace, the Internet-based social networking system, is very popular with children under eighteen, with a member base of over fifty million people. MySpace users commonly list all of their personal data, including personal photographs for anyone to view.

Parent/child relations and Internet access are likely to remain the primary focus of home computer use in the foreseeable future. Efforts to regulate aspects of computer communication, including the Communications Decency Act in 1996, and the Child Online Protection Act of 1998, were halted in a series of constitutional challenges upheld in the Supreme Court of the United States. One solution identified in the primary source, a regulatory framework to govern Internet marketers, remains a remote prospect. The Internet remains essentially unregulated and the onus of protective action against unwanted or undesirable media influence through the Internet continues to rest with families who use a home computer.

FURTHER RESOURCES

Books

Boni, William C., and Gerald L. Kovacich. *I-Way Robbery: Crime on the Internet.* Boston: Butterworth-Heinemann, 1999.

Darrell, Keith B. *Issues in Internet Law.* Phoenix: Amber Books, 2006.

Lanford, Duncan. *Internet Ethics.* New York: Palgrave MacMillan, 2000.

Web sites

Federal Bureau of Investigation. "A Parent's Guide to Internet Safety." 2006 <http://www.fbi.gov/publications/pguide/pguidee.htm> (accessed June 29, 2006).

Home Office, United Kingdom. "Child Protection." 2006 <http://police.homeoffice.gov.uk/operational-policing/

crime-disorder/child-protection-taskforce> (accessed June 30, 2006).

Internet Content Rating Association. "Contact ICRA." 2006 <http://www.icra.org/contact> (accessed June 30, 2006).

That Loveable Sitcom Dad Who Likes to Nibble Bats

Review

By: Caryn James

Date: March 5, 2002

Source: James, Caryn. "That Loveable Sitcom Dad Who Likes to Nibble Bats." *The New York Times* (March 5, 2002).

About the Author: Caryn James is the chief television critic for the *New York Times*. She has also worked as a *Times* film reviewer and the editor for the *Book Review*. James also wrote her first novel, *Glorie*, in 1999.

INTRODUCTION

In 1969, the metal band, Black Sabbath made its debut. The lead singer for this metal band, Ozzy Osbourne would become a cultural icon at the beginning of his career for the gothic imagery and erratic antics used during his performing. In recent years, however, the singer became a symbol of good parenting due to his family's appearance in the reality series "The Osbournes," televised on MTV.

Ozzy Osbourne was born in Birmingham, England as John Michael Osbourne. Early in his life, he dropped out of high school and served time in prison for burglary. However, his love for music led him to form several unsuccessful bands, until 1969 when the band he had been playing with called Polka Tulk changed their name to Black Sabbath. The group began touring and producing albums that created a following due to their occult-inspired imagery and controversial on-stage behavior. Despite successes with heavy metal anthems such as "Paranoid" and "War Pigs", conflict between members of the band led to Osbourne's departure from the group in 1977. He briefly rejoined the group again, only to be fired by the band in 1978. At this point, not only had Osbourne lost his recording contract, his first marriage also ended in 1979.

Ozzy Osbourne and his family, the stars of *The Osbournes,* appearing at a promotion at the Virgin Megastore in Holly-wood, California. From left to right: Ozzy, Sharon, Kelly, and Jack Osbourne. FRAZER HARRISON/GETTY IMAGES. REPRODUCED BY PERMISSION.

Upon the separation between Osbourne and Black Sabbath, the band's manager, Don Arden, chose to focus his energies on promoting Osbourne and ended his managing of the band. Arden's daughter, Sharon, also began to take an interest in Osbourne's career. In 1980, Osbourne released the recording, "Blizzard of Ozz," which included his signature song, "Crazy Train." Known as the "madman of rock," Osbourne often appeared on stage under the influence of drugs and alcohol. In 1982, while on tour with his second album "Diary of a Madman," Osbourne bit the head off of a bat that had been thrown on stage. This act gained Osbourne new notoriety and publicity, although he claimed later that he thought the bat was a toy at the time. In addition, Osbourne urinated on the Alamo memorial shrine leading him to be banned from performing in San Antonio for several years.

Osbourne experienced personal tragedy in 1982 after the accidental death of his collaborator and gui-

tarist Randy Rhodes. Also in 1982, Osbourne married Sharon. By 1983, Sharon took control of Osbourne's career by buying out his contract from her father for approximately $1.5 million and leading to a twenty year estrangement between father and daughter. Shortly thereafter, the Osbournes began to start their family. In 1983, the couple had their first daughter, Aimee. The next year Kelly was born, followed by Jack in 1985.

Sharon continued to manage Osbourne's career and helped to facilitate a shift in the public perception of the rocker during the 1990s. In 1994, Osbourne received his first Grammy Award for best metal performance for "I Don't Want to Change the World" and in 1996, Sharon launched Ozzfest, an annual touring festival of heavy metal and hard rock bands. Osbourne reunited with Black Sabbath in 1997 to produce the album "Reunion" and the group toured Europe with Ozzfest. By 2000, Osbourne had been awarded his second Grammy Award for his perform-ance of "Paranoid" with the band.

◼ PRIMARY SOURCE

As the cameras follow a family moving into its new Cali-fornia house, we see the boxes all neatly labeled: "Pots & Pans," "Linens," "Devil Heads." Then we meet the characters in this newest reality series. There's Sharon, the practical mom; Jack, the bored teenage son; Kelly, the pink-haired teenage daughter; and Dad, a heavy-metal icon who screams "rock 'n' roll!" at the camera.

The whole family uses a word that has to be bleeped all the time; it's sweet when families develop that affection-ate shorthand language. As it trails Ozzy Osbourne and his family through their everyday lives, MTV's new series "The Osbournes" plays like a hilarious real-life version of "The Addams Family," tongue in cheek and mischie-vously funny.

The trick is in its mocking spirit, evident in the theme song—a crooning 50's-style cover of the Osbourne song "Crazy Train"—and the satiric sitcom credits that intro-duce the family, including "Ozzy Osbourne as the Dad." The idea of Ozzy Osbourne playing Ozzie Nelson may be an easy joke, but it's a good one.

We see Dad at home waiting for the cable guy. Of course, this home has a huge red-carpeted staircase out of "Gone With the Wind" and crucifixes as an essential part of the décor. ("We'll never be able to sell it," Sharon says of the house.) Soon Dad is having trouble with the remote for the new television and like any middle-aged father has to call his teenage son to help. The screen is enormous and the remote the size of a small laptop com-puter, but still, fathers and sons everywhere can identify.

Dad walks around the house in black track pants and a T-shirt that shows the tattoos up his arms, but eventually he has to go to work. That means appearing on the "Tonight" show. Jay Leno drops by the make-up room while Mr. Osbourne is having his eyeliner put on and asks for an autographed CD for his nephew.

Mr. Osbourne projects an endearing personality, playing the loving, beleaguered father to the hilt. At a large dinner at a restaurant, when his daughter complains that he can never hear her, he says: "You have not been standing in front of 30 billion decibels for 35 years. Just write me a note." When the children are about to go out for the night, he says in a pleading tone: "Don't drink, don't take drugs, please. And if you have sex, wear a condom." And he means it when he tells the family, "I love you all, I love you more than life itself, but you're all"—expletive—"mad." Aging rock stars don't fade away; they just learn to make fun of their age.

Their father's career leaves the children with unusual con-cerns the series has yet to address. How do teenagers rebel when Dad is famous for eating bats? The Osbourne children haven't strayed far from the parental turf yet; they haven't done the obvious thing of turning Republican and joining a country club. Like any teenagers, they fight and threaten to tell on each other, though in a child-of-Hollywood way. When Kelly swats Jack, he says, "That's on camera, Kelly, I'm showing that to Mom!"

This clever series can be plumbed for meaning: it reveals the way hard rock has been absorbed into the main-stream, and it skewers the self-importance of most real-ity television. But most of all it's a timely joke that works. The Osbournes have arrived, and they have a devil's head over their front door to prove it.

◼

SIGNIFICANCE

In 2000, the Osbourne family appeared on MTV's celebrity home tours show, "Cribs." Following the taping of the show, Sharon met with MTV executives and pitched the idea of planting several cameras in the Osbourne house and creating the first reality sitcom. The family was paid approximately $200,000 for the first season. The show became an instant success by bringing in approximately 5.3 million viewers per episode. The show included Osbourne's fatherly advice to his children, and the show frequently bleeped the family's prolific use of profanities. MTV executives asserted that the show represented a shift in family values from strictness and rules to honesty and openness.

Participation in the show catapulted the entire family (except oldest daughter Aimee who chose not to live in the house during taping) into stardom as MTV's target audience of twelve– to twenty-four–year olds were introduced to the aging rocker and older viewers familiar with Osbourne's reputation tuned into the show. The family received numerous endorse-ment deals and was signed on to additional seasons at approximately $2–5 million per season. In addition, the Osbournes were invited to events also attended by the President of the United States and were invited to meet the Queen of England. Although the first season seemed reasonably comedic by concentrating on issues such as Osbourne trying to operate the remote control or dogs that refused to be housebroken, the second season became more reality than sitcom by dealing with Sharon's cancer treatment and Kelly's handling of stardom.

The show ran from March 2002 to March 2005.

FURTHER RESOURCES

Periodicals

Dempsey, John. "MTV auds go gaga for Ozzy's oddball antics." *Variety*. April 1, 2002.

Hay, Carla. "The Osbournes: The First Family of Rock-'n'Roll." *Billboard*. December 20, 2003.

Poniewozik, James. "Ozzy knows best." *Time, Canadian Edition*. April 15, 2002.

The Family Movie Act of 2004

Legislation

By: United States Congress

Date: June 16, 2004

Source: *Library of Congress*. "Family Entertainment and Copyright Act of 2004." 2004 <http://thomas.loc.gov/cgi-bin/query/z?c108:H.R.4586.RH:> (accessed June 120, 2006).

About the Author: The United States Congress is the law-making branch of the federal government.

INTRODUCTION

Although artistic creation is frequently its own reward, artists often create in the hope of profiting from their work. Writers, composers, and film makers invest their time and effort in the expectation that they will be rewarded if their creation is appreciated by others. In most developed nations, this reasonable expectation is guaranteed by copyright law. A copyright, literally the right to reproduce or copy a work, is guaranteed to the work's creator by the U.S. Constitution for a length of time, which varies depending on the type of work. The framers of the Constitution recognized that copyright law provides an incentive for creativity, since it guarantees ownership and control to a work's creator.

In contrast to U.S. law, other countries have weak or poorly enforced copyright laws. In such countries, name-brand merchandise is frequently copied and sold at extremely low prices; commercial software in particular is often sold for a few dollars a copy, giving software developers little incentive to enhance their products. China, the world's most populous nation, was forced to tighten its copyright laws in 2001 to gain admittance to the World Trade Organization. Copyright enforcement in China remains lax, however, and in 2005 was the world's largest supplier of illegally copied, or bootleg software; analysts estimated that ninety percent of the software in use in China at that time was unlawfully copied.

Copyright law specifically prohibits another party from duplicating and reselling a copyrighted product; consumers may not legally make copies of a DVD and resell them, and the motion picture industry aggressively prosecutes merchants who traffic in stolen movies. But copyright law is less clear regarding whether a consumer may make changes to a copyrighted work he has purchased. More specifically, does a consumer who has purchased a licensed copy of a movie or song have the right to alter it for his own enjoyment?

In 2001, a Los Angeles firm called ClearPlay announced a new type of filtering software. When installed on a home DVD player, the software allowed viewers to select specific types of content to filter; the software would then instruct the DVD player to skip past or mute the objectionable content. ClearPlay's technology was designed for parents who wanted to let their children view a wide variety of movies without being exposed to explicit language, violence, or sexuality.

ClearPlay's technology appeared to avoid the legal difficulties of some other solutions to this dilemma. CleanFlicks, a Utah-based firm, purchases licensed movies on DVD, edits the content and sells the edited versions; the Directors Guild of America has filed suit against the firm, which countersued. CleanFlicks argued that it purchases and owns an original copy of each edited DVD it produces, guaranteeing studios the same income they would normally receive. Hollywood producers argue that editing their movies violates their legal right to control the form of their product. In response to this David-and-Goliath battle between Hollywood and movie editors, Congress weighed in, passing the Family Movie Act of 2004, which was passed the following year as part of the Family Entertainment and Copyright Act of 2005.

◼ PRIMARY SOURCE

Family Movie Act of 2004

108th CONGRESS

2d Session

H. R. 4586

[Report No. 108-670]

To provide that making limited portions of audio or video content of motion pictures imperceptible by or for the owner or other lawful possessor of an authorized copy of that motion picture for private home viewing, and the use of technology therefor, is not an infringement of copyright or of any right under the Trademark Act of 1946.

IN THE HOUSE OF REPRESENTATIVES

June 16, 2004

Mr. SMITH of Texas (for himself and Mr. FORBES) introduced the following bill; which was referred to the Committee on the Judiciary …

A BILL

To provide that making limited portions of audio or video content of motion pictures imperceptible by or for the owner or other lawful possessor of an authorized copy of that motion picture for private home viewing, and the use of technology therefor, is not an infringement of copyright or of any right under the Trademark Act of 1946.

Be it enacted by the Senate and House of Representatives of the United States of America in Congress assembled,

SECTION 1. SHORT TITLE.

This Act may be cited as the 'Family Movie Act of 2004'

SEC. 2. EXEMPTION FROM COPYRIGHT INFRINGEMENT FOR SKIPPING OF AUDIO OR VIDEO CONTENT OF MOTION PICTURES.

Section 110 of title 17, United States Code, is amended—

(1) in paragraph (9), by striking 'and' after the semicolon at the end;

(2) in paragraph (10), by striking the period at the end and inserting '; and'; and

(3) by inserting after paragraph (10) the following:

'(11)(A) the making of limited portions of audio or video content of a motion picture imperceptible by or for the owner or other lawful possessor of an authorized copy of that motion picture in the course of viewing of that work for private use in a household, by means of consumer equipment or services that are operated by an individual in that household and serve only such household; and

'(i) are operated by an individual in that household;

'(ii) serve only such household; and

'(iii) do not create a fixed copy of the altered version; and

'(B) the use of technology to make such audio or video content imperceptible, that does not create a fixed copy of the altered version.'

SEC. 3. EXEMPTION FROM TRADEMARK INFRINGEMENT FOR SKIPPING OF AUDIO OR VIDEO CONTENT OF MOTION PICTURES.

'Section 32 of the Trademark Act of 1946 (15 U.S.C. 1114) is amended by adding at the end the following:

'(3)(A) Any person who engages in the conduct described in paragraph (11) of section 110 of title 17, United States Code, and who complies with the requirements set forth in that paragraph is not liable on account of such conduct for a violation of any right under this Act.

'(B) A manufacturer of technology that enables the making of limited portions of audio or video content of a motion picture imperceptible that is authorized under subparagraph (A) is not liable on account of such manufacture for a violation of any right under this Act. Such manufacturer shall ensure that the technology provides a clear and conspicuous notice that the performance of the motion picture is altered from the performance intended by the director or copyright holder of the motion picture.

'(C) Any manufacturer of technology described in subparagraph (B) who fails to comply with the requirements of subparagraph (B) with respect to a motion picture shall be liable in a civil action brought by the copyright owner of the motion picture that is modified by the technology in an amount not to exceed $1,000 for each such motion picture.'

SEC. 4. DEFINITION.

In this Act, the term 'Trademark Act of 1946' means the Act entitled 'An Act to provide for the registration and protection of trademarks used in commerce, to carry out the provisions of certain international conventions, and for other purposes', approved July 5, 1945 (15 U.S.C. 1051 et seq.).

SIGNIFICANCE

The Family Movie Act was eventually combined with other legislation addressing movie copyright issues to form the Family Entertainment and Copyright Act of 2005, which President Bush signed into law. It provides an exemption to federal copyright for the sale and use of software that selectively filters portions of a copyrighted work; this exemption applied only in cases where no permanent copy of the edited version is created. As passed, the law appears to protect ClearPlay's filtering system and similar products, but not CleanFlicks and other firms that produce permanently altered copies of a movie.

The fundamental purpose of copyright law is to protect the commercial value of a created work; one simple test of reasonable use is whether that use will reduce sales or the artist's potential income from the copyrighted work. For example, purchasing one music CD and making copies for six friends clearly reduces the chance that those friends will buy their own copies, thus reducing the artist's income potential.

In the present case, editing companies operate a system that leads to additional sales of a copyrighted work and additional income for the copyright holder. While this fact does not address the underlying issue of altering and copying a protected work, it does provide some support for the firms' claims that their actions are noninfringing. Supporters of ClearPlay and other movie-filtering systems also argue that studios have always offered edited versions of their films for use on commercial airline flights; to object to someone else editing the same movie for a similar reason appears disingenuous.

In 2005, in an ironic twist to the case, actor and producer Mel Gibson sued CleanFlicks for editing three minutes from his blockbuster film, *The Passion of the Christ*. As of 2006, the cases against ClearPlay and CleanFlicks remained unresolved. At least one other producer of edited feature films left the business the previous year under mounting legal pressure from Hollywood studios.

FURTHER RESOURCES

Books

Moul, Charles, ed. *A Concise Handbook of Movie Industry Economics*. Cambridge, UK: Cambridge University Press, 2005.

Schechter, Roger, and John Thomas. *Intellectual Property: The Law of Copyrights, Patents and Trademarks*. St. Paul, MN: Thomson/West Group, 2003.

Van Tassel, Joan. *Digital Rights Management: Protecting and Monetizing Content*. Woburn, MA: Focal Press, 2006.

Periodicals

Edwards, Cliff, *et al.* "Daggers Drawn over DVDs." *Business Week*. (Oct 6, 2005):92–96.

Goodman, Ellen. "Screen Screams: Why Are the Super-Sanitizers Winning the Culture Wars?" *The Oregonian*. (August 7, 2005).

Pascopella, Angela. "Lights, Camera … Oh, Do You Have a License?" *District Administration*. 38 (2003): 15.

Web sites

Cinematical. "Gibson Sues CleanFlicks." June 9, 2006 <http://www.cinematical.com/2005/11/21/gibson-sues-cleanflicks/> (accessed June 19, 2006).

Recording Industry Association of America. "Brief History on Copyright Laws." <http://www.riaa.com/issues/copyright/history.asp> (accessed June 20, 2006).

Washington Times. "Film Ratings for Violence Labeled as Meaningless." 2005 <http://www.washingtontimes.com/national/20050503–122314-4473r.htm> (accessed June 19, 2006).

Car in Every Garage; Sitcom in Every Cul-de-Sac

Newspaper article

By: David Carr

Date: April 2, 2006

Source: Carr, David. "Car in Every Garage; Sitcom in Every Cul-de-Sac." *New York Times*. (April 2, 2006).

About the Author: David Carr is a journalist employed by the *New York Times*, one of the nation's largest newspapers with a daily circulation of over one million copies. Carr specializes in articles that examine media issues.

INTRODUCTION

The sitcom is an entertainment format that has been popular in North America since the early days of commercial radio in the 1920s. Sitcom is a truncation of the term *situation comedy*, a device that in modern television is defined as a comedy production that relies upon recurring characters that are centered in a fixed environment, such as a home, workplace, or public institution. The storyline of a typical sitcom will often emphasize the features of day to day life as opposed to those surrounding a unique or unusual event.

The sitcom has been a staple of weeknight television programming in the United States since the inception of network television in the late 1940s. The history of the television sitcom in many respects mirrors the progression of American attitudes on a variety of social issues. The first long running American sitcom was "The Burns and Allen Show," where the featured performers George Burns and Gracie Allen reprised elements of their successful radio comedy programs in a made for television situation.

In the 1950s, the popular long running sitcoms "Ozzie and Harriet" and "Leave it to Beaver" symbolized many elements of "the American dream"—a pleasant, spacious home in the suburbs, a cheerful and lively family structure, and relative economic success. These programs enjoyed continued popularity through syndication long after their weekly production ceased.

Beginning in 1969, the sitcom was often at the leading edge of public debate concerning the changes being experienced in every aspect of an American society increasingly driven by the trends and the tastes of the Baby Boomer generation. "The Brady Bunch" was the first television show to deal with the dynamics of a

Actors Oscar Nunez, Noah Matthews and Greg Pitts (left to right) at the *Sons and Daughters* premiere in Los Angeles, California, March 6, 2006. AP IMAGES.

blended family. "The Mary Tyler Moore Show," which first aired in 1970, was a groundbreaking sitcom that featured Moore's character as a single career woman in her thirties determined to advance herself in the then male-dominated world of television news production. The 1971 series "All in the Family" explored recurring themes of gender relations, race, and sexuality in ways that had never previously been displayed in the sitcom format. Such programs were both topical and enduring in their appeal to a wide segment of the American television audience.

The sitcom was taken in a new direction in 1989 with the creation of "The Simpsons", the first animated production to be aired in prime time. The "Simpsons" became the longest running sitcom in the history of American television.

The sitcom is not a format unique to American television. A number of British sitcoms were exported to the United States and achieved favorable ratings when re-broadcast, particularly on the national public television network, PBS. The most notable of these

programs was the series "Fawlty Towers", produced in 1975. In contrast to the American sitcoms noted here, "Fawlty Towers" did not deal with pressing social issues; it was programming clearly intended as pure entertainment.

PRIMARY SOURCE

THE show opens with a familiar scene: post-coital 30-somethings in a pillowed two-shot. Immediately you know: this is another sitcom about attractive, sarcastic, socially active urbanites blessed with really good apartments and no shortage of dates.

"What did you say your name was?" he asks. Hmm, they might be a bit more socially active than most.

"Tammi, with an i," she coos. An i. Sounds racy.

Just then a baby's foot juts into the picture. And from behind the man comes word, "I peed," from a young boy in the same bed. The camera pulls back to a set right off the shelf from Bed, Bath & Beyond. As the boy trips off down the hall of the split-level, we know that we are not in Manhattan—or Boston or Chicago—anymore. We are in that unnamed middle place where most of America lives.

The show is "Sons & Daughters," a new comedy on ABC. In it, a well-housed extended family seems constantly on the verge of going nuclear. Cameron and Liz Walker, who as it turns out are far from single, have parents who may divorce on their anniversary, a doddering aunt who believes they are going to hell because Liz is Jewish and siblings whose marriages are happy but sexless. It seems like such a nice neighborhood, but the mortgage on the human soul is a bit dear.

That opening scene does more than just show where the Walkers live, though; in a sense, it demonstrates where television as a whole resides this season. Because now, as never before in recent memory (and TV memory is always recent), sitcoms, hour-long dramas, reality shows and all the rest of it have taken up residence at a safe commuting distance from the cities that so recently spawned all those sexy, friendly scenarios.

Just a few years ago, for a television show or film to set up house out in suburbia and depict it as a place tinged with emotions too dark for a Tupperware party seemed like a daring, provocative move. Movies like "The Ice Storm" and "American Beauty" won over critics by refusing to pretend that at a reduced population density all is sweetness and light. "Married With Children" and "The Simpsons" subverted the suburban ideal in broadly comic ways and then of course, along came "The Sopranos," in which the guy next door isn't just a mobster; he's a head case.

By last season, the success of "Desperate Housewives" showed that suburban gothic wasn't just for cable subscribers with a taste for the macabre; it appealed just as easily to the most mainstream audiences, even the fraternity boys in whose lad magazines the shows' starlets undressed.

And this season, the balance has tipped—hard. A staggering number of programs, just like the people who watch them, now live in the land of the two-car garage. Along with a change of address, the shows are registering a change of subtext, too. The little Walker kid with the weak bladder is a reminder that seduction and consummation, the fundamental arc of most television, sometimes result in actual reproduction.

Left behind in this great migration, the urban, urbane ensemble shows that were so recently popular now look like curios in reruns, with their conjured families and quaint city rituals. Well, perhaps the search for Mr. or Mrs. Big had to end sometime.

In a sense, it's all just a variation on television's eternal project: marooning various tribes and letting them slug it out. The good people of "Gilligan's Island" do it, the mechanical and human astronauts of "Lost in Space" do it, and even educated fleas on "Survivor" do it. So why not the residents down at the end of the cul-de-sac?

Actually, that's where so many of TV's roots were first planted. "Father Knows Best," "The Donna Reed Show," "Dennis the Menace" and most remarkably "Leave It to Beaver," all offered tidy life lessons on even tidier lawns. But at some point along the way television, like the kids who grew up in its glow, reached early adulthood.

Suddenly the cramped confines of tenement life, with people and storylines stacked on top of each other like cordwood, looked a lot sexier than Harper Valley. There were still plenty of station wagons on the small screen, but the shows that seemed to set the pace—shows like "Cheers," "N.Y.P.D. Blue," "L.A. Law," "Seinfeld," "Ally McBeal," "Frazier," "Homicide" and "Friends"—were all situated within city limits.

That arrangement proved to have a lot of advantages. It made it easier for characters to stay single longer, and dating is always good for dramatic or comedic churn. And whenever the action fell to a lull, or the writing got a little thin, the city itself was there to fill in the gaps, a full-fledged character that always looks great and always gets top billing. Maybe "Sex and the City" didn't really give the two subjects equal billing, but it came close: Carrie chose the latter over the former on more than one occasion.

During the subway years, invoking the suburbs became a way to show that a show (or a movie) was in on the joke—that it didn't really believe all that white-picket-fence fairy-tale happy-family nonsense about life amid the crabgrass. So what if John Cheever, John Updike, Richard Ford and so many others had so beautifully proven the point, so many times over, so many years before? Situating "The Simpsons" in Springfield, the same town in which Father Knew Best, was a way of commenting on Springfield—or Springfields, generic towns with generic names in generic states. On "Married With Children" the title itself was a sarcastic joke—something that was once supposed to sound appealing, repurposed as a code phrase for "kill me now."

The joke was on those boring, homogeneous suburbs, and the people in the city were telling it in the glamorous cocktail lounges, penthouses, and private jets where of course all real city dwellers spend their free time.

Yet today no one's snickering—certainly not network executives—at prime time's predominance of well-groomed lawns. Among the many offerings are "Weeds," "Big Love," a new season of "The Sopranos," dark takes all, along with fluffier but no less toxic shows like "Laguna Beach," and "The O.C." Not to mention all those home-makeover shows, all those nanny shows, half of those wife-swap shows, and "The Real Wives of Orange County," a three-fer attempt to combine reality, desperation, and geography into a ratings hit.

So what changed? How did the youthful possibilities of new job, new guy, new apartment get replaced by a sense of grown-up obligations of mortgages, braces, and college tuition? And how did we end up, in the first half of 2006, in a neighborhood crowded to overflow with pot-dealing PTA moms, hardware-store owners in multiple marriages, and tattooed, Wiccan home-swappers?

Unquestionably, and self-consciously, Tony Soprano led the way: it's no accident that during his show's opening credits he leaves the city, hits the tollbooth, cruises through streets of tightly packed houses and finally up the driveway to his very own McMansion. "I think it is really important that the story takes place in the suburbs," said Carolyn Strauss, the president of HBO, who was talking on a cellphone right after dropping her kids off. "Tony is an aspirational guy who was approaching 40 and his business was troubled. He has problems with his kids and his marriage, everything that many people go through in America—except he was a mob boss."

National demographics have played an important role. Locked in S.U.V.s waiting for a familiar exit to loom up out of the sea of brake lights, half the country now lives in suburbs. Small wonder that they might respond to exaggerated versions of themselves in weekly rotation. "With the suburbs," Ms. Strauss added, "there is a sort of shorthand that goes with it."

That goes for the people who make it as much as the people who write it. "I live on a street in Pasadena where the houses are cheek to jowl and you can't help but hear the little dramas that go on next door," said Mark V. Olsen, who, along with Will Scheffer, created "Big Love," HBO's new series about polygamy among the patios. "Mark and I both grew up in places like that," Mr. Scheffer said of its suburban setting. "It is part of our personal oeuvre." And they write what they know: while the youngest of the three wives on "Big Love" does not mind sharing a husband, she draws the line and says she needs her own car. This is the suburbs after all.

But the most important factor may turn out to be creative ennui. "Between 'Ally McBeal,' 'Frazier' and 'Sex and the City,'" said Marc Cherry, executive producer and creator of "Desperate Housewives," "it seemed like the whole urban thing had been done. It's only natural that writers wanting to do something fresh would turn their attention elsewhere. Why not do something about the suburbs?"

As Robert Greenblatt, president of entertainment of Showtime Networks said, "we all once believed in the bucolic ideal. I think we know by now that a lot of things went on behind those manicured lawns."

We also know by now that a lot of viewers, and a lot of Emmys, lie in wait.

Whatever the case, it's clear that television's long drive out of town has turned into a traffic jam, and it may not clear for a while. Stephen McPherson, the president of ABC Entertainment, gave the green light to "Desperate Housewives" then found himself inundated by similar pitches after the show soared in the ratings. "When we said yes to 'Desperate Housewives,' we weren't saying that we wanted something that was set in the suburbs," he said. "In the same way that there were a lot of mediocre imitations of 'Seinfeld' and 'Friends,' people need to find the next thing, not try to mimic what has already succeeded."

SIGNIFICANCE

The sitcom has endured as one of the most popular forms of American television programming, to a large degree due to the ability of sitcom producers to remain at or ahead of the curve that constitutes American tastes and public opinion. As the newspaper article outlines, popular sitcoms in the 1990s often portrayed urban environments as the backdrop to the comedic storyline. The trend in sitcoms since 2000 has been the increased depiction of situation comedies set in non-urban centers.

Data available through the United States Bureau of Census confirms a demographic basis for the shift in the type of locales used as the setting for television sitcoms. Migration data collected between 2000 and 2005 confirms that while the population of the United States grew by over five percent during this period, the population of the largest American cities declined in total by over three percent. Virtually all of this migration occurred from the large cities to the suburban and exurban areas of the country, where it is estimated that as of 2006, almost fifty percent of Americans lived.

The suburbs are defined as the outlying and primarily residential area of a larger city; the exurbs are those regions situated beyond the suburban area, often free standing in terms of municipal services and structure and connected to the larger city through rapid transit systems. It is clear from the census data that the population of the United States is decentralizing at a faster rate than at any previous time in American history.

Programming such as "Desperate Housewives" and "Weed" are set in a suburban environment; the suburbs and their conceptual extension, the exurbs, are now more important to American society than in any other previous time. As with the earlier sitcom interest in social issues, the geography and the life associated with the fast growing suburban and exurban regions is now a sitcom feature. An incontrovertible truth of American television programming since the commercial inception of the media has been that successful sitcoms provide an American audience with a reflection of how America sees itself.

A significant distinction between the suburban sitcoms of an earlier generation, such as "Leave it to Beaver", and the modern offerings is the nature of the content. The 1950s and 1960s sitcoms that were set in suburbia presented a safe, conservative, and seemingly idyllic existence when contrasted with city life. There were no apparent social problems experienced by the characters in the earlier sitcoms. The modern productions usually portray suburban lifestyles as possessing the diversity and the often-dysfunctional behavior previously associated with urban living. In an indirect fashion, the sitcom continues to reflect a segment of contemporary American living as it has always done.

The significance of the increase in attention paid by the producers of sitcoms to the suburban setting is likely to influence American perceptions about their own country's composition for an indefinite period. According to the A.C. Neilson Company, the average American adult watches over four hours of television per day. As reality television shows of various types and crime or justice themed shows dominate television ratings, the sitcoms are by default one of the few types of mainstream television that seek to depict the environment in which some Americans actually live; the sitcom is the closest portrayal to "real life" that a viewer can find in popular network programming.

FURTHER RESOURCES
Books

Dalton, Mary R. and Laura R. Linden, ed. *The Sitcom Reader: America Viewed and Skewed.* New York: State University of New York Press, 2005.

Marc, David. *Comic Visions: Television Comedy and American Culture (Second Edition).* Malden, Massachusetts: Blackwell , 1997.

Morreale, Joanne. *Critiquing the Sitcom: A Reader (The Television Series).* Syracuse, New York; Syracuse University Press, 2002.

Web sites

Washington State University/Edward R. Morrow School of Communication. "Sitcom: What it is, How it Works." 2005 <http://www.wsu.edu:8080/~taflinge/sitcom.html> (accessed July 27, 2006).

8 The Family in Times of Conflict and Change

The Family in Times of Conflict and Change

The family is an enduring social unit, even in times of conflict or when faced with substantial adversity. This chapter looks at wartime families, immigrant families, refugee families, and slave families. Immigration tests a family's resources, but it also proves that the basic social unit of the family can transcend national and cultural contexts. Since the concept of family is so often defined and influenced by its surroundings, immigrants are often faced with the challenge of reconciling the family structures, laws, and customs of their home country with those of their new country. Also, many immigrant families must face prolonged physical separation from family members.

This chapter also looks at families affected by conflict and war. Whether aiding a war effort on the home front or fleeing war on the battlefront, the family is affected by tumultuous surroundings. Contrasted here are the efforts of the homefront family, the planning of a victor garden or the rolling of bandages, with the violence and horror of the family caught in war. "Diary of the Great Deportation" describes the plight of several Jewish families during the Holocaust in the final weeks before the liquidation of the Warsaw ghetto.

Finally, slavery fractionated families and influenced African-American family identities for generations. Two sources in this chapter feature images and personal narratives of slaves and former-slave families. "A Family Divided" features a correspondence between white family members divided by differing views on the institution of slavery.

A Slave Auction in South Carolina

Editorial cartoon

By: Anonymous

Date: c.1820

Source: Corbis Corporation

About the Author: The illustration of a South Carolina slave auction is a part of the collection of images maintained by the Corbis Corporation, a worldwide provider of visual content materials to advertisers, broadcasters, designers, magazines, media organizations, newspapers, and producers. The artist is unknown.

INTRODUCTION

The practice of slavery took root in the American colonies after 1620. By the second half of the century, colonies such as Maryland and Virginia had developed as prosperous agricultural economies that were primarily supported by labor-intensive farming, particularly in the cultivation of tobacco and other commodities grown for export.

Convict laborers and indentured servants had been brought from England to America, but the availability of this type of labor was limited. The importation of black slaves, first from the West Indies and then from Africa, soon became a central feature of the economy. In 1640, Maryland was the first American colony to institutionalize slavery. By 1690, there were over 200,000 American slaves.

The American colonies quickly became a vital component of an international economic structure built upon the slave trade. Africans, both male and female, who had been captured by rival tribes, were sold by local chieftains to European slave traders. The traders then transported the slaves, in foul and often deadly conditions, to America, where they were offered for sale. Slave labor was an essential part of the intensive farming needed to grow and harvest export crops, the most important of which were tobacco, sugarcane, rice, and cotton.

Slavery soon fell out of public favor in the North, beginning with Vermont's constitutional ban on the practice in 1777; by 1804 all Northern states had followed suit. A number of antislavery movements arose in both England and America in the late 1790s, and the political pressure applied by these groups led to a

ban on the Atlantic slave trade by both countries in 1807. This did not outlaw American slavery, however, and the domestic sale of slaves continued. By 1820, there were approximately 700,000 slaves in the South; in South Carolina, Maryland, and Virginia, the slave population outnumbered that of whites.

Slave auctions were a regular feature of life in southern cities, principally Charleston, South Carolina; Richmond, Virginia; and New Orleans. Although records are incomplete, the last slave sale in the United States likely occurred in South Carolina in 1865.

PRIMARY SOURCE

A SLAVE AUCTION IN SOUTH CAROLINA

See primary source image.

SIGNIFICANCE

The slave auction was one of the most significant and enduring public symbols of the practice of slavery in the United States. George Washington, a slave owner for his entire adult life, frequently participated in slave auctions during his career as a gentleman farmer in Virginia, prior to his entry into military and then political life. Washington's will freed the approximately 100 slaves that he owned at the time of his death in 1799. Thomas Jefferson, although he was a frequent critic of slavery who tried without success to end the practice, owned hundreds of slaves who worked the farming operations at his Virginia estate. When Jefferson died in 1827, most of his slaves were sold to pay his debts.

Slave auctions were, by their nature, public. They were vital aspects of the slave economy, representing an opportunity to profit from the sale of surplus labor as well as an efficient means to acquire it. Auctions were "one-stop shopping," in which a number of slaves could be compared by prospective owners in a single viewing.

Auction proceedings were invariably an emotionless and strictly economic exercise—at least for the auctioneer, buyers, and sellers. This entirely commercial attitude stood in stark contrast to the slaves' enormous stakes in the proceedings. It was common for entire family units—husband, wife, and children—to be sold as individual "components." The distress and trauma caused by separation from family members, often permanently, is reflected in this illustration.

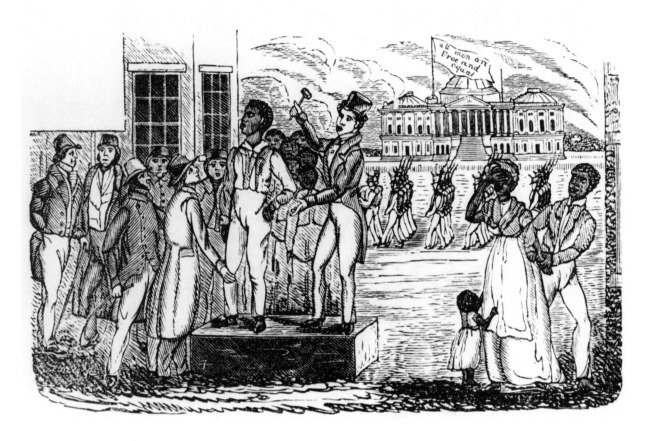

PRIMARY SOURCE

A Slave Auction in South Carolina: A slave is being sold at an auction while a family of ex-slaves looks on in despair, South Carolina. © CORBIS.

The auction was dehumanizing in other respects, as well. Each slave offered for sale was liable to be physically inspected by a prospective purchaser as one would inspect a farm animal. Teeth, build, demeanor, and potential for demanding physical labor were all explored in demeaning ways. Slaves were often made to jump or dance to display their physical capabilities.

Ironically, the auctions were conducted and attended by self-professed Christians whose churches might be located within 100 yards of the auction house. Many southern churches held a theological rationale for slavery: Noah's curse that his son Ham's descendents, popularly believed to be the black African peoples, would always be 'servants of servants.' Jefferson Davis, president of the Confederate States (1861–1865), echoed this belief with his pronouncement that slavery was sanctioned by the Bible. Interestingly, the powerful northern abolitionist movement

was also fueled by Christians, beginning with the Quakers in 1775.

The public slave auction was an element of the "peculiar institution", as slavery came to be euphemistically described. Its characterization as unusual or eccentric was a kinder image than that of forced labor and the auctioned sale of human beings. The expression was also capable of a double meaning—the word "peculiar" is derived from the Latin *peculium*, meaning private property.

FURTHER RESOURCES
Books

Thomas, Hugh. *The Slave Trade: The History of the Atlantic Slave Trade, 1440–1870*. New York: Touchstone, 1997.

Wiencek, Henry. *An Imperfect God: George Washington, His Slaves and the Creation of America*. New York: Farrar, Straus, and Giroux, 2003.

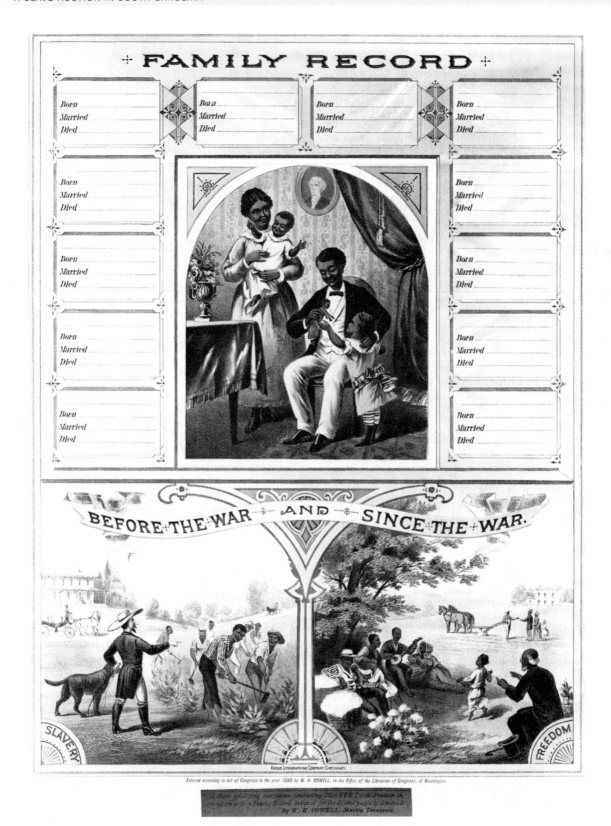

A form for a family tree with illustrations depicting how life for African Americans changed for the better as a result of the Civil War and the end of slavery. © CORBIS. REPRODUCED BY PERMISSION.

Web sites

Eyewitness to History. "Slave Auctions." 2002 <http://www.eyewitnesstohistory.com/slaveauction.htm> (accessed June 27, 2006).

University of Virginia. "Imaging Slavery in Mark Twain's Books." 2002 <http://etext.virginia.edu/railton/wilson/slavery/mtslavhp.html> (accessed June 27, 2006).

A Family Divided

Book excerpt

By: John G. Fee

Date: c. 1861

Source: Fee, John G. "A Family Divided." In *Autobiography of John Fee.* University of North Carolina at Chapel Hill, 1861.

About the Author: John G. Fee (1816–1901), abolitionist and evangelist, lived in the slave state of Kentucky. In his later years, he worked for Berea College and the Christian Missionary Association of Kentucky.

Civil War General R. Ingolls stands on the steps of his house with his family, May 1865. © BETTMANN/CORBIS.

INTRODUCTION

Slavery put severe pressures on blacks as well as whites who opposed the system of bondage. Slaves saw their families frequently ripped apart as members were sold at auction. Whites who viewed slavery as morally wrong and who came from slaveowning familes faced a choice between their conscience and continued family ties. Slavery destroyed all sorts of family relationships.

The creation and continuation of slave families benefited both owners and slaves. Family units were at the core of a slave's personal life and provided slaves with a supportive environment for dealing with oppression, a basis for community development, and an opportunity for creating African-American culture. Enslaved men and women chose spouses from their own plantation community or from slaves on neighboring farms. They participated in marriage ceremonies and raised children in two-parent households.

Yet slave marriages had no legal standing and could be dissolved at the discretion of the master. Additionally, parents were not given rights over their children comparable to those possessed by free people over their offspring. At any time, a child could be sold away from parents and wives could be sold away from husbands. Separation from family members was a slave's worst fear.

Whites feared that they would not go to heaven. While the first anti-slavery societies began in the 1770s, abolition became a major social movement only in the nineteenth century, and only because of the Second Great Awakening; this religious movement taught that individuals could obtain salvation by doing good deeds. Fighting the evils of slavery could guarantee admission to heaven. Accordingly, while it often required considerable courage and considerable risk to do the good deeds, a godly person such as John G. Fee had no real choice. When reviewing this source one should keep in mind the time and context in which it was written, as some language used would not be considered appropriate today.

■ PRIMARY SOURCE

Intelligence came to me that my brother had advised my father to sell the woman referred to, for the reason that there were more women in the family than were needed.

I said to my wife: "I cannot redeem all slaves, nor even all in my father's family, but the labors of Julett and her husband contributed in part to the purchase of the land I yet own in Indiana, and to sell those lands and redeem her will be in some measure returning to her and her husband what they have toiled for." My wife said: "Do what you think is right." I took my horse, rode twenty-five miles to my father's house and spent the night. In the morning of the next day I sought an opportunity when my father was alone, and having learned that he would sell, asked what he would take for Julett. He fixed his price. I said: "Will you sell her to me if I bring to you the money?" He said yes. I immediately rode to Germantown and borrowed the requisite amount of money by mortgaging my remaining tract of land for the payment. Whilst there I executed a bill of sale, so that without delay my father could sign it, before he even returned from the field at noon. I tendered to him the money and the bill of sale. He signed the bill of sale, and took the money. I immediately went to "Add," the husband of Julett, and told him I had bought Julett and should immediately secure by law her freedom. I said to him: "I would gladly redeem you but I have not the means." He replied: "I am glad you can free her; I can take care of myself better than she can." I went to the house, wrote a perpetual pass for the woman, gave it to her, and said, "You are a free woman; be in bondage to no man." Tears of gratitude ran down her sable cheeks. I then told her that at the first county court day I would take her to the clerk's office, where her height could be taken and she be otherwise described, and a record of her freedom made. This was just before the amendment to the State Constitution that forbade emancipation in the State. At noon my father came in and told my mother of the transaction. My mother was displeased,—did not want to spare the woman from certain work for which she was fitted. My father came to me and requested that I cancel the contract and give up the bill of sale. I said to him, "Here is my horse, and I have a house and lot in Lewis County; I will give them to you if you so desire; but to sell a human being I may not." He became very angry and went to the freed woman and said to her, "When you leave this house never put your foot on my farm again, for I do not intend to have a free nigger on my farm." The woman, the wife and mother, came to me and said, "Master says if I leave here I shall never come back again; I cannot leave my children; I would rather go back into slavery." I said, I have done what I regarded as my duty. To now put you back into slavery, I cannot. We must simply abide the consequences. The woman was in deep distress and helpless as a child. Although I had my horse and was ready to ride, I felt I could not leave the helpless one until a way of relief should open. After a time Julett came to me and said, "As long as mistress shall live I can stand it; I would rather stay." I said, "You are a free woman and must make your own decision. If my father will furnish to

you a home, and clothe and feed you, and you shall choose as a free woman to stay, all well; but to sell you back into slavery, I cannot." To this proposition to furnish a home to the freed woman my father agreed. There was now a home for the freed woman, and this with her husband and children and grand-children.

That day of agony was over and eventide had come. I spent the night. The next morning just as I was about starting back to my home, my father said to me, "Julett is here on my premises, and I will sell her before sundown if I can." I turned to him and said, "Father, I am now that woman's only guardian. Her husband cannot protect her,—I only can. I must do as I would be done by; and though it is hard for me to now say to you what I intended to say, yet if you sell that woman, I will prosecute you for so doing, as sure as you are a man." I saw the peril of the defenseless woman. I would gladly have cast from me the cup of a further contest, but I saw that to leave her, though now a free woman, was not the end of obligation. I felt forcibly the applicability of the words, "Cursed be he that doeth the work of the Lord negligently, and cursed be he that keepeth back the sword from blood." Jer. 48:10. I mounted my horse and rode twelve miles where I could get legal counsel,—counsel on which I could rely. I found that if I left the woman on my father's premises without any public record of her having been sold, the fact of her being then on his premises would be regarded as "prima facie" evidence that she was his property and that he could sell her. I also found that in as much as he had sold her to me, I could, by law, compel him to do that which was just and right,—make a record of the fact of sale. I rode back twelve miles, told my father what was his legal obligation, and asked him to conform to it. He said he would not. I then said to him, "It will be a hard trial for me to arraign my father in a civil court, for neglect of justice to a helpless woman, and also for a plain violation of law; but I will do so, as sure as you are a man, if you do not make the required record of sale." After hesitancy and delay he made the record. These were hours of distress to me, to my father, to my mother, and to the ransomed woman; but the only way to ultimate peace, was to hold on rigidly to the right; though in so doing I had, in the Gospel sense, to leave father, mother, brother, sisters, houses, lands,—all, for Christ's sake. I was conscious that no other motive impelled me.

SIGNIFICANCE

The end of slavery brought dramatic changes for African-American families. Individually and with friends and family, thousands of enslaved men, women, and children ran away from their owners and made their way to the relative safety of Union lines. Blacks were then encouraged to legitimize relationships that they had established in plantation marriage ceremonies. African-American families were transformed from female-centered structures existing within white patriarchal households to two-parent nuclear families led by black men.

African-American families were also the basis of black institutions that formed after the Civil War. Schools, churches, and other community organizations became the centers of black family life. Black men headed these institutions, but black women kept them running. In some African-American families, black women withdrew from the labor force to concentrate on household and child-care responsibilities. In family structure and family activities, black families were becoming much like white families.

FURTHER RESOURCES
Books

Hudson, Larry E. *To Have and to Hold: Slave Work and Family Life in Antebellum South Carolina.* Athens, Ga.: University of Georgia, 1997.

Jones, Jacqueline. *Labor of Love, Labor of Sorrow: Black Women, Work, and the Family from Slavery to the Present.* New York: Basic Books, 1985.

Stevenson, Brenda E. *Life in Black and White: Family and Community in the Slave South.* New York: Basic Books, 1997.

When I Journeyed from America

Song Lyrics

By: Harriet M. Pawlowska

Date: c. 1910

Source: Pawlowska, Harriet M., ed. *Merrily We Sing: 105 Polish Folks Songs.* Boston: Bay Back Books, 1961.

About the Author: Harriet Pawloska's volume on Polish folk songs has been widely cited by other writers chronicling the voyages of immigrants to America.

INTRODUCTION

The United States has long been seen as a land of opportunity. Since the first European explorers landed in North America men and women have frequently arrived in search of economic gain; much of the original mapping of North America occurred during Spanish, French, and British searches for treasure. Most of these treasures, including the mythical golden cities of Cibola, were never found.

While the legend of the golden cities persists even today, few foreigners travel to the United States to search for treasure. But many do move to America in the hope of finding higher-paying jobs than are available in their home country. Such a move frequently means relocating the entire family, but in some cases it requires a long stay away from family, followed by a trip back home to deliver accumulated earnings. For some families, such an arrangement is merely a stepping stone to an eventual move, after the father has amassed enough money to fund the trip. For others, an absentee father is simply a hard fact of economic life.

Workers traveling to the United States are neither the first nor the only laborers who leave home for long periods of time. Sailors, away from home for many months at a time, face challenges in maintaining a home life. Entertainers, whose work requires them to travel many months each year, sometimes struggle to re-integrate with their families and communities when they return home. Soldiers have historically left home for long periods of time, and in World War II many civilians were drafted and sent overseas. Oil field workers drilling in Alaska frequently work two-week shifts, followed by a plane flight home and two weeks off. In each of these situations a family member is forced to pursue balance between economic and social needs. In some cases, this balance can be achieved, but in other cases dislocated parents find that their time away from home has cost more than they expected.

■ **PRIMARY SOURCE**

When I journeyed from Amer'ca,
And the foundry where I labored...
Soon I came to New York City,
To the agent for my passage...
Then I left Berlin for Krakow;
There my wife was waiting for me.
And my children did not know me,
For they fled from me, a stranger.

"My dear children, I'm your papa;
Three long years I have not seen you."

■

SIGNIFICANCE

As real estate prices in large cities continue to climb, workers have begun buying homes farther from

A family of Polish refugees displaced by World War II hold out their landing cards for inspection upon arrival in New York City, December 27, 1949. © BETTMANN/CORBIS.

the cities, resulting in increased commute times. Other workers find themselves facing temporary situations in which it is more practical to temporarily endure a lengthy commute than to relocate permanently. These factors have given rise to the so-called Extreme Commuter.

While most Americans consider thirty to forty-five minutes a reasonable daily commute, some employees now travel much farther to work each day. Leaving at 4:00 or 5:00 a.m., they endure commutes of up to two hours each direction. This drive, when tacked onto both ends of a normal work day, means that some leave home before their small children wake up and return home just before the kids go to bed. And while two-hour commutes remain the exception, by 2006 approximately fifteen percent of American commuters were driving more than forty-five minutes each way.

Beyond the time and expense of such lengthy trips, sociologists suspect that this type of lifestyle is unhealthy over the long term. Beyond the sheer time demands, such arrangements place inordinate stress on family relationships, making normal family life difficult. In some cases, homes grow accustomed to functioning without the commuter, only to face difficulty on weekends when he or she is home all day.

As commutes have grown longer and gasoline prices continue to climb, urban planners have begun rethinking the design of communities. In contrast to typical city-suburb arrangements, in which virtually every trip requires the use of a car, "Urban Villages" are designed to connect with urban work areas by light rail, allowing commuters to avoid rush-hour traffic. These new living areas also include movies, shopping, and restaurants and are specifically designed to encourage foot, bicycle, and roller blade traffic.

Designers hope these new hybrid communities will provide the benefits of suburban living without the extensive commuting such lifestyles typically involve.

Migrant workers remain a fixture of American life in the twenty-first century. Most current migrant workers are Mexican citizens rather than Europeans. Migrant farm workers often follow crop harvests across the United States, moving their families with them then and returning home for the winter. In other cases, laborers come to the United States alone, locating near the border to simplify trips home. As of 2006, Mexican immigration was becoming a major political issue.

FURTHER RESOURCES

Books

Fox, Jonathan, and Gaspar Rivera-Salgado, eds. *Indigenous Mexican Migrants in the United States*. Dallas: Center for U.S.-Mexican Studies, 2004.

Maruggi, Edward Albert. *Mushrooms, Sausage, and Wine: Life with an Immigrant Father*. Pitsford, New York: Winston Publishing, 1997.

Neal, Peter, ed. *Urban Villages: The Making of Community*. London: Spon Press, 2003.

Periodicals

Spector, Mike. "Mass Transit is Gaining Riders, and Cachet, as Gas Prices Climb." *Wall Street Journal* (June 20, 2006): D2.

Stodooska, Monika, and Carla Almeida. "Transnationalism and Leisure: Mexican Temporary Migrants in the U.S." *Journal of Leisure Research* 38 (2006):143–167.

Web sites

Outside Magazine Online. "Crude Reality." <http://outside.away.com/outside/features/200402/200402_anwr_1.html> (accessed July 10, 2006).

Public Broadcasting Service. "Mexican Immigrant Labor History." <http://www.pbs.org/kpbs/theborder/history/timeline/17.html> (accessed July 10, 2006).

USA Today. "Think Your Commute is Tough?" November 29, 2004 <http://www.usatoday.com/news/nation/2004-11-29-commute_x.htm> (accessed July 10, 2006).

The Family War Effort

Illustration

By: Thomas Theodor Heine

Date: 1915

Source: Corbis

About the Artist: Thomas Theodore Heine, who was trained as a painter and worked for illustrated papers such as *Die Jugend*, cofounded *Simplicissimus*, a magazine that published satirical commentary on German society and politics. Heine's artwork during World War I targeted the class that encouraged nationalism and militarism in Germany. He was an outspoken critic of the Nazi party and was forced to flee Germany in 1933 when Hitler came to power.

INTRODUCTION

To understand the complex factors that led to World War I, Germany's rise to power in the nineteenth century must be considered. At the close of the Franco-Prussian war in 1871, Prussia and the German kingdoms unified into a single nation under Kaiser Wilhelm I. The war was a humiliating defeat for France, which lost its Alsace and Lorraine territories to Germany.

By 1888, Germany had undergone a massive industrialization, and the kaiser had been succeeded by his son. Wilhelm II was decidedly militaristic and sought to increase Germany's armed forces, with a specific goal: to exceed Britain's navy. By 1890, Germany had become the strongest economic and military power in Europe; under the policy of *weltpolitik*, or world politics, it sought to exert global influence commensurate with its economic and military might.

To this end, Germany engaged in a series of alliances with surrounding nations. By 1910, its rapid economic development led to more wealth per capita than any other European state. But alliances proved unstable. In 1890, as Tsar Nicholas II assumed the Russian throne, Germany declined to renew the Reinsurance Treaty that had bound the two nations since 1887. Russia then entered into a treaty with France, Germany's foe, in 1892.

Europe began to divide itself with secret alliances. Germany allied with Austria-Hungary and Turkey to comprise the Central Powers. The Entente Powers consisted of France, Britain, and Russia. Clashes in European colonies began to affect the political situation in Europe. Fueled by these conflicts, between 1910 and 1914, German military expenditures rose by seventy-three percent and conscription increased the German military by 170,000 men.

On June 28, 1914, the heir to the Austro-Hungarian empire, Archduke Franz Ferdinand, and his wife were assassinated by a Serbian nationalist. Within a month, Austria-Hungary declared war on Serbia. As an ally of Serbia, Russia began to mobilize its army.

■ **PRIMARY SOURCE**

The Family War Effort: This illustration appeared in 1915 in the German periodical *Simplicissimus*, a publication that took a satirical look at German politics and society. The illustration depicts a group of women preparing armaments as part of the war effort. © STAPLETON COLLECTION/CORBIS.

■ **PRIMARY SOURCE**

THE FAMILY WAR EFFORT

See primary source image.

■

SIGNIFICANCE

After defeating France in 1871, Germany had been united and a sense of pride swept the country.

This nationalism grew stronger as Germany underwent its rapid industrialization and began to rival older, established countries' economies. But the alliance system began to isolate Germany diplomatically, leaving it with a feeling that it was encircled by its enemies.

In 1913, Crown Prince Wilhelm published the book, *Germany in Arms*, which lauded Germany's rise to power and cautioned the German people against getting too comfortable in their newfound prosperity. The crown prince asserted that those who truly loved Germany and believed in its future had to be ready to fight, arguing that war would benefit Germany.

After declaring war on Russia, France, and Belgium, Kaiser Wilhelm II addressed the German people in Berlin. In his speech, he declared that Germany's enemies sought to humiliate the nation and that its opponents were preparing to attack, forcing Germany to go to war. Reaction to the Kaiser's declaration of war was enthusiastic willingness to participate on the part of the average German citizen.

FURTHER RESOURCES

Web sites

BBC. "World Wars: World War I ." January 3, 2002 <http://www.bbc.co.uk/history/worldwars/wwone/> (accessed June 15, 2006).

First World War.com. "Primary Sources: Crown Prince Wilhelm on the Prospect of War, 1913." September 27, 2003 <http://www.firstworldwar.com/source/crownprincewilhelm1913.htm> (accessed June 15, 2006).

PBS. "The Great War: And the Shaping of the 20th Century." <http://www.pbs.org/greatwar/chapters/index.html> (accessed June 15, 2006).

This was seen as aggression toward Germany, which declared war on Russia in August. In the following days, Germany also declared war on France and Belgium, and Austria-Hungary declared war on Russia. The Great War had begun.

There's Cheer in the Pictures from Home

Advertisement

By: Eastman Kodak Company

Date: November 21, 1918

Source: Eastman Kodak Company. "There's Cheer in the Pictures from Home." Ellis Collection of Kodakiana, Duke Special Collections Archive. Courtest of The Library of Congress.

There's Cheer in the Pictures from Home

To a homesick boy at the front, a picture of Dad pushing the lawnmower in the old front yard is worth more than the Croix de Guerre.

Pictures of Mother—how much they mean to him now! And of kid sister—perhaps she is "wearing her hair up" by this time—all the old, familiar scenes around the village—yes, and that little girl with the big blue eyes, that lives around the corner—these will mean a world of comfort to the boy who is lonesome among a million strangers.

The Y. M. C. A., the Red Cross, the Knights of Columbus and kindred organizations are doing a world of good in ministering to the bodies and minds of our boys. But in their hearts, homes are first. Cheerful letters and cheerful pictures from home—these will keep their hearts light and their courage high.

EASTMAN KODAK COMPANY, Rochester, N. Y., *The Kodak City*

PRIMARY SOURCE

There's Cheer in the Pictures from Home: A World War I era advertisement encourages sending photos of home to soldiers overseas. The personal camera was still a rare luxury in 1918. THE LIBRARY OF CONGRESS.

About the Author: The Ellis Collection of Kodakiana was created by Wayne P. Ellis (d. 1994). A Pennsylvania engineer and collector of photographs, Ellis concentrated on advertising and marketing items. He acquired virtually every Eastman Kodak ad that appeared in general interest magazines up to the 1980s.

INTRODUCTION

The invention of photography made it possible for ordinary people to afford accurate likenesses of themselves and their loved ones. It was a privilege that had been formerly reserved only for the rich. Photography soon became an enormously popular pastime as families filled photographic albums.

Eastman Kodak began in 1882, when George Eastman invented a machine that did not require photographers to apply fresh chemicals to a metal plate in order to take a single picture. By making photography simple, he began the age of amateur photography. Before Eastman, the photographic process involved using dangerous chemicals to produce a slightly wet exposure on a glass photographic plate. In 1888, Eastman introduced the Kodak, the first camera aimed at the consumer market. It was a small, handheld machine that contained a roll of film with 100 exposures that cost $10 to develop at Eastman Kodak laboratories. With the Kodak, anyone who could press a button could take a photograph. By 1896, 100,000 Kodak cameras had been manufactured.

During World War I, photography was promoted as a way of boosting morale. The fighting ended on November 11, 1918, shortly before the publication of this advertisement for Eastman Kodak cameras.

PRIMARY SOURCE

THERE'S CHEER IN THE PICTURES FROM HOME
See primary source image.

SIGNIFICANCE

The snapshots taken with Kodak cameras are a rich mine of information about families of the past.

U.S. soldiers with cameras in the World War I-era. © UNDERWOOD & UNDERWOOD/CORBIS.

The photographs that a family accumulates are a record not only of what the family members looked like but also of many aspects of family life. They offer clues about how families have changed over time. Despite the suggestion in the Kodak advertisement, photographs of ordinary activities such as mowing the lawn are quite rare. Most pictures depict a special event such as a wedding or vacation. Others show posed family members in front of a house or seated in a room. The arrangement of people, with the honored person typically seated in bygone years, shows the values and expectations of the family.

The popularity of photography in documentng the family rose with the evolving technology. The rise of digital cameras has made it possible to take photographs without wasting film. As a result, more photographs are being taken as photographers can easily edit out a bad shot. While not all of these photographs are developed, a large number are being saved in computer files. In 2003, the *Digital Photography Review* estimated that over fifty million digital cameras were sold worldwide in 2003. Digital historians of the future are likely to have more family images to examine.

FURTHER RESOURCES
Books

Cameron, Ardis, ed. *Looking for America: The Visual Production of Nation and People.* Malden, Mass.: Blackwell, 2005.

West, Nancy Martha. *Kodak and the Lens of Nostalgia.* Charlottesville: University Press of Virginia, 2000.

Learn to Speak, Read, and Write the Language of Your Children

Poster

By: Anonymous artist, Works Progress Administration

Date: 1936–1941

Source: Anonymous. *Learn to Speak, Read, and Write the Language of Your Children.* New York City Federal Art Project/Works Progress Administration, 1936–1941.

About the Author: The Works Progress Administration (WPA) hired thousands of artists and designers to work in government-sponsored jobs as part of a mas-

sive relief package designed by the Franklin D. Roosevelt administration to help the economy recover from the Great Depression.

INTRODUCTION

Jewish immigration to the United States began with a small flow in the 1820s; there were approximately 3,000 Jewish persons in the United States at that time. By 1860, the population had increased to 150,000 Jews, largely through immigration. The emigration of Gaelic and English-speaking Irish migrants was far greater in the 1840s and 1850s; between 1846 and 1855, nearly two million Irish emigrated to the United States, largely pushed by the potato blight that ruined the primary food for the poor and rural farmers. Faced with the choice between starvation and immigration, two million chose to leave. When Jewish immigrations began to leave eastern Europe in increasing numbers in the early 1880s, the push factor was *pogroms*, formal and informal campaigns to persecute people of Jewish descent. Triggered in Russia by the mistaken belief that a Jewish person had killed Tsar Alexander II, the new tsar unleashed a sanctioned wave of violence and rights restriction that forced many Jews to face a difficult choice as had the Irish: stay and face horrible conditions, or leave for the unknown?

Most Jews migrating to the United States before the 1880s were Sephardic Jews, descended from ancestors on the Iberian peninsula. The eastern European Jews who migrated in large numbers from the early 1880s to the mid 1920s, however, were Ashkenazi Jews, Yiddish speakers and of German descent. In 1900, active persecution of Romanian Jews began, leading to an influx of immigrants from that country as well. By the end of the great migration of these Jewish immigrants, more than two million people from Russia and eastern Europe filled the United States, bringing a cultural richness, a cheap source of industrial labor, and a host of challenges to society and government.

Whereas Irish immigrants had spoken English in reasonable numbers, the Russian, Polish, Hungarian, Romanian, and other eastern Europeans spoke little if any English. Without English language skills, the new immigrants were destined for unskilled positions, largely working in factory settings. Clustered in large cities such as Chicago and New York, the new immigrants quickly became the subject of scorn by native-born Americans and older immigrants, who often resented the problems that such wide-scale immigration brought: overcrowded neighborhoods and schools, increased crime, and job competition.

פרייע קלאסען איז ענגליש!

לערנט לעזען, שרייבען און רעדען
די שפראך פון אידערע קינדער.

פארבערייטונג צו
ווערען א בירגער.
אלע סקול געגען-
שטענדע.ספעציעלע
קלאסען פאר געביל-
דעטע אוימלענדער.

אינפארמאצ'ע וועגען די קלאס-
ען קענט איהר קריגען אין..

FREE CLASSES
IN ENGLISH!

LEARN TO SPEAK, READ
& WRITE THE LANGUAGE
OF YOUR CHILDREN.
NATURALIZATION PREP-
ARATION. ALL SCHOOL
SUBJECTS. SPECIAL
CLASSES FOR EDUCAT-
ED FOREIGN BORN.

INFORMATION
& CLASSES AT.

WPA ADULT EDUCATION PROGRAM BOARD OF EDUCATION CITY OF N.Y.

FEDERAL ART PROJECT N.Y.C.

PRIMARY SOURCE

Learn to Speak, Read, and Write the Language of Your Children: A poster advertising free lessons in English for European Jewish immigrants. The advertisement targets older immigrants, mentioning that their U.S.-born children speak fluent English. Such classes were intended to help older immigrants better assimilate. THE LIBRARY OF CONGRESS.

Social reformers, however, worked to assimilate the immigrants and a new immigration law, the National Origins Quota Law of 1924, changed the procedures for legal U.S. immigration, sharply limiting eastern European immigration and favoring northern Europeans. By the 1930s, as the Great Depression created economic chaos and exacerbated poverty not only in immigrant slums and tenements but on farms, in small towns, and across income and ethnic lines, the children of immigrants slowly improved their language and education through enrollment in public schools. The lack of jobs helped children in some ways; parents permitted children to enroll in school rather than having them work in the factories as low-paid unskilled workers.

In 1936, the Works Progress Administration began subsidizing jobs for artists, using their talent to create public campaigns for education and health. This poster, written in English and Yiddish, appeals to immigrant parents and asks them to take advantage of free English and other courses as part of an American assimilation campaign.

■ **PRIMARY SOURCE**

LEARN TO SPEAK, READ, AND WRITE THE LANGUAGE OF YOUR CHILDREN

See primary source image.

■

SIGNIFICANCE

By and large, Jewish immigrants clustered in the Lower East Side of New York City, where overcrowded conditions led to large families living in two-room apartments, butcher shops, grocery stores, street peddlers, bakeries, and houses of worship in close proximity. Federal and state government worked to help society absorb the immigrants, issuing citizenship materials in Yiddish, Russian, and other languages, while schools swelled with the children of immigrants eager to gain a free education to move up through society.

As this poster notes, parents were part of the later campaigns in the 1930s. Earlier public campaigns in World War I had encouraged immigrants to take free night classes to learn English and to attend night school in other subjects, but the new campaign appealed explicitly to parents in terms of their relationship to their children, noting the difference and the divide between first and second generation immigrants. "Learn to Speak, Read, and Write the Language of Your Children" was not just a campaign, but

Night school students of all ages, many of them immigrants, stand in a large group saluting the American flag, New York, New York, April 25, 1941. © BETTMANN/CORBIS.

an appeal to fears that the children of immigrants were separating from their parents, assimilating into American society in a way that left parents behind. Government-sponsored English classes, the campaign implies, could help parents catch up.

That such a poster was created in the late 1930s by a government-funded Works Progress Administration project speaks to the ongoing need to help immigrants to mesh with American society. The stress to speak English also set the tone for future waves of immigration: In 2006, the United States Congress considered a bill making English the official language of the United States, as bilingual programs in education—largely aimed at Spanish-speaking children—have provoked debates about the role of language integration and immigration in modern times.

FURTHER RESOURCES
Books

Friedman-Kasaba, Kathie. *Memories of Migration: Gender, Ethnicity, and Work in the Lives of Jewish and Italian Women in New York, 1870–1924.* Albany: State University of New York Press, 1996.

Hindus, Milton. *The Jewish East Side: 1881–1924*. New Brunswick, N.J., and London: Transaction Publishers, 1996.

Smith, Jason Scott. *Building New Deal Liberalism: The Political Economy of Public Works, 1933–1956*. New York: Cambridge University Press, 2005.

Watkins, TH *The Hungry Years: A Narrative History of the Great Depression in America*. New York: Henry Holt & Company, 2000.

Periodical

Marshall, Edward. "Good Metal in Our Melting Pot, Says Miss Wald." *The New York Times*, November 16, 1913.

Web sites

National Archives and Records Administration. "A New Deal for the Arts." <http://www.archives.gov/exhibits/new_deal_for_the_arts/index.html> (accessed July 3, 2006).

United States Department of Labor. "Compensation from before World War I through the Great Depression." 2001 <http://www.bls.gov/opub/cwc/cm20030124ar03p1.htm> (accessed July 3, 2006).

A Slavery Family in North Carolina

Interview

By: Tanner Spikes

Date: 1936

Source: Federal Writer's Project

About the Author: Tanner Spikes, an elderly woman who had been a slave during her childhood, related her memories of slavery to an interviewer for the Federal Writer's Project in the 1930s. Spikes's account is one of the few interviews with African Americans who could remember slave life.

INTRODUCTION

The state of the black family under slavery has been the subject of considerable debate and study. Inevitably, the analysis turns to the issue of control. While slave owners had ultimate authority over slave families, the slaves challenged them in a variety of ways. This power struggle affected family life in ways that scholars are just beginning to understand.

Some researchers claim that the roots of matriarchy and illegitimacy seen in many present-day African American families began in a system that denied slaves the right to marry and severely curtailed men's authority over their children. Senator Daniel Patrick Moynihan's 1965 report that linked the problems of blacks in inner cities—including drug abuse, high crime rates, and skyrocketing unemployment—to female-headed households is the most famous example of this scholarly link. Other scholars disagreed, but despite the controversy, it is clear that slave parents, whether mothers or fathers, had a very limited ability to protect and care for their children.

As research has moved beyond questions of authority and family structure to consider the complicated relationship between slave families and those who claimed ownership of them, scholars have been helped by the slave narratives. Although these first-hand accounts are plagued by methodological problems—such as the nature of the questions posed by the interviewers, the interviewers' race (usually white), and bias (reflected in the decision to give black responses in dialect)—they remain valuable sources for the study of the slave family. When reviewing this source one should keep in mind the time and context in which it was written, as some language used would not be considered appropriate today.

▇ PRIMARY SOURCE

A Slavery Family

An interview with Tanner Sikes, 77 years of age, of 43 Bragg Street, Raleigh, North Carolina.

"My mammy had fifteen chilluns which wus all borned on Doctor Fab Haywood's plantation here in Wake County. My mammy 'longed ter him, but my daddy 'longed ter a Mr. Wiggins in Pasquotank County. I think that Dr. Haywood bought him just 'fore de war. Anyhow, we took de name of Wiggins.

"Mammy's name wus Lucinda an' pappy's name wus Osburn. I doan 'member seein' many Yankees on Dr. Haywood's place. I doan reckon many comed dar. Anyhow, we had a gyard.

"I 'members a corn shuckin' what happened 'fore de war wus over, an'what a time dem niggers did have. Dey kisses when dey fin' a red year an' atter dat dey pops some popcorn an' dey dances ter de music of de banjo which Uncle Jed am a-playin'. Dey dances all night de best I can 'member.

A slave family in South Carolina, 1862. THE LIBRARY OF CONGRESS.

"I seed a few Yankees, but dey wus just lookin' fer something ter eat. We ain't knowed nothin' 'bout freedom, but de Yankees tol' us dat we ort ter be free, dey also said dat we ort ter have meat an' stuff in de smokehouse. My mammy sez dat dey ain't got good sense an' she tells mares what dey said.

"De Yankees has done tuck all de rations so dar ain't nothin' lef' fer de niggers ter take but mammy tells Marse Haywood what dey sez anyhow. Marse Haywood sez dat iffen he ketch any niggers in his smokehouse dat he'll skin 'em alive. He also sez dat we ain't free an' dat we ain't never gwine ter be free.

"De nex' year, atter de war, wus a hard year. We ain't had nothin' ter eat but hard tack an' 'lasses an' sometimes not half enough of dat. My pappy still farmed fer Marse Haywood, but hit ain't as good as it is in slavery days.

"Seberal years atter dat, while we wus livin' on Davie Street, I met Frank Spikes an' I married him. I can't tell yo' much 'bout our love-makin' case hit warn't much, but he always called me 'honey gal' an' he axed me ter marry him in de kitchen while I wus washin' dishes. He jist puts his arms 'round me an' he sez, 'I wants ter marry yo', honey gal.'

"Well we gits married by de Baptist preacher in Raleigh fifty odd years ago an' we lives tergether till dis past March, when he dies.

"Other boys comed ter see me but I ain't loved none of dem but Frank. He ain't never whupped me but onct an' dat wus fer sassin' him, an' I reckin dat I needed dat.

"We have five chillns an' I'se stayin' wid my daughter since he died, but I misses him, yes mam, I misses him purty awful."

SIGNIFICANCE

As part of the New Deal's Works Progress Administration work relief programs, the Federal Writer's Project transcribed former slaves' memories about their lives in bondage, the first and only such interviews ever conducted. These memoirs greatly expanded the knowledge and study of slavery.

The value of the narratives, however, was not recognized for decades. In the era before the development of African American history, many historians ignored them, believing that black history was of little significance and that oral history should not be privileged over written sources. Numerous accounts written by whites, in fact, testified to the benefits of plantation living for blacks.

The interviews were finally published in 1945, when B.A. Botkin edited a handful of them for *Lay My Burden Down: A Folk History of Slavery*. Many Southern reviewers, however, saw the book as an attack and an attempt to challenge the elevated position of whites in Southern race relations. They denounced the work as unreliable, irrelevant folklore. With the rise of the civil rights movement in the 1960s and 1970s, however, the black experience came to be viewed as part of the struggle for freedom in American history. In the 1970s, the narratives were published in their entirety, making them readily available to the public.

FURTHER RESOURCES

Books

Berlin, Ira, Marc Favreau, and Steven F. Miller, eds. *Remembering Slavery: African Americans Talk about Their Personal Experiences of Slavery and Freedom*. New York: The New Press, 1998.

Davis, Charles T., and Henry Louis Gates, Jr. *The Slave's Narrative*. New York: Oxford University Press, 1985.

Jones, Jacqueline. *Labor of Love, Labor of Sorrow: Black Women, Work, and the Family from Slavery to the Present*. New York: Vintage, 1985.

Diary of the Great Deportation

Book excerpt

By: Abraham Lewin

Date: c. 1940

Source: Lewin, Abraham. *A Cup of Tears: A Diary of the Warsaw Ghetto*. Institute for Polish-Jewish Studies, 1988.

About the Author: Abraham Lewin was born in Warsaw in 1893, where he became a history teacher. Lewin and his daughter are presumed to have died before the end of World War II in 1945. He kept a diary that recorded the horrors of life under Nazi occupation and subsequent deportations to the death camps, which he called the "great deportation." The last entry in Lewin's diary was dated January 15, 1943.

INTRODUCTION

In 1939 Adolph Hitler addressed his commanders as they prepared to invade neighboring Poland. His orders were clear and concise: The army was to kill every man, woman, and child of Polish descent. Hitler's justification for this was simple: Germany needed more space. On September 1 German troops swept into Poland from the west, north, and south, crushing the light resistance and marking the formal beginning of World War II.

Life in German-occupied Poland was miserable both for Jews and gentiles. Educated professionals were rounded up and shot, all vestiges of Polish culture and language were banned or destroyed, and by war's end more than two million non-Jewish Poles had been deported in cattle cars to perform forced labor. For the first year and a half of its existence, the infamous Auschwitz death camp was filled almost entirely with non-Jewish Poles, and by war's end almost two million of them had been killed there and in other camps.

Polish Jews fared even worse. Adults were required to wear white armbands with a blue Star of David on them. Jews were required to identify their businesses as Jewish-owned, and special permits were required to purchase a business from a Jew. Jews were eventually forced to deposit their money in special bank accounts that capped withdrawals at 250 zloty [Polish unit of currency] per week. Jewish stores were confiscated by the government and sold to new own-

A family of Jewish refugees flees the city of Memel after it passes into Nazi Germany control, April 6, 1939. Uniformed Nazis are laughing and jeer at them. © BETTMANN/CORBIS.

ers. With their financial resources largely depleted, many Jews were soon battling starvation.

As the Nazis expanded their control throughout Europe, Jews in Poland were forced into tiny ghettos. Rural Jews were relocated to these urban areas, which were typically enclosed by high fences and barbed wire. Jews captured in other countries were also transported to Polish ghettos, worsening the already overcrowded conditions. Sealed from the outside, the ghettos subsisted on starvation rations distributed by the Nazis—only 253 calories per person a day.

The Warsaw Ghetto eventually housed close to 400,000 Jews in crowded, unsanitary conditions; death rates from starvation and disease eventually reached 4,000–5,000 per month. Phone lines were cut, mail was interrupted, and the ghetto quickly became a maximum-security prison with Jews often forced to perform involuntary labor in support of the war. Those found outside the camp without permission were shot.

By 1942 the massive number of Jews under Nazi control had become troublesome, and a comprehensive extermination plan was developed. Under this "final solution," execution camps would be built in eastern Poland to carry out thousands of executions daily. Beginning July 22, the Warsaw ghetto was raided and weeks of deportations began. Some Jews avoided capture by hiding, while others claimed marriage to non-Jews or police officers. More than 300,000 Jews were eventually sent from the Warsaw ghetto to their deaths in the camps.

■ **PRIMARY SOURCE**

Diary of the Great Depression

Thursday, 23 July—Tishebov

Disaster after disaster, misfortune after misfortune. The small ghetto has been turned out on to the streets. My nephew Uri arrived at half past seven.

The people were driven out from 42–44 Muranowska Street during the night.

Garbatko, 300 women, 55 children. Last Tuesday in the night. Rain has been falling all day. Weeping. The Jews are weeping. They are hoping for a miracle. The expulsion is continuing. Buildings are blockaded 23 Twarda Street. Terrible scenes. A woman with beautiful hair. A girl, 20 years old, pretty. They are weeping and tearing at their hair. What would Tolstoy have said to this?

On Zamenhof Street the Germans pulled people out of a tram, and killed them on the spot (Muranowska Street).

Friday, 24 July, Six in the Morning

The turmoil is as it was during the days of the bombardment of Warsaw. Jews are running as if insane, with children and bundles of bedding. Buildings on Karmelicka and Nowolipie Streets are being surrounded. Mothers and children wander around like lost sheep: where is my child? Weeping. Another wet day with heavy skies: rain is falling. The scenes on Nowolipie Street. The huge round-up on the streets. Old men and women, boys and girls are being dragged away. The police are carrying out the round-up, and officials of the Jewish community wearing white armbands are assisting them.

The death of Czerniakow yesterday at half past eight in the Jewish community building. As for the reasons: during the ceremony at Grzybowska Street, he said: *"szlag mnie I tak trafi, prozse pani"* (I'll die anyway, Madam).

The round-up was halted at three o'clock. How Jews saved themselves: fictitious marriages with policemen. Guta's marriage to her husband's brother. The savagery of the police during the round-up, the murderous brutality. They drag girls from the rickshaws, empty our flats, and leave the property strewn everywhere. A pogrom and killing…

[Text cut off page.]

…has never been seen.

Merenlender's visit. She and her father were taken the first day. In what kind of train-wagons area the prisoner's kept? According to her they will not even last a night. Many buildings have received an order to present themselves on their own. The manager of 30 Swietojerska Street, Nadzia, gave himself up. People get attacks of hysteria; 11,000 people have been rounded up; 100 policemen held hostage. One of them let himself down on a rope, fell, and was badly wounded. The policeman Zakhajm has been shot. Terrifying rumours about the night. Will there be a pogrom?

Schultz is dismissing 100 Jews. His explanation for his action. The great hunger in the ghetto. Someone saves his sister and a four-year-old child, passing her off as his wife. The child does not give the secret away. He cries out: "daddy!" I am trying to save my mother with a paper from the Jewish Self-help Organization [ZTOS]….

Wednesday, 29 July

The eighth day of the "action" that is continuing at full strength. At the corner of Karmelicka Street—a "wagon." People are thrown up on to it….

"Workshop-mania." Will that save people? The Germans thank the police for their "productive efforts." It is said that they are going to put the police to "work" in other locations. How are the Jews listening to the loudspeakers? … So far eight Jewish policemen have committed suicide. Conditions in the streets get worse every day. Many Jews with identity papers from the Jewish Self-help Organization have been arrested.

A bulldog that had been taught to attack only Jews with armbands in Warsaw-Praga. A Jew was seized by him.

How do Jews hide? In couches, in beds, cellars, attics. The Rozencqajgss were set free for 500 zloty. A memorandum has been handed to the authorities, offering a ransom in return for the halting of the expulsion. No reply has yet been received.

No Germans appear until four in the afternoon. The Jews do everything in an orderly fashion. Each day about 1 per cent of those rounded up, between 60 and 70 people, are killed. They throw loaves of bread into the wagons. Those at the front grab even two or three of them, those at the back get none at all. The savage round-ups in the streets will go on until 1 August. Then those who are not working will receive orders. Children will not be separated from their mothers. Someone called our policemen "gangsters." …

Thursday, 30 July

The ninth day of the "action" that is continuing with all its fearfulness and terror. From five in the morning we hear through the window the whistles of Jewish police and the movement and the running of Jews looking for refuge. Opposite my window, in Nowy Zjazd Street, a policeman chases a young woman and catches her. Her cries and screams are heartbreaking. The blockade on our building. How was the Rajchner family saved? How did I save Mrs. Minc?

Today the post office was opened again. Brandstetter was seized yesterday afternoon by the Germans. He was released at the *Umschlagplatz* [German: "place of change"; train station where Poles were assembled for deportation]. Dr. Fusweg's wife was seized, as was Kilma. They were freed this morning.

From midday yesterday onwards the shooting has not stopped next to our building....

Friday, 31 July

... A woman called Mydlarska jumped up into the wagon after her husband had been taken. In our courtyard a woman threw herself from the third floor—she was starving. Today about 3,000 people were taken away from Walicow and Grzybowska Streets. No attention was paid to identity papers[.] *Zay gezunt! Zay gezunt!* [Goodbye! Goodbye!] a young Jew shouts from the wagon.

The calamity of the "dead souls." 120,000 fictitious food-coupons *(bony)*.

Saturday, 1 August

Outside there is destruction by the sword, and inside there is terror. "The 11th day of action" that gets progressively more terrible and brutal. Germans are in the process of emptying whole buildings and sides of streets. They took about 5,000 people out of 20–22 and other buildings on Nowolipie Street. The turmoil and the terror is appalling. There is a general expulsion of all the occupants of Nowolipie Street between Karmelicka and Smocza Streets. The awful sight; people carrying packages of pillows and bedclothes. No one thinks of moving furniture. Fajnkind says to his sister-in-law: "Hide yourself and your beautiful child! Into the cellar!"

The nightmare of this day surpasses that of all previous days. There is no escape and no refuge. The round-ups never cease. Sagan and Chilinowicz, Sztain, Zolotow, Karcewlcz, Prync, Opoczynski have been seized. Mothers lose their children. A weak old woman is carried on to the bus. The tragedies cannot be captured in words.

The rabbi from 17 Dzlelna Street has been seized and apparently shot. Children walking in the street are seized. The property of those who have been expelled is grabbed by neighbours who are left, or by the new tenants, the "shop"-workers.

Fifty of the customers, 10 staff were removed from the official's kitchen at 30 Nowolipie Street. People who have hidden are shot. I spent the whole day at 20 Nowolipki Street and didn't go to eat, so was saved....

SIGNIFICANCE

As reports of mass executions leaked out of the camps, Jews in the Warsaw Ghetto quickly recognized the peril of their situation. Knowing that deportation meant almost certain death, they determined to fight back. In April, as Nazi troops entered the ghetto to round up more Jews they were met with a hail of gunfire, hand grenades, and incendiary weapons the Jews had smuggled in. After sustaining numerous injuries and deaths the Germans quickly retreated.

The Jewish victory was short-lived. After escaping the ghetto, the German troops were ordered to burn it to the ground. As the residents fled some were shot while others were loaded on train cars for shipment to the camps. A few escaped and continued their battle through the buildings and alleys of Warsaw for close to a month. In early May the Germans used poison gas against the last holdouts, and most of the remaining ghetto residents were killed.

The pursuit of Jewish extermination continued throughout the war. In 1943 Heinrich Himmler, head of the SS and Gestapo, addressed a gathering of Nazi SS officers in Poznan, Poland. His presentation began with a detailed discussion of German armament factories; he then turned to what he described as a "very difficult subject," the ongoing effort to eliminate the Jewish race. In his speech, which can be heard online today, Himmler lamented the softness of many Germans who were reluctant to complete the plan. He reminded the SS officers why the extermination was so important, as well as why it was morally defensible. He also noted that officers unwilling to comply had already been executed. After making his case, he went on to the balance of his three-hour speech.

FURTHER RESOURCES
Books

Gutman, Israel. *Resistance: The Warsaw Ghetto Uprising.* New York: Houghton-Mifflin, 1994.

Kurzman, Dan. *The Bravest Battle: The Twenty-Eight Days of the Warsaw Ghetto Uprising.* Philadelphia, PA: Da Capo Press, 1993.

Rotem, S´imha. *Memoirs of a Warsaw Ghetto Fighter: The Past within Me.* New Haven, Connecticut: Yale University Press, 2002.

Periodicals

Einwohner, Rachel L. "Identity Work and Collective Action in a Repressive Context: Jewish Resistance on the 'Aryan Side' of the Warsaw Ghetto." *Social Problems.* 53 (2006): 38–56.

Nordholt, Annelies Schulte. "Re-Enacting the Warsaw Ghetto." *Journal of Modern Jewish Studies.* 3(2004):183–194.

Scott, A. O. "Surviving the Warsaw Ghetto against Steep Odds." *New York Times.* 152 (December 27, 2002): E19.

Web sites

The Holocaust History Project. "Heinrich Himmler's Speech at Poznan." <http://www.holocaust-history.org/himmler-poznan/index.shtml> (accessed June 14, 2006).

Public Broadcasting Service. "The Warsaw Ghetto Uprising (April 19–May 16, 1943)." <http://www.pbs.org/wgbh/amex/holocaust/peopleevents/pandeAMEX103.html> (accessed June 14, 2006).

Service on the Homefront

Poster

By: Anonymous

Date: March 3, 1942

Source: *Library of Congress.* "By the People, For the People: Posters from the WPA, 1936–1943." <http://memory.loc.gov/ammem/wpaposters/wpahome.html> (accessed July 23, 2006).

About the Author: The United States Library of Congress is the nation's official library, with responsibility for collecting and organizing historically significant documents, photographs, and digital media.

INTRODUCTION

In 1940, Europe was consumed with war. Under the Lend-Lease Act signed in March 1941, the United States provided arms to its allies in Europe. However, the nation continued its isolationist foreign policies adopted after World War I. Remnants of the Great Depression still permeated American society as approximately eight million people were still unemployed. In addition, the U.S. military in 1939 was the eighteenth largest in the world and not prepared for a large-scale conflict. On December 7, 1941, the Japanese launched a surprise attack on U.S. bases in the Pacific. The most damaging attack was at Pearl Harbor, Hawaii; the two-hour attack dealt a blow to the military arsenal housed there by damaging eighteen warships, destroying 164 aircrafts, and killing 2,400 service members and civilians. On December 8, President Roosevelt asked Congress to declare war on Japan. Following the declaration, the allies of Japan, Germany, and Italy declared war on the United States, thus leading to a two-front war—one in the pacific and one in Europe. In an address on December 9, 1941, President Roosevelt stated, "We are not at war. We are now in it—all the way. Every single man, woman, and child is a partner in the most tremendous undertaking of our American History.

PRIMARY SOURCE

SERVICE ON THE HOMEFRONT

See primary source image.

SIGNIFICANCE

Roosevelt's philosophy of a total war meant that all aspects of society and all levels of the economy needed to be mobilized in order to out-produce and overwhelm the enemy. As such, the U.S. economy shifted into a war production economy and the majority of resources were channeled into war production. Existing industries began to support the war by changing production to assist in the speedy raising, arming, and outfitting of the U.S. military. Roosevelt called the nation an "Arsenal of Democracy" and the government began campaigns to handle the shortages caused by the war. In 1942, the Food Rationing program began and farmers, families, and individuals were admonished to use spare land to develop victory gardens.

Shortly after the attack on Pearl Harbor, the Japanese invaded Burma. By gaining control over the southeast Asian country, the Japanese effectively cut off the major resource for rubber. The shortage of rubber, as well as the need to mobilize and arm the military quickly, led to salvage and recycling campaigns beginning in 1942. Everyday trash had a value to the war effort and the government encouraged Americans to cut back on certain consumer goods and recycle other materials. Metal, paper, rubber, and old rags were used in war production. Shortages of copper, needed for assault or communication wire on the battlefield, led to pennies being made out of steel. The shortage of nickel affected the production of the five-cent piece. Steel and aluminum that was salvaged from old cars, bed frames, radiators, pots, and tins were used to make everything from ammunition to ships. Even household waste fat was recycled to use the glycerin, a key ingredient in explosives ammunition.

In October 1942, the Conservation Division of the War Production Board created a program to mobilize school-aged children to participate in the salvage program, "Get in the Scrap." Communities were encouraged to activate "junior commandos" to scour their assigned areas for scrap metal that could be used to keep the war factories running. The greatest need was for iron and steel to make guns, tanks and jeeps. Rubber was also a necessity and could come from old tires,

PRIMARY SOURCE

Service on the Homefront: This World War II-era poster promotes the idea that every family member can aid the war effort. THE LIBRARY OF CONGRESS.

A poster promoting wartime recycling of scrap paper and other materials. © SEATTLE POST-INTELLIGENCER COLLECTION; MUSEUM OF HISTORY AND INDUSTRY/CORBIS.

tubes, and garden hoses. The War Production Board announced that one tire could provide the rubber needed to make twelve gas masks. One pail could provide three bayonets and one copper pot made eighty-four rounds of ammunition for the automatic rifle.

From 1940 until the Japanese surrender in 1945, the United States produced 300,000 aircrafts, 86,000 tanks, and 12.5 million rifles. The shipyards were stocked with 107 aircraft carriers and 352 destroyers. As a result of the massive mobilization of the American economy into war production, the United States supplied a great majority of the war supplies used by the Allies in the war and produced twice the amount of materials as the Japanese, Germans, and Italians. Initiatives such as the salvage and recycling programs allowed civilians to feel that they played a vital role in the victory.

FURTHER RESOURCES
Web sites

National World War II Museum. "History of World War II." <http://www.ddaymuseum.org/education/history_war.html> (accessed July 22, 2006).

Southern Methodist University. "Victory Garden Insect Guide 1944." <http://digitallibrary.smu.edu/cul/gir/ww2/pdf/p0025.pdf> (accessed July 22, 2006).

Southern Methodist University. "Victory Garden Leader's Handbook 1943." <http://digitallibrary.smu.edu/cul/gir/ww2/pdf/p0159.pdf> (accessed July 22, 2006).

Plant a Victory Garden

Photograph

By: Anonymous

Date: 1943

Source: Corbis

About the Photographer: This photograph is part of the collection of the Corbis Corporation, headquartered in Seattle, with a worldwide archive of over seventy million images.

INTRODUCTION

In 1940, war spread across Europe. Although the United States provided arms to its allies, it continued the isolationist foreign policies adopted after World War I. As the United States continued to emerge from the Great Depression, there were still approximately eight million unemployed, and the economy was run by New Deal programs. On December 7, 1941, however, the Japanese launched a surprise attack on American forces in Pearl Harbor, Hawaii. The attack, which lasted almost two hours, damaged or sank eighteen warships, destroyed 180 aircraft, and killed more than 2,300. On December 8, President Roosevelt asked Congress to declare war on Japan. Following the declaration, Japan's allies, Germany and Italy, declared war on the United States, thus leading to a two-front war—the Pacific and Europe.

The American economy shifted into overdrive and a majority of resources were channeled into the war effort. Existing industries changed production to arm and outfit the U.S. military and the government began campaigns to address the shortages caused by the war. In 1942, the food rationing program began to avoid public anger over shortages. Coupons were distributed based on family size. Red stamps rationed meats, butter, fats, and oils. Blue stamps rationed canned and frozen fruits and vegetables, bottled juices, and dried beans.

Plant a Victory Garden: A World War II-era poster advocating family gardening and conservation as means of aiding the war effort. © SWIM INK 2, LLC/CORBIS.

When it became apparent that the rationed amount would not feed an entire family, the "Food for Victory" campaign was launched to maximize food production around the nation. The campaign encouraged families to eat leftovers, grow their own fruits and vegetables, and preserve those foods not used immediately. The government encouraged farms to increase production, and backyards and baseball fields were tilled and planted as part of the war effort. Urban areas established community gardens, and schools cultivated their own plots as well. This freed food production for distribution to service members, allies, and workers on the front lines.

By 1943, state and local committees were created to encourage the creation of victory gardens, and the Department of Agriculture published pamphlets with information on garden care and insect control as well as canning and preserving food. Gardeners were provided with special victory garden fertilizer through the Department of Agriculture and War Production Board. Newspapers printed pictures of successful gardens and magazines published recipes that used preserved food.

PRIMARY SOURCE

PLANT A VICTORY GARDEN
See primary source image.

A child makes use of a ration book to get supplies for his family, 1943. During World War II, many basic supplies were rationed out by the government. © CORBIS.

SIGNIFICANCE

The Office of War Information printed a poster that encouraged the American people to "Do more with less, so they'll have more." Victory gardens and food rationing made more canned goods available for troops on the front lines. The victory garden symbolized the war effort on the homefront, an idea echoed in a 1943 Department of Agriculture publication, which asserted that each successful garden was a blow to the enemy.

Gardeners were admonished to avoid abandoning an "army" of vegetables to the "enemy" of weeds, because every bit of food was needed to win the war. Even squandering or misusing seeds was considered unpatriotic, and insects that could destroy crops were described as "Japanazis." People were also encouraged to share tools and not purchase items that would take steel away from war production.

By 1945, there were approximately twenty million victory gardens around the United States. The gardens produced around one billion tons of fruits and vegetables, or about forty percent of American consumption.

FURTHER RESOURCES

Web sites

D-Day: The National World War II Museum. "History of World War II." <http://www.ddaymuseum.org/education/history_war.html> (accessed June 15, 2006).

Southern Methodist University Digital Library. "Victory Garden Insect Guide." <http://digitallibrary.smu.edu/cul/gir/ww2/pdf/a0034.pdf> (accessed June 15, 2006).

———. "Victory Garden Leader's Handbook." <http://digitallibrary.smu.edu/cul/gir/ww2/pdf/a0005.pdf> (accessed June 15, 2006).

Family in Fallout Shelter

Photograph

By: Unknown

Date: May 19, 1955

Source: Bettmann / Corbis.

About the Author: This photograph resides in the Bettmann Archives of Corbis Corporation, an image group headquartered in Seattle with a worldwide archive of over seventy million images.

INTRODUCTION

At the end of World War II in 1945, the United States was the world's most powerful nation, the sole country possessing atomic weapons. Though several world powers had joined the race to harness atomic power for military use, the United States had prevailed, testing its first fission weapon in July 1945 and dropping two atomic bombs on Japan the following month. America began producing an arsenal of atomic weapons after the war, confident that it would maintain its atomic monopoly for up to a decade. Just four years later, however, Soviet scientists matched the American achievement, detonating their own atomic weapon and achieving parity in the atomic age. American citizens began to recognize their vulnerability as the Soviet military began constructing its own atomic arsenal.

In 1953, President Eisenhower made his famous Atoms for Peace speech at the United Nations. In that speech, he noted that the United States had exploded more than forty atomic and nuclear weapons as part of its weapons development programs. While the short-term effects of atomic weapons were well documented, scientists were just beginning to understand the long-term dangers they posed. In particular, the danger posed by nuclear fallout was beginning to become evident.

When a nuclear weapon is detonated, tons of radioactive debris including ash, dust, and unspent nuclear fuel are propelled high into the atmosphere. Much of this debris falls back to earth near the detonation site but some of it is carried away by upper level winds, spreading contamination over a vast area. One 1954 thermonuclear weapon test in the South Pacific created an unexpectedly large fallout cloud, contaminating several nearby islands as well as U.S. naval vessels nearby. The crew of a Japanese fishing boat was heavily irradiated and one crew member eventually died, creating a diplomatic confrontation with Japan. The event became the most serious U.S. radiological incident of the Cold War (1946–1991).

As the potential for a Soviet nuclear attack rose, Americans began an intensive program to prepare for such a possibility. Underground radiation shelters, stocked with survival supplies, were constructed throughout the nation. While these bunkers were primarily intended for government officials and local authorities, some public buildings also built shelters. Several thousand Americans constructed fallout shelters in their homes or beneath their property, reinforcing the shelters with steel or concrete and stocking them with survival supplies. The federal Office of

PRIMARY SOURCE

Family in Fallout Shelter: A photo ad for a do-it-yourself fallout shelter from the Walter Kiddie Nuclear Laboratories company, 1955. © BETTMANN/CORBIS.

Civil Defense sold shelter supplies and even provided shelter plans that homeowners could follow, while commercial contractors began offering custom-designed and single-piece fallout shelters for home installation. Many of these old shelters can still be seen today.

PRIMARY SOURCE

FAMILY IN FALLOUT SHELTER

See primary source image.

SIGNIFICANCE

As the American public began to understand the degree of damage a nuclear attack would inflict, the idea of building home fallout shelters lost favor. No U.S. administration ever actively endorsed the construction of extensive fallout shelters. Most focused instead on the assumption that the United States and Soviet arsenals were so large as to render a first-strike unthinkable. Fallout shelters were more widely deployed in Europe and in the Eastern Block than in North America. Switzerland in particular has invested heavily in shelters: Swiss building codes require the inclusion of underground shelters adequate to house the people living or working within each structure. That small nation currently has more than 250,000 shelters along with extensive stores of food and other survival supplies.

While the Cold War fascination with fallout shelters was short-lived, the idea of seeking safety by burrowing underground remains viable, because excavating provides the simplest and least expensive method of creating a radiation-resistant space. In the weeks following the September 11, 2001, terrorist attacks, Americans began reconsidering the potential value of fallout shelters. The possibility that terrorists might gain access to nuclear materials and detonate a dirty bomb, scattering radioactive material over a wide area, caused interest in home fallout shelters to climb. Basic models can be installed in an existing basement at a cost of several thousand dollars; more elaborate systems with a generator, decontamination equipment, and blast-proof doors can top $300,000. As of 2006, the Department of Homeland Security was not recommending that home fallout shelters be constructed.

FURTHER RESOURCES

Books

Fradkin, Philip L. *Fallout: An American Nuclear Tragedy.* Boulder, Colo.: Johnson Books, 2004.

Rose, Kenneth D. *One Nation Underground: The Fallout Shelter in American Culture.* New York: New York University Press, 2001.

Ross, Richard. *Waiting for the End of the World.* New York: Princeton Architectural Press, 2004.

Periodicals

Bethell, Tom. "With Enough Shovels." *American Spectator* 35 (2002): 78–81.

"Gimme Shelter: Underground America." *Bulletin of the Atomic Scientists* 59 (2003): 38–39.

Willard, Rhoda and Anitra Bascom have moved into their basement with bedding, food and battery powered radio to demomstrate FCDA recommendations for fall-out precautions, Colesville, Maryland. © BETTMANN/CORBIS.

Lemley, Brad. "To the End of the World." *Discover* 24 (2003) 66–73.

Web sites

National Security Archive. "The Atomic Bomb and the End of World War II." August 5, 2005 <http://www.gwu.edu/~nsarchiv/NSAEBB/NSAEBB162/index.htm> (accessed June 20, 2006).

Nebraska Studies. "The Family Fallout Shelter." <http://www.nebraskastudies.org/0900/frameset_reset.html?http://www.nebraskastudies.org/0900/stories/0901_0132.html> (accessed June 20, 2006).

Public Broadcasting Service. "Race for the Superbomb." <http://www.pbs.org/wgbh/amex/bomb/timeline/indextxt.html> (accessed June 20, 2006).

Life's Biggest Lemon

News article

By: Nguyen-Vu Nguyen

Date: March 1, 1994

Source: Nguyen, Nguyen-Vu. "Life's Biggest Lemon." *Refugee Magazine*, (March 1, 1994).

About the Author: The United Nations is an international mediation and aid agency. Its various divisions help mediate political disputes, police militarily unstable regions, and work to improve living conditions throughout the world. The Office of the United Nations High Commissioner for Refugees works to protect the rights of refugees and to help them reach safety in another country. Nguyen-Vu Nguyen's family were refugees from Vietnam who immigrated to the United States in the 1980's.

INTRODUCTION

Each year, several million people throughout the world are forced to relocate unexpectedly. In some cases, they move because of war or civil unrest, while in others they are driven out by famine or the risk of political persecution. These involuntary travelers are known as refugees. In 1998, the United Nations estimated refugee numbers worldwide at approximately thirteen million.

Because of its friendly political climate and strong economy, the United States is a desirable destination for many refugees. Both the United Nations and the United States government believe that the best solution for most refugees is a safe return to their country of origin; however, in many situations such a return is either politically impossible or would subject the refugee to extreme danger. In these cases, refugees may apply to be admitted to the United States. The U.S. Department of State sets quotas for the number of refugees admitted each year; in 2005, the United

A Vietnamese-American family portrait. © CATHERINE KARNOW/CORBIS.

States admitted a total of 70,000 refugees, with the total divided among six geographic regions worldwide.

Refugees generally find themselves ripped from anything familiar and thrust into a strange new environment. While the details of each refugee's story vary, most share a common core of experiences. The Center for Victims of Torture in Minneapolis conducted a study of refugee experiences and found that each stage of the refugee experience involves a unique set of stressors, particularly for children and teens.

On the most basic level, refugees lose their material possessions such as homes and land; in many cases, they also lose their social status, economic security, and extended family connections. For children, the loss of familiar surroundings and the supporting community can be a terrifying experience, particularly since such changes are unexpected and difficult for children to understand.

The journey toward safety is often difficult for refugees, with many stops along the way and a great deal of uncertainty. In many cases, refugees are powerless, forced to depend on national and international agencies for food and shelter. Health problems are common, and children and teens are again subjected to extreme stress. Many refugee children are exposed to malnutrition, assault, and death during their flight, and some are separated from their parents. Children are frequently aware of stress among the adults around them but are often not told of the details.

After arriving at a new home, refugee families still face struggles. In many cases, refugees arrive with few resources, little money, and no useful job skills. Housing in their new country may be in high crime areas, and an inability to communicate often hampers efforts to find employment. New housing arrangements may force multiple families or generations to co-habit, further disrupting previously established relationships. Discrimination is also a problem for many refugees as they try to retain aspects of their old culture while also assimilating into their new surroundings.

Although the challenges facing refugees are daunting, many find opportunities to excel; in many cases, the children of refugee parents are able to quickly settle into their new surroundings and begin new lives. They also frequently play a key role in helping their parents connect to the surrounding culture.

PRIMARY SOURCE

In the American South, where my Vietnamese family made our second home, there is a saying: "If life throws you a lemon, make lemonade." That lemon, for us, is our refugee experience. And we have made the largest glass of lemonade from it. July 1981. My father completed his sixth visit to the local government's office. Since his release from the concentration camp, he had gone there monthly to inform the Vietnamese authorities about the details of his life. That weekend, my family packed a change of clothes for what I was told would be "a long journey".

A nine-day voyage on a wooden boat brought us to Malaysia. My family waited at the camp for a year before we were flown to the United States. Like many refugees, we restarted life in America with several disadvantages. We had no relatives here. Everything that was familiar to us was left behind in Viet Nam. Our English was not good enough to tell people at the local Thrift Store that we needed shoes, and the prospect for employment was not at all certain.

After the refugee experience, the task of recreating meaning and purpose in life was the greatest challenge and perhaps most valuable achievement for my family. During those years, waking up and facing life each day were acts of courage for my parents. Life was not prefabricated. One had the option of hiding inside the apartment and drowning under the demands of the new environment. The alternative was to stand up and face life with the ferocity of a hungry canine when it sees its first prey. How much strength and courage my parents have had in order to continue life under such circumstances!

American society is completely foreign to a refugee. It differs from his native culture in language, customs and attitudes. For a person without the support of a family, life can be intolerable. Fortunately, my family has been the source of comfort and protection for all of us ever since we escaped Viet Nam. My parents have always absorbed the hardest financial and emotional shocks. For many summers, my father would take on a second job to earn extra money so that his children could attend camps, take music lessons or join the Little League baseball teams. We never had to interrupt our education to work and support the family. My parents took this burden upon themselves.

In addition, they have acted as a repository of Vietnamese culture for us. As a young refugee looks around, he sees the ubiquitous American culture, but often his own culture is rapidly disappearing. My siblings and I in return have served as our parents' liaison to the larger society. It is through us that they reached out and made friends with other Americans. Twelve years have passed since my family first became refugees. Today, we no longer have to lift crates at warehouses on night shift. There is no more washing dishes or waiting tables at ethnic restaurants. Instead of survival strategies, we now discuss Christian ethics and social issues at our dinner table. Many of my parents' dreams have been fulfilled.

Through the church and work places, my parents have found ways to become contributing members to the American society that embraced them. My father founded a Boy Scouts of America unit for Vietnamese youths in our city. He also teaches Bible classes in the church. My mother, likewise, is socially engaged in her work to assist immigrant students from Mexico, Viet Nam, Somalia, Haiti and Bosnia. She also worked at World Relief to help refugees adjust to their new lives in the United States.

As for my siblings, when asked, "How have your refugee experiences affected your outlook on life and your future aspirations?" my 19-year-old sister thoughtfully responded: "It made me more sympathetic to the needs of people who have difficulties defining their places in society." She taught summer programs to introduce art into the lives of Vietnamese and African American youths. She presently studies English at Amherst College and plans to become a physician specializing in tropical medicine.

My brother is 20 years old and studies biology at Presbyterian College. He finds that our family's refugee experience has deepened his understanding of human suffering. "A homeless man in the street of Boston lacks not only money," he told me. "You often see people giving spare change to these poor folks, but they are afraid to stop and talk." Having once been a refugee, he knows what it is like in the periphery of human society. "This homeless man also needs human companionship, so I stop and talk to him." My brother has also been involved with former President Jimmy Carter's project to build homes for low-income families in urban areas. He hopes to become a missionary doctor.

I, too, realize that the refugee experience has carved deep into my physical and emotional being. To recapitulate, it is the biggest lemon that life has ever thrown me, but I have also made the largest lemonade for myself. Hardships give birth to endurance, and suffering yields greater compassion. Every time I think that any task I have here at Harvard is unmanageable, I am reminded that nothing is as difficult as picking up the pieces of one's life.

Like my father, I see that the refugee experience is only temporary. For our family it lasted a year, but its impact is felt for a lifetime.

SIGNIFICANCE

Whereas voluntary immigration is often undertaken following years of planning and preparation, refugees frequently arrive with little more than their clothing and a few personal effects. For many refugee families, the trauma of being thrown into an unfamiliar setting tends to draw them closer to one another in the earliest days following their arrival, while assimilation difficulties may lead to generational rifts in later years. Like many traumatic events, the experience of being a refugee produces differing results, in some cases strengthening families and in other cases weakening them.

In 2005, a small group of Russian families arrived in a small town in west Texas. Their journey actually began more than a decade earlier when they fled persecution in their home country of Turkey; they soon found that their new home in Russia offered little more in the way of security. Upon arrival in the United States, they were given housing and a meager stipend for several months and encouraged to find employment and learn English.

The refugee children began attending public schools and picked up English fairly quickly, while their parents studied in language classes held at a local church. While hard-working and highly motivated, they faced tremendous challenges finding employment; some of the men found entry-level work in a local bakery, but the labor was mindless and paid little. In a few months, a new group of refugees arrived, beginning the cycle again. Numerous similar refugee communities exist throughout the United States today.

FURTHER RESOURCES
Books
Hathaway, James C. *The Rights of Refugees under International Law*. New York: Cambridge University Press, 2005.

Office of the United Nations High Commissioner for Refugees. *The State of the World's Refugees: Human Displacement in the New Millennium*. New York: Oxford University Press, 2006.

Pipher, Mary. *The Middle of Everywhere: Helping Refugees Enter the American Community*. New York: Harcourt Books, 2002.

Periodicals
Caesar, Mike. "Post-9/11 Law Keeps Colombian Refugees Out of US." *Christian Science Monitor* 32 (2006): 551—568.

Nawyn, Stephanie J. "Faith, Ethnicity, and Culture in Refugee Resettlement." *American Behavioral Scientist* 49 (2006): 1509–1527.

Prothero, Mitch. "A Wellspring of Anger." *U.S. News & World Report* 140 (June 26, 2006): 34—35.

Web sites

Human Rights Watch. "Refugees." <http://hrw.org/doc/> (accessed July 13, 2006).

U.S. Citizenship and Immigration Services. "Refugees." <http://www.uscis.gov/graphics/services/refugees/index.htm> (accessed July 13, 2006).

U.S. Committee for Refugees and Immigrants. <http://www.refugees.org/> (accessed July 13, 2006).

Immigrants Shunning the Idea of Assimilation

Newspaper article

By: William Branigin

Date: May 25, 1998

Source: Branigin, William. *Washington Post*. "Immigrants Shunning the Idea of Assimilation." (May 25, 1998).

About the Author: William Branigin has worked as both a staff writer and as a foreign correspondent with the *Washington Post* for more than twenty years. In 2000, he won the Eugene Katz Award from the Center for Immigration Studies in recognition of excellence in his coverage of immigration issues.

INTRODUCTION

The history of the development of a distinct American society has involved a multitude of different peoples becoming a part of the societal fabric of the nation over a period of more than 350 years. The manner in which these various immigrant peoples integrated themselves into the existing American society from the colonial period to approximately 1960 generally, but never exclusively, conformed to the melting pot theory. The melting pot is the popular American metaphor for assimilation that describes the generally accepted belief that the best immigrant peoples were those who adopted the ways of the American culture that they found on their arrival.

The first colonists in the period after 1620 were predominately Northern European peoples. By the time that the Declaration of Independence was issued in 1776, there existed a relatively homogeneous, English speaking Protestant community along the American eastern seaboard. The immigrant peoples that

followed tended to meld readily into this early American society.

By 1850, concerns about new Irish Catholic immigration that appeared distinct from the American melting pot prompted the formation of the American Party (the Know-Nothings), an organization that was emphatically nativist in its political and cultural outlook. The nativist movement was less pronounced after the Civil War, as waves of immigrants arrived to work in the rapidly expanding American manufacturing sectors. The political recognition of what types of immigrants were desirable for their ability to become a part of the cultural mainstream, and those to be excluded for their differences was made apparent in the 1880s. *The Chinese Exclusion Act of 1882* was followed by a series of legislative enactments to prevent other Asian immigration, and particularly persons from India and Japan, from taking permanent residence in the United States. The Asians were seen as undesirable in that many Americans believed that they would never assimilate themselves into American culture. It is a historical footnote to the attitude of the United States to Oriental persons that in the war years between 1942 and 1945, persons of Japanese ancestry were interned (the majority of whom were American citizens), whereas only a miniscule number of persons of German and Italian heritage were similarly held.

American immigration laws were significantly liberalized beginning in the 1960s and for the first time in American history, the immigration patterns included persons from a diverse range of ethnic, cultural, and religious backgrounds. Mexican, Hispanic and south East Asian peoples now settled in large numbers throughout America, particularly in its urban areas. A wide range of legal and government policy decisions created an environment where the pressure to assimilate into existing American society was less pronounced than in earlier generations.

In 2006, it was estimated that approximately thirty-three million persons living in the United States were born in another country, a population greater than that of Canada.

■ PRIMARY SOURCE

Immigrants Shunning Idea of Assimilation

OMAHA—Night is falling on South Omaha, and Maria Jacinto is patting tortillas for the evening meal in the kitchen of the small house she shares with her husband and five children. Like many others in her neighborhood, where most of the residents are Mexican immigrants, the Jacinto household mixes the old country with the new.

As Jacinto, who speaks only Spanish, stresses a need to maintain the family's Mexican heritage, her eldest son, a bilingual 11-year-old who wears a San Francisco 49ers jacket and has a paper route, comes in and joins his brothers and sisters in the living room to watch "The Simpsons."

Jacinto became a U.S. citizen last April, but she does not feel like an American. In fact, she seems resistant to the idea of assimilating into U.S. society.

"I think I'm still a Mexican," she says. "When my skin turns white and my hair turns blonde, then I'll be an American."

In many ways, the experiences of the Jacinto family are typical of the gradual process of assimilation that has pulled generations of immigrants into the American mainstream. That process is nothing new to Omaha, which drew waves of Czech, German and Irish immigrants early this century.

But in the current immigration wave, something markedly different is happening here in the middle of the great American "melting pot."

Not only are the demographics of the United States changing in profound and unprecedented ways, but so too are the very notions of assimilation and the melting pot that have been articles of faith in the American self-image for generations. *E Pluribus Unum* (From Many, One) remains the national motto, but there no longer seems to be a consensus about what that should mean.

There is a sense that, especially as immigrant populations reach a critical mass in many communities, it is no longer the melting pot that is transforming them, but they who are transforming American society.

American culture remains a powerful force—for better or worse—that influences people both here and around the world in countless ways. But several factors have combined in recent years to allow immigrants to resist, if they choose, the Americanization that had once been considered irresistible.

In fact, the very concept of assimilation is being called into question as never before. Some sociologists argue that the melting pot often means little more than "Anglo conformity" and that assimilation is not always a positive experience—for either society or the immigrants themselves. And with today's emphasis on diversity and ethnicity, it has become easier than ever for immigrants to avoid the melting pot entirely. Even the metaphor itself is changing, having fallen out of fashion completely with many immigration advocacy and ethnic groups. They prefer such terms as the "salad bowl" and the "mosaic," metaphors that convey more of a sense of separateness in describing this nation of immigrants.

"It's difficult to adapt to the culture here," said Maria Jacinto, 32, who moved to the United States 10 years ago with her husband, Aristeo Jacinto, 36. "In the Hispanic tradition, the family comes first, not money. It's important for our children not to be influenced too much by the gueros," she said, using a term that means "blondies" but that she employs generally in reference to Americans. "I don't want my children to be influenced by immoral things."

Over the blare of the television in the next room, she asked, "Not all families here are like the Simpsons, are they?"

Among socially conservative families such as the Jacintos, who initially moved to California from their village in Mexico's Guanajuato state, then migrated here in 1988 to find jobs in the meatpacking industry, bad influences are a constant concern. They see their children assimilating, but often to the worst aspects of American culture.

Her concerns reflect some of the complexities and ambivalence that mark the assimilation process these days. Immigrants such as the Jacintos are here to stay but remain wary of their adoptive country. According to sociologists, they are right to be concerned.

"If assimilation is a learning process, it involves learning good things and bad things," said Ruben G. Rumbaut, a sociology professor at Michigan State University. "It doesn't always lead to something better."

At work, not only in Omaha but in immigrant communities across the country, is a process often referred to as "segmented" assimilation, in which immigrants follow different paths to incorporation in U.S. society. These range from the classic American ideal of blending into the vast middle class, to a "downward assimilation" into an adversarial underclass, to a buffered integration into "immigrant enclaves." Sometimes, members of the same family end up taking sharply divergent paths, especially children and their parents.

The ambivalence of assimilation can cut both ways. Many native-born Americans also seem to harbor mixed feelings about the process. As a nation, the United States increasingly promotes diversity, but there are underlying concerns that the more emphasis there is on the factors that set people apart, the more likely that society will end up divided.

With Hispanics, especially Mexicans, accounting for an increasing proportion of U.S. population growth, it is this group, more than any other, that is redefining the melting pot.

Hispanics now have overtaken blacks as the largest minority group in Nebraska and will become the biggest minority in the country within the next seven years, according to Census Bureau projections. The nation's 29 million Hispanics, the great majority of them from Mexico, have thus become the main focus for questions about how the United States today is assimilating immigrants, or how it is being transformed.

In many places, new Hispanic immigrants have tended to cluster in "niche" occupations, live in segregated neighborhoods and worship in separate churches. In this behavior they are much like previous groups of immigrants. But their heavy concentrations in certain parts of the country, their relatively close proximity to their native lands and their sheer numbers give this wave of immigrants an unprecedented potential to change the way the melting pot traditionally has worked.

Never before have so many immigrants come from a single country—Mexico—or from a single linguistic source—Spanish-speaking Latin America. Since 1970, more than half of the estimated 20 million foreign-born people who have settled in the United States, legally and illegally, have been Spanish speakers.

Besides sheer numbers, several factors combine to make this influx unprecedented in the history of American immigration. This is the first time that such large numbers of people are immigrating from a contiguous country. And since most have flowed into relatively few states, congregating heavily in the American Southwest, Mexican Americans have the capacity to develop much greater cohesion than previous immigrant groups. Today Hispanics, mostly of Mexican origin, make up 31 percent of the population of California and 28 percent of the population of Texas.

In effect, that allows Mexican Americans to "perpetuate themselves as a separate community and even strengthen their sense of separateness if they chose to, or felt compelled to," said David M. Kennedy, a professor of American history at Stanford University.

To be sure, assimilation today often follows the same pattern that it has for generations. The children of immigrants, especially those who were born in the United States or come here at a young age, tend to learn English quickly and adopt American habits. Often they end up serving as translators for their parents. Schools exert an important assimilating influence, as does America's consumer society.

But there are important differences in the way immigrants adapt these days, and the influences on them can be double-edged. Gaps in income, education and poverty levels between new immigrants and the native-born are widening, and many of the newcomers are becoming stuck in dead-end jobs with little upward mobility.

Previous waves of immigrants also arrived unskilled and poorly educated. What has changed, however, is the nature of the U.S. economy, which increasingly requires education and skills to assure an upward path. Although the children of these low-income, poorly educated immigrants may grow up fluent in English, acquire more education than their parents and assimilate in other ways, research shows that "they will lag well behind other students, particularly in college attendance," said Georges Vernez, director of the Center for Research on Immigration Policy at the RAND Corp.

"Today, for instance, native-born Hispanic youths are 30 percent less likely to go on to college after high school and three times less likely to graduate from college than non-Hispanic white students," he told a House hearing last month.

Nationally, Hispanic youths are the most likely to abandon the classroom. Their dropout rate of 29.4 percent is more than double the rate for black Americans and four times higher than the rate for non-Hispanic whites.

Yet the statistics also show that the dropout rate for second-generation Hispanic students is higher than that for first generation youths, suggesting that assimilation does not always work as intended.

Sociologist Rumbaut said his research has shown that the most disciplined, hardest-working and respectful students "tend to be the most recently arrived." They are the ones "who have not been here long enough to be Americanized into bad habits, into a Beavis and Butthead perspective of the world."

Since the children of immigrants tend to adapt much faster than their parents, the result is often tension and divisions within families. Immigrants who arrive as adults to escape poverty tend to view their lives here as an improvement over what they left behind, but their children often compare their circumstances to those of other Americans and find themselves lacking. Some gravitate toward a growing gang culture that offers them an identity and an outlet for their alienation, according to researchers.

In Omaha, police, teachers and social workers attribute rising youth gang activity in part to an influx of Hispanic families from California. Ironically, many left California precisely to escape a violent gang subculture there but ended up spreading the infection.

"A number of families who moved from L.A. brought children who were already involved with gangs," said the Rev. Damian Zuerlein, the parish priest of the nearby Roman Catholic church, Our Lady of Guadalupe, which caters to the community's growing Mexican population.

Omaha now has an estimated 1,800 "hard-core" gang members, police say. Two main competing Hispanic gangs are believed to have several hundred members each.

And, as it is across the nation, the high school dropout rate among Hispanics is a growing concern here. In the 1995-96 school year, the most recent for which statistics are available, 12 percent of Hispanic students dropped out of Omaha public secondary schools, double the rate for non-Hispanic whites. According to Mario Remijio, a teacher at South High School here, many Hispanic teenagers drop out to get jobs under pressure from their parents.

In many cases, argues University of Nebraska sociologist Lourdes Gouveia, the problem is not a lack of assimilation to American culture, but too much of it.

"An attachment to one's home country, culture and language can be very positive" for immigrant children in U.S. schools, contends Gouveia. These attachments "help maintain a sense of identity and self-respect when the family drops in status," as often happens when foreigners immigrate. As a result, the Venezuelan-born Gouveia said, citing studies by Rumbaut and others, students who are the least "assimilated" often do better in school than other immigrants and sometimes top even the native born.

On the other hand, some critics contend, the United States should not be abandoning a concept—the Melting Pot—that has served the country well for generations, helping to maintain unity through two world wars. They worry that the traditional U.S. commitment to assimilation is breaking down from an incessant advance of "multiculturalism."

"On the whole, there is an American national identity that immigrants ought to be encouraged to assimilate into," said John J. Miller, author of a new book on the issue.

For all the concerns, the recent wave of immigration has brought some notable benefits to Omaha. The city is now home to about 20,000 Latinos, the vast majority of them concentrated in South Omaha. By all accounts, the influx has revived that part of the city. New businesses owned by Hispanics and other immigrants have sprouted up, lending an air of vibrancy to South Omaha's main street.

"Ten years ago, this area was dying," said the Rev. Zuerlein. "Stores were closing, and people were moving out."

The wave of immigration also has stirred new ethnic consciousness among longtime Latino residents, notably the assimilated descendants of Mexicans who came to Nebraska in the early part of this century to work on the railroad and harvest beets.

"When I was a kid, the Hispanics here all just about knew each other," said Virgil Armendariz, a Mexican American businessman who grew up in Omaha. "Now there are hundreds of families....Until recently, we were pretty much invisible."

The influx has helped revive long-forgotten Mexican customs, he said, such as the special celebration of the quinceanera, or 15th birthday. "People who were born here are starting to learn more about their culture," Armendariz said.

Next door to the Jacintos, Matt and Sharon Swanson are one of the few native-born families left in the neighborhood. They agree that the immigrant influx has "revitalized" the nearby main drag but say that gang activities, including drive-by shootings and occasional murders, have become a big problem.

"I see a lack of respect for other people's property," said Mickey Dalton, 50, a friend of the Swansons who lives nearby. The neighborhood is destined to turn even more Hispanic, with little prospect for assimilation, he said.

"They're sticking to their own," Dalton said. "When the Czechs moved here, the big push was to learn English. You don't see that so much now. A lot of them don't want to learn English."

At the Guadalupe church recreation hall, several of the young Mexican immigrants who gather weekly say they want to learn the language but find it difficult because they came here in their teens or early twenties and immediately entered a Spanish-speaking milieu. Some say their biggest problems come from Mexican Americans, known as Chicanos, who mock their attempts to speak English.

"I want to join the U.S. Army or Air Force, but because of the language, I can't," said Jose Fernandez, a lean 22-year-old from Guadalajara who briefly attended high school here before dropping out.

"When I'm around Chicanos, I feel ashamed to speak English," said Margaro Ponce, 23, who came to Omaha two years ago to join relatives. "Instead of helping you, they make fun of you," he said in Spanish.

Guillermina Becerra, 22, arrived nearly seven years ago and spent three years at South High, where she took courses in English as a second language. But she made no American friends and never became fluent. "When I went to other classes, I never spoke with anyone," she said. "When I spoke English, I think some people were laughing."

Becerra has four brothers—one of them a U.S. citizen—and two sisters here but is not a legal resident herself. She first entered the country with her sister-in-law's green card. She plans to stay in the United States because of greater "opportunities" here and hopes eventually to legalize her status and become a citizen.

But even if she does, she says, "I think I will still feel like a Mexican."

SIGNIFICANCE

The assimilation of immigrants into American culture and society has been the general standard by which foreign persons have become a part of the American mainstream. The process of assimilation is not by a fixed method, nor does it follow a distinct path. Assimilation was traditionally assumed as desirable by both the existing American society as well as by immigrant persons themselves. For the Americans, immigrant assimilation meant that the newcomers would adopt American ways and adhere to what are broadly described as American values. For the immigrant, the melting pot was the environment where the opportunities for economic, educational, and social advancement were greatest.

Assimilation policies have also been the subject to notable exceptions in American history. An example is the status of the aboriginal peoples of the United States. For the large part of the history of dealings between the United States government and the aboriginal peoples, assimilation of native culture into the larger whole was a formal policy of government. The modern attitude towards American aboriginals has been one to encourage cultural diversity.

In a similar fashion, the establishment of the Mormon people in Utah after 1847 was a recognition that a group distinct from the religious and cultural mainstream could be permitted to pursue a particular lifestyle without significant interference.

The related notions of American ways and American values became increasingly difficult to quantify as the country expanded through the twentieth century. It is this difficulty that has contributed to the ability of many millions of immigrants to remain outside of the traditional melting pot in a fashion that would have been impossible forty years ago. The increasingly multi-cultural nature of American society has meant that cultural diversity is a far more acceptable concept in the minds of its citizens than at any other time in American history.

The American core culture that is stated to be at the heart of American society has traditionally included Christianity, an adherence to Protestant values and its work ethic, the use of the English language, and a legal system built upon the traditions of the Anglo-American law. It is clear that the demographics of modern America are such that of the thirty-three million current American immigrants, few would

neatly fit into the conventional American core culture framework.

The other aspects of traditional American core values are ones that have been embraced by immigrant peoples as diversity and multiculturalism have taken root in the United States. Liberty, equality of opportunity, freedom of religion and expression, and democratic government are all principles that underlie other diverse societies throughout the world. The American legal system has ruled in a number of distinct areas that both the federal and the state governments must take measures to assist immigrant persons in their transition to life in America; the provision of mandatory English as second language programming for immigrant school children is an example. The mandating of similar requirements in 1900 would have been considered absurd; in the American melting pot, it was the immigrant's responsibility to conform to the society where they had chosen to move.

Author Samuel Huntington describes the modern American immigrants as 'ampersands', persons with a built-in duality who are resident in America for primarily economic reasons and thus they are persons who possess no allegiance to the traditional core values of the country.

The terrorist attacks of September 11, 2001, raised the consciousness of many Americans concerning a suspected vulnerability of the nation to further terrorist action from within its recent immigrant population. It is of interest that with approximately thirty-three million residents born outside of the United States, the country has a ratio of one immigrant for every nine residents. In 1900, the ratio of immigrant to native born persons was one in seven.

The primary source article is also significant in the sense that while the Mexican people profiled in Omaha, Nebraska, are perhaps markedly different in their lifestyle and language than mainstream American culture, their attitudes are ones that would be otherwise embraced as decidedly American. The parents secured their citizenship. The father is fully employed and clearly seeks to create a better economic foundation for his family. Theirs is an apparently stable family unit that is self sustaining and it does not require social assistance. These are also hallmarks of the traditional American societal values.

FURTHER RESOURCES
Books

Huntington, Samuel P. *Who are We?: The Challenges to America's National Identity.* New York: Simon and Schuster, 2004.

Jacoby, Tamar, ed. *Reinventing the Melting Pot.* New York: Basic Books, 2004.

Periodical

Hing, Bill. "Vigilante Racism: The De-Americanization of Immigrant America." *Michigan Journal of Race and Law* 7 (Spring 2002): 441–1456.

Web site

Washington Post. "Blending In, Moving Up" June 12, 2006 <http://www.washingtonpost.com/wp-dyn/content/article/2006/06/11/AR2006061100922.html?sub=AR> (accessed June 26, 2006).

Rwanda: Is It Safe to Come Home Yet?

Magazine article

By: Kitty McKinsey

Date: June 2004

Source: McKinsey, Kitty. "Rwanda: Is It Safe to Come Home Yet?" *Refugees Magazine* (June 2004): Issue 135.

About the Author: Kitty McKinnsey is affiliated with the United Nations High Commissioner for Refugees (UNHCR) Regional Office in Nairobi, Kenya. The UNHCR works to improve the safety and living conditions of refugees throughout the world and publishes *Refugees Magazine.*

INTRODUCTION

The Republic of Rwanda, located in East Africa, is a land of tall mountains and deep valleys, with most of the country situated a mile or more above sea level. Ethnically, the country consists of an eighty percent majority of members of the Hutu tribe and a minority made up primarily of the Tutsi people. The country's economy is largely agricultural.

Rwanda's political history remained relatively placid for much of its history, but in 1973, a bloodless coup brought a new military leader to power. In 1978, he was elected president. In 1988, Rwanda became the new home of 50,000 refugees fleeing political violence in neighboring Barundi, and two years later forces consisting largely of exiled Tutsis invaded Rwanda, eventually forcing the adoption of a new power sharing agreement. Following this agreement, the United Nations installed a peacekeeping force in the nation to monitor the situation and prevent further violence.

In mid–1994, the presidents of Rwanda and Barundi died in a plane crash, and after rumors surfaced that the crash had not been accidental, civil unrest soon followed. The following day, the Rwandan Armed Forces (FAR) and the Hutu militia seized control, setting up roadblocks and going house to house killing Tutsis as well as Hutu politicians deemed too conservative. As the killing spread, United Nations forces failed to intervene, concerned that such action would overstep their authorized role as monitors and peace-keepers. Facing little resistance, the massacre quickly spread.

By mid-May, the International Red Cross estimated that 500,000 of Rwanda's nine million residents had been killed, and by July the 100 days of slaughter were estimated to have taken 800,000 lives, with some estimates placing the total even higher. Fearing for their lives, Rwandans poured across the border into neighboring countries such as the Congo; more than two million Rwandans left the country, and many found themselves in refugee camps. Despite United Nations efforts, more than 100,000 are believed to have died of disease in the camps. Other refugees began new lives, taking whatever work they could find in order to survive.

■ **PRIMARY SOURCE**

Rwanda: Is it safe to come home yet?

A decade after Rwanda's genocide, some refugees are only now learning they can go back.

By Kitty McKinsey

The date is etched firmly on Antoine Butera's mind: January 4, 2004. That's the day, more than seven years after he fled the ongoing chaos and slaughter of Rwanda's genocide, that news finally filtered through to the 56-year-old woodworker that it was safe to go home and search for his long-lost family.

Butera had spent those intervening years of exile hiding deep in the rain forests of the Congo river basin, eking out a solitary subsistence living as an odd-job labourer, literally cut off from news of any events beyond the nearest village clearing, fearing that the bloodbath at home continued unabated.

A chance broadcast by a United Nations station, Radio Okapi, picked up by a neighbour earlier this year, alerted Butera that things had in fact altered radically in Rwanda.

A family separated during Rwanda's civil war is reunited after over two years apart. From left to right: father Leonard, mother Marie, and children Angelo, Laurence, and Jean-Paul. Mbongo, Rwanda, November 15, 1996. © CHRISTOPHE CALAIS/IN VISU/CORBIS.

"It was the first time I heard there was peace," the grey-haired man with a grey-flecked beard explained recently as he waited patiently to board a truck taking him back from his long exile. "I was very happy. I prayed to God to show me a path to go home" to search for a wife and nine children who had remained inside Rwanda when he left in 1996 and of whom "I don't even know if they are dead or alive."

More than 2.3 million people had fled the tiny land-locked country at the height of the mass slaughter in 1994, and tens of thousands of others followed in the next few years as political and military instability continued. The great majority returned home by the end of 1996, but currently between 60,000-80,000 remain scattered throughout several neighbouring states. Most live in established refugee camps or are known to local authorities and are expected to be repatriated by the end of 2005.

RAIN FOREST SURVIVORS

But perhaps the most poignant histories are those of the "survivors of the rain forests" like Butera who dis-appeared into the interior of Rwanda's huge neighbour, the Democratic Republic of the Congo, and are rarely heard from again unless and until, like some of the Japanese soldiers who staggered out of the Philippine jungles decades after the end of World War II, they sud-denly and unexpectedly emerge from the triple-canopy foliage.

Survivors tell similar tales of harrowing escapes into the forest in the 1990s as they fled their towns and vil-lages, a knife-edge existence for many years seemingly lost to the world, and even when news finally reaches them of peace in Rwanda, a reluctance sometimes last-ing for years to return to a country where they might be accused of being accomplices to mass murder.

Many of those now repatriating had initially fled to border camps just inside Congo, but then trudged on foot deeper into the Congo basin in 1996, pursued by Rwan-dan and other military forces intent on taking revenge on the *interahamwe* and their followers. Untold thousands were killed or died of exhaustion and illness in a bloody chase across the waist of Africa.

Some walked for thousands of kilometres and, after months of wanderings, crossed the entire continent east to west and reached the Atlantic Ocean. Most settled in the interior where women gave birth by themselves in the forests and sometimes married local Congolese who could provide them with shelter and protection from rape. Many refugees became small-time labourers for local villagers. Some stayed in the forest, in homemade huts of twigs and leaves, foraging for berries and other fruits. Until word began reaching them that things had changed in Rwanda.

THE END

To try to bring closure to one of the last remaining threads from one of history's most traumatic and confused humanitarian crises, UNHCR recently launched a so-called mass information campaign to encourage remaining pockets of Rwandans to leave the forests. The U.N. Radio Okapi also beams similar messages which obviously have influenced some Rwandans like Butera, but is unlikely to persuade an estimated 17,000 and 30,000 hard-core *interahamwe* and their supporters still at large.

The refugee agency established a series of centres on the fringes of the forbidding interior to welcome the several hundred refugees who arrive each week from the forest. They are mainly women and children, most of these youngsters having been born in exile and never even seen "home." They are registered, provided with basic help and moved along a by now well oiled logistical train to transit centres inside Rwanda and then to their home communes.

Former Rwandan soldiers and *interahamwe* militias are separated out and sent for several weeks to a re-education camp where they are indoctrinated into the rules of the "new" Rwanda, with particular emphasis on the fact that separate Tutsi and Hutu ethnicities and mutual animosity are things of the past.

According to Brigitte Bampile, a nurse in the Congolese town of Bukavu who examines returnees, many of the women and children bear the marks of their harsh existence, suffering from malaria, respiratory infections, skin problems, sexually-transmitted disease and AIDS.

And they face other hardships once they get back to their ancestral homeland. Rwanda is the most densely populated state in Africa and one of the world's poorest countries. Ninety percent of the population live off the land, but there is not enough of it for everyone. Tens of thousands of people still need homes. Children born in exile often speak Swahili rather than the local language, Kinyarwanda.

A MINOR MIRACLE

And then there is the shadow of genocide hanging over everyone. "I was told if I came back to Rwanda, I would be put into prison, so I stayed over there," 32-year-old Sebastien Mazimpaka, a Hutu, said before he finally came back to Buremera in southwestern Rwanda, a mixed village of Tutsis and Hutus.

"It's good with the neighbours," according to Lorence Mwitende, a Tutsi neighbour. "But there are other difficulties, just to find something to eat is difficult." She may earn the equivalent of 34-50 U.S. cents a day as a farm labourer, but from that she must feed four children, often with nothing but leaves from a neighbour's manioc plants. Another child died recently because her mother couldn't afford a doctor.

Back at the Rwanda-Congo border, Antoine Butera has just crossed the frontier. In 1994 this ramshackle post and the military bridge across the Ruzizi River was clogged with tens of thousands of frenzied refugees trying to escape the carnage.

In direct contrast on this particular day, the small group of returning refugees is processed in less than one hour with no fuss or delay. An elderly aunt has met the UNHCR convoy with astonishing news. "I've no idea how many convoys she came to meet, but she was there today looking for me," Butera said. "And my whole family is alive and living in Kigali. All nine children and their mother are alive—10 people total!"

In the horror that was Rwanda, that an entire family survived could surely be considered a modest miracle.

SIGNIFICANCE

In the months following the Rwandan killings, numerous foreign governments and aid agencies investigated the events. While the specific causes of the disaster, as well as the responsibility, remained in dispute, a consensus emerged that the Hutu actions constituted genocide, a crime punishable under international law. According to a 1951 treaty, genocide is any attempt to eliminate or destroy a particular ethnic group, race, or religious group; genocide was made a crime following the Nazi atrocities against the Jews during World War II. By targeting a specific ethnic group for murder, the Hutus violated this law.

Refugee families such as those who fled Rwanda often hope to return to their homeland. In 1996, almost half the refugees who left Rwanda returned home, though upon returning they found themselves facing further violence as the two ethnic groups continued to fight in the years since the original violence. Refugees fleeing their home country face numerous hardships in their new homes, often finding themselves in unfamiliar surroundings, and frequently unable to speak the language or obtain employment. In some cases, refugees such as those leaving Rwanda find themselves confined to sparse, overcrowded camps, depending on the benevolence of aid agencies to remain alive.

Children are particularly vulnerable to the stresses of refugee life. Torn from familiar surroundings, children are often unable to understand the reasons for their sudden departure and the loss of friends and possessions. Hunger and health problems frequently combine with uncertainty and physical danger to produce tremendous stresses within families, although some families appear to be strengthened and drawn closer by the shared hardship.

As of 1998, the United Nations estimated that thirteen million individuals were living as refugees throughout the world. While some have begun new lives in new countries, others remain in limbo, existing in temporary shelter and waiting for the day they may return home to begin rebuilding their previous lives.

In 1999, the organization Human Rights Watch released an extensive report on the bloodshed in Rwanda. The report faulted the United Nations as well as the United States, France, and Belgium, each of which had troops in the country, for observing plans for the massacre and failing to take steps to prevent it. Only a handful of those accused of genocide were convicted, and as of 2005, Rwanda was enjoying a tenuous period of peace.

FURTHER RESOURCES
Books

Dallaire, Romeo, and Samantha Power. *Shake Hands with the Devil: The Failure of Humanity in Rwanda*. New York: Carroll & Graf Publishers, 2003 .

Gourevitch, Philip. *We wish to inform you that tomorrow we will be killed with our families: Stories from Rwanda*. New York: Picador/Farrar, Straus, and Giroux; distributed by Holtzbrinck Publishers, 1998.

Prunier, Gerard. *The Rwanda Crisis: History of a Genocide*. New York: Columbia University Press, 1995.

Periodicals

"Rwanda: Genocide Suspects Who Confess to Go Free." *The New York Times* (Feb 17, 2004): A9.

Short, Clare. "The Lessons We Can Learn from Rwanda." *New Statesman* 132 (2003): 20–21.

Strauss, Scott. "Conspiracy to Murder: The Rwanda Genocide and the International Community." *Political Science Quarterly* 120 (2005): 348–350.

Web sites

Human Rights Watch. "History of Rwanda." <http://www.hrw.org/reports/1999/rwanda/Geno1-3-09.htm#TopOfPage> (accessed July 12, 2006).

Public Broadcasting Service. "The Triumph of Evil; How the West Ignored the Warnings of the 1994 Rwanda Genocide." <http://www.pbs.org/wgbh/pages/frontline/shows/evil/> (accessed July 12, 2006).

Revisiting an Immigrant Family

News article

By: Jeffrey Kaye

Date: October 26, 2005

Source: Kaye, Jeffrey. "Revisiting an Immigrant Family." *Online NewsHour.* (26 October 2005).

About the Author: Jeffrey Kaye is an Emmy winner and a former writer for the *Washington Post*. He is a senior producer for a public television station and the News-Hour's Los Angeles correspondent.

INTRODUCTION

Mexican immigration into the United States became a hot-button political issue in the 1990s and the early years of the twenty-first century. Parts of the United States in the southwest, such as portions of New Mexico, Texas, Arizona, and California, had been part of Mexico for centuries before the United States gained power over these areas in the mid–1800s. Many people of Spanish descent stayed in these lands in spite of the power shift, maintaining communities, missions, businesses and family ties that had been in place long before English-speaking settlers began to colonize portions of the Americas.

Many Mexican men migrate to the United States, entering the country legally, to earn money in seasonal jobs, returning home when the work ends. Throughout the 1990s, the number of Mexican immigrant workers increased by 123 percent in the labor force; for U.S. citizens the increase was thirteen percent. With more than 2.9 million new Mexican immigrant workers entering the United States and working during this time, the impact of Mexicans on the labor force and society in the United States was dramatic.

The seven Luevanos children, Mexican immigrants, live with their single mother in a trailer in Mission, Texas, October 1, 2004. © ALISON WRIGHT/CORBIS.

Many Mexican families use "chain migration" to bring families to the United States. First, a male worker enters the United States—legally or illegally—and gains a paid position. While sending money home to his family, he also works to establish legal residency. Once he receives permanent resident status—the so-called "green card"—he can legally apply to bring a spouse and children to the United States. All persons sponsoring immigrants to the United States must earn more than 125 percent of the federal poverty level; many unskilled laborers or those working without documentation are at a disadvantage in bringing family to this country. Once the permanent resident's family enters the United States, each can apply for permanent resident status—and in turn apply to bring their relatives of first order. In this way, extended families slowly move to the United States, maintaining ties and social networks in both countries.

The following news segment highlights changes in immigration policy and status for one family and sheds light on the state of immigration in 2005.

PRIMARY SOURCE

JIM LEHRER: Now, the third of our reports marking our 30th anniversary, we're revisiting some of the stories we've covered over the years to see what's changed. Tonight, the subject is immigration. News-Hour correspondent Jeffrey Kaye, of KCET-Los Angeles, looks at what's become of a Mexican-American family he first met in 1993.

JEFFREY KAYE: Like countless other villages across Mexico, San Diego, Des Alejandria, is a place whose men go north to the U.S. to find jobs and opportunity.

That tradition more than a century old is so ingrained in the culture that there's even an annual holiday, El Dia De Los Alsentas, the Day of the Absent Ones, that pays tribute to its immigrants.

Twelve years ago during the fiesta, to put a human face on the immigration story, we accompanied Francisco Correa on one of his periodic trips from his Los Angeles home back to this village where he was raised. Like a dozen of his brothers and sisters, Correa left here in the '60s and went illegally to the U.S. to find work.

In 1993, Correa, by then a legal resident, his wife Anna Maria and son Paco, the oldest of their four U.S.-born children, were running El Paco's Tacos, the family's restaurant in Huntington Park, a suburb of Los Angeles.

PACO CORREA: That's supposed to be me up there when I was a kid.

JEFFREY KAYE: When you were a kid?

PACO CORREA: Yeah, that's me.

JEFFREY KAYE: We wanted to know what had become of the Correa family. Soon after this interview Paco got a job in the post office. In 1997 the family sold the restaurant.

Five years ago Paco Correa started his own family. He married Celina Marquez, herself an immigrant from Mexico. Their wedding was attended by friends and family members, now spread throughout California and scattered around the country.

PACO CORREA: That's my uncle Julie's older son.

JEFFREY KAYE: Where is he?

PACO CORREA: In Chicago.

JEFFREY KAYE: The Correa family is just one example of the deep roots that migrant workers have planted in the U.S. Francisco's odyssey is part of the family lore.

PACO CORREA: He says the first time he came, you said you came with five people in a Lincoln?

JEFFREY KAYE: In the trunk of a car?

WOMAN: The first time.

PACO CORREA: The first time he came, five people in the trunk in a Lincoln.

JEFFREY KAYE: Today Paco, now 33 and Celina, have a daughter, Natalie. Paco is a dock worker. Celina also works at the port part-time. She's applying for U.S. citizenship, but the family considers itself bi-national.

CELINA CORREA: I love this country very, very much because they give me a lot of opportunities. They give me job. They give family. They give everything—everything, all the opportunities that are awaiting is just in here. But at the same time part of my heart is Mexico.

WAYNE CORNELIUS: It's also no surprise that the family that you profiled is essentially settled in the United States. The incentives for continuing to live in this country still greatly outweigh the desirability of returning to Mexico, even to retire.

JEFFREY KAYE: Immigration expert Wayne Cornelius directs the Center for Comparative Immigration

Studies at the University of California, San Diego. He says there are more migrants living permanently in the U.S. than ever before, an unintended consequence of U.S. policy.

WAYNE CORNELIUS: Because we have tightened border enforcement, there is much less circular migration. People are staying longer in the United States, and the longer they stay here, the more likely it is that they will settle permanently.

Those without papers have to face the very real certainty that if they return for even a short visit, they will have to risk their lives and spend thousands of dollars to regain entry into the United States. And that is enough of a deterrent to keep them bottled up in the United States.

JEFFREY KAYE: Another reason that migrants tend to stay is a vast network of support, both institutional and informal. For instance, most migrants come for work and can find jobs at any number of city-sanctioned day labor sites around the country.

EDDIE (Translated): We crossed the desert for many days and then had to cross a river, all the while keeping an eye out for the Border Patrol. I thank God I got here and can now look for work to support my family.

JEFFREY KAYE: Migrants find that low-paying jobs are plentiful and employers know there's virtually no risk from immigration authorities in hiring illegal immigrants.

WAYNE CORNELIUS: Since the early 1990s, worksite enforcement has virtually collapsed. The number of fines imposed on employers dropped by 82 percent since 1991. In 2003, the most recent year for which we have statistics, only 124 employers throughout the United States were fined for violating immigration laws. That's not much of a deterrent to employers.

JEFFREY KAYE: Besides jobs, illegal migrants can easily obtain public education and health care. Migrants also help each other. Anna Maria now recovering from a broken leg came here as a teen. She says her family often assisted people from their hometown who showed up on their doorstep.

ANNA MARIA: When they come over here, we help you. We help the people.

JEFFREY KAYE: And you've done that?

ANNA MARIA: Yes. We help you. We have to help you. We have to help the people. Sometimes the mothers have 22 people in the house and one toilet. We have to make a line.

JEFFREY KAYE: They're not the only ones putting out the welcome mat. U.S. Banks and other financial institutions eager to hone in on a new market are tailoring services to attract migrants.

WAYNE CORNELIUS: They are actively courting undocumented migrants who are immigrants regardless of legal status, as depositors as customers for home mortgages and to transfer their money back to relatives in Mexico.

JEFFREY KAYE: Celina Correa like many migrants takes advantage of financial services. Living the lives of middle class Americans she and Paco regularly send money back to her family in Mexico.

CELINA CORREA: I just sent $500. Every month it depends my parents how they need like my parent has a heart surgery so very often I just call and I just want to keep an eye so the money he needs for the medicine.

PACO CORREA: I understand her fully because I lived it. I went through all the same feelings that she felt with my family how they helped my grandparents, uncles, aunts, immediate family that I lived with. I see them. And they need help. So I understand why they need it.

JEFFREY KAYE: The support networks are not just within families. Hometown associations throughout the U.S. stage social and fundraising activities to help migrants here and to collect money to send to Mexico.

Mexicans living in the U.S. pump more money into Mexico than foreign businesses. Last year their remittances totaled $16.5 billion, according to Mexico's Central Bank.

As the son and husband of migrants, Paco Correa has strong feelings about immigration, feelings that are unchanged in 12 years.

PACO CORREA: When you catch them, what are you going to do? Put them back? They'll get back. They'll try it again and again and again.

JEFFREY KAYE: Can the border be closed?

PACO CORREA: No. No way. You can't close that border. Not here.

Especially in LA, when you have every other person that you look over your shoulder that has a connection in Mexico. You know, how do I say no to my family? How do I say no to some cousins that are illegal here? How do I say no to my neighbors? You can't.

JEFFREY KAYE: And as long as there are jobs, says Paco Correa, illegal immigrants will come no matter the costs or the legality just as his father did 36 years ago hidden in the trunk of a car.

SIGNIFICANCE

The Correa family's story is not unique and reflects the experience of many Mexican immigrant families in modern times. The 1996 welfare reform eliminated access to many government programs, such as food stamps and Social Security Insurance for legal immigrants, and bars undocumented workers and their families from accessing all government programs except immunizations, emergency health care, and disaster relief. These changes were designed to discourage immigrants from coming to the United States and using government assistance in lieu of work, or as a substantial supplement to work. However, the children of undocumented workers can enroll in public schools and some states and local entities provide access to government programs for legal and undocumented immigrants.

Tighter borders severely affected "circular migration," in which workers cross the border frequently to work in the United States but spend time in their hometown. As the Embassy of Mexico notes in its document "Fostering Circular Migration": "Until the second half of the eighties the traditional pattern of migration from Mexico to the United States was circular. This entailed the fluid crossing of people along the border. Several analysts suggest that, since Mexican migration is essentially economic in nature, increased border enforcement, without sufficient legal avenues to match labor demand and supply, has reduced circularity over the past years." Until the 1980s circular migration was a popular choice for many Mexican families; the father and older sons came north for the harvest season or for other unskilled work for a few months, then returned home, bringing an influx of money into the economy while maintaining ties with his children, spouse, and extended family. As circular migration becomes difficult, more undocumented Mexican immigrants have chosen to settle in the United States, often bringing their families across the border illegally.

While more than seventy percent of Mexican nationals surveyed stated that they would be interested in participating in a temporary guest worker program, over time fewer Mexican workers who enter the United States legally are willing to return to Mexico for fear of being unable to cross the border again to return to their jobs. This leaves many families in limbo: Without legal status in the United States the worker cannot return home easily for visits or apply to bring his or her family to the U.S. Legal immigrants do not face the same hurdles, but unskilled workers are at a strong disadvantage when applying for legal entry; in 2005 the United States distributed 5,000 visas for unskilled laborers to enter the country legally—only two went to Mexican workers.

FURTHER RESOURCES

Books

Ellingwood, Ken. *Hard Line: Life and Death on the U.S.-Mexican Border*. New York: Pantheon Books, 2004.

Haines, David W., and Karen E. Rosenblum, eds. *Illegal Immigration in America: A Reference Handbook*. Westport, Conn.: Greenwood Press, 1999.

Massey, Douglas S. *Beyond Smoke and Mirrors: Mexican Immigration in an Era of Economic Integration*. New York: Russell Sage Foundation Publications, 2003.

Yoshida, Chisa To, and Alan Woodland. *The Economics of Illegal Immigration*. New York: Palgrave MacMillan, 2005.

Web sites

Embassy of Mexico. "Fostering Circular Miration." <http://www.embassyofmexico.org/images/pdfs/Circular%20Migration%2002%2003%202006.pdf> (accessed July 10, 2006).

United States Citizenship and Immigration Services. <http://www.uscis.gov/graphics/index.htm> (accessed July 10, 2006).

Sources Consulted

BOOKS AND WEBSITES

A Century of Lawmaking. "Library of Congress." <http://rs6. loc.gov/ammem/amlaw/lawhome.html> (accessed on June 24, 2006).

Academy of Natural Sciences. "Horsemen of the Mongolian Steppes: Nomadic Life Beyond the Great Wall." <http://www.acnatsci.org/museum/traveling/horse-men.html> (accessed July 12, 2006).

Afterschool Alliance. "Afterschool Outcomes." <http://www. afterschoolalliance.org/after_out.cfm> (accessed June 28, 2006).

Agency for Healthcare Research and Quality. "Agency for Healthcare Research and Quality." <http://www.ahrq. gov> (accessed on June 24, 2006).

Agnes, Flavia. *Women and Law in India.* New Delhi: Oxford University Press, 2004.

Ahron, Constance. *The Good Divorce.* New York: Harper Paperback, 1998.

AIDS Research Institute (ARI). "AIDS Research Institute (ARI)." <http://ari.ucsf.edu> (accessed on June 24, 2006).

Alabama Cooperative Extension System. "Defining Non-traditional Families." October 7, 2002. <http://www. aces.edu/urban/metronews/vol2no1/nontrad.html> (accessed July 22, 2006).

Alderman, Clifford. *Colonists for Sale: The Story of Indentured Servants in America.* New York: Macmillan, 1975.

Aldridge, J., and S. Becker. *Children Caring for Parents with Mental Illness: Perspectives of Young Carers, Parents and Professionals.* Bristol, United Kingdom: Policy Press, 2003.

All Our Families: New Policies for a New Century, edited by Mary Ann Mason, Arlene Skolnick, and Stephen D. Sugarman. New York: Oxford University Press, 2002.

Almanac of Policy Issues. "Domestic Violence." April 2000 <http://www.policyalmanac.org/crime/archive/domestic_ violence.shtml> (accessed July 4, 2006).

Alzheimer Society, Niagara Region. "Young Carers Initiative Niagara." <http://www.alzheimerniagara.ca/YCIN. htm> (accessed June 12, 2006).

American Academy of Child and Adolescent Psychiatry: Facts for Families.. "Children and Watching TV." February 2005 <http://www.aacap.org/publications/factsfam/tv.htm> (accessed June 16, 2006).

American Academy of Pediatrics. "Television and the Family." <http://www.aap.org/family/tv1.htm> (accessed June 16, 2006).

American Association of Child and Adolescent Psychiatry. "Children and Watching T.V." February 2005 <http://www. aacap.org/page/> (accessed June 29, 2006).

American Civil Liberties Union. "ACLU Disappointed the Supreme Court Will Not Hear an Appeal in Case Challenging Florida's Anti-Gay Adoption Law." January 11, 2005. <http://www.aclu.org/lgbt/parenting/ 12438prs20050110.html> (accessed June 20, 2006).

American Civil Liberties Union. "Frequently Asked Questions about the Federal Marriage Amendment and Gay Marriage." February 25, 2004. <http://www.aclu.org/lgbt/ gen/11931res20040225.html> (accessed June 15, 2006).

American Institute of Certified Public Accountants. "Financial Tips for the Sandwich Generation." <http://www.aicpa. org/download/financialliteracy/Sandwich_Generation_ Toolkit/Financial_Tips.pdf> (accessed July 16, 2006).

American Memory Project, Library of Congress. "Your Family Needs Protection Against Syphilis." <http://memory. loc.gov/ammem/wpaposters/wpahome.html> (accessed July 15, 2006).

American Memory. "Library of Congress." <http://memory.loc.gov/ammem/index.html> (accessed on June 24, 2006).

American President. "President James Knox Polk." <http://www.americanpresident.org/history/jamespolk/biography> (accessed June 19, 2006).

American Prospect. "I Plead the Sixth." July 30, 2002. <http://www.prospect.org/print/V13/14/polakow-suransky-s.html> (accessed June 24, 2006).

American Public Media. "Gay Marketing: Stranger to the Closet." June 7, 2005 <http://marketplace.publicradio.org/shows/2005/06/07/PM200506071.html> (accessed June 15, 2006).

American Rhetoric. "American Rhetoric." <http://www.americanrhetoric.com/> (accessed on June 24, 2006).

American Social Health Association. "Sexually Transmitted Diseases." <http://www.ashastd.org> (accessed July 16, 2006).

American Surrogacy Center (TASC). "TASC Articles: Medical." <http://www.surrogacy.com/Articles/> (accessed June 21, 2006).

Amnesty International. "Amnesty International." <http://www.amnesty.org/> (accessed on June 24, 2006).

Andelin, Helen. *Fascinating Womanhood*. New York: Bantam, 1992.

Anderson, Karen. *Wartime Women: Sex Roles, Family Relations, and the Status of Women During World War II*. New York: Berkley Books, 2001.

Antorini, Yun Mi, Fabian Csaba, and Majken Schultz, ed. *Corporate Branding*. Copenhagen: Copenhagen Business School Press, 2005.

Apple, Rima. *Perfect Motherhood: Science and Childrearing in America*. New Brunswick, N.J.: Rutgers University Press, 2006.

Askeland, Lori, ed. *Children and Youth in Adoption, Orphanages, and Foster Care: A Historical Handbook and Guide*. Westport, Conn.: Greenwood Press, 2005.

Atwood, Joan D. and Frank Genovese. *Therapy with Single Parents*. Binghamton, New York: Haworth Press, 2006.

Auerback, Emily. *Searching for Jane Austen*. Madison: University of Wisconsin Press, 2006.

Austen, Jane. *Jane Austen's Letters*. Philadelphia: Pavilion Press, 2003.

Austen, Jane. *Sense and Sensibility*. New York: Penguin Books, 1999.

Baker, Jean H. *Sisters: The Lives of American Suffragists*. New York: Hill and Wang, 2005.

Baker, Leigh. *Protecting Your Children from Sexual Predators*. New York: St. Martin's Press, 2002.

Balmer, John M.T. *Revealing the Corporation: Perspectives on Identity, Image, Reputation and Corporate Branding*. London: Routledge, 2003.

Bancroft, Lundy. *Why Does He Do That? Inside the Minds of Angry and Controlling Men*. New York: Berkeley Publishing Group, 2002.

Bank, Stephen P., and Michael D. Kahn. *The Sibling Bond*. New York, NY: Basic Books, 2003.

Barter, Judith, ed. *Mary Cassatt: Modern Woman*. New York: Harry N. Abrams, 1998.

Bartollas, Clemens. *Juvenile Delinquency*. New York: Allyn & Bacon, 2002.

Basu, Monnayee. *Hindu Women and Marriage Law-From Sacrament to Contract*. New Delhi: Oxford University Press, 2004.

Bauer, M.W., and G. Gaskell, eds. *Biotechnology: The Making of a Global Controversy*. Cambridge, UK: Cambridge University Press, 2002.

Becker, Heather, et al. *Art for the People: The Rediscovery and Preservation of Progressive and WPA-Era Murals in the Chicago Public Schools, 1904–1943*. San Francisco: Chronicle Books, 2002.

Becker, S., J. Aldridge, and C. Dearden. *Young Carers and their Families*. Oxford, United Kingdom: Blackwell Science, 1998.

Behr, Edward. *Prohibition: Thirteen Years that Changed America*. New York: Arcade Publishing, 1997.

Berlin, Ira, Marc Favreau, and Steven F. Miller, eds. *Remembering Slavery: African Americans Talk about Their Personal Experiences of Slavery and Freedom*. New York: The New Press, 1998.

Billings, Dwight B. and Kathleen M. Blee. *The Road to Poverty: The Making of Wealth and Hardship in Appalachia*. New York: Cambridge University Press, 2000.

Binghamton University. "'The Rule of Love': Wife Beating as Prerogative and Privacy." <http://www.binghamton.edu/womhist/vawa/prologuefootnotes.htm> (accessed July 4, 2006).

Blades, Joan and Kristin Rowe-Finkbeiner. *The Motherhood Manifesto: What America's Moms Want—and What To Do About It*. New York: Nation Books, 2006.

Blakeslee, Sandra, and Judith S. Wallerstein. *What About the Kids? Raising Your Children before, during, and after Divorce*. New York: Hyperion, 2003.

Blank, R.H., and J. Merrick. *Human Reproduction, Emerging Technologies, and Conflicting Rights*. Washington, DC: CQ Press, 1995.

Blankenhorn, David. *Fatherless America: Confronting our Most Urgent Social Problem*. New York: Basic Books, 1995.

Bloom, Lynn Z. *Doctor Spock: A Biography of a Conservative Radical*. Indianapolis, IN: Bobbs-Merrill, 1972.

Bock, Gisela, and Pat Thane, eds. *Maternity and Gender Policies: Women and the Rise of the European Welfare States*. London: Routledge, 1991.

Boland, Mary L., and Brette McWhorter Sember. *Visitation Handbook*. Naperville, Ill.; Sourcebooks, 2002.

Boni, William C., and Gerald L. Kovacich. *I-Way Robbery: Crime on the Internet*. Boston: Butterworth-Heinemann, 1999.

Braden, Donna R., and Judith E. Endelman. *Americans on Vacation*. Dearborn, MI: Henry Ford Museum and Greenfield Village, 1990.

Braude, Ann. *Radical Spirits: Spiritualism and Women's Rights in Nineteenth-Century America*. 2nd edition. Bloomington: Indiana University Press, 2001.

Brewer, Priscilla. *From Fireplace to Cookstove: Technology and the Domestic Ideal in America*. New York: Syracuse University Press, 2000.

British Library. "British Library Images Online." <http://www.imagesonline.bl.uk/britishlibrary/> (accessed on June 24, 2006).

Brody, Jane. *New York Times*. "Children, Media and Sex: A Big Book of Blank Pages." January 31, 2006 <http://www.nytimes.com/2006/01/31/health/> (accessed June 28, 2006).

Brooks, Marla. *The American Family on Television: A Chronology of 121 Shows, 1948–2004*. New York: McFarland and Company, 2005.

Broughton, Trev, and Ruth Symes, eds. *The Governess: An Anthology*. Palgrave Macmillan, 1998.

Brown, Alan, and Chris Logan. *The Psychology of the Simpsons: D'oh!* Dallas: BenBella Books, 2006.

Brown, Candy Gunther. *The Word in the World: Evangelical Writing, Publishing, and Reading in America, 1789–1880*. Chapel Hill: University of North Carolina Press, 2004.

Burns, Alisa, and Cathy Scott. *Mother-Headed Families and Why They Have Increased*. Hillsdale, NJ: Lawrence Erlbaum Associates, 1994.

California Research Bureau, California State Library. "State Grounds for Divorce." <http://www.library.ca.gov/crb/98/04/stateground.pdf> (accessed June 21, 2006).

Cambridge University. "Cambridge University, Institute of Public Health." <http://www.iph.cam.ac.uk> (accessed on June 24, 2006).

Cameron, Ardis, ed. *Looking for America: The Visual Production of Nation and People*. Malden, Mass.: Blackwell, 2005.

Canadian Department of Justice. "Section 43 Criminal Code of Canada." 2006 <http://www.justice.gc.ca/en/news/fs/2004/doc_31114.html> (accessed June 26, 2006).

Cardoza, Arlene Rossen. *Sequencing*. Minneapolis, Minn.: Brownstone Books, 1986.

Cassidy, Thomas. *Elder Care*. Sacramento, California: Citadel, 2004.

Cavanaugh, Mary M., Richard G. Gelles and Donileen R. Loseke, eds. *Current Controversies about Family Violence*. Thousand Oaks, Calif.: Sage Publications, 2005.

CBS News. "The History of Housework." April 5, 1999. <http://www.cbsnews.com/stories/1999/04/02/broadcasts/main41492.shtml> (accessed July 7, 2006).

CDC (Centers for Disease Control and Prevention). "CDCSite Index A-Z." <http://www.cdc.gov/az.do> (accessed on June 24, 2006).

Census and Identity: the Politics of Race, Ethnicity, and Language in National Censuses, edited by David I. Kertzer and Dominique Arel. Cambridge, UK: Cambridge University Press, 2002.

Census Bureau. "United States Census Bureau." <http://www.census.gov/> (accessed on June 24, 2006).

Center for Delinquency Prevention. "Preventing Juvenile Delinquency." <http://www.delinquencyprevention.org/> (accessed June 22, 2006).

Centers for Disease Control. "Cohabitation, Marriage, Divorce, and Remarriage in the United States." July 2002 <http://www.cdc.gov/nchs/data/series/sr_23/sr23_022.pdf> (accessed June 19, 2006).

Charities and the Commons. "Child Labor in New York City Tenements." <http://www.tenant.net/Community/LES/kleeck9.html> (accessed June 21, 2006).

CHE Transitions Web Log: Alumni Letters. "Letters from Alumni: Cynthia J. Schmiege." April 14, 2005. <http://blog.lib.umn.edu/sbaugher/CHEtransitions/2005_04.html> (accessed April 15, 2006).

Cheal, David. *New Poverty: Families in Postmodern Society*. Westport, Conn.: Praeger Publishers, 1996.

Chedekel, David. *The Blended Family Sourcebook*. Columbus, OH: McGraw-Hill, 2002.

Child Labor Coalition. "An Overview of Federal Child Labor Laws." <http://www.stopchildlabor.org/USchildlabor/fact1.htm> (accessed June 21, 2006).

Childhood in America, edited by Paula S. Fass and Mary Ann Mason. New York: New York University Press, 2000.

Clare County Library. "Charles Stewart Parnell." <http://www.clarelibrary.ie/eolas/coclare/people/parnell.htm> (accessed July 22, 2006).

Clements, Barbara Evans. *Bolshevik Women*. Cambridge, U.K., and New York: Cambridge University Press, 1997.

Cleveland Journal, April 15, 1905, p. 6. Available at Ohio Historical Center. "Why Divorce is Bad." <http://dbs.ohiohistory.org/africanam/det.cfm?ID=3769> (accessed June 18, 2006).

Clift, Eleanor. *Founding Sisters and the Nineteenth Amendment*. New York: Wiley and Son, 2003.

Columbia University News Service. "Stay-At-Home Mothers Grow in Number." June 23, 2003. <http://www.jrn.columbia.edu/studentwork/cns/2003-06-22/316.asp> (accessed July 21, 2006).

Columbia University. "Children of Mothers Working Full-Time in the First Year of Life Show Lower Cognitive, Verbal Development." January 29, 2004. <http://www.columbia.edu/cu/news/media/02/jeanneBrooks-Gunn/index.html> (accessed July 22, 2006).

Connerly, Charles E. *The Most Segregated City in America: City Planning and Civil Rights in Birmingham, 1920–1980.* Charlottesville, Virginia: University of Virginia Press, 2004.

Connors, Claire and Kirsten Stalker. *The Experiences and Views of Disabled Children and their Siblings: Implications for Practice and Policy.* London: Jessica Kingsley Publishers, 2003.

Coontz, Stephanie. *Marriage, a History: How Love Conquered Marriage.* New York: Viking, 2005.

Cornell Chronicle. "Economists Coin the Term 'Presenteeism' for on the Job Health Slowdowns." April 22, 2004. <http://www.news.cornell.edu/Chronicle/04/4.22.04/presenteeism.html> (accessed July 26, 2006).

Cornell University Law School Legal Information Institute (LII). "United States Constitution, Article I Section 2." <http://www.law.cornell.edu/constitution/constitution.articlei.html#section2> (accessed June 26, 2006).

Cott, Nancy F. *Public Vows: A History of Marriage and the Nation.* Cambridge, UK: Oxford University Press, 1987.

Cowan, Ruth Schwartz. *More Work for Mother: The Ironies of Household Technology from the Open Hearth to the Microwave.* New York: Basic Books, 1983.

Crenson, Matthew D. *Building the Invisible Orphanage: A Prehistory of the American Welfare System.* Cambridge, Mass.: Harvard University Press, 1998.

Crittenden, Ann. *The Price of Motherhood: Why the Most Important Job in the World is Still the Least Valued.* New York: Owl Books, 2002.

Cutrona, Carolyn E. *Social Support in Couples.* Thousand Oaks, Calif.: Sage, 1996.

Dallaire, Romeo, and Samantha Power. *Shake Hands with the Devil: The Failure of Humanity in Rwanda.* New York: Carroll & Graf Publishers, 2003.

Dalton, Mary R. and Laura R. Linden, ed. *The Sitcom Reader: America Viewed and Skewed.* New York: State University of New York Press, 2005.

Dan Quayle: Speeches: Address to the Commonwealth Club of California. "On Family Values." May 19, 1992. <http://www.vicepresidentdanquayle.com/speeches_StandingFirm_CCC_1.html> (accessed June 19, 2006).

Dandekar, Vinayak Mahadev. *The Indian Economy, 1947–92: Population, Poverty and Employment.* New York: Sage, 1996.

Darga, Kenneth. *Sampling and the Census: A Case Against the Proposed Adjustments for Undercount.* Washington, D.C.: American Enterprise Institute , 1999.

Darrell, Keith B. *Issues in Internet Law.* Phoenix: Amber Books, 2006.

Davis, Charles T., and Henry Louis Gates, Jr. *The Slave's Narrative.* New York: Oxford University Press, 1985.

Davis, Don. *One State, Two State, Red State, Blue State.* Shelbyville, Kentucky: Wasteland Press, 2005.

Davis, Michelle Mwiner. *Divorce Busting: A Step-by-Step Approach to Making Your Marriage Loving Again.* New York: Simon and Schuster, 1993.

Deakin, Michelle Bates. *Gay Marriage, Real Life: Ten Stories of Love and Family.* Boston: Skinner House Books, 2006.

Dearden, C., and S. Becker. *Growing Up Caring: Vulnerability and Transition to Adulthood—Young Carers' Experiences.* Leicester, United Kingdom: Youth Work Press, 2000.

Delafield, E. M. *The Provincial Lady in Russia: I Visit the Soviets.* Chicago: Academy Chicago Publishers, 1985.

Delaney, Diane Meier. *The New American Wedding: Ritual and Style in a Changing Culture.* New York: Viking Studio, 2005.

Denoon, Christopher. *Posters of the WPA.* Seattle: University of Washington Press, 1987.

Department of Family and Community Services. "Young Carers Research Project: Final Report." September 2001. <http://www.carersaustralia.com.au/documents/young_carersfinal_report.pdf> (accessed June 12, 2006).

Department of Health and Human Services. "Promoting Responsible Fatherhood." June 9, 2006. <http://fatherhood.hhs.gov/Parenting/hs.shtml> (accessed June 19, 2006).

Department of Justice Canada. "Overview and Assessment of Approaches to Access Enforcement." 2001. <http://www.justice.gc.ca/en/ps/pad/reports/2001-FCY-8/nature2.html> (accessed June 20, 2006).

Department of State Counsel's Office, State of New York. "Definition of "Family" in Zoning By-Laws and Building Codes." 2004. <http://www.dos.state.ny.us/cnsl/family.html> (accessed June 29, 2006).

Dickenson, Donna. *Property, Women and Politics: Subjects or Objects.* New Brunswick, NJ: Rutgers University Press, 1997.

Discovery Health. "Debunking Divorce Myths." <http://health.discovery.com/centers/loverelationships/articles/divorce.html> (accessed June 19, 2006).

Doctors Without Borders. "Doctors Without Borders." <http://www.doctorswithoutborders.org/> (accessed on June 24, 2006).

DOMA Watch. "Your Legal Source for Defense of Marriage Acts Information." <http://www.domawatch.org/index.html> (accessed June 15, 2006).

Douglas, Susan J. and Meredith W. Michaels. *The Mommy Myth: The Idealization of Motherhood and How It Has Undermined Women.* New York: Free Press, 2004.

Douglas, William. *Television Families: Is Something Wrong in Suburbia?.* Mahwah, NJ: Lawrence Erlbaum Associates, 2003.

Dubofsky, Melvyn. *Hard Work: The Making of Labor History.* Champaign, IL: University of Illinois Press, 2000.

Dubois, Ellen Carol. *Feminism and Suffrage: The Emergence of an Independent Women's Movement in America, 1848–1869.* Ithaca, N.Y.: Cornell University Press, 1999.

Duby, Georges, and Michelle Perrot, eds. *A History of Women: Emerging Feminism From Revolution to World War.* Cambridge, MA.: Harvard University Press, 1993.

DuPage County Bar Association. "Significant Amendment of the Illinois Marriage and Dissolution of Marriage Act Should Alleviate Role Confusion." 2000 <http://www.dcba.org/brief/mayissue/2000/art20500.htm> (accessed July 11, 2006).

DuPlessix Gray, Francine. *Soviet Women: Walking the Tightrope.* New York: Doubleday, 1990.

Dychtwald, Ken. *Age Power: How the 21st Century will be Ruled by the New Old.* New York: Penguin USA, 2000.

Eccles, David. *VW Camper—The Inside Story: A Guide to VW Camping Conversions and Interiors 1951–2005.* Ramsbury, Wiltshire, U.K.: Crowood Press, 2005.

Edelman, Hope. *Motherless Mothers: How Mother Loss Shapes the Parents We Become.* New York: Harper Collins, 2006.

Edwards, Jeanette, et al. *Technologies of Procreation: Kinship in the Age of Assisted Conception.* New York: Routledge, 1999.

Ellingwood, Ken. *Hard Line: Life and Death on the U.S.-Mexican Border.* New York: Pantheon Books, 2004.

Embassy of Mexico. "Fostering Circular Miration." <http://www.embassyofmexico.org/images/pdfs/Circular%20Migration%2002%2003%202006.pdf> (accessed July 10, 2006).

Emery, Robert E. *Marriage, Divorce, and Children's Adjustment.* Thousand Oaks, CA: Sage Publications, 1989.

European Commission. "Gender Equality." 2006. <http://www.ec.europa.eu/employment_social/gender_equality/index_en.html> (accessed June 18, 2006).

Evan B. Donaldson Adoption Institute. *Benchmark Adoption Survey: Report on the Findings.* New York: Evan B. Donaldson Institute, 1997.

Eyewitness to History. "Slave Auctions." 2002. <http://www.eyewitnesstohistory.com/slaveauction.htm> (accessed June 27, 2006).

Fashola, Olatokunbo S. *Building Effective Afterschool Programs.* Thousand Oaks, Calif.: Corwin Press/ Sage, 2002.

Fatherhood: Research, Interventions, and Policies, edited by H. Elizabeth Peters and Gary W. Peterson. Binghamton, N.Y.: Haworth Press, 2000.

Federal Bureau of Investigation. "A Parent's Guide to Internet Safety." 2006. <http://www.fbi.gov/publications/pguide/pguidee.htm> (accessed June 29, 2006).

Federal Government Agencies Directory. "Louisiana State University." <http://www.lib.lsu.edu/gov/fedgov.html> (accessed on June 24, 2006).

Federation of American Scientists. "Federation of American Scientists, ProMED Initiative." <http://www.fas.org/promed> (accessed on June 24, 2006).

FedStats. "FedStats." <http://www.fedstats.gov> (accessed on June 24, 2006).

Field, Withrow Alice. *Protection of Women and Children in Soviet Russia.* New York: E.P. Dutton, 1932.

Fields, Denise, and Alan Fields. *Bridal Bargains: Secrets to Throwing a Fantastic Wedding on a Realistic Budget.* Boulder, CO: Windsor Peak Press, 2002.

Fields, Jason. *U.S. Census Bureau.* "America's Families and Living Arrangements: Family Groups by Type and Selected Characteristics." <http://www.census.gov/prod/2004pubs/p20-553.pdf> (accessed July 23, 2006).

Findlaw. "Findlaw/West." <http://public.findlaw.com/library/> (accessed on June 24, 2006).

First World War.com. "Primary Sources: Crown Prince Wilhelm on the Prospect of War, 1913." September 27, 2003 <http://www.firstworldwar.com/source/crownprincewilhelm1913.htm> (accessed June 15, 2006).

Folbre, Nancy. *Who Pays for the Kids?* New York: Routledge, 1994.

Fong, Vanessa. *Only Hope: Coming of Age Under China's One-Child Policy.* Palo Alto, Calif.: Stanford University Press, 2004.

Forbes. "DNA Evidence Clears Wrongly Convicted Man." July 11, 2006 <http://www.forbes.com/business/commerce/feeds/ap/2006/07/11/ap2872434.html> (accessed July 13, 2006).

Fordham University. "Internet Women's History Sourcebook." February 25, 2001 <http://www.fordham.edu/halsall/women/womensbook.html> (accessed July 17, 2006).

Foster, Geoff, Carol Levine, and John G. Williamson, eds. *A Generation at Risk: The Global Impact of HIV/AIDS on Orphans and Vulnerable Children.* New York: Cambridge University Press, 2005.

Foster, Lawrence. *Religion and Sexuality: The Shakers, the Mormons, and the Oneida Community.* Urbana: University of Illinois Press, 1984.

Fox, Jonathan, and Gaspar Rivera-Salgado, eds. *Indigenous Mexican Migrants in the United States*. Dallas: Center for U.S.-Mexican Studies, 2004.

Fox, Renee C., and Judith P. Swazey. *Spare Parts*. New York: Oxford University Press, 1992.

Fradkin, Philip L. *Fallout: An American Nuclear Tragedy*. Boulder, Colo.: Johnson Books, 2004.

Frank, J. *Couldn't Care More: A Study of Young Carers and their Needs*. London: The Children's Society, 1995.

Frank, J., C. Tatum, and S. Tucker. *On Small Shoulders: Learning from the Experiences of Former Young Carers*. London, United Kingdom: The Children's Society, 1999.

Frank, Stephen M. *Life with Father: Parenthood and Masculinity in the Nineteenth-Century American North*. Baltimore and London: Johns Hopkins University Press, 1998.

Franklin, Bob, ed. *The New Handbook of Children's Rights: Comparative Policy and Practice*. London: Routledge, 2001.

Frantz, Klaus. *Indian Reservations in the United States: Territory, Sovereignty, and Socioeconomic Change*. Chicago: University of Chicago Press, 1999.

Freedman, Russell. *Children of the Great Depression*. New York: Clarion Books, 2005.

Freud Museum of London. "1856–2006: 150th Anniversary of Sigmund Freud's Birth." 1999. <http://www.freud.org.uk> (accessed July 20, 2006).

Freud, Sigmund. *The Interpretation of Dreams*. New York: Avon (Reissue Edition), 1980.

Frick, John. *Theatre, Culture and Temperance Reform in Nineteenth Century America*. New York: Cambridge University Press, 2003.

Friedman, Lawrence M. *A History of American Law*. New York: Touchstone, 2005.

Friedman-Kasaba, Kathie. *Memories of Migration: Gender, Ethnicity, and Work in the Lives of Jewish and Italian Women in New York, 1870–1924*. Albany: State University of New York Press, 1996.

Frymer-Kensky, Tikva. *Reading the Women of the Bible: A New Interpretation of their Stories*. New York: Schocken Books, 2004.

Furman, Elina. *Boomerang Nation: How to Survive Living with Your Parents...The Second Time Around*. New York: Simon and Schuster, 2005.

GAO (Government Accountability Office). "Site Map." <http://www.gao.gov/sitemap.html> (accessed on June 24, 2006).

Gaskell, G., and M. W. Bauer, eds. *Biotechnology 1996–2000: The Years of Controversy*. London, UK: Science Museum, 2001.

Gauthier, Anne Helene. *The State and the Family: A Comparative Analysis of Family Policies in Industrialized Countries*. Oxford: Clarendon Press, 1998.

Gelman, Rita. *Tales of a Female Nomad: Living at Large in the World*. New York: Three Rivers Press, 2001.

George Mason University. "P.T. Barnum As a Temperance Speaker." 2006. <http://chrm.gmu.edu/lostmuseum/lm/48> (accessed June 27, 2006).

Gerstmann, Evan. *Same-Sex Marriage and the Constitution*. Cambridge University Press, 2004.

Gilder Lehman Institute of American History. "Woman's Suffrage Broadsides." 2006. <http://gilderlehman.org/collection/docs_archive_WomensSuffrage_Broadsides.html> (accessed June 23, 2006).

Gill, Libby. *Stay-at-Home Dads: The Essential Guide to Creating the New Family*. New York: The Penguin Group, 2001.

Gluck, Sherma B. *Rosie the Riveter Revisited: Women, the War, and Social Change*. Boston: Twayne Publishers, 1987.

Goer, Henci, and Rhonda Wheeler. *The Thinking Woman's Guide to a Better Birth*. New York: Perigee Trade, 1999.

Gold, Richard E. *Body Parts*. Washington, D.C.: Georgetown University Press, 1997.

Goldman, Wendy Z. *Women, the State and Revolution: Soviet Family Policy and Social Life, 1917–1936*. New York: Cambridge University Press, 1993.

Goldsmith, Barbara. *Other Powers: The Age of Suffrage, Spiritualism, and the Scandalous Victoria Woodhull*. New York: Knopf, 1998.

Gordon, Eleanor, and Gwyneth Nair. *Public Lives: Women, Family and Society in Victorian Britain*. New Haven, CT: Yale University Press, 2003.

Gordon, Sandra. *Best Baby Products*, 8th edition. New York: Consumer Reports, 2006.

Gordon, Sarah Barringer. *The Mormon Question: Polygamy and Constitutional Conflict in Nineteenth Century America*. Chapel Hill, NC: University of North Carolina Press, 2001.

Gourevitch, Philip. *We wish to inform you that tomorrow we will be killed with our families: Stories from Rwanda*. New York: Picador/Farrar, Straus, and Giroux; distributed by Holtzbrinck Publishers, 1998.

Government Printing Office. "Defense of Marriage Act." <http://frwebgate.access.gpo.gov/> (accessed June 10, 2006).

GovTrack.us. "S.J. Res. 1: Marriage Protection Amendment." <http://www.govtrack.us/congress/billtext.xpd?bill=sj109-1> (accessed July 26, 2006).

Goyer, Doreen S. and Gera E. Draaijer. *The Handbook of National Population Censuses —Europe*. New York, NY: Greenwood Press, 1992.

Grant, Julia. *Raising Baby by the Book: The Education of American Mothers*. New Haven, Conn.: Yale University Press, 1998.

Grant, Richard. *American Nomads: Travels with Lost Conquistadors, Mountain Men, Cowboys, Indians, Hoboes, Truckers, and Bullriders*. New York: Grove Press, 2003.

Green, Jennifer, and Susan Wisdom. *Stepcoupling: Sustaining a Strong Marriage in Today's Blended Family*. New York: Three Rivers Press, 2002.

Greenstein, Theodore. *Methods of Family Research*. Thousand Oaks, Calif.: Sage Publishing, 2006.

Gregory, James R. and Jack R. Weichmann. *Branding Across Borders: A Guide to Global Branding Marketing*. New York: McGraw-Hill, 2001.

Growing Up With Disability, edited by Carol Robinson and Kirsten Stalker. London: Jessica Kingsley Publishers, 1998.

Guest, Emma. *Children of AIDS: Africa's Orphan Crisis*. London: Pluto Press, 2003.

Gutjahr, Paul. *An American Bible: A History of the Good Book in the United States, 1777–1880*. Palo Alto, Calif.: Stanford University Press, 1999.

Gutman, Israel. *Resistance: The Warsaw Ghetto Uprising*. New York: Houghton-Mifflin, 1994.

Hacsi, Timothy A. *Second Home: Orphan Asylums and Poor Families in America*. Cambridge, Mass.: Harvard University Press, 1997.

Haines, David W., and Karen E. Rosenblum, eds. *Illegal Immigration in America: A Reference Handbook*. Westport, Conn.: Greenwood Press, 1999.

Hammamoto, Darrell Y. *Nervous Laughter: Television Situation Comedy and Liberal Democratic Ideology*. New York: Praeger, 1989.

Handbook of Family Diversity, edited by David H. Demo, Katharine R. Allen, and Mark A. Fine. New York: Oxford University Press, 1999.

Hanson, S. M., et al., eds. *Single-Parent Families: Diversity, Myths, and Realities*. New York: Hawthorne, 1995.

Hanson, Shirley M. H., Marsha L. Heims, and Doris J. Julina, eds. *Single-Parent Families: Diversity, Myths, and Realities*. New York: The Hawthorne Press, 1995.

Harris, Leslie M. *After Fifty: How the Baby Boom Will Redefine the Mature Market*. Ithaca, NY: Paramount Books, 2003.

Harris. J., and Søren Holm, eds. *The Future of Reproduction: Ethics, Choice, and Regulation*. Oxford, UK: Oxford University Press, 1998.

Hartman, Mary, and Lois Banner, eds. *Consciousness Raised: New Perspectives on the History of Women*. New York: Harper & Row, 1974.

Harvard University: Joint Center for Housing Studies. "Publications: Home Ownership." <http://www.jchs.harvard. edu/publications/homeownership/index.html> (accessed July 3, 2006).

Harvard University. "The Quiet Revolution That Transformed Women: Employment, Education and Family." June 2006. <http://www.aeaweb.org/annual_mtg_papers?2006/0106_1645_0101pdf> (accessed June 28, 2006).

Hatcher, Robert A., et al. *Contraceptive Technology*, 18th Revised Edition. New York: Ardent Media, 2004.

Hathaway, James C. *The Rights of Refugees under International Law*. New York: Cambridge University Press, 2005.

Hayden, Dolores. *Building Suburbia*. New York: Vintage, 2004.

Health Resources and Services Administration (HRSA). "Health Resources and Services Administration (HRSA)." <http://www.hrsa.gov> (accessed on June 24, 2006).

Hebrew Union College Skirball Museum. *Ketubbah: Jewish Marriage Contracts of the Hebrew Union College Skirball Museum and Klau Library*. Philadelphia: Jewish Publication Society, 1990.

Hegar, Rebecca L., and Maria Scanapieco. *Kinship Foster Care: Policy, Practice, and Research*. New York: Oxford University Press, 1998.

Heilbrun, Kirk, et al., eds. *Juvenile Delinquency: Prevention, Assessment, and Intervention*. New York: Oxford University Press, 2005.

Her Majesty's Stationery Office. *Annual Abstract of Statistics*. London: Her Majesty's Stationery Office, 1992.

Herbert Hoover Presidential Library and Museum. "Gallery Six: The Great Depression." <http://hoover.archives. gov/exhibits/Hooverstory/gallery06/gallery06.html> (accessed July 11, 2006).

Hewlett, Sylvia Ann. *Creating a Life: What Every Woman Needs to Know About Having a Baby and a Career*. New York: Miramax, 2002.

Heywood, Colin. *A History of Childhood: Children and Childhood in the West from Medieval to Modern Times*. Cambridge, U.K.: Polity Press, 2001.

Hiler, Megan, et al. *An Ornery Bunch: Tales and Anecdotes Collected by the WPA Montana Writers Project*. New York: Falcon, 1999.

Hindman, Hugh D. *Child Labor: An American History*. Armonk, NY: M.E. Sharpe, 2002.

Hindus, Milton. *The Jewish East Side: 1881–1924*. New Brunswick, N.J., and London: Transaction Publishers, 1996.

Hirshfield, Al and Gordon Kahn. *The Speakeasies of 1932*. New York: Applause Books, 2003.

Hobbs, Frank, and Laura Lippman. *Children's Well-Being: An International Comparison [International Population Reports Series (Series P95, Number 80)]*. Washington, D.C.: U.S. Government Printing Office, 1990.

Hoff, Christina. *Who Stole Feminism? How Women Have Betrayed Women.* New York: Touchstone, 1994.

Hoff, Joan. *Law, Gender and Injustice: A Legal History of U.S. Women.* New York: New York University Press, 1991.

Holmes, King K., et al., eds. *Sexually Transmitted Diseases.* New York: McGraw Hill, 1999.

Home Office, United Kingdom. "Child Protection." 2006. <http://police.homeoffice.gov.uk/operational-policing/crime-disorder/child-protection-taskforce> (accessed June 30, 2006).

Horstein, Jeffrey M. *A Nation of Realtors: A Cultural History of Twentieth Century America.* Raleigh, North Carolina: Duke University Press, 2005.

Hostetler, John A. *Amish Society.* Baltimore, MD: Johns Hopkins University Press, 1993.

Hudson, Larry E. *To Have and to Hold: Slave Work and Family Life in Antebellum South Carolina.* Athens, Ga.: University of Georgia, 1997.

Hughes, Kathryn. *The Short Life and Long Times of Mrs. Beeton.* New York: Alfred A. Knopf, 2006.

Hughes, Kathryn. *The Victorian Governess.* London: Rio Grande, 2002.

Hull, Moses. *The Question Settled. A Careful Comparison of Biblical and Modern Spiritualism. By Rev. Moses Hull.* Michigan Historical Reprint Series. Ann Arbor: Scholarly Publishing Office, University of Michigan Library, 2005.

Human Rights Watch. "Human Rights Watch." <http://www.hrw.org/> (accessed on June 24, 2006).

Human Rights Watch. "Child Labor." <http://www.hrw.org/children/labor.htm> (accessed July 21, 2006).

Human Rights Watch. "History of Rwanda." <http://www.hrw.org/reports/1999/rwanda/Geno1-3-09.htm#TopOfPage> (accessed July 12, 2006).

Human Rights Watch. "Refugees." <http://hrw.org/doc/> (accessed July 13, 2006).

Hunter, Susan S. *Black Death: AIDS in Africa.* New York: Palgrave Macmillan, 2003.

Huntington, Samuel P. *Who are We?: The Challenges to America's National Identity.* New York: Simon and Schuster, 2004.

Indiana University Lilly Library. "The Works Projects Administration in Indiana." 1996. <http://www.indiana.edu/~liblilly/wpa/wpa.html> (accessed July 22, 2006).

Institute for Women's Policy Research. "Fact Sheet." 205 <http://www.iwpr.org/pdf/B250.pdf> (accessed July 27, 2006).

International Assisted Reproduction Center. "Fertility Options." 2006 <http://www.fertilityhelp.com/CM/AboutAssistedReproduction/Fertility_Options.asp> (accessed June 21, 2006).

Internet Content Rating Association. "Contact ICRA." 2006. <http://www.icra.org/contact> (accessed June 30, 2006).

Iovine, Vicki, and Peg Rosen. *Girlfriends' Guide to Baby Gear.* New York: Perigee Books, 2003.

Jacoby, Tamar, ed. *Reinventing the Melting Pot.* New York: Basic Books, 2004.

Jagger, Gill and Caroline Wright. *Changing Concepts of Family.* London: Routledge, 1999.

Jakle, John. *The Tourist: Travel in Twentieth-Century North America.* Lincoln: University of Nebraska Press, 1985.

James Joyce Centre. <http://www.jamesjoyce.ie/home/> (accessed July 22, 2006).

Jane Austen Centre. "Jane Austen Centre in Bath, Somerset, England <http://www.janeausten.co.uk/centre/index.html> (accessed June 27, 2006).

Jane Austen Society of North America. "Jane Austen Society of North America." June 26, 2006 <http://www.jasna.org/> (accessed June 27, 2006).

Jewish Women's Archive. "Certificate of Indenture for Henry Barr." <http://www.jwa.org/teach/primarysources/artifacts_01.pdf //> (accessed July 22, 2006).

Johansen, Shawn. *Family Men: Middle-Class Fatherhood in Early Industrializing America.* London: Routledge, 2001.

Jones, Jacqueline. *Labor of Love, Labor of Sorrow: Black Women, Work, and the Family from Slavery to the Present.* New York: Basic Books, 1985.

Jones, James H. *Bad Blood: The Tuskegee Syphilis Experiment.* New York: The Free Press, 1993.

Journal of Family Violence. "Divorce Related Malicious Mother Syndrome." 1995. <http://www.fact.on.ca/Info/pas/turkat95.htm> (accessed June 19, 2006).

Juvenile Justice FYI. "History of America's Juvenile Justice System." <http://www.juvenilejusticefyi.com/history_of_juvenile_justice.html> (accessed June 24, 2006).

Kelly, Mary C. *Private Woman, Public Stage: Literary Domesticity in Nineteenth-Century America.* Chapel Hill: University of North Carolina Press, 2001.

Kelsh, Nick, and Anna Quindlen. *Siblings.* New York: Penguin Books, 1998.

Kertzer David I., and Dominique Arel, eds.*Census and Identity: the Politics of Race, Ethnicity, and Language in National Census.* Cambridge, UK: Cambridge University Press, 2002.

Khazanov, Anatoly. *Nomads and the Outside World.* Milwaukee: University of Wisconsin Press, 1994.

Klepp, Susan, et al. *The Infortunate: The Voyage and Adventures of William Moraley, An Indentured Servant.* University Park, Penn.: Pennsylvania State University Press, 2005.

Krause, Erik Hans. *Unfair to Babies!: A Helpless Infant Can't Go on Strike: It Depends on Your Care.* Rochester, NY:

WPA Federal Art Project, 1938. Courtesy of the Library of Congress.

Kurzman, Dan. *The Bravest Battle: The Twenty-Eight Days of the Warsaw Ghetto Uprising.* Philadelphia, PA: Da Capo Press, 1993.

Kyvig, David E. *Daily Life in the United States, 1920–1940: How Americans Lived during the Roaring Twenties and the Great Depression.* Chicago: Ivan Dee Publisher, 2004.

La Rossa, Ralph. *The Modernization of Fatherhood: A Social and Political History.* Chicago: University of Chicago Press, 1996.

Labor and Labor Movements. "American Sociological Association." <http://www.bgsu.edu/departments/soc/prof/mason/ASA/> (accessed on June 24, 2006).

Lahey, Benjamin, et al., eds. *Causes of Conduct Disorder and Juvenile Delinquency.* New York: Guilford Press, 2003.

Lanford, Duncan. *Internet Ethics.* New York: Palgrave MacMillan, 2000.

Lansdell, Avril. *Wedding Fashions, 1860–1980.* Buckinghamshire, England: Shire Publications, 1983.

Leavitt, Sarah A. *From Catharine Beecher to Martha Stewart: A Cultural History of Domestic Advice.* Chapel Hill, N.C.: University of North Carolina Press, 2002.

Legal Information Institute, Cornell University. "Code of Federal Regulations." <http://www4.law.cornell.edu/cfr/> (accessed on June 24, 2006).

Lehman, Jennifer M. *Gay & Lesbian Marriage and Family Reader: Analyses of Problems & Prospects for the 21st Century.* New York: Richard Altschuler & Associates, 2001.

Lender, Mark Edward, and James Kirby Martin. *Drinking in America: A History.* New York: The Free Press, 1983.

Lerner, Gerda. *The Majority Finds its Past: Placing Women in History.* New York: Oxford University Press, 1979.

Levinson, Ralph, and Michael J. Reiss. *Key Issues in Bioethics: A Guide for Teachers.* New York: RoutledgeFalmer, 2003 .

Levittown Historical Society "Levittown History." <http://www.levittownhistoricalsociety.org/index2.htm> (accessed June 15, 2006).

Lewin, Abraham. *A Cup of Tears: A Diary of the Warsaw Ghetto.* Institute for Polish-Jewish Studies, 1988.

Library of Congress. American Memory Project. "Married Women's Property Laws" 2006 <http://memory.loc.gov/ammem/awhhtml/awlaw3/property_law.html> (accessed June 19, 2006).

Library of Congress. "Library of Congress Online Catalog." <http://catalog.loc.gov/cgi-bin/Pwebrecon.cgi?DB=local&PAGE=First> (accessed on June 24, 2006).

Library of Congress: Thomas. "Family Entertainment and Copyright Act of 2004." 2004 <http://thomas.loc.gov/cgi-bin/query/z?c108:H.R.4586.RH:> (accessed June 120, 2006).

Library of Congress. "American Memory Project." 2006 <http://memory.loc.gov/ammem/awhhtml/awpnp6/d15.html> (accessed July 3, 2006).

Library of Congress. "An American Time Capsule: Three Centuries of Broadsides and Other Printed Ephemera." 2004. <http://memory.loc.gov/cgi-bin/query> (accessed June 27, 2006).

Library of Congress. "By Popular Demand: 'Votes for Women' Suffrage Pictures 1850–1920." October 19, 1998 <http://memory.loc.gov/service/pnp/cph/> (accessed July 3, 2006).

Library of Congress. "By the People, For the People: Posters from the WPA, 1936–1943." <http://memory.loc.gov/ammem/wpaposters/wpahome.html> (accessed July 23, 2006).

Library of Congress. "Emergence of Advertising in America 1850–1920." 2006. <http://jepoch.dth.jp/ww/scriptorium.lib.duke.edu/eaa/ephemera/A00/A0077/A0077-72dpi.html> (accessed June 27, 2006).

Library of Congress. "Votes for Women: Selections from the National American Woman Suffrage Association Collection, 1848–1921." 2006. <http://memory.loc.gov/cgi-bin/query/gt; (accessed June 20, 2006).

Linn-Gust, Michelle. *Do They Have Bad Days in Heaven? Surviving the Suicide Loss of a Sibling.* Albuquerque, NM: Chellehead Works, 2001.

Litt, Jacquelyn S. *Medicalized Motherhood: Perspectives from the Lives of African-American and Jewish Women.* New Brunswick, N.J.: Rutgers University Press, 2000.

Lofas, Jennifer. *Family Rules: Helping Stepfamilies and Single Parents Build Happy Homes.* New York: Kensington Publishing, 1998.

Longman, Phillip. *The Empty Cradle.* New York: Basic Books, 2004.

Los Angeles County Law Library. "California Divorce Pathfinder." <http://lalaw.lib.ca.us/divorce.html> (accessed June 19, 2006).

Lukas, Carrie. *The Politically Incorrect Guide to Women, Sex and Feminism.* Washington, D.C.: Regnery Publishing, 2006.

Lukebill, Grant. *Untold Millions: Secret Truths about Marketing to Gay and Lesbian Consumers.* San Francisco, California: Harrington Park Press, 1999.

Lystra, Karen. *Searching the Heart: Women, Men, and Romantic Love in Nineteenth-Century America.* New York: Oxford University Press, 1989.

Mackert, Mary. *The Sixth of Seven Wives: Escape from Modern Day Polygamy.* North Salt Lake, Utah: DMT Publishing, 2000.

MacNeil/Lehrer Productions, Public Broadcasting Service. "Remembering Dr. Spock." March 16, 1998 <http://www.pbs.org/newshour/bb/health/jan-june98/spock_3-16.html> (accessed July 12, 2006).

Macunovich, Diane J. *Birth Quake: The Baby Boom and Its Aftershocks*. Chicago: The University of Chicago Press, 2002.

Maier, Thomas. *Dr. Spock: An American Life*. New York: Harcourt Brace, 1998.

Making of America. "Cornell University." <http://cdl.library.cornell.edu/moa/> (accessed on June 24, 2006).

Malone, Mary T. *Women and Christianity: From the Reformation to the 21st Century*. Maryknoll, N.Y.: Orbis, 2003.

Maltin, Leonard. *The Great American Broadcast: A Celebration of Radio's Golden Age*. New York: Penguin Putnam, 1997.

Manchester Guardian. "Look, No Brands...." 2000 <http://observer.guardian.co.uk/review/story/0,6903,396082,06.html> (accessed June 30, 2006).

Marc, David. *Comic Visions: Television Comedy and American Culture (Second Edition)*. Malden, Massachusetts: Blackwell , 1997.

Marks, Lara V. *Sexual Chemistry: A History of the Contraceptive Pill*. New Haven, Conn.: Yale University Press, 2001.

Marosy, Jean Paul. *A Manager's Guide to Elder Care and Work*. Westport, Connecticut: Greenwood, 1999.

Marquardt, Elizabeth. *Between Two Worlds: The Inner Lives of Children of Divorce*. New York: Crown Books, 2005.

Martin, Deborah L., ed. *An Annotated Guide to Adoption Research: 1986–1997*. Washington, D. C.: Child Welfare League of America, 1999.

Martin, Jane. *Women and Education 1800–1980*. New York: Palgrave MacMillan, 2004.

Maruggi, Edward Albert. *Mushrooms, Sausage, and Wine: Life with an Immigrant Father*. Pitsford, New York: Winston Publishing, 1997.

Mason, Mary Ann, Arlene Skolnick, and Stephen D. Sugarman, eds. *All Our Families: New Policies for a New Century. 2nd edition*. New York: Oxford University Press, 2002.

Massey, Douglas S. *Beyond Smoke and Mirrors: Mexican Immigration in an Era of Economic Integration*. New York: Russell Sage Foundation Publications, 2003.

Massolini, Maxine. *Blended Families: Creating Harmony as You Build a New Home Life*. Chicago: Moody Press, 2000.

Mattingly, Carol. *Well Tempered Women*. Carbondale, Ill.: Southern Illinois Press, 1998.

Maushart, Susan. *The Mask of Motherhood: How Becoming a Mother Changes Our Lives and Why We Never Talk About It*. New York: Penguin, 2000.

Mayer, Don. *The Sibling Slam Book: What It's Really Like To Have A Brother Or Sister With Special Needs*. Bethesda, Md.: Woodbine House, 2005.

McCormac, Eugene I. *James K. Polk: A Political Biography*. New York: Russell & Russell, Inc., 1965.

McElvaine, Robert S. *The Great Depression: America 1929–1941*. New York: Three Rivers Press, 1993.

McKenzie, Richard B. *Rethinking Orphanages for the 21st Century*. Thousand Oaks, Calif.: Sage, 1999.

McKinzie, Richard D. *The New Deal for Artists*. Princeton, NJ: Princeton University Press, 1973.

McLanahan, Sara, and Gary Sandefur. *Growing up with a Single Parent: What Hurts, What Helps*. Cambridge, Mass.: Harvard University Press, 1994.

Medical News Today. "Working Mothers Healthier Than Full-Time Housewives." May 15, 2006. <http://www.medicalnewstoday.com/healthnews.php?newsid=43421> (accessed July 22, 2006).

Melville-James, Anna. *Guardian Unlimited*. "My Family and Other Vehicles." <http://www.guardian.co.uk/family/story/0,,1748639,00.html> (accessed July 21, 2006).

Merriam, Dwight. *The Complete Guide to Zoning*. New York: McGraw-Hill, 2004.

Michel, Sonya. *Children's Interests/Mother's Rights: The Shaping of America's Child Care Policy*. New Haven, CT: Yale University Press, 1999.

Michigan State University. "Margaret Sanger and the 1920s Birth Control Movement." 2000. <http://www.msu.edu/course/mc/112/1920s/Sanger/index.html> (accessed July 22, 2006).

Miller, Naomi. *Single Parents by Choice: A Growing Trend in Family Life*. New York: Insight Books, 1992.

Mintz, Steven and Susan Kellogg. *Domestic Revolutions: A Social History of American Family Life*. New York: The Free Press, 1988.

Mitchell, Stephen A. and Margaret Black. *Freud and Beyond: A History of Modern Psychoanalytic Thought*. New York: Basic Books, 1995.

Morreale, Joanne. *Critiquing the Sitcom: A Reader (The Television Series)*. Syracuse, New York; Syracuse University Press, 2002.

Moses, Kate and Camille Peri, ed. *Because I Said So*. New York: Harper Collins, 2005.

Mothers and Motherhood: Readings in American History, edited by Rima D. Apple and Janet Golden. Columbus, Ohio: The Ohio State University Press, 1997.

Moul, Charles, ed. *A Concise Handbook of Movie Industry Economics*. Cambridge, UK: Cambridge University Press, 2005.

Murphy, Patrick T. *Wasted: The Plight of America's Unwanted Children*. Chicago: Ivan R. Dee Publisher, 1997.

Musee McCord Museum. "The Cult of Domesticity." June 8, 2006. <http://www.mccord-museum.qc.ca/en/keys/folders/VQ_P1_6_EN> (accessed June 17, 2006).

Museum of Broadcast Communications. "Family on Television <http://www.museum.tv/archives/etv/F/htmlF/familyontel/familyontel.htm> (accessed June 28, 2006).

Nappa, Mike. *Growing Up Fatherless: Healing from the Absence of Dad*. New York: Revell, 2003.

National Adoption Day. "Adoption Statistics." 2003 <http://www.nationaladoptionday.org/2005/media/materials/Background/Adoption%20Statistics%20Factsheet.doc> (accessed June 23, 2006).

National Alliance for Caregiving and United Hospital Fund. *Young Caregivers in the U.S.: Report of Findings*. Bethesda, MD: National Alliance for Caregiving, 2005.

National Archives and Records Administration. "A New Deal for the Arts." <http://www.archives.gov/exhibits/new_deal_for_the_arts/index.html> (accessed July 3, 2006).

National Center for Fathering. <http://www.fathers.com> (accessed July 22, 2006).

National Conference of Commissioners on Uniform State Laws. "Uniform Adoption Act of 1994." 2002. <http://www.law.upenn.edu/bll/ulc/fnact99/1990s/uaa94.htm> (accessed June 23, 2006).

National Fatherhood Initiative. "NFI Research." <http://www.fatherhood.org/research.asp> (accessed June 19, 2006).

National Fatherhood Initiative. <http://www.fatherhood.org> (accessed July 22, 2006).

National Institute on Media and the Family. "MediaQuotient: National Survey of Family Media Habits, Knowledge, and Attitudes." 1999. <http://www.mediafamily.org/research/report_mqexecsum.shtml> (accessed June 29, 2006).

National Joint Apprenticeship and Training Committee. "Apprenticeship Training." <http://www.njatc.org/apprentice.htm> (accessed July 22, 2006).

National New Deal Preservation Association. "New Deal/WPA Art in Cleveland, Ohio." 2006. <http://www.wpamurals.com/cleveland.html> (accessed July 22, 2006).

National Park Service. "Indian Reservations in the Continental United States." <http://www.cr.nps.gov/nagpra/DOCUMENTS/ResMAP.HTM> (accessed July 16, 2006).

Nature. "Double-Helix: 50 Years of DNA." 2003. <http://www.nature.com/nature/dna50/index.html> (accessed July 12, 2006).

Neal, Peter, ed. *Urban Villages: The Making of Community*. London: Spon Press, 2003.

Nebraska Studies. "The Family Fallout Shelter." <http://www.nebraskastudies.org/0900/frameset_reset.html?http://www.nebraskastudies.org/0900/stories/0901_0132.html> (accessed June 20, 2006).

Nellie Mae Education Foundation. "Critical Hours: Afterschool Programs and Educational Success." <http://www.nmefdn.org/CriticalHours.htm> (accessed June 28, 2006).

New Internationalist. "Two Steps Forward, One Step Back." December 1982. <http://www.newint.org/issue118/two.htm> (accessed July 10, 2006).

New York Divorce and Family Law. "Divorce: History of Divorce in New York." 2006. <http://www.brandeslaw.com/grounds_for_divorce/history.htm> (accessed June 21, 2006).

New York Society for the Prevention of Cruelty to Children. <http://www.nyspcc.org> (accessed July 22, 2006).

NICHD - National Institute of Child Health and Human Development. "NICHD - National Institute of Child Health and Human Development." <http://www.nichd.nih.gov> (accessed on June 24, 2006).

Nicholi Armand M. *The Question of God: C.S. Lewis and Sigmund Freud Debate God, Love, Sex, and the Meaning of Life*. New York: Free Press, 2002.

Nichols, Francine, and Sharron Smith Humenick. *Childbirth Education: Practice, Research and Theory*. New York: Saunders, 2000.

Nike Apparel. "Workers and Factories Code of Conduct." March 2005. <http://www.nike.com/nikebiz/> (accessed June 21, 2006).

Noam, Gil G., et al. *Afterschool Education: Approaches to an Emerging Field*. Cambridge, Mass.: Harvard Education Press, 2002.

Nord, David. *Faith in Reading: Religious Publishing and the Birth of Mass Media in America*. New York: Oxford University Press, 2004.

NYTimes.com. "The New Red-Diaper Babies." December 7, 2004. <http://www.nytimes.com/2004/12/07/opinion/> (accessed June 22, 2006).

O'Connell, Martin T. *Children with Single Parents—How they Fare (Census Brief)*. Washington, D.C.: U.S. Census Bureau, 1997.

O'Neill, William. *Everyone Was Brave: A History of Feminism in America (5th edition)*. New York: Quadrangle Books, 1974.

Office of Global Health Affairs. "Office of Global Health Affairs." <http://www.globalhealth.gov> (accessed on June 24, 2006).

Office of the United Nations High Commissioner for Refugees. *The State of the World's Refugees: Human Displacement in the New Millennium*. New York: Oxford University Press, 2006.

Ohio State University. "Aging Families—The Sandwich Generation." <http://hec.osu.edu/famlife/aging/PDFs/Sandwich%20Generation.final.pdf> (accessed July 16, 2006).

Ohio State University. "Family Life." <http://hec.osu.edu/famlife/family/index.htm> (accessed June 18, 2006).

Ong, Paul M. *The Effects of Race and Life-Cycle on Home Ownership: A Study of Blacks and Whites in Los Angeles 1970 to 1980*. Los Angeles: Graduate School of Architecture and Urban Planning, University of California, Los Angeles, 1986.

Oregon State University. "Curriculum Vitae: Leslie N. Richards." <http://www.hhs.oregonstate.edu/faculty-staff/> (accessed June 23, 2006).

Oriard, Michael. *King Football: Sport and Spectacle in the Golden Age of Radio and Newsreels, Movies and Magazines, the Weekly and the Daily Press.* Charlotte: University of North Carolina Press, 2001.

Orr, Deborah. *Slave Chocolate?* New York: McFarland and Company, 2005.

OurDocuments.gov. "Keating-Owen Child Labor Act of 1916." <http://www.ourdocuments.gov/> (accessed July 21, 2006).

Palmieri, Patricia Ann. *In Adamless Eden: The Community of Women Faculty at Wellesley.* New Haven, Conn.: Yale University Press, 1995.

Parmet, Robert. *The Master of Seventh Avenue: David Dubinsky and America's Labor Movement.* New York: New York University Press, 2005.

Paul, Pamela. "Mother Superior." *The New York Times,* (April 16, 2006).

Pawlowska, Harriet M., ed. *Merrily We Sing: 105 Polish Folks Songs.* Boston: Bay Back Books, 1961.

Pegram, Thomas R. *Battling Demon Rum: The Struggle for a Dry America 1800–1933.* Chicago: Ivan R. Dee, 1998.

Perkins, Joan. *Victorian Women.* New York: New York University, 1993.

Peskowitz, Miriam. *The Truth Behind the Mommy Wars: Who Decides What Makes a Good Mother?* Emeryville, Calif.: Seal Press, 2005.

Peters, H. Elizabeth, and Gary W. Peterson, eds. *Fatherhood: Research, Interventions, and Policies.* Bingamton, N.Y.: Haworth Press, 2000.

Peters, Joan. *When Mothers Work: Loving Our Children Without Sacrificing Ourselves.* New York: Perseus Books, 1997.

Pew Research Center. "From the Age of Aquarius To the Age of Responsibility." December 8, 2005. <http://pewresearch.org/assets/social/pdf/socialtrends-boomers120805.pdf> (accessed June 28, 2006).

Phillips, Roderick. *Putting Asunder: A History of Divorce in Western Society.* Cambridge University Press, 1988.

Pinello, Daniel R. *Gay Rights and American Law.* New York: Cambridge University Press, 2003.

Pipher, Mary. *The Middle of Everywhere: Helping Refugees Enter the American Community.* New York: Harcourt Books, 2002.

Politics and Society in Provincial Russia: Saratov, 1590–1917, edited by Rex Wade and Scott Seregny. Columbus, Ohio: Ohio State University Press, 1989.

Pool, Daniel. *What Jane Austen Ate and Charles Dickens Knew: From Fox Hunting to Whist: The Facts of Daily Life in Nineteenth-Century England.* Carmichael, Calif.: Touchstone, 1994.

Prunier, Gerard. *The Rwanda Crisis: History of a Genocide.* New York: Columbia University Press, 1995.

Pudup, Mary Beth, Dwight B. Billings, and Altina L. Waller, eds. *Appalachia in the Making: The Mountain South in the Nineteenth Century.* Chapel Hill: University of North Carolina Press, 1995.

Quayle, Dan. *Standing Firm.* Harpercollins (mm), 1995.

Radio and Television Museum. "Welcome to the Radio and Television Museum." <http://www.radiohistory.org/> (accessed June 20, 2006).

Rall, Ted and Jules Feiffer. *Revenge of the Latchkey Kids: An Illustrated Guide to Surviving the 90s and Beyond.* New York: Workman, 1998.

Ramming, Cindy. *All Mothers Work: A Guilt-Free Guide for the Stay at Home Mom.* New York: Avon Books, 1996.

RAND. "Family Planning in Developing Countries." 1999. <http://www.rand.org/pubs/issue_paper/IP176?index2.html> (accessed June 26, 2006).

Recording Industry Association of America. "Brief History on Copyright Laws." <http://www.riaa.com/issues/copyright/history.asp> (accessed June 20, 2006).

Republic of Singapore. "Changing Contraceptive Choices of Singapore Women." 2000. <http://www.singstat.gov.sg/ssn/feat/2Q99/featapr991.pdf> (accessed June 26, 2006).

Reuters. "Japan Experts Devise New Human Egg Freezing Method." June 19, 2006. <http://www.alertnet.org/thenews/newsdesk/L1994843.htm> (accessed June 22, 2006).

Richards, David. *The Case for Gay Rights: From Bowers to Lawrence and Beyond.* Lawrence, KS: The University Press of Kansas, 2005.

Richardson, Ronald W. and Lois A. Richardson. *Birth Order and You.* North Vancouver, B.C.: Self Counsel Press., 1990.

Riley, Terence. *Un-Private House.* New York: Museum of Modern Art, 2002.

Robert E. Lee Memorial Association. "Indentured Servants and Transported Convicts." <http://www.stratfordhall.org/ed-servants.html> (accessed July 22, 2006).

Robertson, Una A. *The Illustrated History of the Housewife, 1650–1950.* London: Palgrave MacMillan, 1999.

Rogers, Mary Elizabeth. *Mencken: The American Iconoclast.* New York: Oxford University Press, 2005.

Rose, Elizabeth. *A Mother's Job: The History of Day Care, 1890–1960.* New York: Oxford University Press, 1998.

Rose, Kenneth D. *One Nation Underground: The Fallout Shelter in American Culture*. New York: New York University Press, 2001.

Ross, Richard. *Waiting for the End of the World*. New York: Princeton Architectural Press, 2004.

Rotem, Símha. *Memoirs of a Warsaw Ghetto Fighter: The Past within Me*. New Haven, Connecticut: Yale University Press, 2002.

Rothman, Hal K. *Devil's Bargains: Tourism in the Twentieth-Century American West*. Lawrence: University Press of Kansas, 1998.

Rothman, Sheila M. *Living in the Shadow of Death: Tuberculosis and the Social Experience of Illness in American History*. Baltimore, MD: Johns Hopkins University Press, 1995.

Runkel, Hal. *ScreamFree Parenting: Raising Your Kids by Keeping Your Cool*. Duluth, Georgia: Oakmont Publishing, 2005.

Rutgers University. "Stanton and Anthony Paper Project Online." July 2001. <http://ecssba.rutgers.edu/studies/ecsbio.html> (accessed June 21, 2006).

Sabar, Shalom. *Ketubbah: The Art of the Jewish Marriage Contract*. New York: Rizzoli, 2000.

Saetnam, A.R., N. Oudshoorn, and M. Kirejczyk, eds. *Bodies of Technology: Women's Involvement with Reproductive Medicine*. Columbus, OH: Ohio State University Press, 2000.

Safer, Jeanne. *Beyond Motherhood: Choosing a Life without Children*. New York: Pocket Books, 1996.

Salinger, Sharon V. *'To Serve Well and Faithfully': Labor and Indentured Servants in Pennsylvania, 1682–1800*. New York: Cambridge University Press, 1987.

San Diego Union-Tribune. "Commercial Freezing of Human Eggs Has Backers, Opponents." September 29, 2004. <http://www.signonsandiego.com/uniontrib/20040929/news_1c29eggs.html> (accessed June 22, 2006).

Sanders, Robert. *Sibling Relationships: Theory and Issues for Practice*. Hampshire, UK: Palgrave Macmillan, 2004.

Sanger, Margaret. *The Autobiography of Margaret Sanger*. Mineola, N.Y.: Dover Publications, 2004.

Schactman, Tom. *Rumspringa: To Be or Not to Be Amish*. New York: North Point Press, 2006.

Schechter, Roger, and John Thomas. *Intellectual Property: The Law of Copyrights, Patents and Trademarks*. St. Paul, MN: Thomson/West Group, 2003.

Schepard, Andrew I. *Children, Courts and Custody*. New York: Cambridge University Press, 2006.

Schor, Edward L., ed. *Caring for Your School-Age Child Ages 5 to 12*. New York: Bantam Books, 2000.

Schulman, Sarah. *Stagestruck: Theater, AIDS, and the Marketing of Gay America*. Durham, NC: Duke University Press, 1998.

ScienCentral. "Daddy's Brain." June 16, 2006. <http://www.sciencentral.com/articles/> (accessed June 19, 2006).

Senak, Mark S. *Every Trick in the Book: The Essential Gay & Lesbian Legal Guide*. New York: M. Evans and Company, 2002 .

Seume, Keith. *VW Beetle: A Comprehensive Illustrated History of the World's Most Popular Car*. Osceola, Wisc.: Motorbooks International, 1997.

Shanley, Mary L. *Making Babies, Making Families: What Matters Most in an Age of Reproductive Technologies, Surrogacy, Adoption, and Same-Sex and Unwed Parents' Rights*. Boston: Beacon Press, 2002.

Sheppard, Alice. *Cartooning for Suffrage*. Albuquerque: University of New Mexico Press, 1994.

Shields, Carol. *Jane Austen*. New York: Penguin, 2005.

Shippensburg University. "Sigmund Freud: 1836–1939." <http://www.ship.edu/~cgboeree/freud.html> (accessed July 20, 2006).

Shriberg, Elaine Fantle. *Blending Families*. New York: Berkley Publishers, 1999.

Siegel, Susan and David S. Siegel. *A Resource Guide to the Golden Age of Radio: Special Collections, Bibliography, and the Internet*. Yorktown Heights, N.Y.: Book Hunter Press, 2006.

Simkin, Penny, et al. *Pregnancy, Childbirth, and the Newborn, Revised and Updated: The Complete Guide*. New York: Meadowbrook Press, 2001.

Simon Wiesenthal Center. "Simon Wiesenthal Center." <http://www.wiesenthal.com> (accessed on June 24, 2006).

Sivulka, Juliann. *Soap, Sex, and Cigarettes: A Cultural History of American Advertising*. Belmont, Calif.: Wadsworth, 1997.

Smith, Jason Scott. *Building New Deal Liberalism: The Political Economy of Public Works, 1933–1956*. Cambridge, UK: Cambridge University Press, 2005.

Smithsonian Institution Libraries. "The Making of a Homemaker." <http://www.sil.si.edu/ondisplay/makinghomemaker/> (accessed July 18, 2006).

Smolenyak, Megan, and Ann Turner. *Trace Your Roots with DNA: Using Genetic Tests to Explore Your Family Tree*. New York: Rodale Press, 2004.

Social Sciences Virtual Library. "Digilogical." <http://www.dialogical.net/socialsciences/index.html> (accessed on June 24, 2006).

SocioWeb. "Blairworks." <http://www.socioweb.com/> (accessed on June 24, 2006).

Solomon, Dorothy. *Daughter of the Saints: Growing Up In Polygamy*. New York: W. W. Norton and Company, 2003.

Southern Methodist University. "Victory Garden Leader's Handbook 1943." <http://digitallibrary.smu.edu/cul/gir/ww2/pdf/p0159.pdf> (accessed July 22, 2006).

Southern Poverty Law Center. "Southern Poverty Law Center." <http://www.splcenter.org/> (accessed on June 24, 2006).

Spigel, Lynn. *Make Room for TV: Television and the Family Ideal in Postwar America*. Chicago: University of Chicago Press, 1992.

Spock, Benjamin, and Michael B. Rothenberg. *Baby and Child Care*. New York: Pocket Books, 1985.

Spock, Benjamin, and Miriam E. Lowenberg. *Feeding Your Baby and Child*. New York: Duell, Sloan, and Pearce, 1955.

Spock, Benjamin. *A Better World for Our Children: Rebuilding American Family Values*. Washington, DC: National Press Books, 1994.

Spock, Benjamin. *A Teenager's Guide to Life and Love*. New York: Simon and Schuster, 1970.

Spock, Benjamin. *Dr. Spock's The First Two Years: The Emotional and Physical Needs of Children from Birth to Age Two*. Edited by Martin T. Stein. New York: Pocket Books, 2001.

Spock, Benjamin. *Raising Children in a Difficult Time: A Philosophy of Parental Leadership and High Ideals*. New York: Norton, 1974.

Stacey, William. *Black Home Ownership: A Sociological Case Study of Metropolitan Jacksonville*. New York: Praeger, 1972.

Stanford University. "Why the U.S. Led in Education Lessons from Economic History." June 2006. <http://comparativepolitics.stanford.edu/Papers.205-06/Elis_12_June_2006.pdf> (accessed June 29, 2006).

Stanley, Autumn. *Mothers and Daughters of Invention: Notes for a Revised History of Technology*. Metuchen, N.J.: Scarecrow Press, 1993.

Stanton, Elizabeth Cady. *The Woman's Bible*. Boston: Northeastern University Press, 1993.

Stanton, Glenn T. *Why Marriage Matters: Reasons to Believe in Marriage in Post-Modern Society*. Colorado Spring, CO: Pinon Press, 1997.

State of Illinois. "Illinois Marriage and Dissolution of Marriage Act." April 16, 2006. <http://www.ilga.gov/legislation/ilcs/> (accessed July 11, 2006).

State of Louisiana. "House Bill 1631." 1999. <http://www.lafayetteparishclerk.com/download/pdf/hb1631.pdf> (accessed June 21, 2006).

State University of New York at Potsdam. "History of Anti-Alcohol Movements in the U.S." 2006. <http://www2.potsdam.edu.hansondj/controversies/1124913901.html> (accessed June 27, 2006).

State University of New York/Potsdam. "National Prohibition of Alcohol in the United States." <http://www2.potsdam.edu/hansondj/Controversies/1091124904.html> (accessed July 22, 2006).

Stateline. "50-state Rundown on Gay Marriage Laws." November 3, 2004. <http://www.stateline.org/live/> (accessed June 15, 2006).

Stebbins, Michael. *Sex, Drugs, and DNA: Science's Taboos Confronted*. New York: Macmillan, 2006.

Steinberg, Gail, and Beth Hall. *Inside Transracial Adoption*. Indianapolis: Perspective Press, 2000.

Steiner, Leslie Morgan. *Mommy Wars: Stay-at-Home and Career Moms Face off on Their Choices, Their Lives, Their Families*. New York: Random House, 2006.

Stern, Madeline. *Louisa May Alcott: A Biography*. Boston: Northeastern University Press, 1999.

Stevenson, Brenda E. *Life in Black and White: Family and Community in the Slave South*. New York: Basic Books, 1997.

Stiers, Gretchen. *From This Day Forward*. New York: Saint Martins Press, 1999.

Stockton College. "Women in the Victorian Age." April 19, 2002. <http://caxton.stockton.edu/browning/stories/storyReader$3> (accessed July 16, 2006).

Stoll, Elmo. *The Midnight Test*. Aylmer, Ontario: Pathway Publishers, 1990.

Stoll, James, David Luthy, and Elmo Stoll. *Seeking True Values*. Aylmer, Ontario: Pathway Publishers, 1968.

Straus, Murray. *Beating the Devil Out of Them*. Somerset, N.J.: Transaction Publishers, 2001.

Struyk, Raymond J. *Determinants of the Rate of Home Ownership of Black Relative to White Households*. Washington, D. C.: Urban Institute, 1977.

Subbarao, Kalanidhi, and Dian Coury. *Reaching Out to Africa's Orphans: A Framework for Public Action (Africa Region Human Development Series)*. Washington, D.C.: World Bank, 2004.

Sullivan, Mike. *Safety Monitor: How to Protect Your Kids Online*. Chicago: Bonus Press, 2002.

Summers, Randal W., and Allan M. Hoffman, eds. *Domestic Violence: A Global View*. Westpoint: Greenwood Press, 2002.

Syracuse University Library: Media Services. "Television History Archive." 2005. <http://libwww.syr.edu/information/media/archive/main.htm> (accessed June 16, 2006).

Syracuse University. "Fannia Mae Cohen—Education Leader in Labor and Workers Education." 2006. <http://www-distance.syr.edu/long.html> (accessed July 3, 2006).

Szymanski, Anne-Marie. *Pathways to Prohibition: Radicals, Moderates and Social Movement Outcomes.* Raleigh, N.C.: Duke University Press, 2003.

Taylor, Ella. *Prime-Time Families: Television Culture in Postwar America.* Berkeley: University of California Press, 1989.

Thomas, Hugh. *The Slave Trade: The History of the Atlantic Slave Trade, 1440–1870.* New York: Touchstone, 1997.

Thomas. "Library of Congress." <http://thomas.loc.gov/> (accessed on June 24, 2006).

Tiller, Veronica E. Velarde, ed. *Tiller's Guide to Indian Country: Economic Profiles of American Indian Reservations.* Albuquerque, N.Mex.: BowArrow Publishing, 2006.

Toman, Walter. *Family Constellation: Its Effects on Personality and Social Behavior.* New York: Springer, 1976.

Tucker, M. and C. Mitchell-Kernan. *The Decline in Marriage among African Americans.* New York: Russell Sage, 1995.

Turow, Joseph, and Lilach Nir. *Annenberg Public Policy Center, University of Pennsylvania Report Series.* "The Internet and the Family 2000: The View from Parents, the View from Kids." Report 33. May 2000. <http://www.annenbergpublicpolicycenter.org/04_info_society/family/finalrepor_fam.pdf> (accessed June 29, 2006).

TV.com. "The Cosby Show." Septermber 20, 1984. <http://www.tv.com/the-cosby-show/show/481/summary.html?full_summary=1&tag=showspace_links;full_summary> (accessed July 22, 2006).

Twerski, Abraham S., and Charles M. Schulz. *I Didn't Ask to Be in This Family: Sibling Relationships and How They Shape Adult Behavior and Relationships.* New York, NY : Henry Holt & Co., 1996.

Tyler, Gus. *Look for the Union Label: A History of the International Ladies' Garment Workers Union.* Armonk, New York: M.E. Sharpe, 1995.

U.S. Bureau of the Census. <http://www.census.gov> (accessed July 22, 2006).

U.S. Bureau of the Census. *Abstract of the Fourteenth Census of the United States: 1920.* Washington, D.C.: Washington Government Printing Office, 1923.

U.S. Bureau of the Census. "America's Families and Living Arrangements: 2003 Population Characteristics." November 2004. <http://www.census.gov/prod/2004pubs/p20-553.pdf> (accessed June 24, 2006).

U.S.Bureau of the Census. "Historical Income Data." 2006. <http://www.census.gov/hhes/www/income/histinc/histinctb.html> (accessed July 28, 2006).

U.S. Bureau of the Census. "History." May 29, 2003. <http://www.census.gov/acsd/www/history.html> (accessed June 26, 2006).

U.S. Bureau of the Census. "Housing Vacancies and Homeownership." February 17, 2005. <http://www.census.gov/hhes/www/housing/hvs/annual04/ann04t20.html> (accessed July 3, 2006).

U.S. Bureau of the Census. "State Population Increase Projections." 2005. <http://www.census.gov/Press-Release/www/2005/stateproj7.xls> (accessed June 29, 2006).

U.S. Citizenship and Immigration Services. <http://www.uscis.gov/graphics/index.htm> (accessed July 10, 2006).

U.S. Citizenship and Immigration Services. "Refugees." <http://www.uscis.gov/graphics/services/refugees/index.htm> (accessed July 13, 2006).

U.S. Committee for Refugees and Immigrants. <http://www.refugees.org/> (accessed July 13, 2006).

U.S. Department of the Interior. "Workforce Diversity." 2005. <http://www.doi.gov/diversity/8women.htm> (accessed June 18, 2006).

U.S. Department of Justice. *Criminal Victimization in the U.S., 1991.* Washington, D.C: U.S. Department of Justice, 1992.

U.S. Department of Justice. "Office on Violence Against Women." <http://www.usdoj.gov/ovw/> (accessed July 4, 2006).

U.S. Department of Justice. "Policing on Indian Reservations." July 2001. <http://www.ncjrs.gov/pdffiles1/nij/188095.pdf> (accessed July 16, 2006).

U.S. Department of Labor. "Compensation from before World War I through the Great Depression." 2001. <http://www.bls.gov/opub/cwc/cm20030124ar03p1.htm> (accessed July 3, 2006).

U.S. Department of Labor. "Frequently Asked Questions about Newborns' and Mothers' Health Protection" <http://www.dol.gov/ebsa/faqs/faq_consumer_newborns.html> (accessed July 10, 2006).

U.S. Department of Labor. "Apprenticeship." <http://www.dol.gov/dol/topic/training/apprenticeship.htm> (accessed July 22, 2006).

U.S. Food and Drug Administration. "Birth Control Guide." December 2003. <http://www.fda.gov/fdac/features/1997/babytabl.html> (accessed July 22, 2006).

U.S. House of Representatives. "The United States House of Representatives." <http://www.house.gov/> (accessed on June 24, 2006).

U.S. Library of Congress. "The History of Household Technology with Constance Carter." <http://www.loc.gov/rr/program/journey/household.html> (accessed July 1, 2006).

U.S. Senate. "The United States Senate." <http://www.senate.gov/> (accessed on June 24, 2006).

UNAIDS. "UNAIDS Research." <http://www.unaids.org/en/Issues/Research/default.asp> (accessed on June 24, 2006).

UNAIDS: Joint United Nations Programme on HIV/AIDS <http://www.unaids.org/en/> (accessed June 24, 2006).

United Nations News Centre. "By Surmounting a Few Production Humps, Camel Milk Could Bring in Billions."

April 19, 2006. <http://www.un.org/apps/news/> (accessed July 12, 2006).

United Nations Office of the High Commissioner for Human Rights. "United Nations." <http://www.ohchr.org/english/> (accessed on June 24, 2006).

United Nations. "International Conference on Population and Development." <http://www.un.org/popin/icpd2.htm> (accessed June 11, 2006).

University of California, Los Angeles. "Divorce Research Homepage." 2001. <http://jeffwood.bol.ucla.edu/> (accessed June 18, 2006).

University of Maryland. "National Public Broadcasting Archives." <http://www.lib.umd.edu/NPBA/index.html> (accessed June 19, 2006).

University of Michigan News Service. "U.S. Husbands are Doing More Housework While Wives are Doing Less." <http://www.umich.edu/news/index.html?Releases/2002/Mar02/chr031202a> (accessed July 10, 2006).

University of North Texas: Department of Radio, Television and Film. "Radio and Television History Sites." <http://www.rtvf.unt.edu/links/histsites.htm> (accessed June 16, 2006).

University of Pittsburth. "Superstitions: Pregnancy, Childbirth, and Postnatal Care." <http://www.pitt.edu/~dash/superstition.html> (accessed July 10, 2006).

University of San Diego: History Department. "Television's Golden Age." <http://history.sandiego.edu/gen/recording/television6.html> (accessed June 16, 2006).

University of San Diego. "Golden Age of Radio, 1935–1950." <http://history.sandiego.edu/gen/recording/radio2.html> (accessed June 20, 2006).

University of Tennessee College of Law. "Tennessee Family Law/Divorce Guide." June 2003. <http://www.law.utk.edu/library/divo2.htm> (accessed June 18, 2006).

University of Texas: THSA Online. "Works Project Administration." 2001. <http://www.tsha.utexas.edu/handbook/online/articles/WW/ncw1.html> (accessed July 22, 2006).

University of Texas. "The Divorce Dilemma." 2006. <http://www.utexas.edu/features/2006/divorce/> (accessed June 26, 2006).

University of Utah. "Polygamy." 2006. <http://www.media.utah.edu/UHE/p/POLYGAMY.html> (accessed June 20, 2006).

University of Virginia. "Imaging Slavery in Mark Twain's Books." 2002. <http://etext.virginia.edu/railton/wilson/slavery/mtslavhp.html> (accessed June 27, 2006).

University of Virginia. "Mid-Century Women's Rights Movement: Selected Texts." 2004. <http://etext.lib.virginia.edu/railton/uncletom/womanmov.html> (accessed June 20, 2006).

University of Washington. "In Touch / Blended Families." 2004. <http://www.washington.edu/admin/hr/benefits/worklife/carelink/intouch/intouch_blnded-fam.pdf> (accessed June 18, 2006).

University of Wisconsin. "Parenting the Preschooler." 1999. <http://www.uwex.edu/ces/flp/p/pdf/punishment.pdf> (accessed June 27, 2006).

University of Wisconsin. "Women, Feminism, and Sex in Progressive America." 2003. <http://us.history.wisc.edu/hist102/lectures/lecture14.html> (accessed June 23, 2006).

Upjohn Institute for Employment Research. "Black-White Segregation, Discrimination, and Home-Ownership." August 2001. <http://www.upjohninst.org/publications/wp/01-71.pdf> (accessed July 3, 2006).

Urban Institute. "Beyond the Two Parent Family." May 2001. <http://www.urban.org/url.cfm?ID=310339> (accessed June 21, 2006).

Venker, Suzanne and Laura Schlessinger. 7 *Myths of Working Mothers: Why Children and (Most) Careers Just Don't Mix*. Dallas, Texas: Spence Publishing, 2004.

Victoriana. "The Golden Age of Carriages." <http://www.victoriana.com/lady/buggy.html> (accessed July 16, 2006).

Virginia Tech University: Center for Digital Discourse and Culture. "Feminist Theory." 1999. <http://www.cddc.vt.edu/feminism/> (accessed July 10, 2006).

Virtual Campus of Public Health. "Virtual Campus of Public Health." <http://www.campusvirtualsp.org/eng/index.html> (accessed on June 24, 2006).

Waite, L. J. and M. Gallagher. *The Case for Marriage: Why Married People Are Happier, Healthier and Better Off*. New York: Doubleday, 2000.

Waller, Altina L. *Feud: Hatfields, McCoys, and Social Change in Appalachia, 1860–1900*. Chapel Hill: University of North Carolina Press, 1988.

Wallerstein, Judith S. *The Unexpected Legacy of Divorce*. New York: Hyperion, 2001

Wardlow, Daniel L., ed. *Gays, Lesbians, and Consumer Behavior: Theory, Practice, and Research Issues in Marketing*. Binghamton, NY: The Haworth Press, 1996.

Warner, Judith. *Perfect Madness: Motherhood in the Age of Anxiety*. New York: Riverhead Hardcover, 2005.

Washburn University School of Law. "Survey of Kansas Law: Family Law." 2004. <http://classes.washburnlaw.edu/maxw/publications/surveyoflaw1984.htm> (accessed June 19, 2006).

Washington State University/Edward R. Morrow School of Communication. "Sitcom: What it is, How it Works." 2005. <http://www.wsu.edu:8080/~taflinge/sitcom.html> (accessed July 27, 2006).

Waterman, Barbara. *Birth of an Adoptive, Foster or Step-mother: Beyond Biological Mothering Attachments.* London: Jessica Kingsley, 2004.

Watkins, Elizabeth S. *On the Pill: A Social History of Oral Contraceptives, 1950–1970.* Baltimore, Md.: Johns Hopkins University Press, 1998.

Watkins, T.H. *The Hungry Years: A Narrative History of the Great Depression in America.* New York: Henry Holt & Company, 2000.

Watson, James, and Andrew Berry. *DNA: The Secret of Life.* New York: Knopf, 2004.

Wattes, Jane. *Single Mothers by Choice : A Guidebook for Single Women Who Are Considering or Have Chosen Motherhood.* New York: Three Rivers Press, 1994.

Weiner, Lynn Y. *From Working Girl to Working Mother: The Female Labor Force in the United States, 1820–1980.* Chapel Hill, N.C.: University of North Carolina Press, 1985.

Wellcome Library for the History and Understanding of Medicine. "The guide to history of medicine resources on the Internet." <http://medhist.ac.uk/> (accessed on June 24, 2006).

Welter, Barbara. *Dimity Convictions: The American Woman in the Nineteenth Century.* Athens, Ohio: Ohio University Press, 1976.

West, Nancy Martha. *Kodak and the Lens of Nostalgia.* Charlottesville: University Press of Virginia, 2000.

Westminster College. "VW History." <http://people.westminstercollege.edu/staff/bknorr/html/history.htm> (accessed July 21, 2006).

Wheeler, Marjorie Spruill, ed. *One Woman, One Vote: Rediscovering the Woman Suffrage Movement.* Troutdale, OR: New Sage Press, 1995.

White House. "White House Office of Communications." <http://www.whitehouse.gov/news/> (accessed on June 24, 2006).

Wiencek, Henry. *An Imperfect God: George Washington, His Slaves and the Creation of America.* New York: Farrar, Straus, and Giroux, 2003.

William, Douglas. *Television Families: Is Something Wrong in Suburbia?* Mahwah, NJ: Lawrence Erlbaum Associates, 2003.

Wilson, James Q. *The Marriage Problem: How Our Culture has Weakened Families.* Toronto: Harper Collins Canada, 2003.

Wisconsin Historical Society. "Brewing and Prohibition." http://www.wisconsinhistory.org/turningpoints/tp-051/?action=more_essay> (accessed June 19, 2006).

Withrow, Alice. *Protection of Women and Children in Soviet Russia.* New York: E.P. Dutton, 1932.

Wolf, Alison. Prospect Magazine. "Working Girls." April 2006. <http://www.prospect-magazine.co.uk/article_details.php?id=7398> (accessed July 22, 2006).

Wolf, Naomi. *Misconceptions: Truth, Lies, and the Unexpected on the Journey to Motherhood.* Garden City, N.Y.: Anchor, 2003.

Woloch, Nancy. *Women and the American Experience.* Boston: McGraw-Hill, 2000.

Wood, Elizabeth A. *The Baba and the Comrade: Gender and Politics in Revolutionary Russia.* Bloomington: Indiana University Press, 2001.

World Health Organization. "World Health Organization." <http://www.who.int/en> (accessed on June 24, 2006).

Yalin, Emily. *Our Mother's War: American Women at Home and at the Front During World War II.* New York: Free Press, 2004.

Yew, Lee Kuan. *From Third World to First: The Singapore Story 1965–2000.* New York: Harper Collins, 2000.

Yoshida, Chisa To, and Alan Woodland. *The Economics of Illegal Immigration.* New York: Palgrave MacMillan, 2005.

Youngner, Stuart J., Renee C. Fox, and Laurence J. O'Connell, eds. *Organ Transplantation: Meanings and Realities.* Madison: University of Wisconsin Press, 1996.

Zal, H. Michael. *The Sandwich Generation: Caught between Growing Children and Aging Parents.* Philadelphia, PA: Perseus Publishing, 1992.

Zelizer, Viviana. *Pricing the Priceless Child: The Changing Social Value of Children.* Princeton, NJ: Princeton University Press, 1994.

Zill, N. and M. Gallagher. *Running in Place: How American Families Are Faring in a Changing Economy and an Individualistic Society.* Washington, D.C.: Child Trends, 1994.

Index

Boldface indicates a primary source.
Italics indicates an illustration on the page.

tuberculosis poster, 292, *293*
World War II homefront poster,
    418–420, *419*
World War I, 405–409, *406, 408*
World War II
    background, 418
    salvage and recycling, 418–420, *419,
    420*
    Victory Gardens, 420–423, *421*
    working women, 103–105
World Wide Web. *See* Internet
Worth, Thomas, 162–164, *163*
WPA. *See* Works Progress
    Administration

X

X-rays, chest, 294
Xiaoping, Deng, 311

Y

Yamada, Masahiro, *154*
Yankencheck, Diane, 198
Yew, Lee Kuan, 300, 302
Yoder, Wisconsin v., 56
Young, Brigham, 167, *167*, 168, 234
Young adults, 154–157

*A Young Lady, of Good Family and
    Education, Desires an Engagement
    as Governess* (Anonymous),
    231–233
Young Pioneer Organization of the
    Soviet Union, 179, 180
"Your Family Needs Protection
    Against Syphilis" (Anonymous),
    290–292

Z

Zoning by-laws, 26–31